FILTON COLLEGE

A0051266

Biology
A Functional Approach
Students' Manual
Second Edition

LEARNING RESOURCES CENTRE
FILTON COLLEGE
FILTON AVENUE
BRISTOL BS34 7AT
TEL: 0117 9092224
Return on or before the last date stamped below.

14 MAR 2005
20 OCT 2006
31 OCT 2006
18 JAN 2007
01 DEC 2009
28 FEB 2011
5 DEC
-8 JUN 2016
4.1.18
31 OCT 2022

Biology: A Functional Approach
A0051266

Nelson

D1471179

Nelson Thomas Ltd
Delta Place
27 Bath Road
CHELTENHAM
GL53 7TH
United Kingdom

© M.B.V. Roberts 1974; M.B.V. Roberts, T.J. King 1987

First published by Thomas Nelson and Sons Ltd 1974
Second edition published 1987

ISBN 0-17-448035-0
NPN 20 19 18 17 16 15 14 13

All rights reserved. No paragraph of this publication may be reproduced, copied or transmitted save with written permission or in accordance with the provisions of the Copyright, Design and Patents Act 1988, or under the terms of any licence permitting limited copying issued by the Copyright Licensing Agency, 90 Tottenham Court Road, London W1T 4LP.

Any person who does any unauthorised act in relation to this publication may be liable to criminal prosecution and civil claims for damages.

Printed and bound in China

574.08
A0057264

Preface to the Second Edition

The purpose of this manual is to provide a repertoire of practical investigations and homework questions suitable for Advanced Level biology students. It is designed to be used with *Biology: A Functional Approach* and its complementary series of slides. However, the manual is self-contained and can be used independently of its parent book.

In this second edition we have taken account of the changes that have occurred in the A-level syllabuses since the book was originally published in 1974. We have increased the emphasis on experimental work, whilst retaining the best of the descriptive investigations. There are now more experiments on enzymes, metabolism, ecology and plant physiology. We have increased the proportion of structured questions, in line with current A-level examinations. The large tables of data and the classification of organisms, suitably amended, have been moved into the fourth edition of *Biology: A Functional Approach*. This has allowed us to revise the appendix and to include, amongst other things, advice on project work and a detailed list of suitable projects.

In compiling this manual we lay little claim to originality. Most of the laboratory investigations have been attempted before and many of the questions and problems have featured in past examination papers. In selecting material we have been greatly influenced by what we, in our respective schools, have found useful.

Broadly speaking, practical work in biology falls into four categories: direct observation, dissection, microscopic study, and experimental work. There are, of course, no hard and fast distinctions between these disciplines, and a full investigation of a biological problem often involves all four. We hope that in this manual the correct balance has been achieved. We make no apology for including a fair amount of morphological work, for a functional approach is only meaningful if it is based on sound structural principles, and nowhere can these principles be better acquired than in the laboratory.

Whatever the approach and whatever the techniques, the ultimate purpose of practical work is to explore and investigate the world of living things. Wherever possible, we have tried to present each unit of work in such a way that it can be seen as a genuine scientific investigation and not merely as an exercise to be done for the purpose of passing an examination.

All the investigations are designed to fit into clearly defined periods of time. Most of the experimental investigations can be carried out in 1½ hours. The times for microscopic work and dissection will vary according to the aptitude and ability of the student. We have deliberately omitted experiments that are unduly time-consuming, expensive or capricious. It would, of course, be impossible for all the work suggested here to be completed in a two-year course, but we have included more than can be covered in the time so as to give teachers and students some degree of choice. We hope that some of the investigations may stimulate students to carry out project work on their own.

Many of the homework questions involve interpretation of biological phenomena and analysis of data. In the belief that learning to express ideas clearly and succinctly is an essential part of a biologist's training, we have also included a number of questions requiring the writing of a short essay. On the other hand, we have not included many questions demanding purely descriptive answers, on the grounds that such questions can easily be set by individual teachers.

In preparing this manual we have not had any one syllabus in mind, but the range of laboratory investigations and homework questions should make it suitable for students following the most recent Advanced Level syllabuses of the various universities and examining boards in Great Britain and the Commonwealth, and for students pursuing introductory biology courses in universities and colleges of further education.

When writing a book of this kind, one is very dependent on the constructive advice of one's friends and colleagues. This we have had in full measure, and a list of all those who have helped us is given below. In thanking them we must make it clear that we alone are responsible for the many imperfections which doubtless remain. We hope that teachers and students will not hesitate to point these out to us as they use the manual at home and in the laboratory.

M.B.V. Roberts
T.J. King
August, 1987.

Acknowledgements

The authors and publisher wish to thank the following who helped in the preparation of the first and second editions of this book.

Robin Bertaut
John Bradley
Prof. A.D. Bradshaw
Peter Bright
Chris R. Brown
Tony Brown
Nigel Bruce
Miss Gene Cox
Dr. David Custance
Mark Davies
Miss Liz Edgar
John Emmerson
Graham Fergusson
Dr. Richard Gliddon
Paul Goldsmith
John Haller
Jack Halliday
Dr. Jack Hannay
Malcolm Hardstaff
Beverley Heath
Keith Hicks
Tony Hillier
Tony Hollander
Peter Holway
David Howard
Charles Hughes
Dr. Barrie Juniper
Dr. David Kerridge
Miss Grace Monger
Mrs. Jill Muir
Jay Nicholson
Neil Paffard
Dr. Mary Peach
Ms Gail Perry
Tom Piper
Nigel Purchon
Mrs. Morag Putman
Dr. Rory Putman
Ivor Radford
Mrs. Jeanette Radford
Tim Robinson
Jo Rodgers
Chris Rouan
Nick Screaton
Ianto Stevens
Mrs. Hazel Smith
Miss Lynn Thompson
Michael Ward
Stephen Wood
Robert Wright

Examination questions

We wish to thank the following examining bodies for permission to reproduce, either direct or in modified form, certain questions from their past examination papers. The sources are acknowledged in the manual by the abbreviations shown in parentheses: Associated Examining Board (*AEB*); Biological Sciences Curriculum Study of the American Institute of Biological Sciences (*BSCS*); Cambridge Colleges Joint Examination (*CCJE*); Cambridge Local Examinations Syndicate (*CL*); Joint Matriculation Board (*JMB*); New South Wales Department of Education (*NSW*); Oxford and Cambridge Schools Examination Board (*O and C*); Oxford Colleges Joint Examination (*OCJE*); Oxford Delegacy of Local Examinations (*OL*); Public Examinations Board of South Australia (*SA*); Schools Board of Tasmania (*SBT*); University of London (*UL*); Victorian Universities and Schools Examinations Board (*VUS*); Joint Matriculation Board—Nuffield (*JMB—N*); Hong Kong University (*HK*), Welsh Joint Education Committee (*W*); Northern Ireland Examinations Board (*NI*); Southern Universities Joint Board for School Examinations (*SU*).

The authors would like to thank the publishers, particularly Mr David Warlock, Miss Elizabeth Johnston, Mrs Donna Evans and Mr Pat McGuire for their unfailing courtesy and efficiency during the production of the two editions of this complex book.

A005266
19/12/05
£20.50
574

Note to teachers and technicians

Sources of Equipment and Materials

Most of the laboratory equipment and materials specified in this manual are obtainable from the following biological suppliers in the United Kingdom:
Griffin and George, Gerrard Biological Centre, Worthing Road, East Preston, West Sussex BN16 1AS. Telephone 0903 772071; Telex 87323-FSIG Biology.
Philip Harris Biological Ltd., Oldmixon, Weston-super-Mare, Avon BS24 9BJ. Telephone 0934 413063; Telex 449248 Harris G.
Irwin Desman Ltd., 294 Purley Way, Croydon, Surrey CR9 4QL. Telephone 01-686 6441; Telex 946422.
The University Marine Biological Station, Millport, Isle of Cumbrae, KA28 0EG, Sootland. Telephone 047553 581.
Specimen Department, The Laboratory, Citadel Hill, Plymouth, PL1 2PB, England. Telephone 0752 21761.

Media for chick tissue culture can be obtained from Flow Laboratories, Victoria Park, Heatherhouse Road, Irvine, Scotland.

Marine specimens are generally available from Marine Biological Laboratories such as those at Plymouth and Oban.

Requirements for Individual Investigations

A list of requirements is given at the end of each investigation: apparatus first, then chemicals, and finally prepared microscopic slides and biological materials.

The following abbreviations are used for the microscopic slides:

WM	whole mount	LS	longitudinal section	VS	vertical section
TS	transverse section	HS	horizontal section	VLS	vertical longitudinal section

Some of the investigations involve the use of electron micrographs. Electron micrograph prints are available from Philip Harris Biological Ltd., and electron micrograph transparencies are included in the *Biology: A Functional Approach* slide sets. Electron micrographs can often be supplied by University and/or Polytechnic departments on polite request.

Safety

Experiments involving the use of micro-organisms, the sampling of blood and other body fluids, or where the pupil acts as a subject, are potentially hazardous. Such experiments should be carried out under close supervision. Detailed advice is given in the Association for Science Education booklet entitled *Safeguards in the School Laboratory*. Copies are available from:
The Association for Science Education, College Lane, Hatfield, Herts AL10 9AA.

In addition Local Authorities have issued their own codes and regulations, and teachers are advised to consult these before embarking on any potentially hazardous experiments, particularly those involving the sampling of blood and other body fluids.

Since going to press, the Department of Education and Science has effectively banned from schools the sampling of blood and other body fluids. However, we have retained these procedures in the Students' Manual so that students can see how they are carried out even though they may not carry them out themselves.

Dissection and the Use of Live Animals

Some people object on ethical grounds to experiments on live animals and physiological preparations, and even to the dissection of dead animals. The various Examination Boards have their own policies on these matters and teachers are advised to familiarise themselves with the current guidelines published by the Board.

A joint statement entitled *The Use of Animals and Plants in School Science*, issued by the Associated for Science Education, the Institute of Biology, and the Universities' Federation for Animal Welfare, outlines the problems and should be read by all teachers. It is available from the Association for Science Education at the address given above.

Contents

Chapter 33: Associations between Organisms

Chapter 34: Evolution in Evidence

Chapter 35: The Mechanism of Evolution

Chapter 36: Some Major Steps in Evolution

Chapter 37: Classification and Diversity of Organisms

Appendices

1 Introducing Biology

Background Summary

1 **Biology**, the study of life and living organisms, is divided into numerous subjects which include **zoology**, **botany**, **microbiology** (bacteriology and virology), **anatomy**, **physiology**, **biochemistry**, **cytology** (cell biology), **heredity** (genetics), **molecular biology**, **behaviour** and **ecology**.

2 **Agriculture**, **forestry** and **medicine** are aspects of applied biology; and **biotechnology**, the application of biology to manufacturing industry, is of growing importance.

3 Properties shared by all living organisms are: **movement** (which may be internal), **responsiveness**, **growth** by internal assimilation, **reproduction** (involving replication of nucleic acid), **release of energy** by hydrolysis of adenosine triphosphate, and **excretion**.

4 **Scientific method** starts with an observation which leads to the formulation of a **hypothesis**. Predictions made from the hypothesis are tested by **experiment**. Every experiment must be accompanied by an appropriate **control**, i.e. a standard with which the experimental result(s) may be compared.

5 The number of known species of organisms runs into millions, so a system of classification (**taxonomy**, **systematics**) is essential.

6 Organisms as a whole are divided into **kingdoms** which are further divided into groups and sub-groups (see page 369).

7 **Viruses** do not fit into any of the kingdoms. They have a simple structure and are on the borderline between living and non-living things.

8 Basic biological concepts include survival, adaptation, a close relationship between structure and function, and evolution.

Investigation 1.1
Using the 'Scientific Method'

Requirements
A selection of biological objects, each showing one or more readily observable phenomena which could be investigated e.g. apple (fruit), sycamore fruit, plant galls, plant with distinctive flowers, plant with diseased leaves, fern with spores, green hydra, snail, fanworm, bird's skeleton.

Scientific method starts with an observation: you observe an organism and may notice something interesting about it. Scientists are always on the lookout for interesting phenomena to investigate. The next step is to suggest a hypothesis to explain the observation. From the hypothesis various predictions may be made, and these can then be tested by experiment.

In this exercise you will be presented with a number of biological objects on which you can make your own observations and suggest testable hypotheses.

Procedure

1 Draw up a table with the headings shown in Table 1.1. Make the columns as wide as possible.

2 Examine a selection of biological objects presented to you by your teacher. In each case observe *one* interesting phenomenon, formulate a hypothesis to explain it, make a prediction from your hypothesis and suggest an experiment to test the prediction. Fill in the table as you go along.

3 Go out of doors and find four interesting biological phenomena worthy of investigation. Add them to your table.

Observation	Hypothesis	Prediction	Experimental test
1. An apple is shiny.	The shiny layer is the waxy cuticle.	If you remove the wax the shininess should disappear.	Apply a wax solvent (e.g. xylene) to the surface of the apple and observe the result.
2. A plant has yellow patches on its leaves.	The yellowing is caused by lack of nitrogen.	If you deprive a plant of nitrogen it should develop yellow leaves.	Grow two plants, one (the control) in a solution containing all necessary nutrients, the other in a solution containing all nutrients except nitrogen.

Table 1.1 Table for recording observations and their investigation using the scientific method. Two examples are given to show you how to fill in the table.

For consideration

(1) Which of your hypotheses would be particularly difficult to test experimentally, and why?
(2) Which experimental tests would need a control, and what should the control be in each case?
(3) Give two examples of biological investigations, not necessarly connected with the observations that you have made in this exercise, in which the scientific method, as described here, would be inappropriate.

Note: Some of the observations which you have made could lead on to a project. For advice on projects *see* Appendix 5, page 389.

Investigation 1.2
An exercise in observation: bacteria in yoghurt

Requirements
Monocular microscope with high magnification (×400 or ×1000)
Microscope slide
Bacteriological loop or nichrome wire
Bunsen burner

Crystal violet (0.5 per cent in distilled water)
Ethanol
Lugol's Iodine (1 g of iodine and 2 g of potassium iodide, in 100 g water)
Dilute carbol fuchsin
Distilled water

Natural yoghurt or stale milk

To make carbol fuchsin: dissolve 5 g of basic fuchsin in 25 g of phenol by heating over a boiling water bath and shaking — alternatively, reflux and use a magnetic stirrer. Then mix well with 50 cm^3 of 95 per cent ethanol, add 500 cm^3 water, and filter to make a stock solution. Dilute this solution ten times with distilled water to produce the bacteriological stain known as dilute carbol fuchsin.

The testing of hypotheses by experiment is an important part of the scientific method. Yet the accurate observation and recording of phenomena also plays an important part in biology. Branches of biology such as anatomy, classification, ecology and palaeontology rely heavily on description of what is seen.

To illustrate the value (and difficulty) of observation, let us try to observe the bacteria responsible for fermentating milk to yoghurt. To show up the bacteria under the microscope, we shall stain them with the Gram stain, widely used in medical microbiology to help identify bacteria which cause infections.

Procedure

1 Place a small sample of yoghurt or stale milk in the centre of a microscope slide. Add two drops of distilled water. With a bacteriological loop (a nichrome wire) mix the milky liquid with the water and then spread out the film thinly over the surface of the slide.
2 Allow the film to dry in air. You may hold the slide high above a bunsen flame to accelerate drying (care!). Fix the film by passing it, slowly, face downwards, through the flame.
3 Cover the film with crystal violet stain, and leave it for 30 seconds.
4 After 30 seconds pour off any excess stain, and wash off the rest with Lugol's iodine. Leave the iodine solution on the surface of the slide for a further 30 seconds.
5 Wash twice with ethanol, and then with water.
6 You may wish to apply a second stain e.g. dilute carbol fuchsin. If so, apply two drops of dilute carbol fuchsin and note the time on a watch which records in seconds. After twelve seconds (no more!) wash off the second stain with distilled water.
7 Allow the slide to dry, and examine the film under the high power of a monocular microscope (magnification ×400) without a coverslip. (For advice on using a microscope *see* Appendix 3, page 381).
8 Imagine that you were discovering these bacteria for the first time. Write a careful description of what you have seen so as to inform other scientists of your discovery.

For consideration

(1) What makes you think that the structures which you have seen are bacteria?
(2) Are these bacteria the only ones present in stale milk? Are you justified in believing that these are the bacteria responsible for the conversion of fresh milk to stale milk?
(3) Devise an experiment to test whether or not milk contains living organisms.
(4) Staining bacteria is very important in medicine. Why?

Investigation 1.3
Testing a hypothesis: the number of bacteria in fresh and stale milk

Milk contains bacteria derived from the udder of the cow. We suspect that these bacteria might reproduce rapidly in milk: that is our *hypothesis*. From this we can predict that stale milk should contain significantly more bacteria than fresh milk. How can we test this prediction experimentally?

Method

When a bacterium encounters favourable conditions for growth on nutrient agar, it divides again and again by binary fission to form a 'colony'. By the time that the colony becomes visible to the naked eye it contains hundreds of thousands of individuals.

The problem is that stale milk, and possibly also fresh milk, may contain so many bacteria that if it was spread over an agar plate the bacterial colonies would form a continuous sheet. It would be impossible to count colonies individually. We can overcome this problem by serial dilution.

In serial dilution, the milk is diluted ten times, a hundred times, a thousand times and so on, and samples of each dilution are spread over agar plates. In some of the dilutions, the colonies which form are sufficiently separated to be counted individually. Then the number of colonies can be multiplied by the dilution to obtain an estimate of the total bacterial population in the sample.

Bacteria are almost everywhere and so precautions must be taken to avoid contamination. The glassware, petri dishes and so on must be sterilised.

CAUTION:
Culturing bacteria is potentially hazardous. Wash your hands thoroughly before and after the experiment. Do not put your fingers near your mouth or nose while handling the bacterial cultures. Keep all bottles, test tubes and petri dishes closed except when you *must* open them, and once the lids of the petri dishes have been sealed with sellotape, keep them sealed. At the end of the practical session swab the bench with disinfectant.

Requirements

Bunsen burner
Cotton wool
Incubator
Marker for writing on glass
Disinfectant for cleaning bench
Matches
Petri dishes (sterilised, containing nutrient agar) ×6
Pipettes (sterilised, 1 cm^3 graduated) ×8
Spreader (glass or metal)
Test tubes (sterilised) ×6
Test tube rack

Distilled water, 100 cm^3
Ethanol (70 per cent)

Fresh milk
Stale milk of same type allowed to stand for 24 hours at room temperature

Procedure

1 You are provided with six sterilised test tubes plugged with cotton wool. Label them F1, F2, F3, S1, S2 and S3, F means fresh and S means stale.

2 You are provided with six sterile petri dishes, each containing nutrient agar suitable for bacterial growth. Write on the base of each plate your initials, and one of the codes F1, F2, F3, S1, S2 or S3. Do not open any of the dishes.

3 Transfer 9.9 cm^3 of sterile distilled water from the flask provided to each of the six test tubes, using the following technique:
(a) with your left hand, raise the cotton wool plug from the flask containing sterile distilled water;
(b) holding the sterile 10 cm^3 graduated pipette in your right hand, suck up 9.9 cm^3 of sterile distilled water;
(c) replace the plug on the flask and remove the cotton wool plug from a test tube;
(d) transfer the 9.9 cm^3 of water to the test tube;
(e) replace the plug.

4 Using a sterile pipette, transfer 0.1 cm^3 of fresh milk to tube F1. Replace the plug. Swirl the tube. Tube F1 now contains a ×100 dilution.

5 Using a different sterile pipette, transfer 0.1 cm^3 from tube F1 to tube F2. Tube F2 now contains a ×10 000 dilution.

6 Using a different sterile pipette, transfer 0.1 cm^3 from tube F2 to tube F3. Tube F3 now contains a ×1 000 000 dilution.

7 Using the same pipette as in Step 5, transfer 0.1 cm^3 of ×100 diluted milk from tube F1 to the centre of the agar in the sterile petri dish labelled F1. When you do this, open the lid of the petri dish as little as possible and replace it rapidly.

8 Dip a nichrome wire or a glass spreader in 70 per cent ethanol and pass it through a Bunsen burner flame. Allow it to cool. Open the petri dish and rapidly spread the milk as evenly as possible over the surface of the plate.

9 Using the same pipette as in Step 6, transfer 0.1 cm^3 of ×10 000 diluted milk from F2 to the agar in petri dish F2 and spread it as in Step 8.

10 Using a newly sterilised pipette, transfer 0.1 cm^3 of ×1 000 000 diluted milk from F3 to the agar in petri dish F3 and spread it as in Step 8.

11 Repeat the whole procedure, using the stale milk, tubes S1 to S3 and sterile petri dishes S1 to S3.

12 Sellotape the lids to the dishes and incubate them upside down at 35 °C for 28–48 hours. Distinct colonies should then be visible.

13 *Without removing the lids*, examine the bacterial growth on the agar. Count and record the numbers of bacterial colonies, where possible. Multiply the number of colonies by the dilution to obtain an estimate of the total bacterial population in the milk.

For consideration

(1) Have you obtained enough evidence to prove the hypothesis that bacteria reproduce in milk?
(2) In what ways could you have improved the experiment? What are the major sources of error?
(3) Why were the petri dishes incubated, and why did they have to be incubated *upside down*?
(4) Although the bacteria which you have cultured in this experiment are harmless, you have had to take stringent safety precautions. Why were these precautions necessary?

Reference: N.P. Green, G.W. Stout, D.J. Taylor, *Biological Science 1*, Cambridge University Press, 1984.

Questions and Problems

1 What are the basic properties of living things? What arguments would you present to show that (a) a crystal, and (b) a candle flame are not alive, and that an oak tree is alive?

2 What characteristics of life are exploited in:
(a) the use of flashing signs; (b) giving a green plant extra light; (c) manuring soil; (d) the use of a carrier pigeon; (e) making wine?

3 'The body was found in the neighbouring water meadows. Beside it was a rusty and bloodstained iron bar. At the inquest it was stated that the victim was Fortescue-Watson, a member of Merlberry College, and that death resulted from a series of blows on the back of the head with a blunt instrument.'

'The police searched the area of the crime and the only clue they found was two sets of footprints in the mud; one of these fitted the victim's shoes, while the other had been made by shoes with steel quarter heels and a hole in the left sole. A search was made, and a pair of shoes belonging to Snooks, a member of the same school, was found to fit the footprints.'

'An examination of Snook's clothes was then made and showed recent mud stains on the trousers, seeds of a weed currently in flower in the water meadows in the turn-ups, and on the jacket bloodstains which had been treated, but not obliterated, by the application of ammonia.'

(a) Discuss how far the police investigations in this story illustrate the method of science, and point out any differences in method between these investigations and those carried out by a scientist studying natural phenomena in a laboratory.
(b) Do you consider that, on the evidence given, Snook's guilt is proved? If not, explain why you consider the evidence to be insufficient. What other investigations should the police carry out?

4 Put forward hypotheses to explain the following observations, and suggest how you might test your hypotheses experimentally:
(a) Plants are sometimes seen to droop.
(b) Woodlice are generally found under logs or stones, rarely in the open.
(c) The cut shoot of a water weed often exudes a continuous stream of bubbles.
(d) Mosses occur in greater abundance on north-facing than south-facing walls.
(e) In a certain type of malaria, fever occurs at regular 48-hour intervals.

5 Explain fully how you would test the hypothesis that:
(a) the apical bud is essential for vertical growth of the main stem of a flowering plant;
(b) vitamin B_1 (thiamine) is required for the growth of hens;
(c) the milk yield of cows is stimulated by music;
(d) snails can detect sounds;
(e) people are less likely to have a heart attack if they eat margarine instead of butter.

6 Design an experiment to determine whether:
(a) biological washing powders remove stains more efficiently than non-biological powders;
(b) people can tell the difference between butter and margarine.

7 From your own observations give one example of (a) an animal, and (b) a plant that is strikingly adapted to a particular way of life.

8 (a) Write down two uses in manufacturing industry of each of the following: (i) yeast, (ii) bacteria, (iii) enzymes, (iv) fish, (v) trees.
(b) Choose one of the uses in your list and discuss it in more detail.

2 Structure and Function in Cells

Background Summary

1 Cells were first described in 1665 by Robert Hooke and are now known to be of almost universal occurrence in organisms.

2 The **cell theory** states that the cell is the basic unit of an organism, the whole organism being little more than a collection of independent cells; the **organismal theory** states that the whole organism is the basic unit, the cells being incidental sub-units.

3 Cells may be observed with various kinds of microscope, e.g. optical (light); phase-contrast, polarising and electron microscopes. A typical **light microscope** magnifies about 800 times and has a resolving power of approximately 0.2 μm. The **transmission electron microscope** can magnify objects 300 000 times and has a resolving power of approximately 1.0 nm. (Compare the naked eye whose resolving power is about 0.1 mm.) The more recently developed **scanning electron microscope** is useful for studying surface structures.

4 The main parts of a typical cell are the **nucleus, cytoplasm** and **cell membrane (plasma membrane)**. The nucleus contains **chromosomes** which carry the **genes**. The cytoplasm contains various membrane-bound **organelles**.

5 Structures characteristic of animal cells: **nuclear membrane, nuclear pores, nucleolus** and **chromatin granules**; **cytoplasmic matrix (cytosol)** containing **microtrabeculae, endoplasmic reticulum, glycogen granules, ribosomes** and/or **polyribosomes (polysomes), Golgi body, secretory vesicles** and **zymogen granules, mitochondria, lysosomes, centrioles, pinocytic** and **phagocytic vesicles, microfilaments** and **microtubules; cell membrane** (plasma membrane) sometimes with **microvilli**.

6 Some animal cells and unicellular organisms possess **cilia** or **flagella**. Cilia and flagella contain microtubules in a 9+2 arrangement. They move by bending, in which process the microtubules slide alongside each other.

7 Typical plant cells differ from animal cells in lacking cilia, flagella and centrioles; and in possessing **chloroplasts, starch grains** (instead of glycogen), **sap vacuole** and **cellulose wall**.

8 In plant cells a **primary wall** of cellulose is laid down on the inside of the **middle lamella** (mainly calcium pectate). After the cell has expanded a further **secondary wall** of cellulose may be laid down inside the primary wall. The secondary wall may be absent locally, giving rise to a **pit**, and adjacent cells may be linked by **plasmodesmata**.

9 Cell structures can be separated by **differential centrifugation** and then studied individually to ascertain their functions.

10 The type of cell summarised above is described as **eukaryotic**. In contrast, the cells of bacteria and 'blue-green algae' (cyanobacteria) have a simpler structure lacking membrane-bound organelles. Such cells are described as **prokaryotic**.

11 A typical bacterial cell has a **cell membrane, cell wall, nucleoid, plasmids, ribosomes, mesosome** and sometimes **chromatophores, capsule** and **flagella**. The prokaryotic flagellum is simpler than the eukaryotic flagellum and moves by rotating rather than bending.

12 According to the **fluid-mosaic model**, the plasma membrane consists of a **lipid bilayer** with globular protein molecules in or on it. Some of the protein molecules are **glycoproteins** with carbohydrate chains projecting from them.

13 Though basically similar, cells show considerable diversity in their contents, shape and functions. In all cases there is a close relationship between cell structure and function.

Investigation 2.1
Structure of cells

CAUTION:
Certain infectious diseases can be transmitted through saliva. Avoid any contact with another person's saliva. Do not share a spatula with anyone else. For alternative sources of epithelial cells which avoid possible health hazards associated with the collection of human cheek cells, see *Education in Science*, November 1987, page 28.

The various structures that are crammed into a theoretical diagram of a generalised cell are not all visible in any one cell. So to piece together the structure of a 'typical' cell it is necessary to look at more than one type of cell.

To see a particular structure it may be necessary to stain the cell. The choice of stain is important because certain stains are specific to certain structures; thus acetocarmine stains the nucleus and its contents, iodine solution stains starch grains, and so on.

Procedure

ANIMAL CELL: GENERAL STRUCTURE

1 Gently scrape the inside of your cheek with a sterilised spatula and mount the scrapings in a drop of water on a microscope slide. Cover with a coverslip. Observe under the microscope. (If you have not used a microscope before, *see* Appendix 3, page 381.)

2 Locate a single cell and examine it under high power. Many of the cells

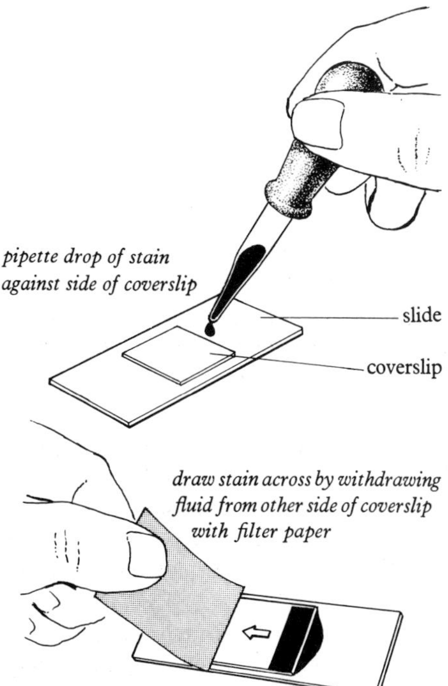

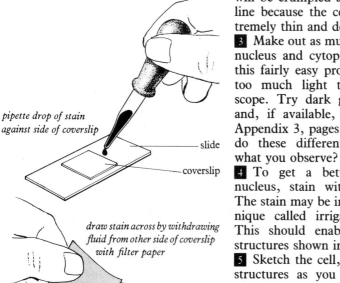

Figure 2.1 The technique of irrigation.

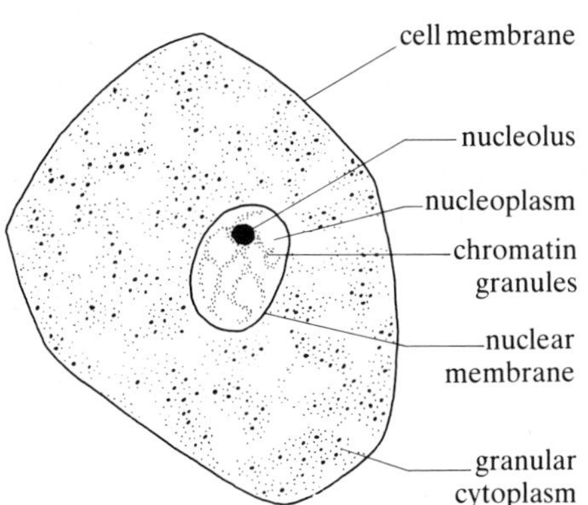

Figure 2.2 A cheek cell as seen under the high power after staining with e.g. methylene blue.

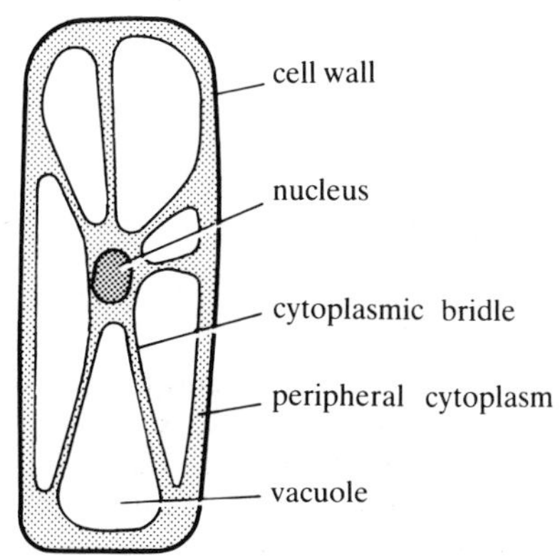

Figure 2.3 Staminal hair cell of *Tradescantia*. The nucleus is suspended in the centre of the cell by thin bridles of cytoplasm. Streaming of the cytoplasm, indicated by movement of the granules, can often be seen in these bridles and in the peripheral cytoplasm.

will be crumpled and irregular in outline because the cell membrane is extremely thin and delicate.

3 Make out as much as you can of the nucleus and cytoplasm. You will find this fairly easy provided you don't let too much light through the microscope. Try dark ground illumination and, if available, phase contrast (*see* Appendix 3, pages 382 and 383). How do these different techniques affect what you observe?

4 To get a better picture of the nucleus, stain with methylene blue. The stain may be introduced by a technique called irrigation (Figure 2.1). This should enable you to see the structures shown in Figure 2.2.

5 Sketch the cell, putting in as many structures as you have been able to observe. Label: nucleus, nuclear membrane, nucleoplasm, chromatin granules, nucleolus, granular cytoplasm, cell membrane.

PLANT CELL: GENERAL STRUCTURE

1 Strip off a piece of epidermis from one of the inner 'fleshy scales' of an onion, mount in iodine solution and observe one cell under low and high powers.

2 Identify the nucleus. Observe the distribution of granular cytoplasm surrounding the vacuole. Also notice: cellulose cell wall, nucleoli (how many?), chromatin granules. The onion is a plant organ but it does not contain chloroplasts: explain. What can you say about the 3-dimensional shape of the cells?

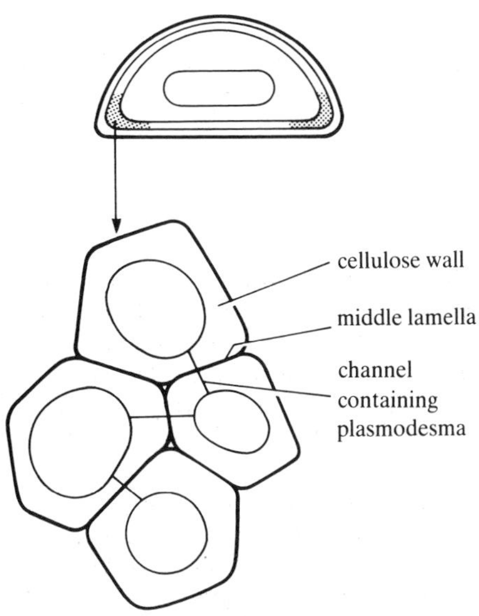

Figure 2.4 Transverse section of pine needle. The cells at the corner have thick cellulose walls perforated by channels connecting adjacent cells.

CHLOROPLASTS

Mount a small leaf of the moss *Mnium* in water and examine its cells under high power. The cells are so packed with chloroplasts that little else can be seen. What is the green colour of the chloroplasts caused by?

CYTOPLASMIC STREAMING

Streaming of the cytoplasm can be seen in cells of the staminal hairs of *Tradescantia*. Open up one of the flowers and remove a stamen. Mount the stamen in water and examine a hair under high power. Adjust the illumination carefully or, better still, use phase contrast. Can you make out the structures shown in Figure 2.3? What might be the function of cytoplasmic streaming? Make drawings to illustrate.

CELL WALL AND MIDDLE LAMELLA

Examine the large cells at the corners of a transverse section of a pine needle (Figure 2.4). Notice the thick cellulose walls which have been laid down in layers. The thin line separating the cellulose walls of adjacent cells, the middle lamella, is clearly visible. What does it represent? Fine channels in the cellulose walls connect adjacent cells: they contain plasmodesmata.

STARCH GRAINS

Many plant cells store starch in the form of starch grains (amyloplasts). Nowhere can these be better seen than in a potato, a swollen stem (stem tuber) which is an example of a plant storage organ.

1 Scrape some tissue from the cut surface of a potato and mount in water. Observe starch grains under high power.

2 Now irrigate with iodine solution and watch the starch grains turn blue. Notice that the starch grains are located inside tightly packed hexagonal cells.

FLAGELLUM

1 Examine *Euglena* or some other comparable unicellular flagellate, under high power, using low illumination or phase contrast, and watch the flagellum in action.

2 Irrigate with Noland's solution which fixes flagella and stains them blue.

Requirements
Slides and coverslips
Spatula
Optical microscope, if possible with phase contrast
Filter paper
Small scissors

Sucrose solution (5 per cent)
Iodine solution
Methylene blue solution
Schultz' solution or FABIL
Noland's solution
Janus B green stain (for details of biological stains, *see* pages 402–3)

TS pine needle

Onion
Moss (*Mnium* sp.)
Tradescantia flowers
Potato
Euglena
Celery stick

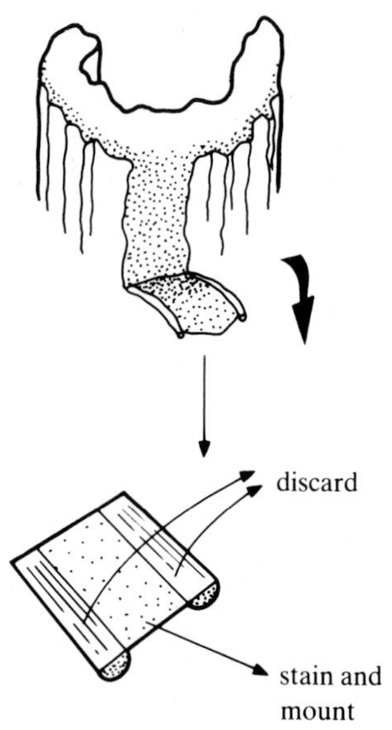

Figure 2.5 How to obtain celery tissue for studying mitochondria.

MITOCHONDRIA

1 Make a transverse cut across a stick of fresh celery, about two-thirds of the way down from the leaves. Carefully peel back two 'strings', together with the tissue in between them (Figure 2.5).

2 Cut off a length of about 1 cm of the strip and remove the strings from either side. Place the remaining tissue in a drop of 5 per cent sucrose solution on a slide with the inner side uppermost. Put on a coverslip and observe under high power.

3 Observe a single cell, noting the cytoplasm which may show streaming movements. If you keep the illumination low you should see small particles in the cytoplasm: these are mitochondria.

4 Irrigate with 2 drops of Janus green and watch the mitochondria over several minutes. The mitochondria should stain blue and then gradually become decolorised.

5 Janus green is an oxidation-reduction indicator. Normally in cell respiration oxygen is reduced by hydrogen atoms to form water. However, in the presence of Janus green, the dye is reduced and changes from blue to colourless. What conclusions can you draw about the function of mitochondria from the way they stain with Janus green?

For Consideration

(1) From your observations made in this investigation, draw up a table comparing the structure of animal and plant cells.

(2) Make a list of the structures visible in the electron microscope which you have been *unable* to see in this investigation.

Investigation 2.2 Fine structure of cells

In the last investigation everything you saw was seen through the light microscope. The purpose of this second investigation is to see what cells look like in the electron microscope. Since it is unlikely that you will have access to an electron microscope, you will do this by looking at prepared electron micrographs.

Procedure

1 First look at Figure 2.6. This is a diagram, based on electron micrographs, of a generalised animal cell. It shows the main structures which you would expect to see in most animal cells and it will help you to interpret the electron micrographs.

2 Now examine an electron micrograph of a section through part of an animal cell. Using Figure 2.6 to help you, identify as many structures and organelles as you can. If the structures are lettered, state what each letter stands for.

What structures included in Figure 2.6 are *not* visible in the micrograph and why?

3 From the scale bar in Figure 2.6, estimate the approximate magnification of your electron micrograph. How many times more magnified is it than the cheek cell which you examined in Investigation 1.1?

4 Examine a high-resolution electron micrograph of a single mitochondrion cut in longitudinal section. Notice how much more detail can now be seen. Using Figure 2.7 to help you, identify as many parts of the mitochondrion as you can, particularly the bounding membranes with space between, cristae and matrix. If the various parts of the mitochondrion are lettered, state what

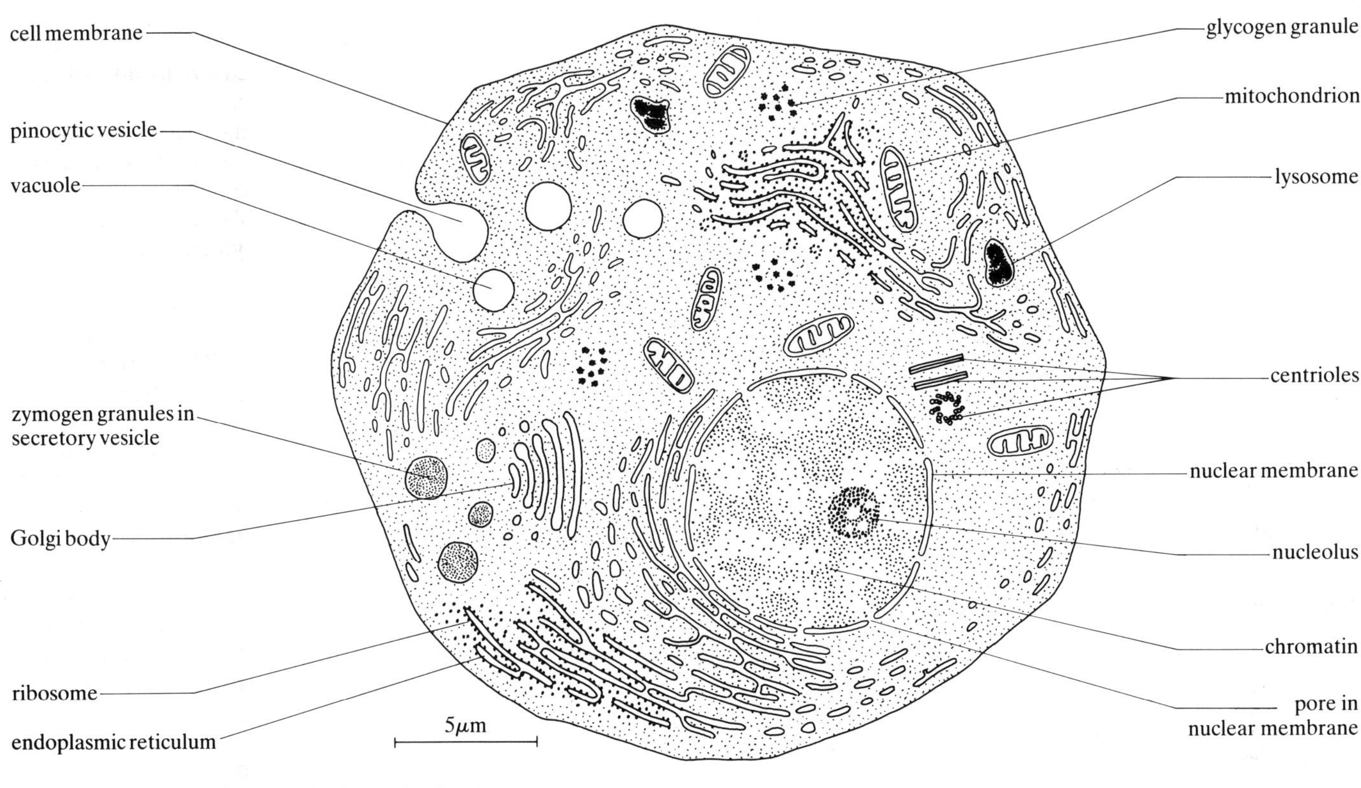

Figure 2.6 Diagram of a generalised animal cell as seen in the electron microscope.

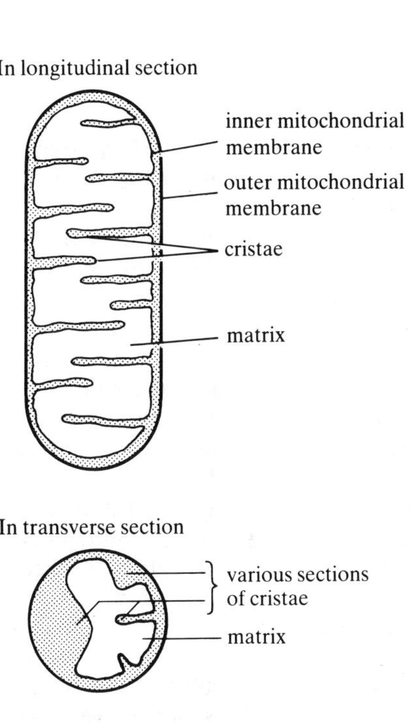

Figure 2.7 Diagrams showing the detailed structure of a mitochondrion.

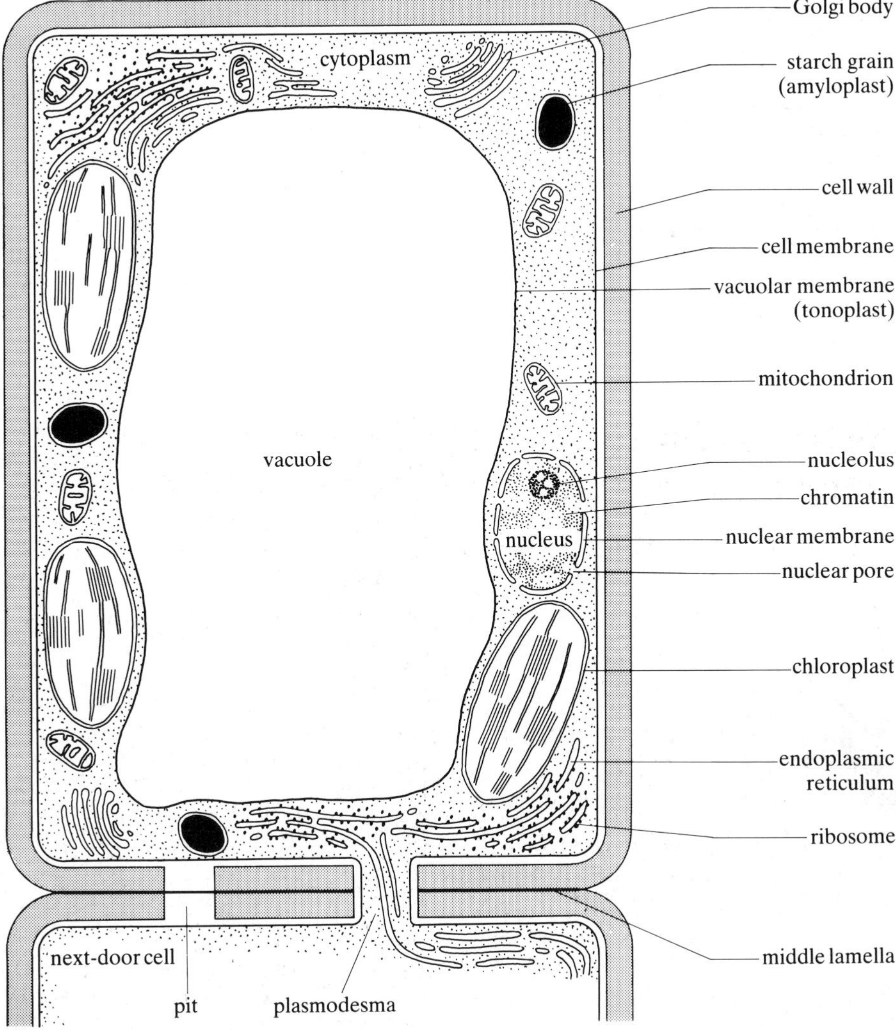

Figure 2.8 Diagram of a generalised plant cell as seen in the electron microscope.

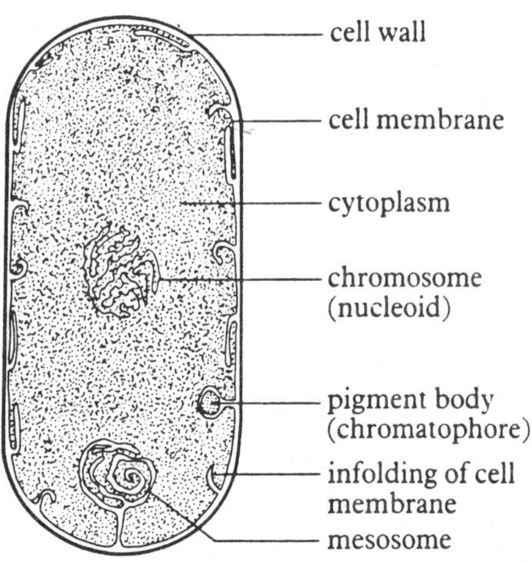

Figure 2.9 Diagram of a bacterial cell as seen in the electron microscope.

Requirements
Electron micrographs of sections through an animal cell (e.g. liver, pancreas), mitochondrion, plant cell and bacterial cell.

each letter stands for. What is the function of the mitochondrion? In what respect is its structure suited to perform this function?

5 Examine an electron micrograph of a section through part of a plant cell. Use Figure 2.8 to help you identify the various structures and organelles.

What structures included in Figure 2.8 are *not* visible in your micrograph, and why?

6 Examine an electron micrograph of a section through a bacterium. This is a prokaryotic cell with a simpler internal structure than the eukaryotic animal and plant cells which you have just been looking at. Use Figure 2.9 to help you identify the various structures in the bacterial cell.

For consideration

(1) Make a table comparing the *fine* structure of a typical animal cell and a typical plant cell as deduced from the electron micrographs which you have examined.

(2) In the same way make another table comparing the structure of a prokaryotic cell and a eukaryotic cell.

Investigation 2.3
Diversity of cells

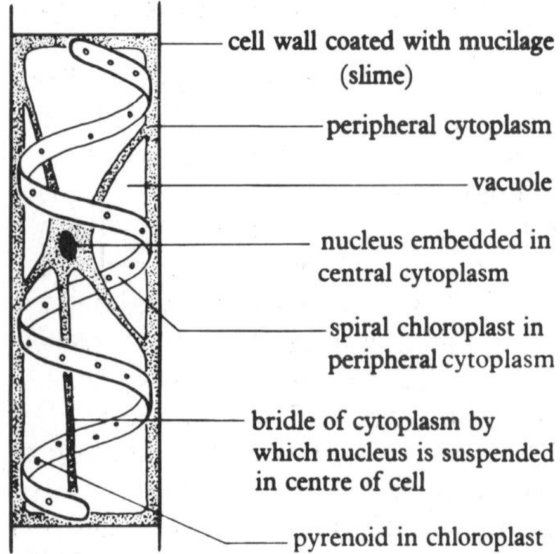

Figure 2.10 Diagram of a cell of the filamentous green alga *Spirogyra*. To what extent does your own specimen conform to this diagram?

In the previous investigations we were concerned with those features which are common to cells in general. In this investigation we will examine four cells which depart from the common pattern.

BLOOD CELLS

1 Examine white blood cells in a prepared smear of human blood. Observe the granulocytes (*see* page 161). In life they move by amoeboid locomotion and engulf bacteria by phagocytosis. What other unusual feature is apparent in these cells?

2 While looking at the blood smear notice the red blood cells. How do they differ from typical animal cells?

PIGMENT CELLS

Look carefully at a prepared slide of frog's skin under high power. Immediately beneath the epidermis you will see black pigment cells (chromatophores). What special features do these cells possess? What is their function?

SPIROGYRA CELL

1 Mount a filament of the fresh water alga *Spirogyra* in water and observe under low and high powers. The filament consists of a chain of elongated cells joined together end to end.

2 Observe one of its cells in detail. Using Figure 2.10 to help you, identify the cell wall, spiral chloroplast(s) with pyrenoids, cytoplasm, nucleus suspended in centre of vacuole by cytoplasmic bridles. What is the three-dimensional shape of the cell?

3 Investigate the detailed structure of the cells by staining three separate slides with (1) acetocarmine for the nucleus, (2) methylene blue for the cell wall, and (3) iodine solution for starch grains near the pyrenoids. The cell wall contains mucilage (slimy): why is this useful?

YEAST CELL

Yeast (*Saccharomyces*) is a unicellular fungus which grows naturally on the surface of fruit.

1 Pipette a small drop of yeast suspension onto a slide and add a drop of iodine solution. Cover with a coverslip. On a second slide mount a drop of the yeast in lactophenol. Observe both slides under high power. What

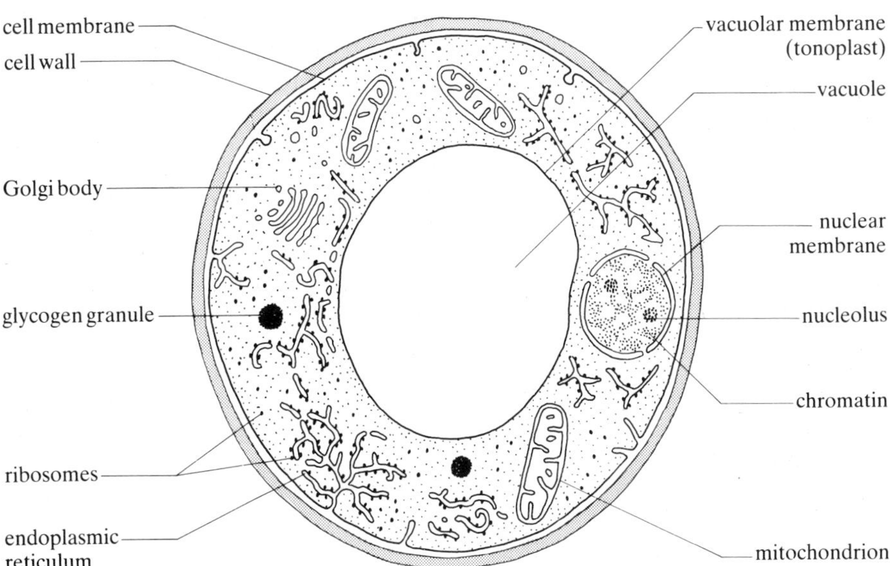

Figure 2.11 Diagram of a cell of yeast (*Saccharomyces*) as seen in a thin section in the electron microscope.

Requirements
Microscope
Slides and coverslips
Filter paper

Iodine solution
Methylene blue solution
Acetocarmine
Lactophenol

Human blood smear stained with Leishman's or Wright's stain
WM or VS frog skin

Spirogyra
Yeast suspension

can you see? How does each stain help you to make out details of the cells?

2 Figure 2.11 is a diagram, based on electron micrographs, of a yeast cell. Which of the structures labelled in the diagram can you see in your own specimens? Why do you see *less* than is shown in the diagram?

3 Yeast reproduces by budding: one or more buds grow out from the parent cell and eventually break away. Can you see any yeast cells budding?

4 In what respects does the yeast cell resemble (a) an animal cell, and (b) a plant cell? What conclusions do you draw from the comparison?

For consideration

(1) Some cells are specialised to carry out specific functions within an organism. Of the cells which you have examined in this investigation, which is (a) the most specialised, and (b) the least specialised? Explain the reasoning behind your choices.

(2) Yeast is a fungus. Fungi used to be placed in the plant kingdom but are now regarded as a separate kingdom. Do you think this is sensible? Explain your answer.

Investigation 2.4
Effect of temperature on the movement of pigment through cell membranes

In beetroot cells the red anthocyanin pigment occurs in the vacuoles. Each vacuole is surrounded by a tonoplast membrane and outside it, the cytoplasm is surrounded by the plasma membrane.

These membranes are too thin to be seen but we can draw certain conclusions about their structure by studying their properties. In this investigation we shall see how temperature affects the rate at which the anthocyanin pigment leaves the cells.

Procedure

1 Using a bunsen burner on a mat, a tripod and a gauze, heat 200 cm^3 of distilled water to 85 °C in a 250 cm^3 beaker.

2 Whilst the water is heating, with a syringe place 10 cm^3 of distilled water (at room temperature) into each of ten test tubes in a test tube rack. Label the tubes 85, 80, 75, 70, 65, 63, 60, 55, 50 and 45 respectively.

3 Cut a beetroot cylinder to a length of 5 cm. Place it in the beaker of water at 85 °C, and note the time. After exactly one minute use forceps to transfer the cylinder to the test tube of cold water marked 85. Note the time.

4 As the distilled water in the beaker cools, repeat Step 3, using a fresh cylinder each time, at the following temperatures: 80 °C, 75 °C, 70 °C, 65 °C, 63 °C, 60 °C, 55 °C, 50 °C and 45 °C.

Requirements
Test tube rack
Test tubes × 10
Marker for writing on glass
Graduated syringe (10 cm^3)
Measuring cylinder (200 cm^3)
Beaker (250 cm^3)
Bunsen burner, mat, tripod and gauze
Ceramic tile
Cork borer
Razor blade
Thermometer (0–100 °C)
Clock/watch
Colorimeter which takes standard test tubes
Forceps

Tap root of beetroot (Cut ten cylinders with a cork borer. Wash the cylinders overnight in running tap water. Transfer them before the practical to a beaker of water)

5 Leave each cylinder in its test tube of cold distilled water for exactly 30 minutes.

6 After 30 minutes have elapsed, shake the test tube and then remove the beetroot cylinder. At the end of the experiment you should have ten test tubes containing water which is stained red with anthocyanin pigment.

7 Using a colorimeter (*see* Appendix 3), compare the amounts of red pigment which have diffused out of the cylinders. Present the results in a table. Plot a graph of colour density (optical density) against temperature.

For consideration

(1) At normal temperatures (e.g. 20 °C) what prevents the anthocyanin pigment from diffusing out of the cells?

(2) Explain your results in terms of the current theory of the structure of cell membranes. If you wish, offer several alternative explanations.

(3) What implications do these results have for bacteria living in hot springs at 80 °C?

(4) Speculate on the value to beetroots of having this anthocyanin pigment in the vacuoles of their cells.

(5) Comment on the accuracy of the experiment. How could it be improved?

Questions and Problems

1 Explain the difference between the cell theory and organismal theory. List the evidence for and against each.

2 What is the difference between magnifying power and resolving power of a microscope? How do the optical and electron microscopes compare as regards magnification and resolution, and how would you explain the difference?

3 Distinguish between (a) chromatin granules and chromosomes; (b) rough and smooth endoplasmic reticulum; (c) ribosomes and polyribosomes (polysomes); (d) cell membrane and cell wall; (e) leucoplast and chloroplast.

4 Figure 2.12 is an electron micrograph of part of a liver cell of a rat.
(a) Name the structures labelled A, B, C and D.
(b) From the scale bar provided, estimate the magnification of this micrograph.
(c) Suggest one function of D.
(d) Why do structures E and F differ in shape?

5 Figure 2.13 is an electron micrograph of a section through a group of plant cells. A cell wall has been labelled.
(a) How many cells (or parts of cells) are visible in this electron micrograph? How can you tell?
(b) Identify the structures labelled A to E.
(c) What lies between structures A and B?
(d) Name one structure, visible but not labelled, which is also found in animal cells.
(e) Name three structures which you would expect to see in plant cells but which are absent from this electron micrograph.

6 The current hypothesis explaining the structure of the cell membrane postulates that the lipid (fat) part of the membrane consists of two layers of lipid molecules whose polar (water-soluble) ends point outwards and hydrocarbon chains inwards.
(a) What physico-chemical evidence supports this idea?
(b) What can you say about the *non*-lipid components of the membrane?

7 What features do the following cells possess over and above those that are common to cells generally: (a) chromatophore; (b) spermatozoon; (c) smooth muscle cell; (d) *Euglena*; (e) musculo-epithelial cell of *Hydra* or *Obelia*? In each case explain how the cell is adapted to perform its particular functions.

8 Certain cells have processes projecting from them. Give examples of such cells and in each case relate the presence of their extensions to the functions which these cells perform.

9 Describe the structure, functions and interactions of cell organelles other than the nucleus. (*CCJE*)

10 What is the evidence that cell membranes exist? (*OCJE*)

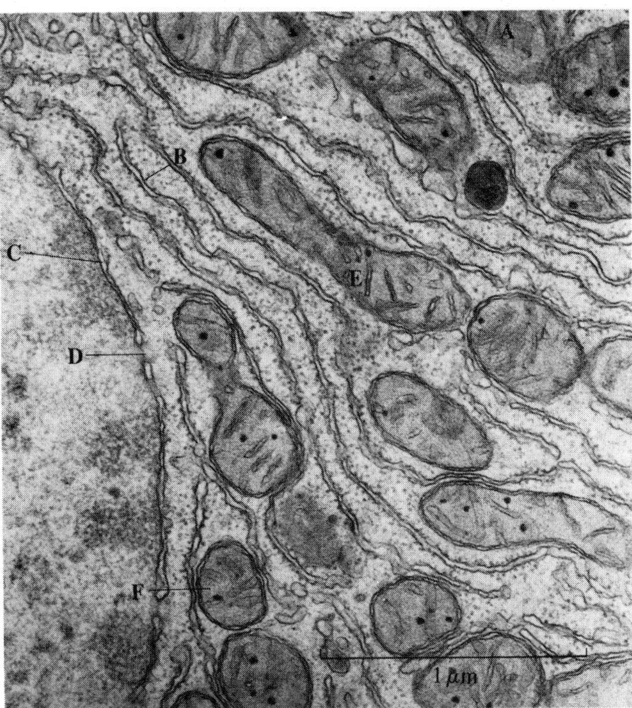

Figure 2.12 An electron micrograph of part of a liver cell. (Dr A.R. Lieberman, University College, London)

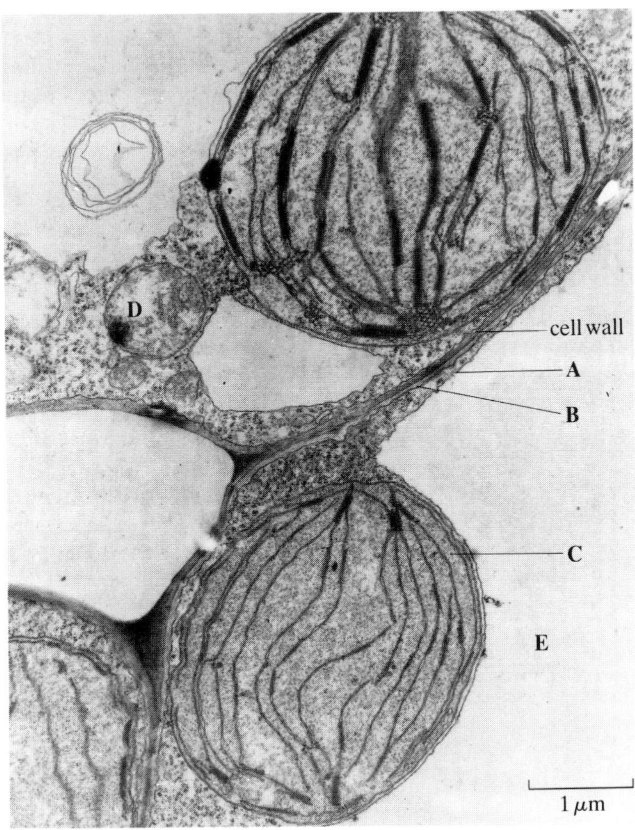

Figure 2.13 Electron micrograph of part of a plant tissue. (Dr Barrie Juniper, University of Oxford)

3 Tissues, Organs and Organisation

Background Summary

1 Cells are united to form **tissues**, and different tissues are united to form **organs**.

2 **Animal tissues** may be classified into epithelial, connective, skeletal, blood, nervous, muscular, and reproductive; **plant tissues** into meristematic, epidermal, parenchymatous, photosynthetic (chlorenchymatous), mechanical and vascular.

3 **Epithelial tissue** illustrates how a tissue is constructed. The different types of epithelium are: cuboidal, pavement (squamous), columnar, ciliated, glandular, stratified and transitional. Glandular epithelium may be invaginated and folded to form different kinds of **glands**.

4 **Connective tissue** consists of cells and fibres embedded in an organic ground substance (**matrix**). It is classified into areolar, collagen (white fibrous), elastic (yellow elastic) and adipose (fatty) tissue.

5 **Skeletal tissue** (cartilage and bone) is also composed of cells embedded in a matrix but in this case the matrix is harder.

6 **Blood** consists of red and white cells (corpuscles) and platelets suspended in a fluid (**plasma**).

7 **Muscular tissue** is divided into visceral (smooth), cardiac (heart) and skeletal (striated) muscle.

8 Most animal tissues have their counterparts in plants. Thus plant **epidermal tissue** is equivalent to epithelium, **mechanical tissues** (collenchyma and sclerenchyma) to skeletal tissue. Plant **vascular tissue** is equivalent to the circulatory system of animals. **Photosynthetic tissue** (also called **chlorenchyma**) is unique to plants.

9 The chief differences between animal and plant tissues (and between animals and plants generally) can be related to their different methods of nutrition.

10 Organs are generally interrelated to form **organ systems** in which several different organs co-operate and work together to fulfil a single overall function.

11 In organisms three different **levels of organisation** are recognised: the unicellular, tissue and organ levels. Most animals are organised on an organ basis; some animals (e.g. *Hydra* and *Obelia*) and most plants are constructed on the tissue level; and a wide range of organisms are unicellular.

12 **Unicellular organisms**, though consisting of only one cell, are by no means simple as is shown by an examination of *Paramecium*. *Paramecium* displays an astonishingly high degree of structural complexity.

13 Some organisms, e.g. sponges, can be regarded as **colonies of cells** showing little or no co-operation and integration between cells.

14 The **multicellular state** carries with it several advantages but it also carries certain disadvantages.

15 Organisms show various types of symmetry, the most common being **radial symmetry** and **bilateral symmetry**. Some organisms show varying degrees of asymmetry.

Investigation 3.1
Examination of some basic animal tissues

The purpose of this laboratory work is to introduce you to animal tissues which you will encounter repeatedly in later microscopic studies.

Animal tissues can be investigated by mounting a small piece of living tissue on a slide and then observing it unstained or stained; by making a permanent preparation of it; or by examining a prepared slide. In this investigation we shall use prepared slides.

Procedure

SIMPLE EPITHELIUM

1 Examine a whole mount of a piece of pavement (squamous) epithelium. Notice the shape of the cells and how they fit together.

2 Examine a section of thyroid gland and observe the cuboidal epithelial cells lining the follicles (*see* page 178). In common with other types of epithelium, the cells rest on a non-living basement membrane.

3 Examine a section of kidney and notice cuboidal cells lining the tubules and collecting ducts (*see* page 140).

4 Your slide of thyroid or kidney should also show pavement epithelial cells in section. These will be seen lining small blood vessels and, in the case of the kidney, Bowman's capsules. The cells are generally so flat that except in the region of the nuclei they appear as no more than a thin line (Figure 3.1).

5 Examine a section of mammalian small intestine (*see* page 82) and ob-

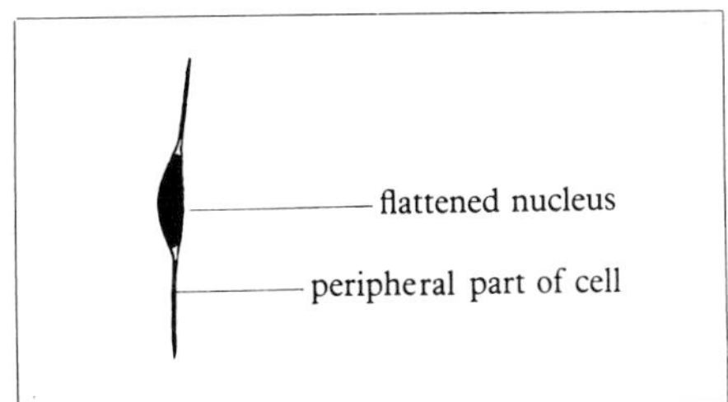

Figure 3.1 A typical pavement epithelial cell as it appears in section under the optical microscope.

serve the cells lining the villi under high power. Notice columnar epithelial cells interspersed with goblet mucus-secreting cells (*see* below).

6 Examine a representative columnar cell in detail, noting its shape and brush border on its free surface (Figure 3.2A). What does the brush border consist of?

7 Examine a section of gall bladder under high power. Notice the columnar epithelium lining the cavity. How does it differ from the columnar epithelium lining the small intestine?

8 Examine a section of trachea and observe its inner lining under high power. Notice cilia projecting from the free surface of columnar epithelial cells (Figure 3.2B). This is an example of ciliated epithelium. As in the small intestine, mucus-secreting goblet cells are also present (Figure 3.2C, D).

9 Examine a goblet cell in detail, if necessary using oil-immersion. The mucus droplets accumulate at the free end of the cell, giving rise to a clear cup-shaped region – which is why they are called goblet cells. The goblet appearance is accentuated by the fact that the end of the cell containing the mucus may be swollen, the base of the cell being constricted. The exact shape of the cells depends on their age and whether or not active secretion has taken place (Figure 3.2C, D).

10 If secretory cells are present in an epithelial tissue, the latter qualifies as glandular epithelium. Glandular epithelium is even better demonstrated by the large intestine (colon or rectum) where goblet cells greatly outnumber the supporting columnar epithelial cells. Examine a section of the wall of the colon or rectum, and see for yourself.

11 Glands are formed by invagination of glandular epithelium. Examine a crypt of Lieberkühn in the mammalian small intestine as a representative simple tubular gland (*see* page 82), and glands in the skin of the frog as representative simple saccular glands (Figure 3.3). What kind of epithelial cells line these glands and what are their functions?

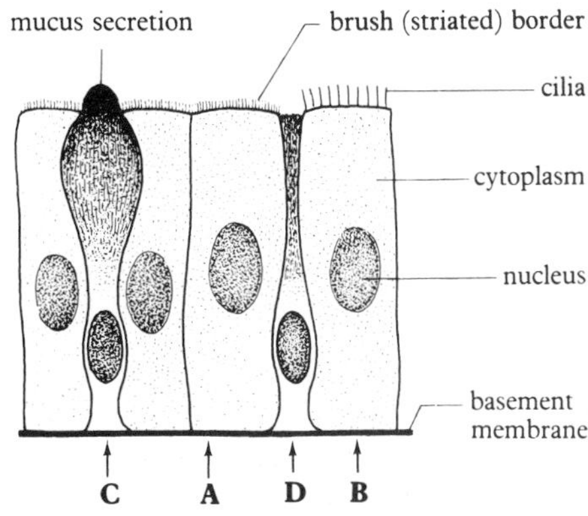

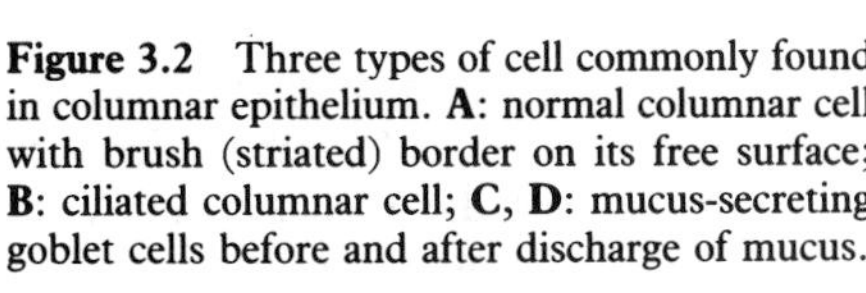

Figure 3.2 Three types of cell commonly found in columnar epithelium. **A**: normal columnar cell with brush (striated) border on its free surface; **B**: ciliated columnar cell; **C, D**: mucus-secreting goblet cells before and after discharge of mucus.

STRATIFIED EPITHELIUM

1 Examine a prepared vertical section of frog skin and observe the epidermis (Figure 3.3). This is composed of stratified epithelium. Notice the formative (Malpighian) layer at the base, above which are successive layers of increasingly flattened cells. You will find the nuclei easy to detect but the cell membranes are more difficult to see.

2 Examine a vertical section through the wall of the mammalian bladder. How does its inner lining differ from the epidermis of the frog? It is known as transitional epithelium: the cells are approximately the same size and can change their shape according to circumstances. Transitional epithelium lines tubes and cavities that are liable to stretching.

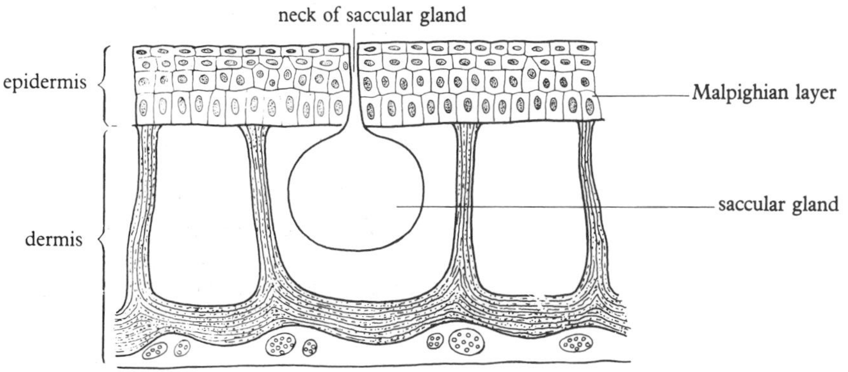

Figure 3.3 Vertical section of frog skin showing location of saccular gland and epidermis.

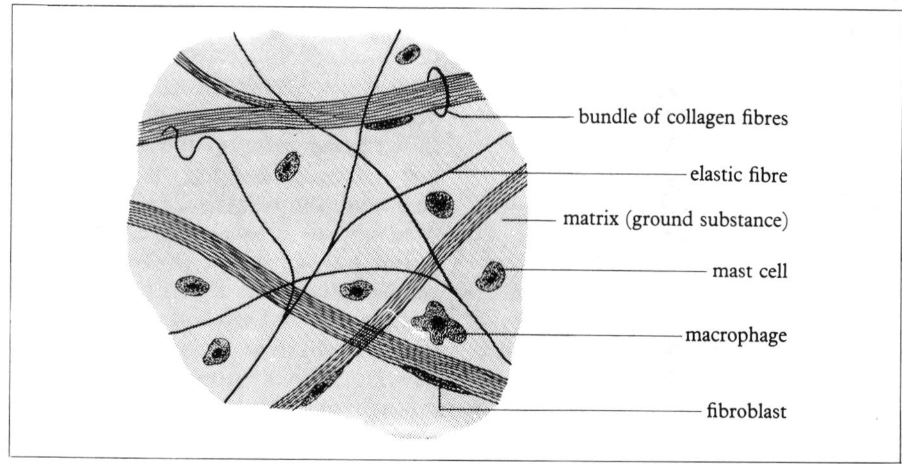

Figure 3.4 Areolar connective tissue as it appears in a typical microscopic preparation.

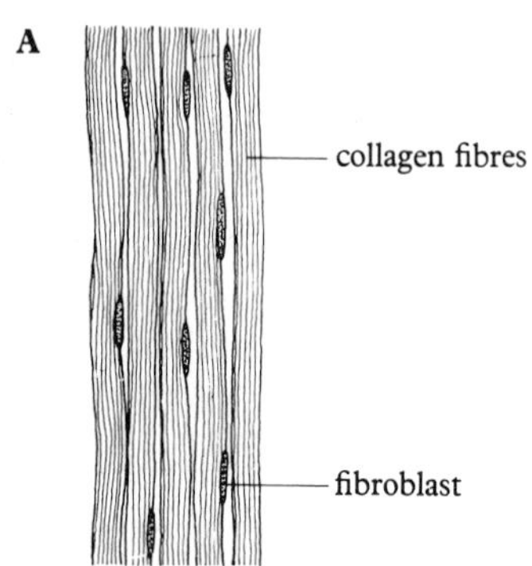

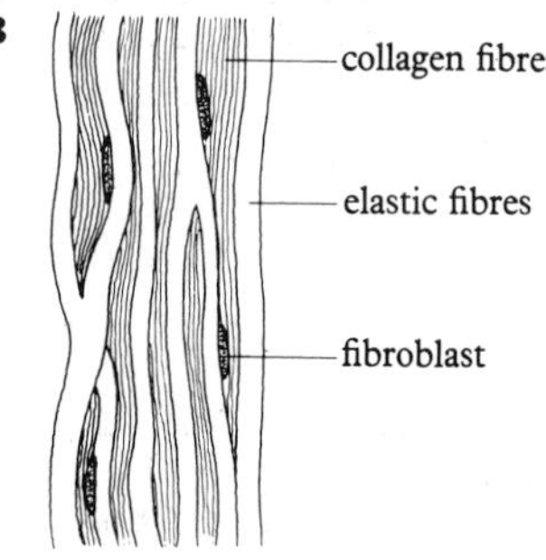

Figure 3.5 Longitudinal sections of **A** tendon, and **B** ligament.

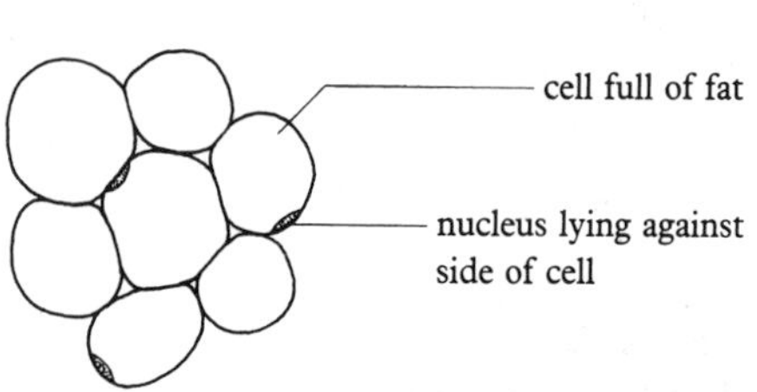

Figure 3.6 Fat cells as they appear in a typical section of adipose tissue.

CONNECTIVE TISSUE

1 Examine a slide of areolar tissue (Figure 3.4). Notice the matrix (ground substance), bundles of collagen (white) fibres, and irregular network of elastic (yellow) fibres. Try to distinguish fibroblasts (which produce the fibres), mast cells and macrophages. Spherical fat cells may also be seen.

2 Examine longitudinal sections of tendon and ligament (Figure 3.5). The tendon consists of densely packed parallel bundles of collagen fibres between which are rows of fibroblasts. The ligament is composed mainly of elastic fibres.

How does the composition of these two structures relate to their respective locations and functions in the body?

3 Examine a section of adipose tissue, e.g. in the dermis of mammalian skin, (*see* page 150). Notice clear fat-filled cells, little cytoplasm discernible, flattened nucleus lying against edge of cell (Figure 3.6).

CARTILAGE

1 Examine a section of hyaline cartilage, e.g. in the wall of the trachea, and note the chondroblasts in the matrix (Figure 3.7). The chondroblasts produce the matrix. Does the grouping of the cells give any clues as to how they have been formed?

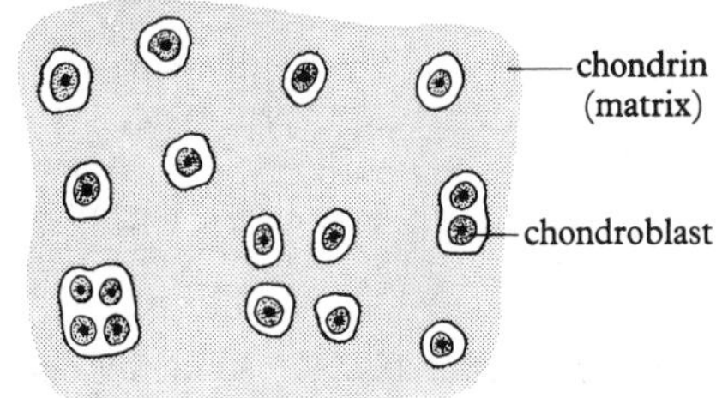

Figure 3.7 Hyaline cartilage as it appears in a typical microscopic section.

2 Examine sections of fibro-cartilage (cartilage containing collagen fibres) and elastic cartilage (cartilage containing elastic fibres). Compare these structurally and functionally with hyaline cartilage.

BONE

1 Examine a transverse section of compact bone and observe the Haversian pattern (Figure 3.8). In each unit (known as an osteon or Haversian system) observe the central Haversian canal surrounded by concentric lamellae. Also note lacunae and canaliculi which house the bone-forming osteoblasts and their fine processes.

2 To gain a three dimensional picture of bone examine longitudinal as well as transverse sections. Make a three dimensional diagram of a single osteon, based on your observations.

VISCERAL (UNSTRIATED, SMOOTH) MUSCLE

1 Examine a whole mount of smooth muscle from e.g. bladder. Observe under high power noting long thin muscle fibres. Each fibre is a single cell with an elongated nucleus (Figure 3.9).

2 Smooth muscle is present in the wall of various organs and structures which move or change shape. Look again at a section of small intestine and find smooth muscle in its wall. What is the function of the muscle in this situation?

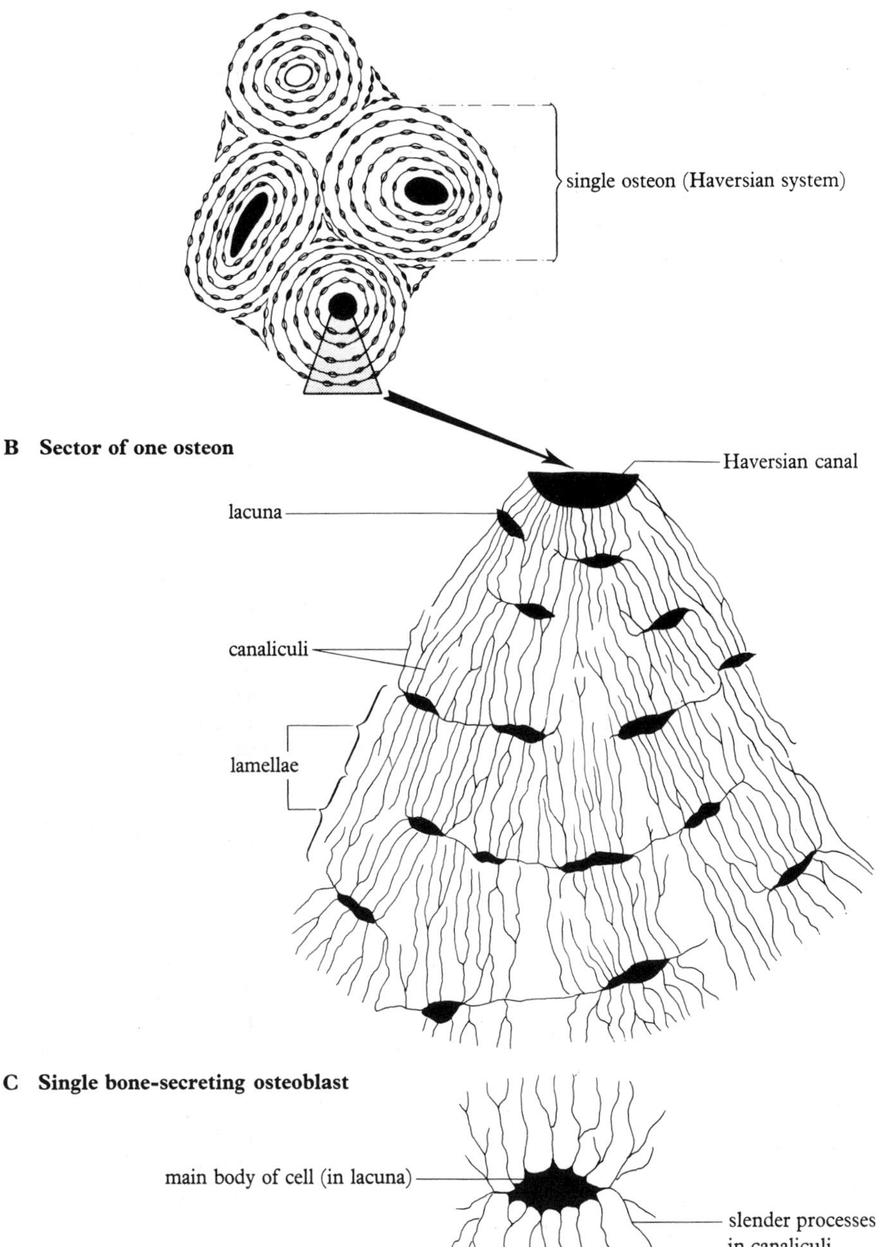

Figure 3.8 Structure of compact bone as seen in transverse sections.

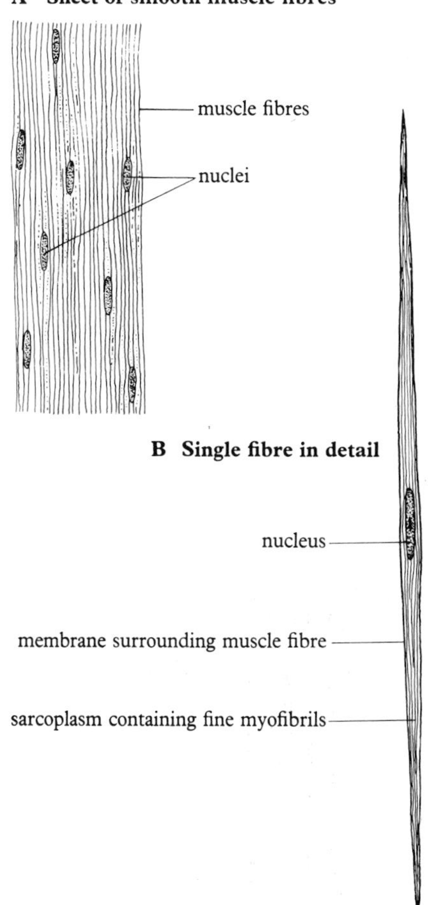

Figure 3.9 Structure of visceral (smooth) muscle as seen in longitudinal section.

For Consideration

(1) How is the structure of each of the animal tissues which you have investigated related to the functions which it performs?
(2) Do you think it is valid to classify epithelial tissue rigidly into columnar, ciliated and glandular? Base your answer on observations which you have made in this investigation.

Note: The microscopic structure of cardiac muscle is dealt with on page 111, and skeletal (striated) muscle on page 196. Nerve tissue is on page 171.

Requirements
Microscope (if possible with oil-immersion and phase contrast)

Prepared slides:
Section of thyroid gland
Section of kidney
Pavement (squamous) epithelium
VS frog skin (with epidermis intact)
TS mammalian small intestine
Section of gall bladder
TS trachea
TS colon or rectum
Areolar tissue
LS tendon
LS ligament
Adipose tissue
Hyaline cartilage
Fibro-cartilage
Elastic cartilage
TS and LS compact bone
Visceral (smooth) muscle

Investigation 3.2
Examination of some basic plant tissues

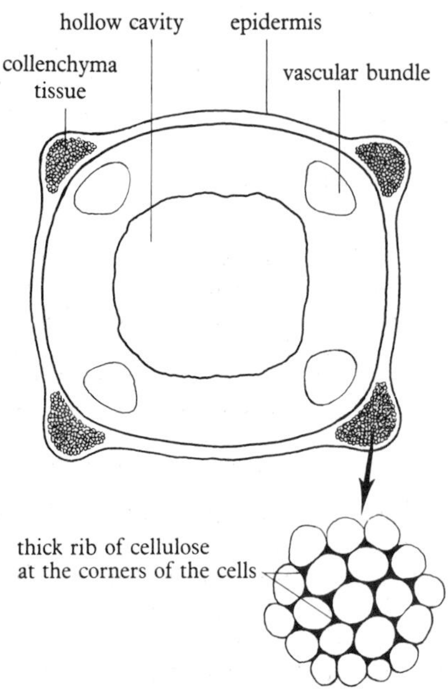

Figure 3.10 Collenchyma tissue in a transverse section of the stem of deadnettle.

Requirements
Microscope
Slides and coverslips
Razor blade
Petri dishes

Dilute glycerine (propan-1,2,3-triol)
Iodine solution
Schultz' solution
FABIL

Leaf and stem with easily removable epidermis
Onion
Tomato or grape
Potato tuber
Leafy moss plant
Deadnettle stem (fresh or preserved)
Macerated woody twig

Woody twig can be macerated as follows by Franklin's method:

Cut into strips approximately 1 × 10 mm and immerse in a mixture of equal parts of glacial ethanoic acid (acetic acid) and '20 volume' hydrogen peroxide. Either boil under reflux for an hour or maintain at 60 °C for 24 hours (times depend on material). Shake vigorously to disintegrate the tissues. Decant off the fluid and wash with several changes of water. Neutralise with a little ammonium hydroxide and store in 70 per cent ethanol.

The object of this investigation is to introduce you to plant tissues which you will encounter repeatedly in later microscopic studies.

Plant tissues can be investigated by mounting a piece of the living tissue or a thin section of it, on a slide and observing it stained or unstained; by making a permanent preparation of it; or by examining a prepared slide. In this investigation you will make your own temporary slides.

Procedure

EPIDERMIS

1 Strip off a piece of epidermis from the lower side of a leaf (e.g. privet, laurel, holly, iris, geranium) and mount it in glycerine or iodine solution. Examine the shape and form of the epidermal cells. In passing notice stomata (air pores) lined with guard cells. They are dealt with in detail on page 98.

2 Compare the leaf epidermis with the inner epidermis of an onion scale and a piece of epidermis removed from the side of a smooth stem.

3 How does plant epidermal tissue compare with the epithelia of animals? Make a table to illustrate the similarities and differences.

PARENCHYMA

1 Remove a small amount of pulpy tissue from just beneath the skin of a tomato or grape. Place it on a slide in a drop of water and spread it out with needles. Put on a coverslip and examine the parenchyma cells.

2 Irrigate with fresh Schultz' solution and notice cellulose walls, nuclei, and vacuoles. How would you describe the shape of the cells?

3 Compare with sections of potato tuber mounted in Schultz' solution. What does this tell us about the functions of parenchyma tissue?

PHOTOSYNTHETIC TISSUE

Mount a small leaf of moss in a drop of water on a slide and examine the chloroplast-packed photosynthetic tissue (chlorenchyma) making up the leaf's structure (*see* also page 99).

COLLENCHYMA

1 Examine transverse and longitudinal sections of collenchyma tissue. This is particularly abundant at the four thickened corners of deadnettle stem (Figure 3.10). If you cut your own sections mount them in FABIL. (Instructions for cutting sections are given on pages 98 and 126.) FABIL clears the material and stains the cellulose light purple.

2 From your examination of transverse and longitudinal sections, reconstruct the shape of an individual collenchyma cell.

3 Observe how the collenchyma cells fit together to form the tissue, and notice the thick cellulose ribs at the corners of the cells.

SCLERENCHYMA

1 Mount a very small amount of macerated woody tissue in FABIL solution and examine it under low and high powers. FABIL stains lignin (wood) red to brown. Look for slender sclerenchyma fibres with tapering ends. These give mechanical strength to plant stems.

2 In addition observe tubular lignified elements (vessels and tracheids). These contribute to mechanical strength and also conduct water and mineral salts from roots to leaves (vascular tissue).

If you want to make permanent preparations of any of these tissues, you should stain with safranin and light green (*see* page 380).

For Consideration

(1) Which tissue (if any) in animals is functionally equivalent to each of the plant tissues which you have investigated? What are the structural similarities between them?

(2) All the tissues you have examined in this investigation are found in the stem of a herbaceous plant such as sunflower or lupin. Whereabouts in the stem would you *expect* to find each tissue if it is to fulfil its function with maximum efficiency?

Investigation 3.3
Unicellular level of organisation: *Paramecium*

Paramecium is a single-celled organism which has to carry out within one cell all the functions that in a multicellular organism are performed by numerous different cells. Accordingly it possesses a high degree of internal organisation which will become apparent as you examine it.

Procedure

1 Mount a drop of water containing *Paramecium* on a slide; put on a coverslip and examine under the low power of the microscope. Can you make a rough estimate of *Paramecium's* speed of swimming? Can you see cilia beating? What happens when the organism hits an obstacle?

2 Slow the organisms by mixing a drop of *Paramecium* culture with an equal amount of methyl cellulose. Alternatively they can be trapped in the fine meshwork obtained by pulling lens paper to pieces. Watch the cilia beating in a wave-like (metachronal) rhythm.

3 Make a thorough examination of a single specimen under high power. Use Figure 3.11 to help you observe as much as possible of its internal organisation. In particular look for the contractile vacuoles. Can you see the contractile vacuoles discharging?

4 Irrigate your slide with either 1 per cent methyl green in ethanoic acid, or acetocarmine. Both fix the organisms and stain the nuclei, green in the case of the first stain, red in the second. The micronucleus will be difficult to see because it is usually covered by the macronucleus.

5 Feed *Paramecium* on yeast suspension stained with Congo Red.

On a slide make a vaseline enclosure just large enough to fit under a coverslip. Place within the enclosure one drop of *Paramecium* culture. Shake the stained yeast suspension. Dip a mounted needle into the suspension to a depth of about 1 cm and then stir the drop of culture on the slide with it. Put on a coverslip and press gently.

Watch the feeding process and note the contribution of the cilia. Stained yeast cells should be visible in food vacuoles within 5 minutes.

Trace the movement of the food vacuoles and notice any change in colour of the stain. Congo Red is red in

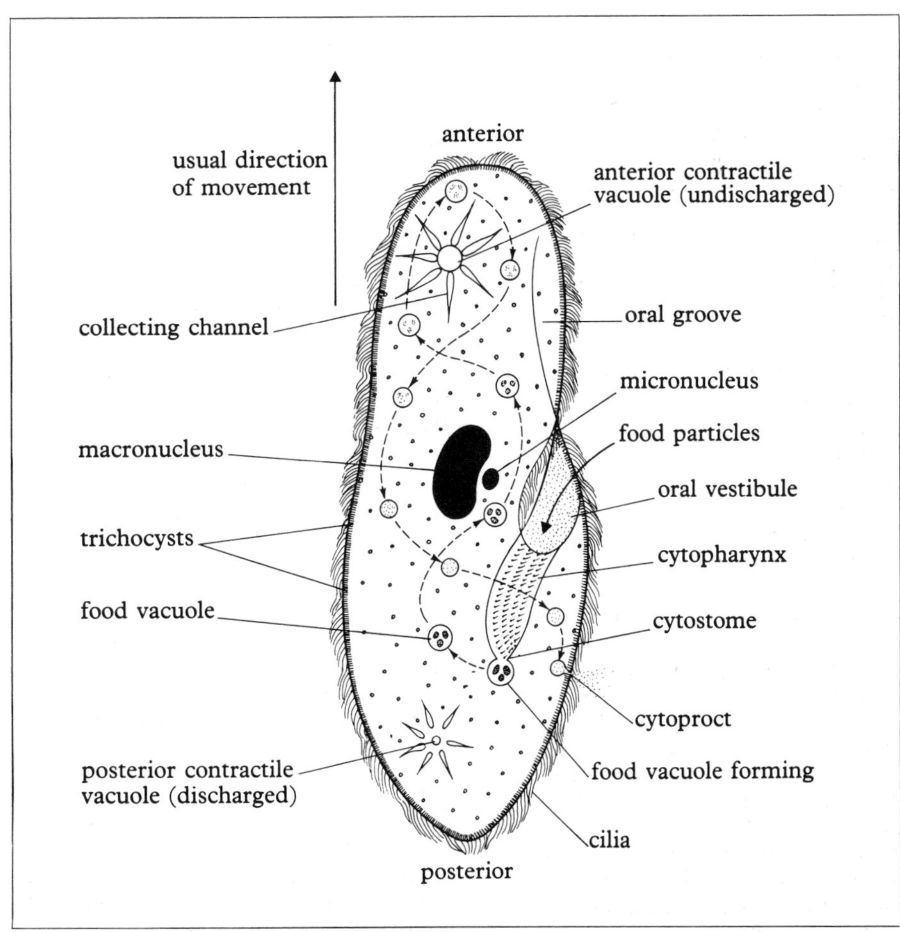

Figure 3.11 *Paramecium.* All the structures shown in this diagram can be detected under the light microscope if the correct procedures are adopted (*see* text).

Requirements
Microscope
Slides and coverslips
Lens paper
Filter paper
Mounted needle

Vaseline
Acidified ethanol for cleaning slides
Methyl cellulose
Methyl green (1 per cent solution using 1 per cent ethanoic acid)
Acetocarmine
Silver nitrate (2 per cent aqueous solution)
Canada balsam

Stained yeast suspension made by mixing the following thoroughly, then boiling the mixture gently for 10 minutes:
Yeast (fresh baker's yeast or dried yeast) (3 g)
Congo Red (30 mg)
Distilled water (10 cm^3)
Paramecium

an alkaline medium and blue in an acid medium: it changes from red to blue at between pH 5 and 3.

6 Beneath the sculptured pellicle the basal bodies of the cilia are interconnected by fine threads (kinetodesmata). Something of this sub-pellicular apparatus can be seen by staining with silver nitrate.

Clean a slide with acidified ethanol and dry it thoroughly. Spread a drop of the culture on the slide and dry it at room temperature. Cover the smear with a 2 per cent aqueous solution of silver nitrate and leave for 6–8 minutes. Then rinse the smear thoroughly with distilled water and place the slide on a white background in bright daylight. This reduces the silver nitrate with the result that the preparation turns brown to the naked eye. When reduction is complete dry the slide and then put on a drop of Canada balsam and a coverslip.

Find a specimen which has stained satisfactorily and view it under high power. The large dots along the lines of the kinetodesmata are basal bodies, the smaller dots in between are trichocysts. Small dots between the kinetodesmata are probably junctions in the pellicular lattice.

For Consideration

(1) What structures in the human are equivalent to those which you have observed in *Paramecium*?
(2) Does the behaviour of *Paramecium* show any obvious similarities to that of higher animals?

Reference: D. Patterson, 'The Behaviour of Cilia and Ciliates', *Journal of Biological Education*, Vol. 15, No. 3, 1981.

Investigation 3.4
Some other unicellular organisms

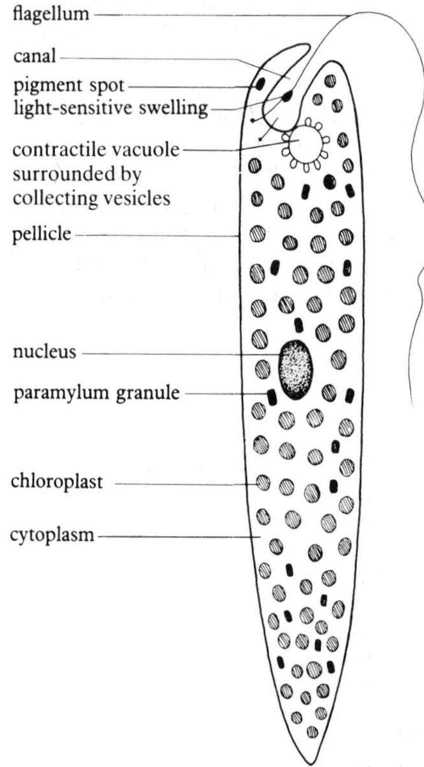

Figure 3.12 *Euglena.* The arrangement of the chloroplasts varies between different species.

Paramecium, which you examined in the last investigation, has many unicellular relatives which occur in freshwater ponds and ditches. In this investigation we shall look at some of them.

Procedure

EUGLENA

1 Examine the unicellular flagellate *Euglena* by pipetting a very small drop of culture onto a slide and covering it with a coverslip. Watch the organism's method of locomotion and record your observations.

2 Observe a stationary specimen under high power. How many of the structures shown in Figure 3.12 can you see? Be honest! Try to make out the pigment spot, flagellum and chloroplasts. How would you account for the difference between *your* observations and the diagram in Figure 3.12?

3 How do you think *Euglena* feeds? In some older texts the canal is referred to as a gullet. However, there is no evidence that *Euglena* takes in particulate food either through the canal or any part of the body surface. But in the absence of light *Euglena* feeds saprotrophically on *soluble* organic food which it absorbs through the pellicle.

4 Observe *Euglena* swimming. It swims towards light. The mechanism guiding it towards light depends on the opaque pigment spot working in conjunction with the light-sensitive swelling at the base of the flagellum. From your observations on the way *Euglena* swims, can you offer an explanation as to how the light-directing mechanism works?

5 With filter paper carefully withdraw water from beneath the coverslip. Unable to swim freely by flagellate locomotion, the organisms may resort to a worm-like wriggling movement (euglenoid locomotion). What sort of structures might be responsible for this type of movement?

6 If you want to examine the flagellum in detail, irrigate with Noland's solution. This fixes flagella and stains them blue.

CHLAMYDOMONAS

1 Examine *Chlamydomonas*, another unicellular flagellate, under high power and observe two flagella, cellulose cell wall, two small contractile vacuoles, cytoplasm, cup-shaped chloroplast, pigment spot, pyrenoid (Figure 3.13).

2 More detailed information may be obtained by staining: irrigate with acetocarmine to see the nucleus, with Noland's solution to see the flagella, and with iodine solution to see starch grains close to the pyrenoid.

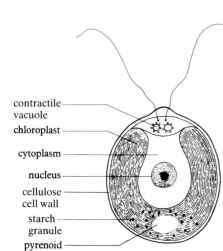

Figure 3.13 *Chlamydomonas.*

VORTICELLA

1 Examine the stalked ciliate *Vorticella* under both low and high powers (Figure 3.14). This unicellular organism is a common sessile inhabitant of dirty ditches, where it is found attached to weeds and stones; it is also commonly found attached to the head region of the fresh water shrimp *Gammarus*, and other animals. Watch the stalk contract and coil up when the organism is disturbed.

2 Examine a single specimen in detail. Observe the cilia whose beating draws small food particles into the oral groove, elongated macronucleus; undulating membrane of fused cilia in the cytopharynx; food vacuoles, contractile stalk.

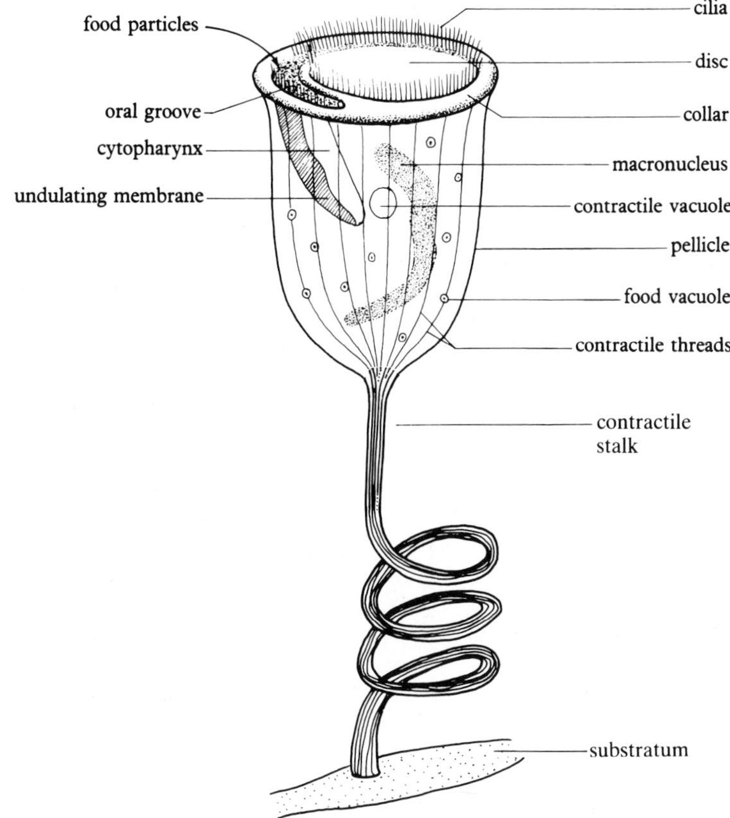

Figure 3.14 *Vorticella.*

AMOEBA

1 You will be provided with an *Amoeba* in a drop of water on a slide under a coverslip supported by a strip of paper. Examine under low and high powers (Figure 3.15). Notice how this unicellular organism changes in shape as it moves. Notice flowing of the granular endoplasm, the clear ectoplasm, pseudopodia, food vacuoles (how are they formed?). If you are lucky you may see the contractile vacuole collapsing periodically.

2 Irrigate with acetocarmine which fixes the *Amoeba* and stains the nucleus.

A VARIETY OF UNICELLULAR ORGANISMS

Examine a drop of water from a pond or ditch – the dirtier the better. Look out for the organisms which you have already examined in Investigations 3.3. and 3.4. In addition you may see others. Decide whether each one is flagellated, ciliated or amoeboid and, if possible, identify it (see below).

Small multicellular organisms may also be seen, e.g. rotifers, tardigrades, nematodes and crustaceans.

For consideration

The organisms which you have been examining are small and vulnerable. What hazards do they face in their natural environment, and how do you think they manage to survive?

References: J. Clegg, *The Observers' Book of Pond Life*, Warne, 4th ed, 1980; H. Mellanby, *Animal Life in Fresh Water* Methuen, 6th ed, 1975. Both these books contain useful accounts, with means of identification, of fresh water unicellular organisms.

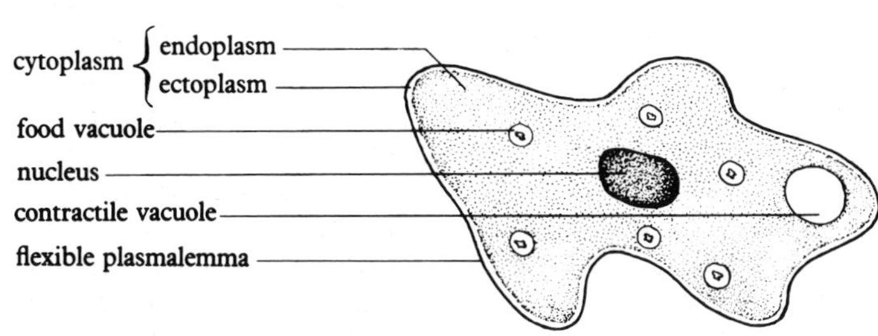

Figure 3.15 *Amoeba.*

Requirements
Microscope
Slides and coverslips
Filter paper

Noland's solution
Iodine solution
Acetocarmine

Euglena
Chlamydomonas
Vorticella
Amoeba

Investigation 3.5
Tissue level of organisation: *Hydra*

Hydra shows some degree of cellular specialisation. Seven different types of cell are structurally integrated into two distinct tissue layers, the ectoderm and endoderm, and the activities of some of the cells are coordinated by a nerve net. However, behaviour tends to be very simple and slow and, apart from the ovary and testis, there are no organs.

Procedure

1 Examine living green *Hydra* either in a watchglass under a binocular microscope, or the low power of a monocular microscope.

Use Figure 3.16 to help you identify mouth, tentacles, foot, body wall surrounding enteron. The ectoderm is colourless; the endoderm is green because it contrains mutualistic green protists (zoochlorella). Depending on the time of year, you may see buds developing into new individuals; or, alternatively, testes near the tentacles and/or ovaries towards the foot.

2 Separate the cells of a specimen whose intercellular material has been partially dissolved in boric acid, by teasing it into pieces with fine needles. Put on a coverslip and gently press it so as to cause further separation of the cells. Examine under high power. How many types of cell can you discern? In particular look out for large musculo-epithelial cells.

3 Mount a live specimen in water under a coverslip and irrigate with 1 per cent ethanoic acid. This should cause discharge of some of the nematoblasts which can then be examined under high power. Irrigating with methylene blue may help you to see them more clearly.

4 Examine a prepared transverse or longitudinal section of *Hydra*. Observe the different cells of the ectoderm and endoderm under high power and notice

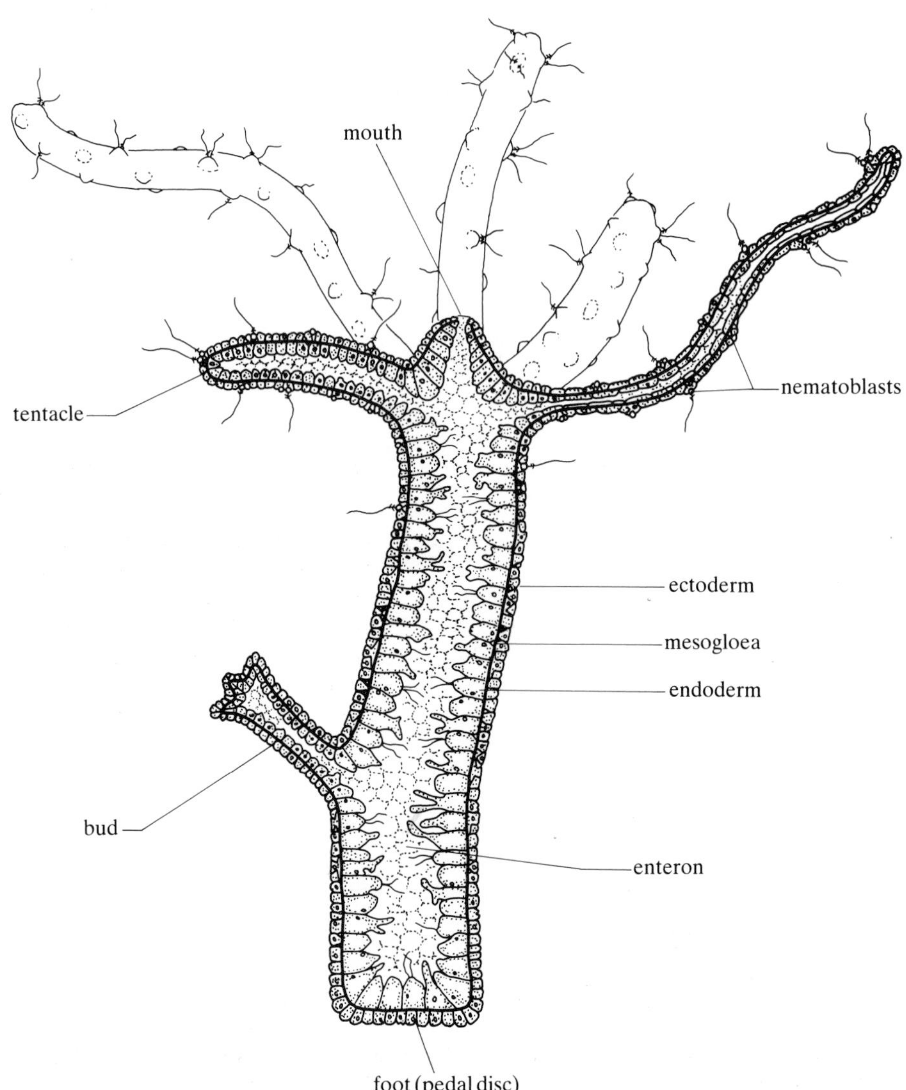

Figure 3.16 General structure of *Hydra* as seen in sectional side view.

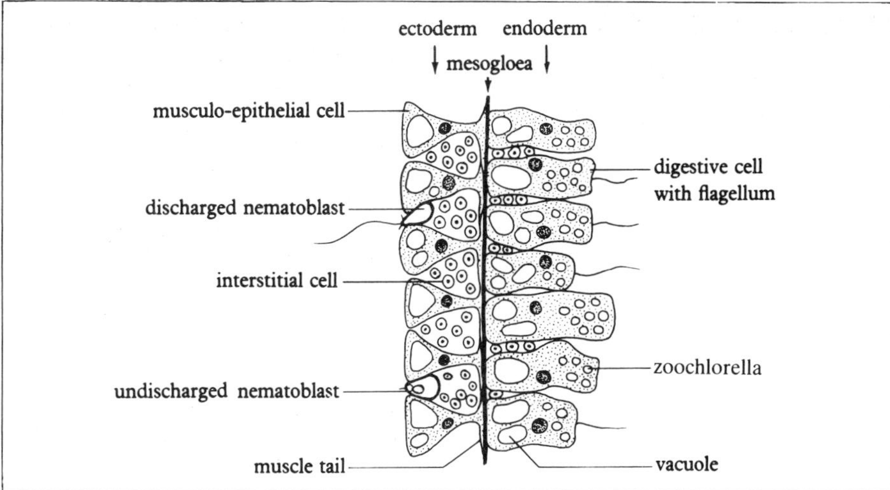

Figure 3.17 Body wall of the green hydra *Chlorohydra viridissima* as it appears in a typical longitudinal section.

Requirements
Microscope
Binocular microscope
Watchglass
Slides and coverslips
Mounted needles

Ethanoic acid (1 per cent)
Methylene blue

Hydra macerated with boric acid
TS or LS *Hydra*
Live green hydra
Daphnia

the non-cellular mesogloea in between (Figure 3.17). Can you make out the direction in which the muscle tails of the musculo-epithelial cells are orientated in the ectoderm and endoderm?

5 Investigate the feeding behaviour of a live specimen of *Hydra* by feeding it with live water fleas (e.g. *Daphnia*). With your knowledge of *Hydra*'s structure in mind, try to interpret the sequence of events that takes place.

For Consideration

(1) In what respects would you consider *Hydra* to be more advanced than *Paramecium* and less advanced then the human? In what sense is the word advanced being used in this context?
(2) *Hydra* is described as radially symmetrical. What does this term mean?

Questions and Problems

1 (a) Figure 3.18 shows various planes in which a tubular structure, such as a blood vessel, with a wall of uniform thickness might be cut in a microscopic section. In each case the plane of the section depends on the orientation of the structure relative to the cutting blade. Draw simple sketches showing the appearance of the tube when sectioned in each of the planes a–j.
(b) Imagine that the structure instead of being tubular is a hollow ovoid (Figure 3.19). What will be its appearance when sectioned in planes k–o?

2 (a) What criticisms would you level against classifying epithelial tissue into cuboidal, pavement, columnar, ciliated, glandular and stratified epithelia? Can you suggest any alternative classifications?
(b) In some classifications of tissues, cartilage, bone and blood are included with connective tissue; and in plants parenchyma is included with mechanical tissue. Do you think this is justified?
(c) What general principle emerges from your answers to questions (a) and (b)?

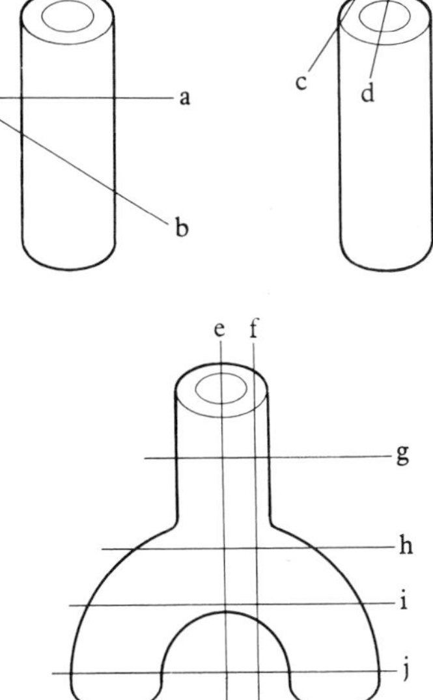

Figure 3.18 Various planes in which a tubular structure might be cut.

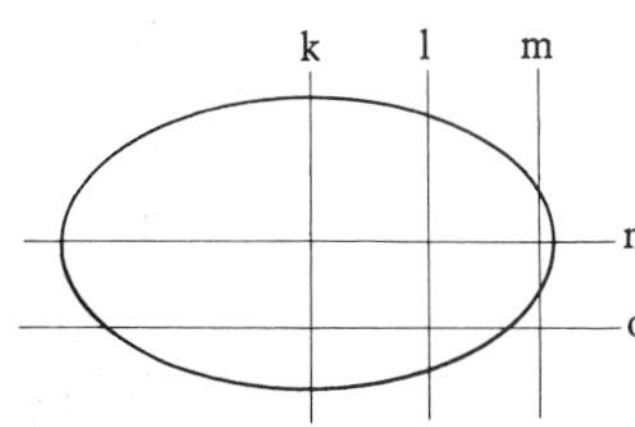

Figure 3.19 Various planes in which a hollow ovoid structure might be cut.

A

B

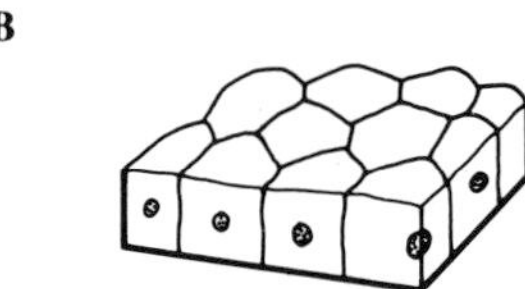

C

D

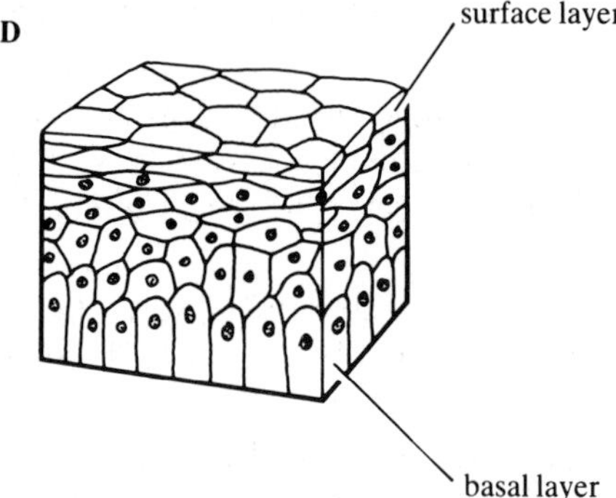

Figure 3.20 Four different types of epithelial tissue.

3 Figure 3.20 shows four different types of epithelial tissue.
(a) (i) Name the four types of epithelial tissue.
(ii) Give a location in the mammalian body where each of these epithelial tissues occurs.
(b) Describe two ways in which tissue C may be modified, and give one function of each modification.
(c) Briefly explain the functions of the basal and surface layers of tissue D.
(*UL modified*)

4 Figure 3.21 is a transverse section of hard (compact) bone.
(a) Name the parts labelled A–D.
(b) Name one function in living bone of each of the parts labelled B, C, D and E.
(c) Draw structure A as it would appear in a *longitudinal* section.
(d) What would have had to be done to the bone before the section could be cut? Explain your answer. (*UL modified*)

5 Compact bone tissue of mammals and sclerenchyma tissue of plants have a number of features in common. What are these features? Suggest a functional explanation for the similarities.

6 By means of a table compare a typical animal, as exemplified by a mammal, with a typical plant, as exemplified by an angiosperm (flowering plant).

7 The chief differences between animals and plants can be related to their different methods of nutrition. Explain.

8 Discuss the evidence for considering a sponge to be (a) a colony of single cells, and (b) a simple multicellular animal.

9 Which structures in (a) *Hydra* and (b) *Paramecium* are functionally equivalent to the following structures in the human:
(i) skin (ii) mouth (iii) anus (iv) kidney (v) limbs.

10 Make a list of the advantages and disadvantages of being (a) unicellular and (b) multicellular.

11 (a) With the aid of simple diagrams, explain the difference between radial and bilateral symmetry.
(b) Give an example of an organism which is:
(i) radially symmetrical externally and internally;
(ii) radially symmetrical externally but slightly bilaterally symmetrical internally;
(iii) bilaterally symmetrical externally and internally;
(iv) bilaterally symmetrical externally but slightly asymmetrical internally;
(v) asymmetrical externally and internally.

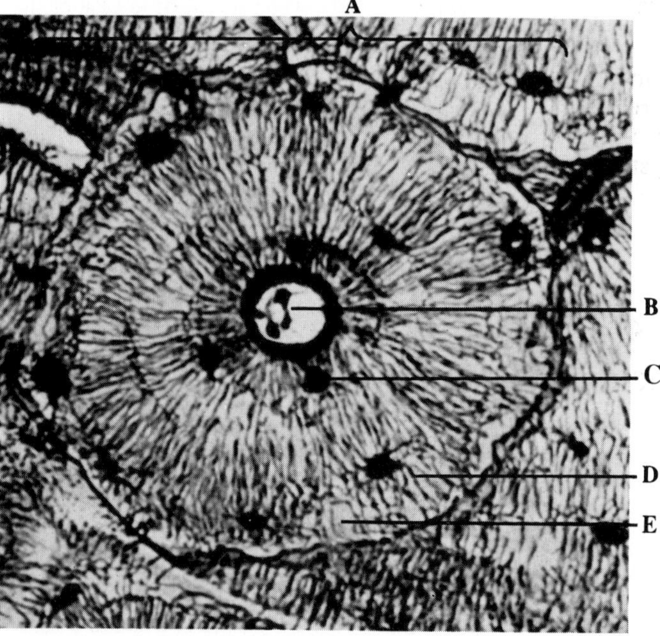

Figure 3.21 Transverse section of hard (compact) bone. (*Gene Cox*)

4 Movement in and out of cells

Background Summary

1 Materials move in and out of cells by diffusion, osmosis, active transport, phagocytosis, and pinocytosis.

2 **Diffusion** is the net movement of molecules (or ions) from a region of high concentration to a region of lower concentration.

3 Diffusion satisfies the metabolic needs of small organisms whose **surface-volume ratio** is large and where the diffusion distance is small. Larger organisms, whose surface-volume ratio is small, and where the diffusion distance is great, have special ways of acquiring essential materials and transporting them within the body.

4 In **facilitated diffusion** protein carriers in the cell membrane help to move the molecules or ions down concentration gradients.

5 **Osmosis** is the one-way net diffusion of solvent (particularly water) across a selectively permeable membrane. It is particularly important to cells because the cell membrane is selectively permeable.

6 The osmotic movement of water can be expressed in terms of **osmotic pressure**. This is the tendency of a solution to take in water across a selectively permeable membrane.

7 An animal cell immersed in water or a **hypotonic solution** swells and may burst unless it has a means of disposing of the water that enters by osmosis. In a **hypertonic solution** the cell shrinks and the cell membrane crinkles. A plant cell immersed in water or a hypotonic solution becomes **turgid**. If immersed in a hypertonic solution the protoplast shrinks and **plasmolysis** occurs. (The protoplast membranes are selectively permeable but the cellulose wall is fully permeable.)

8 As a way of expressing water movement, osmotic pressure is increasingly being replaced by the **water potential** concept. For practical purposes water potential may be regarded as the capacity of a system to give out water, and it is given a negative sign. The component of the water potential which is caused by the presence of solutes is called the **osmotic potential**. The symbol for water potential and related energy potentials is ψ, the Greek letter psi.

9 The water relations of a plant cell can be summarised as follows:

$$\psi_{cell} = \psi_s + \psi_p$$

where ψ_{cell} is the water potential of the cell (usually negative), ψ_s is the osmotic potential of the sap (negative), and ψ_p is the **pressure potential** – that is the inward pressure exerted by the cell wall against the protoplast (zero or positive).

10 The water potential of a plant tissue can be determined by balancing it with an external solution which produces no mass or volume change in the tissue. The osmotic potential can be determined by balancing it with an external solution that produces incipient plasmolysis.

11 **Active transport**, the movement of molecules or ions against a concentration gradient, is an energy-requiring process involving the use of protein carriers in the cell membrane.

12 Certain substances can be taken into cells by invagination of the cell membrane to form vesicles. The general term for this is **endocytosis**.

13 **Phagocytosis** is the intake of large particles by invagination of the plasma membrane. The contents are then digested and absorbed.

14 **Pinocytosis** also involves invagination of the plasma membrane, but on a smaller scale than phagocytosis. It provides a means by which liquids and macromolecules may be brought into cells.

15 Substances such as enzymes, hormones, antibodies and cell wall precursors can be shed from cells by vesicles fusing with the cell membrane and emptying their contents to the exterior. The general term for this is **exocytosis**. The vesicles are often derived from the Golgi body.

Investigation 4.1
Cells and osmosis

The cell membrane is selectively permeable and if a cell is placed in a solution whose solute concentration differs from that of the cell's contents, water either enters or leaves the cell. It enters if the external solution is hypotonic, it leaves if the external solution is hypertonic. In plant cells the cellulose wall is fully permeable to both water and solutes.

Procedure

RED BLOOD CELLS

1 Place a drop of blood on each of four slides, labelled A–D. To A add a drop of distilled water; to B, C and D add a drop of 0.75 per cent, 1.0 per cent and 3.0 per cent salt solution.

2 Observe the red blood cells under high power for some period of time. Watch what happens and interpret your observations as fully as you can.

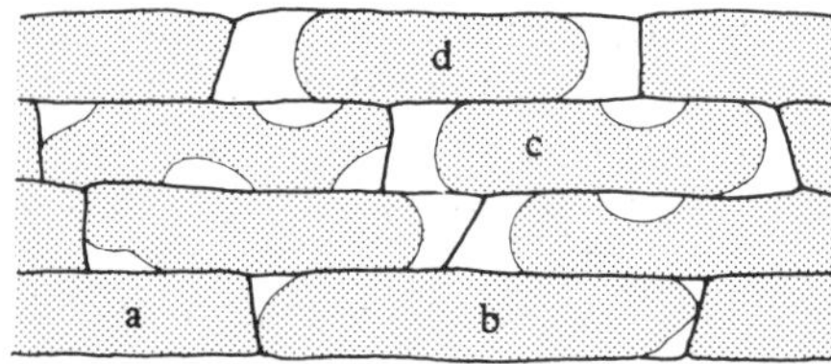

Figure 4.1 Appearance of onion epidermal cells in a hypertonic external solution. Cell **a** is unplasmolysed; **b**, **c**, and **d** show progressive plasmolysis with the protoplast shrinking away from the cell wall.

Requirements
Slides and coverslips ×4
Pipettes ×5
Filter paper

Distilled water
Sodium chloride solutions (0.75, 1.0 and 3 per cent)
Sucrose solution (1.0 mol dm^{-3})
Defibrinated blood
Onion bulb or rhubarb stem
Cladophora

Note: Blood is usually available from the local abattoir.

PLANT EPIDERMIS

1 Strip off two small pieces of epidermis from a plant stem or leaf. (The epidermis from the inner surface of an onion scale, or the red pigmented epidermis from a rhubarb stem are recommended).

2 Mount one piece in water and the other in a strong solution of sucrose (1.0 mol dm^{-3}).

3 Compare the two slides at intervals and interpret your observations. Look for plasmolysis and compare with Figure 4.1. If you are using rhubarb epidermis can you say where the red pigment is located within the cell?

4 Irrigate the piece of epidermis, which you mounted in sucrose, with distilled water. Use filter paper to draw the water beneath the coverslip, and look down the microscope as you do so. Observe what happens and interpret your result.

FILAMENTOUS ALGA

1 Mount one small piece of the filamentous alga *Cladophora* in water, and a second piece in a strong sucrose solution (1.0 mol dm^{-3}).

2 Compare the two slides and interpret your observations. Do you find it easier to observe plasmolysis in the algal cells than in the plant epidermal cells, and if so why?

3 Mount one piece of *Cladophora* in a 1.0 mol dm^{-3} solution of sucrose, and a second piece in a 1.0 mol dm^{-3} solution of sodium chloride. Compare how long it takes for plasmolysis to occur in each solution. Which one works faster? Can you suggest a reason? What does this tell us about the nature of osmosis? Why is it better to do this experiment using *Cladophora* rather than plant epidermal tissue?

For Consideration

What is the relevance of your observations on the osmotic properties of cells to the organisms concerned?

Investigation 4.2
Osmotic relations of red blood cells

Like any other cell, red blood cells are enclosed in a selectively permeable membrane. If a red blood cell is placed in a hypotonic solution, water enters by osmosis and the cell swells. In extreme cases, i.e. when the external solution is markedly hypotonic to the cell's contents, the blood cell bursts and its haemoglobin is released (haemolysis). The purpose of this investigation is to examine the effect of hypotonic solutions on mammalian red blood cells and to investigate the mechanical properties of the cell membrane.

Procedure

1 Place 10 cm^3 of sodium chloride (NaCl) solution into a series of five test tubes, one tube each of the following strengths: 0.1, 0.3, 0.5, 0.7, 0.9 per cent.

The 0.9 per cent NaCl has about the same concentration as mammalian blood; the other solutions are hypotonic.

2 To each test tube add 0.1 cm^3 of defibrinated blood with a micropipette. It is most important to stir the blood thoroughly before pipetting it so as to ensure uniform distribution of the cells. Leave the tubes standing for a while and examine them at intervals.

3 In some of the test tubes the contents will be cloudy: what does this indicate? In others the contents will be clear: what does this indicate?

In certain of the test tubes a clearing may develop in a restricted region at the top of the tube if you leave it long enough. What is this caused by? What is the colour of this clear liquid? Explain fully.

Plainly, haemolysis has occurred to a greater or lesser extent in some of the tubes. From looking at the tubes what can you conclude about the extent of haemolysis in each case?

4 Using a haemocytometer, estimate the number of red blood cells per mm^3 in each tube. Start with a sample of blood from the tube containing 0.9 per cent NaCl, which you know has not undergone haemolysis, and then go on to the other tubes.

The technique for counting red blood cells is described on page 106. Mix the blood thoroughly before you suck it into the haemocytometer pipette. There is no need to dilute the blood any more than it has been diluted already.

If you have not got a haemocytometer, a rough estimate of the red cell concentration can be obtained by pipetting a small volume of blood onto a slide, covering it with a coverslip and counting the number of cells visible in the high-power field of view.

5 Centrifuge the remaining blood in the tubes until the contents are clear. (About three minutes should be sufficient.) In each case examine the amount of sediment at the bottom of the tube, and the colour of the supernatant. Conclusions?

Results

Assuming that no haemolysis has occurred in the 0.9 per cent NaCl and that the blood in this tube gives a normal blood count, calculate the number of haemolysed cells per mm^3 of blood in the other tubes. In each case this figure can be obtained by subtracting the number of intact cells present in the sample from the number in the 0.9 per cent NaCl.

Now calculate the percentage of cells haemolysed in each tube:

$$\text{percentage haemolysis} = \frac{a}{b} \times 100$$

a = no. of haemolysed cells per mm^3
b = no. of intact cells per mm^3 in 0.9 per cent NaCl

Plot percentage haemolysis (vertical axis) against the strength of the NaCl solutions.

For Consideration

(1) Can you account for the shape of your curve?
(2) Why don't all the red blood cells haemolyse at the same NaCl concentration?
(3) Do you think the results of this experiment might have any medical significance?
(4) What light does this investigation throw on the properties of blood plasma?
(5) How are the properties mentioned in answer to (4) maintained in the human body?

Requirements
Microscope
Haemocytometer with accessories
(Slide and coverslip if no haemocytometer is available)
Test tubes (to fit centrifuge) ×10
Test-tube rack
Pipette (for 1.0 cm^3 of blood)
Micropipette (for 0.1 cm^3 of blood)
Rod for stirring blood
Labels or wax pencil
Centrifuge

Sodium chloride solutions (0.1, 0.3, 0.5, 0.7, 0.9 per cent, each student requires 10 cm^3 of each solution)
Defibrinated blood (1.0 cm^3 per student)

Note: Blood is usually available from the local abattoir.

Investigation 4.3
Water potential of potato tuber cells: the weighing method

If a plant cell is in equilibrium with an external solution of such a concentration that there is no net loss or gain of water, the water potential of the external solution will be equal to the water potential of the cell.

Use of this fact can be made in estimating the water potential of a plant tissue. Samples of tissue are immersed in a range of external solutions of different strengths. The solution that induces neither an increase nor a decrease in the volume or mass of the tissue has the same water potential as that of the cells in the tissue.

The cells to be investigated in this experiment are those of the potato tuber. Changes in mass will be used as an indication of whether the cells are taking up or losing water.

Procedure

1 Label six specimen tubes: distilled water, 0.1, 0.2, 0.3, 0.4, 0.5 mol dm^{-3}.

Place approximately one-third of a tube of distilled water in the first, and an equal volume of each of a series of sucrose solutions of different strengths (molarities) in the remainder. Each tube should be firmly stoppered.

2 Using a cork borer and razor blade, prepare six solid cylinders of potato. Each cylinder should be approximately 10 mm diameter and 12 mm long. Slice up each cylinder into six discs of approximately equal thickness. Place each group of discs on a separate piece of filter paper.

3 Weigh each group of discs. (In each case weigh them on the piece of filter paper, then weigh the filter paper alone, and subtract the one from the other to get the mass of the discs). Record the mass of each group.

4 Put one group of discs into each of the labelled tubes and as you add each group, record its mass. Stopper the latter firmly and leave for not less than 24 hours.

Requirements
Specimen tubes with stoppers ×6
Cork borer of 1 cm diameter
Labels or wax pencil
Razor blade
Filter papers
Balance (preferably rapid-weighing)

Distilled water
Sucrose solutions (0.1, 0.2, 0.3, 0.4, 0.5 mol dm^{-3})

Potato tuber

5 After about 24 hours remove the discs from each tube. Remove any surplus fluid from them quickly and gently with filter paper, using a standardised procedure for all of them. Then re-weigh them. Record the new mass of each group of discs.
6 Graph your results by plotting the percentage change in mass (change in mass multiplied by 100 divided by original mass) against the molarity of the sucrose solutions. The latter, being the independent variable, should be on the horizontal axis; the former on the vertical axis.
7 Calculate the water potential of the potato cells as follows. Find the point on your graph corresponding to a percentage mass change of zero. The molarity of sucrose corresponding to this zero mass change can now be read from the horizontal axis. From Table 4.1 find the water potential of a sucrose solution of that molarity. That is the water potential of your sample of potato cells. Express your result in kPa.

Molarity (mol dm^{-3})	**Osmotic potential** (kPa)
0.05	−130
0.10	−260
0.15	−410
0.20	−540
0.25	−680
0.30	−860
0.35	−970
0.40	−1120
0.45	−1280
0.50	−1450
0.55	−1620
0.60	−1800
0.65	−1980
0.70	−2180
0.75	−2370
0.80	−2580
0.85	−2790
0.90	−3000
0.95	−3250
1.00	−3500

Table 4.1 Relationship between molarity and osmotic potential of sucrose solutions.

For Consideration

(1) Criticise this method of finding the water potential of plant cells. How might it be improved?
(2) What was the reason for dividing each cylinder into six discs, and why was it necessary to standardise the procedure for drying the discs?
(3) With what kind of plant tissue might it be possible to use a change in volume rather than mass for estimating the water potential?
(4) How does the value of the water potential differ from the osmotic potential of the solution in the vacuole?
(5) In constructing your graph did you join up the points with straight lines or a smooth curve? Justify whichever technique you used.

Investigation 4.4
Water potential of potato tuber cells: the density method

Suppose we take a drop of coloured sucrose solution and transfer it to a sucrose solution of equal strength in which plant tissue has been suspended for some time. What will happen to the drop? It depends on the density of the drop compared with that of the surrounding solution. The drop will rise if the tissue gained water from the solution, making the solution more dense. The drop will fall if the solution gained water from the tissue, making the solution less dense. If the drop neither rises nor falls, its water potential is equivalent to that of the solution and the tissue suspended in it.

The cells to be investigated in this experiment are those of the potato tuber, but most plant tissues are suitable. The roots of salt marsh species (halophytes) are particularly interesting since they may have lower water potentials than the tissues of mesophytes. Why?

Procedure

1 Label seven test tubes: 0.10, 0.15, 0.20, 0.25, 0.30, 0.50, 1.00 mol dm^{-3}. Using a separate graduated syringe in each case, place 5 cm^3 of the appropriate sucrose solution in each tube.
2 From the test tube containing 0.1 mol dm^{-3} sucrose, pipette 3 cm^3 into another test tube and label it, leaving 2 cm^3 in the original tube. Place the tubes in the test tube rack so that the 3 cm^3 tube is directly *behind* the 2 cm^3 tube. Repeat the procedure with all the other sucrose solutions in turn, using a different pipette in each case. You will now have two rows of seven labelled

test tubes, with those containing 2 cm^3 of sucrose solution at the front.

3 Place *one drop* of methylene blue into each of the *front* test-tubes. This will colour the solution but will not significantly affect its water potential.

4 Using a cork borer and a razor blade, prepare a solid cylinder of potato tuber about 7 mm in diameter and 60 mm long. Slice the cylinder into thirty discs of approximately equal (2 mm) thickness.

5 Note the time. Place four of the potato discs into each of the seven 3 cm^3 test-tubes of sucrose solutions. Manipulate the discs so that they are all covered with sucrose solution in each tube.

6 After at least 40 minutes, pour off the fluid from the 3 cm^3 tube labelled 0.1 mol dm^{-3} into a clean test tube. This tube of decanted solution should be placed in the test-tube rack in the position previously occupied by the tube containing the potato discs immersed in 0.1 mol dm^{-3} sucrose.

7 Use a teat pipette to collect a small quantity of blue sucrose solution from the 0.1 mol dm^{-3} sucrose tube which contains 2 cm^3 sucrose solution. Now, *with great care*, introduce a *single* drop of this blue fluid into the tube behind it, the tube containing the decanted fluid which had been in contact with the potato slices. The drop should be *released carefully into the centre of the liquid* about 5 mm below the surface.

8 Watch the drop. Note whether it remains in the same place, or rises, or sinks. Repeat with another drop, and continue until you are quite certain that you have made the correct observation about the behaviour of the drop.

9 Repeat Steps 6, 7 and 8 with the other six sets of tubes, using a clean pipette for each sucrose concentration.

10 Present your results in the form of a table.

Requirements
Test-tube rack (double row) or two test-tube racks (single row)
Test tubes ×21
Marker for writing on glass
Graduated pipettes (3–5 cm^3) ×7
Graduated syringes (5 cm^3 or 10 cm^3) ×7
Teat pipettes ×7
Cork borer (c. 7 mm diameter)
Razor blade
Ceramic tile

Sucrose solutions (0.1, 0.15, 0.2, 0.25, 0.3, 0.5, 1.0 mol dm^{-3}, at least 5 cm^3 of each)
Methylene blue

Potato tubers

For consideration

(1) From your understanding of the factors which cause water to leave or enter plant tissues, explain what has been happening in each of the sucrose concentrations. In each case account for the behaviour of the blue drops.

(2) A 1.0 mol dm^{-3} solution of sucrose has a water potential of −3510 kPa. From your results, estimate the approximate water potential of the potato tissue.

(3) Are your results estimates of the water potentials of the potato cells, or the water potentials of the solutions in their vacuoles? Explain your answer.

(4) Suggest improvements to the experimental technique in order to estimate the water potential of potato tissue more accurately.

Investigation 4.5
Osmotic potential of cell sap of plant epidermal cells

The water potential of a plant cell (ψ_{cell}) is related to the osmotic potential of the sap ψ_s and the pressure potential (ψ_p):

$$\psi_{cell} = \psi_s + \psi_p$$

Use can be made of this in determining the osmotic potential of plant tissue. The cells are placed in a range of external solutions of different concentrations. The one which plasmolyses the cells to the extent that the protoplasts just lose contact with the cellulose walls (incipient plasmolysis) can be regarded as having the same osmotic potential as the cell sap. This is because, under these circumstances, no inward pressure is exerted by the cellulose wall, i.e. $\psi_p = 0$ and $\psi_{cell} = \psi_s$.

In practice the cells of a piece of plant tissue, such as the epidermal tissue to be used in this experiment, plasmolyse at different rates. For practical purposes we can regard incipient plasmolysis as the condition in which half the cells are visibly plasmolysed.

Procedure

1 Remove one of the fleshy scale leaves of an onion. With a razor blade cut the inner epidermis into six squares of approximately 5 mm side. With fine forceps peel off each square of epidermal cells and place it in distilled water in a petri dish.

2 Label six stoppered tubes and into each one place approximately 10 cm^3 of sucrose solution of the following concentrations: 0.3, 0.4, 0.5, 0.6, 0.7 and 1.0 mol dm^{-3}.

3 Put two pieces of epidermis into each tube. Stopper the tubes, and gently shake the contents so as to bring all parts of the epidermis into full contact with the solution. Leave the tissue in the solutions for about 20 minutes.

Requirements
Microscope
Razor blade
Petri dish
Specimen tubes with stoppers ×5
Graph paper

Distilled water
Sucrose solutions (0.3, 0.4, 0.5, 0.6, 0.7, 1.0 mol dm^{-3}, 10 cm^3 of each)

Onion scale or alternative (see note below)

Note: Suitable alternatives to onion include the pigmented epidermis of red cabbage, rhubarb or *Rhoeo*. The experiment may also be carried out using the filamentous alga *Cladophora* (*see* Investigation 4.1, page 34). Use the same range of sucrose solutions as with onion. For each solution count the number of plasmolysed cells out of 50 in a single filament. *Reference*: C. Rouan, 'Plasmolysis Experiments with Cladophora', *Journal of Biological Education*, Vol. 15, No. 2, 1981.

4 After 20 minutes remove one piece of epidermis from each tube and mount it in a drop of the solution in which it has been immersed. Observe under low power. If cells are not clearly visible in any of the epidermal pieces, try using the second piece.

5 Count *all* the cells visible within the low power field of view. Now count all those that are plasmolysed: include all cells which show a visible separation of the protoplast from the cell wall, however slight this may be. If the reading for a particular sucrose solution is markedly at variance with the others, use the second piece of epidermis.

6 Plot a graph of percentage plasmolysis (vertical axis) against molarity of sucrose solution (horizontal axis).

7 From your graph read off the molarity of sucrose that corresponds to 50 per cent plasmolysis. This solution may be regarded as having the same osmotic potential as the cell sap of the tissue. From Table 4.1 you can work out the osmotic potential in kilopascals (kPa) corresponding to this molarity.

For Consideration

(1) Explain the shape of your graph.
(2) Why should the pieces of epidermis be placed in distilled water before being put into the experimental solutions?
(3) What are the major sources of inaccuracy in this method of determining the osmotic potential of plant cells?
(4) Suggest a better method which overcomes the objections raised in your answer to (3).
(5) Why don't all the cells in the same tissue have the same osmotic potential?

Investigation 4.6
Differential ion movement into red cabbage epidermal cells

Different ions move through cell membranes at different rates. The rate at which an ion passes across a membrane depends on its solubility in lipids and the availability of protein carrier molecules able to recognise the ion and take it across the membrane by facilitated diffusion or active transport.

The anthocyanin pigment which colours the contents of the vacuoles of red cabbage epidermal cells is sensitive to pH. It is red under neutral and acidic conditions, but blue under alkaline conditions. If the balance of ions in the vacuole changes, its colour may change. Ammonium chloride is a weakly acidic compound, but it is completely dissociated into ammonium and chloride ions, which can move across the cell membrane independently. A change in the colour of the anthocyanin pigment may be used as an indication of the movement of these ions.

Requirements
Microscope
Slides and coverslips ×3

Ammonium chloride solution (1.0 mol dm^{-3})

Red cabbage

Procedure

1 Tear a red cabbage leaf into two, twisting it at the same time. Select a protruding flap of upper or lower epidermis and pull it away from the underlying tissues. It should be as thin as possible.

2 Place the thin flap of epidermal tissue on a microscope slide. Add a drop of water and carefully place a coverslip over the top. Examine under the low and high power of the microscope. In the parts of the tissue which are one cell thick the cells will appear as red blobs separated by clear cell walls.

3 Obtain another epidermal strip and tear it in half. Put each of the two strips on a different microscope slide. To one strip add a drop of water, and to the other a drop of 1.0 mol dm^{-3} ammonium chloride. Add coverslips to both tissues. Mark the slides and leave them for at least five minutes.

4 Examine the tissues again on both slides, and compare them. In each case record the colour and shape of the cell contents.

For consideration

(1) What can you say about the water potential of the ammonium chloride solution?
(2) What evidence suggests that the ammonium and chloride ions do not always migrate together?
(3) Which of the two ions can migrate faster across cell membranes? Speculate on the reasons. (The radius of the ammonium ion is 0.143 nm and that of the chloride ion 0.198 nm.)
(4) Which of the two ions is more likely to be useful to the plant cell, and why?

Questions and Problems

1 It is said that as an object increases in size its surface-volume ratio decreases.
(a) Prove this relationship mathematically for (i) a cube, (ii) a sphere, and (iii) a cylinder.
(b) What is the significance of this principle to organisms? (r = radius; $\pi = 3.142$)

Surface area of a sphere $= 4\pi r^2$ Volume of a sphere $= \frac{4}{3}\pi r^3$

Area of a circle $= \pi r^2$ Circumference of a circle $= 2\pi r$

2 Consider a cylindrical-shaped organism filled with densely packed cells.
(a) What problems are attendant on getting oxygen from the surrounding atmosphere to its innermost cells?
(b) By what means might the delivery of oxygen to these cells be facilitated?

3 Justify the statement that osmosis is a special case of diffusion. What is the relevance of osmosis to (a) a human liver cell, and (b) a parenchyma cell in the stem of a flowering plant?

4 Pieces of well-washed epidermis of the stem of *Lamium album* (deadnettle) were placed in each of five sucrose solutions and the percentage of plasmolysed cells in each solution determined at intervals of time until no further change took place. The results were as follows:

Molar concentration of sucrose solution (mol dm^{-3})	0.55	0.6	0.65	0.7	0.75
Percentage of cells plasmolysed	0	5	20	80	100

Explain these results and state, with reasons, what conclusions you draw from them.
(*O and C*)

5 The hollow scape (flower stalk) of a dandelion is split longitudinally into six portions of length 3 cm. The strips immediately bend outwards as shown in Figure 4.2 A. The curvature is the same for all six strips.

The strips are now placed in six sucrose solutions of different concentrations. The curvatures adopted by the strips after 15 minutes are shown in Figure 4.2 B–G, together with the concentration of each sucrose solution.
(a) Why do the strips bend outwards as soon as they have been removed from the scape?
(b) Why do the strips bend further outwards in B and C?
(c) Why do the strips bend inwards relative to A in E–G?
(d) Why does strip D remain unchanged relative to A?
(e) What are the limitations of this experiment as a method for measuring the water potential of dandelion scape cells?

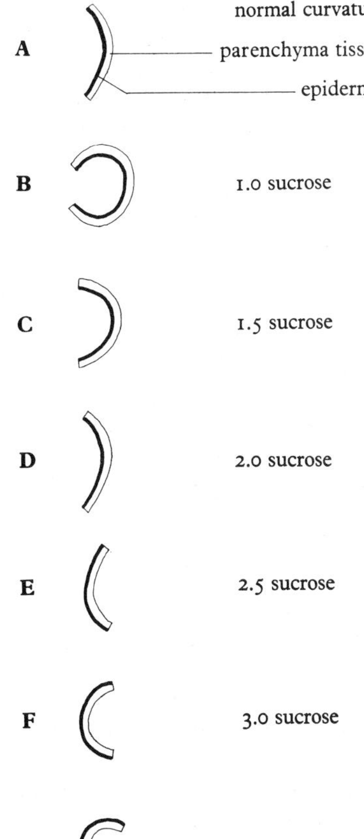

Figure 4.2 The shapes adopted by strips of dandelion scape when immersed in different concentrations of sucrose solution. The sucrose concentrations are expressed in arbitrary units.

6 Mammalian red blood cells are sensitive to a change in salt concentration of the external solution. If they are transferred from plasma to a less concentrated solution they swell and, if they swell sufficiently, they burst; in which case they are said to have haemolysed. In an experiment to find the percentage of human red cells haemolysed at different concentrations of salt solution, the following results were obtained:

Percentage salt concentration (grams per 100 cm^3)	0.33	0.36	0.38	0.39	0.42	0.44	0.48
Percentage red cells haemolysed	100	90	80	68	30	16	0

(a) Plot the results on graph paper, using the horizontal axis for the varying percentages of salt concentration.
(b) Explain why red cells swell and burst when placed in a less concentrated salt solution.
(c) At what percentage salt solution is the proportion of haemolysed to non-haemolysed cells equal?
(d) Suggest a hypothesis to account for the red cells haemolysing over a range of salt concentrations rather than at one particular salt concentration.
(e) Of what significance are these observations as far as the working of the human body is concerned? (*AEB modified*)

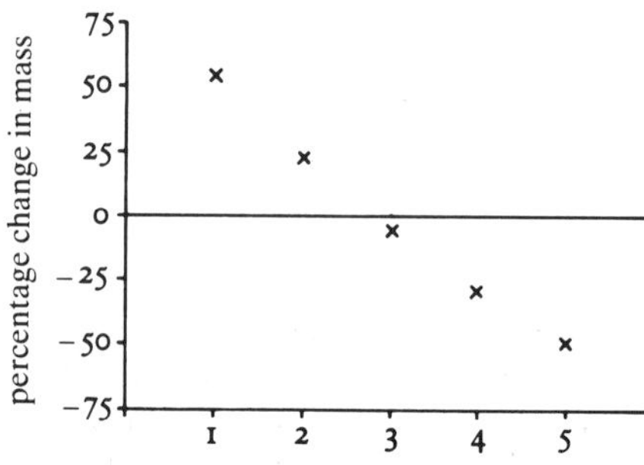

Figure 4.3 Results of experiment on change in mass of sandworms placed in different concentrations of sea water.

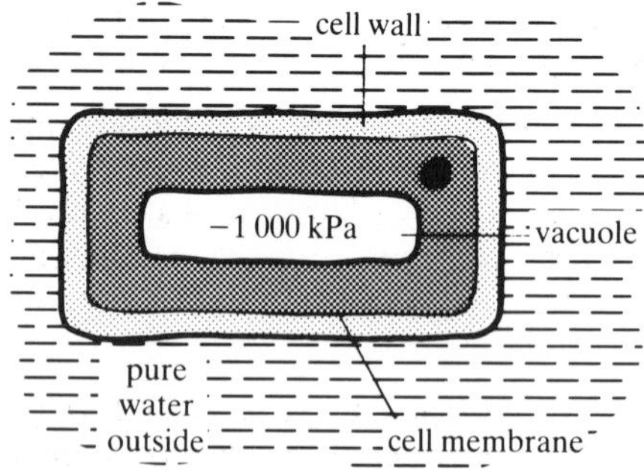

Figure 4.4 A plant cell in equilibrium with pure water.

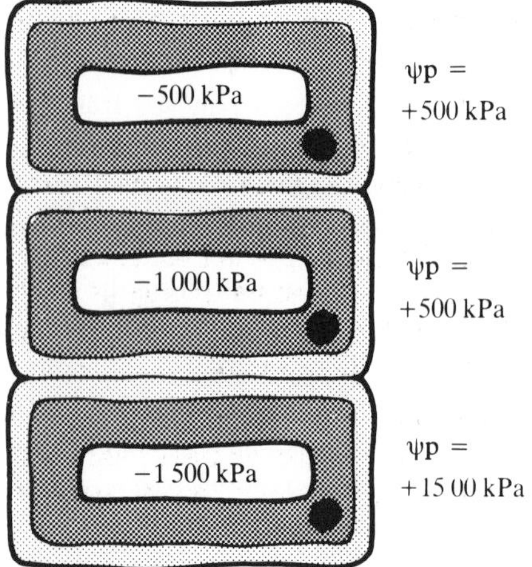

Figure 4.5 Three adjacent cells in a plant tissue. The pressure potentials (wall pressures) which the cell walls are exerting on the cell contents are shown for each cell as ψp on the right hand side of the diagram.

7 A scientist collected a number of sandworms from a beach. Fifty worms of equal mass were selected and equal numbers placed in five different concentrations of sea water. After twelve hours the worms were re-weighed and the average mass for each group was determined. From this the percentage changes in mass were calculated. The results are shown in Figure 4.3. Explain them as fully as possible. *(VUS)*

8 The fully turgid plant cell illustrated in Figure 4.4 has a vacuole with an osmotic potential of −1000 kPa. Yet the cell is in equilibrium with pure water, that is, there is no net gain or loss of water to or from the cell.

(a) State the water potential of this cell.

(b) Calculate the pressure potential (wall pressure).

(c) (i) In which direction would water flow if the cell were transferred to a sucrose solution (0.5 mol dm^{-3}) with a water potential of −1000 kPa?

(ii) Predict the changes in osmotic potential and pressure potential which might occur.

(iii) Under what conditions will the flow of water cease?

9 Figure 4.5 illustrates three adjacent cells in a plant tissue. The osmotic potentials of the contents of their vacuoles are stated, together with the pressure potentials (wall pressures) which the cell walls are exerting on the cell contents.

(a) Calculate the water potential of each cell individually.

(b) In which direction will water travel from cell to cell by osmosis, and why?

(c) Predict the changes in the osmotic potentials and the pressure potentials (wall pressures) of each cell when this movement of water occurs.

(d) Under what conditions will the flow of water cease?

10 Figure 4.6 shows a root hair cell in a section of a root. This cell is in equilibrium with the soil solution surrounding the root; the soil solution has a water potential of −300 kPa.

It rains, diluting the molecules dissolved in the water of the soil solution by three times.

(a) Calculate the probable change in the water potential of the soil solution.

(b) Predict the effect of this change on the flow of water molecules between root hair and soil.

(c) What effect will this have on the osmotic potential and the pressure potential of the root hair cell?

(d) When will the flow of water stop?

11 The following data illustrate the relative absorption by carrot discs of potassium ions at different concentrations of oxygen from an external solution at 23 °C.

Concentration of O_2 (per cent)	2.7	12.2	20.8
Relative absorption of K^+	22	96	100

What explanations can you suggest for the form of the relationship, and what experiments would you carry out to test your suggestions? *(O and C)*

12 (a) What are the similarities and differences between phagocytosis and pinocytosis? What are the functions of each?

(b) In what sense can the contents of a phagocytic vesicle be said to be outside the cell?

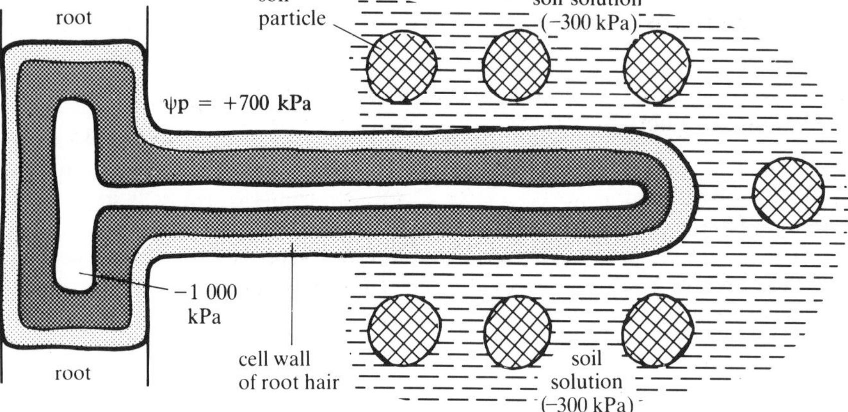

Figure 4.6 A root hair cell in equilibrium with the surrounding 'soil solution'. The pressure potential (wall pressure) which the cell wall is exerting on the cell contents is shown as ψp on the diagram.

5 The Chemicals of Life

Background Summary

1 The principal organic constituents of organisms are carbohydrates, lipids, proteins, nucleic acids and vitamins. Inorganic constituents include acids, bases, salts and water.

2 The importance of **water** as a medium for life derives from its solvent properties, heat capacity, surface tension and its evaporation and freezing properties.

3 **Acids** and **bases** are important in that they determine the **pH** of an organism's body fluids. The correct functioning of cells depends on the pH being kept constant.

4 **Salts**, or their **ions**, perform a wide range of functions in different animals and plants. Many are essential metabolites without which disabilities and death may occur.

5 **Carbohydrates** (general formula $(CH_2O)_n$), are sources of energy and are also important structurally (e.g. cellulose). They are classified into **monosaccharides**, **disaccharides** and **polysaccharides**.

6 Monosaccharides such as glucose can be built up into polysaccharides such as starch and glycogen by condensation, and the latter can be broken down by hydrolysis. The reactions are catalysed by specific enzymes.

7 Starch and cellulose differ in their chemical composition, and this is related to their physical properties and functions in cells. Cellulose, a material of great commercial importance, may become impregnated with **lignin** to form **wood**.

8 Some biological materials, e.g. chitin, are composed of **amino sugars**. An amino sugar is a monosaccharide molecule to which an amino ($-NH_2$) group is attached.

9 **Lipids** include fats and related substances. Fats are compounds of **glycerol** ($C_3H_8O_3$) and **fatty acids** ($R(CH_2)_nCOOH$) which can be united by condensation or split by hydrolysis. They are important sources of energy and also carry out structural roles, e.g. in the cell membrane.

10 Cell membranes contain **phospholipids**, which contain phosphoric acid in addition to glycerol and fatty acids. Many membranes also contain **cholesterol**.

11 Most fatty acids can be synthesised by the body but certain ones, known as **essential fatty acids**, are required in the diet.

12 **Steroids** are a group of lipid-like compounds with important biological functions e.g. the formation of hormones.

13 **Proteins** are composed of numerous **amino acids** ($RCHNH_2COOH$). Amino acids can be combined by condensation to form **polypeptide chains** and ultimately proteins. Polypeptides can be hydrolysed into free amino acids. The sequence of amino acids constitutes the **primary structure** of the protein.

14 The chain of amino acids may be coiled into an **α helix** which constitutes the **secondary structure** of the protein. Further coiling or folding gives the protein its **tertiary structure**. Finally, several polypeptide chains may be combined in the finished protein molecule, giving it its **quaternary structure**.

15 A further aspect of a protein's quaternary structure is that it may be combined with another compound to form a **conjugated protein**. In haemoglobin the protein is combined with a **porphyrin** (haem), and in mucus it is combined with a carbohydrate as a **glycoprotein**.

16 Proteins are classified as **globular** or **fibrous**. The former are usually soluble and perform mainly regulatory functions in the body (e.g. enzymes), whilst the latter fulfil structural roles (e.g. collagen). Certain structures, e.g. microfilaments and microtubules, are formed by the massing together of globular protein molecules.

17 An important function of globular proteins is **buffering**. They owe this function to the presence of both positively and negatively charged groups in the polypeptide chain.

18 About half the known amino acids can be synthesised in the body by **transamination**. The remainder, known as **essential amino acids**, are required in the diet. Most animal and some plant proteins contain a high proportion of essential amino acids and accordingly are of **high biological value** in the diet (**first class proteins**).

19 Proteins in a mixture can be separated by **electrophoresis**. Electrophoresis and/or **chromatography** enables their constituent amino acids to be identified, and when combined with **isotope labelling** it enables the amino-acid sequence to be determined (e.g. insulin). **X-ray crystallography** enables the three-dimensional shape of the protein molecule to be established (e.g. haemoglobin and myoglobin).

20 **Nucleic acids**, like proteins, are very large molecules. Formed from building blocks called **nucleotides**, they are concerned with the formation and expression of genetic material (*see* chapter 30).

21 **Vitamins**, a mixed assortment of chemical compounds, are required by organisms for various metabolic purposes. Some of them function as coenzymes.

22 The chemical substances listed above should be constituents of a balanced diet. Shortage of one or more of them can lead to various **deficiency diseases**.

Investigation 5.1
Identification of biologically important compounds

CAUTION:
Some of the reagents used in these tests are dangerous, especially when hot. You should wear safety spectacles to protect your eyes.

The chemical composition of cells can be investigated in two main ways. One is to grind up the tissue, or extract the juices from it, and perform chemical tests on the material so obtained. Alternatively the tissue can be sectioned, stained with a reagent specific to a certain chemical constituent, and examined under the microscope. This approach has the advantage that the distribution of individual compounds within the cells can be studied in detail.

Procedure

STARCH

1 To approximately 4 cm^3 (quarter of a test tube) of starch suspension add two drops of iodine solution. A blue-black colour indicates the presence of starch.

2 Examine the distribution of starch in a potato tuber by cutting thin sections of the pulp and mounting them in iodine solution. Starch grains stain blue and can be located in the cells.

3 Irrigate a section of potato tuber on a slide with iodine solution. Watch the starch grains turning blue as the iodine reaches them.

SUGARS

All monosaccharide sugars and certain disaccharides will reduce copper (II) sulphate, producing a precipitate of copper (I) oxide on heating. Such sugars are known as **reducing sugars**, and a suitable reagent with which to test them is **Benedict's reagent**. This contains copper (II) sulphate.

1 To approximately 4 cm^3 of glucose in a test tube add an equal quantity of Benedict's reagent. Shake and bring to the boil by heating the test tube in a water bath. A precipitate indicates reducing sugar.

The colour and density of the precipitate gives a rough indication of the amount of sugar present. A green precipitate means relatively little sugar; a brown or red precipitate means progressively more sugar.

2 Cut a cube of apple of side 1 cm. Grind it up in a mortar with a small quantity of water. Transfer the material to a test tube and add water to make up a total volume of approximately quarter of a test tube. Add an equal volume of Benedict's reagent and heat to boiling in a water bath. Record your results and conclusions.

3 The main reducing sugar in apple tissue is fructose. Investigate its distribution as follows. Cut a thin section with a razor blade and mount it on a slide in a few drops of Benedict's reagent. Examine the cells under the microscope. Now heat the slide *gently* over a small flame until the tissue turns brown. Add water if the tissue looks like drying up. Allow the slide to cool and then re-examine the cells.

What changes have occurred in the cells? Is sugar present in all the cells or only certain ones?

4 Sucrose (cane sugar) is a disaccharide which does not reduce copper sulphate. However, it can be detected by first hydrolysing it into its constituent monosaccharides and then testing with Benedict's reagent:

Boil a little sucrose solution with dilute hydrochloric acid, neutralise with sodium hydrogencarbonate then test with Benedict's reagent.

CELLULOSE

1 Cellulose stains purple with Schultz' solution (*see* page 403). Put a drop of the stain onto a small piece of teased-out cotton wool and notice the reaction.

2 Mount a section of plant tissue in Schultz' solution and examine the cells. Note the colour reaction shown by some of the cell walls.

LIGNIN

1 Lignin (wood) stains red with acidified phloroglucinol (*see* page 403). Put some phloroglucinol into a watch glass and add a few drops of concentrated hydrochloric acid. Dip a match stick into this mixture and note the colour reaction.

2 With a razor blade cut thin transverse and/or longitudinal sections of a woody stem. Stain your sections in acidified phloroglucinol in a watch glass for five minutes and then mount in water, or (if you wish to keep them for long) in dilute glycerine. Examine under the low power and observe the distribution of lignin in your section.

LIPIDS

1 Lipids produce a red stain with Sudan III. To some olive oil in a test tube add a small amount of water and shake it up with a few drops of Sudan III. On standing, the oil separates from the water and will be seen to have taken up the red stain.

2 Try this alternative test for lipid: shake some olive oil in a test tube with 5 cm^3 absolute ethanol for one minute; add an equal volume of water. A cloudy white precipitate indicates lipid. The whiteness of the precipitate is proportional to the concentration of lipid in the substance being tested.

3 The presence of lipid in a tissue can be detected as follows. Grind the tissue in a mortar. Transfer it to a test tube containing water, and boil. If lipids are present, oil droplets will escape from the tissue and rise to the surface of the water. Add Sudan III and shake. Allow the oil to settle and notice that, as before, it is stained red. Try this on a fat-containing seed such as castor oil or linseed.

4 Investigate the distribution of fat in a tissue by staining the tissue in Sudan III and then washing with several changes of water and/or 70 per cent ethanol. Any fat present will retain the red colour of the stain. Section a castor oil seed longitudinally and investigate the distribution of fat this way.

PROTEINS

1 To about 2 cm^3 of a solution or suspension of the protein add about six drops of Millon's reagent, and boil. A brick-red colour on the surface of the substance being tested indicates protein. Try this test on some egg albumen. What happens to the albumen when you boil it? Explain your observations.

2 Split open a soaked pea and slice off a thin section. Mount it in Millon's reagent on a slide, and heat gently to boiling. Add water if necessary. Cool and examine under the microscope for the distribution of protein.

> **CAUTION:**
> Millon's reagent is dangerous. Do not boil it for long, inhale its fumes or get it on your skin.

3 Try this alternative test (known as the biuret test) which is suitable for soluble proteins and is safer than Millon's test. Add a little potassium hydroxide to the protein solution till the solution clears; add a drop of copper sulphate down the side of the test tube. Do not heat. A blue ring at the surface of the solution indicates protein; on shaking, the blue ring disappears and the solution turns purple.

INVESTIGATING UNKNOWNS

Investigate the occurrence and distribution of reducing and non-reducing sugars, starch, cellulose, lignin, fat and protein in a variety of plant tissues and organs, e.g. apple, orange, grape, carrot, parsnip, etc. In the case of a complex structure like an orange, test the different components (e.g. skin, matrix, juice, pips) separately.

In some cases it is necessary to carry out your analysis on a solution prepared by grinding up the tissue in a mortar, in other cases it is more appropriate to analyse the solid tissue. Where possible, carry out the tests on microscope slides and examine the distribution of the substance in question under low power.

In addition, try testing commercial food products such as bread, cereals, milk powder, baby food, stock cubes, sauces, soups etc.

For Consideration

(1) Summarise the functions performed by the various chemical substances which you have investigated.

(2) What is the value of obtaining information on the occurrence and distribution of different substances in a plant or animal?

(3) Select one of the plant organs in which you have investigated the distribution of substances. Explain, as far as you can, how the various substances came to be located in their specific situations.

Requirements

Microscope
Test tubes ×10
Test tube rack
Slides and coverslips
Bunsen burner or spirit lamp
Pestle and mortar
Razor blade
Watch glass
Spatula
Safety spectacles

Iodine solution
Benedict's reagent
Schultz' solution
Phloroglucinol (benzene-1,3,5-triol)
Concentrated hydrochloric acid
Dilute hydrochloric acid
Sodium hydrogencarbonate
Sudan III
Millon's reagent
Dilute potassium hydroxide
Copper (II) sulphate solution (1 per cent)
Ethanol (absolute and 70 per cent)
Litmus paper

Starch solution
Potato tuber
Glucose (dextrose)
Sucrose (cane sugar)
Apple
Cotton wool
Woody stem
Match sticks
Olive oil
Castor oil seed
Egg albumen
Soaked peas
Variety of plant tissues and organs and commercial foods

Investigation 5.2

Analysis of amino acids in a protein by paper chromatography

The building blocks of protein are amino acids. This experiment provides an opportunity to determine which amino acids are present in the protein albumen. The protein is first hydrolysed by treating it with the digestive enzyme trypsin; the amino acids are then separated and identified by paper chromatography.

Paper chromatography

The principle behind paper chromatography is as follows. A small amount of solvent is put at the bottom of a jar. A strip of absorptive paper, with a concentrated spot of the mixed amino acids near the bottom, is suspended in the jar so that its end dips into the solvent. The latter moves slowly up the strip of paper, carrying the amino acids with it. As the amino acids travel at different speeds, they separate from one another. The paper is then treated with a reagent which stains the amino acids so they can be detected and identified.

Procedure

This experiment takes several days so it is advisable to draw up a time schedule before you start.

BREAKING DOWN THE PROTEIN

Half fill a test tube with the trypsin solution provided. Now add the protein: either 2 g of egg white, or 5.0 cm^3 of albumen. Finally drop in a crystal of thymol to kill any bacteria. Leave the mixture to incubate at 37 °C for 48–72 hours.

SETTING UP THE CHROMATOGRAPHY APPARATUS

Separation of the amino acids can be carried out in a glass jar of height not less than 30 cm. There should be a cap for covering the open end of the jar to which the strip of chromatography paper can be attached (see below).

1 In a fume cupboard, pour the solvent into the jar to a depth of about 3 cm. Cover the open end of the jar so the atmosphere inside becomes saturated with vapour.

2 Cut a strip of chromatography paper of sufficient length for one end to dip into the solvent to a depth of about 5 mm, and the other end to stick out of the top of the jar by about 2 cm. Handle the paper as lightly as possible and make sure your hands are clean and dry, otherwise amino acids on your skin may get onto the paper.

3 About 4 cm from one end of the strip of paper draw a *pencil* line across the strip. Using a fine pipette place a small drop of the amino acid mixture in the centre of the pencil line. Let this dry, and then place another drop on top of the first, and dry again. Repeat this about six times keeping the spot as small as possible.

4 Lower the strip into the glass jar, pencilled end first, taking care not to let it come into contact with the sides of the jar. Allow the bottom end of the strip to dip about 5 mm into the solvent, then bend the top end over and attach it to the cap (Figure 5.1).

5 The experiment should now be left for not less than eight hours, and not longer than 16.

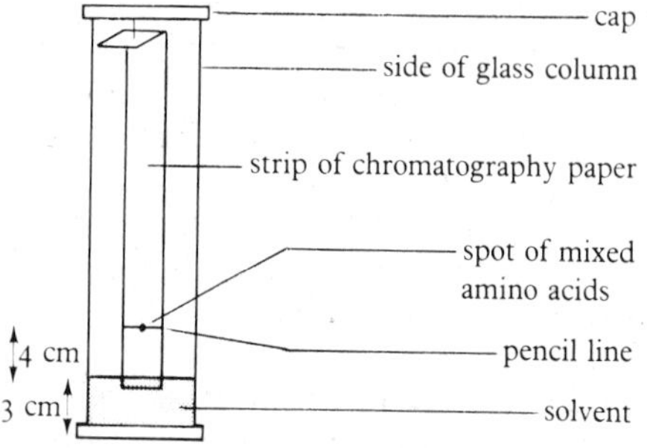

Figure 5.1 Diagram of paper chromatography apparatus for the separation of amino acids.

DEVELOPING THE CHROMATOGRAM (8–16 HOURS LATER)

1 Remove the strip from the jar. The solvent should have risen some 20–25 cm from the pencil line. Draw another line across the strip at the highest point reached by the solvent. Then hang the strip to dry in a warm place.

2 The chromatogram is developed (i.e. the amino acids are stained) by means of a dilute solution of ninhydrin in butan-1-ol.

> **CAUTION:**
> Ninhydrin is poisonous: Use it only in a fume cupboard, and wear protective gloves, do not inhale its fumes, and wash it off immediately if it gets onto your skin.

In a fume cupboard pour a small amount of the ninhydrin reagent into a glass crystallising dish and slowly draw the chromatography paper through the liquid. Ensure that the whole of the area between the two pencil lines is thoroughly soaked.

3 Dry the strip rapidly by holding it close to a source of heat e.g. a hair dryer. Don't use a bunsen flame: ninhydrin is inflammable! If you continue heating it after it is dry, purple spots should appear at points along its length. Continue heating until the spots are as dense as possible.

INTERPRETATION OF THE CHROMATOGRAM

Each purple spot corresponds to one or more amino acids. Certain spots are clear and easily identified; others tend to merge together and are less distinct.

To identify the amino acids we make use of a measurement called the R_f value. R_f stands for relative front. This is the ratio of the distance moved by the spot to the distance moved by the solvent.

$$R_f = \frac{\text{distance moved by spot}}{\text{distance moved by solvent}}$$

Draw a horizontal line through the centre of each spot and calculate the R_f values. By comparing your R_f values with the list given in Table 5.1, try to identify the amino acid responsible for each spot in your chromatogram.

PRESENTATION OF RESULTS

Attach your chromatogram to a sheet of paper and write alongside each spot the name of the amino acid, together with your estimated R_f value.

For Consideration

(1) According to your analysis how many different amino acids are present in albumen?
(2) It is probable that you will have identified between six and eight amino acids with reasonable certainty. But there are known to be 15 (*see* Table 5.1). Why don't they all appear in your chromatogram? (There are several possible reasons.)
(3) One possible reason for (2) is that all 15 amino acids *are* present in your chromatogram but some of the spots may be so close to each other that it is impossible to distinguish between them. How could you extend the chromatographic technique in order to show whether or not this explanation is correct?

Requirements
Large test tube (24 × 150 mm)
Glass jar (approximately 40 cm high × 7 cm diameter, gas jar recommended)
Lid for glass jar
Strip of chromatography paper (approximately 40 cm × 2 cm)
Dropping pipette with fine point
Measuring cylinder (10 cm^3)
Sellotape
Crystallising dish (125 mm diameter)
Incubator at 37 °C
Pencil and ruler

Trypsin solution (10 cm^3)
Thymol crystals
Solvent (200 cm^3, see below)
Distilled water
Ninhydrin reagent (sufficient to fill crystallising dish to depth of 10 mm)

Egg white (2 g) or fluid albumen (5 cm^3)

Make up solvent as follows: 4 parts of butan-1-ol, 1 part glacial ethanoic acid, and 1 part distilled water.
Make up ninhydrin reagent as follows: 1.0 per cent solution of ninhydrin in butan-1-ol.
Make up trypsin solution as follows: Dissolve 2.0 g trypsin in 100 cm^3 of 1.0 per cent sodium hydrogencarbonate.

Amino Acid	Concentration (%)	R_f value
Glutamic acid	16.5	0.30
Aspartic acid	9.3	0.24
Leucine	9.2	0.73
Serine	8.2	0.27
Phenylalanine	7.7	0.68
Valine	7.1	0.60
Isoleucine	7.0	0.72
Alanine	6.7	0.38
Lysine	6.3	0.14
Arginine	5.7	0.20
Methionine	5.2	0.55
Threonine	4.0	0.35
Tyrosine	3.7	0.45
Proline	3.6	0.43 (yellow)
Glycine	3.1	0.26

Table 5.1 The amino acids present in albumen listed in order of decreasing concentrations.

Investigation 5.3
Analysis of amino acids in a protein by paper electrophoresis

The aim of this experiment is to determine which amino acids are present in the protein casein, the major protein in milk. It also illustrates paper electrophoresis, an important technique for separating and identifying organic compounds in mixtures.

Paper electrophoresis

Amino acids are often charged. All have amino ($-NH_2$) and carboxylic acid ($-COOH$) groups attached to the central carbon atom. Many also have amino or carboxylic acid groups as part of the radical (R) which differentiates one amino acid from another. Depending on the pH of the medium, their $-NH_2$ groups may be ionised to $-NH_3^+$, their $-COOH$ groups may be ionised to $-COO^-$, or both types of groups may be ionised at the same time.

When a mixture of amino acids is placed on moist filter paper between two electrodes and the current is switched on, the amino acids with no

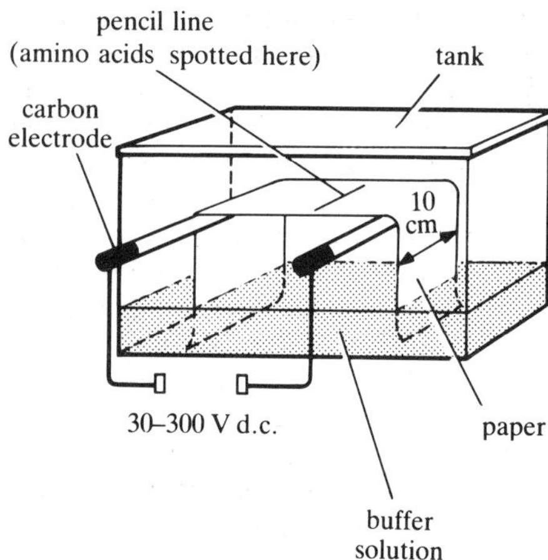

Figure 5.2 Apparatus for paper electrophoresis. Several types of apparatus exist for electrophoresis. In all of them the charged compounds to be separated are placed between the electrodes on a moist medium in a buffer solution which conducts electricity.

net charge will stay in place, the positively-charged molecules will move towards the negative electrode and the negatively-charged molecules will move towards the positive electrode. When the current is switched off, the paper is dried and treated with a reagent which stains the amino acids so that they can be located and identified. Identification is simplified if pure solutions of known amino acids are run simultaneously.

Procedure

1 Take a 30 × 10 cm sheet of filter paper and rule a pencil line across it halfway down, 15 cm from either end. Starting 1 cm from the edge, make nine pencil dots on this line, each 1 cm apart. Number these dots 1–9. Do not finger the paper.

2 Dissolve 5 g of casein hydrolysate in 10 cm^3 of water in a test tube. Stopper the test tube and shake thoroughly. After five minutes, use a dropping pipette with a fine point to pipette drops of this solution onto dots 3 and 6. Do not let the spots become larger than 3 mm diameter.

3 Dry the spots by placing the paper some distance from a blow heater. Then add another drop of casein hydrolysate solution to each spot. Repeat this procedure another eight times.

> **CAUTION:**
> Pyridine is poisonous. Use it only in a fume cupboard and wear protective gloves. Do not inhale its fumes, and wash it off immediately if it touches your skin.

4 Using a separate clean pipette in each case, add solutions of pure amino acids to the remaining dots as follows: 1-arginine, 2-lysine, 4-glycine, 5-aspartic acid, 7-glutamic acid, 8-valine, 9-tryptophan. For each dot, about ten applications of amino acid solution are needed.

5 To moisten the filter paper, first place some buffer solution in a crystallising dish in a fume cupboard. Draw both ends of the filter paper through the buffer so that the paper is wetted at both ends up to 2 cm from the pencil line, but remains dry in the centre.

6 Set up the paper in a tank; an example is shown in Figure 5.2. Moisten the centre of the paper, but not the spots themselves, with buffer solution from a dropping pipette. Replace the top of the tank firmly.

7 Connect the electrodes to a 30–300 volt DC supply. Run the current for half an hour (high voltage) or several hours (low voltage).

> **CAUTION:**
> Do not touch the electrophoresis apparatus whilst the current is flowing.

8 Switch off the current. Remove the paper from the jar, and hang it up to dry in a warm fume cupboard.

9 Stain the amino acids by means of a dilute solution of ninhydrin in propanone.

> **CAUTION:**
> Ninhydrin is poisonous. Use it only in a fume cupboard and wear protective gloves. Do not inhale its fumes, and wash it off immediately if it touches your skin.

In a fume cupboard, pour a small amount of ninhydrin solution into a glass crystallising dish. Slowly draw the electrophoresis paper through the liquid. Ensure that the whole of the area of the paper is thoroughly soaked. Then dry the paper in the fume cupboard and observe the stained amino acids.

10 Write alongside the name of each spot the amino acid responsible.

Requirements
Electrophoresis apparatus with 12 volt power supply
Chromatography paper
Crystallising dish (diameter 12 cm or more)
Blow heater
Dropping pipettes (with fine points) ×10
Pencil and ruler
Glass beakers (50 cm^3) ×8

Amino acids
Buffer solution (pH 3.6)
Ninhydrin reagent (sufficient to fill crystallising dish to depth of 10 mm)
Casein Hydrolysate (available from suppliers)

Make up buffer solution as follows:
Add carefully 13.8 g glacial ethanoic acid and 1.5 g pyridine to 234.7 g distilled water

Make up ninhydrin reagent as follows:
200 mg ninhydrin in 100 cm^3 propanone

Note: Electrophoresis kits are available from suppliers, but home-made versions can be just as satisfactory.

For Consideration

(1) According to your analysis, how many different amino acids occur in casein?

(2) Which amino acids can you say with certainty (a) do occur (b) do not occur in casein?

(3) There are known to be 17 different types of amino acids in casein. Why do they not all appear in your electrophoretogram?

(4) One possible reason for (3) is that all 17 amino acids are present in your electrophoretogram but some of the spots may so close to each other that it is impossible to distinguish between them. How could you extend the electrophoretic technique in order to show whether or not this explanation is correct?

(5) If you altered the pH of the solution, would the pattern of spots obtained be the same? Explain your answer carefully.

(6) Electrophoresis is frequently used to separate whole protein molecules. Why should protein molecules be charged?

Reference: G.D. Brown and J. Creedy, *Experimental Biology Manual*, Heinemann Educational, 1970.

Investigation 5.4
Vitamin C content of a lemon

Requirements
Beaker (100 cm^3)
Beaker (500 cm^3)
Container to collect a small volume of lemon juice
Measuring cylinder (50 cm^3)
Pipette or syringe to measure 2 cm^3 volume
Pipette or syringe to measure accurately volumes up to 1 cm^3
Test tube
Spatula

Distilled water (50 cm^3)
Vitamin C (0.1 per cent solution, fresh, see below)
DCPIP (dichlorophenolindophenol) (0.1 per cent aqueous solution)

Half a lemon

To prepare a fresh 0.1 per cent Vitamin C solution: Add one 50 mg tablet of vitamin C to 50 cm^3 distilled water, crushing the tablet if necessary. Shake well. Allow the suspension to stand for about ten minutes. Shake well again. Allow the solids to settle and then pour off the supernatant solution.

Citrus fruits, such as lemons, contain vitamin C which prevents the deficiency diseases scurvy. Vitamin C is a reducing agent, and decolourises the blue dye dichlorophenolindolphenol (DCPIP). This reaction allows us to estimate the vitamin C content of a lemon.

First we shall estimate the volume of 0.1 per cent vitamin C solution required to decolourise 2 cm^3 of a DCPIP solution. Then we shall determine the volume of lemon juice required to decolourise the same volume of the same DCPIP solution. This provides an estimate of the concentration of vitamin C in lemon juice, in units of mg per cm^3. This figure is then multiplied by the volume of the lemon to obtain the total vitamin C content of the lemon.

Procedure

1 Using a pipette or syringe, place exactly 2.0 cm^3 of DCPIP solution into a test tube.
2 Using a different graduated pipette or syringe, add the vitamin C solution, drop by drop, to the DCPIP solution in the test tube. Shake the tube very gently after the addition of each drop of the vitamin C solution and continue adding drops until the DCPIP solution is decolourised. Record the exact volume of the vitamin C solution which you have added.
3 Repeat this procedure. Average your results to obtain the mean volume of 0.1 per cent vitamin C which decolorises 2 cm^3 of DCPIP.
4 Calculate the mass of vitamin C in this volume of vitamin C solution. The vitamin C solution was made up to contain 0.001 g vitamin C in 1.0 cm^3 water.
5 You now know how much vitamin C is required to decolourise 2 cm^3 of DCPIP. The next step is to find the volume of lemon juice which contains the equivalent mass of vitamin C.
6 First determine the volume of your lemon. Submerge it in water in a 500 cm^3 beaker and mark the level of the base of the meniscus on the side of the beaker. Remove the lemon and add a measured volume of water from a measuring cylinder until the water level reaches the mark. The volume of water added is the volume of the lemon.
7 Cut your lemon in half. Squeeze the juice from half the lemon into a small beaker. Suck up some of the lemon juice into a clean graduated pipette or syringe.
8 Repeat Steps 1 and 2, using lemon juice. Add the lemon juice drop by drop to 2 cm^3 of DCPIP solution in a test tube until it becomes decolourised. Record the exact volume of lemon juice added. It may be that only one or two drops of lemon juice are needed to decolourise the DCPIP. In that case dilute the lemon juice five times and repeat the procedure.
9 Repeat Step 8. Average the two results. You have now found the volume of lemon juice which contains the mass of vitamin C calculated in Step 4.
10 Work out the mass of vitamin C in 1 cm^3 of lemon juice. Multiply by the volume of the lemon in cm^3 to find the vitamin C content of the whole lemon.

For consideration

(1) Discuss any sources of error in this investigation.
(2) Ascorbic acid is a derivative of a hexose sugar. Suggest why it is so abundant in fruits and vegetables.
(3) A typical human needs about 10 mg of vitamin C per day to prevent scurvy and the British government recommends a daily intake of 30 mg. To what extent can these needs be met by a single lemon?

Questions and Problems

1 Describe the experiments you would perform to determine which mineral elements are required for the growth of barley plants, and in what form.

2 Carbon is quadrivalent. Why does this make it ideal as a constituent of biological molecules? Illustrate your answer by referring to the structure of carbohydrates, fats and proteins.

3 (a) What are the physical properties of starch and cellulose, and how are the properties related to the functions of these two compounds in plant cells?
(b) How does a knowledge of the chemical structure of starch and cellulose help to explain their physical properties?

4 (a) Define the word protein.
(b) How can the shape of a protein molecule be determined?
(c) Why is it that fibres of wool are easily stretched but collagen fibres are virtually unstretchable?

5 It was discovered accidentally in the East Indies towards the end of the nineteenth century that fowls fed on cooked polished rice developed paralysis, but when fed on cheaper unhusked rice they recovered. Suggest a hypothesis to explain this. How would you test your hypothesis?

6 The table below shows that animal and plant tissues vary considerably in the relative abundance of the various major classes of constituent chemicals.

	Percentage content				
	Water	Protein	Lipid	Carbohydrate	Minerals
Animal	60	20	15	1	4
Plant	60	5	1	30	4

Why do animals differ from plants in their protein, lipid and carbohydrate content?

7 (a) What is meant by (i) a vitamin, and (ii) an essential amino acid? Make clear the physiological and nutritional differences between them.
(b) Separate samples of young rats were fed on diferent diets as shown below. After a period of 28 days the rats were killed and sections of their limb bones were made and examined. The results are shown below.

Diet given	**Bone section showed**
(i) Kitchen scraps	Normal development
(ii) Maize, calcium carbonate, sodium chloride, yeast, wheat protein, water	Severe rickets
(iii) As in (ii) plus olive oil	Severe rickets
(iv) As in (ii) plus ergosterol	Severe rickets
(v) As in (ii) plus olive oil and ergosterol	Normal development

What can you deduce from these experiments? Explain carefully how you arrive at your conclusions. *(AEB)*

8 Figure 5.3 shows the nutritional information given on the side of a packet of Weetabix.
(a) State the main function or functions of each nutrient listed in the table below Figure 5.3.
(b) What is meant by *available* carbohydrate?
(c) Briefly describe the deficiency diseases caused by lack of the three vitamins listed.
(d) Why is it useful for food manufacturers to give this kind of information?

INGREDIENTS:
Whole Wheat, Malt Extract, Sugar, Salt, Niacin, Iron, Riboflavin (B_2), Thiamin (B_1)

An average serving of two Weetabix (37.5g) provides at least one sixth of the daily recommended requirements for the average adult of the vitamins listed and iron.

TYPICAL NUTRITIONAL COMPOSITION

	Per 100g		Per 100g
Fat	2.0g	Dietary Fibre	12.9g
Protein	10.5g	Vitamins:	
Available Carbohydrate	66.8g	Niacin	10.0mg
Energy	1400kJ	Riboflavin (B_2)	1.0mg
	335kcal	Thiamin (B_1)	0.7mg
		Iron	6.0mg

Figure 5.3 Part of the side of a packet of Weetabix.

9 Polypeptides consist of a linear sequence of amino acids linked by bonds between the amino group of one amino acid and the carboxyl group of the adjacent amino acid. Each polypeptide therefore has one free amino group at the N-terminal end and one free carboxyl group at the C-terminal end. The following results were obtained in an analysis of a certain polypeptide.

Acid hydrolysis gave the following composition

Amino acid	Quantity (mole of amino acid per mole peptide)
Glycine	1
Alanine	1
Serine	2
Valine	1

The N-terminal amino acid was found to be glycine. After partial acid hydrolysis of the polypeptide, five new short polypeptides were produced. These were purified and the amino acids present in each determined. The following amino acids were detected but not in equimolar amounts in every case.

Polypeptide	Amino acids present
A	Alanine, Serine
B	Glycine, Serine
C	Glycine, Serine
D	Serine, Alanine, Valine
E	Serine, Alanine

Suggest structures for each of the polypeptides A, B, C, D and *E*, giving your reasons. How would you confirm your findings? *(CCJE)*

10 Haemoglobin contains four polypeptide chains, 2α and 2β. Normal haemoglobin has the amino acid glutamic acid (R-group: CH_2-CH_2-COOH) at position 6 in the two β chains. In contrast sickle-cell haemoglobin, which causes sickle-cell anaemia, has the amino acid valine (R-group: $CH-(CH_3)_2$) at position 6 in the two β chains.

(a) How, and why, would you expect this amino acid substitution to affect the movement in an electrical field of sickle-cell haemoglobin compared with normal haemoglobin?

(b) How might such a difference be made use of in elucidating the cause of sickle-cell disease?

6 Chemical Reactions in Cells

Background Summary

1 Chemical reactions occurring in cells constitute **metabolism**. Metabolic processes proceed in small steps which together constitute a metabolic pathway.

2 **Metabolic pathways** can be analysed by various techniques, for example enzyme inhibitors, isotope labelling and chromatography.

3 Metabolic reactions may be synthetic (**anabolism**) or breakdown (**catabolism**). The former absorb energy (**endergonic**), the latter release energy (**exergonic**).

4 The energy released by catabolic reactions is required for driving anabolic reactions, for work, e.g. muscular contraction and active transport, and for maintenance purposes.

5 Oxidative breakdown of sugar yields carbon dioxide, water, and energy (**cell respiration**). The chemical products of this catabolic process can be re-synthesised into sugar by green plants (**photosynthesis**). A proportion of the energy from respiration can be used for the establishment of chemical bonds in organic molecules, the rest being lost as heat.

6 To initiate chemical reactions such as the oxidative breakdown of sugar, **activation energy** must be supplied.

7 Chemical reactions in organisms are catalysed by **enzymes**. Enzymes effectively lower the activation energy required to initiate the reaction.

8 **Enzymes are proteins** and their properties are as follows:
(a) They generally work very rapidly
(b) They are not destroyed by the reactions they catalyse
(c) They are inactivated by excessive heat
(d) They are sensitive to pH
(e) They are usually specific.

9 Enzymes work by temporarily combining with substrate molecule(s) to form an **enzyme-substrate complex**. The enzyme molecule has an **active site** to which specific substrate molecules become attached. This **lock-and-key hypothesis** explains many properties of enzymes.

10 When a substrate molecule enters the active site, it may cause the enzyme molecule to change its shape thereby ensuring a closer fit. This is called the **induced fit hypothesis**.

11 Enzymes are inhibited by poisons which either compete with the normal substrate molecules for the active site (**competitive inhibition**), or block the active site (**non-competitive inhibition**). Non-competitive inhibition may be reversible or irreversible. Competitive inhibition is always reversible.

12 In **end-product inhibition** the product of a metabolic reaction itself acts as an enzyme inhibitor, thereby cutting down its own production and preventing itself from accumulating.

13 **Allosteric enzymes** exist in two different shapes, active and inactive. Certain inhibitors, known as **allosteric inhibitors**, lock such enzymes in the inactive state.

14 Many enzymes are assisted in their action by non-protein **cofactors**. These include metal ions (Na^+, Mg^{2+} etc.) and organic molecules comprising **coenzymes** or **prosthetic groups**, the latter being an integral part of the enzyme itself. Coenzymes and prosthetic groups play an important part in transferring chemical groups from one enzyme to another.

Investigation 6.1
Action of the enzyme catalase

CAUTION:
Be careful when handling hydrogen peroxide: it is corrosive and may burn the skin or clothing.

The enzyme catalase breaks down hydrogen peroxide into water and oxygen:

$$2H_2O_2 \rightarrow 2H_2O + O_2$$

Hydrogen peroxide is formed continually as a by-product of various chemical reactions in living cells. It is toxic, and if it were not immediately broken down by the cells it would kill them. Hence the importance of the enzyme. It is, in fact, the fastest enzyme known. In this investigation you will be able to watch the action of catalase in a test tube and compare it with an inorganic catalyst that catalyses the same reaction.

Procedure

1 Pour hydrogen peroxide solution into each of two test tubes to a depth of about two centimetres. Into one of the test tubes sprinkle about 0.1 g of fine sand. Note the result, if any. Into the second test tube sprinkle the same amount of either manganese dioxide powder or iron filings. Observe what happens and test for oxygen with a glowing splint. Make notes on your observations.

2 Pour fresh hydrogen peroxide into a clean test tube to the same depth as before. Now cut a cube of liver, 1 cm square, and drop it into the test tube of hydrogen peroxide. Observe carefully and record what happens.

Requirements
Test tubes ×3
Pestle and mortar
Beaker (250 cm^3)
Thermometer
Bunsen burner, tripod, and gauze
Splint
Spatula

Fine sand
Hydrogen peroxide
Manganese (IV) dioxide (powdered)
Iron filings

Mammalian liver, kidney, blood, and muscle
Potato and apple

3 Repeat Step 2 but this time record the temperature of the hydrogen peroxide before and after adding the liver. Is there any evidence of a rise in temperature? Explain.

4 Take a piece of liver the same size as before and place it in a mortar along with a little fine sand. Grind, and then transfer the ground-up liver (along with the sand which will not interfere with the reaction) to a test tube containing fresh hydrogen peroxide. How does the activity of the ground-up liver compare with the activity observed for the whole piece of liver? Explain fully.

5 Take another piece of liver and put it in a beaker of boiling water for three minutes. Then drop the piece of liver into fresh hydrogen peroxide and find out if the enzyme is still capable of breaking down hydrogen peroxide. Explain your results as fully as possible.

6 Carry out experiments to determine if catalase occurs in other organs and tissues besides liver. Mammalian kidney, muscle, and blood might be tried; also potato and apple. Test ground-up material as well as whole pieces (why?).

For Consideration

(1) Describe an experiment which you could do to find out the precise temperature at which catalase is destroyed.

(2) What conclusions can you draw from these experiments as to how enzymes work, and what further experiments could you do to test your ideas?

Investigation 6.2
Following the progress of an enzyme-controlled reaction

To follow the progress of an enzyme-controlled reaction we must mix together known amounts of substrate and enzyme. Then, at regular intervals, we can measure the amount of substrate which has not yet been acted on by the enzyme.

In this investigation we shall use starch as the substrate and amylase as the enzyme. Amylase breaks down starch into maltose. As an indication of how much starch is still left after given intervals of time, we shall use the iodine test. If there is any starch left it will give a blue colour with the iodine solution. The intensity of the blue colour can be taken as an indication of how much starch is still left: a dark blue colour means that a lot of starch is still present, a light blue colour means that there is comparatively little.

In order to make an accurate estimate of how much starch is present we need to be able to measure the intensity of the blue colour. This is done by means of a colorimeter (*see* page 384).

Procedure

1 Put 10 cm^3 starch solution into one beaker, and 5 cm^3 amylase into another beaker.

2 Label ten test tubes 1–10 and place them in a rack.

3 Put 10 cm^3 iodine solution in each test tube.

4 Pour the 5 cm^3 of amylase into the beaker of starch and mix them together by swirling the beaker.

5 Immediately withdraw 1 cm^3 of the starch–amylase mixture with a syringe, and squirt it into the iodine solution in tube 1. Shake the test tube.

6 After 1 minute take another 1 cm^3 sample of the starch–amylase mixture and squirt it into test tube 2. Repeat this procedure at one minute intervals until samples of the starch–amylase

Test tube	Colorimeter reading	Starch concentration	Logarithm of starch concentration
1			
2			
3			
4			
5			
6			
7			
8			
9			
10			

Table 6.1 Table for presenting the results of Investigation 6.2.

mixture have been added to all the test tubes of iodine solution.

7 Carry out a Benedict's test on the remainder of the starch–amylase mixture (*see* page 42).

8 Use the colorimeter to measure the intensity of the blue colour in each test tube.

9 Find out the value of the starch concentrations which correspond to the colorimeter readings by the following method:

Place 10 cm^3 iodine solution in a test tube and add 1 cm^3 of starch solution to it. Place this mixture in the colorimeter and obtain a reading. Now dilute the mixture to half strength with water and obtain another reading. Repeat with a quarter strength and an eighth strength. Plot a graph of the colorimeter readings (vertical axis) against starch concentrations.

10 By means of the graph convert your series of colorimeter readings into equivalent starch concentrations. Then find the logarithm (base 10) of each starch concentration. Copy Table 6.1 into your notebook and fill it in.

11 Draw a graph of the logarithm of the starch concentration (vertical axis) against time.

Requirements
Colorimeter
Test tubes ×11
Test tube rack
Small beakers ×2
Syringe (1.0 cm^3)
Bunsen burner, tripod and gauze

Starch solution (1.0 per cent)
Amylase solution (0.5 per cent)
Iodine solution (5.0 per cent)
Benedict's reagent

For consideration

(1) Interpret the shape of your graph in terms of the interaction between the starch and amylase molecules.
(2) How could you adapt this experiment to investigate the effect of (a) temperature, (b) pH and (c) substrate concentration on the course of the reaction?
(3) Why is it necessary to convert starch concentrations to log starch concentrations?

Reference: Nuffield Advanced Science, Biology, Practical Guide 2 – *Chemical Reactions in Organisms*, Longman, 1985.

Investigation 6.3
Effect of temperature on the action of an enzyme

Enzymes, being proteins, are readily inactivated by excessive heat. One way of investigating the influence of heat on the action of an enzyme is to expose the enzyme to a given temperature for a known period of time, and then estimate how long it takes to catalyse its particular reaction. In this experiment samples of the enzyme diastase are exposed to different temperatures for exactly five minutes. The time required for each sample to hydrolyse a given volume of starch is then estimated. We shall use iodine as an indicator: in the presence of iodine starch turns blue.

Requirements
Test tubes ×5
Labels or wax pencil
Test tube rack
Pipette (5 cm^3)
White tile
Glass rods ×6
Water baths maintained at 25 °C, 40 °C, 60 °C and 100 °C.

Diastase solution (enzyme) (25 cm^3, 1.0 per cent)
Starch solution (substrate) (25 cm^3, 1.0 per cent)
Iodine solution

Procedure

1 Label five test tubes: room temperature (control), 25 °C, 40 °C, 60 °C, and 100 °C. To each add 5 cm^3 of diastase solution.

2 Place each tube in the appropriate water bath for exactly five minutes. The first tube should be kept at room temperature.

3 At the end of the five-minute period remove the tubes from the water baths, and cool them rapidly to room temperature.

4 Now add to each tube 5 cm^3 of starch solution and mix with a clean glass rod.

5 At intervals of one minute test each tube for the presence of starch: withdraw one drop of the starch-diastase mixture, place it on a white tile, and add one drop of iodine solution. Use one glass rod for each tube and a separate one for the iodine solution.

6 Make a complete record of your observations, noting how long it takes in each case before a blue colour *ceases* to be given when iodine is added to the mixture.

For Consideration

(1) As a method of investigating the effect of temperature on enzyme action, what are the shortcomings of this experiment? What could be done to improve it?
(2) Suggest further experiments you might carry out to examine the effect of temperature on the inactivation of the enzyme.
(3) Interpret your results as fully as you can in terms of what you know about how enzymes work.

Investigation 6.4
Influence of pH on the activity of potato catalase

Catalase occurs in many plant and animal tissues. It breaks down toxic hydrogen peroxide, formed as a by-product of various biochemical reactions, into water and oxygen (*see* page 50).

The activity of most enzymes is influenced by changes in pH. In this experiment, potato discs in solutions of known pH act on hydrogen peroxide, and the rate at which oxygen is evolved is measured. This reflects the activity of the catalase in the potato.

CAUTION:
Be careful when handling hydrogen peroxide: it is corrosive and may burn the skin or clothing.

Requirements
Razor blade
Cork borer
Petri dish
Boiling tube (with rubber bung)
Stand, bosses and clamps
Manometer tube (approximately 2 mm diameter)
Beaker
Syringe (5 cm^3)
Clip
Clock
Wax pencil
Potato tuber

Hydrogen peroxide ('20-volume')
Citric acid phosphate buffers, made up as shown below from Na_2HPO_4 (0.2 mol dm^{-3}) and citric acid (0.1 mol dm^{-3}), to give 100 cm^3 of buffer in each case:

pH	Na_2HPO_4	Citric acid
3.0	20.55 cm^3	79.45 cm^3
4.0	38.55	61.45
5.0	51.50	48.50
6.0	63.15	36.85
7.0	82.35	17.65
8.0	97.25	2.75

Before the experiment, these pHs should be checked with an electrical pH meter.

Procedure

1 With a cork borer cut cylinders of potato tuber tissue about 1 cm in diameter and at least 6 cm long. Place a ruler beside the cylinder. Cut the cylinder into discs 1 mm thick. As the discs are cut, place them under water in a petri dish. You require at least 60 discs.

2 For measuring the rate of oxygen production, use the technique shown in Figure 6.1. First assemble the apparatus. Then remove the rubber bung from the neck of the boiling tube. With a syringe, place into the boiling tube 5 cm^3 of buffer solution at pH 3. Carefully add ten potato discs. Then, with another syringe, add 5 cm^3 of hydrogen peroxide to the boiling tube.

3 As soon as you have added the hydrogen peroxide, replace the bung and make sure it provides an airtight seal.

4 As the reaction begins and oxygen is produced you should see the manometer fluid being pushed down the left hand side of the manometer tube. Time how long it takes for the fluid to rise through a distance of 5 cm in the right hand side of the tube. During this period gently agitate the boiling tube. (Why?)

5 Open the clip at the top of the boiling tube so that the manometer fluid returns to its original position. Time the evolution of oxygen twice more and work out the average reading.

6 Remove the bung and wash out the boiling tube thoroughly.

7 Now carry out five further tests, each with a fresh set of ten potato discs. Follow the same procedure as before but with buffer solutions of pH 4, 5, 6, 7 and 8 in turn. Make sure you use a *clean* syringe each time.

8 For each of your final readings express the rate of the reaction by dividing 100 by the time taken in seconds for a 5 cm rise in the manometer tube. This gives larger numbers suitable for plotting.

9 Plot a graph of the rate of the reaction (vertical axis) against pH.

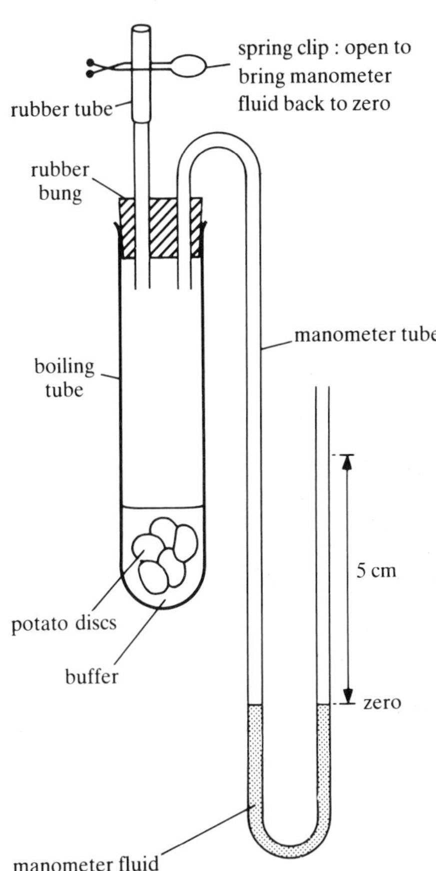

Figure 6.1 Technique for measuring the rate of evolution of oxygen from hydrogen peroxide in the presence of living tissue.

For consideration

(1) What is the relationship between the activity of potato tissue catalase and pH?
(2) Is this relationship relevant to the conditions within the potato cells?
(3) At the molecular level, how does pH affect the efficiency with which the enzyme works?
(4) What is a 'buffer' solution? Why was it valuable to use buffer solutions in this experiment?
(5) List the problems which you encountered during the experiment and suggest how they might have been overcome.
(6) Using the same apparatus, how could you measure the *volume* of gas given off per unit time?
(7) Describe further experiments which could be used to investigate the activity of potato catalase, using the same apparatus.

Investigation 6.5
Specificity of enzymes: sugars metabolised by yeast

In anaerobic conditions yeast cells break down sugar into ethanol and carbon dioxide. This process is called alcoholic fermentation:

$$C_6H_{12}O_6 \rightarrow 2C_2H_5OH + 2CO_2\uparrow + E$$

The process consists of a series of reactions catalysed by specific enzymes. The enzymes present in yeast cells are specific, i.e. they will catalyse the fermentation of certain sugars but not others.

In this experiment you will investigate which of four different 6-carbon sugars can be broken down by yeast. We shall use the evolution of carbon dioxide as an indication that fermentation has taken place. After finding out which sugars can, and cannot, be fermented, the structural formulae of the four sugars can be compared so as to determine the particular configuration of atoms required for the yeast enzymes to work.

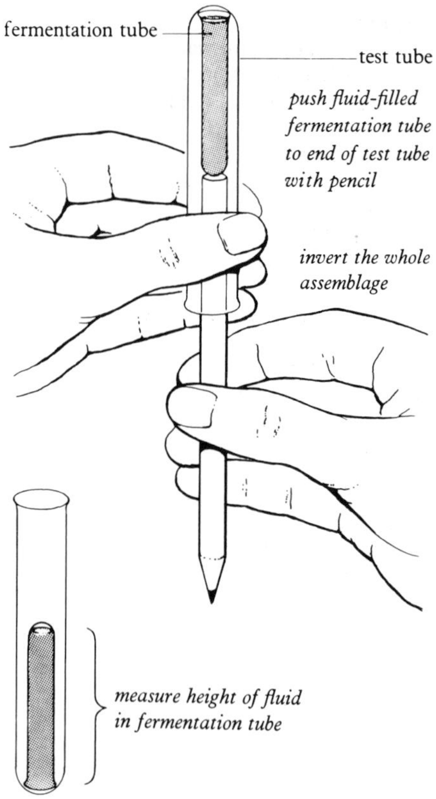

Procedure

1 Label five fermentation tubes 1–5, writing the numbers with a wax pencil upside down near the bottom of each tube.

2 Using a clean syringe or pipette in each case, transfer the following into each fermentation tube:

No. 1: 1 cm^3 distilled water
No. 2: 1 cm^3 glucose
No. 3: 1 cm^3 fructose
No. 4: 1 cm^3 galactose
No. 5: 1 cm^3 sorbose

3 To each tube add 1 cm^3 of yeast suspension and top up with distilled water. N.B. Mix the yeast suspension thoroughly by swirling the flask before adding the yeast to each tube.

4 Set up the fermentation tubes as shown in Figure 6.2. Hold the filled tube in your hand and insert it into an inverted test tube. With a pencil, or some other suitable instrument, push the small tube into the inverted test tube as far as it will go and then invert the whole assemblage. Tap the outer tube firmly to release any bubbles trapped at the mouth of the inner tube.

5 When all the fermentation tubes have been set up, record the height of the liquid in mm in each one. Do this by holding the test tube vertically on a table and placing a millimetre ruler alongside it.

6 Now place all the test tubes in a water bath at 37 °C for at least one hour. Look at the test tubes occasionally to see if anything has happened.

fermentation tube
test tube
push fluid-filled fermentation tube to end of test tube with pencil
invert the whole assemblage
measure height of fluid in fermentation tube

Figure 6.2 Assembling a fermentation tube.

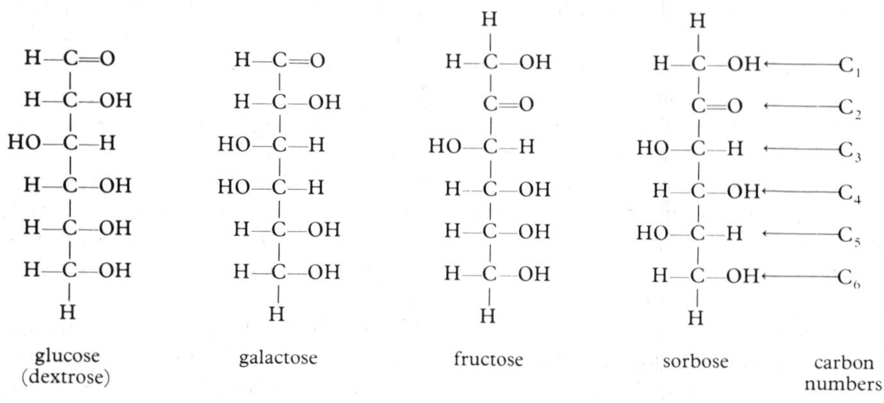

Figure 6.3 The structural formulae of the four sugars studied in Investigation 6.3.

Figure 6.4 The structural formulae of two other sugars.

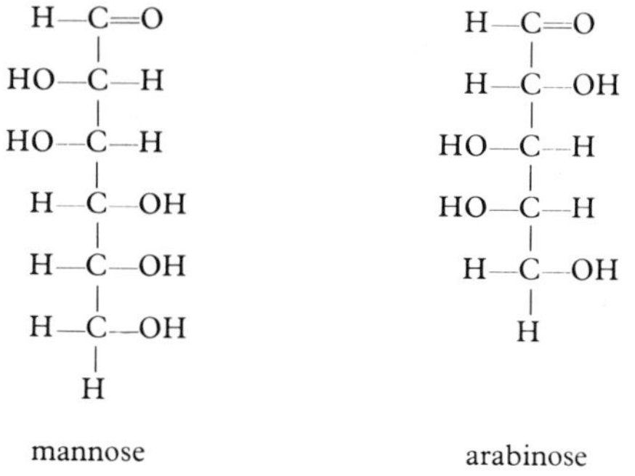

mannose

arabinose

Requirements
Constant-temperature water bath at 37 °C
Polypropylene test tube rack
Fermentation tubes (Durham: 50 × 7.5 mm) ×5
Test tubes ×5
Pipette or syringe (for delivering 1.0 cm^3 quantities)
Wax pencil*
Ruler with mm scale

Flask of brewer's or baker's yeast (10 per cent)
Distilled water
20 per cent solutions of the following sugars: glucose (dextrose), fructose, galactose, sorbose, (mannose) (arabinose)

* Since wax writing tends to melt at high temperatures a non-water soluble felt pen may be preferred.

7 Remove the test tubes from the water bath, and re-measure the height of the fluid in each fermentation tube. If enough gas has collected in the fermentation tube to make it buoyant, you must push it down when taking your reading.
8 Record the difference in height between the initial and final reading for each of the tubes.

For Consideration

(1) Figure 6.3 shows the structural formulae of the four sugars investigated in this experiment. All four have the general formula $C_6H_{12}O_6$, but they differ in the positions of their hydrogen and oxygen atoms, and OH groups, in relation to the carbon atoms. The carbon atoms are numbered 1–6.

From your results, which positions are important, and which ones unimportant, in determining whether or not the yeast enzymes will break down the sugar?
(2) Figure 6.4 shows the structural formulae of two other sugars, mannose and arabinose. Compare these formulae with those of the other sugars, and predict which ones can be fermented by yeast. If time and facilities permit, test your predictions.
(3) Interpret the results of this experiment in terms of what you know about how enzymes work.

Investigation 6.6
Effect of enzyme and substrate concentrations on the hydrolysis of sucrose

The rate at which an enzyme breaks down its substrate depends partly on the relative concentrations of enzyme and substrate in the solution. These effects can be investigated either by comparing the rate at which different amounts of enzyme break down the same quantity of substrate, or by maintaining a constant concentration of enzyme and varying the substrate concentration.

The enzyme sucrase (invertase) hydrolyses the disaccharide sucrose to the monosaccharides glucose and fructose:

$$\underset{\text{Sucrose}}{C_{12}H_{22}O_{11}} + H_2O \rightarrow \underset{\text{Glucose}}{C_6H_{12}O_6} + \underset{\text{Fructose}}{C_6H_{12}O_6}$$

Sucrose does not give a positive test when heated with Benedict's solution, but glucose and fructose both yield a yellow, brown or red precipitate (*see* page 42).

Whether you wish to determine the effect of enzyme concentration or substrate concentration on the rate of a reaction, it is essential to measure the *initial* rate. This is because, in any one test tube, the rate of a reaction declines with time.

Procedure

1 Take eight clean, dry test tubes and number them 1–8. With a syringe, add 1 cm^3 of Benedict's solution to each tube.
2 Make sure that one water bath is set to 38 °C, the other to 50 °C.
3 Add 5 cm^3 of 2 per cent sucrose solution to a test tube and place it in the 38 °C water bath. Add 5 cm^3 of 1 per cent sucrase solution to a test tube and place in the same water bath.
4 Leave both test tubes in the water bath for five minutes to allow their temperatures to reach the temperature of the water in the bath.
5 Have ready eight clean 1 cm^3 syringes, and a stopclock.
6 Simultaneously start the stopclock and pour the sucrase solution into the sucrose solution. Swirl the contents of the test tube and rapidly put it back into the 38 °C water bath.
7 After thirty seconds, remove 1 cm^3 of the reaction mixture with a syringe and squirt it into the test tube labelled 1 in the test tube rack.
8 Repeat this procedure every 30 seconds, placing your samples in test tubes 2–8 in turn.
9 Place test tubes 1–8 in the water bath at 50 °C for five minutes. Watch the test tubes. Record the approximate amount of precipitate formed in each tube.
10 Investigate the influence of enzyme concentration as follows: repeat Steps 1–10 twice, using 0.75 per cent and

0.5 per cent sucrase solutions respectively with 2 per cent sucrose solutions.

11 Investigate the influence of substrate concentration as follows: repeat Steps 1–10 three times, using 0.25, 0.5 and 1 per cent sucrose solutions respectively with 1 per cent sucrase each time.

12 Carry out the following controls. Separately, test a sucrose solution and a sucrase solution for reducing sugars. Heat the solution to be tested with Benedict's reagent in a water bath. Both tests should be negative.

Requirements
Beaker
Bunsen burner
Marker for writing on glass
Matches
Measuring cylinders
Stopclock
Syringes (1 cm^3) ×9
Test tube holder
Test tube rack
Test tubes ×12
Water baths at 38 °C and 50 °C

Benedict's reagent
Distilled water
Sucrase (invertase) solutions (0.5, 0.75, 1 per cent)
Sucrose solutions (0.25, 0.5, 1, 2 per cent)

For consideration

(1) Examine your results. What relationship is there between the initial rate of reaction and either enzyme or substrate concentration?
(2) It may be possible to express your results graphically, by measuring the rate of reaction as 1/reaction time for first reducing sugars to be detected. You may then be able to plot reaction rate (vertical axis) against enzyme or substrate concentration (horizontal axis).
(3) Explain the relationship you obtained in terms of the dynamics of interactions between enzyme and substrate molecules.
(4) Why does sucrose yield a negative Benedicts test whilst the two sugars of which it is composed both give positive tests?
(5) Do you think that the Benedicts solution stops the reaction between enzyme and substrate?

Note: Investigation 6.4 (page 53) on potato catalase can be modified to investigate the effects of enzyme and substrate concentration rather than pH.

Reference: N.P. Green, G.W. Stout, D.J. Taylor, *Biological Science Volume 1*, (Cambridge University Press, 1984)

Investigation 6.7
Synthesis of starch using an enzyme extracted from potato

Potato tubers contain an enzyme capable of synthesising starch from simple substrates. The aim of this investigation is to find out which particular substrates the enzyme can act on to make starch. The results can tell us something about equilibria, enzyme specificity and the energetics of starch synthesis. Starch is a polymer of glucose units. We shall investigate three possible substrates: glucose, glucose-1-phosphate (formed from a reaction between glucose and ATP) and maltose.

Procedure

1 Take one medium-sized potato. Peel it. Cut the peeled potato into small pieces. Put about 20 cm^3 of water into a mortar and add a few pieces of potato. Add a pinch of sand. Grind the potato with a mortar.

2 Pour the liquid part of the extract into two centrifuge tubes, so that each contains an equal volume. Try to prevent sand and solid matter getting into the tubes: any that does so should be distributed roughly equally between the two tubes.

3 Spin the extracts in a centrifuge at 3000 rpm for four minutes (Appendix 3.3). The object is to throw down the starch, cell walls and other solid matter to the bottom of the centrifuge tubes. The starch-free liquid above the deposit should contain the enzyme.

4 Stop the centrifuge. To test whether or not the liquid in the tubes is starch-free, use a teat pipette to withdraw a few drops of the clear, supernatant liquid. Squirt it into a test-tube which contains 1 cm^3 of iodine solution. If a blue colour appears, some starch remains and the potato extract needs to be centrifuged again.

5 Using a teat pipette, withdraw from the centrifuge tubes as much as possible of the clear enzyme solution, without disturbing the deposit beneath. Put this enzyme solution into a test tube.

6 Distribute the enzyme solution equally amongst three test tubes.

7 Label three clean test tubes G-1-P, G and M respectively. Using a separate syringe in each case, place 3 cm^3 glucose-1-phosphate in the G-1-P tube, 3 cm^3 glucose solution in the G tube and 3 cm^3 maltose solution in the M tube.

8 Pour the starch-free enzyme solution from one of the enzyme tubes into the G-1-P tube, containing glucose-1-phosphate. Mix well, note the time, and immediately withdraw one drop of solution with a glass rod. Touch the

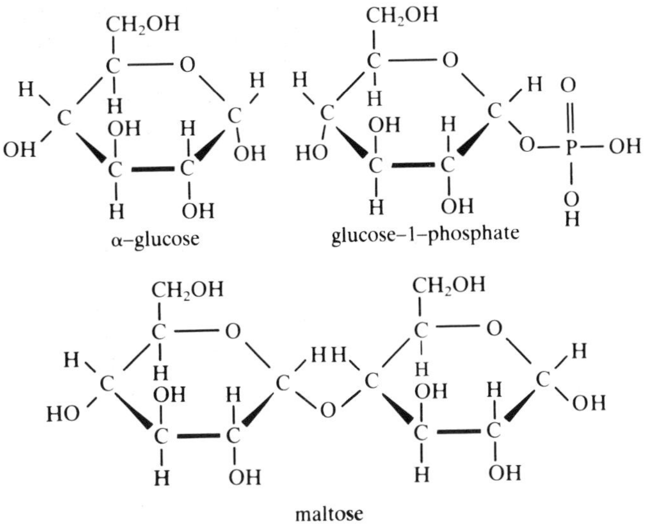

Figure 6.5 The three substrates investigated in Investigation 6.7.

Requirements
Centrifuge and centrifuge tubes
Test tube rack
Pestle and mortar
Marker for writing on glass
Test tubes ×7
Teat pipette
Syringes (5 cm^3) ×3
Glass rod
White tile

Glucose-1-phosphate solution (3 cm^3, 1 per cent)
Glucose solution (3 cm^3, 1 per cent)
Maltose solution (3 cm^3, 1 per cent)
Iodine solution

Potato tuber

drop onto a drop of fresh iodine solution on a white tile, and record the colour produced.

9 Repeat at intervals of one minute *for fifteen minutes*. Record the colour each time. If starch is being made in the test tube a blue colour will eventually appear when a drop of the reaction mixture is added to the iodine solution.

10 Repeat Steps 8 and 9 using the glucose (G) and maltose (M) solutions in turn. In which of the solutions is starch synthesised?

For consideration

(1) The chemical structures of the three substrates are shown in Figure 6.5. What feature of the substrate molecule do you think was recognised by the starch-synthesising enzyme?

(2) The synthesis of polymers such as starch requires metabolic energy. What was the source of this energy in the successful reaction?

(3) The enzyme which was isolated from potatoes is called starch phosphorylase. In the intact potato tuber it is also used to *break down* starch. How did conditions in the test tube differ in a way which favoured starch synthesis? In what circumstances does the enzyme bring about starch synthesis in a potato?

(4) In plant leaves, starch accumulates in chloroplasts. The synthesis of starch requires ATP. Where does this ATP come from?

Questions and Problems

1 Discuss the significance of the first and second laws of thermodynamics in cell biology.

2 More than 1000 different chemical reactions may take place in a single cell. How are confusion and chaos prevented?

3 (a) In what ways do enzymes (i) resemble, and (ii) differ from inorganic catalysts?
(b) Explain how the special properties of enzymes are a consequence of the structure of enzyme molecules. (*JMB modified*)

4 The table shows the activity of an enzyme (in arbitrary units) in relation to pH:

pH	4.5	5.5	6.5	7.5
Units of enzyme activity	3.1	9.6	14.5	10.1

(a) Have you any criticisms of the data?
(b) What general features of enzyme action are illustrated by these figures?
(c) How are the results related to the chemical structure of enzymes?
(d) Give an example of a particular enzyme that might give such results.
(e) Give examples of enzymes which would *not* be expected to give these results. (*JMB modified*)

5 An experiment was carried out to investigate the effect of temperature on the initial rate of an enzyme-controlled reaction. The concentrations of enzyme and substrate were kept constant at all the temperatures investigated. The results are shown below:

Temperature (°C)	**Initial rate of reaction** (mg of products per unit time)
5	0.3
10	0.5
15	0.9
20	1.4
25	2.0
30	2.7
35	3.3
40	3.6
45	3.6
50	2.3
55	0.9
60	0

Plot the results on graph paper. Interpret and explain them as fully as you can.

6 Two types of enzyme inhibitor are recognised. In the first, the extent to which the enzyme-controlled reaction is inhibited depends on the relative concentration of the substrate and inhibitor. In the second, the extent of the inhibition depends only on the concentration of the inhibitor, and cannot be varied by changing the amount of substrate present. From this information, suggest a hypothesis explaining the action of each type of inhibitor.

7 An experiment was carried out to investigate the effect of varying the concentration of substrate on the enzymatic hydrolysis of adenosine triphosphate (ATP). The concentration of enzyme (ATPase) was kept constant at each substrate concentration investigated. The results are shown below.

Concentration of substrate (ATP) (millimol dm^{-3})	**Rate of hydrolysis** (micromol $dm^{-3}\ s^{-1}$)
0.01	0.06
0.02	0.09
0.04	0.15
0.08	0.18
0.17	0.19
0.25	0.19

(a) Plot the results on a graph and interpret them as fully as you can.
(b) Would you expect the shape of the graph to be the same whatever enzyme-controlled reaction was investigated? Explain your answer.

8 Suggest ways in which enzyme inhibitors might be made use of in (a) agriculture, (b) medical practice, and (c) biochemical research.

9 Figure 6.6 is a graph of the reaction velocity (V) of an enzyme-controlled reaction, as a function of the substrate concentration [S] for a fixed amount of enzyme.
(a) Explain in your own words precisely what the graph demonstrates.
(b) How would you account for these relationships?
(c) K_m is called the Michaelis constant. What is the significance of knowing this value?
(CL modified)

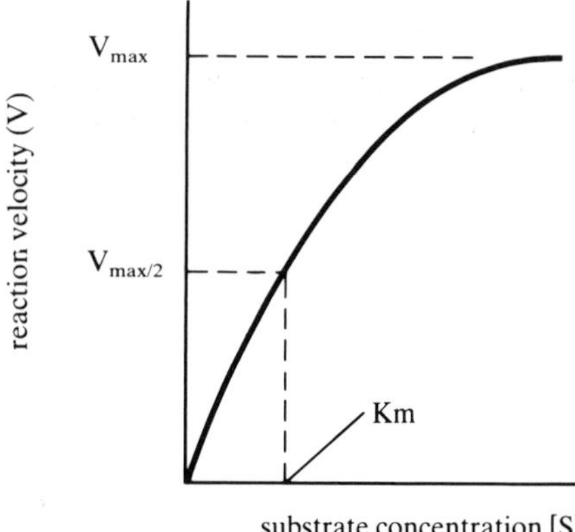

Figure 6.6 Graph of the reaction velocity (V) as a function of the substrate concentration [S] for a fixed amount of ensyme.

7 The Release of Energy

Background Summary

1 Energy is released by **respiration** which occurs in all living cells. It generally involves the oxidation of sugar:

$$C_6H_{12}O_6 + 6O_2 \rightarrow 6H_2O + 6CO_2 + \text{Energy}$$

2 Simple experiments can be carried out to show that oxygen is used and carbon dioxide produced in respiration. In the human, quantitative comparisons of the amount of oxygen and carbon dioxide in inspired and expired air can be carried out by **gas analysis**.

3 Dividing the amount of CO_2 produced by the amount of O_2 consumed gives the **respiratory quotient** (RQ). Knowledge of the RQ gives information on the type of food being respired, and the kind of metabolism that is taking place.

4 The rate of oxygen consumption of small organisms can be measured with a **respirometer.** For humans a **spirometer** can be used. The rate of oxygen consumption provides a measure of the **metabolic rate**. The metabolic rate increases during muscular exercise.

5 Another method of determining the metabolic rate is to estimate the energy released by the organism per unit time. This can be done by measuring heat production using a **calorimeter**.

6 The minimum amount of energy on which the body can survive is the **basal metabolic rate** (BMR). Actual metabolic rates usually exceed the BMR, and depend on the activity of the individual.

7 The energy value of different foods can be determined by means of a **food calorimeter** which measures the amount of heat produced when a given quantity of food is burned.

8 Sufficient energy-containing food must be consumed to maintain the BMR and to satisfy such additional energy needs as the individual's activities and circumstances demand.

9 The immediate source of energy for biological functions is **adenosine triphosphate** (ATP). In the presence of the enzyme ATPase, ATP can be hydrolysed into adenosine diphosphate (ADP) and inorganic phosphate with the release of free energy.

10 In appropriate conditions ATP can be synthesised from ADP and inorganic phosphate. This reaction *requires* energy.

11 Energy for synthesis of ATP comes from the breakdown of **sugar**, stored in cells as **glycogen** (animals) or **starch** (plants). Fat and protein are also potential sources of energy for ATP synthesis.

12 In **aerobic respiration** the step-by-step breakdown of sugar yields energy for ATP synthesis in two ways:
(a) Several of the reactions are exergonic, each releasing sufficient energy for synthesis of a limited number of ATP molecules.
(b) Many of the reactions involve the removal of pairs of hydrogen atoms (dehydrogenation) which are taken up by an acceptor. The hydrogen atoms, or their electrons, are then passed along a series of carriers, the energy released being used for synthesis of ATP. Most ATP is produced this way.

13 Aerobic breakdown of sugar occurs in two main stages: **glycolysis** (sugar → pyruvic acid) followed by **Krebs' citric acid cycle** (also known as the **tricarboxylic acid cycle** or **TCA cycle**). Most of the energy for ATP synthesis is derived from electron carrier systems associated with the Krebs cycle.

14 Evidence suggests that glycolysis takes place in the cytoplasmic matrix (cytosol), Krebs' cycle in the matrix of the mitochondria, and electron transfer in the membranes of the mitochondria. Mitchell's **chemiosmotic theory** helps to explain the role of the mitochondrial membranes in this process.

15 The Krebs cycle is connected with fat and protein metabolism as well as carbohydrate. This enables all three groups of compounds to be used as sources of energy for ATP synthesis and it allows metabolic interconversions between them.

16 In anaerobic respiration pyruvic acid is converted into **lactic acid** (animals and certain bacteria) or **ethanol** (plants and yeasts). Krebs' cycle is omitted and the mitochondria are not involved. Considerably less energy is released in anaerobic than in aerobic respiration.

17 The rate of sugar breakdown is controlled by the relative concentrations of ATP and ADP in the cell, a **negative feedback system**.

Investigation 7.1
Composition of inspired and expired air

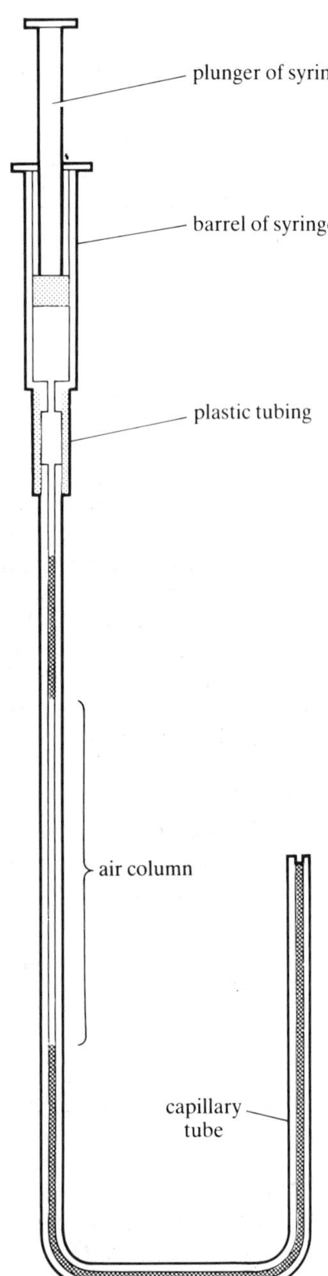

Figure 7.1 J tube for gas analysis. A column of air has been drawn into the straight part of the tube. (Commercial versions of this apparatus have a screw attachment instead of a syringe.)

> **CAUTION:**
> Pyrogallol can be harmful and should be handled with care. Do not spill it, or get it on your skin.

One of the best ways of confirming the general nature of respiration is to compare the amounts of oxygen and carbon dioxide in inspired (i.e. atmospheric) and expired air. This can be done by means of gas analysis. The experiment is even more interesting if we analyse samples of expired air before and after a bout of exercise. How would you *expect* them to differ, and why?

Method

The principle behind the method of analysing the gases in a sample of air is as follows. A sample of the air is drawn into a capillary tube and its volume noted. Potassium hydroxide is then introduced into the tube, absorbing any carbon dioxide present and causing the air to decrease in volume. The new volume is noted. Then potassium pyrogallate is admitted. This absorbs any oxygen present, causing the air to decrease in volume once more. Again the new volume is noted. From the decrease in the volume of air when the potassium hydroxide and pyrogallate are added, the percentages of carbon dioxide and oxygen in the air sample can be calculated.

The tube into which the air is drawn is bent and is called a J tube. Air is drawn into it by means of a syringe at one end (Figure 7.1). The volume of the air sample is expressed as the length of capillary tube which it occupies.

It is important that all the air samples which you collect should be at constant temperature. This is most conveniently achieved by ensuring that all water and reagents drawn into the tube are at room temperature and that any air samples collected are given time to come to room temperature before their volumes are measured. If possible carry out your analyses with the J-tube under water which has equilibrated with room temperature.

To improve the accuracy, at least three samples of air should be analysed and the average taken.

Procedure

ANALYSIS OF ATMOSPHERIC AIR

1 Pour water into a small beaker, a small amount of potassium hydroxide into a second beaker, pyrogallol into a third beaker, and dilute hydrochloric acid into a fourth beaker. Label each beaker so you don't get them muddled up.

2 Push the plunger of the syringe to the far end of the barrel of the J tube. Immerse the end of the J tube in the beaker of water, then carefully pull the plunger until a column of water approximately 5 cm in length has been drawn into the tube.

3 Remove the tube from the water and draw in approximately 10 cm of air. Then draw in water again until the column of air occupies the straight part of the J tube (Figure 7.1). Wait for at least one minute, and do not handle the straight part of the tube where the air is located (why?). Now measure the length of the air column with a ruler.

4 Expel all but about 1 cm of the water from the far end of the J tube and then admit concentrated potassium hydroxide into the tube. Keeping the tip of the J tube in the hydroxide, carefully shuttle the potassium hydroxide backwards and forwards about six times so the air sample is given an opportunity to come into contact with the sides of the tube which have been wetted with the hydroxide. The hydroxide will absorb carbon dioxide from the air sample. Wait for a further minute, then re-measure the length of the air column. In fact you will probably find that the decrease is negligible and difficult to measure.

5 Now expel all but the last 5 *cm* or so of the hydroxide and draw in pyrogallol. Keeping the tip of the J tube in the pyrogallol, shuttle slowly backwards and forwards as before but never expel the last 5 cm of the hydroxide. The pyrogallol will react with the potassium hydroxide still in the tube, forming potassium pyrogallate which will absorb oxygen from the air sample. Wait for another minute, then measure the length of the air column again.

6 Wash out the J tube thoroughly, first with dilute hydrochloric acid and then water.

7 Calculate the percentage of carbon dioxide and oxygen in the air sample.

$$\text{Percentage of } CO_2 \text{ in the air sample} = \frac{a - b}{a} \times 100$$

$$\text{Percentage of } O_2 \text{ in the air sample} = \frac{b - c}{a} \times 100$$

(a = original length before KOH admitted
b = new length after KOH admitted
c = new length after pyrogallol admitted)

A

B

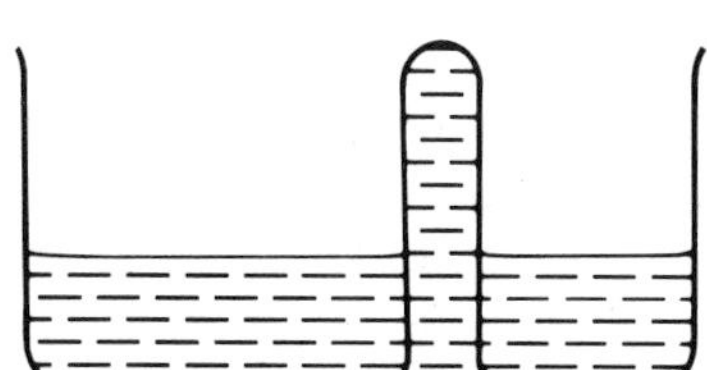

Place large test tube on its side in bowl of water, and allow test tube to fill up with water.

Raise test tube into vertical position in bowl.

C

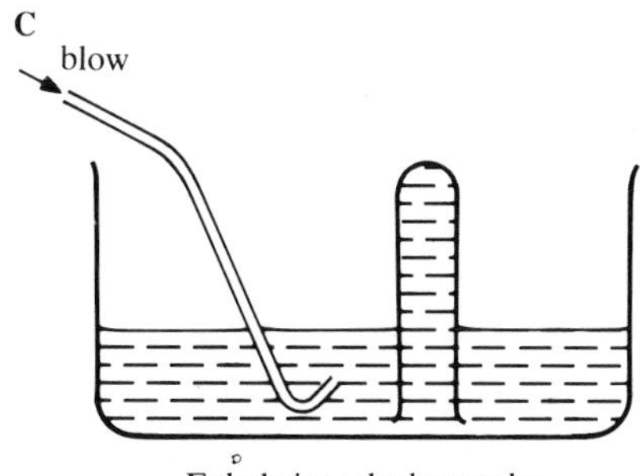

D

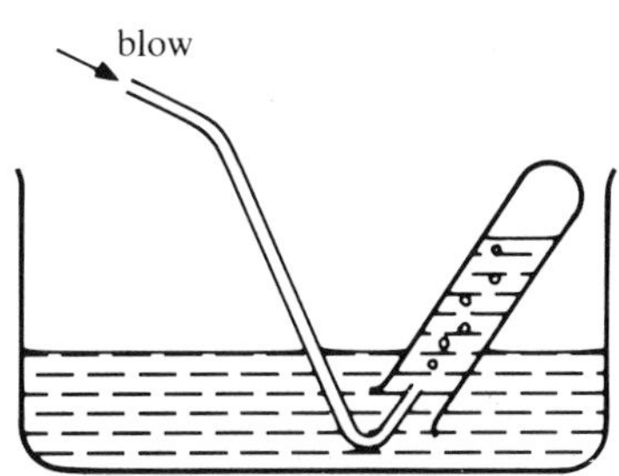

Exhale into the bent tube as shown.

Towards end of breath, insert tip of bent tube into test tube and collect the *last lot* of expired air in the test tube.

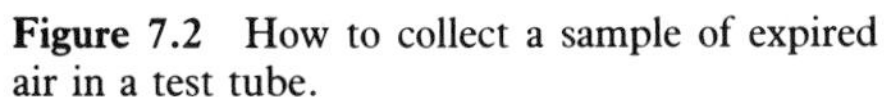

Figure 7.2 How to collect a sample of expired air in a test tube.

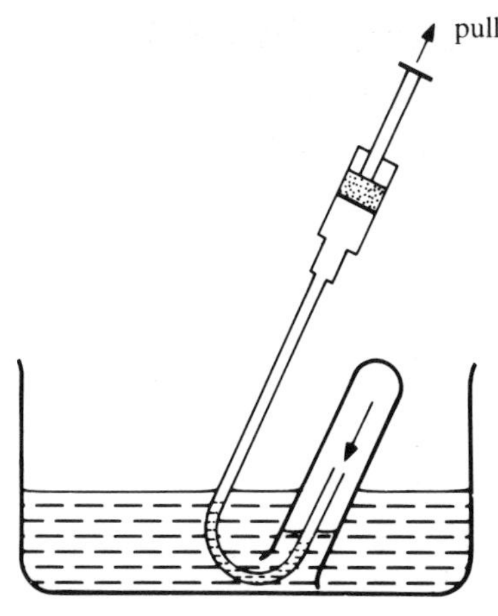

Figure 7.3 Drawing a sample of the expired air into the J tube.

Requirements
J tube (*see* Figure 7.1)
Bent glass tube (*see* Figure 7.2)
Four small beakers
Ruler
Large test tube (24 × 150 mm)
Bowl (large enough for the test tube to be laid down flat in)

Concentrated potassium hydroxide solution
Concentrated benzene-1, 2, 3-triol (pyrogallol, pyrogallic acid)
Dilute hydrochloric acid

Note: It is conventional in gas analysis to use previously prepared potassium pyrogallate (alkaline pyrogallol) for absorbing oxygen. Potassium pyrogallate is unstable and must be made up immediately before the practical session by mixing equal quantities of pyrogallol (pyrogallic acid) and potassium hydroxide. The potassium pyrogallate thus formed must then be covered with liquid paraffin to prevent it taking up oxygen. When the experiment is performed, the end of the J tube has to be inserted through the liquid paraffin before the potassium pyrogallate is sucked up. This is messy and can be avoided by sucking up pyrogallol instead of potassium pyrogallate and allowing it to react with potassium hydroxide still in the J tube, as described in the instructions for this experiment.

ANALYSIS OF EXPIRED AIR IN RESTING CONDITIONS

1 Collect a sample of expired air in a large test tube by the method shown in Figure 7.2.

It is essential that the expired air which you collect for your analysis should come from the *depth* of your lungs. Breathe out into the bent tube but don't insert the tip into the test tube until the very end of your expiration.

2 After you have expired into the test tube wait for several minutes until your expired air comes to room temperature.

3 Now admit approximately 5 cm of water into the J tube. Then insert the tip of the J tube into the upturned test tube and draw in about 10 cm of your expired air (Figure 7.3). Then draw in water again. Measure the length of the column of air.

4 Analyse first the carbon dioxide and then the oxygen in the sample of expired air exactly as you did for atmospheric air. Use *fresh* pyrogallol – not the same lot that you used for the previous analysis (why?).

5 When you have finished wash out the J tube with dilute hydrochloric acid followed by water.

ANALYSIS OF EXPIRED AIR AFTER EXERCISE

1 Perform a bout of vigorous exercise as instructed by your teacher.

2 Immediately after taking the exercise collect a sample of expired air from the depth of your lungs and analyse it as before. It is important that the air should be at room temperature before you analyse it so don't measure the length of the air column in the J tube until you have given it time to come to room temperature.

3 Do not forget to wash out the J tube when you have finished.

RESULTS

Copy Table 7.1 into your notebook and fill in your results. Interpret your results as fully as possible.

	Atmospheric Air	Expired air resting	Expired air exercise
CO_2 (%)			
O_2 (%)			

Table 7.1 Table for recording the results of Investigation 7.1.

For consideration

(1) You will have found it very difficult to measure accurately the percentage of carbon dioxide in atmospheric air. Why was this, and how might the J tube be improved so as to achieve a better result?
(2) What sources of error might there be in the way you measured the percentage of oxygen in this experiment? How could you minimise the errors?
(3) What other gases (besides the ones investigated in this experiment) are present in the air we breathe? What is their significance, if any, in respiration?

Investigation 7.2
Oxygen consumption in humans

CAUTION:
Experiments involving prolonged breathing in and out of a spirometer can be dangerous and should only be done under close supervision by a teacher.

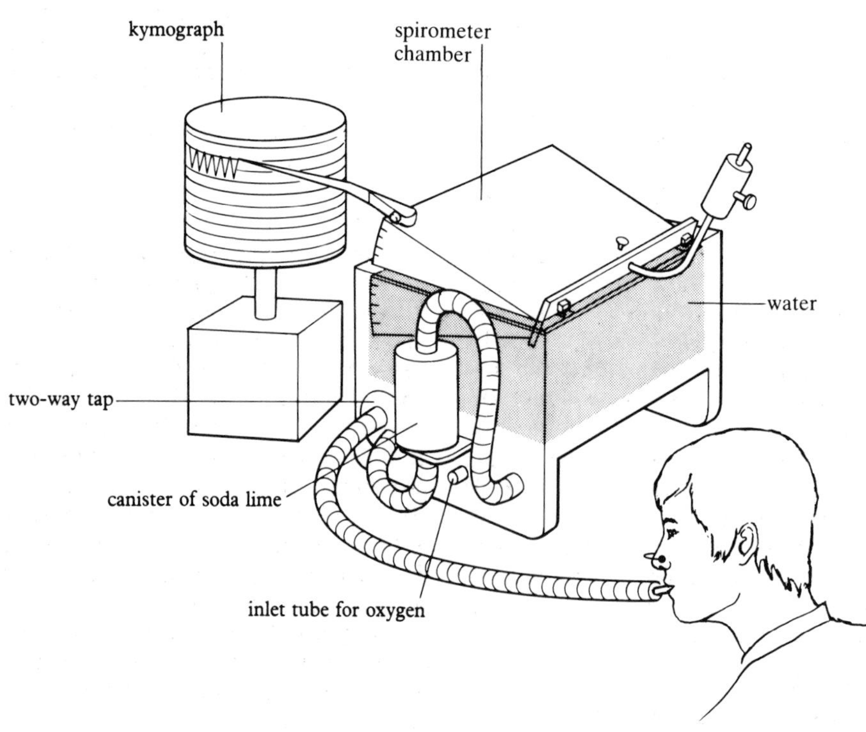

Figure 7.4 A recording spirometer in use. The horizontal lines on the kymograph represent 250 cm^3 divisions.

For the cells of the body to maintain their vital activities, a continual expenditure of energy is required. This energy comes from the oxidative breakdown of food. Estimating oxygen consumption gives a measure of the metabolic rate. In this investigation changes in the metabolic rate will be related to different kinds of activity.

Method

The technique involves the use of a spirometer. The model recommended for this experiment consists of an inverted perspex lid floating in a tank of water (Figure 7.4). The chamber is filled with oxygen and connected to the subject by a rubber mouthpiece at the end of a length of flexible tubing. A canister of self-indicating soda lime is inserted between the mouthpiece and the spirometer chamber so all the carbon dioxide expired by the subject is absorbed. At the side of the spirometer is a two-way tap enabling the subject to be quickly connected to, or disconnected from, the spirometer chamber. The subject's nose must be clipped so that, when connected, the lungs and respiratory tract form a closed system with the chamber and tubing of the spirometer. As the subject breathes in and out, the lid goes up and down in time with his or her breathings, and slowly sinks as oxygen is used up.

The lid is counter-balanced by an adjustable mass which should be set so that the lid falls very slowly when the spirometer chamber is open to the atmosphere. When the chamber is closed off, the lid should remain stationary: if it falls there is a leak in the system.

Changes in the volume of oxygen in the spirometer chamber can be read off the scale attached to the side of the lid. Alternatively, movements of the lid can be recorded by a pen writing on a slowly revolving kymograph drum (*see* Appendix 3, page 384). The drum is fitted with paper calibrated horizontally for volume. It is necessary to know the speed at which the drum rotates so that the rate of oxygen consumption can be measured. The kymograph should be set at a speed of approximately 20 mm min^{-1}.

Procedure for doing an experiment

1 With the two-way tap closed, fill the spirometer chamber with medical-grade oxygen from a cylinder. Make a note of the volume, or if you are using a kymograph, put ink in the pen and bring it into contact with the top of the drum surface.

2 Rinse the rubber mouthpiece in antiseptic and insert it into the subject's mouth. Clip the subject's nose. The two-way tap being closed, the subject is connected to the outside atmosphere and should remain so until he or she has got accustomed to breathing through the mouthpiece.

3 When you are ready to proceed, turn the two-way tap so as to connect the subject with the spirometer chamber. This must be done *at the end of a normal expiration*, so the first movement of the spirometer lid will be downwards.

4 When you have finished, turn the tap at the end of a normal expiration so as to disconnect the subject from the spirometer and re-connect him or her with the atmosphere. If you are not using a kymograph, make a note of the new volume.

5 Determine the subject's oxygen consumption by subtracting the new volume from the initial volume. This can be done using the scale on the lid or, if you are using a kymograph, from your recordings. It is most important that both the initial and final volume are taken at the end of a normal expiration.

Body mass (kg)	Height (cm)										
	120	130	140	150	160	170	180	190	200	210	220
40	1.15	1.20	1.25	1.30	1.36	1.42	1.48	1.55			
45	1.23	1.27	1.32	1.37	1.43	1.48	1.54	1.61			
50	1.30	1.34	1.39	1.44	1.49	1.54	1.60	1.67	1.74		
55	1.37	1.42	1.46	1.50	1.55	1.61	1.67	1.73	1.80		
60	1.44	1.48	1.52	1.57	1.62	1.67	1.73	1.79	1.85	1.92	
65		1.54	1.58	1.63	1.68	1.73	1.79	1.85	1.91	1.97	
70		1.61	1.65	1.70	1.75	1.80	1.85	1.91	1.96	2.02	2.08
75		1.68	1.72	1.76	1.81	1.86	1.91	1.96	2.02	2.07	2.13
80		1.74	1.78	1.82	1.86	1.91	1.96	2.02	2.07	2.13	2.18
85		1.81	1.84	1.88	1.92	1.97	2.02	2.07	2.13	2.18	2.24
90		1.87	1.90	1.94	1.98	2.03	2.08	2.13	2.18	2.24	2.30
95			1.97	2.01	2.05	2.09	2.14	2.18	2.24	2.30	2.36
100			2.03	2.07	2.12	2.16	2.20	2.24	2.30	2.35	2.41
105			2.10	2.14	2.18	2.22	2.26	2.31	2.35	2.41	2.47
110			2.17	2.21	2.24	2.28	2.32	2.36	2.41	2.47	2.53
115			2.23	2.27	2.30	2.33	2.38	2.42	2.47	2.53	2.58
120				2.33	2.36	2.39	2.43	2.48	2.53	2.58	2.63
125				2.39	2.42	2.45	2.49	2.53	2.58	2.63	2.69
130				2.44	2.47	2.51	2.54	2.59	2.63	2.68	2.75
135				2.50	2.53	2.56	2.60	2.64	2.69	2.74	2.81
140				2.55	2.58	2.62	2.66	2.70	2.74	2.80	2.87

Table 7.2 Surface area in square metres (m^2) of humans in relation to height and body mass. (From A. Grinnell and A.A. Barber, *Laboratory Experiments in Physiology*, Mosby, 9th ed, 1976).

Experiments

OXYGEN CONSUMPTION AT REST

1 With the subject sitting as relaxed as possible, connect him or her to the spirometer chamber.

2 Record the subject's breathings for five minutes. Estimate the total oxygen consumption in cm^3 during the five-minute period. What is the oxygen consumption in cm^3 per minute?

OXYGEN CONSUMPTION DURING AND AFTER EXERCISE

1 Refill the spirometer with oxygen. The same subject, with mouthpiece in position and two-way tap open to the atmosphere, should now engage in vigorous exercise (e.g. running on the spot) for 12 minutes.

2 Measure the oxygen consumption during the 9th and 10th minutes. During the 11th and 12th minutes, while the subject continues to exercise, the partner should top up the spirometer with oxygen.

3 After 12 minutes' exercise the subject should rest. As soon as he or she does so, the partner should estimate the oxygen consumption over a further five minutes, i.e. during the subject's recovery period.

4 Estimate the oxygen consumption in cm^3 per minute for the 9th and 10th minutes of exercise, and for the five-minute recovery period.

RESULTS

1 Oxygen consumption gives a measure of metabolic rate. Find the subject's body mass in kilograms and calculate the oxygen consumption in $dm^3\ O_2\ kg^{-1}\ h^{-1}$ (a) in resting conditions, (b) during exercise, (c) during recovery.

2 It has been calculated that for every dm^3 of oxygen consumed by the body, approximately 20.18 kJ of energy are released. Express the subject's metabolic rate in $kJ\ kg^{-1}\ h^{-1}$ (a) in resting conditions, (b) during exercise, (c) during recovery.

3 The energy produced by an animal is most closely related to its surface area. Obtain the subject's surface area from Table 7.2. Express the subject's metabolic rate in $kJ\ m^{-2}\ h^{-1}$ (a) in resting conditions, (b) during exercise, (c) during recovery.

For consideration

(1) How does the oxygen consumption during exercise compare with the resting oxygen consumption? Explain the reason for the difference.

(2) How does the five-minute recovery oxygen consumption compare with the resting oxygen consumption? Why should a high metabolic rate continue after muscular exertion has ceased?

(3) To what extent does the subject's resting metabolic rate, as measured in this experiment, approximate to his or her *basal* metabolic rate?

(4) Why should the metabolic rate be related more closely to surface area than to other parameters such as body mass or height?

Requirements
Recording spirometer with concertina tubing, mouthpiece, nose clip, CO_2-absorber, and recording pen
Eosin or non-clogging ink
Kymograph set at speed of about 20 mm/min
Kymograph paper calibrated horizontally for volume (250 cm^3 divisions)
Oxygen cylinder (medical grade)

Investigation 7.3
Effect of temperature on the oxygen consumption of broad bean seeds

In organisms such as plants and insects, which cannot control their body temperature, the body temperature fluctuates with the temperature of the environment. The respiration rate of such organisms changes accordingly. The aim of this experiment is to compare the rates of respiration of broad bean seeds at different temperatures.

Method

The respiration rate can be estimated by measuring the rate of gas exchange with a **respirometer**. If aerobic respiration is taking place and glucose is the substrate being oxidised, the volume of oxygen taken up equals the volume of carbon dioxide produced. In a closed vessel containing seeds which are respiring, the concentration of oxygen will decrease and the concentration of carbon dioxide will increase. The total volume of gases should remain constant.

If a compound which absorbs carbon dioxide is placed inside the closed vessel, the pressure in the vessel decreases as oxygen is absorbed by the seeds during respiration. The rate at which the pressure falls is a measure of the rate at which the respiring tissue is taking up oxygen. This is the principle behind a simple respirometer.

Two identical closed vessels are used. One contains living seeds and the other (the control) contains dead seeds. The control with dead seeds is necessary because temperature changes alter the pressures of the gases. Any differences in the two vessels can be attributed to gas exchange by the living seeds.

It is not necessary to restrict oneself to seeds in this experiment: other organisms can be used, including small animals such as maggots, mealworms or woodlice.

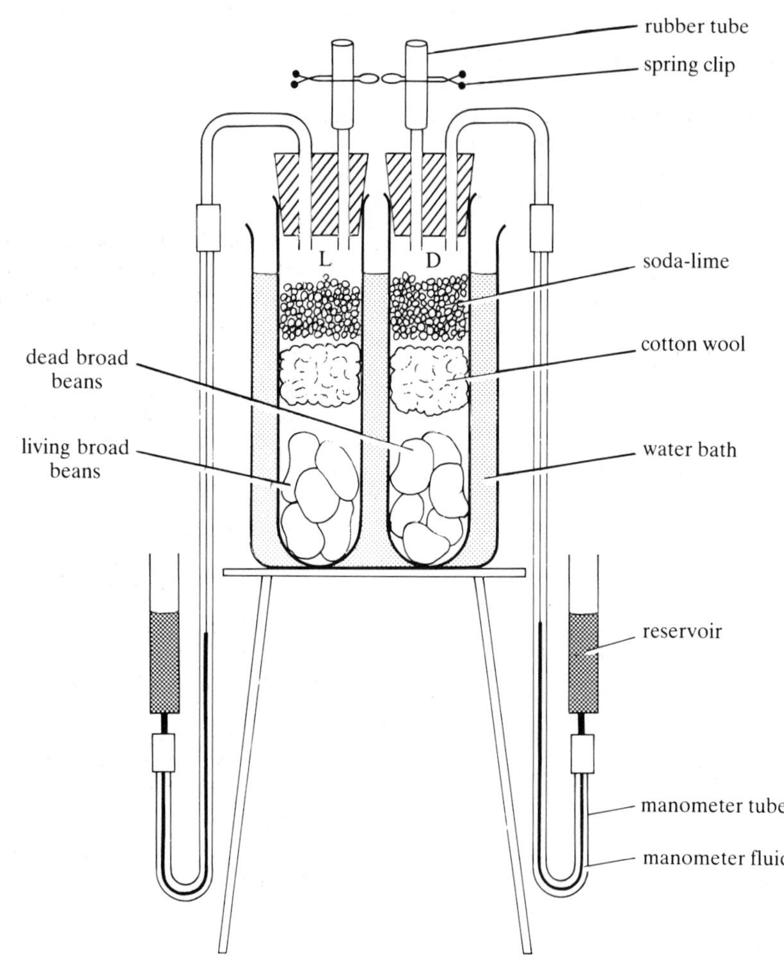

Figure 7.5 A respirometer, with control, for measuring the rate of oxygen uptake by small organisms, in this case broad beans. (*After D.G. Mackean)*

Procedure

1 Fill a beaker half full with cold water. Place it on a tripod and gauze and take the temperature of the water with a thermometer. If it is below 20 °C, heat the beaker gently with a bunsen burner until it reaches 20 °C. Then stop heating. The beaker of water is to serve as a water bath.

2 Label two boiling tubes L and D. Place six living broad bean seeds in tube L and six dead seeds in tube D.

3 Push a plug of cotton wool into each tube (see Figure 7.5). Place an equal mass (5 g) of self-indicating soda-lime on top of the cotton wool in each tube. Place both tubes in the water bath.

4 Pour coloured manometer fluid into the reservoir of one of the manometers. If air bubbles appear in the capillary tube of the manometer, blow down the long arm of the manometer tube to remove them (take care!).

5 Fit the long arm of the manometer tube into the rubber tubing attached to one of the rubber bungs. Fit the bung securely into one of the boiling tubes.

6 Repeat Steps 4 and 5 with the other manometer tube and bung. Your apparatus should now look like Figure 7.5.

7 Open both spring clips. Check that your water bath is at 20 °C. With a felt pen, mark the levels of the menisci of the coloured fluid in both manometer tubes. Close both the spring clips. Note the time.

8 Record the levels of the fluid in the manometers after 5, 10 and 15 minutes. If the level of the manometer fluid attached to boiling tube L does not change, check carefully for leaks and start again.

Requirements
Beaker
Bunsen, tripod, gauze, bench mat
Thermometer
Boiling tubes ×2
Rubber bungs (each with two holes) ×2
Cotton wool
Manometer tubes (capillaries) ×2
Pen for marking glass
Two-way taps ×2

Ice
Self-indicating soda-lime
Manometer fluid
Six broad bean (*Vicia faba*) seeds, soaked in cold water for 24 hours
Six broad bean seeds, soaked in cold water for 24 hours then placed in boiling water for 10 minutes and dipped in disinfectant to kill surface micro-organisms
As alternatives to broad beans, use 20 mung beans or garden peas, or six blowfly maggots.

9 Open both spring clips. Heat the water bath with a bunsen burner until the water temperature reaches 33 °C. Remove the bunsen burner. Allow at least five minutes for the beans to reach this temperature and for the volumes of air in the boiling tubes to stabilise. By this time the water should have cooled to 30 °C. Repeat Steps 7 and 8 at this temperature.
10 Open both spring clips. Pour away the water at 30 °C and replace it with cold tap water. Add a few cubes of ice until the water reaches 8 °C. Allow ten minutes for the beans to reach this temperature and for the volumes of air in the boiling tubes to stabilise. By this time the water in the beaker should have reached 10 °C. Repeat Steps 7 and 8 at this temperature.
11 Plot your data on a graph which shows the volume of oxygen evolved against time for each of the three temperatures.

For consideration

(1) How much faster is the respiration rate at 20 °C than at 10 °C? How much faster is the respiration rate at 30 °C than at 20 °C? In working out these ratios you are calculating two estimates of the Q_{10}. The Q_{10} denotes the extent to which the rate of reaction increases with a 10 °C increase in temperature. The Q_{10} is approximately 2 for a large number of enzyme-controlled reactions. Do your results agree with this?
(2) Explain in terms of the behaviour of individual molecules why the rate of an enzyme-controlled reaction doubles with a 10 °C increase in temperature. (There are two main reasons.)
(3) Suppose the uptake of oxygen suddenly stops but the seeds remain alive. Suggest an explanation.
(4) Glucose is not the only compound which is oxidised in cellular respiration. Some seeds store and respire fat, for example. Imagine that octodecanoic acid (stearic acid) is respired. The equation is:

$$C_{17}H_{35}COOH + 26O_2 \rightarrow 18CO_2 + 18H_2O$$

Suppose that fatty acids are used more in respiration at high temperatures than at low temperatures. How will this affect the results, if at all?

Reference: D.G. Mackean, *Experimental Work in Biology No. 7 – Respiration and Gaseous Exchange*, Murray, 1975.

Investigation 7.4
Multiplication of yeast cells in aerobic and anaerobic conditions

Cell division, like any other vital activity, requires energy, and the rate at which cells divide depends on the amount of energy available. Much more energy is produced by aerobic than by anaerobic respiration, and so we would expect cell division to proceed faster in aerobic than in anaerobic conditions. The following experiment is designed to test this hypothesis.

Procedure

1 Obtain three conical flasks of the following sizes: 50 cm^3, 150 cm^3, and 500 cm^3 (or close equivalents).
2 Pour 50 cm^3 of cider into each flask, and to each one add *one drop* of yeast suspension (make sure that the yeast suspension is mixed thoroughly first).
3 Cover the opening of each flask with four layers of muslin (cheese cloth) held in place by a rubber band. Leave your flasks in a warm cupboard for about a week.
4 One week later: thoroughly mix the contents in each of the three flasks to make sure that the yeast cells are uniformly distributed. For the two larger flasks this can be done by swirling the flasks; in the case of the small flask it can be done by sucking and expelling the contents back and forth with a pipette.
5 After the contents of each flask are thoroughly mixed, remove a sample with a clean pipette, and estimate the concentration of cells using a haemocytometer (*see* page 106).

For counting the cells select a type of square that contains between 8 and 12 cells per square. Count in as many squares as you consider necessary to give a reasonably accurate result, and carry out at least two separate counts for each flask. Express the concentration of yeast cells in each flask as number of cells per cm^3.

Requirements
Microscope
Haemocytometer
Conical flasks (50 cm^3, 150 cm^3, 500 cm^3)
Measuring cylinder (50 cm^3)
Muslin (cheese cloth)
Pipette
Elastic band

Rich culture of brewer's yeast
Uncontaminated dry cider

For Consideration

(1) How would you summarise conditions in the three flasks with reference to the availability of oxygen?
(2) Is our original hypothesis that cell division occurs more rapidly in aerobic than anaerobic conditions confirmed or refuted?
(3) Are there any other possible explanations for the different cell concentrations in the three flasks apart from availability of oxygen?
(4) Which do you consider is the critical factor determining the availability of oxygen: the depth of medium through which the oxygen has to diffuse to the yeast cells, or the surface area of the medium exposed to oxygen – or both?
(5) Can you, from the results of this investigation, make predictions concerning the shape and complexity of organisms in relation to their size? To answer this question think of each flask of cider as an *organism*.

Investigation 7.5
Effect of temperature on the rate of anaerobic respiration in yeast

Requirements
Balance
Beaker (250 cm^3)
Fermentation tubes ×6
Graph paper
Dropping pipettes ×3
Pipette or syringe (3 cm^3) ×3
Ruler with mm scale
Spatula
Stopclock or stopwatch
Test tubes ×6
Water baths (at 20 °C, 35 °C, and 50 °C)

Glucose (3 g)
Dried yeast (2 g)
Yeast extract (1 g)
Water (100 cm^3)

Many yeasts of the genus *Saccharomyces* can grow in the absence of oxygen. Under these conditions yeast respires anaerobically: glucose is converted to carbon dioxide and ethanol through the process of fermentation. The equation for this reaction is:

$$C_6H_{12}O_6 \rightarrow 2\ CO_2 + 2\ C_2H_5OH$$

The rate at which carbon dioxide is produced can be used to measure the rate of fermentation of yeast. In this experiment we shall determine the effect of temperature on the rate of fermentation.

Procedure

1 Set up a culture of yeast in a beaker using 2 g dried yeast, 3 g glucose, 1 g yeast extract and 100 cm^3 water.
2 Place this culture in an incubator or a water bath and leave it for an hour to allow fermentation to get underway.
3 Set up three water baths, at 20 °C, 35 °C and 50 °C. If thermostatically controlled water baths are not available you will need to use a water-filled beaker, supported on a tripod and gauze, over a Bunsen burner.
4 Using a pipette or syringe, transfer 3 cm^3 of the culture to each of six test tubes. Place two tubes in each water bath. Leave them there for five minutes to allow the temperature of their contents to reach the temperature of the water bath.
5 Now you need to fill a fermentation tube and insert it upside down into each test tube. Carry out the following procedure for each tube:
(a) Insert a teat pipette into the culture, suck up some of the culture and fill the fermentation tube to the brim.
(b) Hold the test tube at an angle. Invert the fermentation tube and quickly push it down the wall of the test tube. If the fermentation tube collects an air bubble on the way down remove it, refill it, and try once more.
6 At intervals of ten minutes, record the length of the carbon dioxide bubble within each fermentation tube. Work out the average bubble length for each temperature at each time interval.
7 Draw a graph of average bubble length (vertical axis) against time (horizontal axis). Plot three lines on it, one each for 20 °C, 35 °C and 50 °C.
8 Estimate the rate of fermentation at each temperature by measuring the slope of each line.

For consideration

(1) Give two reasons why the fermentation tubes were necessary in this investigation.
(2) Carbon dioxide is very soluble in water. Why did it accumulate at the end of the tube, instead of dissolving in the water?
(3) In what way does the rate of fermentation vary with temperature? Most enzyme-controlled processes approximately double in rate for each ten degree centigrade rise in temperature. Do your results confirm this general rule, or not?
(4) What lessons might brewers learn from the results of this experiment?

Reference: Revised Nuffield A-level Biology, *Practical Guide 2 – Chemical Reactions in Organisms*, Longman, 1985.

Questions and Problems

1 Without going into experimental details, discuss the principles underlying the different methods by which an organism's metabolic rate may be determined. Assess the advantages and disadvantages of each method.

2 (a) What is meant by respiratory quotient (RQ) and how would you measure it for a small animal like a mouse?
(b) The RQ for carbohydrate is 1.0, for fat 0.7, and for protein 0.9. What would you expect the RQ to be for most animals most of the time?
(c) Under what circumstances would you expect the RQ of an organism to be (i) greater than 1.0, (ii) lower than 0.7, and (iii) somewhere between 1.0 and 0.7?
(d) The graph in Figure 7.6 shows the respiratory quotients of *Zea mais* (maize) and *Ricinus communis* (castor oil) during germination. Account for the difference in shape of the two curves shown on the graph. *(AEB modified)*

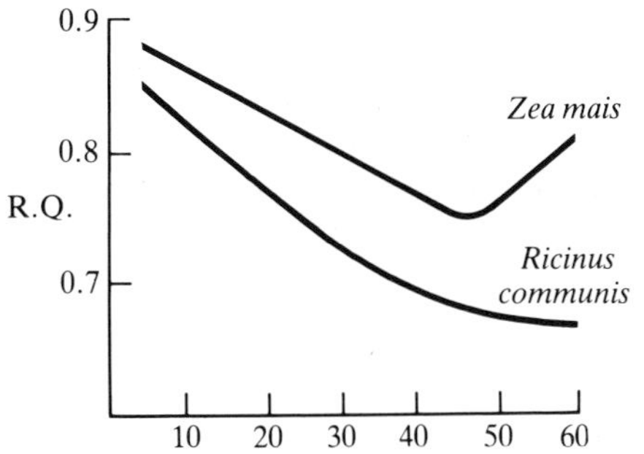

Figure 7.6 The respiratory quotients (RQ) of *Zea mais* and *Ricinus communis* during germination.

3 Refer to a suitable list of the calorific values of various foods:
(a) Make a rough estimate of your own daily energy intake.
(b) How adequate, or otherwise, is your own diet from the energy point of view?
(c) Find out the current cost per unit mass of various types of food. Convert to cost per kilojoule. Assuming a dietary requirement of 10 500 kJ per day, calculate the cost per day of (i) the cheapest and (ii) most expensive meal that satisfies this energy requirement.
(d) Briefly discuss the social implication of your answer to (c) above.

4 The table gives approximate figures for the daily requirement of kilojoules and protein for human males of different age groups. The average body mass for each age group is included for comparison:

Age (years)	**Mass** (kg)	**Kilojoules per day**	**Protein per day** (g)
10–12	35	10 500	70
13–15	49	13 400	85
16–20	63	16 000	100
25	77	13 400	65
45	77	12 200	65
65	77	10 900	65

Explain the variation in energy and protein requirements at different ages. *(JMB modified)*

5 In an investigation of the process of respiration, the liver of a rat was homogenised and treated to remove adenosine triphosphate (ATP). Four flasks were set up as follows:

Flask A 1 cm^3 homogenate + 20 cm^3 glucose solution
Flask B 1 cm^3 homogenate + 20 cm^3 glucose solution + ATP
Flask C 1 cm^3 homogenate + 20 cm^3 distilled water + ATP
Flask D 1 cm^3 distilled water + 20 cm^3 glucose solution + ATP

The concentration of the glucose solutions and the amounts of ATP were the same in each case.

All flasks were then flushed and filled with oxygen, stoppered with a bung fitted with a graduated tube (as shown in Figure 7.7) and placed in a water bath at 20 °C. The tube contained coloured liquid. The position of the meniscus on the right-hand side of the tube was noted at the start of the experiment and again after one hour. The results are shown in the table in the margin.

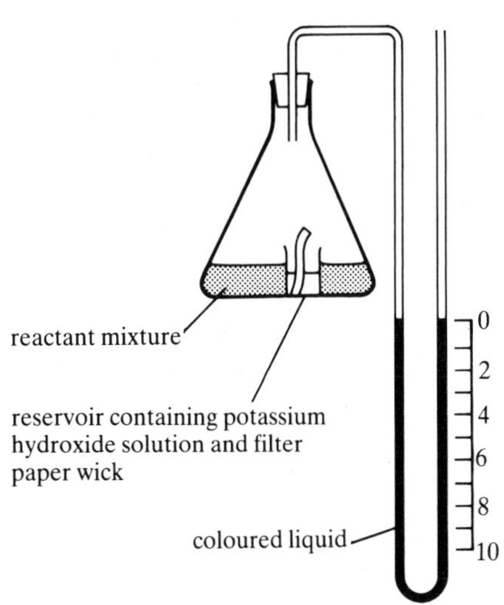

Figure 7.7 Flask for investigating the process of respiration.

Flask	**Position of liquid**	
	At start	After 1 hour
A	1	3
B	0	9
C	1	2
D	2	2

(a) (i) What is the purpose of the potassium hydroxide solution in the reservoir?
(ii) What is the purpose of the filter paper?
(iii) What process occurring during respiration can be measured by this apparatus?
(b) Flask D is a control. Why is it included in the experiment?
(c) Suggest how the addition of ATP in flask B increases the rate of the reaction.
(d) Account for the change in flask C.
(e) The reaction in flask A stopped after 2 hours and that in flask B after 1.25 hours. Why?

(f) What reading would you have expected to observe in flask B after 30 minutes if the temperature of the water bath had been (i) 30 °C and (ii) 60 °C? Why?

(g) Identify two possible sources of error in carrying out this experiment and suggest ways in which error could be minimised. *(AEB)*

6 Give a concise account of how energy is made available in cells. (A detailed account of the Krebs cycle is not required).

7 The following is a summary of the functions of the tricarboxylic acid cycle (the Krebs cycle):

'The tricarboxylic acid cycle (a) serves as a *metabolic hub* into which many *macromolecules* can be *degraded*; (b) enables *interconversions* to be made; and (c) provides *reducing power* for the *electron transport system*'.

Explain the words and phrases in italics.

8 Aerobic breakdown of sugar yields 2880 kJ of energy per mole, whereas anaerobic breakdown of sugar yields not more than 210 kJ per mole. Explain this difference in terms of the chemistry of cell respiration.

9 By what experimental techniques could it be ascertained whereabouts inside a cell the reactions of the Krebs cycle take place?

10 Discuss the circumstances in which (a) carbohydrate, (b) fat, and (c) protein are the substrates for cell respiration; and the circumstances in which (a) carbon dioxide, (b) ethanol, and (c) lactic acid are the end products.

11 The following metabolic pathway represents the first four steps in the Krebs citric acid cycle. Examine it carefully and then answer the questions below:

```
                  1              2                   3                  4
     COOH       COOH           COOH                COOH           COOH
      |          |              |                   |              |
     CH2         CH            CHOH                 CO             CO
      |          ||             |                   |              |
OH—C—COOH  →  C—COOH  →  H—C—COOH  →  H—C—COOH  →  CH2
      |          |              |                   |              |
     CH2        CH2            CH2                 CH2            CH2
      |          |              |                   |              |
     COOH       COOH           COOH                COOH           COOH
 citric acid  cis-aconitic  isocitric acid   oxalosuccinic  α-ketoglutaric
                 acid                             acid           acid
```

(a) The five compounds in the pathway are all acids. To what do they owe their acid properties?

(b) The citric acid cycle is also known as the tricarboxylic acid cycle. Which of the above compounds are (i) tricarboxylic acids and (ii) dicarboxylic acids?

(c) What kind of enzymes are responsible for catalysing each of the steps depicted?

(d) Citric acid is the first acid of the cycle. What do you know about the reaction by which citric acid is formed?

(e) How would you explain the fact that water is removed at step **1** and then added again at step **2**?

(f) Why is isocitric acid so-called?

(g) What happens to the two hydrogen atoms removed from the isocitric acid at stage **3**, and what is the biological usefulness of this?

(h) Why do you think it is necessary for carbon dioxide to be removed from oxalosuccinic acid at stage **4**?

(i) In general terms what happens to the α-ketoglutaric acid in the completion of the cycle?

(j) What sort of techniques would be used to elucidate the steps in a metabolic pathway such as the one outlined above?

12 A human eats the equivalent of 700 grams of carbohydrate per day but turns over about 75 kg of ATP per day. Explain what is happening. *(OCJE)*

8 Gas Exchange in Animals

Background Summary

1 In small or flattened animals the **surface-volume ratio** is large enough for gas exchange to take place by diffusion across the body surface. Larger animals, with a smaller surface-volume ratio, possess special **respiratory surfaces** for gas exchange.

2 In humans air is drawn by expansion of the thorax into the **lungs** where gas exchange occurs by diffusion across a greatly folded and highly vascularised alveolar surface.

3 This may be compared with fishes in which water is pumped over much folded and vascularised **gills**.

4 For efficient gas exchange in aquatic animals a **counterflow system** is better than parallel flow. The gills of bony fishes (teleosts) achieve a more direct counterflow than the gills of cartilaginous fishes, e.g. dogfish.

5 In teleosts, and probably also in the dogfish, the ventilation mechanism, involving the combined actions of a force pump and suction pump, maintains a continuous stream of water over the gills.

6 In insects gas exchange occurs in the **tracheal system**. Air reaches the tissues by diffusion, aided in some species by rhythmical movements of the thorax or abdomen.

7 In mammals and other vertebrates rhythmical breathing movements are coordinated by the **respiratory centre** in the hindbrain, and can be influenced by changes in the level of carbon dioxide, etc.

Investigation 8.1
Dissection of the respiratory apparatus of the rat

CAUTION:
Several serious diseases can be caught from rats. Wear a laboratory coat and thin rubber gloves while you are dissecting, and wash your hands thoroughly afterwards.

Note: This investigation should be combined with Investigation 9.1 on page 78.

In all mammals the respiratory and alimentary tracts cross each other at the back of the pharynx. Air in the nasal cavity is drawn via the naso-pharynx, through the glottis and larynx into the trachea whence it reaches the lungs via the bronchi.

All these structures can be readily seen in a dissection of the rat.

Procedure

1 Pin the animal, ventral side uppermost, to a dissecting board. Open up the thorax by cutting along the dotted lines shown in Figure 8.1. Tie a thread round the xiphoid cartilage and pull it back so as to stretch the diaphragm (Figure 8.2). Note the muscles of the diaphragm and the intercostal muscles between the ribs.

2 Remove the thymus gland from the surface of the heart. Be careful not to damage the underlying blood vessels.

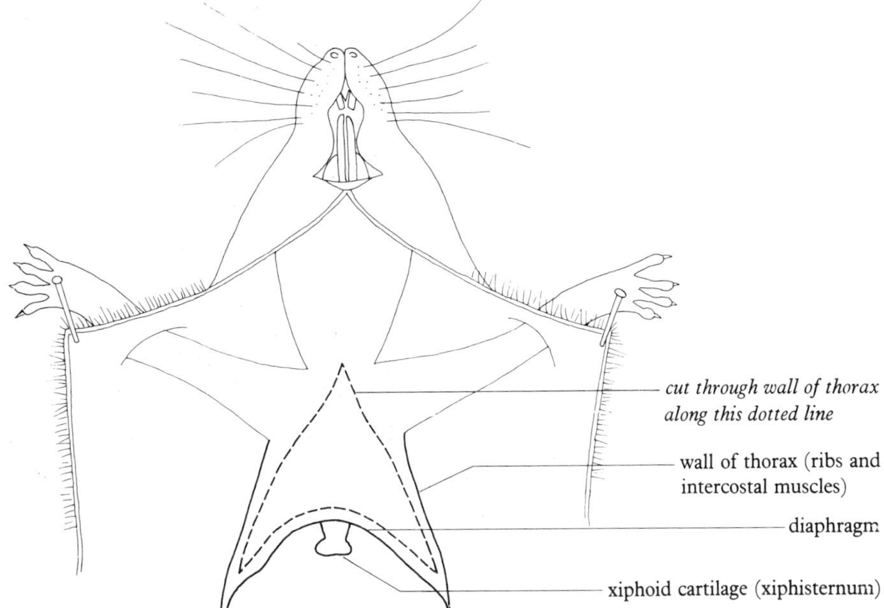

Figure 8.1 How to open up the thorax of the rat.

Identify the heart and lungs. Remove superfluous fat sufficiently to see the pulmonary arteries and veins (Figure 8.2). Also note the phrenic nerve which innervates the diaphragm.

3 With a scalpel cut along the centre of the neck muscles and remove them. (Arrow 1 in Figure 8.2). Be careful not to damage the trachea underneath.

4 Dislocate the lower jaw (mandible) by cutting along the angle of the jaw on both sides of the head. (Arrows 2 in Figure 8.2). *Do not remove the tongue.*

5 Grasp the tongue with forceps and cut along the walls of the pharynx on either side as far back as the glottis. This is the point where the alimentary and respiratory tracts cross.

6 Pull back the tongue and floor of the pharynx and notice the epiglottis guarding the glottis (Figure 8.3). Insert a probe into the glottis and confirm that it enters the larynx and trachea.

7 Just dorsal to the glottis (i.e. on the far side of the glottis as you look at your dissection) is the opening into the oesophagus. Insert your probe into this opening, directing it posteriorly. Note that if you push the point of the probe to one side it distends the wall of the oesophagus.

8 Now identify the soft palate. Immediately below this as you look at your dissection is the nasal cavity. Push a bristle into the nasal cavity from the rear and go on pushing until it comes out of one of the nostrils.

9 Insert the tip of a rubber pipette into the glottis and inflate the lungs. What happens to the respiratory tract when the animal swallows?

10 Follow the trachea down to the thorax. It disappears on the dorsal side of the heart where it divides into a pair of bronchi, one to each lung. To see the connection between the bronchi and the lungs necessitates removing the heart and the great vessels, which you may not want to do at this stage.

Figure 8.2 Stage in the dissection of the respiratory tract and blood supply to the lungs of the rat.

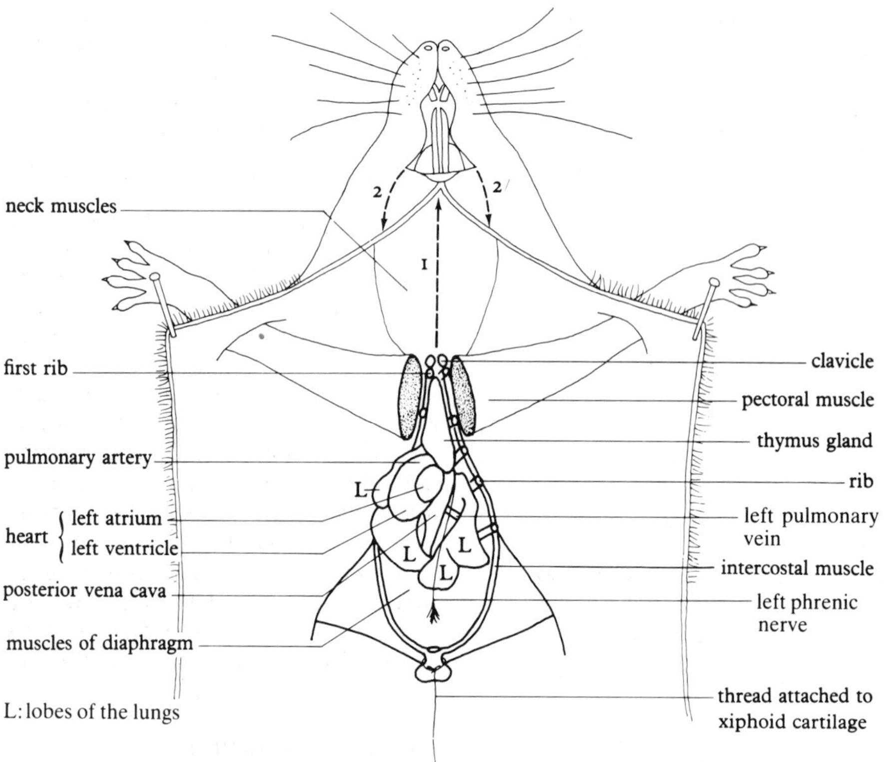

Figure 8.3 The glottis and related structures of the rat.

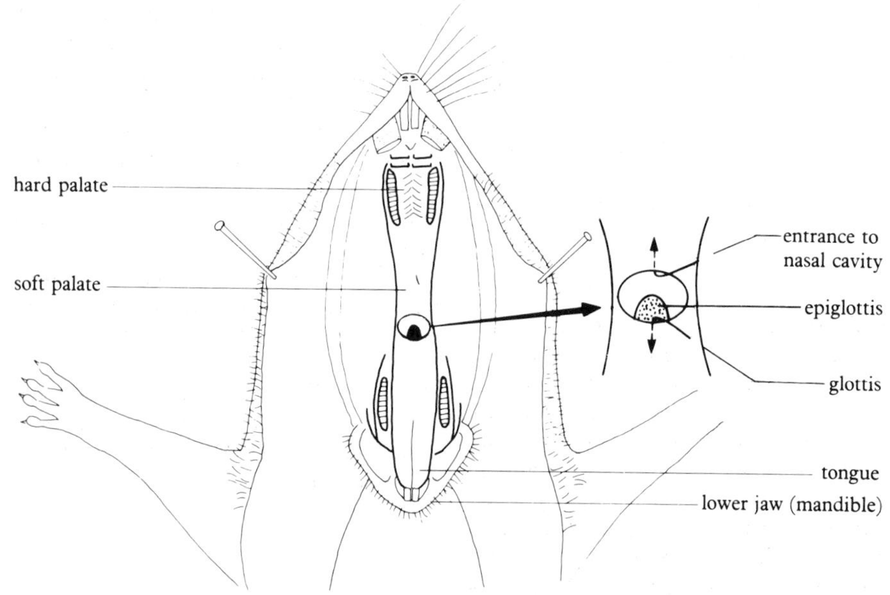

For Consideration

(1) Trace the path taken by a molecule of oxygen from the atmosphere just outside a person's nose to the blood in the pulmonary vein. What structures play a part in the process by which the air is moved?

(2) What are the possible advantages and disadvantages of the fact that the respiratory and alimentary tracts cross each other in the throat?

Reference: H.G.Rowett, *Dissection Guides, III – the Rat*, John Murray, 1951.

Requirements
Dissecting instruments
Bristle
Rubber pipette
Rubber gloves

Fresh-killed or deep-frozen rat

Investigation 8.2
Ventilation of the lungs in humans

What proportion of the total functional capacity of our lungs do we use when we breathe? We can answer this question by recording the breathing movements of a human subject. This kind of information is particularly relevant to athletes who wish to improve their performance and make the best use of their respiratory system.

Method

A spirometer and kymograph are required (*see* page 62). The kymograph should be set at a speed of approximately 30 mm per minute and the recording paper should be calibrated horizontally in 250 cm^3 divisions.

Work in pairs, one student acting as subject, the other as experimenter. Fill the spirometer with oxygen (medical grade). The carbon dioxide absorber (canister of soda lime) should be in position, so the subject will inspire pure oxygen from the spirometer chamber.

Connect the subject, who should be sitting comfortably, to the spirometer. Record the subject's breathings on the kymograph drum for about 30 seconds in order to get used to the apparatus and ensure that the recording pen is writing satisfactorily. Then proceed as follows:

MEASURING LUNG VOLUMES

1 Record about six normal breathings followed by a maximum inspiration and then a maximum expiration. The recordings should look like those in Figure 8.4.

2 From the horizontal divisions on the recording paper, measure the tidal volume, inspiratory reserve volume, expiratory reserve volume and vital capacity. What percentage of the vital capacity does the tidal volume represent?

3 Compare the vital capacities of all the members of your class. What do you think determines the size of a person's vital capacity?

THE EFFECT OF EXERCISE

1 Record the subject's normal resting breathings for one minute, then continue to record for three further minutes while the subject takes vigorous exercise such as running on the spot or pedalling a stationary bicycle. What happens to the size of the subject's inspirations during the period of exercise? What percentage of the vital capacity is represented by the final inspiration at the end of the exercise period? Do the breaths during exercise extend into the inspiratory reserve volume, the expiratory reserve volume, or both?

2 Plot the change in the size of the subject's inspirations as a graph with time on the horizontal axis and volume on the vertical axis.

3 The rate of gas exchange can be expressed as the total volume of air inspired per minute. This is the ventilation rate. It can be calculated by measuring the volume of each inspiration over a one minute period and adding them together. Alternatively it can be estimated from the fact that:

$$\text{ventilation rate} = \text{frequency} \times \text{depth}$$

where frequency is the total number of inspirations carried out during the one minute period, and depth is the average volume of air inspired at each breath during the same one minute period.

Calculate the subject's ventilation rate for each minute from the beginning to the end of your set of recordings. Express the ventilation rate in $dm^3\ min^{-1}$. This is called the respiratory minute volume.

4 Compare your recordings with others in the class. Can you draw any conclusions about the different ways people increase the rate of gas exchange during exercise?

For Consideration

(1) Why is it better to express the ventilation rate as the respiratory minute volume rather than the number of breaths per minute?

(2) How could the residual volume of the lungs be measured? What is the significance of this part of the lungs?

(3) Is there any evidence from the recordings made by your class that during exercise fit people breathe more deeply and at a lower frequency than unfit people? How could you test this hypothesis in detail?

(4) Why do you think the inspiratory reserve volume is so much greater than the expiratory reserve voume?

Reference: Revised Nuffield Biology Practical Guide I – *Gas Exchange and Transport in Plants and Animals*, Longman, 1985.

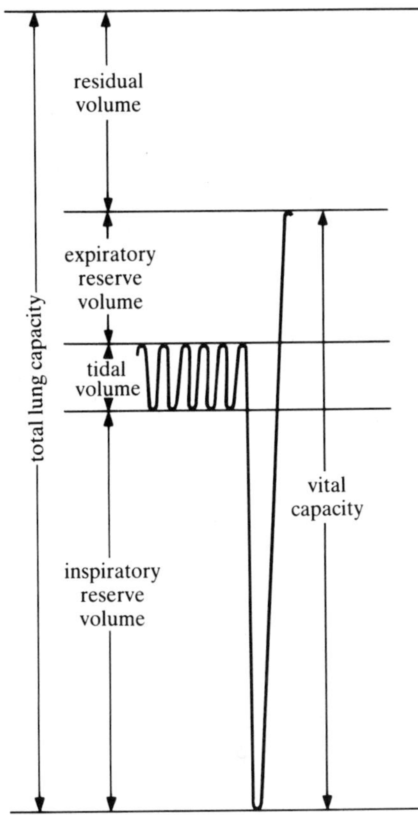

Figure 8.4 Spirometer recording of the breathing movements of a typical human subject.

Requirements
- Recording spirometer with concertina tubing, mouthpiece, nose clip, CO_2-absorber, and recording pen
- Eosin or non-clogging ink
- Kymograph set at speed of about 20 mm min^{-1}
- Kymograph paper calibrated horizontally for volume (250 cm^3 divisions)
- Oxygen cylinder (medical grade)

Investigation 8.3
Microscopic structure of the mammalian respiratory apparatus

Functionally the respiratory apparatus of the mammal can be distinguished into two components, the respiratory surface itself where gas exchange takes place, and the respiratory tract through which air is moved to and from the respiratory surface by the animal's ventilation mechanism.

In its microscopic structure the respiratory surface should show an intimate relationship between the inspired air and the bloodstream; and the respiratory tract should keep the tubes permanently open and prevent anything other than air reaching the respiratory surface.

STRUCTURE OF THE TRACHEA

1 Examine a transverse section of trachea under low and high powers. Use Figure 8.5 to help you identify the various structures in the tracheal wall.

The inner lining is composed of ciliated columnar epithelium interspersed with goblet cells.

2 In some sections mucus glands, opening to the surface by ducts, may be seen in the submucosa immediately beneath the epithelium.

3 Notice the incomplete ring of cartilage embedded in the centre of the wall. Why is the ring incomplete?

4 What are the functions of the cilia, glands and cartilage? Is there anything odd about the epithelial lining? Explain. Can you make out any other tissues in the wall of the trachea? Explain their functions.

Figure 8.5 Diagram of a transverse section through the wall of the mammalian trachea. The epithelial lining consists of several layers of cells. Because of its superficial resemblance to stratified epithelium (*see* page 23) it is known as pseudo-stratified epithelium. The connective tissue on either side of the cartilaginous ring consists of a mixture of collagen and elastic fibres. Some smooth muscle may also be seen, particularly at the free ends of the cartilage.

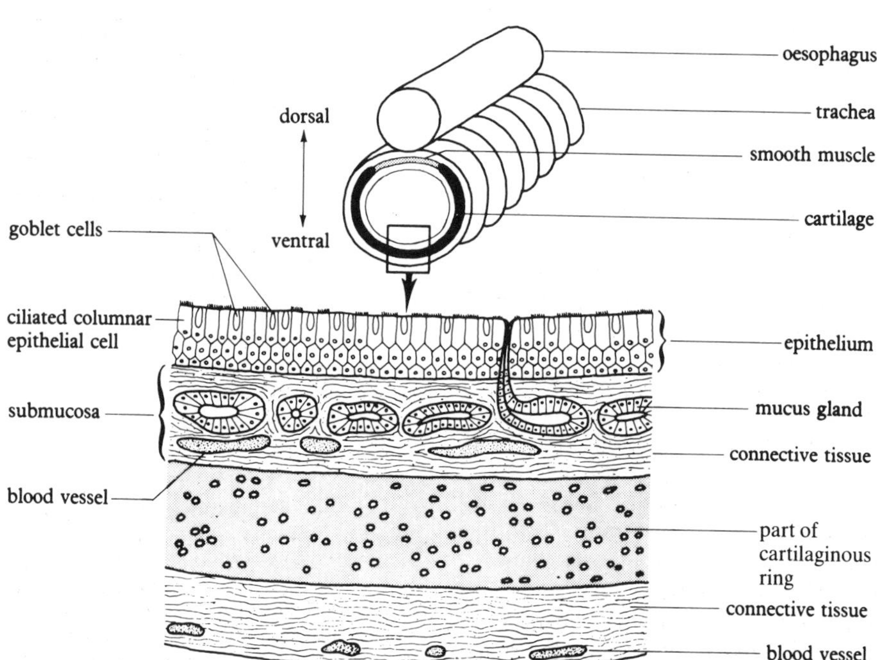

STRUCTURE OF THE LUNG

1 Examine a section of mammalian lung, first under low power and then under high power. Using Figure 8.6 to guide you, identify alveoli, atria, bronchioles, bronchi, pulmonary arteries, veins, and capillaries.

The following notes may help you:

Alveoli and atria have very thin walls of pavement epithelium.

Bronchi can be distinguished from bronchioles as follows: bronchi are larger, and contain glands and cartilage in their walls. Bronchioles are smaller and have no glands or cartilage.

The bronchi and larger bronchioles are lined with ciliated epithelium.

Blood vessels can be distinguished from other cavities by the fact that they contain numerous red blood cells. Arteries can be distinguished from veins by their thicker

Figure 8.6 Semi-diagrammatic section of mammalian lung.

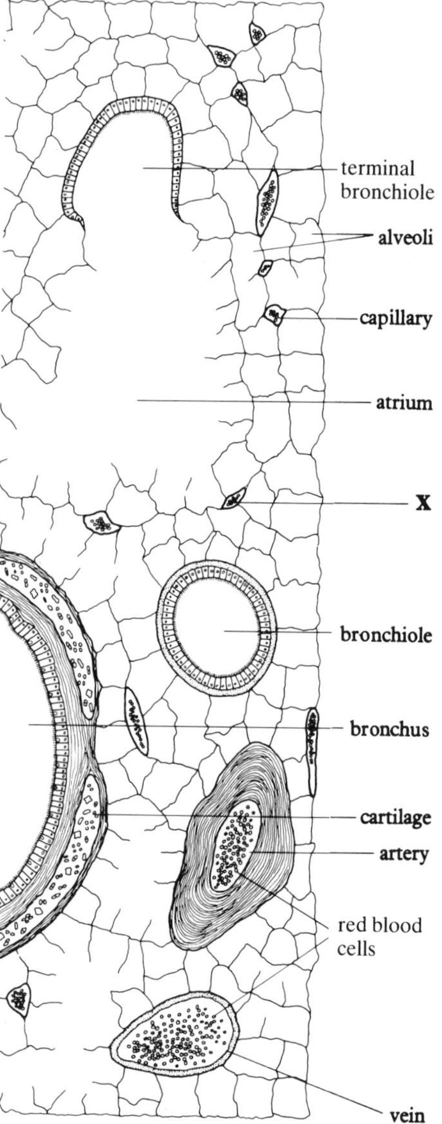

muscular walls. Capillaries are lined with a single layer of pavement epithelium.

2 Notice how numerous the alveoli are in your section. Can you work out their approximate frequency? How could you express their frequency?
3 Using high power (with oil immersion if available), explore the intimate association between a capillary and adjacent alveolus (**X** in Figure 8.5). Can you see that the thin barrier between them is only two cells in thickness? What sort of cells are they? If you have a micrometer eye piece, estimate the thickness of the barrier in micrometers (μm). Is the barrier of uniform thickness or uneven? Explain.
4 Examine an electron micrograph of the alveolar barrier. Identify the flattened regions of the capillary and alveolar epithelial cells abutting against each other with a narrow intercellular space between.

With a ruler measure the thickness of the barrier in millimetres and from the known scale of the micrograph estimate its true thickness in micrometres.

Requirements
Microscope
Oil immersion if available

TS trachea
Section of mammalian lung
EM of section through alveolar barrier

For Consideration

(1) What functions are performed by (a) the ciliated cells, (b) the mucus-secreting cells, and (c) the muscle fibres in the wall of the trachea and bronchi?
(2) Review the ways in which the mammalian lung is adapted to perform its function of ensuring rapid gas exchange.

Reference: W.H. Freeman and B. Bracegirdle, *An Advanced Textbook of Histology*, Heinemann, 1976.

Investigation 8.4
Structure of the gills of the dogfish

In the mammalian lung the numerous alveoli create a very large surface area for gas exchange. A comparable situation is seen in the gills of fishes except that here the large surface area is achieved not by alveoli but by numerous flattened epithelial surfaces. Like alveoli, these have a very good blood supply.

Procedure

1 Examine a thick slice (hand section) of a dogfish cut through the gill region. What structures can you see? Can you judge the level at which the cut has been made? Notice in particular the relationship between the pharyngeal cavity, gill pouches, and gills.
2 Examine a single gill that has been removed from a dogfish (Figure 8.7). You will be able to feel the cartilaginous branchial arch supporting the base of the gill. Projecting from the branchial arch are flattened lamellae. Can you detect the delicate gill plates on each lamella? (Running a needle along the surface of the lamellae may help.) Notice the branchial valve projecting beyond the end of the gill. What is its function?

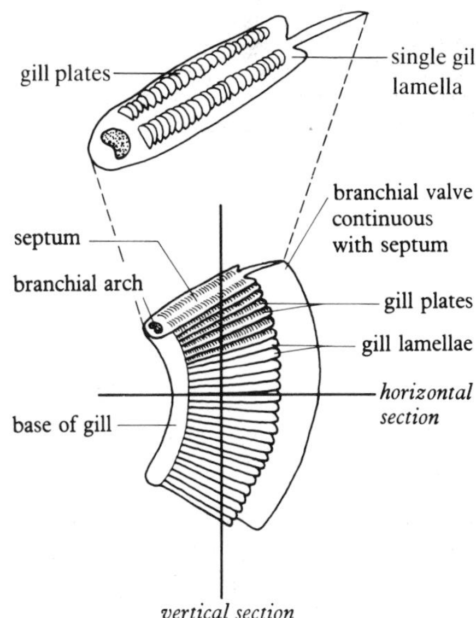

Figure 8.7 Isolated gill of dogfish. The entire gill is known as a holobranch, the portion on each side of the septum being called a hemibranch ('half-gill'). The base of the gill, stiffened by the cartilaginous branchial arch, contains the afferent and efferent branchial arteries which are interconnected by an extensive capillary system in the gill lamellae and plates.

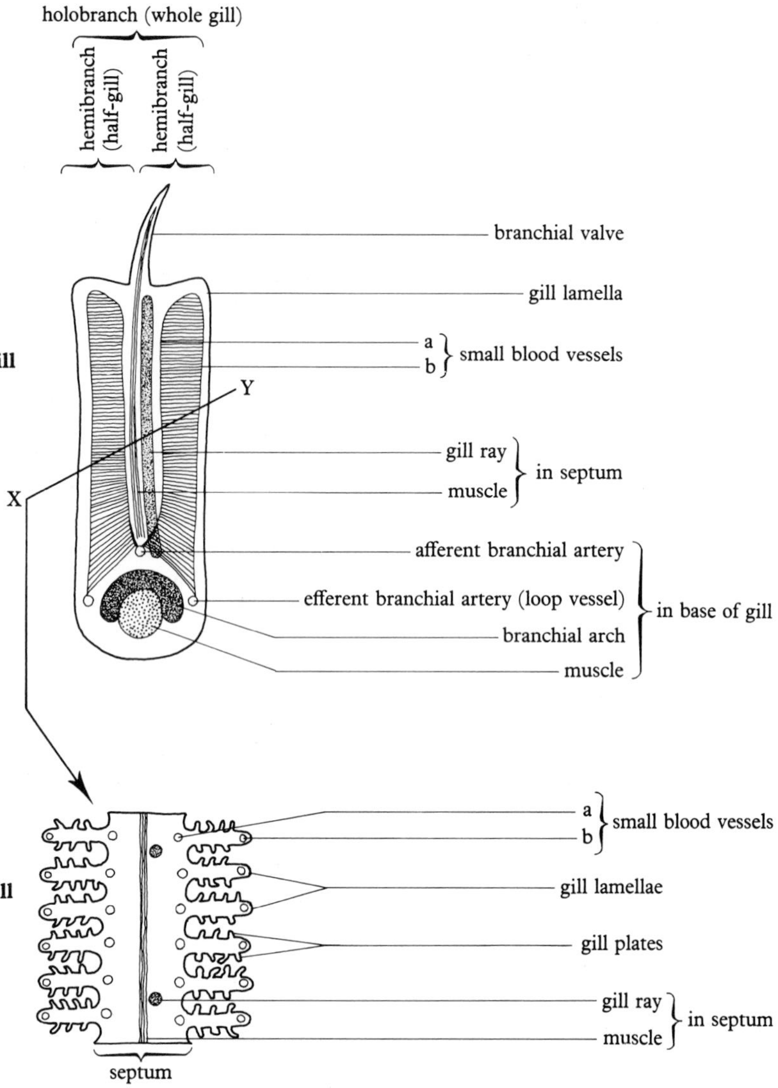

Figure 8.8 Structure of the gill of dogfish. **A**, horizontal section of whole gill (holobranch) showing a pair of lamellae and associated structures. **B**, vertical section of gill cut in the plane X–Y; this is drawn on a larger scale and shows six pairs of lamellae together with the gill plates which project from them: this is how the gills appear in a transverse section of a dogfish embryo. **a** and **b** are small blood vessels: **a** carries deoxygenated blood from the afferent branchial artery in the base of the gill to the lamella, **b** carries oxygenated blood from the lamella to the efferent branchial artery in the base of the gill. Within each lamella **a** and **b** are interconnected by tiny blood spaces which run through the gill plates. Gas exchange takes place during passage of the blood through the lamellae and plates.

Requirements
Microscope
Hand lens or binocular microscope

Hand section through gill region of dogfish
HS dogfish gill
VS dogfish gill

3 Examine the gill under a hand lens or binocular microscope and see the plates in more detail. Approximately how many lamellae are there per gill? How many plates per lamella?

4 Examine under the microscope a prepared slide of a horizontal section through a gill. The section should pass parallel to the lamellae as shown in Figure 8.8A. Identify afferent and efferent branchial arteries and the cartilaginous branchial arch in the gill base; a cartilaginous gill ray may be seen in the septum which is continuous with the branchial valve.

5 Now examine a vertical section, i.e. one which passes at right angles to the lamellae (Figure 8.8B). Gills cut in this plane can be seen in a transverse section of a dogfish embryo.

Identify lamellae and gill plates at right angles to each other; vertical septum running down centre of gill; cartilaginous gill rays in septum; blood vessels.

6 In your vertical section examine the blood vessels in a single gill plate. How many layers of cells are there between the lumen of the vessels and the exterior?

For Consideration

(1) What are the functions of the gill rays and muscles in the septum of the gill?

(2) Compare the respiratory surface of the dogfish with that of the mammal. What particular structures are directly comparable in these two animals? What features of both surfaces facilitate gas exchange?

Investigation 8.5
Tracheal system of insects

The respiratory system of insects is based on a system of tubes, the tracheal system, which distribute gases to all parts of the body. Air enters the tracheal system through openings in the cuticle, the spiracles, which are present on either side of the thorax and abdomen. In this investigation we shall look at the structure of the tracheal system and investigate some aspects of how gases move through it.

Procedure

1 Dissect a cockroach or locust so as to expose the inside of the body cavity (*see* page 364). Can you see the larger tracheal tubes (tracheae)? Attached to the tracheae are a number of thin-walled air sacs. These can be readily seen in a dissection but their function is not fully understood.

2 Tease out a small piece of muscle from the thorax and mount it in a drop of water on a slide. Observe under microscope (low power). Notice that the tracheae branch profusely and have rings of thickening in their walls to keep them open. They terminate as very narrow tracheoles.

3 The tracheae are invaginations of the integument and are therefore lined with cuticle. The rings are composed of chitin, like the rest of the cuticle. Examine the cast-off cuticle of an insect to see how much of the tracheal system is discarded when the animal moults. What part of the tracheal system is *not* lined with cuticle, and what is the significance of this?

4 Fix a live locust on its side to a slab of plasticine or blu-tack as shown in Figure 8.9. Observe the spiracles under a binocular microscope. What shape are they? Can you see them opening and closing? How do they open and close? Do they all open and close in the same way and at the same time? Explain your observations.

5 With the locust still under the binocular microscope, watch the movements of the abdomen. These movements pump air through the tracheal system. How do the pumping movements relate to the opening and closing of the spiracles? Explain your observations.

6 Place a live locust in a transparent 20 cm^3 plastic hypodermic syringe as shown in Figure 8.10. Push the piston in gently so that it almost touches the locust. Count the number of pumping movements per minute for three minutes and take the average.

7 Remove the piston and replace it with a plug of cotton wool. Exhale slowly through the tube into the syringe until as much air as possible has been expelled from your lungs, then replace the piston. Count the number of pumping movements per minute, as before. Has the rate changed? Explain your results.

8 Move the piston to and fro about 10 times so as to replace your exhaled air with fresh air. What happens to the locust's pumping movements now?

For consideration

(1) It is said that the size of insects is limited by their gas exchange system. Why should this be so and what other factors might affect their size?

(2) It has been suggested that in the locust, air is drawn into the tracheal system through the first four pairs of spiracles and leaves via the remaining spiracles. How would you verify this experimentally and what might be the mechanism ensuring such a unidirectional flow of air?

Reference: W.M. Clarke and M.M. Richards, *The Locust as a Typical Insect*, Murray, 1976.

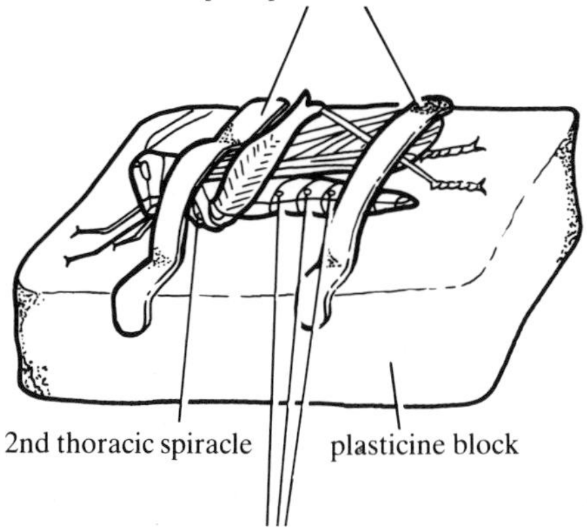

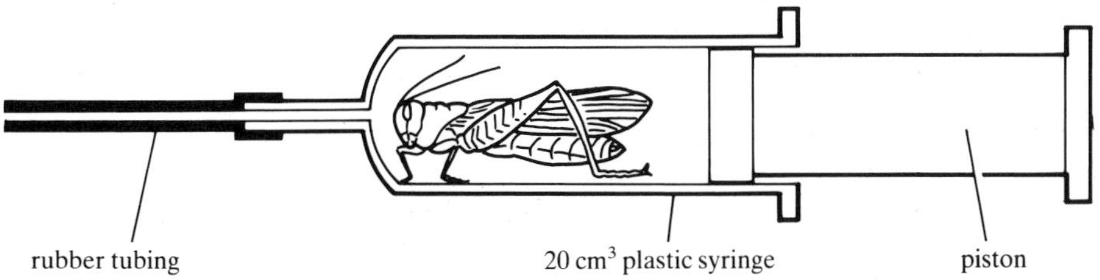

Figure 8.9 A live locust fixed in position for viewing the spiracles under a binocular microscope. (*After W.M. Clarke and M.M. Richards*)

Figure 8.10 A live locust inside a syringe for studying its breathing movements. (*After W.M. Clarke and M.M. Richards*)

Requirements
Slides and coverslips
Microscopes, monocular and binocular
Plasticine or blu-tack
Dissecting instruments
Plastic hypodermic syringe, 20 cm^3 capacity (transparent)
Cotton wool

Live locust
Freshly killed cockroach or locust for dissection
Cast off cuticle of locust or other insect
Live locust

	Air	Water
oxygen content	210	8
diffusion rate	1	10^{-5}
density	1	1000
viscosity	1	100

Questions and problems

1 The table in the margin shows a comparison between a sample of fresh water and air. Oxygen content is given in cm^3 per dm^3; other ratios are in arbitrary units:
With reference to these figures, compare air and water as sources of oxygen for organisms.

2 (a) Explain, *without the use of a diagram*, the meaning of the terms tidal volume, inspiratory reserve volume and expiratory reserve volume.
(b) The table shows the respiratory minute volumes (RMV = tidal volume × breaths per minute) of three healthy young men as they were subjected individually to a progressive decrease in the oxygen content of their inspired air while its carbon-dioxide content was held at a constant level. The RMV was calculated each minute for 10 minutes as shown.

Time (minutes)		1	2	3	4	5	6	7	8	9	10
Oxygen content of inspired air (%)		21	18	16	14	12	10	8	6	5	4
RMV (dm^3 per minute)	Man A	6.6	6.8	6.9	6.9	7.2	8.6	12.9	18.2	21.0	25.5
	Man B	7.4	7.4	7.3	7.3	7.3	7.4	11.5	18.0	19.7	24.4
	Man C	7.0	6.8	6.8	6.8	7.1	8.0	11.6	17.8	19.3	25.1

(i) Give the mean RMV at each oxygen level.
(ii) Plot a graph of mean RMV against oxygen content of inspired air.
(iii) What does your graph show about the effect of oxygen concentration in inspired air on mean RMV?
(iv) Suggest how respiratory movements increase the RMV.
(v) Suggest two reasons why these three men appear not to have the same oxygen requirements.
(vi) Suggest why severe oxygen deficiency (below 4%) suppresses rather than stimulates ventilation.

(c) Explain briefly how the rate of breathing is controlled. *(AEB modified)*

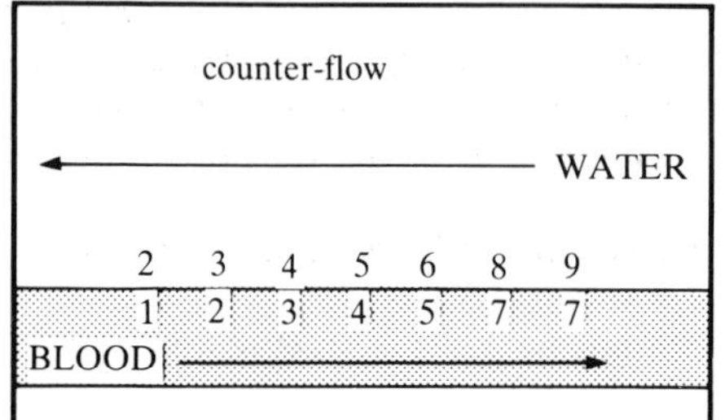

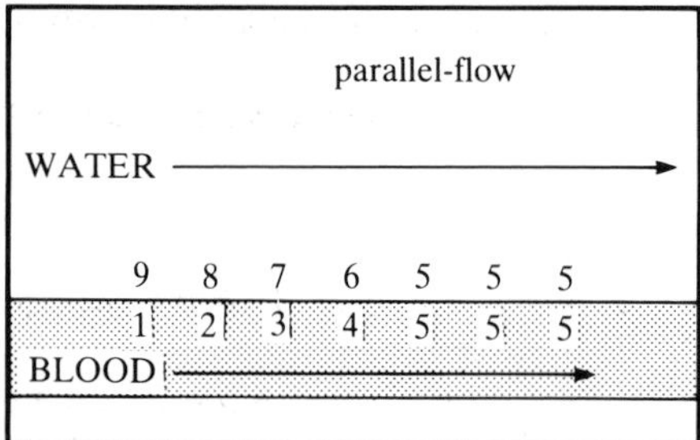

Figure 8.11 Counter-flow and parallel-flow in the gills of fishes.

3 In some fish, water is forced over the gills in the opposite direction to the flow of blood in the gill plates (counter-flow system). In others, water and blood both flow in the same direction (parallel-flow system). In Figure 8.11 the numbers show the relative concentrations of oxygen in the water and in the blood.
(a) Explain, with reference to the illustration, how oxygen is exchanged between the water and the blood in each of these systems.
(b) Which system is more efficient, and why?
(c) How is the structure of a fish gill adapted so as to achieve maximum efficiency in gas exchange? *(W modified)*

Air
pO_2 = 20 kPa
pN_2 = 78.6 kPa

water surface

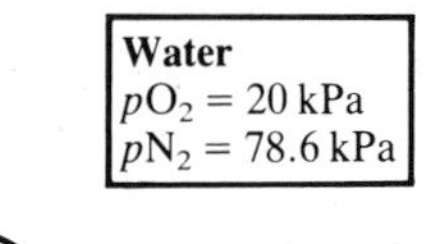

Figure 8.12 Partial pressures of oxygen and nitrogen in air, water, and the gas bubble of an aquatic insect.

4 Certain water bugs and water beetles can remain submerged for a time because, when they dive, they take with them a bubble of air which remains in contact with their gas-exchange system. Figure 8.12 shows the partial pressures (p) of oxygen and nitrogen in the air, in the water and in the gas within the bubble when the insect has been active just below the water surface for a short time.
(a) With what part of the gas-exchange system is the bubble in contact?
(b) Suggest how the bubble is held in position.
(c) Account for the partial pressures of oxygen and nitrogen in the air and in the water.
(d) Account for the differences between the partial pressures of oxygen and nitrogen in the bubble and in the water. *(AEB modified)*

5 Figure 8.13 shows part of the tracheal system of an insect.
(a) Suggest possible functions for the hairs round the spiracles.
(b) What is the function of the rings of chitin round the tracheae?
(c) Why do the tracheoles have no such rings?
(d) By what mechanism might oxygen be conveyed through the tracheal system?
(e) The tracheoles are made up of rows of 'drainpipe' cells – i.e. each individual cell is a hollow cylinder with the nucleus to one side. What is the possible functional significance of this?

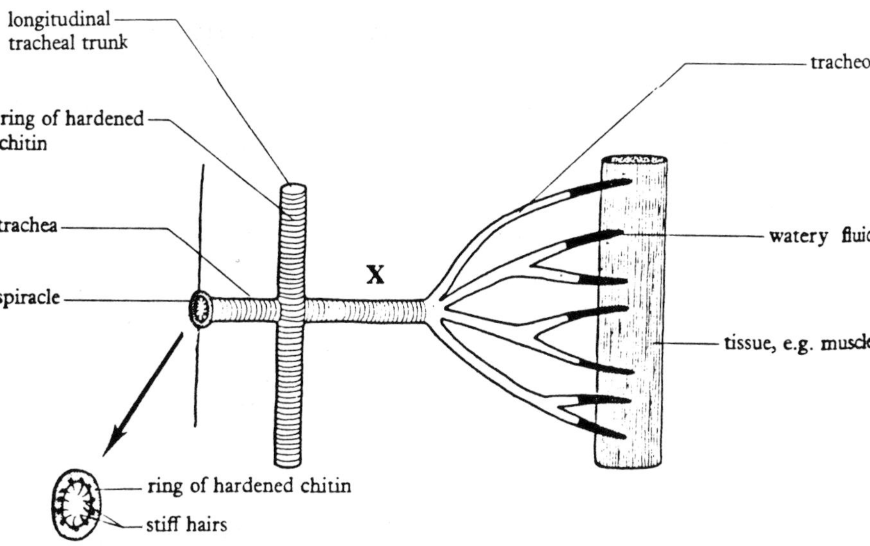

Figure 8.13 Diagrammatic representation of part of the tracheal system of an insect.

(f) What would you expect to happen to the watery fluid in the tracheoles when the muscle is actively contracting?
(g) Of what respiratory significance is your answer to (f)?
(h) What would you expect to happen if the tracheal system was blocked at X?

6 Evidence indicates that groups of nerve cells, collectively known as the respiratory centre, in the hindbrain are involved in the control of breathing in the mammal. Figure 8.14 shows how nerves connect the respiratory centre to the breathing apparatus.
A represents the vagus nerves which transmit impulses (messages) from the walls of the bronchial tubes in the lungs to the medulla.
B represents the intercostal nerves which transmit impulses from the respiratory centre to the intercostal muscles.
C represents the phrenic nerves which transmit impulses from the respiratory centre to the diaphragm.
In addition two other nervous pathways are shown:
D represents nerves which transmit impulses from the walls of certain blood vessels to the respiratory centre.
E represents nerve tracts within the brain which connect the higher centres (cerebral cortex) with the respiratory centre.
Consider the following experiments and their results:
1. A, B and C are cut. *Result*: breathing ceases.
2. A, D and E are cut, but B and C are left intact. *Result*: rhythmical breathing continues but slower and deeper than normal.
3. B, C, D and E are cut. The lungs are inflated by means of a pump and nervous impulses are recorded from A with an oscilloscope. *Result*: as the lung is inflated the frequency of impulses increases.
4. A and E are cut. The concentration of carbon dioxide in inspired air is increased to three per cent. *Result*: ventilation rate increases.
5. Experiment 4 is repeated. After the ventilation rate has increased, D is cut. *Result*: ventilation rate decreases.
6. A and E are cut. The concentration of carbon dioxide in inspired air is increased to five per cent. *Result*: ventilation rate increases.
7. Experiment 6 is repeated. After the ventilation rate has increased, D is cut. *Result*: ventilation rate remains at the increased rate.
(a) What conclusions can you draw about the control of breathing from these results?
(b) (i) Predict the effect of cutting E but leaving all the other nerves intact, and of cutting A and D but leaving B, C and E intact. (ii) If your predictions turned out to be correct, what conclusions would you draw concerning the role of the higher centres in the control of breathing?

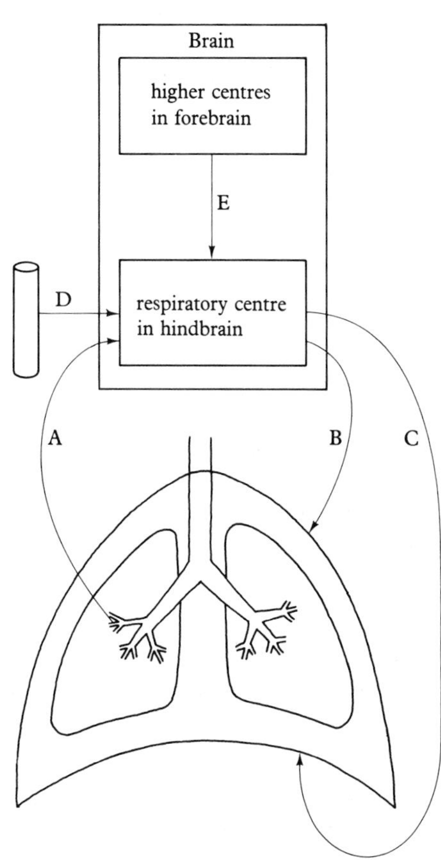

Figure 8.14 Diagram showing neural connections between the respiratory apparatus of a mammal and the respiratory centre in the hindbrain.

7 How is the structure of an animal's respiratory surface, and its ventilation mechanism, related to (a) its size, (b) its activities, and (c) its environment? Illustrate your answer with specific examples.

8 How would you test the hypothesis that feathery structures projecting from the sides of a marine worm are used for gas exchange? *(OCJE)*

9 Heterotrophic Nutrition

Background Summary

1 Heterotrophic nutrition, feeding on organic food, can be classified into three types: **holozoic**, **saprotrophic** and **parasitic**. Saprotrophic nutrition, carried out by many bacteria and fungi, is important in bringing about decay.[1]

2 The problem facing any heterotroph is how to acquire and take in organic food and then break it down into soluble products capable of being absorbed. In most heterotrophs the food is successively **ingested**, **digested**, **absorbed**, **transported** and **assimilated** (i.e. incorporated into the cells). The functions of digestion and absorption are carried out by a **gut** (**alimentary canal**). Indigestible remains are **egested**.

3 **Digestion**, the breaking down of the food into soluble substances takes place by physical and chemical means. The former is achieved by e.g. teeth, gut muscles, and the action of solutions such as bile. Chemical breakdown is achieved by **digestive enzymes**.

4 In general digestive enzymes fall into three groups: **carbohydrases**, **lipases** and **proteases** which attack carbohydrates, fats and proteins respectively. The enzymes work by splitting chemical bonds in the process of **hydrolysis**.

5 Digestion is either entirely **extracellular** (e.g. human), entirely **intracellular** (e.g. *Amoeba* and sponges), or extracellular and intracellular (e.g. *Hydra*).

6 The human gut is differentiated into a series of specialised regions, each showing, in both its coarse and microscopic anatomy, a close relationship between structure and function.

7 In humans physical digestion is achieved by the teeth, stomach contractions, and bile. Movement of food along the gut is achieved by **peristalsis**.

8 Chemical digestion is achieved by enzymes contained in **saliva**, **gastric juice**, **pancreatic juice** and **intestinal juice**, secreted by the salivary glands, stomach wall (gastric glands), pancreas and wall of the small intestine respectively.

9 Secretion is initiated by expectation, reflex stimulation, hormones or direct mechanical stimulation, depending on the gland in question.

10 To aid absorption, the surface area of the absorptive epithelium is increased by **villi**, and the surface area of the individual epithelial cells is increased by **microvilli**.

11 Holozoic organisms can be described in terms of the food they eat as herbivores, carnivores, omnivores, liquid-feeders, and microphagous feeders.

12 **Herbivores** have special adaptations for ingesting and digesting plants, e.g. serrated molar teeth of horse and elephant, mandibles of locust and grasshopper, radula of snail. A number of herbivores harbour cellulase-secreting micro-organisms in the gut.

13 **Carnivores** have adaptations for catching and killing prey (e.g. canine teeth, tentacles, stinging cells) and for crushing and slicing it (e.g. carnassial teeth).

14 Certain specialised plants possess adaptations for trapping and digesting small animals, e.g. butterwort, sundew, Venus fly-trap, pitcher plants. In this way their photosynthetic feeding is supplemented by heterotrophic means.

15 **Liquid feeders** include absorbers (e.g. tapeworm) and suckers (e.g. certain insects). The mouthparts of sucking insects are adapted in different ways to form various types of proboscis.

16 **Microphagous feeders** devour small particles suspended in water which are collected and filtered. They are hence also known as **filter feeders**, e.g. bivalve molluscs.

[1] The term saprotrophic is rapidly replacing the term saprophytic. A saprotroph is *any* organism which feeds on dead organic material.

Investigation 9.1
Dissection of the mammalian alimentary canal

Note: This investigation should be combined with Investigation 8.1 on page 69.

> **CAUTION:**
> Several serious diseases can be caught from rats. Wear a laboratory coat and thin rubber gloves while you are dissecting, and wash your hands thoroughly afterwards.

As food passes along the alimentary canal it is digested physically and chemically and the soluble products of digestion are absorbed into the bloodstream. Solid indigestible matter remains in the gut and is voided. The overall function of the alimentary canal is therefore to process and absorb food. In both its coarse and microscopic anatomy the gut shows a close relationship between structure and function.

Procedure

1 Pin the rat to a dissecting board, ventral surface upwards and head pointing away from you. Make a mid-ventral incision through the skin and cut forward as far as the lower jaw, and backwards to the anus. Cut either side of the urino-genital openings as shown in Figure 9.1. Free the skin from the underlying body wall.

2 Pin back the skin and cut through the body wall as shown in Figure 9.2. Identify all the structures shown in Figure 9.2.

3 Wet your fingers so they slide easily between the organs. Look between the stomach and the liver and find the lower end of the oesophagus where it joins the stomach. Using your fingers to move the organs this way and that, and *without cutting the mesentery by which the gut is suspended in the abdominal cavity*, follow the alimentary canal in the abdomen from oesophagus to rectum.

4 Identify cardiac and pyloric regions of stomach (note spleen clinging to stomach), pyloric sphincter, duodenum, ileum, caecum with short appendix, colon and rectum. The duodenum and ileum together make up the small intestine; the colon and rectum make up the large intestine.

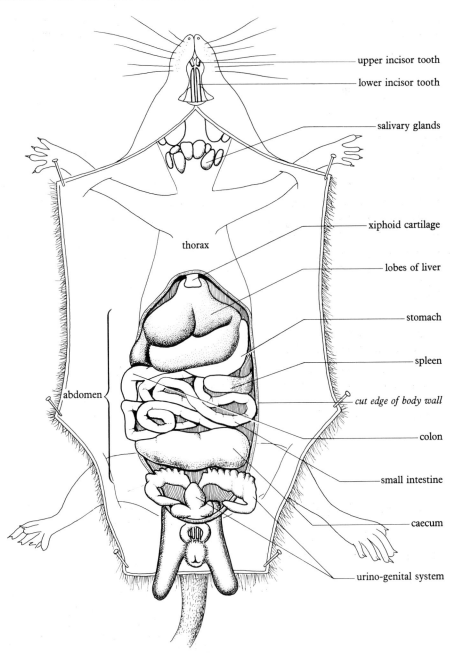

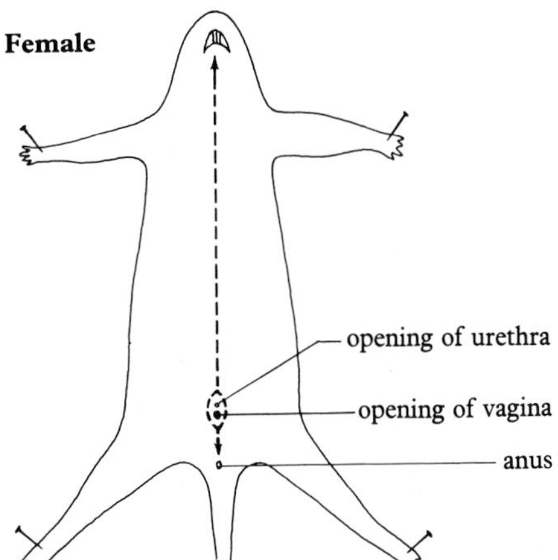

Figure 9.1 Opening up the rat. Cut through the skin as indicated by the dotted line.

Figure 9.2 Contents of abdominal cavity of male rat *in situ*.

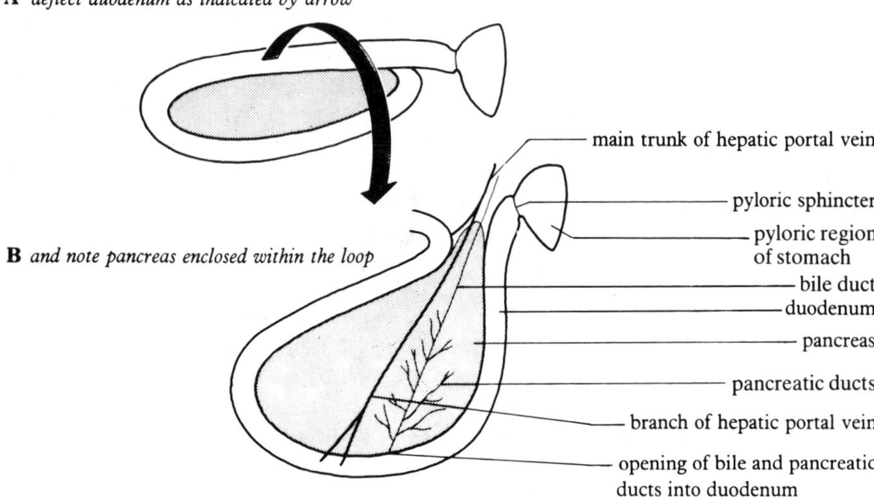

Figure 9.3 Technique for revealing the pancreas, bile duct, and hepatic portal vein of the rat.

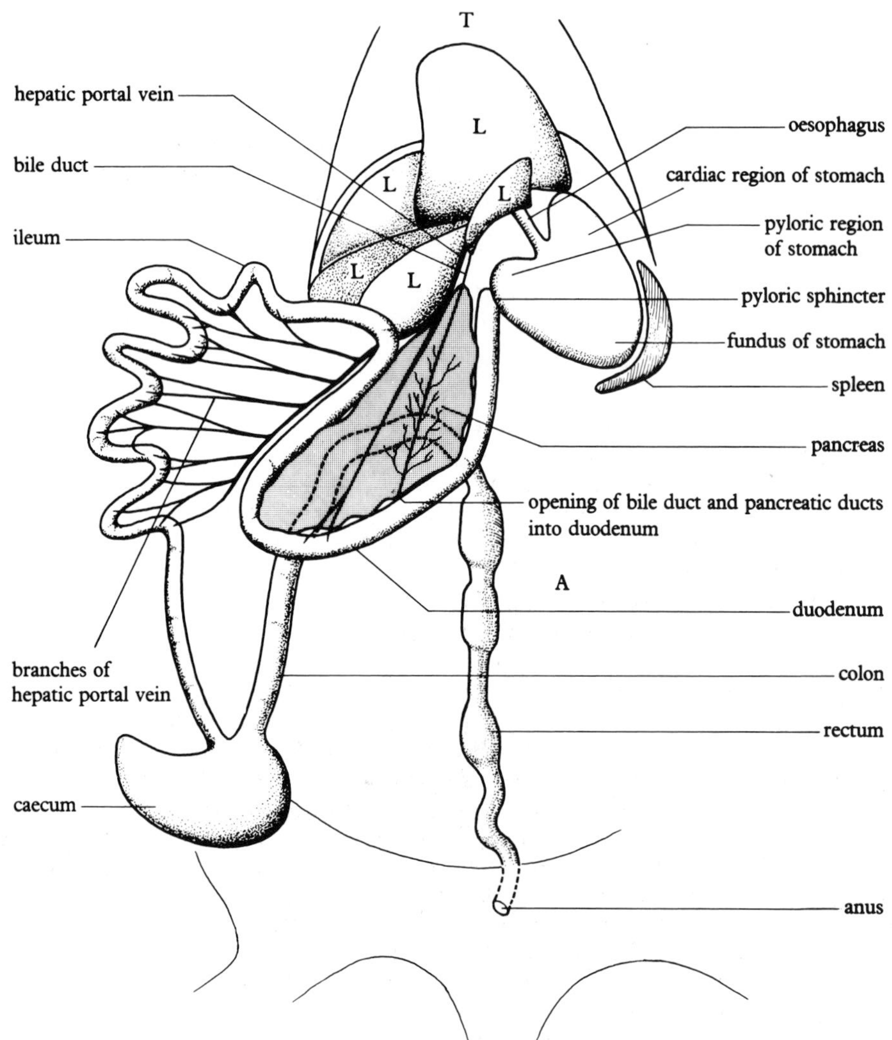

Figure 9.4 Alimentary canal of the rat as seen with the duodenum deflected downwards (*see* Figure 9.3), the stomach pushed to the right, and the ileum spread out to the left. **L**, lobes of liver; **T**, thorax; **A**, abdominal cavity.

5 Push the liver upwards, the stomach to your right and the ileum to your left. Deflect the duodenum downwards towards you as shown in Figure 9.3. This will enable you to see the pancreas within the loop of the duodenum, and the bile duct (white tube) running from liver to duodenum (there is no gall bladder in the rat).

6 Numerous small pancreatic ducts open into the bile duct as it runs towards the duodenum. Running in the same mesentery as the bile duct is the main trunk of the hepatic portal vein which conveys blood from the gut to the liver.

7 Without breaking the mesentery, spread out the ileum to your left and notice numerous branches of the hepatic portal vein in the mesentery (Figure 9.4).

Running alongside the hepatic portals are branches of the anterior mesenteric artery but these are generally obscured by fat.

8 With the liver pushed forward, deflect the whole of the stomach and intestine to your left and stretch the mesentery. Running in the mesentery are three median (unpaired) arteries to the gut (Figure 9.5): coeliac, anterior mesenteric, and posterior mesenteric arteries. All three are branches of the dorsal aorta, the first two arising at about the level of the left kidney, the last where the aorta splits into the leg arteries.

9 Pluck away the fat clinging to the proximal end of the three arteries to show their origin from the dorsal aorta. Trace them to their destinations. What structures do they serve?

10 Arrange the viscera in such a way as to display the whole of the alimentary canal and its blood supply to maximum advantage.

11 If the rat is to be used for further dissection, remove the alimentary canal as follows. Ligature the main trunk of the hepatic portal vein, cut through the oesophagus where it enters the stomach, and cut through the rectum where it disappears under the urino-genital organs. Cut through the suspensory mesenteries so as to remove the whole of the gut, spleen and pancreas. Leave the liver.

Note: After removing the alimentary canal the rat can be deep-frozen or preserved in 'formalin' and used again later for dissecting the excretory and reproductive systems.

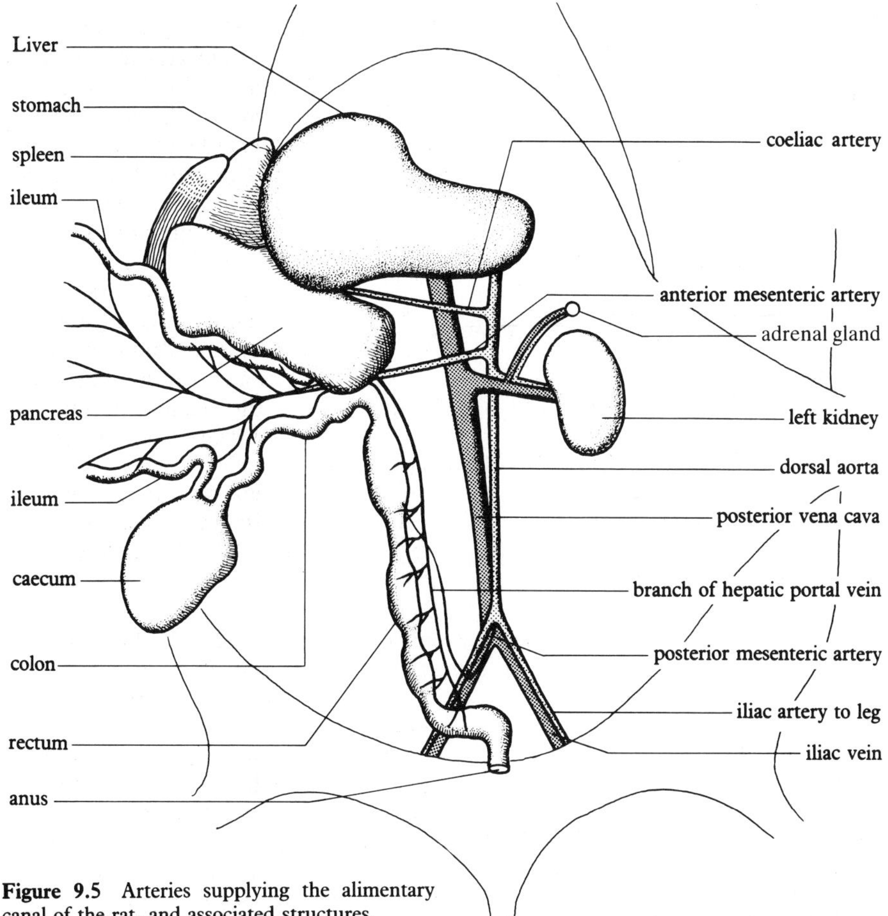

Figure 9.5 Arteries supplying the alimentary canal of the rat, and associated structures.

For Consideration

(1) The veins serving most organs of the body take blood straight to the heart. However those serving the alimentary canal take blood to the liver, after which it flows on to the heart. Why should there be this difference between the venous supply of the alimentary canal and other organs?
(2) Suggest three ways in which the gut of the rat, as you have observed it in your dissection, is adapted to perform its functions.

Requirements
Dissecting instruments
Dissecting board
Dissecting pins
Rubber gloves

Rat, killed immediately before the laboratory session (deep-frozen rats are unsatisfactory for this dissection).

Investigation 9.2
Microscopic structure of the gut wall

Although the mammalian gut shows regional differentiation, its wall can always be distinguished into the seven layers shown in Figure 9.6. The epithelium, showing various degrees of folding, is protective, secretory, and/or absorptive; the mucosa and submucosa consist of connective tissue, blood vessels, etc.; the muscularis mucosa is composed of two thin layers of smooth muscle, an inner circular layer, and an outer longitudinal layer; the external muscle coat is made up of thick layers of circular and longitudinal muscle; and the serosa is composed of connective tissue continuous with the mesentery by which the gut is attached to the body wall.

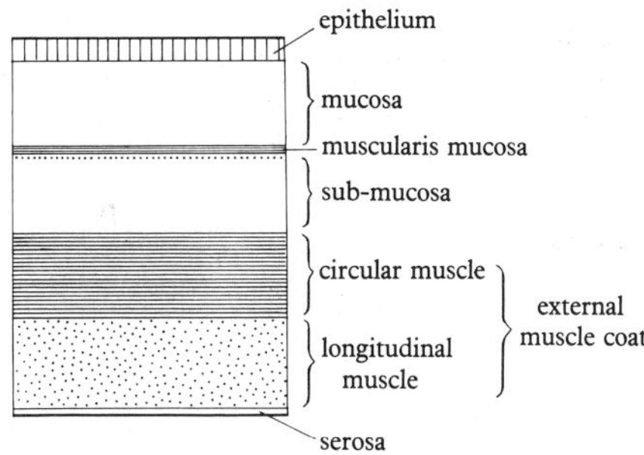

Figure 9.6 The principal layers in the wall of the alimentary canal.

Procedure

SMALL INTESTINE

1 Examine a transverse or longitudinal section of the ileum under low power. Identify the various layers of the wall using Figure 9.7 to help you.

2 Examine your section under high power and answer these questions:
(a) What sort of cells occur in the epithelium lining the villi and crypts of Lieberkühn and what are their functions?
(b) In what ways is the epithelium adapted for absorption of the products of digestion?
(c) What functions are performed by the various muscles which are visible in your section?
(d) In what other respects is the wall of the ileum adapted to perform its various functions?

3 Examine a section of the wall of the duodenum (Figure 9.7). How does this differ from the ileum?

4 Look at an electron micrograph of a section through an epithelial cell of the small intestine. Notice in particular numerous microvilli projecting from the free surface of the cell. In what plane(s) have they been cut? Identify other structures in the micrograph. If the structures are lettered, state what each letter stands for.

STOMACH

1 Examine a vertical section of the wall of the stomach. Identify the various layers of the wall (Figure 9.8A) and compare with the ileum.

2 Examine a gastric gland in detail. Towards the surface where it opens into the gastric pit it will be cut in longitudinal section, but deeper down

Figure 9.7 Microscopic structure of the wall of the mammalian small intestine.

A Sections of the wall of ileum and duodenum

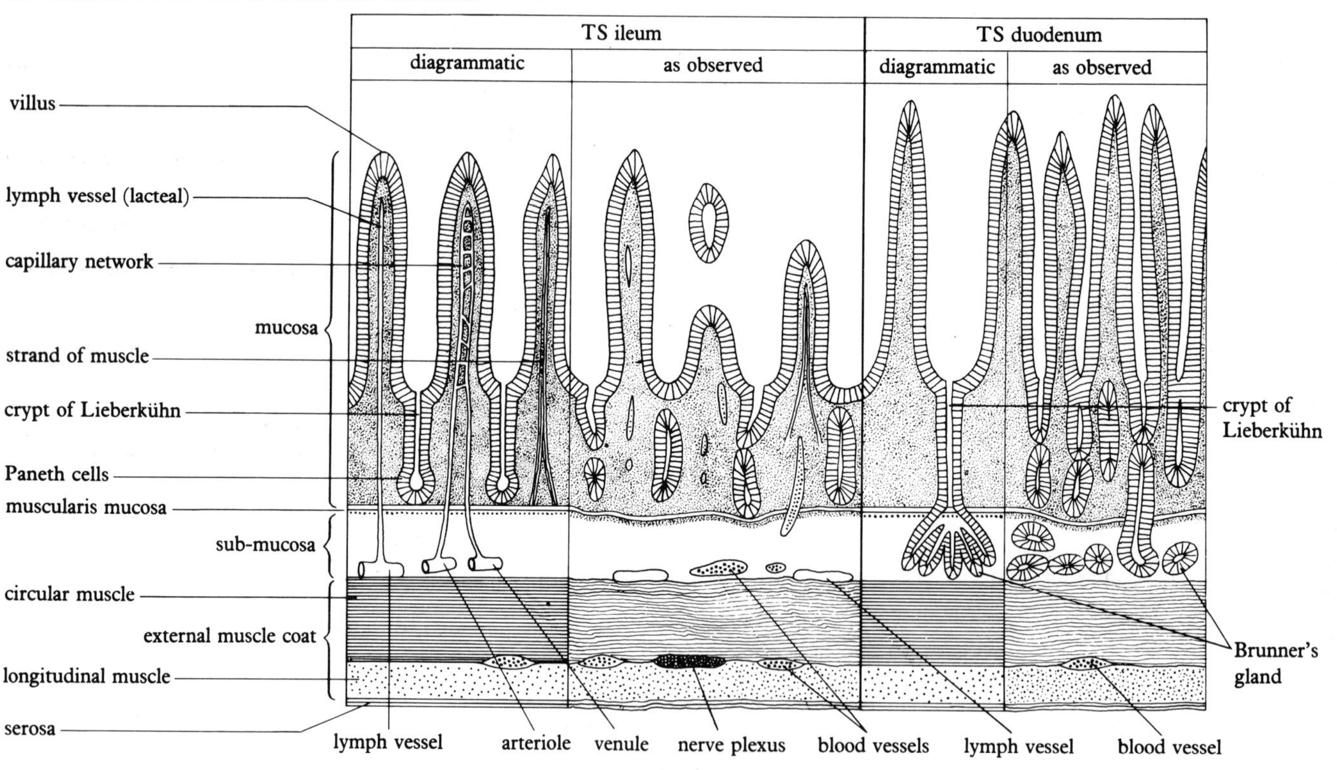

B Epithelial lining of villus

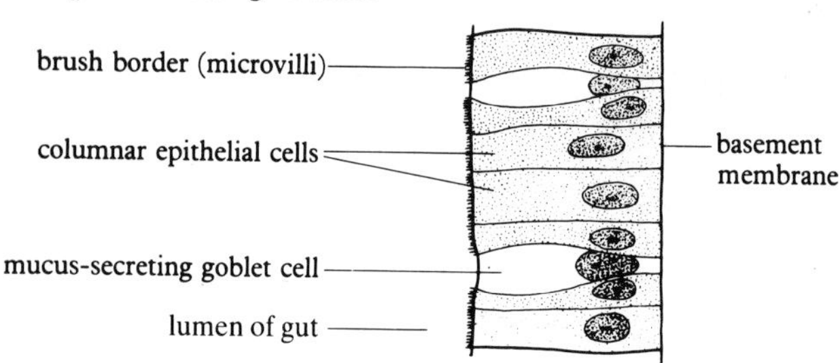

C Paneth cells lining base of crypt of Lieberkühn

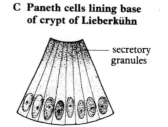

D Cells lining Brunner's gland

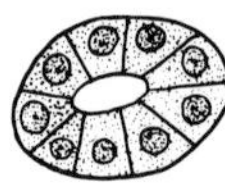

where the glands twist and turn they will have been cut transversely and obliquely (Figure 9.8B).

3 Identify the epithelial cells lining the gastric glands, noting: mucus-secreting cells lining the neck and gastric pit, pear-shaped parietal (oxyntic) cells at intervals along most of the length of the gland, and closely-packed chief (peptic) cells lining the deeper part of the gland (Figures 9.8B and C).

(a) What are the functions of these cells?

(b) In what ways is the wall of the stomach adapted to perform its functions?

OTHER REGIONS OF THE GUT

If available, examine sections or photomicrographs of the tongue, oesophagus, colon and rectum and compare them with the stomach and small intestine with respect to their epithelial lining and muscles. In particular notice:

1 Tongue: taste buds (flask-shaped bundles of sensory and supporting cells) embedded in stratified epitheium; striated muscles are seen deeper down (*see* page 196).

2 Oesophagus:inner lining of stratified epithelium; outer layer of striated circular muscles.

3 Colon and rectum: wall contains simple tubular glands lined by numerous goblet cells.

While examining the above sections relate structure to function where possible.

For Consideration

(1) From your observations of different regions of the alimentary canal, construct a *generalised diagram* of a section through the wall of the gut, indicating the component tissues of each layer.

(2) In what respects is the structure of the wall of different parts of the gut adapted to perform its particular functions?

Requirements
TS or LS ileum
TS or LS duodenum
VS wall of stomach
Sections or photomicrographs of tongue, oesophagus, colon, rectum.
Electron micrograph of epithelial cell of small intestine

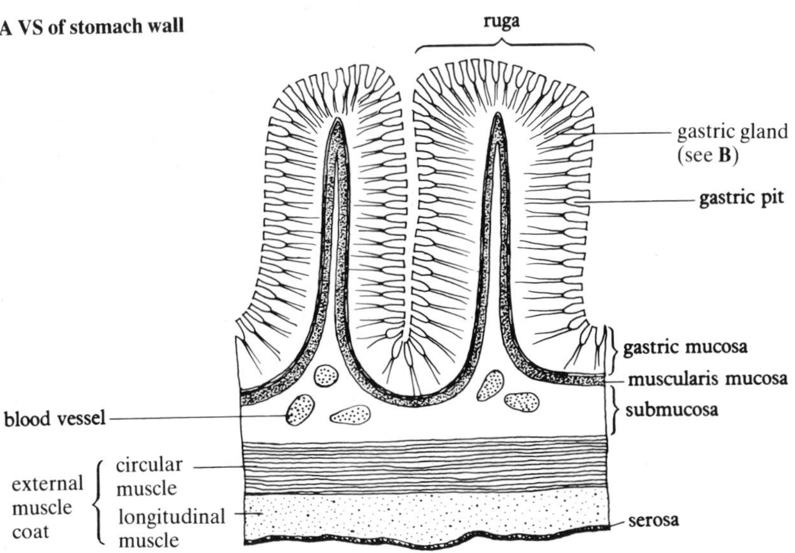

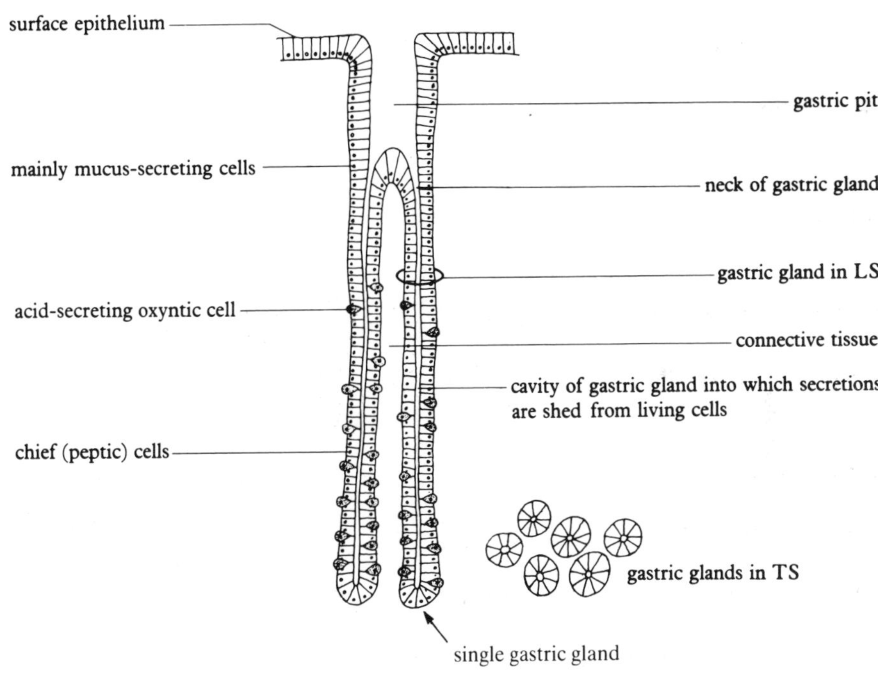

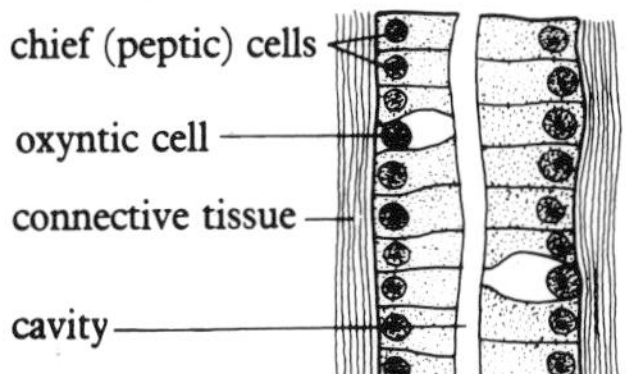

Figure 9.8 Microscopic structure of the wall of the mammalian stomach.

Investigation 9.3
Digestion of starch in humans

CAUTION:
Because of the risk of infection, do not let your mouth come into contact with a test tube containing someone else's saliva.

Requirements
Test tubes × 12
Test tube rack
Measuring cylinder (20 cm^3)
Water bath (250 cm^3 beaker)
Bunsen burner with tripod and gauze
Wax pencil

Starch suspension
Dextrose (glucose)
Iodine solution
Benedict's reagent
Hydrochloric acid (1.0 mol dm^{-3})
Paraffin wax

Starch is a polysaccharide which has to be broken down into free sugar molecules before absorption can take place.

The purpose of this experiment is firstly to test the hypothesis that saliva contains an enzyme which breaks down starch to sugar; and secondly to investigate the properties of the enzyme and the conditions under which it works most effectively.

Starch is mixed with saliva under various conditions and after a given period of time the mixture is tested for starch with iodine solution and for sugar with Benedict's reagent. (For details of these tests *see* page 42).

It is of course important to set up the necessary controls and to carry out standard tests on starch and sugar with which to compare the experimental results. The sugar used should be a reducing sugar, e.g. glucose.

Procedure

1 Collect 20 cm^3 of uncontaminated saliva in a measuring cylinder: the flow can be increased by chewing paraffin wax.[1]

2 Transfer one quarter of the saliva to a test tube and place this in a boiling water bath for 15 minutes. Transfer a further quarter to another test tube: add four drops of hydrochloric acid (1.0 mol dm^{-3}), mix well and leave for at least 15 minutes. Keep the rest of the saliva untreated at room temperature.

3 Now set up six pairs of test tubes as follows. Label each test tube with its code number, using a wax pencil.

Pair A (1) 4 cm^3 sugar only
(2) 4 cm^3 sugar only
Pair B (3) 4 cm^3 starch only
(4) 4 cm^3 starch only
Pair C (5) 4 cm^3 untreated saliva only
(6) 4 cm^3 untreated saliva only
Pair D (7) 4 cm^3 starch plus 2 cm^3 untreated saliva
(8) 4 cm^3 starch plus 2 cm^3 untreated saliva
Pair E (9) 4 cm^3 starch plus 2 cm^3 pre-heated saliva
(10) 4 cm^3 starch plus 2 cm^3 pre-heated saliva
Pair F (11) 4 cm^3 starch plus 2 cm^3 acidified saliva
(12) 4 cm^3 starch plus 2 cm^3 acidified saliva

4 Leave the test tubes for at least 10 minutes before you proceed further (why?).

5 Test the contents of each pair of test tubes (a) for starch by adding two drops of iodine solution and (b) for sugar by heating with one-eighth test tube of Benedict's reagent. Do the starch test on the first of each pair of test tubes, and the sugar test on the second of each pair.

6 It is important to be able to compare the results: this is why separate test tubes are used and it is also why the same quantities of substrate, saliva and test-reagent must be used in each case. To facilitate comparison place the test tubes in a rack in numerical order.

7 Record your results in a table, indicating which test tubes give a positive and which ones a negative result for starch and sugar. It is possible that some may give a result in between: if so, say so.

For Consideration

(1) What is the purpose of testing test tubes 1 to 6?
(2) In which test tubes have you actually tested the hypothesis that saliva contains an enzyme which breaks down starch to sugar? Does the hypothesis turn out to be correct? Would you say it was proved?
(3) Which test tubes provide information on the properties of the enzyme?
(4) What tentative conclusions can be drawn as to the chemical nature of the enzyme and what further experiments could be done to confirm these conclusions?
(5) What is the name of the enzyme in saliva and what compound does it produce from starch?

[1] If you cannot produce 20 cm^3 of saliva, make do with 10 cm^3 and halve all subsequent quantities and reagents.

Investigation 9.4
Digestion of egg white

In the gut proteins are hydrolysed by two main enzymes, pepsin and trypsin. Pepsin is present in the stomach where conditions are markedly acidic. Trypsin, on the other hand, is present in the small intestine where conditions are alkaline. Presumably these two enzymes work best at acidic and alkaline pH respectively. In this investigation we shall test this hypothesis, using egg white as the substrate for the enzymes.

Requirements
Boiling tubes ×4 (or more)
Boiling tube rack
Pipettes or syringes (for measuring 10 cm^3) ×2
Pipettes or syringes (for measuring 1.0 cm^3) ×2
Wax pencil
pH indicator paper (Universal indicator paper)
Incubator (at 37 °C)

Iodine solution
Pepsin solution (20 cm^3, 1.0 per cent)
Trypsin solution (20 cm^3, 1.0 per cent)
Hydrochloric acid (2 cm^3, 0.1 mol dm^{-3})
Sodium carbonate (2 cm^3, 0.2 mol dm^{-3})

Egg white (boiled egg albumen)

Procedure

1 With a wax pencil label four boiling tubes P2, P9, T2 and T9 respectively.

2 Set up the boiling tubes as follows. Use separate graduated pipettes or syringes for the acid, alkali and the two enzymes:

P2 (pepsin at pH 2): 10 cm^3 pepsin solution and 1.0 cm^3 hydrochloric acid

P9 (pepsin at pH 9): 10 cm^3 pepsin solution and 1.0 cm^3 sodium carbonate

T2 (trypsin at pH 2): 10 cm^3 trypsin solution and 1.0 cm^3 hydrochloric acid.

T9 (trypsin at pH 9): 10 cm^3 trypsin solution and 1.0 cm^3 sodium carbonate.

Shake each boiling tube so as to mix the contents thoroughly.

3 Set up any further boiling tubes which you consider to be necessary as controls. Label them appropriately.

4 With pH indicator paper check the pH of the contents of each boiling tube. If necessary adjust the pH by adding acid or alkali, drop by drop.

5 To each boiling tube add a strip of solid egg white. Place the tubes in an incubator at 37 °C and leave them for about 24 hours.

6 After 24 hours examine the contents of each tube: observe the appearance of the egg white *and* the surrounding solution. Record and interpret your results.

For consideration

(1) Do your results support the hypothesis that pepsin and trypsin work best in acid and alkaline conditions respectively?

(2) What controls did you set up, and why?

(3) How could you test the effectiveness of the enzymes at each pH *quantitatively*?

(4) How could you extend the experiment to determine the optimum pH for the action of each of these enzymes?

Investigation 9.5
Digestion of fat

In humans, fats are acted on in the duodenum by two agents, bile salts and lipase. The bile salts are constituents of bile which comes from the liver via the gall bladder. Lipase is a constituent of pancreatic juice which is produced by the pancreas.

In this investigation you are invited to explore the action of these two agents and assess their roles in digestion. The investigation differs from previous ones in that here you will *not* be given detailed instructions, only general guidance as to how to proceed.

General guidance

When fats are hydrolysed, fatty acids and glycerol are released. The presence of acid, creating a relatively low pH, may be used as an indication that hydrolysis has occurred. You can demonstrate the formation of acid by using the pH indicator phenolphthalein: at a pH of above 10 phenolphthalein is pink, but below pH 8.4 it is colourless. If phenolphthalein is added to a test tube in which fat is being hydrolysed, the colour of the contents should change gradually from pink to colourless as fatty acids accumulate. Sodium carbonate should be added to the fat-lipase mixture beforehand to ensure that the pH is above 10 to start off with.

Procedure

With phenolphthalein as your indicator, design and carry out experiments to test some or all of the following hypotheses:

1 Lipase can hydrolyse fat.

2 Bile salts cannot hydrolyse fat.

3 Lipase is more effective if the fat has been acted on by bile salts.

4 Lipase is inactivated by excessive heat.

Requirements
Water bath (boiling)
Stop clock
Test tubes
Beaker (for washing pipette)
Pipette (for delivering up to 5 cm^3 quantities)

Bile salts (5 per cent)
Lipase solution (5 per cent, fresh)
Phenolphthalein
Sodium carbonate solution, (0.2 mol dm^{-3})
pH paper

Fat (e.g. butter)

Other items may be requested by individual students

You are provided with the basic requirements for testing these hypotheses, but if you need any other items you should ask for them.

Write up the results of your experiments and draw such conclusions as you can.

For consideration

(1) Do you think that using phenolphthalein is a satisfactory way of showing that fat has been hydrolysed? Can you suggest a better way?
(2) Consider your experiments very critically in the light of the hypotheses which you have been trying to test. Are your conclusions justified and have your hypotheses *really* been confirmed? What further experiments should be carried out?

Investigation 9.6
Structure and origin of human teeth

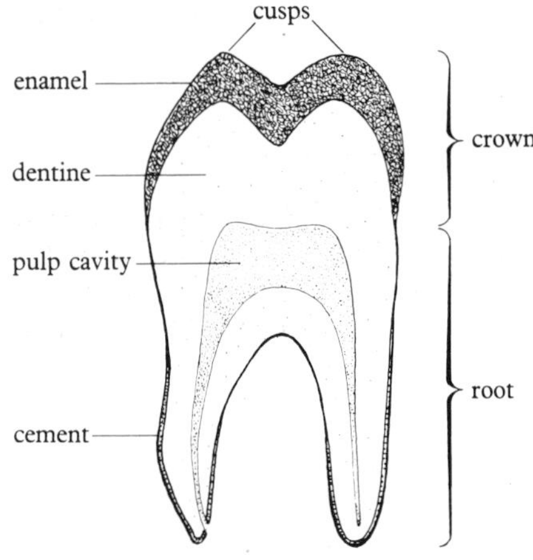

Figure 9.9 Vertical section of a human molar tooth.

Requirements
Microscope

VS tooth
Teeth of dogfish or shark
Skin of dogfish
VS dogfish skin (placoid scales)

In mammals, unlike most other vertebrates, the teeth are differentiated (heterodont). Typically there are cutting incisors, piercing canines, and grinding pre-molars and molars (cheek teeth). In this investigation we shall look at human teeth and consider their possible evolutionary origin.

Procedure

1 Study the external structure of human teeth by (a) looking at your own teeth in a mirror, (b) feeling the surface of your teeth with the tip of your tongue, and (c) observing teeth that have been extracted by a dentist.
2 Notice how the different types differ: thus incisors are more or less chisel-shaped with single roots, canines are pointed and single-rooted, whilst the premolars and molars have two or more cusps on the surface of the crown and are double-rooted. Can you ascribe different functions to these teeth in the human?
3 All these teeth have the same internal structure (Figure 9.9): hard enamel on the outside, then a layer of somewhat softer dentine, and in the centre a pulp cavity containing blood vessels and nerve fibres. The tooth is attached to the jaw bone by cement.

Examine a vertical section of a tooth and verify its structure. Note the distinction between crown and root.
4 In their microscopic structure teeth bear a striking similarity to the placoid scales of the dogfish to which they are no doubt related in evolution.

Examine a piece of dogfish skin and notice the placoid scales. Examine a vertical section of the skin under the microscope and observe one of the scales in detail. To what extent does it resemble a mammalian tooth?
5 Observe, and feel, the placoid scales in and around the mouth of a dogfish. How are they orientated with respect to the antero-posterior axis of the fish? Explain.

The teeth of dogfish, sharks, etc., are, in fact, nothing more than greatly enlarged placoid scales which project from the skin covering the jaws and lining of the mouth cavity.

For consideration

The teeth of lower vertebrates are numerous and are constantly replaced. In contrast, mammals have relatively few teeth at any given time, and they only have two sets in the course of post-natal life. First there are the milk teeth, consisting of incisors, canines and pre-molars, but no molars; these are later replaced by the permanent teeth characteristic of the adult. Consider the advantages and disadvantages of the mammalian dentition, and its pattern of replacement, compared with lower vertebrates.

Investigation 9.7
Teeth and skulls of different mammals

In this exercise we shall look at the teeth of a selection of mammals, noting in particular the way the teeth are adapted both in the relative numbers of each type and in their structure, to deal with particular kinds of diet.

It is a convenient convention to summarise a mammal's complement of teeth in the form of a dental formula. In this the number of teeth of each type belonging to the upper jaw is written above the number of teeth of each type belonging to the lower jaw. Since the jaws of all mammals are symmetrical about the mid-line, the number of teeth of each type represented is scored on one side only. The tooth types are designated by their initial letters. Thus the dental formula of the human adult is:

$$i\frac{2}{2},\ c\frac{1}{1},\ p\frac{2}{2},\ m\frac{3}{3} = \frac{8 \times 2}{8 \times 2} = 32$$

CARNIVORES

1 Examine the skull of a dog and note the teeth (Figure 9.10). Verify that the dental formula is:

$$i\frac{3}{3},\ c\frac{1}{1},\ pm\frac{4}{4},\ m\frac{2}{3} = \frac{10 \times 2}{11 \times 2} = 42$$

2 Whatever you may feed your own dog on, it is supposed to be a meat-eater (carnivore). How are the teeth adapted to deal with such food? What is the exact function of each type of tooth?

3 Notice the large carnassial teeth. These are the last pair of pre-molars in the upper jaw and the first pair of molars in the lower jaw. What are they for?

4 Close the upper and lower jaws together. Note how the upper and lower teeth fit (occlusion). What is the importance of this?

5 Look at an individual molar tooth. Notice that the surface of the crown bears a series of triangular cusps. Such cusps are typical of the cheek teeth of primitive mammals. They have been modified for different purposes in the course of mammalian evolution.

6 Look at Figure 9.10 and note the points of attachment (i.e. the origin and insertion) of the masseter and temporal muscles. What happens to the jaws when these muscles contract?

7 Investigate the articulation between the upper and lower jaws, and notice also the stout condyles for articulation with the first vertebra. What part do these structures play in the action of the teeth?

8 If available, compare the skull and teeth of the dog with those of other carnivores such as cats.

OMNIVORES

An omnivore lives on a mixed diet of animal and plant material.

1 Examine the skull of an adult man and pig, both omnivores, and compare their teeth with those of the dog. Note that the cusps are lower and more rounded than the dog's.

2 The dental formula of the pig is:

$$i\frac{3}{3},\ c\frac{1}{1},\ pm\frac{4}{4},\ m\frac{3}{3} = \frac{11 \times 2}{11 \times 2} = 44$$

Does this agree with your specimen?

HERBIVORES

Feeding on plants presents special problems, particularly the necessity for grinding the food. Why is this necessary? In a grass-eater like the horse,

Figure 9.10 Skull and teeth of dog, a carnivore. The arrows indicate the positions of the masseter and temporal muscles.

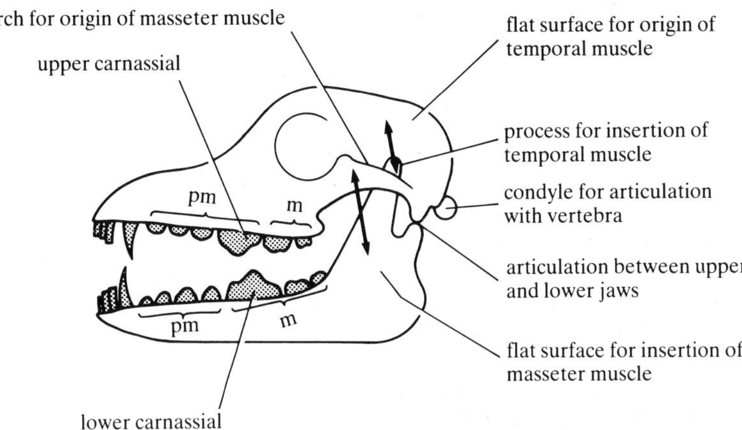

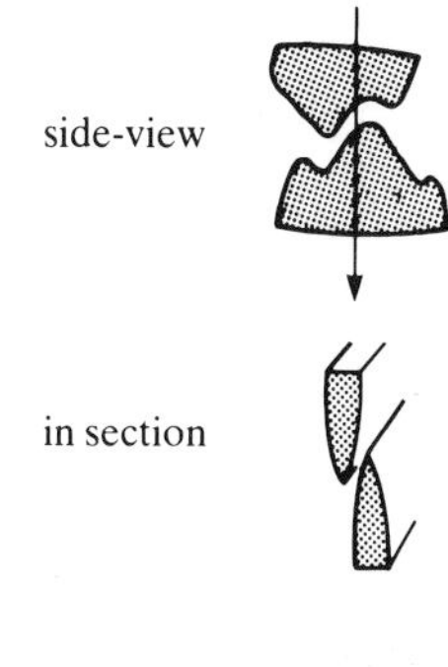

A Molars in longitudinal section

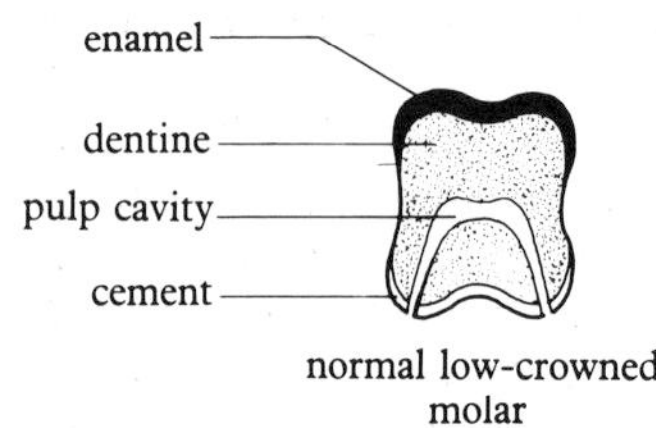

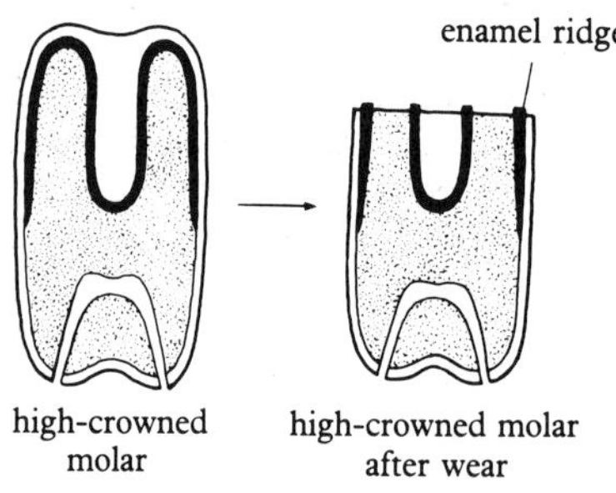

B Crown surface

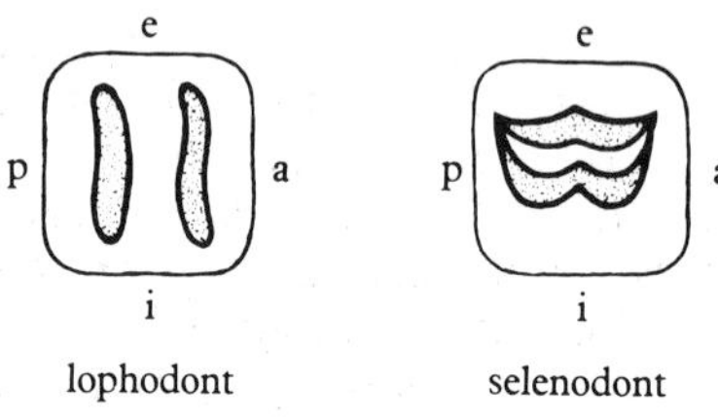

C Action of molars

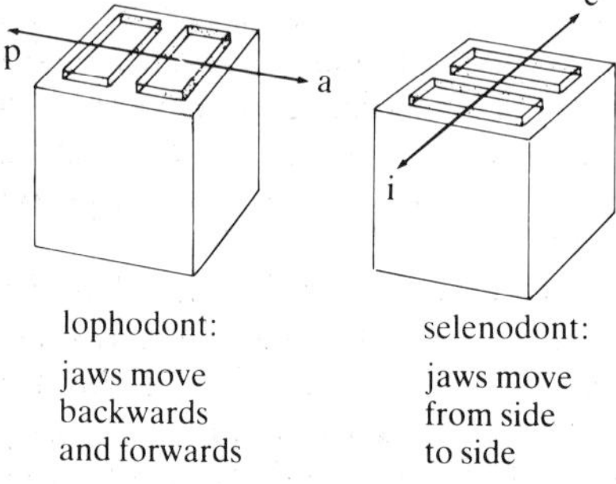

Figure 9.11 Molar teeth of herbivore. In **B** and **C**: **a**, anterior; **p**, posterior; **e**, external; **i**, internal. In **C** the arrows indicate the direction of movement of the upper and lower jaws relative to each other. Note that the maximum grinding effect is achieved by the lophodont tooth being moved backwards and forwards, and the selenodont tooth from side to side.

the incisors are used for cutting and the cheek teeth for grinding.

The cheek teeth of herbivores show varying degrees of elongation of the crown to allow for wear. This is achieved by growth of the cusps as shown in Figure 9.11A. The cusps are covered with cement. With continued wear, the tops of the cusps are worn away. Since the cement and dentine are softer than the enamel, they wear away more quickly, thus leaving a series of enamel ridges on the surface of the crown. This makes the cheek teeth ideally suited to grinding tough plant food.

The cheek teeth of herbivorous mammals are thought to have evolved from a primitive type of tooth which bore six cusps. The cusps have fused, and undergone other modifications to give two types of teeth (Figure 9.11B):

(a) Lophodont teeth. The cusps are fused to give two ridges running at *right angles* to the antero-posterior axis. Examples are tapir, rhinoceros, elephant and horse.

(b) Selenodont teeth. The cusps are modified into crescent-shaped ridges running *parallel* to the antero-posterior axis. Examples are ox, sheep and deer.

1 Examine the skull of tapir or rhinoceros, which show the lophodont condition in a comparatively unmodified form. What sort of jaw movements would be expected to make best use of these teeth? The horse shows a rather modified version of the lophodont condition. In what respects is it modified?

2 The lophodont pattern can be seen particularly clearly in the elephant. Apart from the tusks (which are elongated upper incisors), the elephant's teeth are reduced to a few enormous molars, each bearing numerous enamel ridges.

3 Examine the lower jaw of, e.g. sheep. The pre-molars and molars display the selenodont condition very clearly. What kind of jaw movements would make best use of these teeth? Do the jaws of sheep and cows display such movements?

4 Examine the upper jaw of e.g. sheep. Note that the upper incisors and canines are absent. They are replaced by a hardened upper lip which the lower incisors bite against.

5 Compare the skull of a typical herbivore, e.g. sheep, with that of the dog. To what extent are the features shown in Figure 9.10 different in the herbivore's skull, and why?

GNAWERS

These include rodents, e.g. rats, mice and beavers. The most striking feature of their teeth is the large chisel-like incisors which are adapted for gnawing. Their effectiveness is admirably demonstrated by the beaver, which uses them to cut down trees for building dams.

1 Examine the skull of a rodent such as rat. Note reduction in the total number of teeth. The dental formula of the rat is:

$$i\frac{1}{1}, c\frac{0}{0}, pm\frac{0}{0}, m\frac{3}{3} = \frac{4 \times 2}{4 \times 2} = 16$$

Does this agree with your specimen?

2 Examine the incisors and note how long they are. The teeth of most mammals cease to grow at a certain stage. This is because the opening into the pulp cavity constricts, so isolating the tooth from its blood supply. The incisors of rodents, however, have a persistent pulp cavity, which enables them to continue growing throughout life. This enables the teeth to maintain their length despite constant wearing.

3 Notice the gap behind the incisors. This is called the diastema; here food is rolled into a ball before being swallowed. What do you think the cheek teeth are used for?

4 Examine the skull of a rabbit. This is not a rodent, but it has a similar dentition. Compare its teeth with those of the rat. In what respects are they similar, and different? How do their diets differ?

OTHER TYPES OF MAMMAL

Many species of mammal eat particular types of food for which their teeth are suited. The following skulls, if available, are particularly worth looking at.

1 Some mammals, known as insectivores, feed on insects. Examples include moles, hedgehogs and shrews. A diet of insects does not necessitate having teeth of different types, and the insectivore probably possesses the most primitive type of mammalian dentition: a uniform set of small teeth with pointed cusps. How do the teeth compare with the dog's?

2 Dolphins and certain types of whales eat squid and fish which are taken alive and swallowed whole. If available, examine the teeth of, e.g. dolphin. Note the large number of sharp peg-like teeth. Their main function is to prevent the fish escaping from the jaws.

Requirements
Skulls, or photographs of skulls, of the following:

dog	sloth
cat, tiger	rat, beaver
hedgehog, mole	rabbit
dolphin	rhinoceros, tapir
walrus	horse
pig	elephant
man	ox, sheep, deer

3 Certain mammals feed on shelled molluscs. An example is the walrus. Its large upper canines ('tusks') are used not only for fighting, but also for digging up clams. The shells are crushed with its flattened back teeth.
4 Now consider the sloth. This tropical, tree-living mammal lives on soft fruit. Its peg-like teeth, which lack enamel, are quite adequate for this kind of diet.

For Consideration

(1) Select one of the carnivores and one of the herbivores which you have investigated in this practical, and compare their skulls and teeth from a structural and functional point of view. Relate their dentitions to their diets.
(2) Which do you consider to be the most primitive kind of mammalian cheek teeth from which the others may have been derived in the course of evolution?
(3) The teeth of fishes, amphibians and reptiles are, in the main, numerous, all alike, and pointed. There are no cusped teeth of the molar type. What general effects do you think such a dentition has on the feeding habits of these lower vertebrates? Give examples.
(4) What functions are performed by chewing (mastication) and what are the consequences of its *not* taking place?

Investigation 9.8 Mouthparts of insects

Insects employ a wide variety of feeding techniques, involving the use of mouthparts which are adapted to suit the type of food eaten. In this investigation we shall start by looking at the locust or cockroach whose mouthparts, adapted for biting and chewing, illustrate the basic pattern. We shall then look briefly at the more specialised mouthparts of other insects.

Procedure

COCKROACH

1 Remove the head from a dead cockroach (or locust) and boil it gently in a test tube containing a little potassium hydroxide solution until it is soft and semi-transparent. (Put a few fragments of broken pottery in the test tube to prevent 'bumping'). It is normally necessary to boil for approximately five minutes. This facilitates the removal of the mouthparts later.
2 Wash the head in several changes of water. Hold the head down, dorsal surface uppermost, on a white tile, and cut off the labrum ('upper lip') which shields the mouthparts.
3 Now remove each of the mouthparts by grasping them *at their base* with small forceps and pulling them gently but firmly from their attachment to the head. Remove the mandibles first, then the two maxillae, and finally the labium. Notice the hypopharynx adhering to the inner surface of the labium. This forms the floor of the pharynx and is pierced by the opening of the salivary duct. Separate the hypopharynx from the labium.
4 Mount the mouthparts in dilute glycerine and examine under low power. Compare with Figure 9.12.
5 Make a permanent preparation as follows. Dehydrate the mouthparts by placing them in a covered watchglass of 70 per cent ethanol for five minutes, then 90 per cent (five minutes), then two changes of absolute ethanol (five minutes each). Clear in xylene or clove oil (at least five minutes) and mount in Canada balsam under a supported coverslip.
6 Observe the mouthparts of a live specimen. Present it with a small speck of bread on the end of a needle and observe the mouthparts working. Notice that the bread becomes moistened with saliva. What are the functions of the different components of the cockroach's mouthparts?

OTHER INSECTS

Either make your own slides or examine prepared slides of the heads of some or all of the following insects:
1 **Mosquito**: a proboscis sheath envelops six slender processes – suction food tube, hypopharynx with salivary tube, and two pairs of sharp stylets for piercing skin. In your preparation some or all of these will probably have come out of the sheath. Note also the pair of short sensory palps.

A Head showing positions of mouthparts

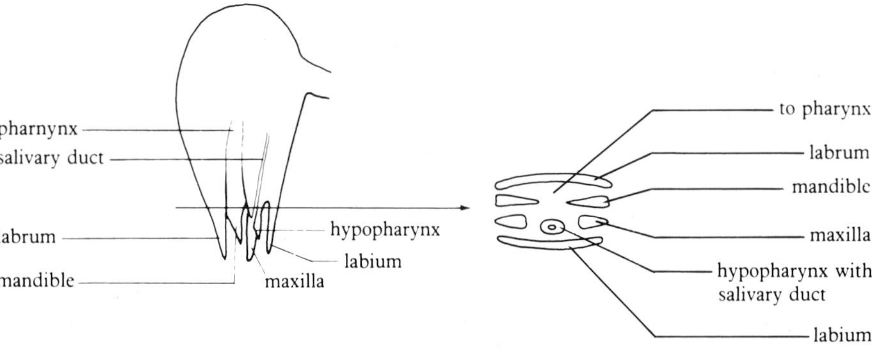

B Individual mouthparts in detail
mandible

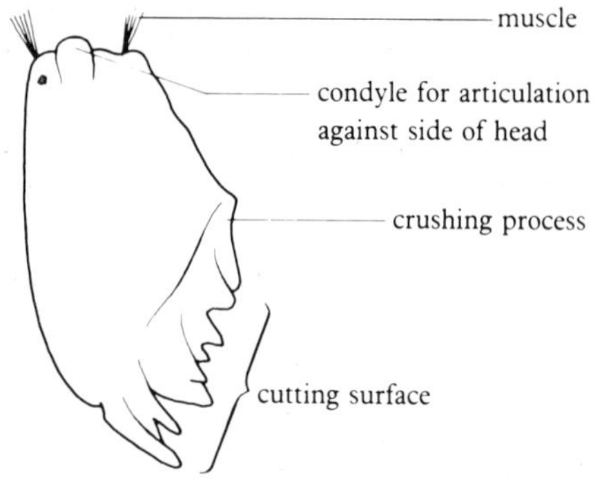

maxilla

foot forming hinge against side of head
stem
lacinia
galea
maxillary palp (sensory)

labium

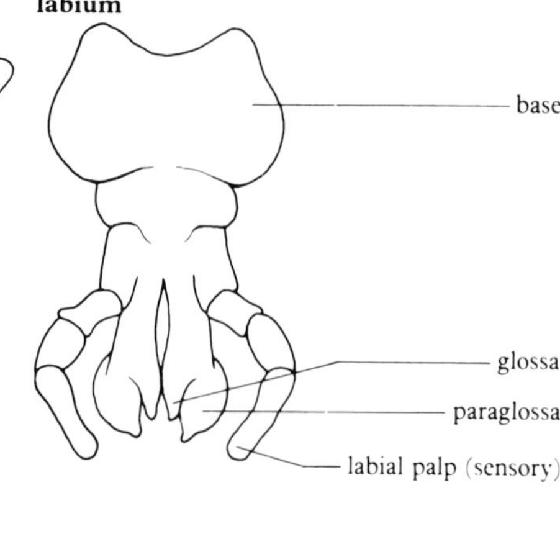

Figure 9.12 Mouthparts of cockroach.

2 **Aphid**: here the proboscis sheath encloses three slender processes – suction food tube, which also contains the salivary tube, and one pair of stylets for piercing plant tissues.
3 **Butterfly**: mouthparts reduced or absent except for palps and long, flexible proboscis for probing flowers.
4 **Honey bee**: in this case the suction food tube is surrounded by four supports which together form a flexible, probe-like proboscis; the mandibles are spatulate and used for moulding wax in building the comb.
5 **Housefly**: numerous pseudotracheal tubes in a pair of expanded lobes at the end of the labium form a filtering device which leads to the food tube.

For Consideration

Choose one of the above insects and speculate on how its mouthparts may have evolved from the kind of arrangement seen in present-day locusts and cockroaches.

Requirements
Broken pottery fragments
Test tube
White tile
Dissecting instruments
Slides and coverslips
Watchglasses
Microscope
Binocular microscope

Potassium hydroxide solution (5 per cent)
Dilute glycerine
Ethanol (70 per cent)
Ethanol (90 per cent)
Absolute ethanol
Xylene or clove oil
Canada balsam

Fresh-killed or preserved cockroach or locust
Live cockroach or locust
Prepared slides of mosquito (head), aphid, butterfly (head), honey bee (head) and house fly (head)

Questions and Problems

1 Make a list of the pathway by which food substances reach the cells of (a) a mammal, and (b) a named invertebrate.

2 Explain each of the following statements:
(a) If you stand on your head it is still possible for food to pass upwards into your stomach.
(b) When food touches the back of the pharynx it is difficult not to swallow.
(c) When food touches the back of the pharynx swallowing normally occurs, but if the back of the pharynx is touched with a feather vomiting occurs.
(d) Secretion of gastric juice may start before the food reaches the stomach.
(e) If the bile duct is blocked (for example by gall-stones in obstructive jaundice), digestion of fats is impaired.

3 Trace what happens to a ham sandwich from the moment it is taken into the mouth to the absorption of its chemical constituents into the bloodstream.

4 Explain how it is that a man whose stomach has been removed in the surgical operation of gastrectomy may continue to eat and digest a fairly normal diet. What special precautions do you think a gastrectomised man should observe in his eating habits?

5 Junket is prepared by warming milk with a commercial substance called rennet to a temperature of about 36 °C. What is happening chemically and what is the biological significance of this process?

6 (a) By means of diagrams show how a globular protein is broken down in the alimentary canal.
(b) How is the body able to digest protein without digesting itself?

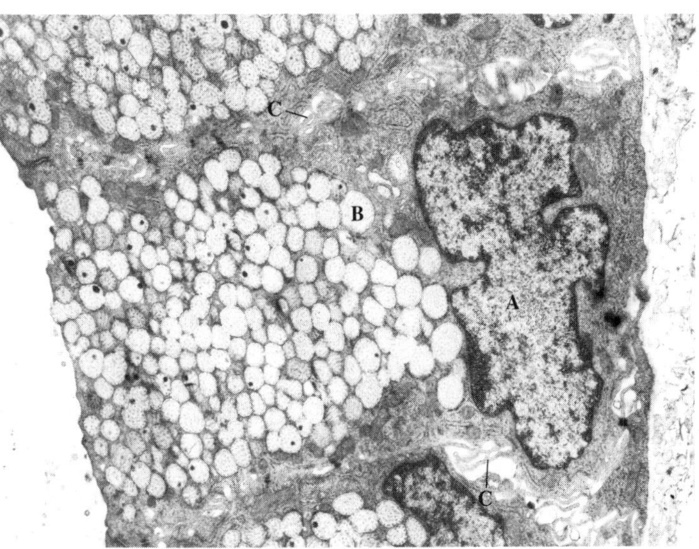

Figure 9.13 (*See Question 7*) Electron micrograph of section through epithelium lining a gastric gland of a mouse. (*Dr Elizabeth Tudor, Monash University, Australia*).

7 Figure 9.13 is an electron micrograph of a section through the epithelium lining a gastric gland of an adult mouse. The plane of the section is perpendicular to the free surface of the epithelium.
(a) Name structure A. Why does it appear distorted?
(b) (i) Name structure B and describe how it was formed.
(ii) Suggest *two* possible functions for structure B.
Of your two suggestions which is more likely to be correct, and why?
(c) Structure C is part of the membrane between adjacent epithelial cells. Suggest reasons why it is folded and why there appear to be gaps between the cells.

8 Glucose, galactose, and fructose are examples of hexose sugars, having the empirical formula $C_6H_{12}O_6$. Xylose and arabinose are pentose sugars, having the empirical formula $C_5H_{10}O_5$. Results from experiments on the rate of absorption of these sugars by pieces of living intestine and by pieces of intestine poisoned with cyanide are given in the margin. The rates are shown as relative to the rate for glucose.

Comment fully on these results. (*JMB Nuffield*)

	Rate of absorption	
	By living intestine	By poisoned intestine
glucose	1.00	0.33
galactose	1.10	0.53
fructose	0.43	0.37
xylose	0.30	0.31
arabinose	0.29	0.29

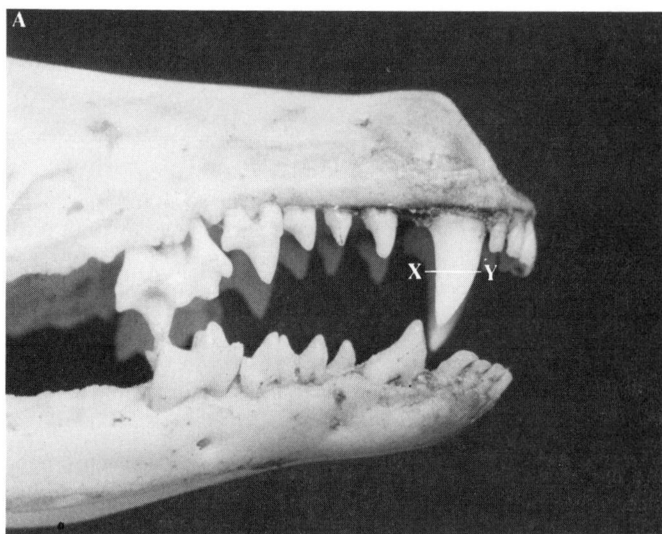

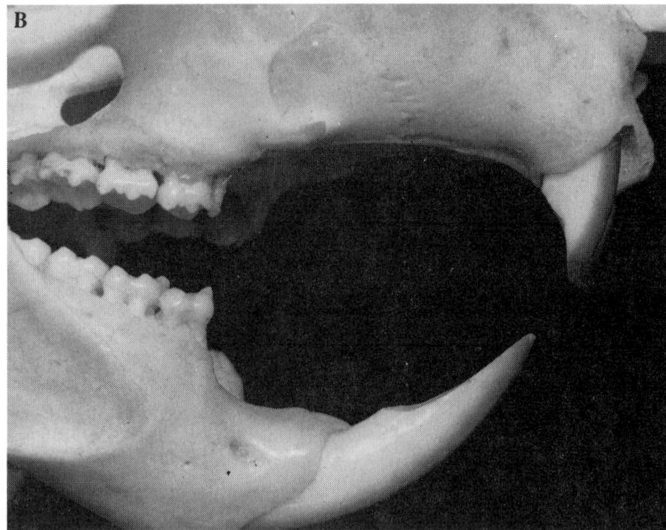

Figure 9.14 The teeth of (A) hedgehog and (B) squirrel. (*B.J.W. Heath*)

9 Figure 9.14A shows the teeth of a hedgehog, and Figure 9.14B shows the teeth of a squirrel.
(a) Draw and label a transverse section of a canine tooth at the level indicated by the line X—Y in Figure 9.14A.
(b) Describe how the dentitions of the two animals differ.
(c) Find out as much as you can about the diets of these two animals and explain how each dentition is adapted to the diet.

10 (a) What is the chemical structure of cellulose and how must this structure be altered in order for cellulose to be assimilated by an animal?
(b) It is known that snails can digest cellulose. How would you investigate the source of the enzyme that achieves this?

11 A comparison was made of the relative amounts of amylase present in the saliva produced by three separate human groups, the Tswana of Botswana, the Bushmen of the Kalahari Desert, and Europeans. The amylase activity, expressed in arbitrary units, was as follows:

Tswana 248 Bushmen 22 European 101

(a) Describe the method by which the amylase activity of the three groups might have been assessed.
(b) What does the data suggest about the diets of the three groups?
(c) Suggest two alternative hypotheses to explain how the three groups may have come to differ from each other in this respect.
(d) Briefly outline *one* investigation which might be carried out to discover which of your two hypotheses is correct.

LEARNING RESOURCE CENTRE
FILTON COLLEGE
FILTON AVENUE
BRISTOL
BS34 7AT

0117 9092228

10 Autotrophic Nutrition

Background Summary

1 Autotrophic nutrition, the synthesis of organic compounds from inorganic sources, takes place by **photosynthesis** in plants and **chemosynthesis** in certain bacteria.

2 Photosynthesis and chemosynthesis play an important part in the **carbon cycle**: carbon dioxide is built up into complex carbon compounds by photosynthesis and chemosynthesis; it is subsequently released back into the atmosphere by respiration.

3 The raw materials of photosynthesis are carbon dioxide and water; the major products are carbohydrate and oxygen. Sunlight is the source of energy and **chlorophyll** traps the light energy.

4 Experiments can be performed to show that the external conditions required for photosynthesis are carbon dioxide, water, light, and a suitable temperature. The effect of light and other factors on the rate of photosynthesis of an aquatic plant such as *Elodea* can be investigated quantitatively by means of a **photosynthometer**.

5 Experiments show that photosynthesis is subject to the **law of limiting factors**, i.e. when a chemical process depends on more than one condition being favourable, its rate is limited by that factor which is nearest its minimum value.

6 Probably the most important single factor controlling the rate of photosynthesis is light, and plants exhibit a wide variety of adaptations for securing adequate illumination.

7 The **absorption spectrum** of chlorophyll indicates that red and blue light are absorbed most, and the **action spectrum** for photosynthesis shows that these are the most effective wavelengths in photosynthesis.

8 The photosynthetic pigments in a green leaf can be separated and identified by chromatography. The pigments are **chlorophyll a** and **chlorophyll b** plus the accessory pigments **xanthophyll** and **carotene**. A further pigment, **phaeophytin**, is a breakdown product of chlorophyll. The function of the accessory pigments is to increase the range of wavelengths from which plants can harvest energy.

9 At dawn and dusk there is a critical level of illumination when photosynthesis and respiration proceed at the same rate and there is no net gain or loss of carbohydrate (**light compensation point**).

10 Photosynthesis occurs in the **chloroplasts** where chlorophyll is located. Studies on the fine structure of the chloroplast show that the chlorophyll molecules are laid out on pairs of parallel membranes (**thylakoids**) which are organised into **grana**, thereby providing maximum surface in a minimum volume.

11 The chloroplasts are mainly in the **leaves** whose anatomy shows a close relationship between structure and function. Loosely packed **photosynthetic cells** (**palisade** and **spongy mesophyll**) carry out photosynthesis and the epidermis is pierced by numerous **stomata** for gas exchange. Other tissues are responsible for strengthening and transport.

12 Evidence indicates that photosynthesis is a two-stage process, the first requiring light and the second capable of occurring in the dark. The function of the **light stage** is to produce ATP, and to split water (the **Hill reaction**), thus providing hydrogen atoms for the subsequent reduction of carbon dioxide. In the **dark stage** the carbon dioxide is reduced and carbohydrate synthesised via the **Calvin cycle**.

13 In the light stage electrons are removed from chlorophyll and either passed back to chlorophyll via a series of carriers with the production of ATP (**cyclic photophosphorylation**), or combined with hydrogen ions (from the splitting of water) to form hydrogen atoms for the dark reactions (**non-cyclic photophosphorylation**). The hydrogen atoms are transferred to the dark stage by NADP in the final step of a process which involves the transfer of electrons through two chlorophyll pigment systems (**photosystems I** and **II**).

14 In the dark stage carbon dioxide is fixed, reduced by the hydrogen formed in the light stage, and built up, by a complex series of enzyme-controlled reactions, into carbohydrate using energy from the ATP and reduced NADP formed in the light stage.

15 Within the chloroplast the light reactions take place on the thylakoid membranes where the chlorophyll is located, the dark reactions in the stroma. Mitchell's chemiosmotic theory helps to explain how ATP is formed in the membranes.

16 **C3 plants** fix carbon dioxide into a 3-carbon compound (phosphoglyceric acid). **C4 plants**, in contrast, fix carbon dioxide into a 4-carbon compound (oxaloacetic acid), a rapid reaction which enables such plants to build up a store of fixed carbon dioxide for subsequent conversion to carbohydrate.

17 In C3 plants the substrate for carbon dioxide fixation (ribulose bisphosphate) sometimes combines with oxygen instead of carbon dioxide, resulting in **photorespiration**.

18 From carbohydrate intermediates formed as a result of photosynthesis, other organic molecules are synthesised. These include amino acids formed by transamination. For synthesising amino acids a source of nitrogen is required, which for most plants is nitrate or ammonium ions from the soil.

19 Some autotrophic bacteria undergo photosynthesis but most are chemosynthetic. In chemosynthesis organic compounds are synthesised from inorganic raw materials, the necessary energy coming from the oxidation of, e.g. iron (II) salts, nitrates (nitrate (V)) and nitrites (nitrate (III)).

20 Chemosynthetic bacteria are important in the **nitrogen cycle**, the process in which nitrogen compounds circulate in nature. **Nitrifying bacteria** obtain energy for synthesis by

converting ammonium compounds, released from animal and plant protein during decay, into nitrites and nitrates. Nitrates are then assimilated by plants.

21 The nitrogen cycle also includes **denitrifying bacteria** which convert nitrates into nitrites, ammonia or free nitrogen.

22 **Nitrogen-fixing bacteria**, either free in soil or mutualistic in the roots of certain plants, can convert atmospheric nitrogen into (eventually) protein.

Investigation 10.1
Effect of light intensity on the rate of photosynthesis

A convenient way of investigating the effect of light intensity on the rate of photosynthesis is to measure the evolution of oxygen from an aquatic plant at different levels of illumination. In this experiment we shall use Canadian pondweed, *Elodea*, from whose cut stem gas may be seen emerging as a stream of bubbles.

A simple way of estimating the oxygen evolved by *Elodea* is to count the number of bubbles given off per unit time. If this method is used it is important to select a piece of *Elodea* which is exuding bubbles of approximately equal size at a constant rate.

A more accurate method is to estimate the volume of gas given off by the plant in a given time, using a photosynthometer. That is what we shall be doing in this investigation.

Apparatus

The apparatus consists of a capillary tube, flared at one end for collecting the gas, and connected at the other end via a plastic tube to a 2 cm^3 syringe (Figure 10.1). Gas evolved by the plant over a known period of time is collected in the flared end of the capillary tube. It is then drawn into the capillary tube by the syringe, and its volume recorded in terms of the length of the capillary tube that it occupies. This is repeated at different light intensities.

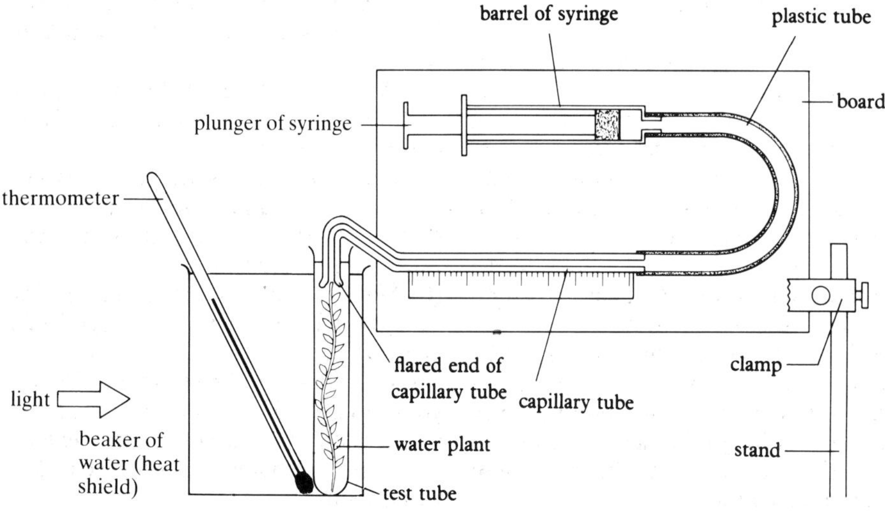

Figure 10.1 Apparatus for investigating the effect of light intensity on the rate of photosynthesis of a water plant such as *Elodea*.

The plastic tube serves as a place to deposit the gas after it has been collected and pulled through the capillary tube.

Procedure

1 Cut a piece of well-illuminated *Elodea* about 10 cm long, and make sure bubbles are emerging from the cut end of the stem. Place it, bubbling end upwards, in a test tube containing the same water that the pondweed has been kept in.

2 Fill the apparatus with tap water as follows. Remove the plunger of the syringe, and direct a gentle stream of water from a tap into the barrel until the whole of the syringe and plastic tube are full of water. Then replace the plunger and gently expel water from the flared end of the capillary tube until the plunger is almost at the end of the syringe. Make sure the whole apparatus is full of water and that there are no air bubbles in the capillary tube. In soft-water areas it is advisable to add a pinch of hydrogencarbonate powder to the water. Why?

3 Place the end of the capillary tube in the test tube in such a way that the bubbles emerging from the piece of *Elodea* accumulate in the flared end. Stand the test tube in a beaker of water to prevent the temperature of the plant from increasing during the experiment. Check the temperature of the water in the beaker from time to time during the experiment.

4 With the room darkened, position a light source 5 cm from the plant. A bench lamp with 40W bulb will do, though a lantern slide projector is better. (Why?).

5 Wait for the plant to come into equilibrium with this light intensity. Then collect the gas given off during a given period of time (five minutes is generally sufficient). Then draw the bubble of gas into the capillary tube by gently pulling the plunger of the syringe. Measure its length and record this together with the distance of the plant from the light source.

6 Now repeat the process with the light source at increasing distances from the plant, e.g. 10, 15, 20, 25, 30, 40, 80 cm. In each case measure the amount of gas evolved in a standard period of time. Record your readings.
7 Repeat Step 6, moving the lamp gradually *closer* to the plant.

Results

The intensity of light falling on a given object from a constant source is inversely proportional to the square of the distance between them. In other words:

$$\text{Intensity} \propto \frac{1}{d^2}$$

where d is the distance between the light source and the object.

Work out the light intensity as $\frac{1}{d^2}$ $\left(\text{or, more conveniently, } \frac{1000}{d^2}\right)$ for each distance used in your experiment and record this together with the amount of gas given off.

Plot your results on a graph, putting light intensity on the horizontal axis and the amount of oxygen evolved (as length of bubble in mm) on the vertical axis.

FURTHER EXPERIMENT: ANALYSIS OF THE GAS

If you want to analyse the gas given off by *Elodea* for its carbon dioxide and oxygen content, proceed as follows.
1 Place the light as close as possible and collect a large sample of the gas several cm long in the capillary tube. Measure the length of the bubble to the nearest mm. (Do not hold the capillary tube in your hand or the rise in temperature will cause the gas to expand.)
2 Now push the bubble to the open end of the capillary tube until it is about 1 cm from the end. Quickly put the open end into a solution of potassium hydroxide and then pull the bubble to the other end of the tube. Still holding the open end in the potassium hydroxide solution, slowly shunt the bubble back and forth along the length of the tube at least 6 times.
3 Put the end of the capillary tube back in water for 5 minutes, then measure the length of the bubble. Any decrease in length is due to absorption of carbon dioxide by the potassium hydroxide solution.
4 Now repeat Steps 2 and 3 with pyrogallol instead of potassium hydroxide. The pyrogallol reacts with any potassium hydroxide still in the tube to form potassium pyrogallate which then absorbs the oxygen. Record the final length of the bubble in the capillary tube. The further decrease in the length of the bubble is due to the absorption of oxygen by the pyrogallate.

> **CAUTION:**
> Pyrogallol can be harmful and should be handled with care. Do not spill it or get it on your skin.

5 Calculate the percentages of carbon dioxide and oxygen in the sample of gas.

$$\text{Percentage of } CO_2 = \frac{a - b}{a} \times 100$$

where a = original length before potassium hydroxide admitted
b = new length after potassium hydroxide admitted

$$\text{Percentage of } O_2 = \frac{b - c}{a} \times 100$$

where a and b are as explained above,
c = new length after pyrogallol admitted
(For further details of gas analysis see page 60.)
6 Record and interpret your results. Are they what you expected?

For Consideration

(1) What relationship between gas production and light intensity is demonstrated by the results of your experiment with the photosynthometer?
(2) What difficulties, if any, did you encounter in the course of the experiment and how did you overcome them?
(3) Consider any sources of inaccuracy in the technique used, and explain how they might be overcome.
(4) Why did you move the lamp gradually further away from the plant, and then closer again?
(5) How might the procedure be modified to investigate the influence of carbon dioxide concentration on the rate of photosynthesis?
(6) How would you use *Elodea* to investigate whether or not photosynthesis obeys the law of limiting factors?
(7) What effect did respiration have on your results? Were you measuring the rate of photosynthesis or the extent to which photosynthesis exceeded respiration?

Requirements
Photosynthometer (Figure 10.1. The capillary tube bore should be not more than 1 mm. The rubber plunger of the syringe should be greased so that it moves easily inside the barrel.)
Test tube
Beaker (400 cm^3)
Thermometer
Lamp with 40W bulb (or other suitable light source)
Metre rule

Potassium hydroxide solution (40 per cent)
Benzene-1,2,3-triol (pyrogallol, pyrogallic acid)
Sodium or potassium hydrogencarbonate powder

Canadian pondweed, (*Elodea canadensis*) or similar pondweed (healthy, illuminated, bubbling)

Investigation 10.2
Effect of hydrogen-carbonate concentration on the rate of photosynthesis

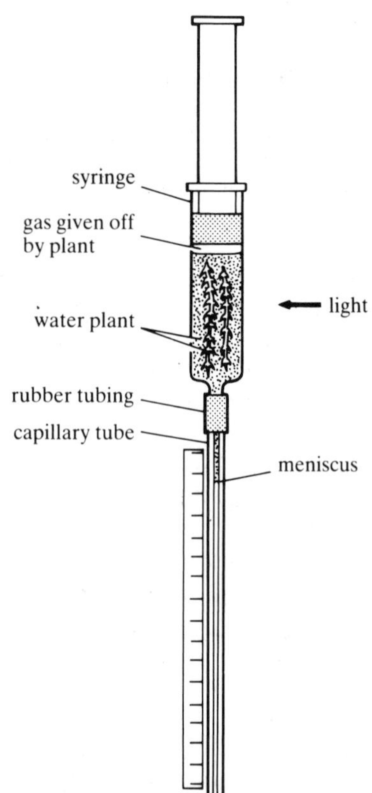

Figure 10.2 Apparatus for investigating the effect of hydrogencarbonate concentration on the rate of photosynthesis of a water plant such as *Elodea*. (*After Freeland*)

Requirements
Small beakers ×5
Capillary tubing (30 cm long, 1 mm internal diameter)
Clamp, stand and boss
Lamp with 100W bulb
Pen for marking glass
Pipette or plastic syringe (10 cm^3)
pH indicator papers
Razor blade
Rubber tubing (to join nozzle of syringe to capillary tubing)
Ruler
Plastic Syringe (20 cm^3)

Distilled water (500 cm^3)
Sodium hydrogencarbonate solutions (0.0100, 0.0125, 0.0166, 0.0250, 0.0500 and 0.1000 and dm^{-3})

Canadian pondweed (*Elodea canadensis*) or similar pondweed (healthy, illuminated, bubbling)

Carbon dioxide is often in short supply for the plants which grow in ponds and lakes. The gas is very soluble in water but once in solution it only diffuses slowly. Lack of carbon dioxide may therefore be one of the factors which limits the growth rate of aquatic plants such as Canadian pondweed under natural conditions.

One source of carbon dioxide is the hydrogencarbonate ion, which rapidly dissociates into carbon dioxide when added to water. In this practical we shall investigate the effect of adding sodium hydrogencarbonate on the photosynthetic rate of Canadian pondweed. We shall use a different type of photosynthometer from the one used in Investigation 10.1. It is illustrated in Figure 10.2.

Procedure

1 Attach a capillary tube to the nozzle end of a 20 cm^3 syringe by means of rubber tubing. Push the end of the capillary tube to the tip of the nozzle of the syringe, and make sure that the rubber tubing provides an airtight seal.

2 Using a razor blade, cut three portions of *Elodea* stem, each from the top end of a different shoot.

3 Remove the plunger from the syringe. Introduce the plants into the barrel of the syringe, with their cut ends facing up, away from the nozzle.

4 Clamp the syringe vertically, nozzle downwards, over a beaker.

5 Place a finger over the open end of the capillary tube. Fill the barrel of the syringe to the brim with tap water. Replace the plunger, catching any excess water in the beaker. Gently push in the plunger of the syringe until the top of the water in the barrel reaches the 20 cm^3 mark. No air should be trapped between plunger and water.

6 Clamp a lamp with the end of its 100W bulb exactly 8 cm from the syringe. The distance is critical and must be exactly the same in each experiment that you perform.

7 Switch the lamp on. Very carefully raise the plunger of the syringe to pull the meniscus to a point near the top of the capillary. Mark the position of the meniscus. Your set-up should now look like Figure 10.2.

8 Measure the distance travelled by the meniscus during the next three minutes. Repeat several times. Record your results, and average the distance the meniscus moved in each three-minute interval.

9 Repeat Steps 5 to 8 with the same *Elodea* shoots in sodium hydrogencarbonate solutions of 0.0100, 0.0125, 0.0166, 0.0250, 0.0500 and 0.1000 mol dm^{-3}.

10 Plot a graph of the rate of photosynthesis (average meniscus movement in mm) on the vertical axis against the concentration of sodium hydrogencarbonate (mol dm^{-3}) on the horizontal axis.

For consideration

(1) How might your results be affected by the expansion and contraction of the air which accumulates in the apparatus?
(2) Examine the graph. Does the supply of carbon dioxide limit the rate of photosynthesis?
(3) What environmental factors might limit the rate of photosynthesis at high hydrogencarbonate concentrations?
(4) Does this method measure the rate of photosynthesis of the pond weed, or the net rate of photosynthesis (i.e. photosynthesis minus respiration?)
(5) In the upper layers of ponds and lakes, even in temperate regions, the pH of the water increases markedly during the day and decreases at night. Why do you think this happens?

Reference: P.W. Freeland, *Problems in Practical Advanced Level Biology*, Hodder and Stoughton, 1985.

Investigation 10.3
Separation of photosynthetic pigments by paper chromatography

The pigments involved in photosynthesis can be separated and identified by paper chromatography. Absorptive paper containing a concentrated spot of leaf extract is dipped in a suitable solvent. The various pigments have different solubilities in the solvent with the result that as the solvent ascends the absorptive paper it carries the pigments with it at different rates. In this way they become separated from one another and can be identified by their different colours and positions.

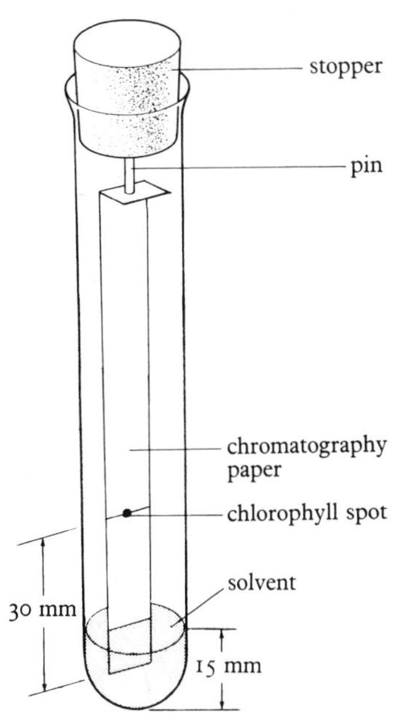

Figure 10.3 Set-up for the chromatographic separation of photosynthetic pigments

Requirements
Large test tube (24 × 150 mm)
Stopper to fit test tube
Pin
Chromatography or filter paper
Scissors
Rack for test tube
Pigment solution (see below)
Solvent (5 cm^3) (see below)

Prepare pigment solution as follows:
Grind up fresh leaves of, e.g. nettle, killed by rapid immersion in boiling water, with pure propanone. Filter.
Make up solvent as follows: Add one part 90 per cent propanone (acetone) to 9 parts petroleum ether (boiling point 80–100 °C).

Procedure

1 Cut a strip of chromatography paper (filter paper will do) of sufficient length to almost reach the bottom of a large test tube and of such width that the edges do not touch the sides of the tube.

2 Rule a pencil line across the strip of paper 30 mm from one end. Fold the other end through 90° and by means of a pin attach it to the stopper as shown in Figure 10.3. Make sure that the lower end of the strip almost reaches the bottom of the tube and that the edges do not touch the sides.

3 Remove the paper from the boiling tube and, using the head of a small pin as a dropper, place a drop of the pigment solution at the centre of the pencil line. Let the drop dry, then place a second small drop on the first. Repeat this process for about 15 minutes, building up a small area of concentrated pigment: the smaller and more concentrated, the better. Drying the spot can be hastened each time by gently warming with the heat from a lamp.

4 While preparing your pigment spot, pour some solvent (a mixture of propanone and petroleum ether) into the boiling tube to a depth of not more than 15 mm. Seal the tube with a stopper for about 10 minutes so the atmosphere inside becomes saturated with vapour.

5 Now suspend the strip of paper in the boiling tube. The bottom edge of the paper should dip into the solvent, but make sure the pigment spot is not immersed.

6 The solvent will ascend rapidly and the pigments will separate in about 10 minutes. When the solvent is approximately 20 mm from the top of the paper, remove the strip, rule a pencil line to mark the solvent front, and dry the paper.

Name	Colour	R_f
Carotene	Yellow	0.95
Phaeophytin	Yellow-grey	0.83
Xanthophyll	Yellow-brown	0.71
Chlorophyll a	Blue-green	0.65
Chlorophyll b	Green	0.45

Table 10.1 Colours and R_f values of the pigments found in a typical leaf. (R_f values for propane/ether mixture).

7 Your chromatogram is now complete and you can proceed to identify the pigments. If you are lucky you should be able to detect the five pigments listed in Table 10.1. They can be identified by their colours and R_f values.

8 Measure the distance from the pencil line to the leading edge of each clearly detectable pigment, and work out the R_f value for each one.

$$R_f = \frac{a}{b}$$

where a = distance moved by substance from its original position.
b = distance moved by solvent from same position.

Compare your results with the information given in Table 10.1.

For Consideration

(1) How could you ascertain if there are more pigments present in a leaf than the ones you have identified?
(2) What is the functional significance of the fact that there are several pigments, not just one?
(3) By what means might you be able to improve the clarity of your chromatogram?

AN ALTERNATIVE TECHNIQUE

A quicker and more complete separation of photosynthetic pigments can be achieved by **thin layer chromatography**. Instead of absorptive paper, a glass or plastic slide (or aluminium sheet) coated with silica gel is used. The gel is spotted and then the slide or aluminium sheet is placed vertically in a beaker or Coplin jar containing solvent at the bottom. For a suitable technique see P.W. Freeland, *Problems in Practical Advanced Level Biology* Hodder and Stoughton, 1985.

Investigation 10.4
Structure of leaves

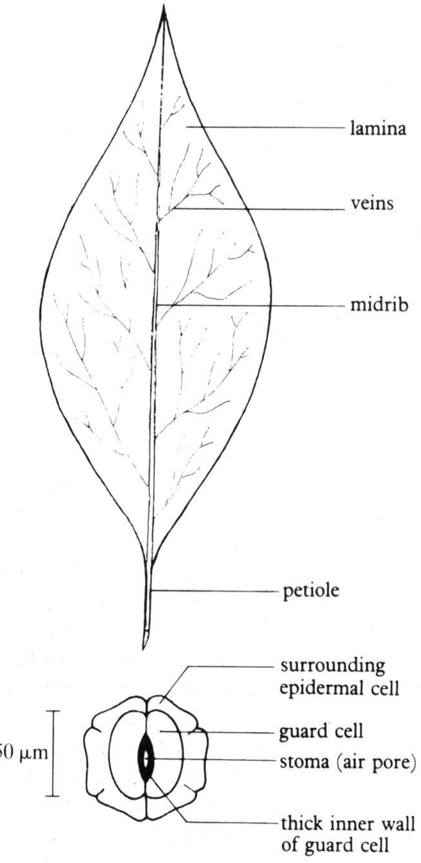

Figure 10.4 External features of a generalised dicotyledonous leaf.

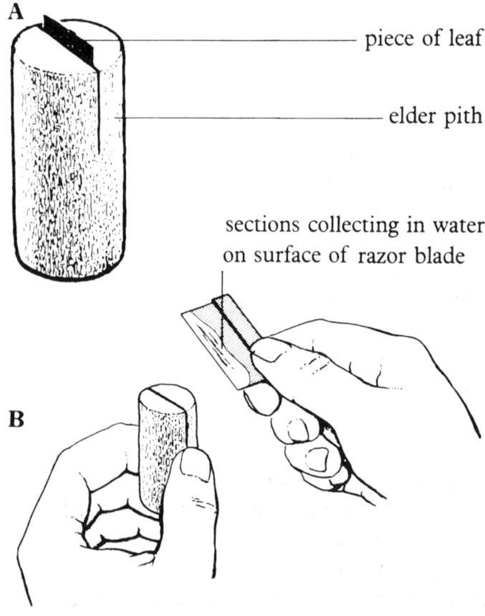

Figure 10.5 Technique for cutting sections of a leaf. **A** shows how the piece of leaf is mounted in elder pith prior to sectioning. **B** shows the actual sectioning procedure.

The leaf is the plant's organ of photosynthesis. As such it would be expected to contain photosynthetic tissue in such a position as to secure optimum illumination of the chloroplasts. The leaf must obviously be in functional connection with the rest of the plant, the transport tissues bringing water and mineral salts to the photosynthetic tissues and taking the products of photosynthesis away from them.

Procedure

EXTERNAL STRUCTURE

1 Study the external features of a leaf of a representative dicotyledon (e.g. privet, laurel, holly, etc.) and monocotyledon (e.g. lily, grasses, etc.). Dicotyledons generally display a network of veins, monocotyledons parallel veins.

2 Note the terminology in Figure 10.4A. Why is the upper surface of the leaf a darker green and more shiny than the bottom surface? What are the functions of the midrib and veins?

3 With small forceps strip off a piece of epidermis from the upper and lower surfaces of the leaf. (Ivy-leaved toadflax is recommended.) Mount in water, outer side of the epidermis uppermost, and put on a coverslip. Examine under the microscope noting epidermal cells in surface view, stomata, and guard cells. To what extent do the stomata resemble the generalised diagram in Figure 10.4B?

INTERNAL STRUCTURE

1 Cut transverse sections of a dicotyledonous leaf. Holly is recommended since it is available throughout the year and is comparatively easy to cut. As the leaf is thin it must be mounted in a firm position while the sections are cut: do this by inserting the piece of leaf into a vertical slit made down the centre of a piece of moistened elder pith or carrot tuber (Figure 10.5). Hold the pith or carrot in one hand and cut your sections rapidly and smoothly with a sharp razor blade held in the other hand. Place the sections in a dish of water.

2 Select one or two thin sections, including at least one that is cut through the midrib, and mount them in water on a slide. Transfer the sections with a fine brush, not with forceps which may damage them.

3 Examine the lamina of the leaf on either side of the midrib. Using low power, identify the various layers labelled on the right hand side of Figure 10.6A.

4 Examine the cells in detail under high power.

Upper epidermis: one or more layers of rectangular cells, generally with thick cuticle. Few, if any, stomata. No chloroplasts.

Palisade mesophyll:
One to three cells thick, dense green due to presence of numerous chloroplasts; cells elongated at right angles to leaf surface; narrow intercellular air spaces appear as dark lines flanking many of the cells.

Spongy mesophyll:
Cells rounded or sausage-shaped; fewer chloroplasts; extensive intercellular air spaces.

The palisade and spongy mesophyll together make up the photosynthetic tissue (chlorenchyma) in the leaf.

Lower epidermis: single layer of cells with relatively thin cuticle. There are generally many stomata perforating the lower surface of the leaf and your section may be cut through several pairs of guard cells. These are sunk below the general surface of the epidermis (Figure 10.6B). The guard cells are the only epidermal cells that have chloroplasts. What is the functional significance of this?

5 Now examine the vascular bundles in the flat part of the leaf (*not* the midrib). The vascular bundles may have been cut through transversely or obliquely. The upper part consists of water-conducting xylem tissue; the lower part consists of food-conducting phloem tissue. Thick-walled sclerenchyma fibres may be seen immediately beneath the phloem. If the bundle is cut obliquely, spirally thickened xylem elements may be seen (Figure 10.6C).

6 Examine the midrib and observe how this differs from the rest of the leaf. Note two main types of tissue:

Vascular tissue: large vascular bundle(s) in centre; phloem is generally confined to the underside of the xylem but in some plant species it surrounds the xylem.

Strengthening tissue: variable amount of parenchyma tissue surrounds vascular area; collenchyma immediately beneath lower epidermis; sclerenchyma close to phloem.

7 Irrigate your sections with iodine solution. All lignified walls will be stained yellow and any starch present will be stained dark blue. If no starch is present what is the explanation?

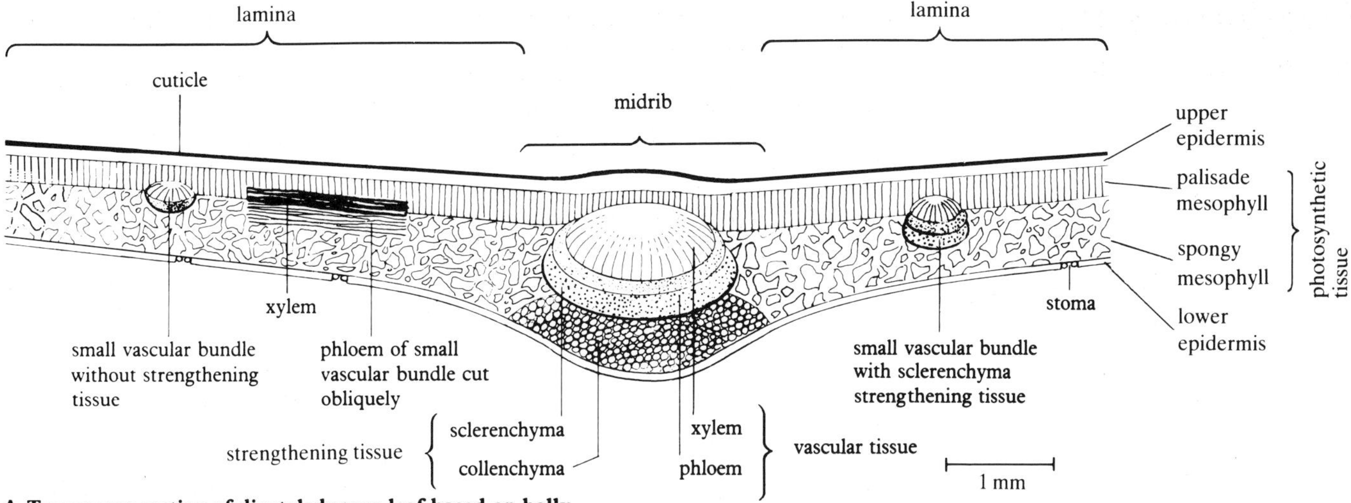

A Transverse section of dicotyledonous leaf based on holly

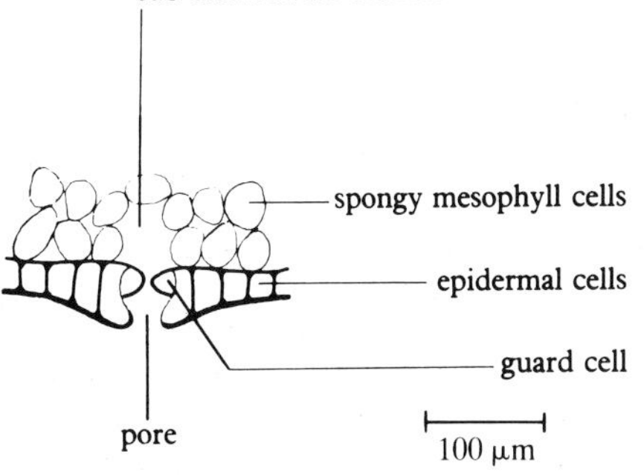

B Generalised stoma

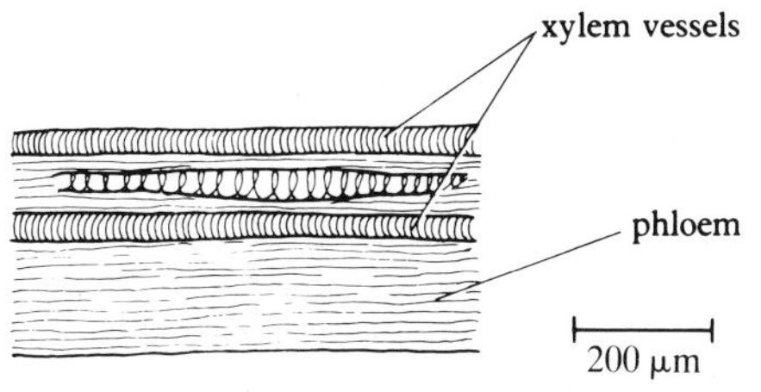

C Detail of vascular bundle cut obliquely

Figure 10.6 Structure of dicotyledonous leaf based on holly.

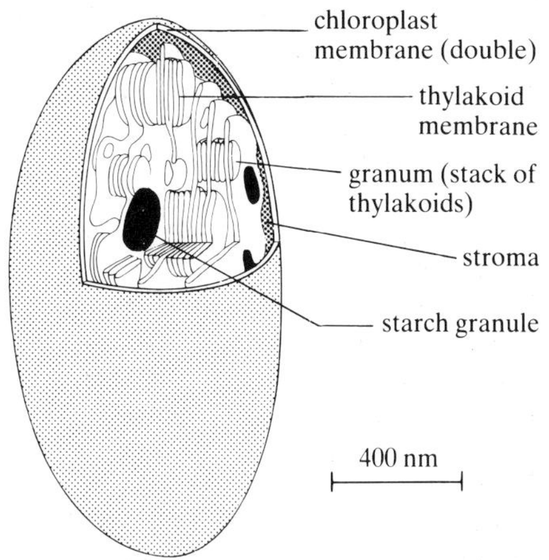

Figure 10.7 Three-dimensional diagram of a generalised chloroplast.

8 Mount another section in Sudan III. This stains fat and is a good way of showing up the cuticle.

9 Stain another section with FABIL (*see* page 402). The staining reaction varies but generally xylem elements stain brown, sclerenchyma pink, cellulose pale blue, cytoplasm and nuclei dark blue, starch black.

FINE STRUCTURE OF CHLOROPLAST

1 Examine an electron micrograph of a section through a chloroplast. Compare the section with the appearance of a chloroplast as seen under the light microscope. Why the difference? (It's not just a matter of size.)

2 Using Figure 10.7 to help you, identify the various structures in the micrograph. If the structures are lettered, state what each letter stands for. Notice in particular the thylakoid membranes, grana and stroma. The photosynthetic pigments are located in the thylakoid membranes.

FURTHER INVESTIGATIONS

1 Although the leaves of all dicotyledons are basically similar, they differ in various details. Investigate the internal structure of other species of dicotyledons of your own choice. How do they differ from one another and how would you explain the differences?

2 Cut transverse sections of a monocotyledon leaf, e.g. lily, iris, etc. How does its internal structure differ from that of the dicotyledon leaf? Why the differences?

For Consideration

(1) If you are an artist, try to draw a three-dimensional diagram of the dicotyledonous leaf which you have studied in this investigation. Include the vascular and strengthening tissues as well as the photosynthetic tissue.

(2) Most of the leaf's photosynthesis goes on in the palisade mesophyll. In what respects are the palisade cells adapted for photosynthesis (a) in their arrangement within the leaf, and (b) in the structure of each individual cell?

(3) How does the microscopic structure of the leaf permit gases to diffuse readily between the outside air and the photosynthetic cells?

Requirements

Slides and coverslips
Dish for sections
Fine brush
Safety razor blade
Small forceps
Elder pith and/or carrot tuber

Iodine solution
Sudan III
FABIL

Fresh leaves of dicotyledon and monocotyledon (holly recommended for the dicotyledon)
Ivy-leaved toadflax
Electron micrograph of section through chloroplast

Investigation 10.5
Compensation point of a plant

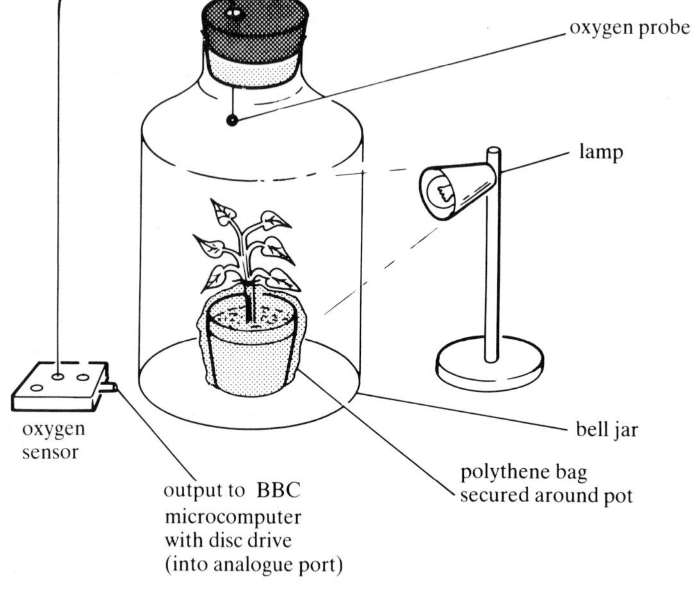

Figure 10.8 Apparatus for determining the compensation point of a *Pelargonium* plant. The microcomputer must be programmed with the appropriate program disc. This will allow it to store and display the observations. If the microcomputer is linked to a printer, the stored data can be printed out in the form of a table or a graph.

Requirements

*BBC Model B microcomputer, fitted with analogue converter, disc drive and printer
*Oxygen probe, oxygen sensor and connecting box
*Software for accumulation of data, display on screen, integration of oxygen output

Bell jar
Elastic bands
Lamp with 100W bulb
Polythene bag
Vaseline
Photographic light meter

Pelargonium plant (potted, in soil)

*Available from Philip Harris Biological Ltd.

Note: A similar experiment can be carried out using the filamentous green alga *Zygnema cylindrica* or the cyanobacterium (blue-green alga) *Anabaena cylindrica*. See A.J. Love and R.M. Spragg, 'Assessing photosynthetic oxygen liberation using a BBC microcomputer', *Journal of Biological Education*, Vol. 20, No. 2, 1986.

At the compensation point, the rate of photosynthesis of a plant equals its respiration rate so that the plant is in 'carbon balance'. To determine the compensation point of a plant under standard conditions, its oxygen output can be measured at a range of light intensities from zero to bright light. The light intensity at which there is no net oxygen input or output is the compensation point.

Now that appropriate sensors and software are available, the most elegant way of determining a light compensation point is to use a microcomputer to record and analyse the data.

Procedure

1 Obtain a potted *Pelargonium* plant and set it up as shown in Figure 10.8. Make sure that the polythene bag is secured around the pot.

2 Switch on a lamp with a 100W light bulb close to the plant. Wait for five minutes. Then record the pattern of oxygen concentration in the closed jar for ten minutes.

3 After ten minutes, obtain a screen dump of the data and use the software to integrate the oxygen output of the plant over the ten minutes. Use a photographic light meter to determine the average light intensity which reached the plant. Record both these values.

4 Repeat these measurements with the lamp at distances of 20, 40 and 80 cm from the bell jar containing the plant.

5 Switch off the light and determine the net oxygen exchange of the plant in the dark.

6 If you have time, you may be able to alter the distance of the lamp from the bell jar until there is no net oxygen exchange.

7 Plot a graph of the net integrated oxygen input or output over ten minutes (vertical axis) against the light intensity (horizontal axis). Read off the graph, and record, the light intensity at which there is no net oxygen exchange. This is the compensation point of the *Pelargonium* plant under these conditions.

For consideration

(1) Which wavelengths of light does the light sensor measure? Are they the same as the optimal wavelengths which a plant uses in photosynthesis?
(2) Why was the soil beneath the *Pelargonium* plant enclosed in a polythene bag?
(3) In what ways would you expect the compensation points of a 'sun plant' and a 'shade plant' to differ?

Questions and Problems

1 The highest yield of wheat ever recorded on an agricultural scale in Great Britain is said to have been one of 11.7 tonnes of grain per hectare obtained in lowland Scotland. In this region the total energy of sunlight and infra-red radiation received per unit of ground surface during the period March to July is (in an average year) 1.1×10^4 joules per square centimetre. Make a *rough* estimate of the percentage of this energy converted into chemical energy in the grain. Outline briefly what would have happened to the rest of the energy.

(Note: 1 hectare = 10^4 square metres; the heat given out by the combustion of dry carbohydrate is about 1.8×10^4 joules per gram.) *(CCJE)*

2 How would you demonstrate:
(a) that carbon dioxide is necessary for photosynthesis,
(b) that red and blue light are more effective than yellow light in photosynthesis,
(c) that chlorophyll is required for photosynthesis,
(d) that photosynthesis occurs in the chloroplasts,
(e) that the oxygen evolved in photosynthesis is derived not from carbon dioxide but from water?

3 A plant's rate of photosynthesis can be estimated by the following alternative methods:
(a) measuring the rate of carbon dioxide uptake,
(b) measuring the rate of evolution of oxygen gas,
(c) measuring increase in the dry mass of leaves during a given period,
(d) measuring the amount of carbohydrate formed in the leaves during a given period.
Compare the relative merits of each method.

4 Account for the following:
(a) In dropping its leaves a deciduous tree loses its photosynthetic equipment, and yet it survives the winter.
(b) The CO_2 content of the air in early spring has been found to be slightly higher than in the late summer.
(c) Crops planted in the vicinity of certain factories have been observed to show more rapid and prolific growth than those planted in identical soil elsewhere.
(d) It is customary for the windows of greenhouses to be whitewashed in summer.

5 The effect of temperature on the rates of (a) apparent photosynthesis (net CO_2 uptake in the light) and (b) respiration (CO_2 produced in the dark) was determined. The results, expressed as mg CO_2, taken up or released, per gram dry mass of leaf per hour, are given in the following table:

Rate (mg CO_2 g^{-1} h^{-1})	Temperature (°C)						
	7	10	15	19	22	28	31
Uptake (apparent photosynthesis)	1.3	2.3	2.8	3.1	2.8	2.5	1.8
Release (respiration)	0.3	0.6	0.7	1.2	1.8	2.1	2.7

(a) Calculate the rates of true photosynthesis at each temperature, assuming that the rate of respiration in the light is equal to the rate of respiration in the dark.
(b) Plot on a graph the results for apparent photosynthesis, true photosynthesis and respiration.
(c) Comment briefly on these observations. *(O and C)*

6 Results of experiments to measure the rate of photosynthesis under different conditions are shown in the graphs in Figure 10.9.
(a) Explain the effect of variation in the carbon dioxide concentration on the rate of photosynthesis.
(b) In what way is the rate of photosynthesis dependent on temperature?
(c) What general principle is illustrated by the results of changing the light intensity?
(d) What conclusions can you draw from these experiments concerning the nature of the process of photosynthesis? *(AEB modified)*

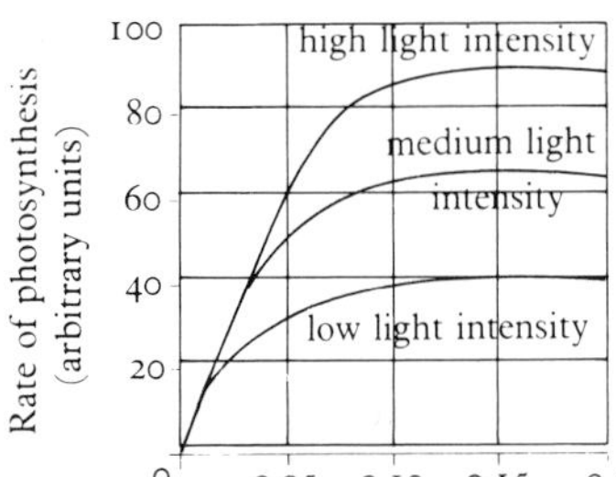

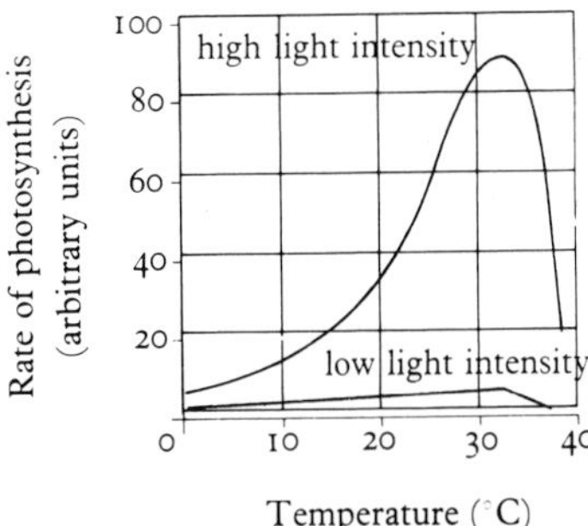

Figure 10.9 Results of experiments in which the rate of photosynthesis was measured under different conditions. The rate of photosynthesis is expressed in arbitrary units.

7 In the aquatic moss *Fontinalis antipyretica*, a determination was made of the rate of photosynthesis when the plant was submitted to differences in temperature, carbon dioxide concentration and light intensity. The results of these experiments are set out below, the figures within the body of the table representing the photosynthetic rate in arbitrary units from values of 0 to 15.

Conc. of CO_2 (%)	**Temperature** (°C)	**Light intensity** (lux)							
		250	500	750	1000	1500	2500	4000	5500
0.10	25	1.8	3.6	5.0	6.1	8.2	11.3	13.8	14.8
	15	1.6	3.0	4.4	5.2	7.0	8.8	10.3	11.0
0.01	25	1.2	2.4	3.2	3.6	4.0	4.2	4.4	4.6
	15	1.1	2.2	2.9	3.4	3.8	3.9	4.0	4.1

(a) Plot the results on graph paper.
(b) What do these data reveal about the nature of the photosynthetic mechanism?
(c) Describe one further piece of experimental evidence which supports the conclusions you have drawn in (b). *(O and C)*

8 Figure 10.10 is a scanning electron micrograph of part of a leaf.
(a) Name the layers of the leaf labelled A–D.
(b) Between some of the cells in the leaf numerous connections are visible. What are these called and what is their function?
(c) In which layers of the leaf do most of the cells lack chloroplasts?
(d) In which layer of the leaf do the cells contain most chloroplasts?
(e) Name structure E. Of what value is it to the leaf?
(f) There is a vein in the leaf. Where is it and what are its functions?

9 Figure 10.11 is a transmission electron micrograph of a section through a chloroplast.
(a) From the scale bar provided, work out the magnification of this micrograph.
(b) Name the parts of the chloroplast labelled A and B, and outline the principal events which occur in each part.
(c) Speculate as to the nature of structure C.

10 The effect of the length of the dark intervals between flashes of light on the amount of synthesis per flash was measured at two different temperatures with these results:

Amount of photosynthesis per light flash (arbitrary units)

Temperature (°C)	Length of dark intervals (seconds)					
	0.02	0.06	0.1	0.2	0.3	0.4
1.0	2.1	3.5	4.0	4.6	4.8	5.0
24.0	5.0	5.1	5.0	4.9	5.0	5.0

The amount of photosynthesis is given in arbitrary units and in all cases the light flash was 1.0×10^{-5} seconds. Comment on these results in relation to your knowledge of the effects of other factors on photosynthesis and consider their significance in relation to the mechanism of the process. *(O and C)*

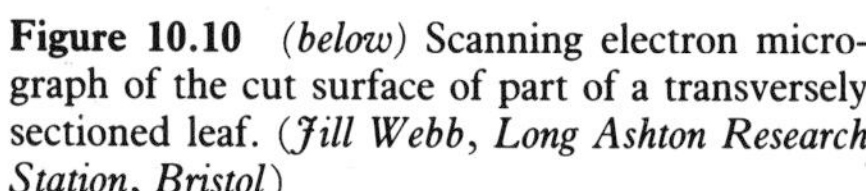

Figure 10.10 *(below)* Scanning electron micrograph of the cut surface of part of a transversely sectioned leaf. *(Jill Webb, Long Ashton Research Station, Bristol)*

Figure 10.11 *(below right)* Transmission electron micrograph of a section through a chloroplast. *(Prof. Rachel Leech, University of York)*

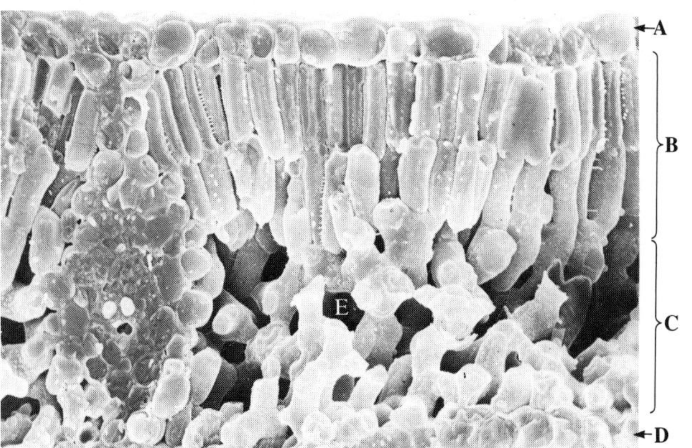

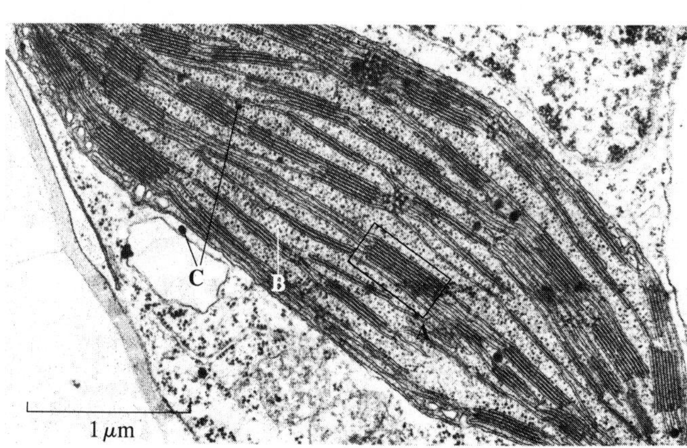

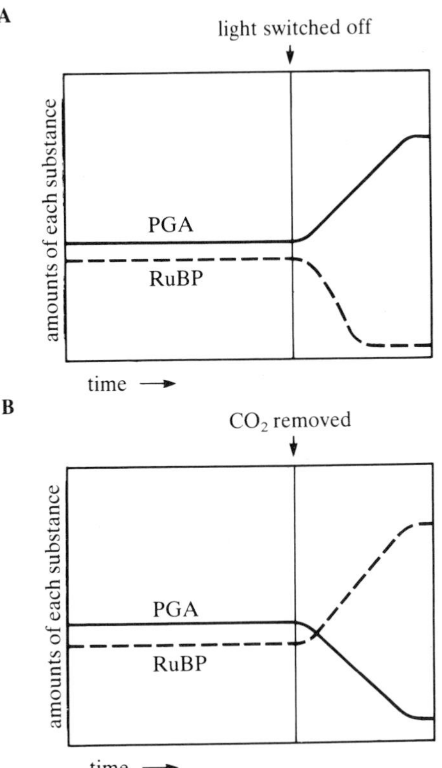

Figure 10.12 The effect of **A** switching the light off, and **B** removing carbon dioxide, on the relative amounts of phosphoglyceric acid (PGA) and ribulose bisphosphate (RuBP) formed by a green protist.

11 Experiments were carried out on cultures of a unicellular green protist to investigate the effect on the formation of phosphoglyceric acid (PGA) and ribulose bisphosphate (RuBP) of (A) switching the light off, i.e. suddenly putting the organisms in darkness, and (B) depriving the organisms of carbon dioxide. The results are summarised in Figure 10.12.

(a) Explain why PGA rises and RuBP falls after the light is switched off (graph A), and why PGA falls and RuBP rises after carbon dioxide is removed (graph B).

(b) What do you think would happen to the levels of PGA and RuBP if the experiments were continued for longer?

12 Photosynthesis involves the removal of electrons from chlorophyll, the splitting of water, the production of ATP, and the reduction of carbon dioxide. Explain concisely how these four processes are linked and whereabouts they take place.

13 An experiment was carried out in which the enzyme RuBP carboxlase was labelled in sections of a C4 grass, *Digitaria brownii*, and a C3 grass, *Danthonia bipartita*. In the C4 plant the enzyme was found in the bundle sheath cells but not in the mesophyll cells, whereas in the C3 plant the enzyme was found in all the mesophyll cells.

(a) In which stage of photosynthesis is the enzyme RuBP carboxlase involved?

(b) Where in the chloroplast would you expect to find molecules of this enzyme?

(c) Which reaction does this enzyme catalyse?

(d) Account for the distribution of the enzyme in the two species in terms of what you know about the relationship of carbon dioxide fixation to leaf anatomy in C4 and C3 plants.

(e) At high temperatures and light intensities the photosynthetic rate is higher in C4 than in C3 plants. Account for this in terms of the biochemical and structural features of their leaves.

14 Two Australian species of saltbush (*Atriplex* sp.), one a C3 plant and the other a C4 plant, were placed under the same conditions and their rates of carbon dioxide output or intake were measured. The data below show their rates of net photosynthesis (carbon dioxide uptake in the light), respiration (CO_2 release in the dark), and photorespiration (increase in photosynthesis in oxygen-free air in the light), at three different temperatures.

	Carbon dioxide flux (mg CO_2 exchanged per dm^3 of leaf surface per hour)					
	C3			C4		
	20 °C	30 °C	40 °C	20 °C	30 °C	40 °C
Net photosynthesis	27	29	17	24	31	32
Respiration	2.5	4	8	1.7	3	5.3
Photorespiration	5	11	10	0	0	0

(a) Plot these data on the same piece of graph paper.

(b) What does the term 'net photosynthesis' mean? How does net photosynthesis differ from the actual rate of photosynthesis?

(c) Work out the actual rate of photosynthesis for both plants at each of the three temperatures.

(d) Explain the meaning of the term photorespiration.

(e) To what extent do the data illustrate the relative photosynthetic efficiency of the two species?

(*Data from:* G. Hofstra and J.D. Hesketh, *Planta*, No. 85, 1969.)

11 Transport in Animals

Background Summary

1 The volume of an animal is generally too large for diffusion alone to supply the needs of the tissues, and as a result transport systems have been developed. These range from water-filled canals to blood-filled circulatory (vascular) systems.

2 Mammalian blood is composed of **red** and **white blood cells** (**erythrocytes** and **leucocytes** respectively) and **platelets** suspended in **plasma**. Dissolved food substances are transported in the plasma, oxygen by the red blood cells.

3 Red blood cells are non-nucleated, biconcave discs. Their shape increases their surface-volume ratio. They contain **haemoglobin** which has a high affinity for oxygen, as is shown by **oxygen dissociation curves** for blood.

4 Haemoglobin's affinity for oxygen is lowered by the presence of carbon dioxide. Thus loading of haemoglobin with oxygen is favoured in the lungs, whereas unloading is favoured in the tissues.

5 **Myoglobin** (**muscle haemoglobin**) and **foetal haemoglobin** have a higher affinity for oxygen than adult haemoglobin. The invertebrate blood pigments **chlorocruorin**, **haemoerythrin** and **haemocyanin** have comparable affinities to haemoglobin though their total oxygen capacities are generally lower.

6 The lowering of haemoglobin's affinity for oxygen in the presence of carbon dioxide is explained by the mechanism of carbon dioxide carriage in the blood. Due to the presence of the enzyme **carbonic anhydrase**, most of the carbon dioxide enters the red blood cells in the tissues. Hydrogen ions resulting from the carriage of carbon dioxide are quite readily taken up by haemoglobin which, therefore, acts as a buffer.

7 The haemoglobin molecule consists of four **haem groups** each of which is linked to a **polypeptide** (**globin**). The combination of one haem group with oxygen facilitates the combination of the remainder, with the movements of the globin chains playing a crucial part in this.

8 The mammalian circulation with its heart, arteries, capillaries, and veins is well adapted for delivering oxygen at high speed to the tissues.

9 The heart is divided into four chambers: two **atria** and two **ventricles**. Blood is propelled through the heart by a series of electrical and mechanical events which constitute the **cardiac cycle**. The ventricles have thick muscular walls, and **valves** prevent blood flowing in the wrong direction.

10 The heart beat is initiated by the **sino-atrial node** (pacemaker) which, though it has an innate rhythm, is influenced by its nerve supply. The sympathetic nerve accelerates the heart, the vagus slows it.

11 Despite variations in the frequency with which it beats, the heart automatically pumps into the arteries the same amount of blood as it receives from the veins.

12 **Cardiac muscle** has a similar microscopic structure to that of skeletal (striated) muscle but adjacent fibres are interconnected. It contracts repeatedly without fatigue.

13 **Arteries** and **veins** are adapted in their structure and properties for carrying blood away from/back to the heart.

14 **Capillaries** are narrow and thin-walled and come into intimate association with the tissue cells. Exchanges take place between the capillary blood and neighbouring tissues via **tissue fluid** between the cells.

15 The mammal has a **double circulation**, blood flowing through the heart twice for every complete circuit of the body. The heart is completely divided into right and left sides. In contrast, fishes have a **single circulation** with an undivided heart. Amphibians have a double circulation with a partially divided heart. Octopuses and squids have a single circulation with two sets of hearts.

16 The circulation of most animals, with tubular blood vessels, is described as a **closed circulation**. This contrasts with the **open circulation** of insects where blood flows through large cavities and sinuses. In insects the only blood vessel as such is the single tubular heart.

Investigation 11.1
Looking at red blood cells

To look at, red blood cells are amongst the simplest of cells. They lack a nucleus and their cytoplasm is less elaborate than that of most cells. And yet at the chemical level they perform the specialised job of taking up oxygen in the lungs and transporting it to the tissues. Bear this in mind as you examine them.

The experiment involves making a slide of your own blood. You can also use a prepared slide of human blood.

Procedure

1 Put an elastic band round one of your fingers. Clean the skin of your finger by rubbing it with cotton wool soaked in ethanol.

1

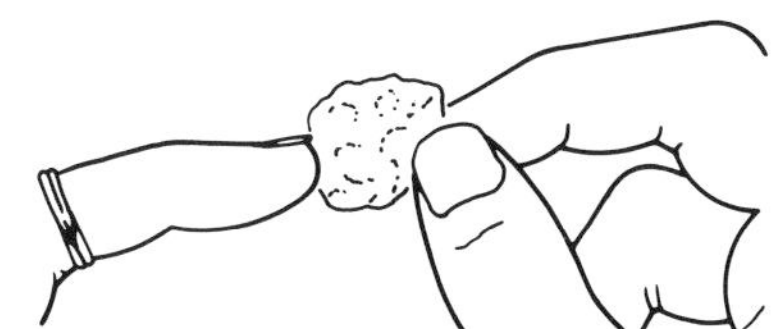

Sterilise the end of your finger by swabbing it with cotton wool soaked in ethanol.

2

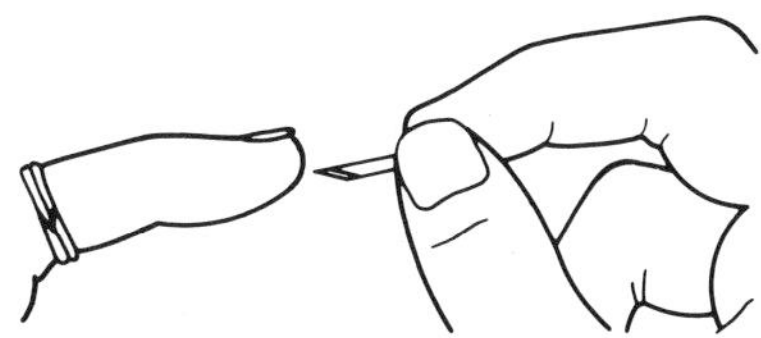

With a sterile lancet prick the tip of your finger with a firm jab, so a drop of blood comes out.

3

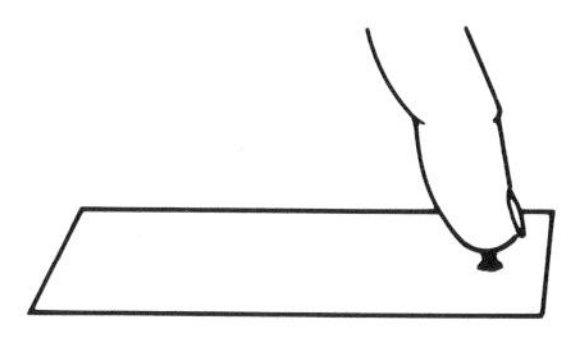

Place the drop of blood at one end of a microscope slide.

4

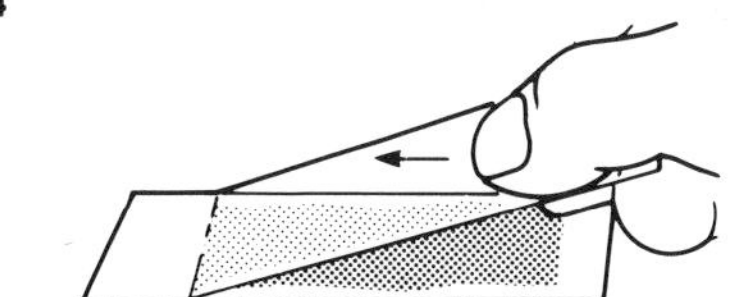

With another slide spread the blood over the surface of the slide so it forms a smear.

5

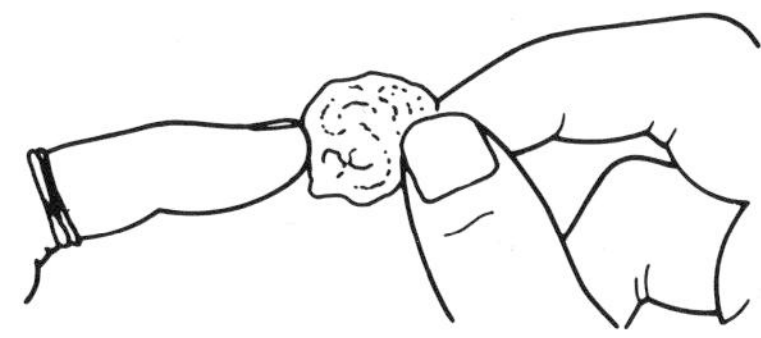

Sterilise the end of your finger with ethanol again.

Figure 11.1 How to make a blood smear for examining under the microscope.

CAUTION:
Because of the risk of infection, you should sample only your own blood. Do not touch anyone else's blood. The lancet must be sterile and used only once. Throw it away afterwards in the receptacle provided.

Requirements
Microscope
Micrometer eyepiece and stage micrometer or transparent scale (*see* page 378)
Slides and coverslip
Elastic band
Sterile lancet
Cotton wool
Receptacle for used lancets (e.g. empty beer can)

Ethanol (absolute)

Frog's blood
Slide of human blood smear
Scanning and transmission electron micrographs of red blood cells

2 Using a sterile lancet, obtain a drop of blood and smear it on a slide by the technique outlined in Figure 11.1.
3 Let the blood smear dry, then examine it under the microscope: low power first, then high power. You will see large numbers of red blood cells. What colour are they, and why?
4 Examine a single red blood cell in as much detail as you can. Can you get any clues as to its shape from its appearance under the microscope? What can you say about its internal structure?
5 Using a micrometer scale (*see* page 378), measure the diameter of a red blood cell. How does this compare with the width of most animal cells? What limits the size of red blood cells?
6 Examine a prepared slide of frog's blood under the microscope. How do the frog's red blood cells differ from a human's? Which do you think are more efficient at carrying oxygen, and why?
7 Examine transmission and scanning electron micrographs of red blood cells. What information does each provide about the shape and internal structure of the cells?

Some interesting calculations

1 Each human red blood cell has a volume of 87 μm^3, and contains spherical haemoglobin molecules each of volume 87 nm^3. Assume that these haemoglobin molecules are packed like spheres in a box, so that in a regular lattice they only occupy half the cell volume. Calculate the number of haemoglobin molecules in a single red blood cell.
2 Each haemoglobin molecule can carry four oxygen molecules. Calculate the number of oxygen molecules a single red blood cell contains when its haemoglobin is saturated with oxygen.
3 There are 5.5×10^6 erythrocytes per mm^3 of blood. Each time your heart beats, about 60 cm^3 of oxygenated blood is pumped from the left ventricle into the aorta and then to the capillaries of the body. Calculate the number of oxygen molecules carried by the blood which leaves the left ventricle with each contraction, assuming that all the haemoglobin molecules are saturated with oxygen.
4 Assume that the heart beats 72 times a minute. Calculate the number of oxygen molecules supplied to the tissues each day.
5 Calculate the oxygen demand of the tissues. Assume for simplicity that the oxygen is all required to oxidise glucose and that this is the body's only source of energy. The equation for aerobic respiration is given below:

$$C_6H_{12}O_6 + 6O_2 \rightarrow 6CO_2 + 6H_2O + 2880 \text{ kJ mol}^{-1}$$

Six moles of oxygen are required to release 2880 kJ of energy. A normal healthy human adult needs a daily energy intake of about 12 000 kJ. How many moles of oxygen does the body need each day to satisfy its energy requirements? How many *molecules* of oxygen does this represent? (Avogadro number = 6×10^{23}).
6 Compare your estimate of the oxygen supplied (Q4) with your estimate of the oxygen required (Q5), and discuss any discrepancy. Note any assumptions which you have made at each stage of these calculations.

For consideration

(1) Make a list of as many different reasons as you can think of why it is better to have haemoglobin inside cells rather than free in the plasma.
(2) In the electron microscope red blood cells show little internal organisation. Comment on this.
(3) What is the relevance of the calculations which you carried out on oxygen supply and demand?

Investigation 11.2
The number of red cells in human blood

Since it is obviously impossible to count all the blood cells present in a circulatory system, one resorts to sampling – that is, one counts the cells in a representative volume.

A device for sampling cells in this way is the haemocytometer, a modified microscope slide. Although in this investigation the haemocytometer is used for counting blood cells, it can be used for counting any cells that are uniformly distributed on the surface of the slide (*see* page 320, for example).

In the present experiment a measured volume of blood is diluted a known number of times. The red blood cells are counted in a known volume of the diluted blood, from which the number of cells per mm^3 of undiluted blood may be calculated.

Apparatus

The haemocytometer consists of a special slide with a ruled area in the centre, a coverslip and two graduated pipettes with rubber tubing.

The slide is a delicate piece of equipment: be careful not to scratch it; wipe it only with lens paper. Ensure that both the slide and coverslip are clean: if necessary wash them in distilled water followed by propanone; when the propanone has evaporated rub them with lens paper.

Examine the slide under the low power of the microscope and locate the ruled area in the centre. The middle of the ruled area consists of a grid 1 mm^2 in area. We will call this the type-A square (Figure 11.2). If you use the ×10 objective and ×10 eyepiece, the type-A square should just about fill your field of view.

Notice that the type-A square is subdivided by triple lines into 25 type-B squares, each of which has an area of $\frac{1}{25}$ mm^2. Each type-B square is further subdivided by single lines into 16 type-C squares, each of which has an area of $\frac{1}{400}$ mm^2.

The surface of the slide between the two deep grooves is 0.1 mm lower than the rest of the slide on either side of the grooves. So when the coverslip is put on, its lower surface clears the ruled surface of the slide by 0.1 mm. The volume subtended by the type-A square is therefore 0.1 mm^3; the volume subtended by a type-B square is 0.004 mm^3; and the volume subtended by a type-C square is 0.00025 mm^3.

The pipette for red blood cells is the one with the mark 101 above the bulb. The other pipette, with the mark 11 above the bulb, is used for white cells.

The pipettes must be cleaned and dried immediately after use. Wash by sucking distilled water (or, if necessary, ethanoic acid) into the pipette; dry with propanone.

Figure 11.2 Neubauer haemocytometer slide.

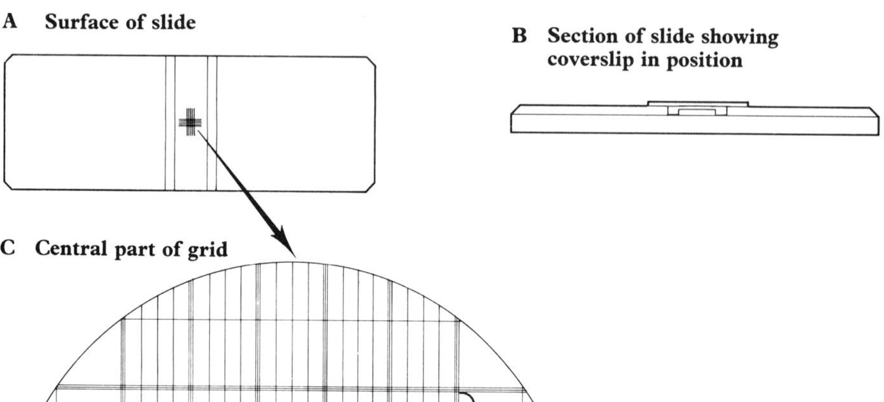

> **CAUTION:**
> Because of the risk of infection you should sample only your own blood. Do not touch anyone else's blood. The lancet must be sterile and used only once. Throw it away afterwards in the receptacle provided.

Procedure

1 Obtain a large drop of blood by pricking the end of your thumb or finger with a sterile lancet. First sterilise your skin by swabbing it with ethanol. Do not squeeze the blood out too hard for this will force out a lot of tissue fluid which will dilute the cells.

2 With the rubber tubing attached to the pipette, suck the blood up to the '1' mark. Quickly dry the tip of the pipette. If the 1 mark has been passed, touch the tip of the pipette with filter paper until the blood drops back to the 1 mark.

3 Now suck up three per cent sodium chloride (NaCl) solution until the contents of the pipette reach the 101 mark. If the 101 mark is passed, the pipette must be emptied and the procedure started again.

4 Remove the rubber tubing from the pipette. Close the two ends of the pipette with thumb and finger and rock the pipette for at least a minute. When the blood and NaCl are thoroughly mixed, blow out six drops so as to expel excess NaCl solution. Your blood sample is now diluted 1 in 100.

5 Place the coverslip in the centre of the slide. Put one drop of diluted blood from the pipette onto the slide alongside the coverslip in the area between the two deep grooves. The blood should be drawn under the coverslip by capillary action. Wait five minutes to allow the red blood cells to settle. If the blood flows into the grooves, clean the slide and put on another drop.

6 Place the slide under the microscope and adjust the illumination so the grid and the red blood cells can be clearly seen. If the cells are very unevenly distributed, clean the slide and start again.

7 Count the red blood cells in 100 type-C squares. Record your results by ruling out 100 squares and writing the number of cells in each square.

Note: In each square count all the cells which lie entirely within it, plus those which are touching or overlapping the top and left-hand sides. Do not include those touching or overlapping the bottom and right-hand sides even if they are within the square.

8 Calculate the average number of red blood cells in a type-C square. Bearing in mind the volume represented by a type-C square, and the dilution factor, calculate the number of cells per mm^3. A typical figure might be 5 million per mm^3. How does your figure compare with this?

Assuming that the total volume of blood in the body is 5 litres, calculate the number of red blood cells in the entire circulation.

Requirements

Haemocytometer (slide, coverslip, pipette and rubber tubing)
Sterile lancet
Lens paper
Receptacle for used lancets
Small beaker

Sodium chloride solution (0.75 per cent)
Distilled water
Ethanoic acid
Propanone (acetone)
Ethanol and cotton wool

For Consideration

(1) Under what circumstances might you find the red blood cell count to be (a) unusually high, (b) unusually low?

(2) Nowadays in hospitals, blood counts are carried out by techniques which make it unnecessary for a person to count the cells. How do you think these techniques work, and what are their advantages?

Investigation 11.3
Dissection of the mammalian circulatory system

The mammal has a double circulation with a completely divided heart. The right side of the heart receives deoxygenated blood from the great veins which it pumps to the lungs. The left side receives oxygenated blood from the lungs which is then pumped into the aorta.

The entire system is a dynamic transport device. Both in the structure of its individual units (heart, arteries, capillaries, veins etc.) and in its overall layout, we see a close relation between structure and function.

CAUTION:
Several serious diseases can be caught from rats. Wear a laboratory coat and thin rubber gloves while you are dissecting, and wash your hands thoroughly afterwards.

Procedure

1 If it has not already been done, open up the thorax as described on page 69.

2 Remove the thymus gland to expose the heart and pluck away fat from

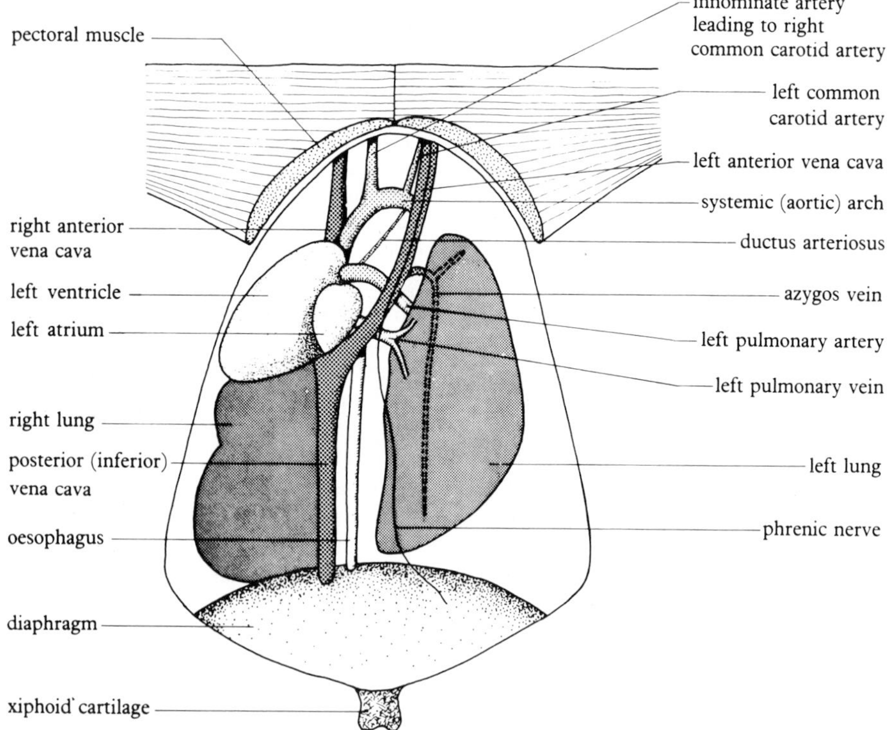

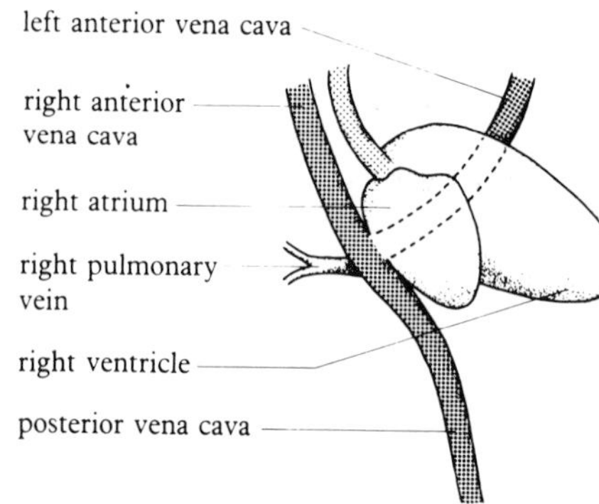

Figure 11.3 Contents of thorax of rat.

around the great vessels. Be careful not to damage the ductus arteriosus, a slender strand linking the pulmonary artery and aorta: it is a relic of a vessel which was present in the embryo (function?).

3 Push the heart to your left and identify the structures shown in Figure 11.3A.

4 Push the heart to your right and identify the point where the venae cavae enter the right atrium (Figure 11.3B). Mentally reconstruct the flow of blood through the heart and great vessels.

5 Carefully trace the right anterior vena cava and innominate artery from the thorax up into the neck, removing all the muscle which now is obscuring these vessels. (Arrows, Figure 11.4).

6 Remove the pectoral muscle and clavicle, taking great care not to cut any blood vessels underneath. This will reveal the origin of the subclavian and internal jugular veins.

7 Trace the innominate artery forwards and notice the origin from it of the right subclavian artery. The innominate continues forward as the right common carotid artery.

8 Now repeat the above steps on the left side of the body. On this side there is no innominate artery, the left subclavian arising from the systemic arch. To see the left subclavian you will probably need to deflect the left anterior vena cava to your right.

9 Finally trace the arteries and veins forwards to the jaw as shown in Figure 11.5.

10 Identify the structures shown in Figure 11.5. What is the function in relation to the circulation of the nerves shown in the inset to Figure 11.5?

11 Follow the dorsal aorta through the thorax into the abdominal cavity. In the thorax it gives off a series of intercostal arteries.

12 Blood is returned to the heart from the thoracic wall by the azygos veins. Trace the azygos veins back to the heart. Also note the posterior vena cava running close to the dorsal aorta.

13 If it has not already been done, open up the abdominal cavity, identify the coeliac, anterior mesenteric and posterior mesenteric arteries (all branches of the dorsal aorta), and remove the gut (*see* pages 78–81).

14 Pluck away the fat obscuring the posterior vena cava and dorsal aorta and investigate the branches of each.

15 Trace the iliac arteries and veins into the hind legs, noting their branches.

Note: In carrying out Steps 14 and 15 do *not* use a dissection guide. Try to follow the arteries and veins to their destinations in a genuinely exploratory way. Bear in mind that William Harvey, who discovered the circulation, did not have a dissection guide!

For Consideration

(1) In your dissection you will have noticed that the veins generally have a wider diameter and a darker colour than the arteries. Can you suggest reasons for this difference?

(2) Suggest explanations of the asymmetrical origin of the subclavian arteries on the two sides of the body.

(3) By what series of blood vessels does blood flow from the heart to (a) the brain, (b) the right forelimb, (c) the liver, (d) the left kidney, and (e) the left hindlimb?

(4) By what series of blood vessels is blood returned to the heart from (a) the sides of the head, (b) the left forelimb, (c) the lungs, (d) the intercostal muscles, and (e) the gut?

Reference: H.G. Rowett, *Dissection Guides, III The Rat*, Murray, 1970.

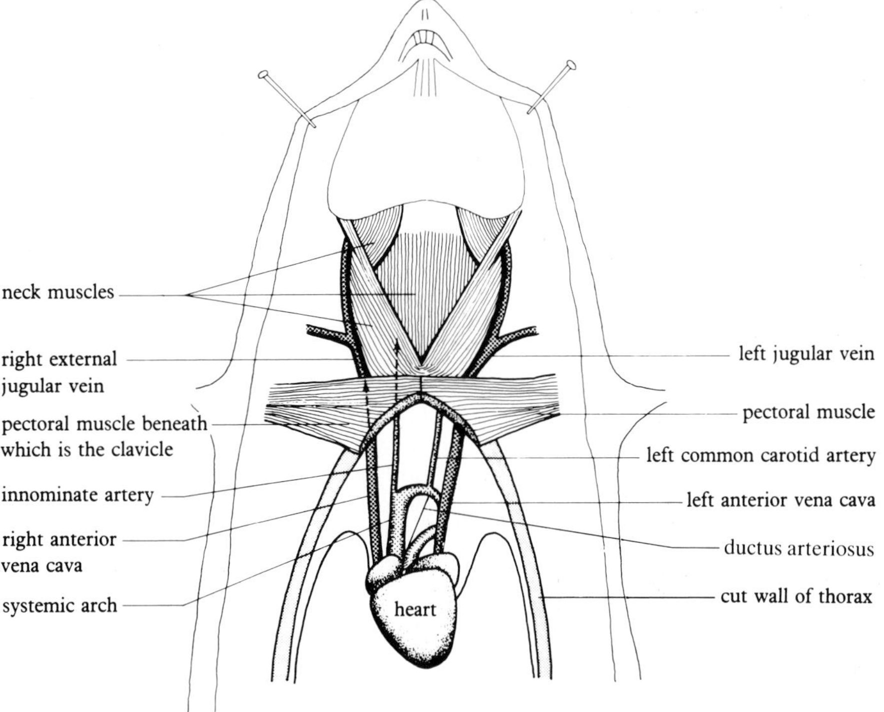

Figure 11.4 Dissection of the anterior circulation of the rat before removal of pectoral and neck muscles.

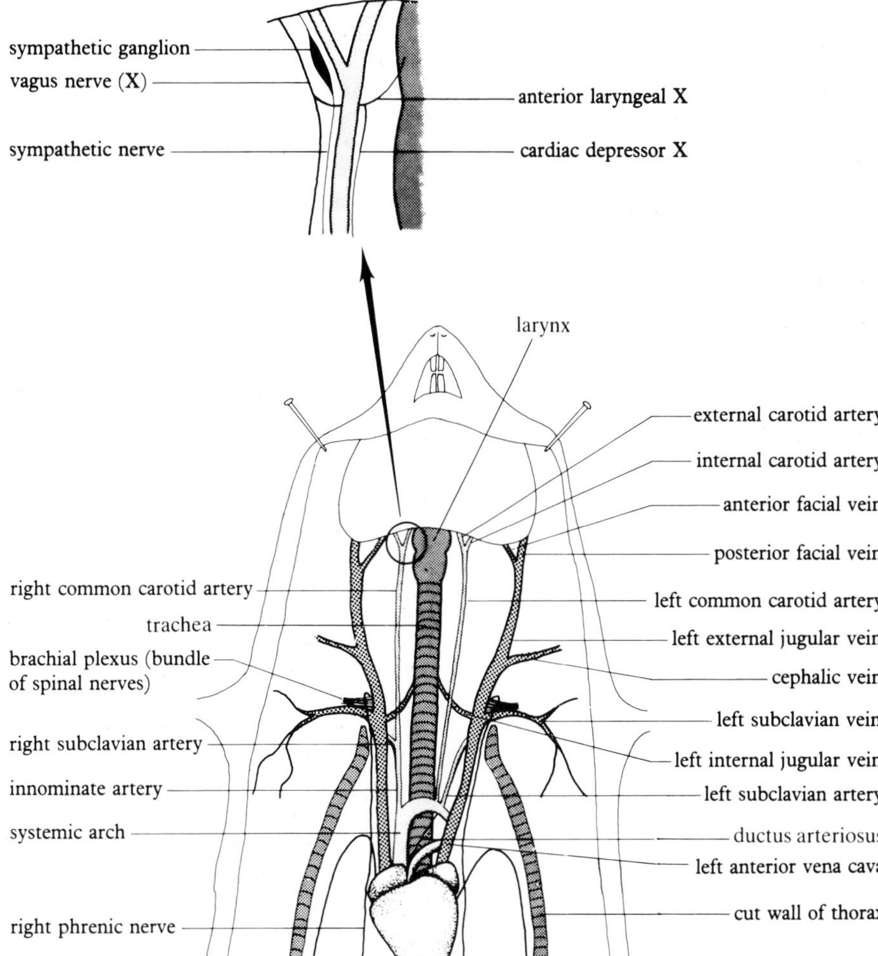

Figure 11.5 Dissection of the heart and anterior circulation of the rat after removal of pectoral and neck muscles.

Requirements
Dissecting instruments
Hand lens or binocular microscope
Rubber gloves

Freshly killed rat

Investigation 11.4
Structure and action of the mammalian heart

The mammal has a double circulation, that is, blood flows twice through the heart for every complete circuit of the body. Deoxygenated blood from the tissues enters the right atrium from the great veins (venae cavae). From the right atrium blood flows into the right ventricle whence it is pumped to the lungs via the pulmonary artery. Having been oxygenated in the lungs blood is returned to the heart via the pulmonary veins; after entering the left atrium the blood flows into the left ventricle whence it is pumped to the body via the aorta.

Two main questions arise in connection with the heart: how is the blood propelled from it, and how is the blood kept moving in the right direction. Keep these questions in mind as you examine the heart.

Procedure

For this experiment use the heart of a pig, sheep or ox.

1 Distinguish between the dorsal and ventral sides of the heart. The ventral side is more rounded (convex) than the dorsal side, and the thick-walled arteries arise from this side (Figure 11.6).

2 Identify right and left atria, right and left ventricles; pulmonary artery and aorta (systemic arch) arising from right and left ventricles respectively; anterior and posterior venae cavae opening into right atrium; pulmonary veins opening into left atrium; coronary vessels in heart wall (function?).

3 Insert the end of a rubber tube leading from a tap, into the anterior vena cava. Clamp the posterior vena cava. Run water into the vena cava and note its flow through the heart. From which blood vessel does the water emerge? This is the pulmonary artery. Explain fully.

4 Now run water into the pulmonary vein and note the vessel from which it emerges. This is the aorta.

5 Expose the interior of the left ventricle by a longitudinal cut through the ventral wall of the ventricle (*see* right-hand dotted line in Figure 11.6). At the top of the ventricular cavity to your left observe the opening into the aorta guarded by semilunar (pocket) valves. To your right observe the atrioventricular opening guarded by bicuspid (mitral) valve; note that the latter has two flaps attached to the ventricular wall by tendinous cords and papillary muscles (function?).

6 Turn the heart upside down and run water into the ventricle through the slit which you have cut. Notice the impeding action of the bicuspid valve. In life it prevents the backflow of blood from ventricle to atrium.

7 Now turn the heart the right way up; run water into the cut end of the aorta and note the impeding action of the semilunar valves. What are the functions of the semilunar valves?

8 Cut open the left atrium and aorta by continuing your ventricular cut upwards. Observe details of the bicuspid valve and the pocket-like semilunar valves. Also notice the opening into the coronary artery from the aorta just above the semilunar valves. This important artery takes oxygenated blood to the wall of the heart.

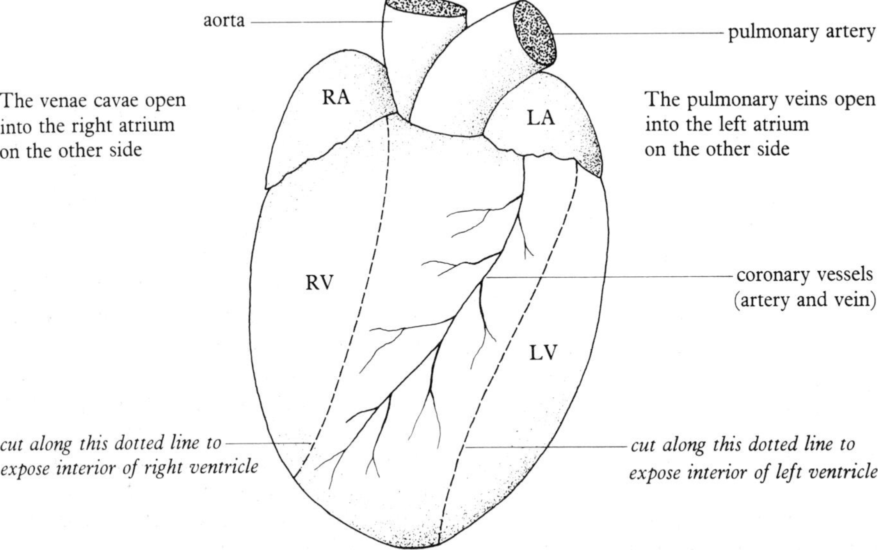

Figure 11.6 Ventral view of mammalian heart. This is the more convex side of the heart and shows the attachment of the aorta and pulmonary artery to the ventricles. The veins are on the other side. **RA**, right atrium; **LA**, left atrium; **RV**, right ventricle; **LV**, left ventricle.

9 Expose the interior of the right ventricle by a longitudinal slit through the ventral wall (*see* left hand dotted line in Figure 11.6). Observe the atrioventricular opening guarded by tricuspid valve (three flaps); semilunar valves guarding the extrance to the pulmonary artery.

10 Pour water into the pulmonary artery and note the impeding action of the semilunar valves exactly as on the other side of the heart.

11 Slit open the right atrium and pulmonary artery by continuing your ventricular slit upwards. Observe the valves in detail as you did on the other side of the heart. In addition note the opening of the coronary vein on the left hand side of the atrium (the right as you view it from the ventral side).

12 In the inter-atrial septum you may see a small oval depression, the fossa ovalis. This is a relic of the foramen ovale which connects the right and left atria in the embryo. (Function of foramen ovale in the embryo?)

13 Examine the openings of the pulmonary veins and venae cavae into their respective atria. Are there any valves guarding these openings and what might be their functions?

14 Finally notice the relative sizes of the four chambers of the heart and the relative thickness of their walls. Which is the largest chamber, and which one has the thickest wall? Explain the reason for any differences observed.

For Consideration

(1) Trace the sequence of events that takes place as blood flows through the heart from the venae cavae to the pulmonary artery, and from the pulmonary veins to the aorta.

(2) Can you think of any functional reason why the atrio-ventricular valve has three flaps on the right hand side of the heart but only two flaps on the left?

(3) Consider the consequences of a blood clot occurring at various points along the length of the coronary artery and its branches.

Reference: C. Rouan, 'The Heart – a different approach', *Journal of Biological Education*, Vol. 15, No. 3, 1981.

Requirements
Dissecting instruments
Tap and rubber tubing
Clamps for sealing of blood vessels

Heart of pig, sheep or ox

Investigation 11.5
Structure and properties of cardiac muscle

When the heart beats the muscle contracts more or less synchronously: a wave of contraction spreads rapidly over the heart wall so that all the muscle fibres contract at about the same moment. The wave of contraction is spread not by nerves but by the heart muscle (cardiac muscle) itself.

Procedure

1 Take your pulse rate by placing your finger over your radial artery at the wrist. How many times is your heart beating per minute? Assuming a constant rate, how many beats will your heart have undergone by the time you are sixty? From these considerations what predictions can you make about the properties of heart (cardiac) muscle?

2 Clench your fist repeatedly, at the same rate as your heart-beat, for one minute. What does your hand feel like afterwards? What does this suggest about the way cardiac muscle differs from skeletal muscle?

3 Examine a section of cardiac muscle under the microscope, low power first then high power. Note the network of muscle fibres interconnected by bridges, and the other structures shown in Figure 11.7. The muscle fibres consist of chains of muscle cells, each containing a single nucleus. The muscle cells are separated from one another by intercalated discs and the fibres are striated, i.e. they have alternating dark and light bands running across them as in skeletal (striated) muscle. Which of these features, if any, confirm your predictions regarding the structure of cardiac muscle?

4 Studies with the electron microscope show cardiac muscle to have a similar fine structure to that of skeletal (striated) muscle (*see* page 196). Examine an electron micrograph of cardiac muscle in which the fibres have been sectioned longitudinally. You will now be able to see the alternating dark and light bands very clearly. Notice that the intercalated discs correspond

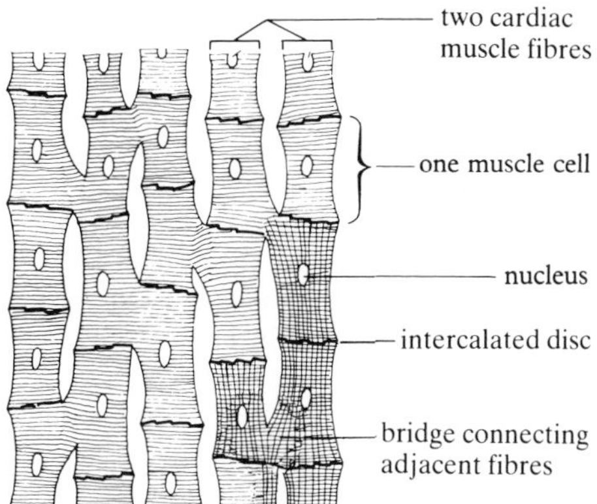

Figure 11.7 Longitudinal section of cardiac muscle as seen under the light microscope.

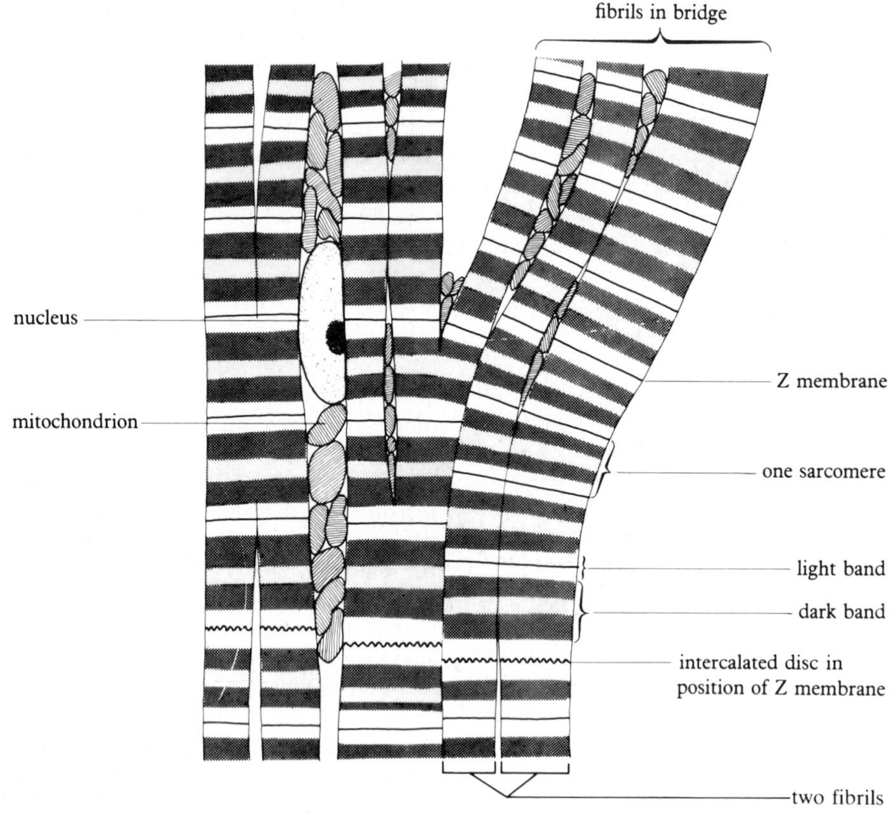

Figure 11.8 Detail of fibrils as seen in the electron microscope.

in position to the Z membranes. Use Figure 11.8 to help you identify these and other structures in the electron micrograph. If the structures are lettered, state what each letter stands for.

For consideration

(1) In the electron micrograph of cardiac muscle you will have noticed numerous mitochondria. Why are there so many?
(2) The fine structure of cardiac muscle is similar to that of skeletal muscle. Is this coincidence or is there a more fundamental reason?

Requirements
Microscope

Section of cardiac muscle
Electron micrograph of cardial muscle

Investigation 11.6
Microscopic structure of blood vessels

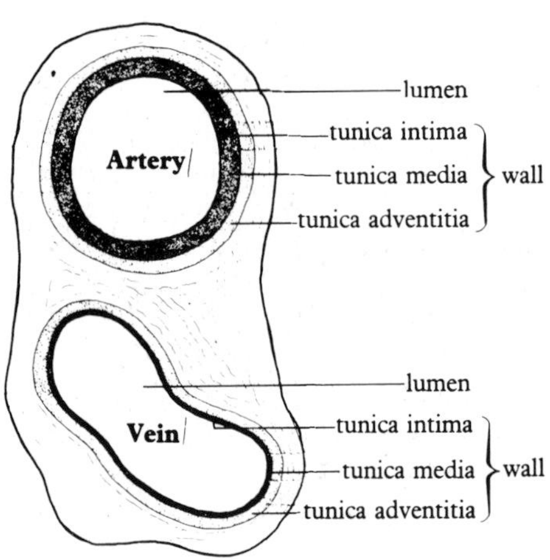

Figure 11.9 Transverse sections of an artery and vein to show the main layers in their walls.

Before beginning this investigation think of the jobs which arteries, veins and capillaries have to do and see if you can predict their structure.

Procedure

1 Examine transverse sections of a large artery and vein under the microscope. Notice the layers of tissue in their walls (Figure 11.9).
2 Examine the layers in detail (Figure 11.10). They are as follows:

Tunica intima: thin, lined with pavement endothelium and composed of delicate collagen and elastic fibres mainly disposed longitudinally.

Tunica media: thicker, consisting of tough circular elastic fibres and smooth muscle interspersed with collagen fibres. In appropriately stained sections the elastic fibres appear as wavy lines.

Note: The tunica media of arteries is much thicker than that of veins and contains much more smooth muscle.

Tunica adventitia: varies in thickness, contains a mixture of irregularly arranged elastic and collagen fibres and blood vessels (vasa vasora).

Note: The tunica adventitia of arteries contains mainly elastic fibres; the tunica adventitia of veins contains mainly collagen fibres.

3 Compare the artery and vein with regard to the relative amounts of elastic fibres, collagen fibres and smooth muscles in their walls. How will the differences affect their functional properties? How do living cells in the walls of the artery and vein obtain oxygen? Do your observations agree with Table 11.1?
4 Examine a transverse section of a smaller artery. How does it differ from the large artery? As arteries get smaller their walls become thinner and contain progressively less elastic tissue relative to smooth muscle. (Functional explanation?) The smallest arterioles have

A Large artery e.g. aorta

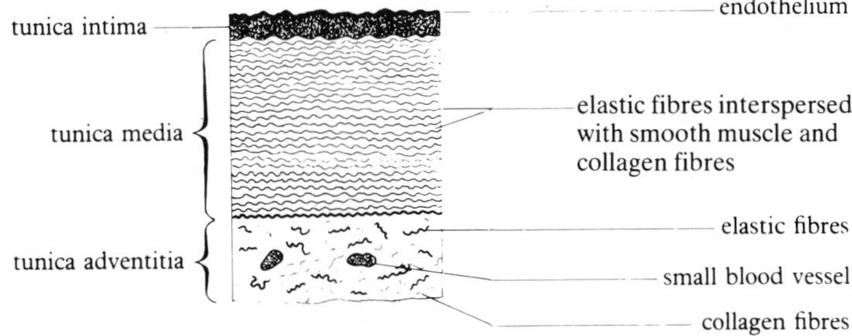

B Large vein e.g. vena cava

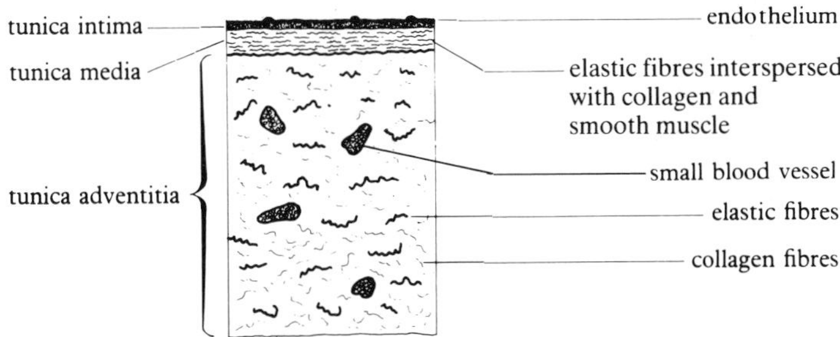

C Medium sized artery

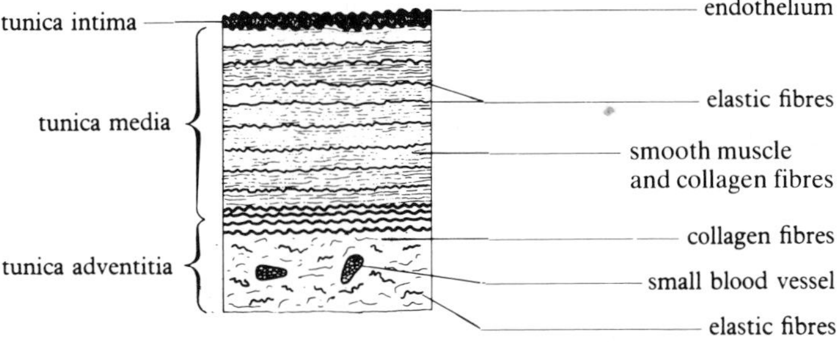

Figure 11.10 Detailed microscopic structure of the walls of artery and vein.

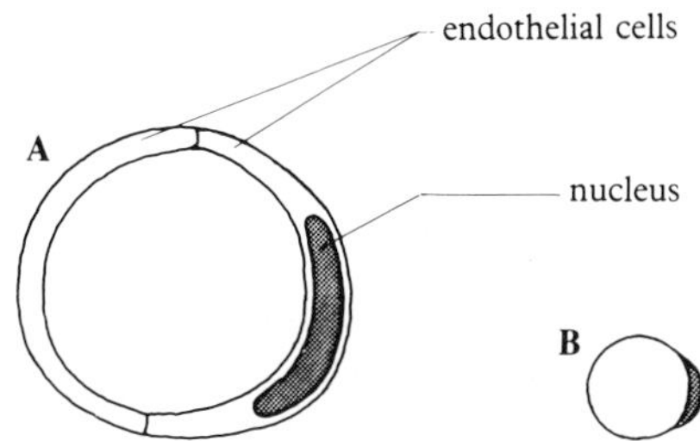

Figure 11.11 Microscopic structure of a capillary as seen in transverse section, A on a large scale, B as it appears in a typical slide under the microscope.

Requirements
TS large artery
TS large vein
TS smaller artery
Section of e.g. lung, kidney or thyroid gland for capillaries
Electron micrograph of capillary

Tadpole or young fish in watchglass, anaesthetised with urethane. (Place the animal in a 3–5 per cent solution of urethane until movement ceases.)

an endothelium surrounded by a layer of smooth muscle, then a thin layer of connective tissue.

5 Examine a capillary in a microscopic section of an organ such as lung, kidney or thyroid gland. Notice that the wall consists of a single layer of pavement epithelial cells (Figure 11.11). Significance?

6 Examine an electron micrograph of a section through a capillary wall. Locate one or more endothelial cells. Notice that the cell is bulbous in the vicinity of the nucleus, but flattened peripherally.

7 Examine the tail of a tadpole or young fish, under the microscope. Notice red blood cells flowing through capillaries in single file. Compare the velocity of blood-flow in a capillary with that in an artery. Is there any difference? Explain.

For Consideration

(1) In Table 11.1 the structure of a typical mammalian artery is compared with that of a vein. On the assumption that your own observations agree with the information given in the table, comment on the functional significance of each of the differences.

(2) Arterioles have an endothelium surrounded by a layer of smooth muscle, then connective tissue. Venules, on the other hand, have an endothelium surrounded by connective tissue, but there is no muscle present. Why the difference?

(3) How do capillaries manage without any muscle or connective tissue in their walls? Which of your observations made during this investigation help you to answer this question?

Artery	Vein
Smaller overall diameter	Larger overall diameter
Narrower lumen	Wider lumen
Thicker wall with greater overall content of elastic fibres	Thinner wall with smaller overall content of elastic fibres
Tunica intima thicker	Tunica intima thinner
Tunica media thicker and more muscular	Tunica media thinner and less muscular
Tunica adventitia thinner with high elastic fibre content relative to collagen	Tunica adventitia thicker with low elastic fibre content relative to collagen
Vasa vasora situated further away from inner surface of wall	Vasa vasora penetrate closer to inner surface of wall

Table 11.1 Comparison between typical mammalian artery and vein. The vasa vasora are small blood vessels situated in the wall of the artery and vein.

Investigation 11.7
Properties of blood vessels

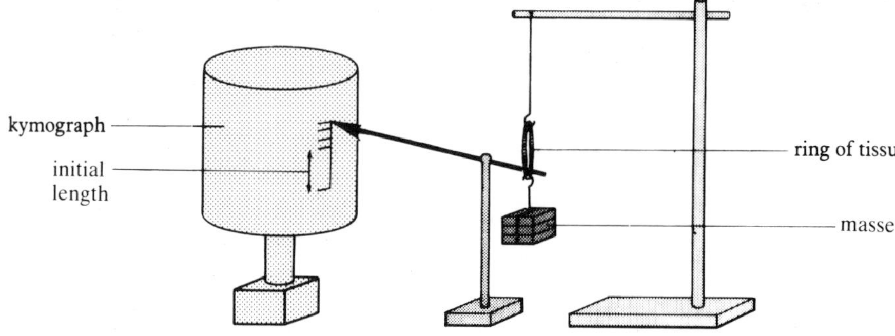

Figure 11.12 Technique for recording and measuring changes in length of a ring of tissue with increasing load. After adding each mass the new length acquired by the tissue is recorded by manually rotating the kymograph.

Pumped by the muscular action of the heart, the blood is propelled round the body in tubular blood vessels. The latter include, in the order in which blood flows through them: arteries, arterioles, capillaries, venules and veins. In this investigation we shall relate some of the physical properties of these vessels to their functions.

Procedure

1 Using the heart from the previous investigation, cut out a ring from the aorta and another from one of the venae cavae. Suspend the artery-ring from a hook on a stand and attach it to a lever as shown in Figure 11.12.[1]

2 Record the initial length of the artery-ring. This can be taken as the distance moved by the lever point when the other end of the lever is moved through the length of the ring.

3 Load the ring with increasing masses, 10 g at a time. Record the increase in length each time until no further change takes place.

4 Remove the masses one at a time, and record the decrease in length each time until no further decrease is given.

5 Repeat Steps 1 to 4 with the vein-ring. Make your kymograph recordings at the same level as the artery recordings so that they can be readily compared.

6 Plot your results on graph paper in whatever way best illustrates the differences between the artery and vein.

7 Calculate the total percentage increase in length achieved by loading (a) the artery and (b) the vein.

[1] If a kymograph is not available use a graduated scale or ruler mounted on a stand for recording changes in length.

For consideration

(1) How do the artery and vein compare with regard to (a) percentage increase in length on loading, (b) ability to return to their original length on unloading?

(2) How do their elastic properties relate to the stresses and strains which arteries and veins are likely to experience in life?

(3) In this experiment we have taken no account of the *time* it takes for the artery or vein to acquire their new lengths when they are loaded or unloaded. How could you investigate this aspect of their properties?

(4) In an experiment masses were hung on blood vessel rings until they broke. Here are the results for three specific vessels: dorsal aorta 5000 g, pulmonary artery 3500 g, vena cava 800 g. Comment.

(5) How do the results of this experiment fit in with your observations on the microscopic structure of arteries and veins?

Requirements
Kymograph (stationary)
Stand with lever and hook (*see* Figure 11.12)
Masses (10 g)
Ring of large artery and vein

Investigation 11.8
Action of the frog's heart

The amphibian heart is basically similar to the mammal's except that there is only one ventricle and blood enters the right atrium via an additional chamber, the sinus venosus. Evidence suggests that the latter serves as the pacemaker and that its intrinsic rhythm can be modified by impulses reaching it from the vagus and sympathetic nerves. The rate at which the heart beats is known as the cardiac frequency. In this investigation we shall investigate factors affecting the cardiac frequency.

Technique

A kymograph (*see* Appendix 3, page 384) is used for recording the beating heart. The heart is attached to a lever which writes on the drum. The drum should revolve at approximately 5 mm s^{-1}. If you have a time marker, a time tracing can be made on your drum along with your heart records. If you have not got a time marker, a time scale can be constructed from the time taken for the drum to do a complete revolution. The heart is attached to the lever by a thread with a hook at the end[1].

[1] If no kymograph is available the cardiac frequency can be estimated by counting the number of heartbeats per minute. For ease of counting, the heart may be attached to a lever and the beats recorded by making a mark on a sheet of paper every time the lever rises. The microbalance described on page 385 makes an admirable lever for this purpose.

Preparing the frog

You should be provided with a 'double pithed' frog, i.e. one whose brain and spinal cord have been destroyed. The animal is therefore dead but its heart will remain physiologically active for several hours provided it is kept well doused with Ringer's solution.

> **Note:** Pithing is a skilled procedure and must be carried out by an experienced teacher or technician, *not* by the student.

1 Pin the frog, ventral side uppermost, to a piece of cork. Cut away the skin from the pectoral region and identify the xiphisternum (xiphoid cartilage) just behind the bony part of the pectoral girdle (Figure 11.13A).

2 Carefully cut round the perimeter of the xiphisternum and remove it. This will create a window in the body wall through which the heart may be seen. *Warning:* there is a large superficial vein just behind the xiphisternum: be careful not to cut it.

3 Cut away the pericardial membrane surrounding the heart and force the latter out of the window so it is completely exposed. Now insert the hook into the thick muscle at the tip of the ventricle (Figure 11.13B).

4 Attach the thread to the lever by means of a small piece of plasticine. Position the lever on its stand, if necessary counter-balancing it with plasticine,

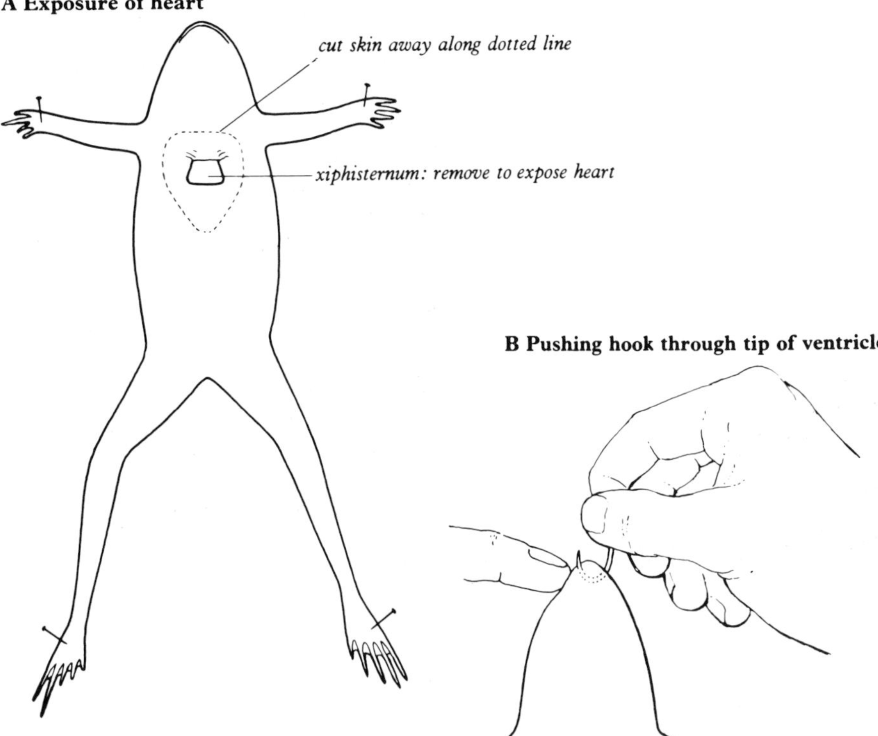

Figure 11.13 Preparing a frog for recording the heart-beat. In B the heart and hand are not on the same scale.

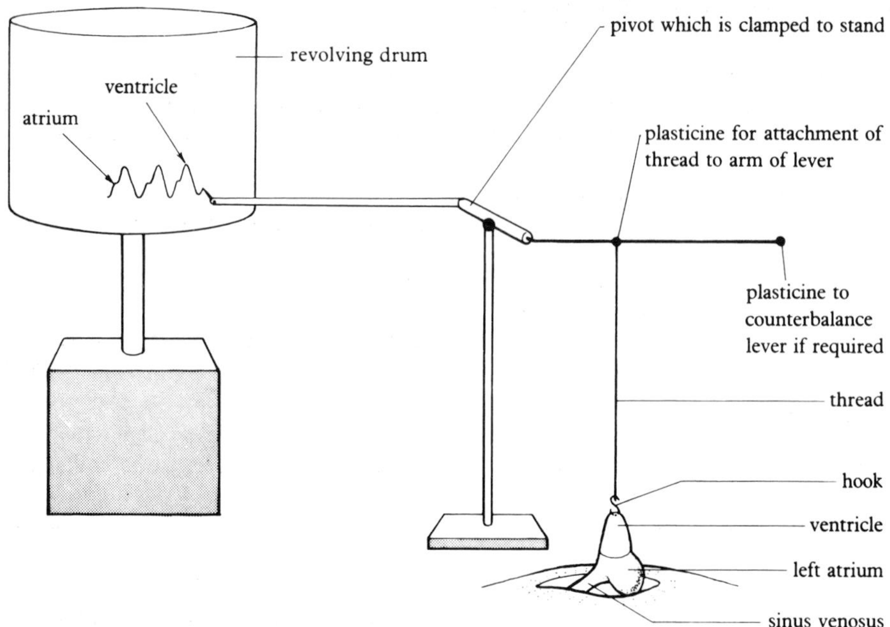

Figure 11.14 Recording the heart beat of the frog.

Requirements
Dissecting instruments
Kymograph set at approximately 5 mm s^{-1}
Time marker (if available)
Heart lever, thread and hook (the microbalance described on page 385 can be used as the lever in this experiment)
Recording pen
Plasticine
Blunt rod

Frog Ringer's solution (at room temperature, ice-cold, 30 °C and 40 °C, *see* page 403)
Acetyl choline, 1 in 5000 and 1 in 1000
Adrenaline, 1 in 10 000 and 1 in 1000

Pithed frog (as an alternative to the frog, the African clawed toad, *Xenopus laevis*, may be used.)

so the heart is fairly well stretched and the lever horizontal. The writing point should give an excursion of about a centimetre every time the heart contracts. The writing point should be directed towards the base of the drum. The drum should be as high as possible on its spindle. (Figure 11.14).

Experiments

1 NORMAL BEATING OF THE HEART
Record about 12 complete heart cycles at room temperature round the base of the drum. If there is not too much friction between the writing point of the lever and the paper, you should be able to distinguish the contractions of the atria and ventricle (*see* Figure 11.14). How do the contractions compare with one another? Explain any differences.

2 EFFECT OF TEMPERATURE ON CARDIAC FREQUENCY
Have available Ringer's solution at the following temperatures: ice-cold, 30 °C and 40 °C. Record about six normal contractions (at room temperature). Then, with the kymograph still running, pipette ice-cold Ringer's solution onto the heart. With a pencil or pen make a mark on the drum corresponding to the moment that the Ringer's is applied. Record the effect until the heart beat returns to normal. Repeat the experiment with Ringer's solution at 30 °C and 40 °C. Explain your results.

3 RESPONSE OF THE HEART TO DRUGS
Record about six normal contractions, then pipette a drop of 1 in 5000 acetyl choline onto the sinus venosus of the heart. If this produces little or no change try 1 in 1000. When the heart has returned to normal wash it with Ringer's solution and repeat the experiment with 1 in 10 000 and 1 in 1000 adrenaline. Does the heart respond differently to acetyl choline and adrenaline? Explain fully.

4 EFFECT OF HIGH TEMPERATURE ON VARIOUS REGIONS OF THE HEART
Record normal contractions. Then bring the tip of a blunt rod, heated to 40 °C, close to (a) the ventricle, (b) left atrium, (c) right atrium, (d) sinus venosus. In each case record the effect, if any, on the cardiac frequency. Explain your results.

Results

From each set of recordings which you have made, calculate as accurately as possible the cardiac frequency as the number of heart beats per minute.

For Consideration

(1) Did you encounter any particular difficulties, or obtain any unexpected results, in the course of this work? How did you, or would you, cope with such situations?
(2) What light is thrown by the drug experiment on the normal working of the heart? Can you think of a better way of investigating this aspect of the physiology of the heart?
(3) Summarise the results of the experiment in which you investigated the effect of temperature on the cardiac frequency. Relevance to real life?

Note: Some people object on ethical grounds to experiments on pithed frogs. As an alternative to carrying out this practical investigation, a film, video recording or computer simulation program may be preferred.

Questions and Problems

Percentage saturation of haemoglobin with oxygen	Partial pressure of oxygen (kPa)
97	13.33
96	10.66
93	7.99
84	5.33
72	3.99
50	2.66
19	1.33

1 The table in the margin gives figures to show the percentage oxygen saturation of adult haemoglobin at different partial pressures of oxygen in a human. Other conditions such as temperature were kept constant. The partial pressures of oxygen are expressed in kilopascals (kPa).
  (a) Plot these data in a suitable form
  (b) On the *same* graph sketch oxygen dissociation curves for the following:
    (i) an increase in carbon dioxide (labelled P),
    (ii) an increase in temperature (labelled Q).
    (iii) foetal haemoglobin (labelled R).
  (c) Explain the significance of curves P and Q for gas exchange in an active muscle.
(UL modified)

2 Comment on the following:
  (a) Red blood cells are shaped like biconcave discs and lack a nucleus.
  (b) The haemoglobin of the lugworm *Arenicola* has an oxygen dissociation curve well to the left of that of a human.
  (c) The oxygen dissociation curve of the pigeon's haemoglobin is situated well to the right of that of a human.
  (d) Breathing coal gas for more than a few seconds is generally fatal.
  (e) Approximately 95 per cent of the CO_2 released from the tissues in a mammal is returned to the lungs in combination with the red blood cells.

Animal	**Oxygen capacity** (cm^3 O_2 per 100 cm^3 of blood)
human	20.0
seal	29.3
llama	23.4
crocodile	8.0
frog (*Rana esculenta*)	9.8
carp	12.5
mackerel	15.7
electric eel	19.75
toadfish	6.2

3 (a) The oxygen capacity of an animal's blood is the amount of oxygen carried in the blood when it is saturated. The table on the left gives the oxygen capacity of the blood of various vertebrates. In all cases the blood contains haemoglobin. Comment on the figures.
  (b) Most invertebrates have blood with low oxygen capacities (generally ranging from 0.1 to 2.5 cm^3 O_2 per 100 cm^3) but there are two notable exceptions: the lugworm *Arenicola* has a capacity of 8.0 and the cuttlefish *Sepia* has a capacity of 7.0 cm^3 O_2 per 100 cm^3. Comment.

4 (a) Give an illustrated account of the structure of the mammalian heart.
  (b) Consider what would happen if (i) the right side of the heart were to beat more powerfully than the left side; (ii) a blood clot develops inside one of the coronary vessels; (iii) the heart is totally denervated.

5 Suggest explanations for each of the following, all of which relate to the human heart:
  (a) The beginning of ventricular systole is accompanied by first a slight increase in atrial pressure and then a marked decrease.
  (b) The onset of ventricular diastole is accompanied by a sudden slight increase in aortic pressure.
  (c) At the commencement of ventricular systole and diastole, thud-like sounds can be heard through a stethoscope applied to the chest.
  (d) Blood leaves the heart with uneven flow but by the time it reaches the capillaries it flows evenly.
  (e) In certain types of disease the ventricles beat at a slower rate than the atria.

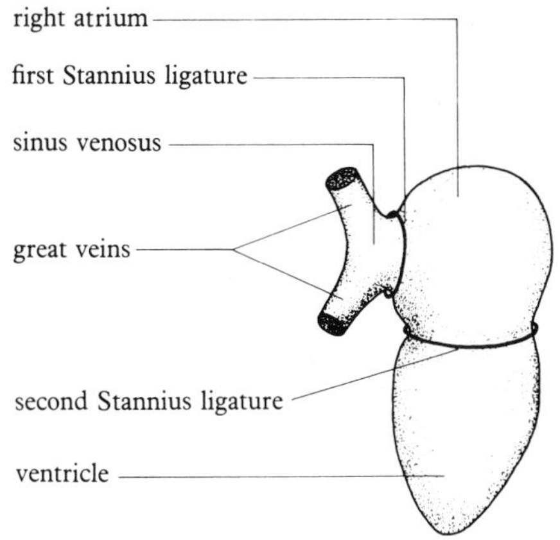

Figure 11.15 Side view of frog's heart showing the position of the first and second Stannius ligatures. The threads are tied firmly but not so tight as to impede the flow of blood.

6 One of the earliest experiments on the initiation of the heartbeat was carried out by Stannius on the frog's heart. This is basically similar to the mammalian heart except that there is only one ventricle and the great veins, instead of opening direct into the right atrium, open into a vestibule-like sinus venosus (Figure 11.15). The heartbeat starts at the sinus venosus and then spreads via the atria to the ventricle. Stannius found that if he tied a ligature round the junction between the sinus venosus and right atrium, the atria and ventricle stopped beating, but the sinus continued to beat at its normal rate. However, after about half-an-hour the atria and ventricle started beating again, but at a slower rate than the sinus. Stannius next tied a second ligature, this time between the atria and ventricle. The result was that the ventricle stopped beating, but the sinus venosus and atria continued to beat at the same rate as before. However, after about an hour the ventricle started beating again extremely slowly, much more slowly than the atria.
  (a) Explain Stannius's observations in terms of modern knowledge of how the heart works.
  (b) How does the cardiac mechanism of the frog compare with that of a mammal?

7 Figure 11.16 shows how the mean pressure and velocity of the blood changes in relation to the cross-sectional area of successive blood vessels in the mammalian circulation. Select two features of the graphs which you consider to be of particular interest, and comment on them as fully as you can.

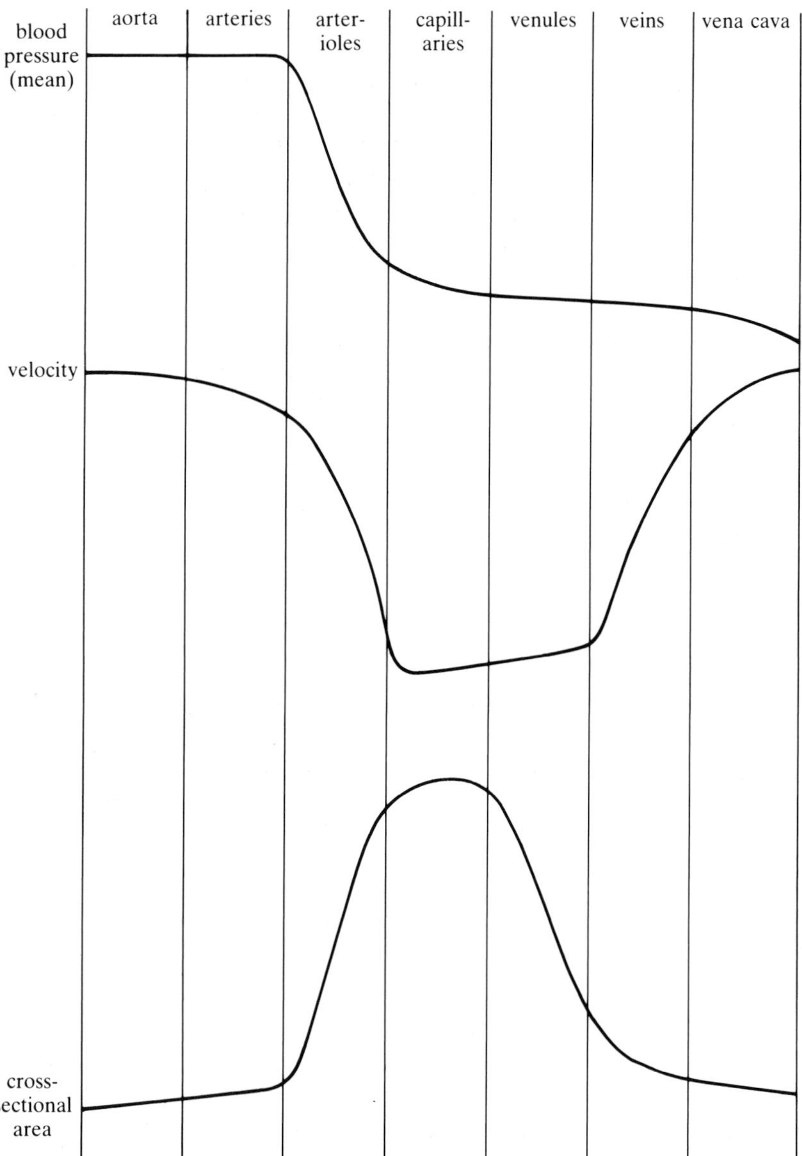

Figure 11.16 Graphs showing the relative changes in the mean pressure and velocity of blood in relation to the cross-sectional area of successive blood vessels in the mammalian circulation.

8 From your knowledge of the structure and functioning of the human heart, lungs and circulatory system, put forward a design for a heart-lung machine that would enable blood to by-pass a person's own heart and lungs, thereby allowing surgical operations to be carried out on these organs. How, precisely, should the machine be connected with the patient?

9 (a) Compare the mechanisms by which blood is returned to the heart from the tissues in a mammal, a fish, and an insect.
(b) How does the composition of an insect's blood differ from that of the mammal? Give reasons for the differences.

12 Uptake and Transport in Plants

Background Summary

1 Plants require carbon dioxide, water, mineral salts and oxygen. In lower plants these are transported by diffusion; in higher plants specialised **vascular tissues** are required.

2 In land plants carbon dioxide is taken up through **stomata** which are located mainly on the underside of the **leaves**. The degree of openness or closure of the stomata can be estimated by means of a **porometer** which measures the resistance to airflow of a leaf.

3 Bordered by **guard cells**, the stomata are controlled by an osmotic mechanism, dependent on the active transport of potassium ions, which ensures that generally they open by day and close by night.

4 The stomata also permit the escape of water vapour from the plant (**transpiration**). Transpiration is an integral part of the mechanism by which water is taken up into the plant from the soil.

5 In the leaves water evaporates from the surfaces of the spongy mesophyll cells into sub-stomatal air chambers, whence it diffuses through the stomata to the outside.

6 The rate of transpiration can be estimated indirectly by measuring the rate of water uptake by a cut leafy shoot, using a **potometer**. The rate of transpiration depends on temperature, relative humidity, air movements, atmospheric pressure, light, and water supply. Some structural features of plants appear to prevent excessive transpiration.

7 To replace the water transpired from the above-ground parts of a plant water, taken up by the roots, flows through the plant in the **transpiration stream**.

8 Water moves through the living tissues of the plant mainly by the **apoplast** (cell walls) and to some extent via the **symplast** (cytoplasm) and **vacuoles**.

9 Water-flow through the plant is maintained by a **water potential gradient**, the water potential being highest in the soil surrounding the roots and lowest in the atmosphere outside the leaves.

10 The **roots** are adapted for the uptake of water. Movement of water from soil to vascular tissues occurs at least in part by osmosis. The existence of **root pressure** suggests that osmosis may be aided by active transport, possibly in the **endodermis** where the **Casparian strip** diverts water and solutes through the symplast.

11 The **stem** is well adapted for carrying the transpiration stream from roots to leaves. Water (and mineral salts) are transported in lignified **xylem elements** (**vessels** and **tracheids**) within **vascular bundles** continuous with the vascular tissues in the roots and leaves. Lateral movement is permitted by **bordered pits** which in certain plants contain a **torus**.

12 How water is drawn through a tall stem, and the water columns prevented from breaking or falling back, may be tentatively explained by **adhesion** and **cohesion** forces developed in the anatomical elements involved.

13 Mineral salts are taken up as ions by **active transport** and pass through the symplast system to the xylem. They are then carried in the transpiration stream to the leaves.

14 Some plants have special methods of obtaining essential elements, particularly nitrogen – e.g. they may harbour mutualistic mycorrhiza or nitrogen-fixing bacteria in their roots, or they may adopt a parasitic or carnivorous habit.

15 Organic compounds manufactured in leaves are **translocated** to the rest of the plant in **sieve tubes** in the **phloem** within the vascular tissues. The structure of the sieve elements shows adaptations for this function.

16 The mechanism of translocation is not fully understood but it may take place by means of **mass flow**, **active transport**, **electro-osmosis**, **surface-spreading** or **streaming** in protein filaments.

Investigation 12.1
Factors affecting the rate of transpiration

The rate at which water enters a plant depends on the rate at which it evaporates from the leaves, i.e. is transpired into the surrounding atmosphere. Any external condition which affects the rate of transpiration will be expected to have a corresponding effect on the rate of water uptake.

In this exercise we shall investigate the effect of various external conditions on the rate at which water enters a leafy shoot.

Method

We shall use a potometer for measuring water uptake by the shoot. The potometer consists of a length of graduated capillary tubing which can be attached to the cut end of the stalk. The capillary tube is filled with water which is continuous with the water columns in the xylem elements in the stalk. The rate at which water traverses the capillary tube is then measured and the rate of water uptake calculated.

Type 1 (with reservoir)

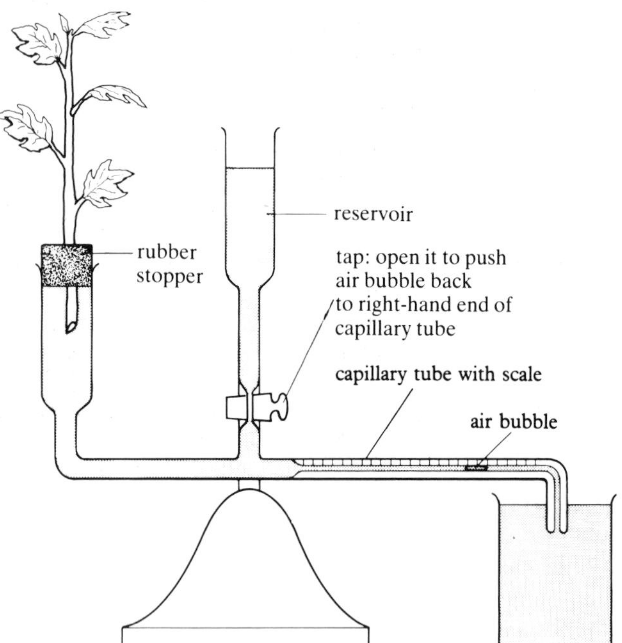

Type 2 (without reservoir)

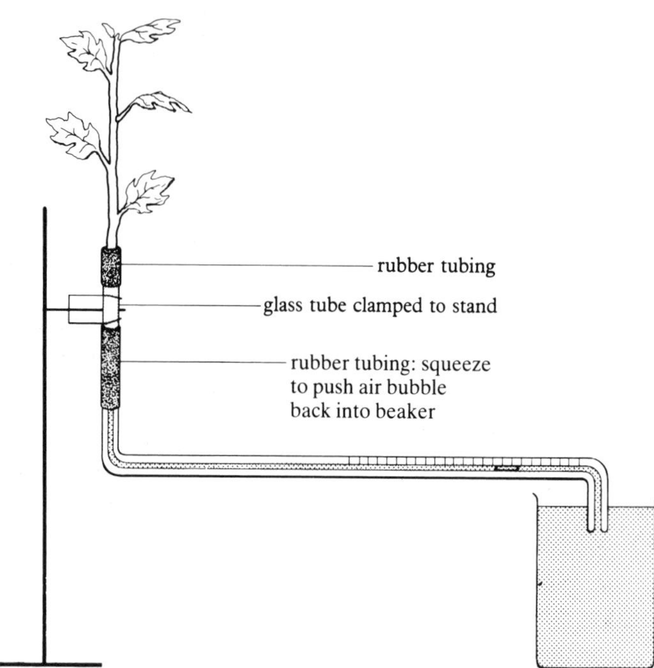

Figure 12.1 Two types of potometer.

Two types of potometer are illustrated in Figure 12.1. In both cases water uptake is measured by timing how long it takes for an air bubble to pass along the graduated capillary tube.

Procedure

SETTING UP THE POTOMETER

1 Immerse the potometer completely in water and make sure it is completely filled. Now put the cut stalk (but *not* the leaves) of your leafy shoot (sycamore is recommended) into the water and cut off the last centimetre of the stalk obliquely *under water*.

2 Pause for a moment and then, with the potometer and stalk still under water, attach the stalk to the potometer as shown in Figure 12.1. The object is to ensure that the water in the xylem elements of the plant is continuous with the water in the potometer: there must be no air bubble in the system.

3 Now remove the plant and potometer from the water and mount them in a fixed position. The end of the capillary tube should rest in a beaker of water and any air bubbles in the capillary tube should be expelled by letting in water from the reservoir (type 1) or squeezing the rubber tubing (type 2).

4 If necessary, smear vaseline on the joints between the stalk and the potometer so as to prevent leakage.

USING THE POTOMETER

1 Perform a trial run with the plant in normal room conditions. Remove the capillary tube from the beaker for a few seconds to allow a bubble of air to enter it. Measure the distance moved by the air bubble in a certain interval of time.

2 Return the bubble to the beginning and repeat the procedure.

In the case of type 1 the air bubble can be returned by carefully letting in water from the reservoir: the same air bubble can then be used again. In type 2 it is necessary to expel the air bubble into the beaker by pressing the rubber tubing: a new one may then be introduced.

3 Continue making trial runs until your plant settles down to a steady rate of transpiration.

Experiments

Investigate the effect on the rate of transpiration of some or all of the following situations:

1 Place the plant in a current of air, created by e.g. an electric fan.

2 Put the plant in a humid environment, e.g. by covering the leaves with a polythene bag.

3 Raise the temperature by putting the plant close to a heat source such as a radiator.

4 Block the stomata on the lower and/ or upper surfaces of the leaves by

Requirements
Potometer (*see* Figure 12.1)
Cutters
Electric fan
Polythene bag
Heat source
Squared paper

Vaseline or silicone grease

Leafy shoot e.g. sycamore

smearing the leaves with vaseline or silicone grease.

5 Remove some or all of the leaves from the plant.

Don't forget that when you investigate the effect of one condition, all other conditions must be kept constant.

Processing your results

1 Express the rate of water uptake in distance moved by the air bubble per unit time (e.g. mm min^{-1}).

2 If you know the volume of water that each division of the scale corresponds to, convert your results to volume of water taken up per unit time (e.g. mm^3 min^{-1}).

3 Make an estimate of the total leaf area of your plant by removing the leaves and laying them on squared paper. This will enable you to express the water uptake in volume per unit time per leaf area (e.g. cm^3 h^{-1} m^{-2}).

For Consideration

(1) What conclusions can you draw from your results?

(2) Will evaporation alone account for the movement of water through a plant? What other forces might be involved?

(3) What effect might the removal of the roots have had on the flow of water through the plant?

(4) Under what circumstances might the rate of water uptake differ considerably from the rate of water loss?

Investigation 12.2
Water loss from the leaves of a plant

The rate of water loss from the leaves of a plant (transpiration) depends on numerous characteristics of the leaves and the environment in which they live. For instance, one might expect the number and distribution of stomata to influence the transpiration rate. Is there a correlation between the mass of water lost from the leaves of a plant and the stomatal frequency and distribution?

Cherry laurel or rhododendron is recommended for this experiment. The investigation is more valuable, however, if two or three different species are compared, and the results related to their habitats. The water loss from a typical mesophyte can be compared with that from a xerophyte. Mesophytes grow where water is reasonably plentiful, but xerophytes grow where the water supply is poor.

Water loss can be determined, as described here, by weighing leaves with an electrical top-pan balance. Alternatively, a sensitive microbalance can be used, as described in Appendix 3 (*see* page 385).

Procedure

ESTIMATING WATER LOSS BY WEIGHING

1 Take several leaves with their stalks (petioles) attached. String them together with thread and weigh them on an electrical top-pan balance. Aim to have a bunch of leaves which weighs about 10 g. This will be about four leaves in the case of cherry laurel. Note the time.

2 Hang this bundle of leaves on a 'washing line' which consists of string suspended between clamp stands.

3 Repeat this procedure with a similar bundle of leaves. On this occasion suspend the bundle on a 'washing-line' in turbulent air from a fan, hairdrier or convector heater.

4 Create two more bundles of leaves. Smear vaseline or silicone grease thinly on the upper surfaces of one group of leaves and the lower surfaces of the other. Weigh each group separately, and hang them up to dry. Be careful during this procedure not to brush vaseline from the leaves onto the balance pan or onto your fingers.

5 If you wish to compare water loss from two species, repeat Steps 1, 2, 3 and 4 with leaves from the other species.

6 If you have enough time and leaves, subject *several* bundles to each treatment. The results can then be analysed statistically to see if the water loss differs significantly between contrasting treatments (*see* Appendix 6, page 393).

7 If a microbalance is used, these procedures can be carried out on single leaves. Before the initial weighing, trace the outline of the leaf on graph paper and determine the surface area. Water loss can then be related to the unit area of the leaf.

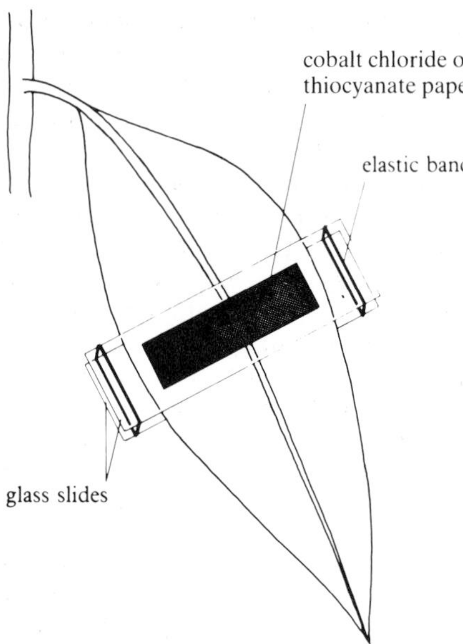

Figure 12.2 Cobalt chloride or thiocyanate 'sandwich' experiment.

Requirements
Electical top-pan balance
Microbalance (Appendix 3) and accessories, such as weights and S-wires
Clamp stands
Convector heater, fan or hairdrier
String
Ruler
Fuse wire
Graph paper
Microscope with high power
Microscope slides
Elastic bands or paper clips
Forceps
Coverslips
Marking pen
Transparent ruler/scale, or micrometer eyepiece graticule and micrometer slide

Vaseline or silicone grease
Anyhydrous cobalt chloride or cobalt thiocyanate paper
Polystyrene cement or nail varnish

Leaves of one or more named tree or shrub species e.g. cherry laurel or rhododendron

8 Reweigh each bundle of leaves (or, if a microbalance is used, reweigh each individual leaf) at least four times, at intervals of about 15 minutes. Record your results.
9 Calculate the percentage decrease in mass at each interval, from the formula:

$$\text{Percentage decrease in mass} = \frac{a - b}{a} \times 100$$

where a = mass at start of experiment and b = new mass.
10 Record your results and conclusions. Does air movement significantly affect the rate of water loss from leaves? Does the water loss from the upper surface of the leaves differ from that from the lower surface?

ESTIMATING WATER LOSS WITH COBALT PAPER

1 Whilst the leaves are drying apply a strip of anyhydrous cobalt chloride or cobalt thiocyanate paper to the upper and lower surfaces of a leaf on an intact leafy shoot (Figure 12.2). Hold the paper in place with two glass slides held firmly together with elastic bands or paper clips. Anyhydrous cobalt paper is blue, but in the hydrated state it is pink. When the leaf surface loses water, the paper will change colour from blue to pink.
2 Estimate the time taken for the cobalt paper to change colour on the upper and lower surfaces of the leaf. Is there any difference? What does the difference indicate?

ESTIMATING STOMATAL FREQUENCY

1 Compare the numbers of stomata per unit area on the upper and lower surfaces of your leaf. To do this, make a replica of the leaf surface with polystyrene cement or nail varnish. Place a drop of cement or nail varnish on the lower surface of the leaf and spread it out with a pin. When dry, peel it off with forceps and place it on a microscope slide under a drop of water. Add a coverslip. Label the slide L.
2 Repeat this procedure with the upper surface of the leaf; in this case, label the slide U.
3 Examine your replicas under low and medium powers. Count and record the numbers of stomata per field of view for both upper and lower surfaces. Survey and count at least four different areas on each replica.
4 By means of a transparent ruler or scale (or a micrometer eyepiece graticule in conjunction with a micrometer slide) estimate the diameter of the field of view (*see* Appendix 2, page 378). From this calculate the area of the field of view. (Area of a circle = πr^2, where π = 3.142 and r is the radius). From this calculate the average number of stomata per unit area (e.g. per mm^2) on each side of the leaf.

For consideration

(1) Do the results of the weighing and cobalt paper experiments agree? Can you explain the results in relation to stomatal frequency?
(2) If you have investigated two different plant species, did you find a relationship between the number of stomata per unit area and the transpiration rate?
(3) What other structural features of leaves, apart from the density of stomata, may influence the rate of transpiration?
(4) In what sorts of environments would you expect to find (a) plants with a large number of stomata per unit leaf area (b) plants with relatively few stomata?

Investigation 12.3
Supply of water to the leaves of broad bean

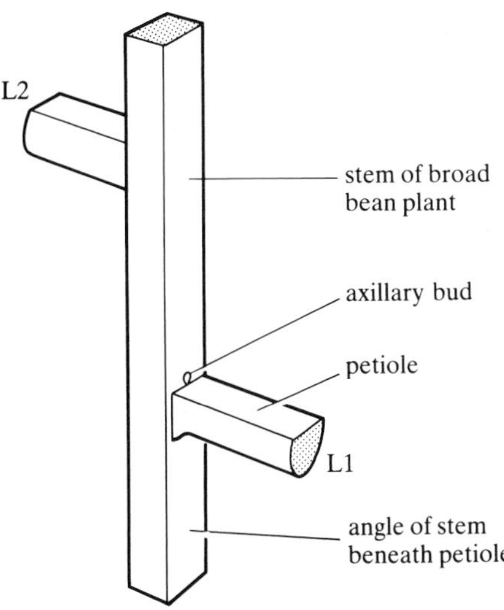

Figure 12.3 Diagram of part of stem of broad bean (*Vicia faba*) showing the distance over which vascular bundles should be dissected.

Requirements
Test tubes ×2
Test tube rack
Beaker
Dissecting instuments (including a blunt scalpel or razor blade)
Ceramic tile
Lens
Plain paper

Stain (75 cm^3, a mixture of equal volumes of 0.1 per cent aqueous eosin and 0.1 per cent aqueous rose Bengal)

Turgid transpiring shoots of broad bean (*Vicia faba*, at least four weeks old, growing in soil) ×2

The water which evaporates from the leaves of a plant is replaced by uptake from the vascular bundles of the stem. The vascular bundles in the stem must branch to provide vascular bundles which run up the petioles of the leaves to the leaf blades. In this investigation you will use a stain to examine the way the vascular bundles are arranged, both in the petiole and in the stem of a broad bean plant (*Vicia faba*).

Procedure

1 Pour the stain into two separate test tubes until each is full to within 2 cm of the rim. Place the test tubes in a rack.
2 Fill a beaker with water. Take two healthy shoots of broad bean. Cut them off at soil level and immediately plunge the cut end into your beaker of water.
3 Take each shoot in turn and cut off obliquely, under water, the base of the stem to within 5 cm of the lowest expanded leaf. Immediately, transfer each shoot to a test tube which contains stain. Make sure that the cut surface is deep in the liquid.
4 Leave the shoots in the stain in a light and well-ventilated place for at least 30 minutes. The stain will travel up through the xylem tissue in the vascular bundles and stain it.
5 After at least thirty minutes, remove one of the shoots from its test tube. It is likely that you will need only one plant. The other plant is there as an emergency reserve, which you may use if you wish.
6 Cut the shoot transversely near the base and examine with a lens the pattern of stained bundles. Draw a diagram which shows the distribution of xylem in the cross-section. Examine and draw in a similar manner a cross-section across a leaf petiole.
7 Using a fairly blunt scalpel or razor blade, begin to scrape on one of the angles of the stem just below a fully expanded leaf (Figure 12.3). Gentle scraping should soon reveal the stained xylem of a major vascular bundle.
8 Once you have seen a stained bundle, use further scraping and dissection to investigate the arrangement of the stained xylem. Write an illustrated report of your findings as you go along.
9 Begin your investigation about 1 cm below a fully expanded leaf (L1 in Figure 12.3) and complete it 1 cm above the next leaf (L2), which will be on the opposite side of the stem from L1.
10 Aim to find the courses of all the stained bundles in the stem between the start and finish points. Pay particular attention to junctions of bundles.
11 If you wish, follow the vascular bundles as far as you can along the petiole and into the leaf. Dissect or scrape for at least 1 cm from the stem, out along the petiole.

For consideration

(1) Suggest the probable pathway by which water molecules pass from the xylem vessels to the cells between the vascular bundles.
(2) If water is continually taken up by the cells between the vascular bundles, why is the dye restricted to the vascular bundles in your sections?
(3) Speculate on the internal factors which determine the pattern of vascular bundles in the leaf petiole and the stem during leaf and shoot development.

Investigation 12.4
Structure of stems

Stems have three main functions: (1) to lift the leaves and flowers into an elevated position, (2) to convey water and mineral salts from the roots to the leaves, and (3) to convey synthesised food materials from the leaves to other parts of the plant. The first function is achieved by various types of strengthening tissue; the second and third functions by conducting tissue inside the vascular bundles.

We shall here be concerned only with the primary tissues of the stem, namely those formed from the dividing cells at the apex of the growing shoot.

Procedure

EXTERNAL STRUCTURE

1 Examine an entire plant so as to appreciate the relationship between the main stem and other structures (Figure 12.4). In particular notice that leaves

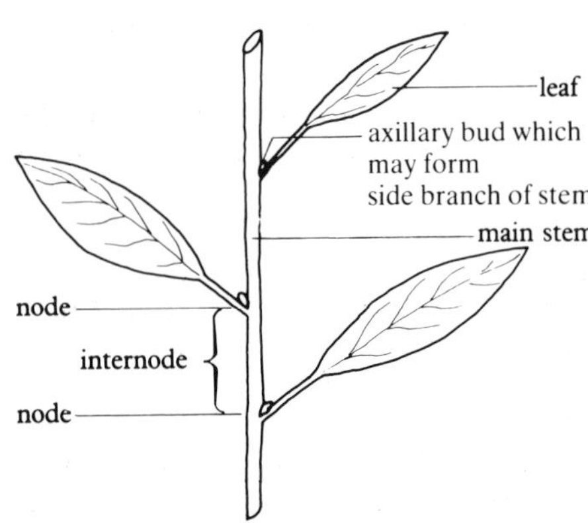

Figure 12.4 The stem and associated structures of a generalised dicotyledonous plant.

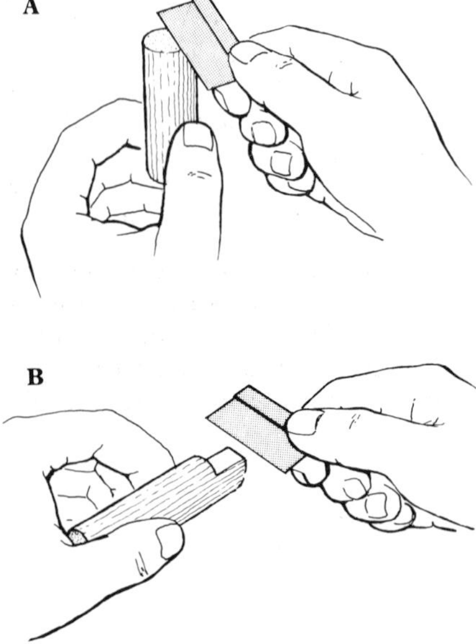

Figure 12.5 Cutting **A** transverse, and **B** longitudinal sections of a plant stem.

and axillary buds arise at intervals (nodes). The region of the stem between two successive nodes is called an internode. The stem may be hairy (function?) and/or pigmented.

2 Strip off a piece of the epidermis and examine under the microscope. Anything interesting?

GENERAL INTERNAL STRUCTURE OF A DICOTYLEDONOUS STEM

For internal structure of the stem, the sunflower, *Helianthus*, is a suitable plant to investigate.

1 With a sharp scalpel square off the ends of a short length of an internode.

2 Cut thin transverse sections of the stem with a sharp razor blade (Figure 12.5A). Hold the piece of stem in one hand and the blade in the other: cut smoothly and rapidly, constantly wetting the blade and surface of the stem with water. As the sections accumulate on the surface of the blade, transfer them to a dish of water with a paintbrush.

3 Select your thinnest sections. Stain them for 5–10 minutes in FABIL, then mount in dilute glycerine. Alternatively the sections can be mounted in the stain.

4 To build up a complete picture of the three-dimensional structure of the stem, and its constituent cells, cut longitudinal as well as transverse sections (Figure 12.5B). Longitudinal sections can be stained and mounted in the same way as transverse sections.

5 Supplement your investigation of stem structure by examining prepared slides.

6 Using Figure 12.6 to help you, identify the following tissues, first in transverse and then in longitudinal section.

Protective and strengthening tissues:

Epidermis: single layer of rectangular cells covering surface of stem.

Collenchyma: about four layers of thick-walled cells immediately beneath epidermis; cells vertically elongated and cellulose walls thickened at corners; constitute outer part of cortex.

Parenchyma: layer of thin-walled packing cells making up the bulk of the cortex, medulla (pith) and medullary rays.

Sclerenchyma: large group of vertically elongated lignified fibres on the immediate outside of each vascular bundle; constitute the pericycle, part of the cortex (N.B. in some stems the pericycle fibres form a continuous ring). Having lignified walls, sclerenchyma fibres are dead and empty.

Conducting (transport) tissues – Vascular bundles:

Phloem: vertically elongated sieve tubes, companion cells, and small-celled parenchyma on the immediate inside of the pericycle fibres.

Xylem: mainly vertically elongated xylem elements (vessels) with thick lignified walls: first-formed xylem elements small in cross-section and located in innermost region of xylem (protoxylem); more recently formed elements larger and located further out (metaxylem). Having lignified walls, xylem elements are dead and empty.

Cambium: several layers of small rectangular cells wedged between xylem and phloem in each vascular bundle; cambium tissue within each vascular bundle (intrafascicular cambium) joined by cambium cells which traverse each medullary ray (interfascicular cambium). Cambium cells divide tangentially to form secondary vascular tissues within the vascular bundles and secondary parenchyma in the medullary rays – *see* page 270).

N.B. In some stems the xylem and phloem form a continuous ring of vascular tissue.

VASCULAR TISSUE IN DETAIL

1 Examine xylem vessels of *Helianthus* or *Cucurbita* (marrow) in longitudinal section under high power. Explore their structure in as much detail as you can. Note lignified walls, open ends, pits, various forms of lignified thickening particularly annular and spiral. (Figure 12.7A).

2 Examine sieve tubes in longitudinal sections of *Helianthus* or *Cucurbita*. Note cellulose walls, sieve plate with pores, cytoplasmic slime (callose) in the immediate vicinity of sieve plate; companion cell(s) with cytoplasm and nucleus (Figure 12.7B).

3 In addition to studying cell detail in longitudinal sections, macerated tissue is recommended. Pieces of stem are treated with a chemical agent which causes the cells to separate from one another.

Take a very small quantity of macerated stem tissue and mount in FABIL.

Observe under low and high power.

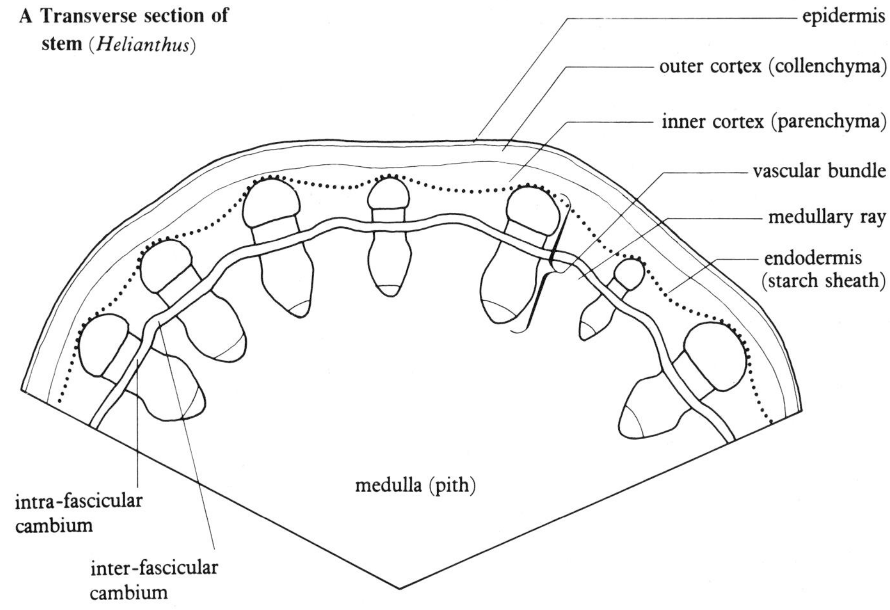

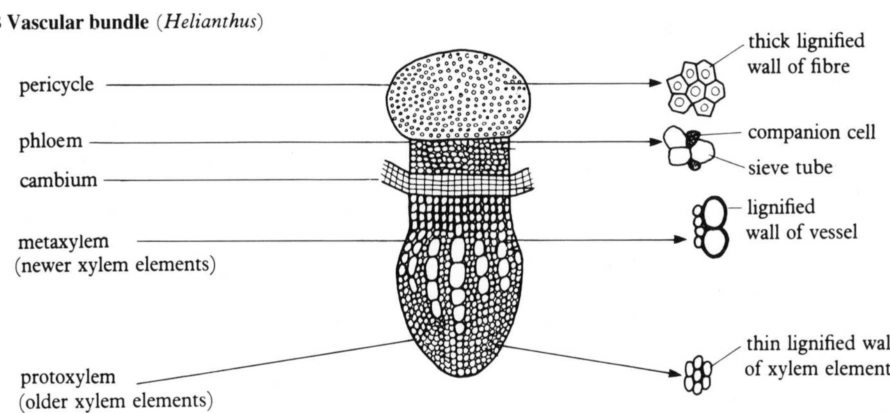

Figure 12.6 Structure of the stem of a dicotyledon, based mainly on the sunflower *Helianthus*. This particular plant is unusual in having an endodermis (starch sheath) in its stem. There is much variation in the detailed arrangement of the pericycle fibres and vascular tissues in other dicotyledons. Thus the pericycle may be separated from the phloem, it may form a continuous cylinder round the stem, or it may be absent altogether. The vascular tissues, too, may form a complete cylinder instead of discrete vascular bundles.

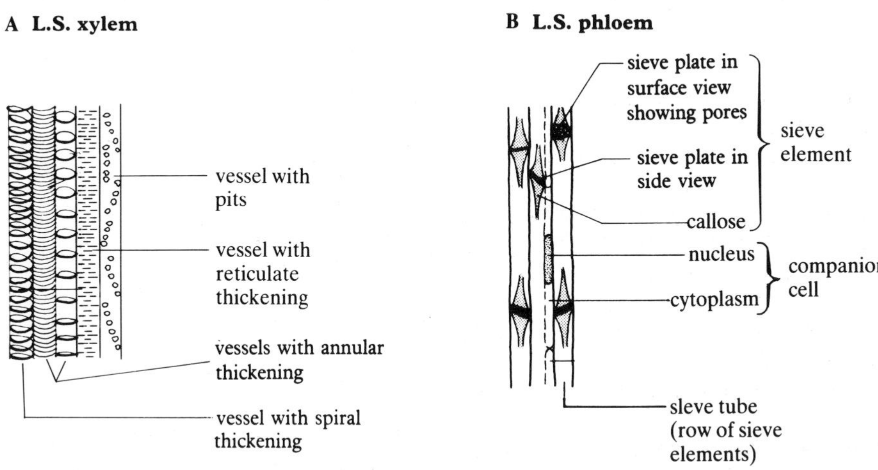

Figure 12.7 Vascular tissues as seen in longitudinal sections of a dicotyledonous stem, based on *Cucurbita*.

COMPARISON WITH MONOCOTYLEDONOUS STEM

1 Cut, stain and mount (or examine prepared) transverse sections of the stem of a typical monocotyledon such as maize, iris or lily.

2 Examine a complete section under low power. Notice that the arrangement of the vascular bundles differs from that seen in the dicotyledon. How would you describe the difference?

3 Examine an individual vascular bundle under high power. Notice that it is basically similar to that of the dicotyledon: phloem towards the outside of the stem, xylem towards the inside. However, there is no cambium. (Consequences?).

For consideration

(1) Summarise the ways in which the structure of the dicotyledonous stem is adapted to perform its functions.

(2) Dicotyledonous stems get much taller and can support much heavier masses than monocotyledonous stems. Explain the reason for this difference in terms of their internal structure.

References: C.J. Clegg and Gene Cox, *Anatomy and Activities of Plants*, Murray, 1978; A.R. Noel, Improvements in Botanical Microtechnique, *School Science Review*, Vol. 48, No. 64, 1966.

Requirements
Slides and coverslips
Dish for sections
Fine brush
Stiff razor blade

Iodine solution
FABIL
Dilute glycerine (25 per cent, aqueous)

Entire plant with leaves and axillary buds
Stem of sunflower (*Helianthus*) and marrow (*Cucurbita*, fresh or in 70 per cent ethanol)

Stem of monocotyledon, e.g. maize, iris
TS and LS *Helianthus* and *Cucurbita*
TS monocotyledon
Macerated stem tissue

Stem tissue macerated as follows (Franklin's method): Cut stem into small pieces about the size of half a matchstick. Immerse in a mixture of glacial ethanoic acid and 20 vol. hydrogen peroxide in equal parts. Maintain at 60 °C for 24 hours or boil under reflux for 1 hour. Tissues should then disintegrate with vigorous shaking or stirring. Wash by decantation, neutralise with a little ammonium hydroxide, and store in 70 per cent ethanol.

Investigation 12.5
Structure of roots

In addition to providing a firm anchorage, roots absorb water and mineral salts from the soil, and transport these to the stem. The root system of a plant must, therefore, provide an adequate surface area for absorption, and it will also be expected to contain vascular tissues which link up with those in the stem. In addition food reserves may be stored in the roots.

In this investigation we shall be concerned only with the primary tissues, namely those that are derived from the dividing cells at the apex of the growing root.

Procedure

EXTERNAL STRUCTURE

1 Examine the radicle of a seedling of mustard, cress or pea. The apex of the radicle is smooth, but further back it is covered with root hairs. (Function?). Further back still it is smooth again. The apex is the youngest part of the root. How do you account for the fact that root hairs are confined to a zone just behind the apex?

2 The radicle develops into the taproot, or main root, from which lateral roots sprout. Are any lateral roots visible in your seedling?

3 Mount a radicle in iodine solution without crushing it and examine it under the microscope. Note that each root hair is a single cell.

4 Examine a maize or wheat seedling. In this case there is no radicle as such, the taproot being replaced by a bunch of fibrous roots characteristic of grasses.

INTERNAL STRUCTURE

1 Cut transverse sections of a young primary root, i.e. one that has not laid down secondary tissues. Buttercup or broad bean are recommended. As the root is flexible it must be held in a firm position while the sections are cut: do this by inserting a short length of the root into a vertical slit made down the centre of a piece of moistened elder pith or carrot tuber (*see* Figure 10.5, page 98). Hold the pith or carrot in one hand and cut your sections rapidly and smoothly with a sharp razor blade held in the other hand. Place the sections in a dish of water.

2 Select one or two thin sections and, transferring them with a fine brush, mount them in a drop of iodine solution on a slide.

3 Examine your sections under the microscope and, using Figure 12.8 as a guide, identify the following tissues, starting at the outside and working inwards:

Outer cell layer: in the root-hair zone this is the piliferous layer; further back in older parts of the root the piliferous layer withers and is replaced by the outermost cortical cells which constitute the exodermis. The latter may become corky due to deposition of suberin in the cell walls.

Cortex: extensive area of parenchyma (packing) cells which may contain stored starch grains (stain blue-black with iodine solution).

Endodermis: single layer of cells marking the inner boundary of the cortex. Note thickened radial walls (Casparian strip) and stored starch grains (the endodermis is also known as the 'starch sheath').

Pericycle: indistinct layer of parenchyma cells immediately inside the endodermis. May become lignified in older roots. Function?

Vascular tissues: enclosed within the endodermis and pericycle, water-conducting xylem tissue and food-conducting phloem tissue. Xylem generally star-shaped, with phloem lying between the 'spokes' of the star. The first elements to form are located in the 'spokes' of the star (protoxylem); xylem elements in the centre of the star develop later (metaxylem). Wedged between protoxylem and phloem are small groups of cambium cells. These give rise to secondary vascular tissue in older roots (*see* page 270).

4 Examination of the vascular tissues is aided by staining sections in acidified phloroglucinol (eight drops of phloroglucinol plus three drops of concentrated hydrochloric acid) which stains lignin red. Alternatively FABIL may be used (*see* page 402).

For Consideration

(1) In what ways is the structure of the root adapted to perform its functions?
(2) Stems are generally stiff and erect, but roots are flexible. Explain this difference in terms of their internal structure.

Requirements
Slides and coverslips
Elder pith and/or carrot tuber
Dish for sections
Fine brush
Section lifter
Safety razor blade

Iodine solution
Benzene-1,3,5-triol (phloroglucinol)
Concentrated hydrochloric acid
FABIL

Seedling of mustard, cress or pea
Seedling of maize or wheat
Fresh roots e.g. broad bean or buttercup

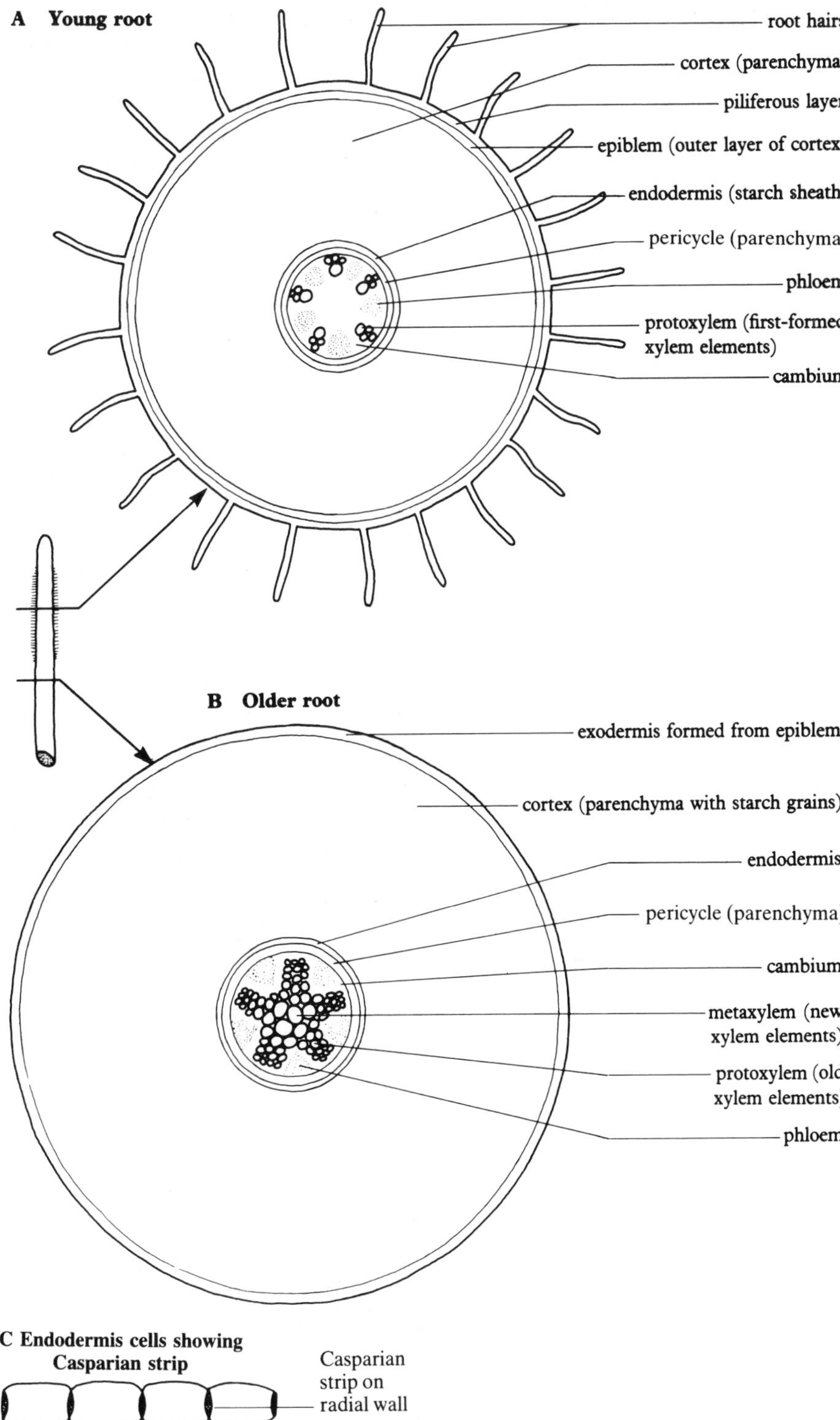

Figure 12.8 Transverse sections of dicotyledonous root, based on buttercup *Ranunculus*, **A**, young part of root in the root hair zone just behind the tip; **B**, older part of root further back; **C**, endodermis cells from above, showing suberised thickenings (Casparian strips) on the radial walls.

Investigation 12.6
Rate of translocation of sucrose in a stolon of potato

One of the functions of translocation in the phloem sieve tubes is to move the products of photosynthesis to storage organs. Such is the case with the potato plant, *Solanum tuberosum*. In early summer sucrose is translocated from the leaves to the developing tubers – the 'new potatoes'. Each tuber is situated at the end of a stolon which grows out from the base of the main stem.

To estimate the rate of translocation in the stolon we need to know (1) the volume of sucrose which enters the tuber in a given period of time, and (2) the cross-sectional area occupied by sieve tubes in the stolon.

In this investigation we shall determine these two values, and then use them to calculate the rate of translocation of sucrose in the stolon.

Plant and organ	Translocation rate ($cm\ h^{-1}$)	Experimenters
Potato tuber stem	225	Dixon & Ball
Potato tuber stem	105	Crafts
Yam tuber stem	220	Mason & Lewin
Bean (*Phaseolus*) petiole	28	Birch-Hirschfield

Table 12.1 Some measured rates of phloem transport in plant organs. The values in the table are figures calculated on the basis that the solutes in the sieve tubes make up two per cent of the mass of the translocated solution. (Adapted from M.J. Canny, *Biological Reviews*, Vol. 35, 1960.)

Requirements
Balance
Cotton wool
Microscope with high power
Stage micrometer
Eyepiece graticule
Microscope slides
Coverslips
Safety razor blade

Benzene-1,3,5-triol (phloroglucinol)
Concentrated hydrochloric acid

Potato tuber with attached stem through which it was supplied with sucrose

Procedure

In summer, before the growing season for potatoes has ended, dig up from the soil a potato with its living stem attached. Find out when the gardener planted the 'seed potato' from which your tuber is derived.

DETERMINATION OF THE VOLUME OF SUCROSE ENTERING THE TUBER PER UNIT TIME

1 Clean the potato, remove the soil carefully, blot the outside of the potato tuber with cotton wool, and weigh the potato on a balance.

2 Assume that 80 per cent of the mass of the potato is water. How much does the dry matter in the potato weigh? About 20 per cent of this dry mass is starch. Calculate the mass of starch in the tuber.

3 All the starch in the tuber is derived from sucrose transported down the phloem into the tuber. Calculate the length of time for which the tuber has been accumulating starch. Assume that the tuber arises at the end of an underground stem about thirty days after planting. How much starch has the tuber accumulated each day? Each hour?

4 The figure for the mass of *starch* accumulated by the potato tuber each hour is an estimate of the mass of *sucrose* which entered the tuber each hour. Some of the sucrose which enters the tuber, however, will not be stored but will be used in cellular respiration. This will provide the ATP to provide the energy and the materials such as cellulose to build the new storage cells. Assume that 25 per cent of the sucrose which entered the tuber has been used in this way. Recalculate the mass of sucrose which reaches the tuber each hour. This new estimate will be higher than the previous one.

5 What volume of liquid does your figure represent? Imagine that the sucrose is a 2 per cent solution (i.e. that there are 2 g sucrose in every 100 cm^3 of liquid). Calculate the volume of sucrose solution which must have passed down to the tuber each hour.

DETERMINATION OF THE CROSS-SECTIONAL AREA OCCUPIED BY SIEVE TUBES IN THE STOLON

1 Cut several thin cross-sections of the tuber stem with a sharp razor blade. Place them on a microscope slide, and add phloroglucinol and hydrochloric acid to stain lignin pink. Add a coverslip.

2 Use a stage micrometer to calibrate an eyepiece graticule under the highest power of your microscope (*see* page 378).

3 Place your tuber stem cross-sections under the low power of the microscope and examine them. Notice that the bundles of xylem and phloem are arranged in a ring, as in a stem, instead of in the centre, as in a root (*see* page 125 and page 127).

4 Look at one vascular bundle under high power. Measure the distance across the phloem area in two directions at right angles. Average the two estimates. Assuming that the area covered by the phloem is rectangular, calculate the cross-sectional area of the phloem in this bundle.

5 It has been suggested that only a fifth of this cross-sectional area consists of the sieve tube elements themselves. Thus divide by five your estimate of the cross-sectional area of the phloem in one bundle. The result represents the area of sieve tube elements in a bundle. Multiply by the number of bundles in the cross-section.

HOW TO CALCULATE THE RATE OF TRANSLOCATION OF SUCROSE IN THE STOLON

You have determined the volume of sucrose transported and the cross-sectional area of the phloem sieve tubes. Now, volume = length × area. To calculate the length of phloem sieve tube which empties per hour, divide the volume of sucrose which enters the tuber per hour by the cross-sectional area through which it has travelled. This is the rate of phloem transport, that is the rate at which sucrose is translocated in the stolon.

For consideration

(1) Compare your estimate of the rate of translocation with those in Table 12.1. How close is your estimate to the ones in the table? If the correspondence is not exact, discuss possible reasons for the differences.
(2) Of what practical use might these determinations be?
(3) Outline the possible factors which might determine the rate at which a tuber fills up with starch, and its ultimate size.

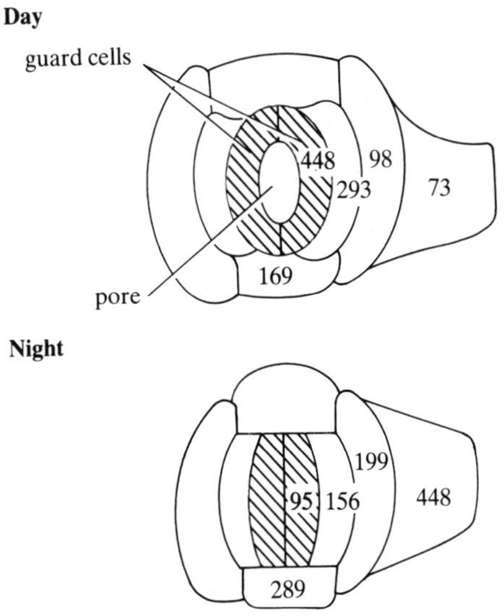

Questions and Problems

Day

guard cells

448 98 293 73 169

pore

Night

199 95 156 448 289

Figure 12.9 The stomatal complex of *Commelina communis*.

1 The stomatal complex of *Commelina communis* consists of a pair of guard cells associated with six subsidiary cells. The stomatal pore is closed at night and open during the day. The concentrations of potassium ions within the cells of the stomatal complex were measured with an ion probe and the results are shown in Figure 12.9.

(a) Compare the concentrations of potassium ions in the cells in the stomatal complex in the day and in the night.

(b) Imagine that it is night and the stoma is closed. In which direction do the potassium ions move when day breaks?

(c) What processes provide the energy for the movement of the potassium ions across the cell membranes?

(d) In what way does the flow of potassium ions affect the water potential of the cells which they enter? What effect does this have on the direction of water movement between the cells in the complex?

(e) The hormone abscisic acid, produced in water-stressed leaves, closes the stomatal pore.

(i) What is meant by the term 'water stress'?

(ii) Suggest a hypothesis to explain how abscisic acid produces its effect.

2 How would you measure the rates of transpiration and water absorption of a sunflower plant? These rates were determined over two-hour periods for plants subject to natural daily variation in the environment and given an adequate supply of water. Comment on the results which are given below and suggest possible explanations.

Process	Grams per plant and time of day							
	1100–1300	1300–1500	1500–1700	1700–1900	1900–2100	2100–2300	2300–0100	0100–0300
Transpiration	33	44	52	46	27	16	10	4
Absorption	20	30	41	46	32	22	15	12

3 A potted hydrangea plant was put out for a period of one hour in each of the following conditions in the order given, and the transpiration in each hour measured. The air temperature was 18 °C throughout the experiment:

Conditions	Relative humidity (per cent)	Transpiration (g)
(a) Still air, in light shade	70	1.2
(b) Moving air (fan) in light shade	70	1.6
(c) Still air, in bright sunlight	70	3.75
(d) Still air, dark (moist chamber)	100	−0.20

Experimental error: ±0.05 g

Suggest explanations of these results. *(O and C)*

4 The diagrams in Figure 12.10 show the relative humidities and temperatures inside and outside a hypothetical leaf.

(a) Write down the numbers of the diagrams in order, from the leaf with the lowest transpiration rate to the leaf with the highest transpiration rate. Explain your answer.

(b) What is 'guttation'? Which of the leaves illustrated in the diagram might be exhibiting guttation?

(c) Explain why a leaf may reach a higher temperature than the surrounding air.

Figure 12.10 The relative humidity (RH) and temperature (°C) inside and outside a leaf. The leaf is tinted.

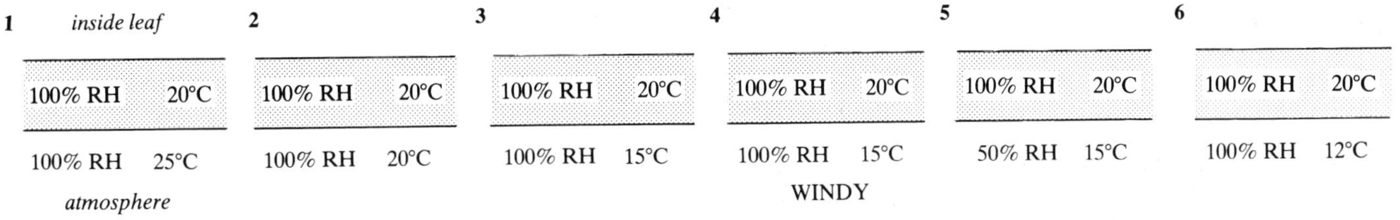

	1	2	3	4	5	6
inside leaf	100% RH 20°C	100% RH 20°C	100% RH 20°C	100% RH 20°C	100% RH 20°C	100% RH 20°C
atmosphere	100% RH 25°C	100% RH 20°C	100% RH 15°C	100% RH 15°C WINDY	50% RH 15°C	100% RH 12°C

5 The rate of transpiration of maize plants was compared with the rate of evaporation of water from a porous-pot atmometer over a 24-hour period with the following results:

	Water lost per hour (cm^3)	
Period (h)	Porous pot	Maize leaves (per m^2)
7–9	3.8	91
9–11	6.6	160
11–13	8.1	218
13–15	9.5	248
15–17	9.4	195
17–19	9.0	179
19–21	6.6	124
21–23	3.8	8
23–1	3.4	18
1–3	1.5	18
3–5	0.7	13
5–7	0.9	23

Explain these results as fully as you can. *(O and C)*

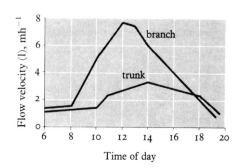

Figure 12.11 Changes in the linear velocity of flow of sap through the xylem in the trunk and in one of the small branches at the top of a tree.

6 (a) Explain fully how the properties of water molecules help to explain the passage of water up a tree.
(b) The linear velocity of flow of sap through the xylem of a tree was measured in $m\,h^{-1}$ in the trunk and in one of the small branches at the top of the tree. Measurements were taken at two-hourly intervals during a summer day. The results are shown in Figure 12.11.
(i) What difference would you expect in the circumference of the trunk measured at 1400 hours when compared with that measured at 1800 hours? Briefly explain your answer.
(ii) What light do these results shed on the mechanism by which water passes up the tree? *(JMB modified)*

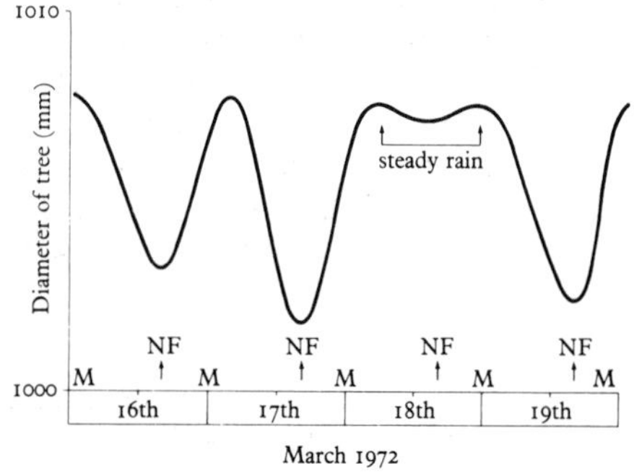

Figure 12.12 Changes in the diameter of the trunk of a large tree during the course of four days in March 1972. **M**, midnight; **NF**, nightfall.

7 Using very sensitive recording equipment, a scientist observed that the diameter of certain very large tree trunks changed from day to day. The graph in Figure 12.12 shows the results he obtained when he recorded the changes in one of these trunks over a period of about four days. What conclusions would you draw from his results? *(VU modified)*

8 Briefly explain each of the following phenomena:
(a) Stomata generally open during the day and close at night.
(b) There are generally fewer stomata on the upper side of a leaf than the lower side.
(c) When transplanting a plant it is advisable to remove some of the leaves.
(d) The stump of a severed tree trunk may exude copious quantities of fluid after cutting.
(e) On warm humid evenings water may be seen to drip from the edges of the leaves of certain plants.

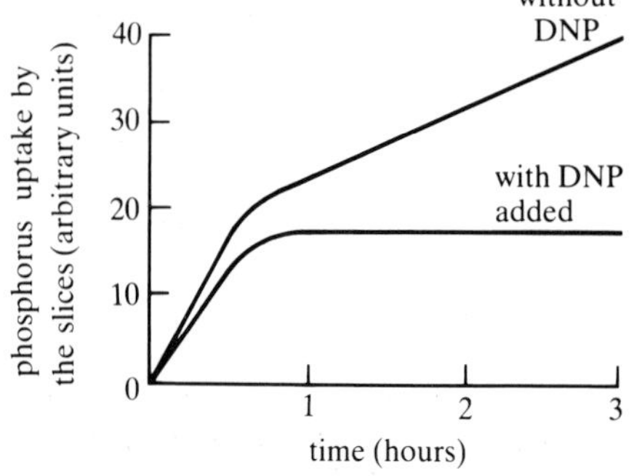

Figure 12.13 Graph showing the effect of dinitrophenol (DNP) on the uptake of phosphorus by slices of carrot.

9 Slices of storage root of carrot were washed in water for twenty-four hours. Two batches of slices were then taken; one was incubated in a mineral nutrient solution containing phosphate ions, the other in a similar solution to which dinitrophenol (DNP) had been added. DNP inhibits enzymes concerned in the synthesis of ATP. The phosphorus uptake by the slices was determined at intervals of time and the results are shown on the graph in Figure 12.13.
(a) What can be deduced from these results with respect to the process of phosphorus uptake by the slices?
(b) Suggest two conditions other than inhibitors which might produce an effect similar to the lower curve in Figure 12.13. Explain your answer. *(JMB Nuffield)*

10 A series of experiments was carried out to investigate the influence of temperature, oxygen concentration, and transpiration rate on the uptake of phosphate by barley plants. All plants, at a comparable level of development, were grown in a standard culture solution bubbled either with a constant stream of air or with an oxygen-nitrogen mixture. Unless otherwise stated, the temperature was 15 °C. The results are shown at the top of the next page.

Experiment 1
(bubbled with air)

Total phosphate uptake (μg per plant)	Temperature (°C)
10.1	0.0
14.0	5.0
20.6	10.0
29.6	15.0
43.0	20.0
60.2	25.0

Experiment 2
(bubbled with an oxygen–nitrogen mixture)

Total phosphate uptake (μg per plant)	Oxygen concentration in bubbles (%)
0.5	0.0
8.6	2.0
15.1	4.0
20.0	6.0
23.8	8.0
26.7	10.0
28.2	12.0
28.6	14.0
29.0	16.0
28.7	20.0

Experiment 3
(bubbled with air)

	Low humidity	High humidity
Mean transpiration rate in g per plant per 24 hours.	18.0	1.4
Total phosphate uptake μg per plant.	29.2	30.5

(a) Represent the data of experiments 1 and 2 graphically. State, giving reasons, what you conclude from these three experiments about the uptake of phosphorus.
(b) What other factors will influence the rate at which phosphate is absorbed by these plants? *(O and C)*

11 A ringing experiment is carried out in which a girdle of bark (corky cells plus phloem tissue) is removed from a woody stem, leaving only the xylem tissues connecting the upper and lower parts of the plant (Figure 12.14A).
(a) After a time the bark immediately above the ring develops the swollen appearance shown in Figure 12.14B. Put forward hypotheses to explain this phenomenon. How would you test your hypotheses?
(b) Eventually the plant dies. Explain in detail the reason why death occurs.

A Immediately after cutting the ring

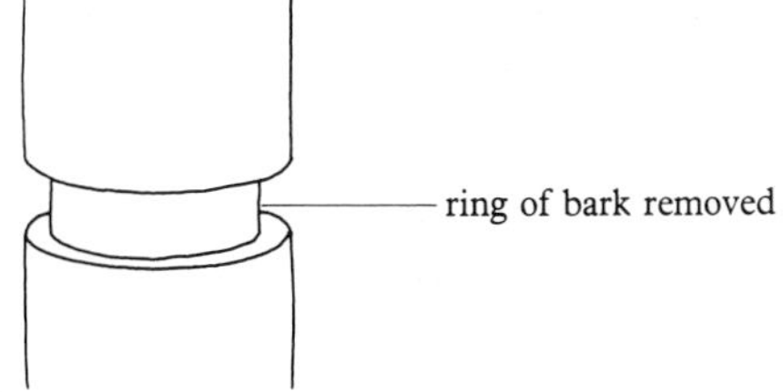

B Appearance later

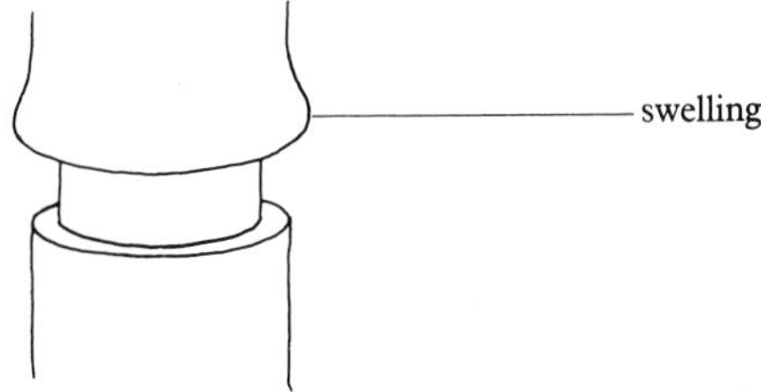

Figure 12.14 Ringing experiment on a woody stem.

12 Carbon dioxide whose normal carbon has been replaced by the radioactive isotope ^{14}C is introduced into a leaf half way up a bean plant from which all other leaves have been removed. Estimations of the distribution of the ^{14}C throughout the plant are made at five-minute, two-hour and ten-hour intervals from the start of the experiment.

The experiment is repeated with another similar plant from which a ring of tissue, including the phloem, has been removed just below the leaf. Both plants are exposed to full illumination throughout the experiments. What would you expect the distribution of the ^{14}C to be in each case? Explain your reasoning.

(Use arbitrary units adding up to 10 for the quantities of ^{14}C).

13 The following table shows the results of an experiment on the effects of phosphate fertiliser and mycorrhizal infection by a mutualistic fungus on the growth of tomato plants.

Relative phosphate level in soil	**Infection of plants by fungus** (%)	**Mean dry mass of plant** (g)	**Phosphate concentration in roots** (μmol per g)
0.25	91	3.9	62
0.25	0	0.8	33
0.5	82	3.8	68
0.5	0	1.3	25
1	77	3.4	93
1	0	1.2	36
2	64	4.8	140
2	0	3.6	26

(a) Under what circumstances is mycorrhizal infection most advantageous to tomato plants? Speculate on possible reasons for this.
(b) When might infection with the fungus be a *disadvantage* to the plants? *(OCJE)*

13 The Principles of Homeostasis

Background Summary

1 *'The constancy of the internal environment is the condition for free life.'* This principle was first enunciated by Claude Bernard in 1857. Maintenance of a constant internal environment is **homeostasis**.

2 By 'free life' is meant the ability of an organism to inhabit a wide range of environments.

3 The 'internal environment' is the immediate surroundings of the cells. In animals this consists of **tissue fluid** (also known as **intercellular** or **interstitial fluid**) which bathes the cells.

4 Tissue fluid consists of plasma minus proteins and is formed by ultra-filtration from the capillaries. Excess tissue fluid passes into **lymphatic vessels** where it constitutes **lymph**.

5 The following features of an animal's internal environment normally need to be kept constant:
(a) its chemical constituents, e.g. glucose, ions, etc.
(b) its osmotic pressure
(c) its carbon dioxide content
(d) its temperature.
Nitrogenous waste products and other toxic substances are usually eliminated altogether.

6 The principles of homeostasis can be illustrated by the control of blood sugar in the mammal. A rise in the sugar level results in the secretion of **insulin** from the islets of Langerhans in the pancreas and this brings about metabolic disposal of excess blood sugar in the liver. Failure of the pancreas to perform this function results in diabetes melitus.

7 In general homeostatic control processes work as follows: any deviation from the norm (**set point**) sets into motion the appropriate **corrective mechanisms** which restore the norm (**negative feedback**).

8 Various mechanisms help to minimise deviations from the set point, thereby dampening down fluctuations and improving the efficiency of the homeostatic system.

9 In certain circumstances a deviation from the norm may result in a further deviation (**positive feedback**).

10 One of the most important homeostatic organs in the body is the **liver**. Its homeostatic functions include the regulation of sugar, lipids and amino acids, elimination of haemoglobin from used red blood cells and the production of heat.

11 The structure of the liver, showing an intimate association between the liver cells, blood vessels and bile channels, is admirably adapted to perform its numerous functions.

Investigation 13.1
Microscopic structure of the pancreas

The pancreas is a gland with a dual function:
(1) It secretes digestive enzymes (which ones?) into the pancreatic duct which conveys them to the duodenum. In this capacity the pancreas is functioning as a ducted exocrine gland. The enzymes secreted by the exocrine portion of the gland play no direct part in the homeostatic control of blood sugar.
(2) It secretes the hormones insulin and glucagon into the bloodstream. In this capacity the pancreas is functioning as a ductless endocrine gland, or gland of internal secretion.

Knowing these two functions of the pancreas, can you make any predictions about its microscopic structure?

Procedure

1 Examine a section of pancreas under low power. The bulk of it is made up of numerous secretory cells, together with blood vessels and branches of the pancreatic duct (Figure 13.1A).

2 Go over to high power and notice that these secretory cells are arranged in small groups surrounding a narrow duct (Figure 13.1B). This unit of structure is called an acinus.[1] As well as having prominent nuclei, the cells have a highly granular cytoplasm indicative of their secretory function. They secrete digestive enzymes and represent the exocrine portion of the pancreas.

3 Return to low power and notice that here and there amongst the cells mentioned above are bunches of cells that look different from the rest. These are the islets of Langerhans; a typical section might show about six islets.

[1] The term acinus can be applied to any exocrine gland. It is a group of secretory cells associated with a branch of the duct.

Three features should enable you to pick them out:

(a) They are generally stained differently from the rest of the pancreas; for example in a section stained with haematoxylin and eosin (*see* page 379) the cytoplasm of the islet cells is a lighter pink than the surrounding enzyme-secreting cells.

(b) The islet cells are arranged differently from the enzyme-secreting cells: in irregular chains rather than small groups (Figure 13.4C).

(c) The diameter of a typical islet is approximately 200 μm (0.2 mm), 6–8 times that of a group of enzyme-secreting cells.

The islets of Langerhans secrete the hormones insulin and glucagon and represent the endocrine portion of the pancreas.

4 Examine an islet of Langerhans under high power (Figure 13.1C). Notice irregular chains of hormone-secreting cells with lightly-stained cytoplasm and prominent nuclei. Between the chains of secretory cells are capillaries lined with pavement endothelium: flattened nuclei of endothelial cells will be seen in places.

5 In suitably stained preparations two different kinds of secretory cell may be detected in the islets of Langerhans: β cells which secrete insulin and α cells which secrete glucagon. The β cells are the more numerous of the two and fill the interior of the islet; the α cells are fewer, larger, more densely stained and occur in the peripheral part of the islet.

6 In examining an islet of Langerhans notice particularly the intimate association between the hormone-secreting cells and capillaries, a basic requirement of any endocrine organ.

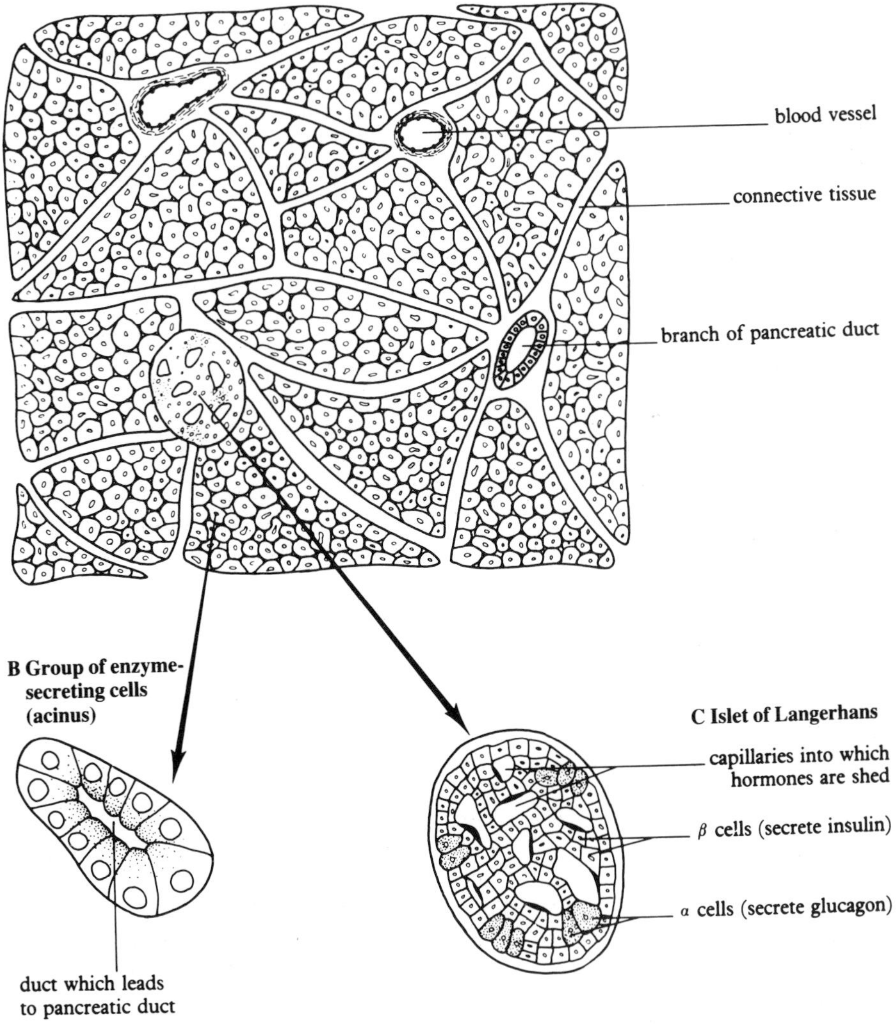

Figure 13.1 Microscopic structure of the pancreas. The β cells secrete insulin. The α cells secrete glucagon, a hormone whose actions are the opposite of those produced by insulin.

For consideration

(1) How is the microscopic structure of the pancreas adapted to perform its particular functions? Remember to include its exocrine as well as its endocrine functions.

(2) Homeostatic mechanisms can be analysed in terms of receptors, control mechanisms and effectors. How does the pancreas fit into such a scheme?

(3) If you were to examine a section through an islet of Langerhans in the electron microscope, what special features would you expect to see?

Requirements

Microscope

Section of pancreas (haematoxylin and eosin will do)

If available, section of pancreas stained with e.g. aldehyde fuchsin to show alpha and beta cells

Investigation 13.2
Microscopic structure of the liver

The liver has many functions of which we can single out two principal ones:
(1) It secretes bile into the bile duct which carries it via the gall bladder to the duodenum. Bile plays no direct part in the control of blood sugar, but it is associated with certain other homeostatic functions (which?).
(2) It regulates the amounts of blood sugar, lipids and amino acids by removing them from the bloodstream or adding them to it, as appropriate.

Knowing these two general functions of the liver, can you make any predictions about its microscopic structure?

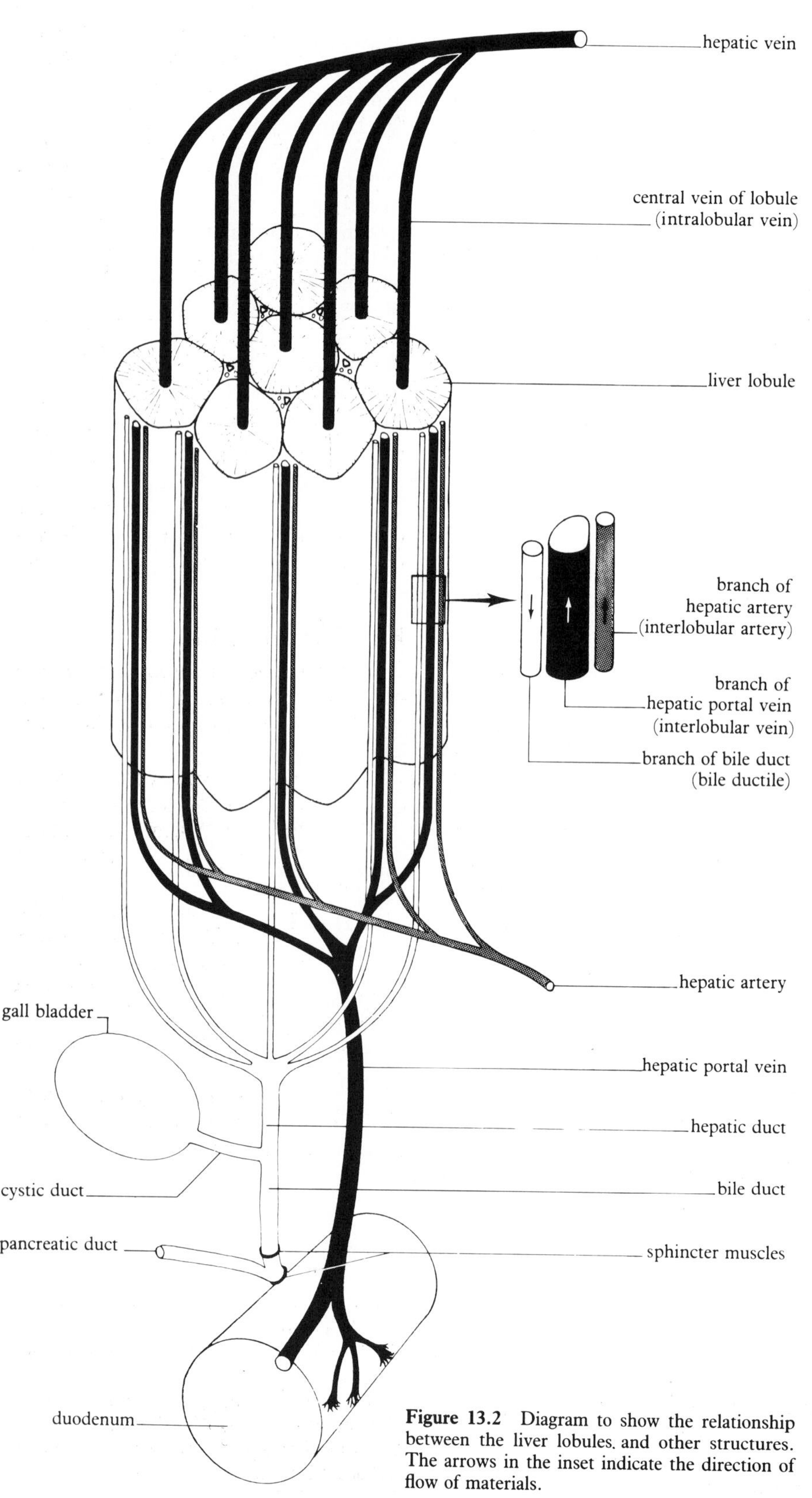

Figure 13.2 Diagram to show the relationship between the liver lobules. and other structures. The arrows in the inset indicate the direction of flow of materials.

Procedure

Before examining it, recall that the liver receives a dual blood supply: oxygenated blood is taken to it via the hepatic artery, blood rich in food substances via the hepatic portal vein from the gut (*see* page 80). Blood is drained from the liver via the hepatic vein (Figure 13.2).

1 Examine a transverse section of liver under low power (Figure 13.3A). You will see it to consist of numerous closely packed lobules, each roughly 1.0 mm in diameter. A lobule is composed of radiating rows of cells arranged round a central (intralobular) vein, a tributary of the hepatic vein. In pig's liver the lobules are completely encased in connective tissue and can therefore be easily distinguished from each other. In the livers of most other mammals connective tissue is confined to the corners of the lobules.

2 Now look at the edges of the lobules: here, wedged between one lobule and the next, are various tubes cut in cross-section. In good sections they can be identified by their size and walls when viewed under high power (Figure 13.3B):
(a) Interlobular vein (branch of hepatic portal vein): large lumen, thin endothelial lining.
(b) Interlobular artery (branch of hepatic artery): much smaller lumen, thicker walls.
(c) Bile ductile (branch of bile duct): intermediate in size between (a) and (b), lining of cuboidal or columnar epithelium.
Blood cells may be seen in (a) and (b).

3 Now examine the radiating rows of cells inside one of the lobules under high power (Figure 13.3C). These are the liver cells, each row comprising a liver cord. Notice that the liver cells are of a regular cuboidal shape, have prominent nuclei and granular cytoplasm. Glycogen droplets may be seen in suitably stained sections.

4 Between the liver cords are clearly visible channels: these are sinusoids, small capillaries which connect the

A Transverse section showing four complete lobules

connective tissue capsule surrounding lobule (pig only)

one complete lobule in TS (about 1 mm diameter)

central (intralobular) vein

liver cells and associated structures

interlobular artery, vein and bile ductile

B Edge of lobule

interlobular vein

interlobular artery

bile ductile

connective tissue

C Centre of lobule

central (intralobular) vein

nucleus of endothelial cell lining sinusoid

sinusoid (blood channel)

row of liver cells (liver cord)

canaliculus (bile canal)

Figure 13.3 Microscopic structure of the liver.

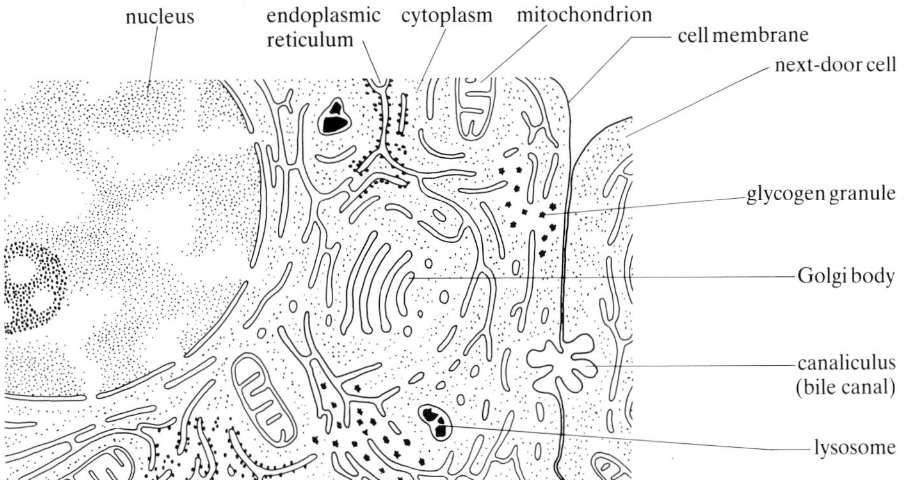

Figure 13.4 Part of a liver cell as seen in the electron microscope.

interlobular arteries and veins at the edge of the lobule with the intralobular vein in the centre. Blood flows from the former to the latter via the sinusoids and in so doing comes into close association with all the liver cells.

The sinusoids are lined with pavement endothelium whose flattened nuclei may be visible in places. Phagocytic Kupffer cells may be seen.

5 Where would you expect to see canaliculi (bile canals)? If you are not sure, look at Figure 13.3C. Can you see any in your section? They are narrow intercellular spaces between the liver cells; they do not have an epithelial lining and are difficult to see under the light microscope.

6 Examine an electron micrograph of a section through two adjacent liver cells. Look for canaliculi between the cells. From the magnification of the micrograph, work out the widest diameter of the canaliculus. Using Figure 13.4 to help you, identify other structures in the micrograph, particularly glycogen granules. These are characteristically star-shaped in electron micrographs.

For Consideration

(1) How is the microscopic structure of (a) the pancreas and (b) the liver adapted to perform its particular functions?

(2) Homeostatic mechanisms can be analysed in terms of receptors (detectors), control mechanisms and effectors. How do the pancreas and liver fit into such a scheme?

(3) The basic functional unit of the liver is the lobule. But in most exocrine glands the basic functional unit is an acinus, i.e. a branch of the duct and its associated secretory cells. Bearing this in mind, what comprises an acinus in the liver?

(4) Do you think it is right to regard the liver as an exocrine gland? Is this an adequate description of it?

Requirements

TS liver (haemalum and Van Gieson's stain recommended)

If available, TS liver stained for glycogen by periodic-acid Schiff technique

Electron micrograph of section through two adjacent liver cells

Questions and Problems

1 Compare and contrast the composition of blood, tissue fluid, and lymph. How would you explain their similarities and differences?

2 (a) How many biological and non-biological situations can you think of that involve control by feedback mechanisms?
(b) What do you understand by an *efficient* homeostatic process? In physiological circumstances homeostatic processes involve the use of a receptor, control centre, and effector. Discuss the extent to which shortcomings in these three components can influence the efficiency of the overall process.

3 (a) When a speech is made using a public address system a howl is sometimes heard from the loudspeakers. How would you explain this? Draw an analogy between this and events that sometimes occur in biological situations.
(b) Imagine that the mechanism which initiates the human body's cooling processes (sweating, etc.) breaks down completely. Under these circumstances what will be the result of the body temperature being raised by 2 °C?

4 What physiological events would you expect to follow the injection of a small quantity of glucose into the bloodstream of a healthy mammal? What would be the result of injecting glucose into the bloodstream of a pancreatectomised animal, i.e. one from which the pancreas had been removed?

5 Discuss the possible circumstances in which:
(a) more blood sugar may be found in the hepatic portal vein than in any other vessel,
(b) more blood sugar may be found in the hepatic vein than in the hepatic portal vein;
(c) the blood sugar level in the general bloodstream may depart dangerously from the normal;
(d) sugar is present in the urine. (*O and C modified*)

6 (a) Make a list of the effects on the body's homeostatic mechanisms of surgically removing the whole of the liver.
(b) Under experimental conditions removal of the liver from a mammal results in an increase in the amounts of amino acids in the blood and the absence of urea. Discuss possible reasons for this and suggest further experiments which might be carried out to test your explanations. (*O and C modified*)

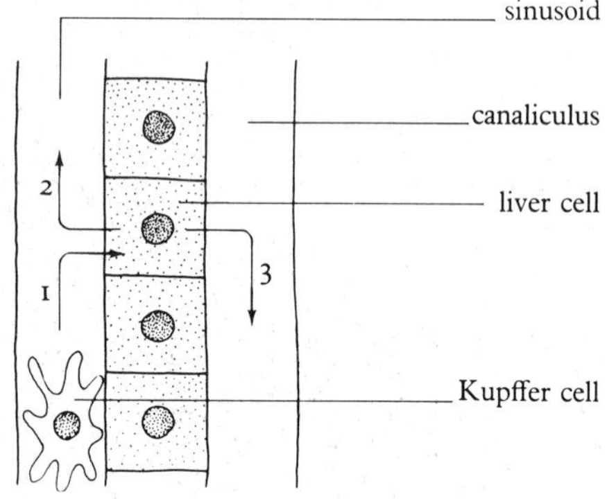

Figure 13.5 Diagram showing the relationship between cells and channels in a mammalian liver lobule.

7 Figure 13.5 shows highly magnified the relationship between cells and channels as seen in a transverse section of a mammalian liver lobule:
(a) The sinusoid contains blood; what vessels does the blood come from and what vessel does it drain into?
(b) What enters the liver cells from the blood in the sinusoid (arrow 1)?
(c) What is shed into the sinusoid from the liver cells (arrow 2)?
(d) What is shed into the canaliculus from the liver cells (arrow 3)?
(e) What function is performed by the Kupffer cells?

8 Read the following passage which describes the way insulin was discovered.

In October 1920, Banting conceived his Great Idea. He had read that blockage of the pancreatic ducts led to degeneration of the trypsin-producing tissue but not the islet tissue of the gland. Lack of a hypothetical islet tissue secretion (insulin) was supposed to cause diabetes and many workers had tried to treat this with pancreatic extracts. It was suggested that their failure was due to the destruction of the 'insulin' by the trypsin of the pancreas during extraction. Banting's Great Idea was that this could be avoided by ligating the ducts in a dog, waiting for some weeks for the gland to degenerate, and then removing the remaining islet tissue, and extracting the insulin.

Frederick Banting was a rough, tough young Canadian, aged 29, who was struggling to make a living as a small town GP when his idea struck him with all the force of a religious revelation. Ignorant of research methods, he took it to J.J.R. Macleod, professor of physiology in Toronto, an expert on sugar metabolism. Macleod knew that Banting's idea was not original, but new techniques had appeared and his enthusiasm might produce something of interest.

So in May 1921, Macleod gave him laboratory space, a student assistant (Charles Best), and six weeks to get results. He planned Banting's experiments and showed him how to operate on dogs. After a month he went on holiday to Scotland. Banting and Best struggled on in sweltering heat, and produced some depancreatised diabetic dogs and some with ligated ducts to be used for insulin extracts. Then came the first experiments, and the extracts did reduce the high blood sugar levels in the diabetic dogs. Banting and Best were jubilant. The idea was working! But a control experiment using an extract of normal pancreas worked just as well.

Astonishingly, they refused to accept the evidence and reported the result as poor. (How often have research workers put some cherished idea above the facts of Nature!) Then Banting had another idea – also at 2 am. Why not use fetal pancreas, in which trypsin production had not yet developed? Sure enough, extracts of fetal calf pancreas worked beautifully.

Meanwhile, Macleod had returned to find his young protégés triumphant. He planned further experiments and it finally emerged that extracts of normal, adult pancreas worked perfectly well. The protracted, laborious and chancy method imposed by Banting's idea was unnecessary, and was, in fact, based on a fallacy. The normal pancreas contains not active trypsin but an inactive precursor with no effect on insulin. Success was really due to the extraction with cold alcohol suggested by Macleod.

Banting, in the excitement of the progress, was unaware that his idea had been exploded, and remained certain that it was the keystone of the work. It was his blind faith in it that had indeed started the research and sustained its momentum. Thus he failed to recognise the essential contributions of Macleod, and of J.B. Collip, the biochemist who produced the first clinically usable preparations of insulin.

(From G. Macfarlane, 'Right for the wrong reason', *New Scientist*, 10 May, 1984)

Discuss this passage with particular reference to (a) the importance of controls in scientific investigation, and (b) the use, and abuse, of the scientific method.

9 Figure 13.6 is an electron micrograph of a section through part of two adjacent liver cells.
   (a) Make a rough sketch of the micrograph, showing and labelling the following structures: cell membrane, canaliculus, glycogen granule, mitochondrion, lysosome.
   (b) Name one organelle, not listed above, which you would expect to be present in a liver cell. State its function as precisely as possible.
   (c) Numerous mitochondria are visible in the micrograph. Suggest one specific hepatic function for which they would be required and explain their role in enabling the liver to fulfil this function.

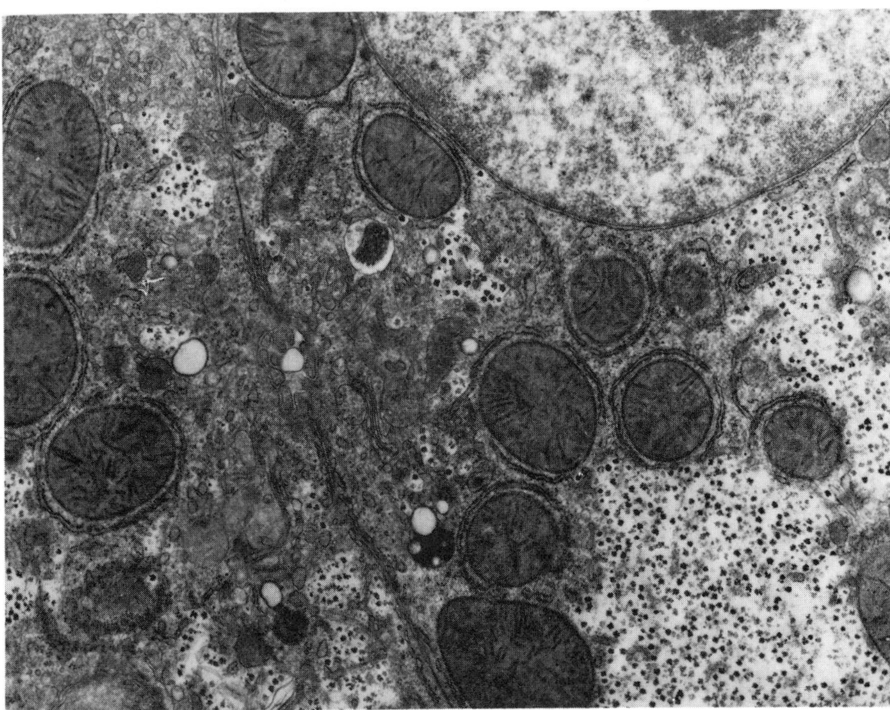

Figure 13.6 Electron micrograph of a section through part of two adjacent liver cells.

14 Excretion and osmoregulation

Background Summary

1 **Excretion** is the removal from the body of the waste products of metabolism: these are predominantly nitrogenous compounds. **Osmoregulation** is the process by which the osmotic pressure of the blood and tissue fluids is kept constant.

2 In the mammal both functions are performed by the **kidney**, the basic unit of which is the **nephron**. Plasma minus protein passes from the blood vessels of the **glomerulus** into the cavity of Bowman's capsule. Some of the constituents of the glomerular filtrate are then selectively reabsorbed across the walls of the **tubules** into the bloodstream. The remaining renal fluid passes into the ureter, whence it passes to the bladder.

3 The blood pressure in the glomerulus, and the fine structure of the barrier between the glomerular capillaries and cavity of Bowman's capsule, are consistent with the view that renal fluid is formed by **ultra-filtration**.

4 Analyses of renal fluid at different points along the tubules in the frog indicates that water and glucose are selectively reabsorbed in the proximal convoluted tubule, chloride in the distal tubule. Urea is eliminated altogether and is actively secreted into the proximal tubule from the surrounding blood vessels.

5 Comparable experiments on the mammalian kidney suggest that in mammals chloride, as well as water, glucose and amino acids, are reabsorbed in the proximal tubule. Over two thirds of the water in the glomerular filtrate is reabsorbed in the proximal tubule. Urea is actively secreted into the tubule.

6 Evidence suggests that water is reabsorbed mainly by osmosis, glucose and salts by diffusion and active transport. There is a close association between the epithelium of the tubule and capillaries, and the fine structure of the tubule epithelial cells is consistent with their function of active absorption.

7 Further water is reabsorbed from the **collecting ducts** by the high osmotic pressure in the medullary region of the kidney. This high osmotic pressure is achieved by the loop of Henle conserving salts on the principle of a **hair-pin countercurrent multiplier**.

8 Reabsorption of water by the kidney is controlled homeostatically by the osmotic pressure of the blood acting through the intermediacy of **anti-diuretic hormone** (**ADH**, also known as vasopressin) secreted by the posterior lobe of the **pituitary gland**. In conditions of high internal osmotic pressure ADH causes retention of water by the kidney.

9 The body fluids of **marine invertebrates** are isotonic with sea water and such animals have no osmoregulatory devices.

10 **Freshwater and estuarine animals**, including freshwater fishes, counter the osmotic influx of water that inevitably results from their internal osmotic pressure (OPi) being greater than the external osmotic pressure (OPe) by eliminating excess water and actively taking up salts from the external medium.

11 In **marine vertebrates** OPi is less than OPe. Such animals counter the resulting osmotic outflux of water by eliminating excess salts and retaining water.

12 **Migratory fishes** (salmon, eel) present a special problem since in the course of their life cycle they move from one extreme of aquatic environment to the other (fresh water to sea water, and vice versa). **Intertidal** and **brackish-water animals** also face the problem of an ever-changing osmotic environment.

13 **Terrestrial animals** are liable to water loss by evaporation. They possess a variety of structural and physiological techniques for preventing excessive water loss.

14 A variety of water-conservation devices, equivalent to those seen in animals, have been developed by plants, particularly **xerophytes** and **halophytes**.

15 **Ionic regulation** in animals is achieved by hormones which regulate the uptake of ions in the gut and their elimination by the kidneys. In plants ionic regulation is carried out mainly by selective absorption and elimination by individual cells.

16 In animals **acid-base balance**, and hence pH, is controlled by elimination of carbon dioxide by the lungs, the buffering action of the blood, and elimination of hydrogen ions by the kidneys.

Investigation 14.1
Examination of the mammalian kidney

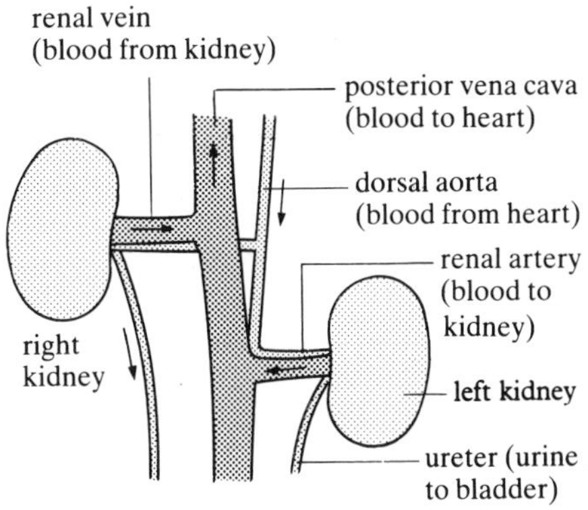

renal vein
(blood from kidney)
posterior vena cava
(blood to heart)
dorsal aorta
(blood from heart)
renal artery
(blood to
kidney)
right
kidney
left kidney
ureter (urine
to bladder)

Figure 14.1 Kidneys and their blood supply *in situ* (rat).

Requirements
Binocular microscope
Enamel dish
Syringe (2 cm^3)
Syringe (5 cm^3)
Thread

Sodium chloride solution (1.0 per cent)
Warm latex solutions (yellow, red and blue)

Rat for dissection (demonstration dissection showing kidneys ureters and blood supply will do)
2 Fresh kidneys from butcher (one should be lamb's kidney still encased in fat with connecting blood vessels and ureter in place – ask the butcher not to slice through the kidney)

The kidney is the mammal's principal organ of excretion and osmoregulation. It performs these functions by 'purifying' the blood that flows through it. The blood is first filtered to form renal fluid. Useful substances are reabsorbed back from the renal fluid into the bloodstream, while unwanted substances are eliminated as urine.

In this investigation we shall look at the coarse structure of the kidney and its associated structures.

Procedure

1 Look at a dissected rat (or other mammal, *see* page 81), note that the kidneys are asymmetrically disposed towards the anterior end of the abdominal cavity (Figure 14.1).

2 Observe the good blood supply: renal artery bringing blood to the kidney from the dorsal aorta runs close to the larger, thinner-walled, renal vein, which takes blood from the kidney to the posterior vena cava.

3 Locate the thin thread-like ureter which leads from the indented inner side of the kidney to the bladder. The route by which urine passes from the bladder to the exterior is dealt with on page 228.

4 Fill a 2 cm^3 syringe with warm yellow latex, then put on the needle. Press the plunger of the syringe until one drop of latex emerges. Insert the needle into the kidney horizontally until its tip reaches the pelvis (see below). Press gently on the plunger of the syringe and watch the latex flowing down the ureter into the bladder.

5 Remove a kidney from the body (or use a kidney of pig, sheep or cow from the butcher). Slice through the kidney horizontally (Figure 14.2) and notice: light-coloured cortex towards the outside, darker medulla towards the inside, much blood, pyramids (onto which open the collecting ducts), pelvis.

The pelvis is the cavity where the urine collects before flowing down the ureter to the bladder.

6 Obtain a fresh lamb's kidney from the butcher, still enclosed in fat. Remove the fat, taking care not to damage the ureter, renal artery or vein. Inject the kidney with latex, using the following technique:

Gently massage the kidney in warm saline (1 per cent salt solution) so as to empty the vessels of their contents. Using separate 5 cm^3 syringes, inject
(a) the ureter with warm yellow latex, then tie a thread round it,
(b) the renal artery with warm red latex, then tie a thread round it,

Allow the latex to cool. As it does so it will harden like rubber.

7 Slice your injected kidney horizontally with a sharp razor blade. Observe the distribution of the latex. The yellow latex should have filled the pelvis and collecting ducts, the red latex the arteries and the blue latex the veins. Examine thin slices under a binocular microscope.

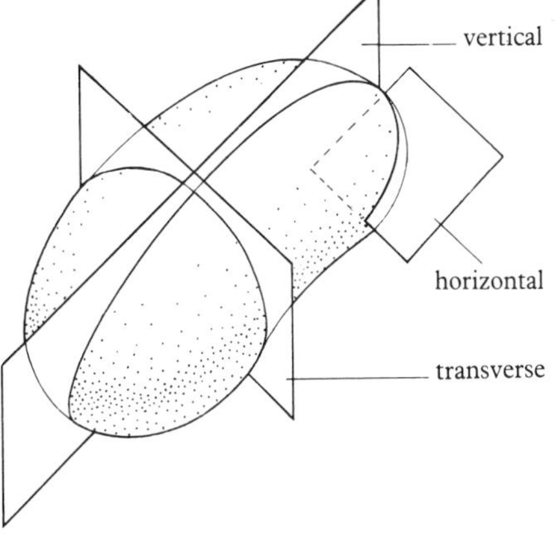

Figure 14.2 Whole kidney showing the different planes in which it may be sectioned.

For consideration

(1) What can you say about the pattern of collecting ducts in the kidney? What is their role in the overall functioning of the kidney?
(2) How could you use the latex-injection technique to estimate the total length of blood vessels in the kidney?

Investigation 14.2
Microscopic structure of the mammalian kidney

The formation and processing of renal fluid are carried out by the nephrons, of which each kidney in a human contains about 1.5 million. Each nephron consists of a Bowman's capsule containing a bundle of capillaries called the glomerulus, and a long differentiated tubule which leads to a collecting duct. (Bowman's capsule and glomerulus together comprise a Malpighian corpuscle).

Blood is filtered across the walls of the glomerular capillaries into the cavity of Bowman's capsule (capsular space). The glomerular filtrate, (renal fluid), consists of plasma minus proteins. As the renal fluid flows along the tubule of the nephron useful substances are selectively reabsorbed back into the bloodstream, whilst harmful substances that escaped filtration are secreted from the blood into the tubule.

Obviously, to achieve this, there must be a close association between the nephron and its blood supply. Bear this in mind as you look at the microscopic structure of the kidney.

Procedure

Examine a prepared horizontal or transverse section of mammalian kidney. First hold it up to the light and examine it under a lens and note the demarcation between cortex and medulla.

Figure 14.3 shows on a distorted scale how the nephrons and collecting ducts are disposed relative to the cortex and medulla. Have this diagram in mind as you look at the cortex and medulla under the microscope.

Figure 14.3 Horizontal section showing the positions of the nephrons and associated structures.

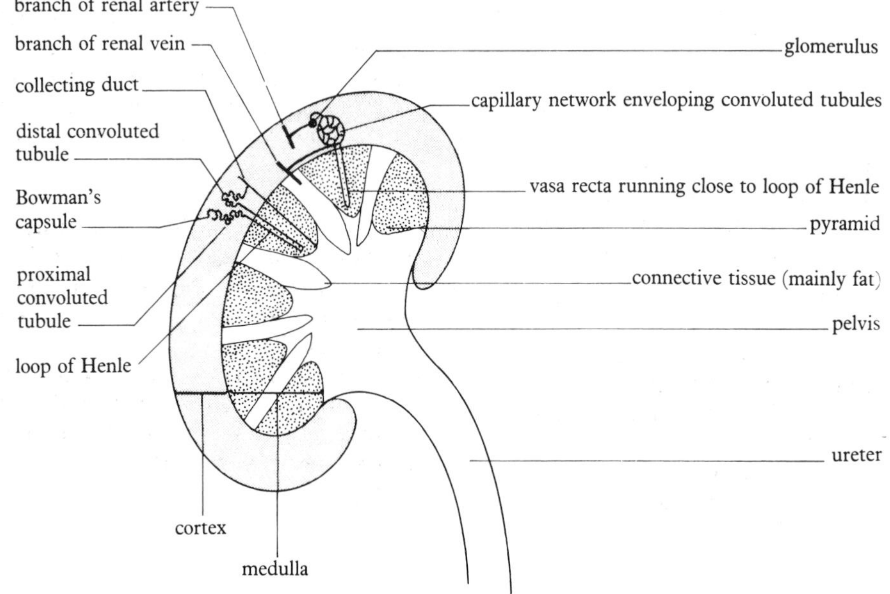

CORTEX

1 Examine the cortex under low power. Notice that it contains Bowman's capsules, numerous tubules in section, and capillaries.

2 Examine several capsules under high power. Select one that most resembles Figure 14.4A in its general appearance. The capsule contains a glomerulus and you may see afferent and efferent arterioles which take blood to and from it. Notice the gap between the bunch of glomerular capillaries and the outer epithelium of the capsule: this is the capsular space into which blood is filtered to form renal fluid. The renal fluid then passes along the tubules and so eventually to the collecting ducts.

3 The tubular structures visible in a section of the cortex are a mixture of proximal and distal convoluted tubules and collecting ducts (Figure 14.4B). The three can be distinguished as follows:

Proximal tubule:
outer diameter about 60 μm,
large lining cells,
cell membranes between adjacent cells not visible,
relatively few nuclei visible in cross section of tubule,
small irregular lumen,
brush border,
three times as long as distal tubule so more plentiful in section.

Distal tubule:
outer diameter 20–50 μm,
smaller lining cells,
cell membranes between adjacent cells not visible,
more nuclei visible in cross section of tubule,
large regular lumen,
no brush border visible,
shorter than proximal tubule so less plentiful in section.

Collecting duct:
outer diameter 25–60 μm,
wall similar to distal convoluted tubule except that cell membranes between adjacent cells are clearly visible.

4 Pay special attention to the proximal tubule, particularly its brush border (function?) and its proximity to capillaries. What blood vessels are the capillaries derived from?

A Bowman's capsule and glomerulus (Malpighian corpuscle)

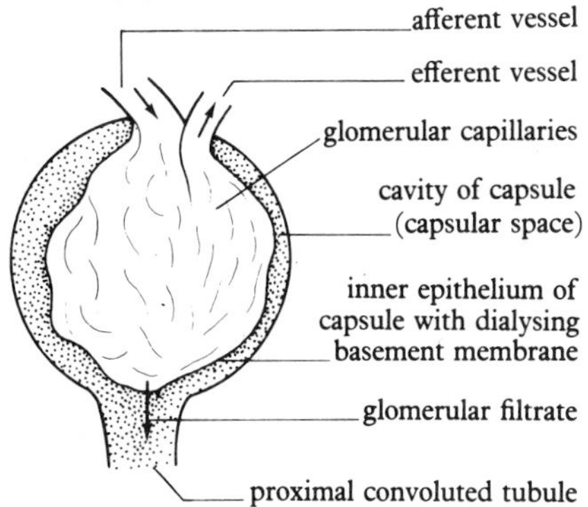

B Tubules and capillaries in cortex

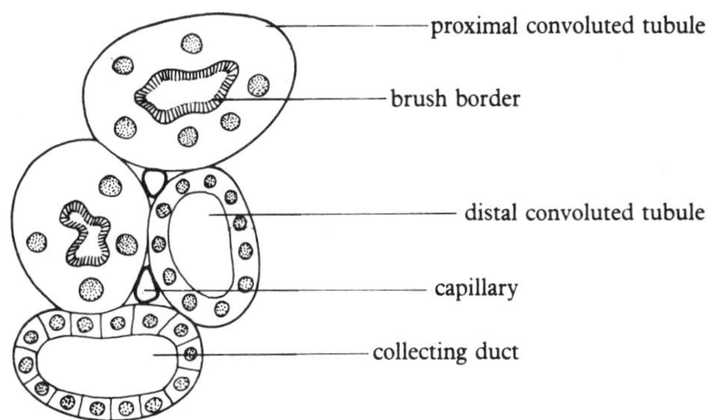

C Tubules and capillaries in medulla

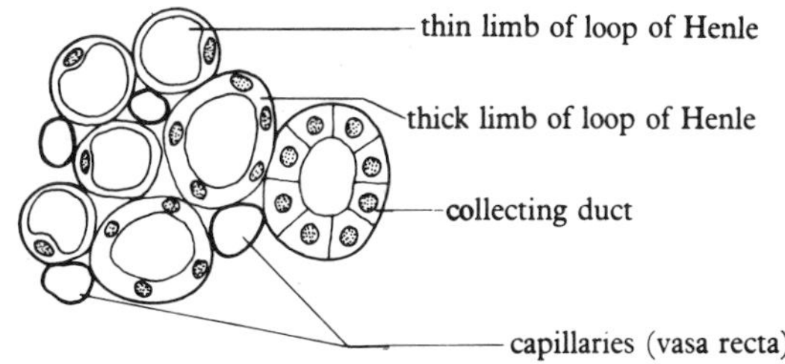

Figure 14.4 Microscopic structure of the kidney. The Malpighian corpuscle is idealised; rarely would a section pass through the afferent and efferent vessels *and* the proximal tubule.

Requirements
Microscope

TS or HS kidney
Section of injected kidney

MEDULLA

1 Now examine the medulla under high power. This part of the kidney contains the loops of Henle which connect the proximal with the distal convoluted tubule. Notice the descending and ascending limbs of the loops of Henle and the long straight capillaries, vasa recta, running parallel with them. They are shown in transverse section in Figure 14.4C. Why are the tubules and blood vessels long and straight in this part of the kidney?

2 Descending and ascending limbs and collecting ducts can be distinguished as follows:

Descending limb: (except the lowest third)
outer diameter 14–20 μm,
lining of thin pavement epithelium,
nuclei flattened and bulging into lumen; (known as thin limb).

Ascending limb: (plus lowest third of descending limb)
outer diameter 30–35 μm,
lining of cuboidal epithelium,
cell membranes between adjacent cells not visible,
rounded nuclei,
(known as thick limb).

Collecting duct:
outer diameter 50–200 μm,
lining cells cuboidal to columnar,
cell membranes between adjacent cells clearly visible,
rounded nuclei.

N.B. The wall of the thin limb is confusingly similar to that of the capillaries (vasa recta). However, the capillaries can usually be distinguished by the fact that they contain red blood cells.

3 To appreciate the vascular nature of the kidney examine a section in which the blood vessels have been injected. In particular notice the vasa recta and the intimate association between the proximal convoluted tubule and capillaries.

For Consideration

(1) In what respects is the structure of the kidney, *as you have observed it in this investigation*, adapted to perform its functions of excretion and osmoregulation?

(2) From a study of single transverse and horizontal sections, how could you make a rough estimate of the number of Malpighian corpuscles in the entire kidney?

Investigation 14.3
Variation in the concentration of chloride in urine

> **CAUTION:**
> Because of the risk of infection you should use only your own urine for this investigation. Do not touch anyone else's urine.

Requirements
Large test tubes (with stoppers) ×2 (for urine samples)
Labels
Burette (25 cm^3)
Pipette (2 cm^3)
Pipette (10 cm^3)
Porcelain bowls ×2
Glass rod

Methylbenzene
Silver nitrate (50 cm^3, 0.1 mol dm^{-3})
50 per cent v/v nitric acid)
Potassium thiocyanate (50 cm^3, 0.1 mol dm^{-3})
Ammonium iron (III) sulphate (iron alum)

One of the kidney's functions is to regulate the osmotic pressure of the blood and tissue fluids. It does this by selectively eliminating varying amounts of water and salts depending on their levels in the body. In this investigation you will estimate the quantity of chloride in the urine in different conditions.

Method

The method involves reacting the chloride present in the urine sample with a known quantity of silver nitrate, and then titrating the unprecipitated silver nitrate (i.e. the silver nitrate which has not been used up in the reaction) against potassium thiocyanate. From this the amount of chloride in the urine sample can be calculated.

The reactions are as follows:

(1) Chloride in the urine sample reacts with silver nitrate, forming a white precipitate of silver chloride:

$$NaCl + AgNO_3 \rightarrow NaNO_3 + AgCl$$

(2) Potassium thiocyanate from the burette reacts with unprecipitated silver nitrate, forming a white precipitate of silver thiocyanate:

$$KCNS + AgNO_3 \rightarrow KNO_3 + AgCNS$$

(3) The first excess drop of potassium thiocyanate reacts with iron(III)sulphate (indicator), forming red iron(III) thiocyanate:

$$Fe^{3+}(\text{sulphate}) + KCNS \rightarrow FeCNS + K(\text{sulphate})$$

Collecting the Urine Samples

This should be done before the laboratory session. You will need two large test tubes with stoppers.

1. Urinate about an hour before a meal. With your meal consume plenty of salt but no water.
2. One hour later collect a sample of your urine in one of the tubes: at least 5 cm^3 are required. Label this sample 'fed urine'.
3. Now drink as much water as possible.
4. One hour later collect a further urine sample in the second tube. Label this 'watered urine'.
5. Add 2–3 drops of methylbenzene to each specimen to prevent bacterial action.

Laboratory Procedure

1. Measure fed urine (2 cm^3) into a porcelain bowl. Add silver nitrate solution (10 cm^3), stirring well with a glass rod. Any chloride in the urine produces a white precipitate of silver chloride.
2. Allow the mixture to stand for five minutes to ensure maximum coagulation of the precipitate.
3. Add a small spatula-end of iron(III) sulphate, the indicator. Titrate any unprecipitated silver with 0.1 mol dm^{-3} potassium thiocyanate from a burette: run the thiocyanate in carefully, stirring gently all the time until a red colour, permanent for 15 seconds, is produced.
4. Repeat with another 2 cm^3 sample of fed urine. Then do the same for your watered urine. In each case make a note of the volume of thiocyanate required to produce the red colour.

Calculation

From your readings calculate the quantity of chloride in fed and watered urine. In each case express your result as mg chloride per 100 cm^3 urine. The calculation is carried out as follows:

Suppose the volume of potassium thiocyanate (KCNS) required to precipitate the unused silver nitrate ($AgNO_3$) is x cm^3.

This is equivalent to x cm^3 $AgNO_3$ since both are 0.1 mol dm^{-3} solutions.

Then $10 - x$ cm^3 $AgNO_3$ has been precipitated by the chloride in 2.0 cm^3 urine.

Now 1000 cm^3 mol dm^{-3} $AgNO_3$ is equivalent to 35.5 g chloride.

Therefore 1.0 cm^3 mol dm^{-3} $AgNO_3$ is equivalent to $\frac{35.5}{1000}$ g chloride, and 1.0 cm^3 0.1 mol dm^{-3} $AgNO_3$ is equivalent to $\frac{35.5}{1000} \times \frac{1}{10}$ g chloride.

So $10 - x$ cm^3 0.1 mol dm^{-3} $AgNO_3$ is equivalent to $\frac{35.5}{1000} \times \frac{1}{10} \times (10 - x)$ g chloride.

This is the amount of chloride in 2.0 cm^3 urine. Convert to mg per 100 cm^3.

For Consideration

(1) Compare your results for fed and watered urine and explain the difference between them in terms of the functioning of the kidney.

(2) Suppose that samples of your blood had been taken at the same time as your two urine samples. What would you expect the chloride content of the blood samples to be? Explain why.

Investigation 14.4
Action of the contractile vacuole of a protist

The contractile vacuole, found in unicellular organisms, is a comparatively simple osmoregulatory device. As quickly as it enters by osmosis, water is collected into the vacuole, which swells and, when full, discharges its contents through a temporary pore in the cell membrane.

If the function of the contractile vacuole is to eliminate excess water from the cell, it stands to reason that decreasing the solute concentration of the external medium should increase the activity of the contractile vacuole, and increasing the solute concentration of the medium should decrease the activity of the contractile vacuole. In this investigation we will test this prediction. For convenience we shall examine the action of the contractile vacuole in the suctorian *Podophrya*.

THE ORGANISM

Podophrya is a ciliate, but it only possesses cilia in the juvenile (larval) stage. The free-swimming ciliated larva settles down and develops into a non-ciliated, sessile adult. The adult suctorian (Figure 14.5), has a 'body' with a single nucleus. It has a non-contractile stalk by which it is attached to the substratum, and an array of tentacles with sucker-like ends with which it catches prey. If, for example, *Paramecium* touches the tentacles it is held by the suckers and its contents are absorbed (via the tentacles) into the suctorian's body.

Podophrya lends itself well to studies on the contractile vacuole. The two contractile vacuoles, easily identified from their glistening appearance, discharge relatively frequently while the organism, being sessile, will remain steady under the microscope.

Procedure

1 Place two small squares of filter paper on a clean slide as indicated in Figure 14.6. Saturate each piece with *Podophrya* culture solution and fill the area between them with the same solution. The purpose of the filter paper is to support the coverslip and provide a reservoir of solution.

2 With small forceps transfer a short piece of silk thread which has *Podophrya* attached to it into the culture solution between the filter-paper squares. Now put on a coverslip so that it rests on the two pieces of filter paper.

3 Examine your slide under medium power of a microscope, arranging the illumination in such a way that there is no chance of the temperature of the *Podophrya* increasing. (N.B. Avoid using a microscope with a substage lamp).

4 Locate *Podophrya* attached to the silk thread, and identify a contractile vacuole under high power. Focus on the contractile vacuole and keep watching it for at least five minutes. Can you learn anything about the mechanism of discharge from your observations?

5 By observing the contractile vacuole over a period of time, estimate its frequency of discharge. While you are doing this keep the filter paper saturated with culture solution.

Requirements

Filter paper (preferably strips about 15 mm wide)
Fine pipette
Small forceps
Slide and coverslip
Microscope and lamp (*not* substage illumination)
Micrometer eyepiece or transparent ruler
Fine cotton thread

Distilled water
Sucrose solutions (0.05, 0.1 and 0.5 mol dm^{-3})

Podophrya on silk thread in culture solution

Prepare *Podophrya* as follows: Tease out short *fine* fibres from a small piece of undyed silk fabric and float on surface of *Paramecium* culture (about 200 cm^3) in crystallising dish. Add culture of *Podophrya*. In 2 or 3 days larvae of *Podophrya* settle on threads and grow rapidly. After a further week fully grown adults should be ready for observation. Maintain culture by feeding with *Paramecium* every 2–3 days.

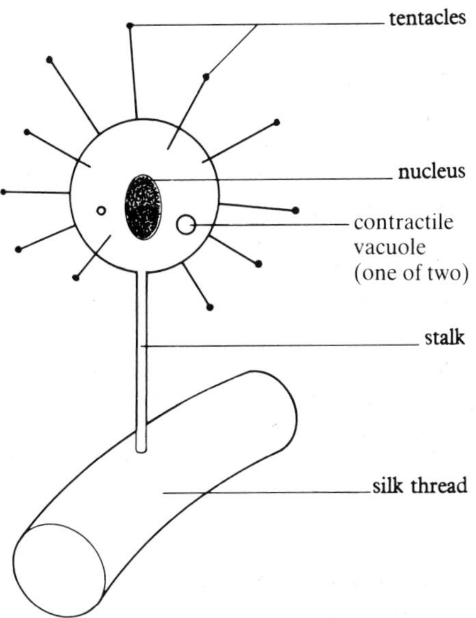

Figure 14.5 *Podophrya* in the adult condition.

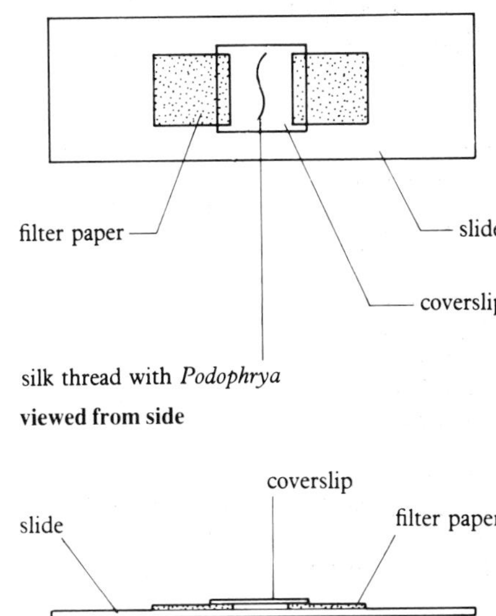

Figure 14.6 Method for mounting *Podophrya*.

6 Now replace the culture solution under the coverslip with distilled water. This can be done by adding distilled water to one of the two pieces of filter paper and withdrawing the solution from the other with dry filter paper. Do this for sufficiently long to ensure that the liquid is completely changed. Re-estimate the frequency of discharge of the contractile vacuole.

7 Now replace the distilled water with sucrose solution (0.05 mol dm^{-3}) by the same technique. Estimate the frequency of discharge as before. If there is no noticeable difference, try stronger sucrose solutions, e.g. 0.1 or 0.5 mol dm^{-3}.

8 Finally make an approximate estimate of the diameter of the animal's body and of a fully inflated contractile vacuole.

For Consideration

(1) How does the frequency of discharge compare in the culture solution, distilled water, and 0.05 mol dm^{-3} sucrose solution? Interpret your results as fully as you can.

(2) Assuming that the organism's body and contractile vacuole are spherical, estimate the volume of liquid discharged per unit time in distilled water. How long would it take for a contractile vacuole to discharge a volume of liquid equal to the volume of the organism's body?

Reference: Revised Nuffield Advanced Biology, *Practical Guide 3: Cells, tissues, and organisms in relation to water*, Longman, 1985.

Investigation 14.5
Comparison of water loss of arthropods in dry and humid air

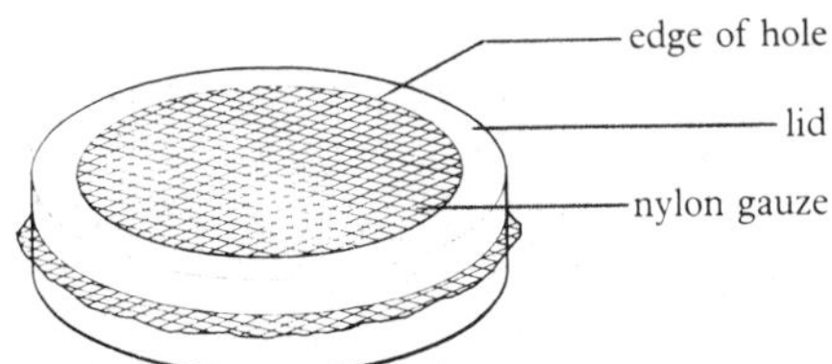

Figure 14.7 Box in which to place small arthropods for estimating changes in mass.

Requirements
Balance
Plastic boxes (with hole in lid, Figure 14.7) ×4
Nylon gauze
Watch glasses ×4

Anhydrous calcium chloride

Woodlice ×20
Mealworms ×20

The ecological distribution of animals, like plants, is closely related to their ability to control water loss. Some animals, for example mammals and insects, have marked powers of water retention and are, therefore, able to exploit habitats which are denied to animals whose water retaining capabilities are not so good.

In this investigation the water-retaining ability of the mealworm, an insect, is compared with that of the woodlouse, a terrestrial crustacean. Other small animals can be compared by the same method. Water loss is estimated by measuring changes in mass.

Procedure

1 Obtain four small plastic boxes with lids. The diameter of the box should be about 5 cm and a large hole of about 4 cm diameter should be cut in the lid. Label the boxes 1–4.

2 Place ten woodlice in each of boxes 1 and 2 and a similar number of mealworms in boxes 3 and 4. Cover the hole in each box with a single layer of nylon gauze trapped under the lid (Figure 14.7). Then invert the box so the animals are resting on the gauze.

3 Weigh each box and its contents. Record the mass.

4 Place boxes 1 and 3 over a watch glass containing anhydrous calcium chloride; place boxes 2 and 4 over watch glasses containing water. In all cases make sure that the contents of the watch glass do not touch the gauze. Note the time.

5 Re-weigh the boxes and their contents at 15-minute intervals at least four times during the laboratory session. Then return the animals to their stock jars.

Results

Calculate the percentage decrease in mass of the animals in each of the four boxes at each interval of time (*see* page 122). Plot the results for all four boxes on one sheet of graph paper: loss in mass on the vertical axis, time on the horizontal axis.

For Consideration

(1) What assumption have we made in this investigation? Is this assumption justified?

(2) What ecological conclusions do you draw from your results? (Beware of concluding more than is justified.) Are your conclusions supported by the occurrence of woodlice and mealworms in their natural habitats?

(3) Is one of the two species investigated better at controlling water loss than the other? What structural and/or physiological features might explain the differences observed?

(4) To what extent do the results of this experiment relate to the behaviour of woodlice and mealworms?

Questions and Problems

1 Explain the effect that each of the following will have on the quantity and composition of urine: (a) drinking a large amount of water; (b) eating a very salty meal; (c) a hot dry day; (d) consuming a large quantity of carbohydrate; (e) high arterial pressure; (f) low arterial pressure; (g) sleep (h) prolonged muscular exertion; (i) removal of the pancreas; (j) destruction of the posterior lobe of the pituitary gland.

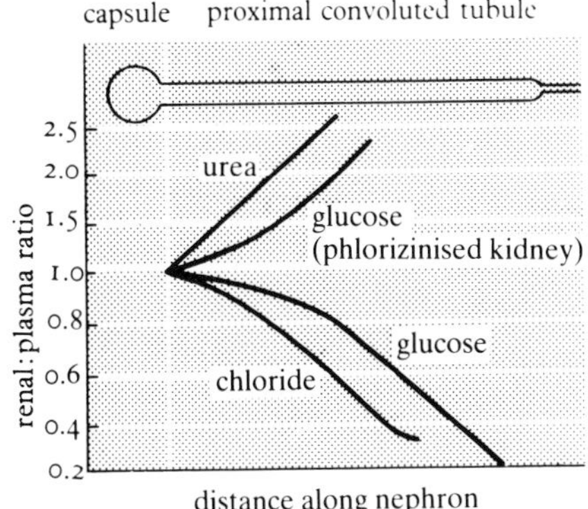

Figure 14.8 Graphs showing the renal-plasma ratio for various constituents of renal fluid in the nephron of a mammal.

2 In experiments on the mammalian kidney, samples of renal fluid from different regions along the length of the proximal convoluted tubule have been withdrawn and analysed. The results, expressed in terms of the renal–plasma ratio for each constituent, are shown graphically in Figure 14.8. (The renal–plasma ratio is the amount of the particular constituent in the renal fluid divided by the amount of the same constituent in the blood plasma.) The graph also includes a curve for glucose absorption in a phlorizinised kidney, one that has been treated with phlorizin which renders the tubules incapable of absorbing glucose.

(a) Explain each of the curves.

(b) In what respects do the results of comparable experiments on amphibian kidneys differ from the mammal?

3 The following table shows the composition of plasma, filtrate, and urine in a mammal.

Component	**Plasma** *(g per 100 cm³)*	**Filtrate** (g per 100 cm³)	**Urine** (g per 100 cm³)
Urea	0.03	0.03	2.00
Uric acid	0.004	0.004	0.05
Glucose	0.10	0.10	0.00
Amnio acids	0.05	0.05	0.00
Salts	0.72	0.72	1.50
Proteins	8.00	0.00	0.00

Comment on these data. *(SBT modified)*

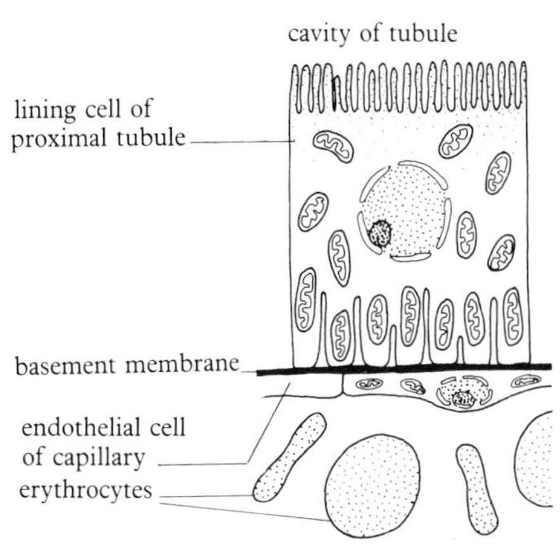

Figure 14.9 Diagram based on an electron micrograph of the proximal convoluted tubule of a mammal.

4 The diagram in Figure 14.9 has been reconstructed from electron micrographs of a mammalian kidney tubule. It shows one cell of the proximal convoluted tubule, together with part of an adjacent capillary.

Fluid entering the proximal tubule from Bowman's capsule contains water, salts, glucose, amino acids and excretory substances. More than 80 per cent of the water is reabsorbed in the proximal tubule and there is normally no glucose or amino acids, and a greatly reduced sodium content in the fluid which is passed on to the loop of Henle.

Using the information given, together with your own biological knowledge, write short answers on the following:

(a) What do you suggest is the mechanism responsible for the reabsorption of water in the proximal tubule? Explain your answer.

(b) The reabsorption of glucose and amino acids is described as taking place 'against a concentration gradient'. What does this mean?

(c) If the kidney is cooled for a time, glucose and amino acids appear in the urine. How would you explain this?

(d) In what ways is the structure of the tubule cell particularly suited to its function of absorption? *(CL modified)*

5 The loops of Henle are located in the medulla of the kidney. Blood flowing through this region of the kidney does so in long U-shaped capillaries, the vasa recta, which run close to and parallel with the loops of Henle. Blood flowing through the vasa recta represents only about one per cent of the blood that flows through the kidney. The vasa recta are derived from the efferent arterioles serving the glomeruli.

What can you say about:

(a) the pressure of blood in the vasa recta?

(b) the viscosity of the blood in the vasa recta?

(c) the rate of flow of blood through the vasa recta?

(d) the osmotic pressure of the blood in the vasa recta?

What light is thrown by your answers on the function of the vasa recta?

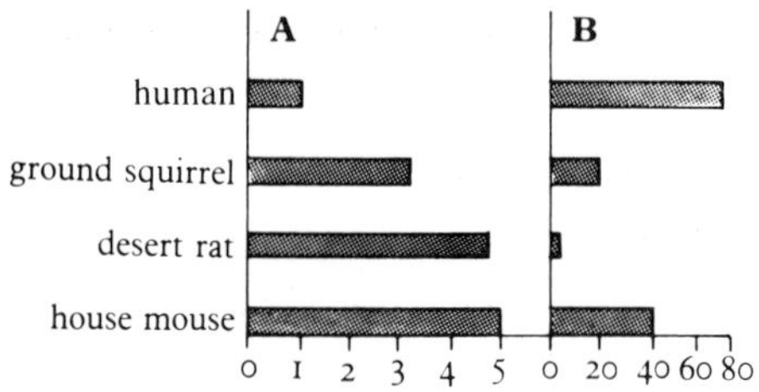

Figure 14.10 Summary of data on the composition of the urine and faeces of four different species of mammal. **A**, urine salt content (arbitrary units); **B**, water content of faeces (per cent).

6 Figure 14.10 summarises the results of experiments carried out to determine the composition of the urine and faeces of four different species of mammal. Explain the data as far as you can in physiological and ecological terms. *(SA modified)*

7 Comment on each of the following statements:

(a) Miners eat salt tablets or drink salted beer.

(b) Sea birds such as the herring gull secrete salts twice as concentrated as in sea water from nasal glands, and marine reptiles such as turtles secrete salts from glands close to the eyes.

(c) Certain salt-marsh plants secrete salt onto the surface of the leaves from salt glands.

(d) Mammals which can produce the most concentrated urine have the longest loops of Henle.

(e) It is dangerous for a human to drink a large quantity of sea water.

8 You are given the following information concerning the kidney of three different animals, together with their respective environments, the nature of their nitrogenous waste, and the type and quantity of urine produced. Study the information and then describe how the structure and product of the kidney is adapted to the osmotic environment in which the animal lives:

Animal	**Environment**	**Kidney**		**Nitrogenous waste**	**Urine relative to blood**
		Glomerulus	**Tubule**		
Trout	freshwater	large	long	ammonia	hypotonic, copious
Herring	sea	nil	short	trimethylamine oxide	isotonic, scanty
Lizard	land	small	very long	uric acid	hypertonic and scanty

How would you characterise the structure and product of the human kidney on the above chart? *(AEB modified)*

9 An experiment was carried out on the Pacific shore crab *Hemigrapsus* to determine the relationship between the solute concentration of the blood and that of the surrounding water. Specimens were subjected to different external salinities, and, after being given time to come to equilibrium with the medium, blood samples were taken and their solute concentration determined. The results were as shown below:

(a) Plot the results on a graph, putting solute concentration of blood on the vertical axis and solute concentration of water on the horizontal axis.

(b) Interpret the results as fully as you can.

(c) What particular chemical substances will contribute to the solute concentration of (i) sea water, and (ii) the blood of the crab?

Solute concentration (arbitrary units)	
Water	Blood
0.1	0.1
0.15	1.0
0.2	1.1
0.3	1.2
0.4	1.3
0.5	1.35
1.0	1.4
1.5	1.6
2.0	2.0

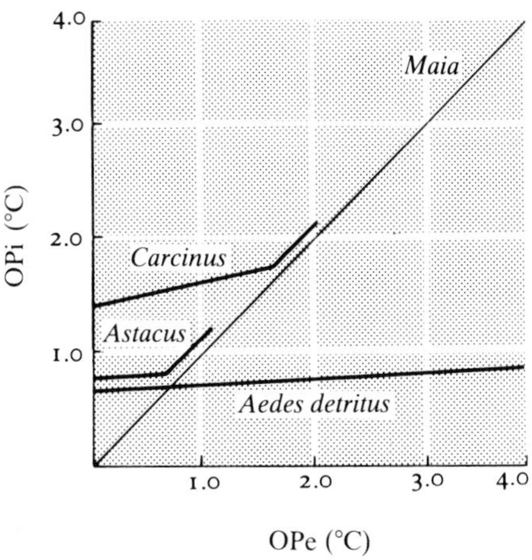

Figure 14.11 Relationship between the osmotic pressure of the blood (OPi) and the external medium (OPe) for four different arthropods. The osmotic pressure is expressed as depression of the freezing point in °C.

10 Figure 14.11 shows the relationship between the osmotic pressure of the blood (internal OP = OP_i) and of the external medium (external OP = OP_e) in four different arthropods: the marine spider crab *Maia*, the estuarine shore crab *Carcinus*, the freshwater crayfish *Astacus*, and the larva of the mosquito *Aedes detritus* which inhabits salt marsh pools.
(a) Explain what each curve shows.
(b) Relate the information which the curves show to the habitat of each animal.
(c) Discuss the anatomical and physiological basis of the curves.

11 To what extent are the methods employed by terrestrial animals and plants to prevent excessive water loss comparable with those seen in plants?

12 (a) What structural features enable plants characteristic of dry habitats to (i) increase the thickness of the boundary layer of still air over the plant surface, (ii) store and conserve water?
(b) What features of the life cycles of dry-land plants allow them better to withstand periods of drought?
(c) In the early afternoon on hot summer days, many crop plants exhibit 'midday closure' of their stomatal pores. Suggest a reason for this.

13 Typical C3 plants lose about 500 molecules of water for every molecule of CO_2 fixed. For typical C4 plants the figure is 330 molecules lost per CO_2 fixed, and for plants with crassulacean acid metabolism (CAM plants), about 100 molecules per CO_2 fixed.
(a) Explain the meaning of the term crassulacean acid metabolism.
(b) What is the difference between a CAM plant and a C4 plant?
(c) What special features of CAM plants enable them to lose less water per carbon dioxide molecule fixed than a C3 plant?

14 The CO_2 output from leaves of a succulent crassulacean plant maintained in total darkness was found to vary as shown in the following table:

	Time (hours)	**CO_2 output** ($\mu l\ h^{-1}\ g^{-1}$ fresh mass)	**Time** (hours)	**CO_2 output** ($\mu l\ h^{-1}\ g^{-1}$ fresh mass)
4.00 p.m.	0	80	44	50
	4	30	48	30
	8	7	52	23
	12	8	56	32
	16	82	60	51
	20	104	64	48
	24	80	68	38
	28	30	72	28
	32	23	76	21
	36	60	80	29
	40	68		

Comment on these results. Can you suggest any explanation for them? Suggest further experiments to investigate the situation. (*OCJE*)

15 Temperature Regulation

Background Summary

1 Organisms cannot withstand fluctuations in body temperature beyond what is compatible with the functioning of their enzymes.

2 On the basis of their ability to regulate their body temperature animals are classified into **homoiothermic** and **poikilothermic** or, more usefully, **endothermic** and **ectothermic**.

3 Heat is lost or gained by **radiation**, **evaporation**, **conduction** and **convection**. The problem in temperature regulation is to overcome, control, or make use of these physical processes.

4 Endothermic animals (e.g. mammals) have various structural and physiological ways of coping with excessive cold and heat, many of them involving the **skin**.

5 Physiological responses are controlled by a **thermoregulatory centre** in the **hypothalamus** of the brain which responds to changes in the temperature of the blood.

6 In endotherms physical (non-metabolic) mechanisms maintain a constant body temperature when the environmental temperature ranges between a high and low **critical temperature**. This is the body's **efficiency range**. Above the high critical temperature, and below the low critical temperature, the metabolic rate rises.

7 It has been found that the low critical temperature is significantly lower for arctic than for tropical animals. A human's low critical temperature is about 27 °C, that of the arctic fox −40 °C.

8 Some endothermic animals cut down excessive heat loss from exposed structures by means of a **countercurrent heat exchange system**.

9 Many animals regulate their body temperature by **behavioural means**. In ectothermic animals this is the only method. **Migration** and **hibernation** may be regarded as ways of avoiding unfavourable environmental temperatures.

10 A few animals and many plants are **temperature-tolerant**, i.e. they are able to tolerate wide temperature fluctuations.

11 Plants have a number of structural features which help them to withstand heat. To some extent plants are cooled by **transpiration**, in some cases markedly so.

Investigation 15.1
Effect of temperature on the heartbeat of *Daphnia*

Daphnia, the 'water flea', is a small freshwater crustacean which lacks physiological methods of maintaining a constant body temperature. This means that if the environmental temperature changes, its body temperature does so too. This being so, its metabolic rate will be expected to rise or fall accordingly. In this investigation we shall test the hypothesis that as the environmental temperature rises, the metabolic rate rises too. We shall use the rate at which the heart beats (cardiac frequency) as a measure of the metabolic rate. Fortunately *Daphnia* is comparatively transparent, which enables the workings of its internal organs, including the heart, to be seen clearly under the low power of the microscope (Figure 15.1).

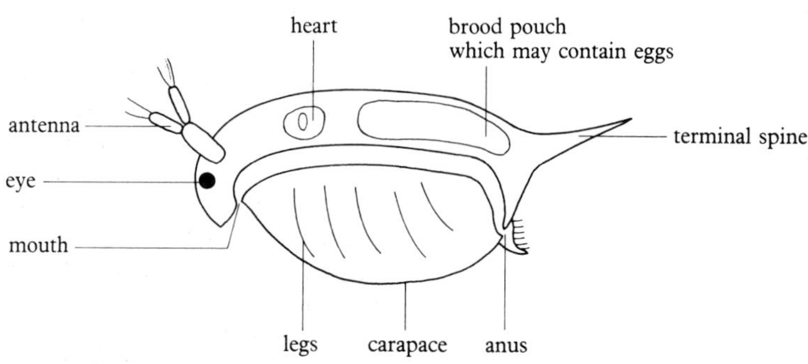

Figure 15.1 Side aspect of *Daphnia* as seen under low power to show the position of the heart.

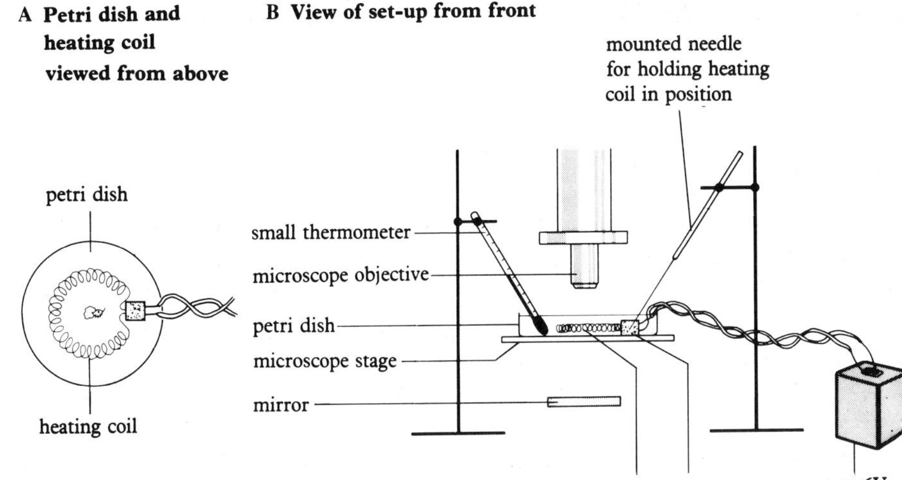

Figure 15.2 Experiment on the effect of temperature on the heartbeat of *Daphnia*.

Procedure

SETTING UP THE EXPERIMENT

1 Select a large specimen and transfer it by means of a pipette to the centre of a small petri dish. Remove excess water from around the specimen, so it is temporarily stranded.

2 Now smear a little silicone grease onto the floor of the petri dish and, using a mounted needle, push the posterior end of the animal into the grease so it is firmly anchored in position. Now fill the petri dish with water.

3 Place the petri dish on the stage of a microscope and observe the animal under low power. The beating heart is located on the dorsal side just above the gut and in front of the brood pouch (Figure 15.1). Do not confuse the beating of the heart with the flapping of the legs which lie within the carapace on the ventral side.

4 Surround the animal with a circular heating coil and clamp it in position. Also clamp a thermometer in position so that its bulb is in the water (Figure 15.2).

ESTIMATING THE CARDIAC FREQUENCY

A convenient way of doing this is to time, by means of a stopwatch, how long it takes for the heart to beat 50 times. The heart may be beating sufficiently slowly for every pulsation to be counted. If, however, it is beating too rapidly, count by making a mark on a sheet of paper at every tenth beat. Do several practice runs to get used to the technique.

When you feel ready, proceed with the experiment as follows:

1 Replace the water in the petri dish with ice-cold water. Estimate the cardiac frequency and note the temperature.

2 Now connect the heating coil with a 4 or 6 volt battery so as to gradually heat up the water in the dish. Estimate the cardiac frequency at 5 °C intervals, noting the temperature each time.

If the temperature of the water rises too quickly, disconnect the heating coil from the battery and, if necessary, add a few ice chippings.

3 Present your results in a table, recording the cardiac frequency at each temperature.

4 Plot your results on a graph, temperature along the horizontal axis and cardiac frequency along the vertical axis.

For Consideration

(1) What conclusions do you draw from your results? Would you conclude that *Daphnia* has no means of controlling its body temperature?
(2) What criticisms can you make of the experimental technique?
(3) Did you reach the upper lethal temperature in your experiment? If not, what would you expect it to be? Explain fully.
(4) Would you expect to get the same sort of results with any 'cold-blooded' animal?
(5) How would you carry out the same investigation on a human subject? In what respects would you expect the results to differ from those obtained with *Daphnia*?

Requirements
Small petri dish
Mounted needle
Heating coil plus stand and clamp
Small thermometer plus stand and clamp
4V or 6V battery
Stopwatch
Pipette (10 or 25 cm^3)
Rubber pipette

Iced water
Silicone grease

Daphnia

Investigation 15.2
Microscopic structure of skin

Though important in temperature regulation, the skin performs many other functions as well. For example, it contains numerous sensory devices and is therefore important in reception of stimuli, informing the body of environmental changes at the surface. Its toughness affords the body physical protection. Hairs, nails and the keratinized outer layer of the skin contain protein, so the skin can be said to contribute towards nitrogenous excretion. Moreover, its impermeability makes it an effective water-proofing layer, thus giving it a passive role in osmoregulation: the fact that we can go swimming in water of any salinity without osmotic effects bears witness to this last function. The skin is therefore important in protection against, and adjustment to, changing external conditions.

Procedure

Examine a vertical section of hairy skin (for example, human scalp). First distinguish between the superficial epidermis, the deeper, more extensive dermis, and (strictly not part of the skin) the hypodermis (subcutaneous tissue) (Figure 15.3). Now examine each in turn.

1 EPIDERMIS

The epidermis is composed of stratified epithelium (*see* page 23). Cells formed by proliferation of the basal Malpighian layer get pushed outwards, flattening as they do so (stratum spinosum, so-called because under high power the cells sometimes have a 'prickly' appearance); eventually they become granulated and die (stratum granulosum), then clear (stratum lucidum) and finally the cells become converted into scales of keratin (stratum corneum) which flake off (stratum disjunctum). The strata granulosa and lucida represent stages in the keratinisation of the cells. The stratum corneum is tough and impermeable, thus conferring on the epidermis its protective and water-proofing properties.

In your section of skin, the nuclei of the Malpighian layer and stratum spinosum should be clear, but the cell membranes will probably be difficult to make out. The stratum granulosum should be apparent, but the stratum lucidum, unless it stands out as a clear bright line, may be difficult to see.

Cells of the Malpighian layer may be pigmented, containing melanin towards their outer surface. Function?

2 DERMIS

First notice that the surface of the dermis is folded to form a series of ridges, the dermal papillae. Receptors sensitive to touch are located in the dermal papillae, but these will only be

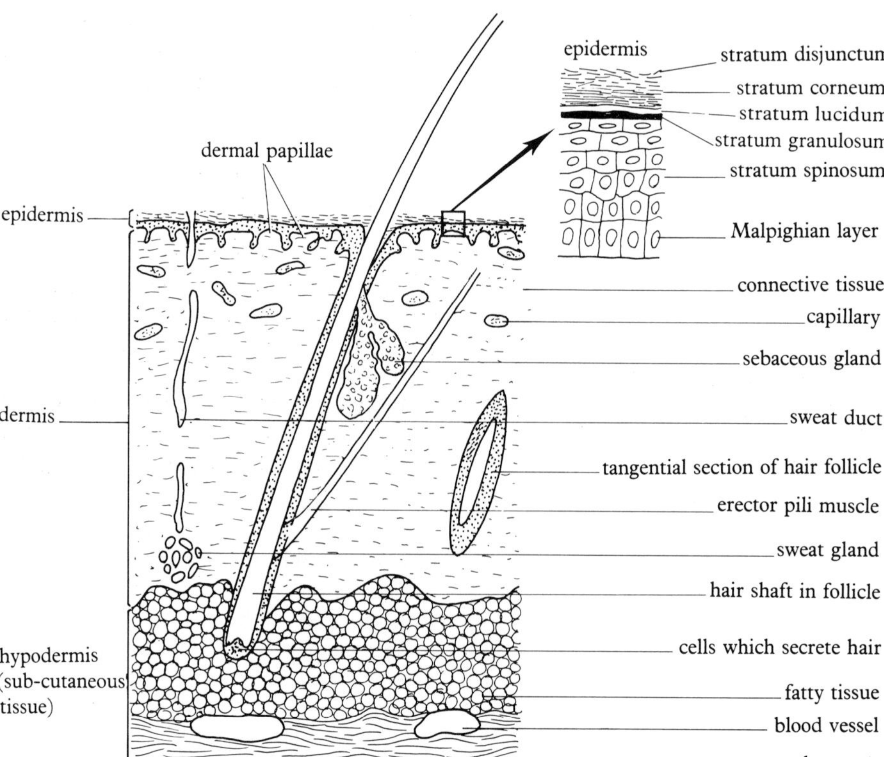

Figure 15.3 Microscopic structure of human skin (scalp).

seen with special staining techniques.

The rest of the dermis is made up of loose connective tissue, mainly collagen fibres, but some elastic fibres too. Note: capillaries (red blood corpuscles may be seen in them), sweat glands and their ducts, hairs in hair follicles with erector pili muscles and sebaceous glands. Functions? What sort of glands are the sweat and sebaceous glands?

Few sections will be as complete as the one drawn in Figure 15.3. Seldom will a hair follicle be cut throughout its full length: more often it will be cut tangentially as shown on the right hand side of the drawing. Similarly sweat ducts seldom appear complete in a section. The organisation of the dermis must therefore be reconstructed by searching the entire section for clues and, if necessary, examining several different sections.

3 HYPODERMIS (SUB-CUTANEOUS TISSUE)

Hypodermis means 'beneath the dermis'; it is not strictly part of the skin. It consists of a layer of adipose tissue (subcutaneous fat) of variable thickness, beneath which is a layer of smooth muscle and blood vessels.

The adipose tissue as well as providing an insulating layer against heat loss, allows the skin to move freely on underlying structures.

4 RECEPTORS IN THE SKIN

Here is a simplified summary of the distribution and functions of skin receptors:

In epidermis:

Free nerve endings: derived from branched nerve fibre – sensitive to pain.

In dermal papillae:

Meissner's corpuscles: Branched nerve endings embedded in connective tissue – sensitive to touch.

In rest of dermis:

Krause's end bulbs: Bundle of branched nerve endlings enclosed in connective tissue capsule – thought to be sensitive to cold.

Ruffini's endings: Tree-like system of nerve endings terminating as flattened discs, supported by connective tissue – thought to be sensitive to warmth.

Free nerve endings: wrapped round base of hair follicle – sensitive to movements of hair.

Pacinian corpuscle: Unbranched nerve ending encapsulated in thick multi-layered covering of connective tissue – sensitive to pressure.

Only the Pacinian corpuscles can be seen properly without special staining methods. The others are visible in methylene blue or silver preparations.

5 COMPARISON WITH THE SKIN OF AN ECTOTHERM

Observe, and feel, the skin of a live frog. What structures would you predict to be present (and not present) in the skin?

Now examine a vertical section of the skin of the frog. Are your predictions correct? In what respects is the frog skin (a) similar to, and (b) different from mammalian skin? Explain the differences.

For Consideration

(1) How much of the surface of human skin can be removed without feeling pain and without bleeding?

(2) What areas of the skin would you expect to: (a) lack hair follicles, (b) have a particularly thick layer of subcutaneous fat, (c) have little or no subcutaneous fat, (d) have a particularly thick stratum corneum, (e) have numerous Meissner's corpuscles, (f) have a particularly large number of sweat glands?

(3) In sunbathing, what causes the skin to develop: (a) a pink colour; (b) a brown tan; (c) blisters?

(4) Why is it a good thing for sunlight (in moderation) to fall on the skin? What are the dangers of excessive sunlight falling on the skin?

Requirements

VS hairy skin (e.g. scalp)
VS skin stained to show receptors (if available)
Common frog
VS frog skin

Questions and Problems

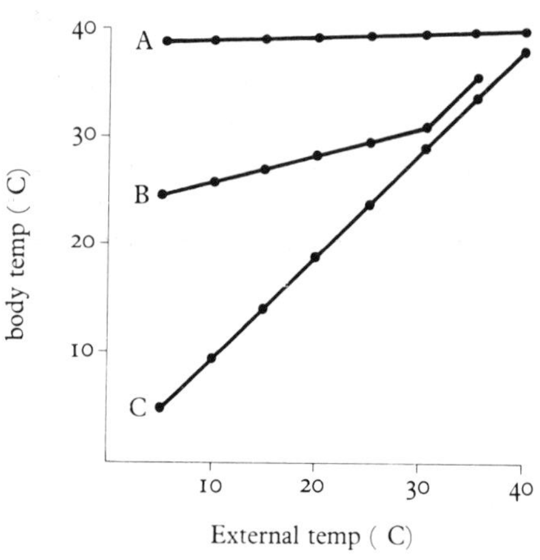

Figure 15.4 Relationship between the external temperature and body temperature for three different animals. **A**, cat; **B**, spiny anteater *Echidna*; **C**, lizard.

1 Comment on the graph shown in Figure 15.4 and discuss reasons for the difference in the three curves.

2 Why is it that: (a) the skin is red in hot weather, white in cold weather, and blue in very cold weather; (b) in prolonged exposure to severe cold the living cells at the tips of the fingers may die ('frostbite'); (c) for bodily warmth a 'string' vest is particularly effective; (d) during a fever a body temperature of less than about 40 °C is treated by covering the patient with extra blankets, but if the temperature exceeds about 40 °C ice packs are placed in contact with the patient?

3 It has been observed that in many animals the veins that bring blood back from exposed extremities (such as the hands and feet in humans) run close to, and parallel with, the artery that takes blood to these structures. In some cases, such as the flippers of whales, the artery may be completely surrounded by the veins. What do you think is the significance of this arrangement?

4 Graph A in Figure 15.5 shows how the rate of heat production by a naked human body varies with the temperature of the surrounding air. Graph B shows how the rate of heat loss from a naked human body varies with the temperature of the surrounding air. Explain the form of each graph. (*JMB*)

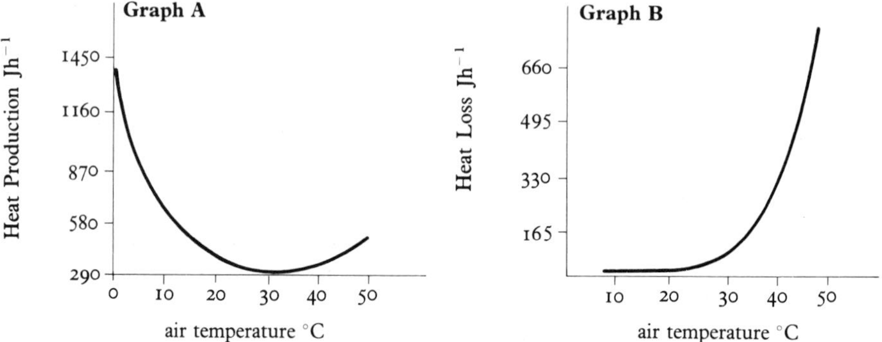

Figure 15.5 Relationship between air temperature and **A** heat production, **B** heat loss in human.

5 Figure 15.6 shows the results of an experiment carried out by Pugh and Edholm on two human volunteers, A and B. A is fat (i.e. has much subcutaneous adipose tissue), whereas B is thin. Both subjects had their body temperatures recorded at intervals while immersed in water at 16 °C. This was done first with the subjects lying still, and then while the subjects were swimming.
(a) Interpret the results as fully as you can.
(b) Criticise the data on which the graphs are based.

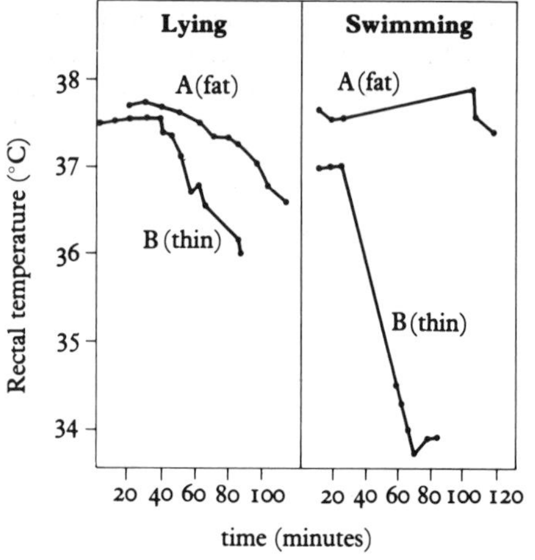

Figure 15.6 Results of Pugh and Edholms' experiment on the body temperature of two human subjects, one thin, the other fat, immersed in water at 16 °C.

6 Within a given species of animal, the average size of individuals tends to be smaller in warmer climates and larger in colder climates (Bergmann's principle), whereas the extremities, such as ears and tail, tend to be longer in warmer climates and shorter in colder climates (Allen's principle). Can you explain these generalisations? Would it be justified to call these two generalisations laws?

7 On a still sunny day it often happens that the tar on roads melts in the sun, and car roofs become too hot to touch. Comment on the fact that in these circumstances the leaves of plants are usually within 12 °C of the air temperature, even in full sunlight. (*CCJE*)

8 The graph in Figure 15.7 shows the effect of environment temperature on the metabolic rate of (a) a monkey and (b) a polar bear cub. Comment on these results.

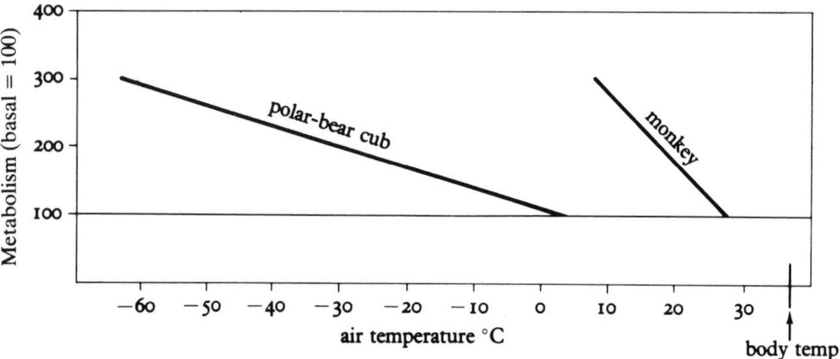

Figure 15.7 Effect of environmental temperature on metabolic rate of monkey and polar-bear cub. Metabolism is expressed as oxygen consumption ($cm^3\ O_2\ h^{-1}$).

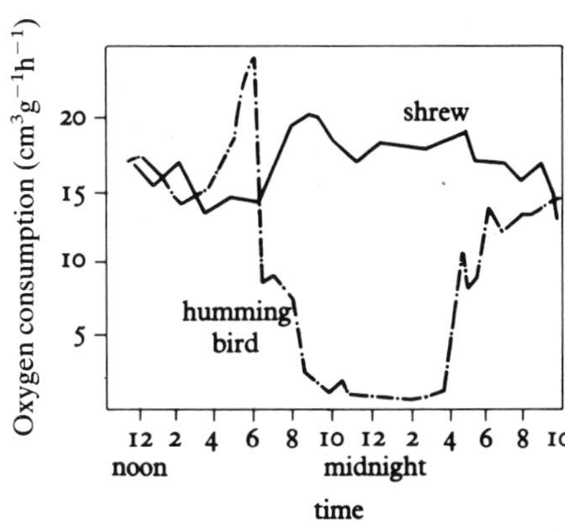

Figure 15.8 Oxygen consumption of a humming bird and a shrew over a 24-hour period. (*After Pearson*)

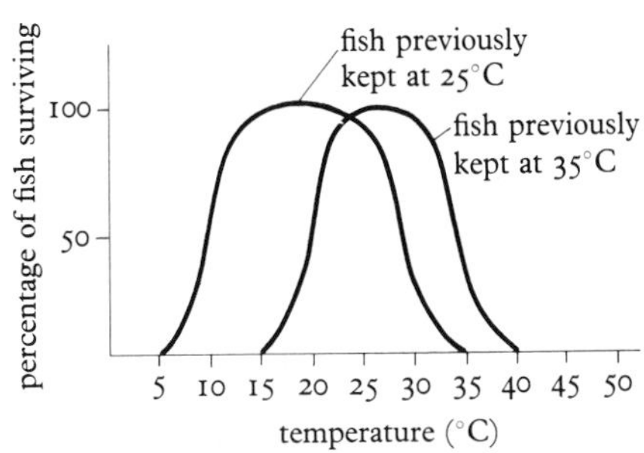

Figure 15.9 The effect of temperature on the survival rate of two groups of fish, one previously kept at 25 °C, the other at 35 °C.

9 In humans there is little evidence for acclimatisation to adverse temperatures. Humans have mastered the climate 'by the creation of a *milieu intermediaire* rather than by physiological adjustment'. (*HE Lewis*) Discuss. (*CCJE*)

10 The graph in Figure 15.8 shows the oxygen consumption of a humming bird and a shrew over a period of 24 hours. Explain the differences between the two curves.

11 A tortoise (*Testudo sulcata*), previously kept at room temperature (20 °C) was exposed to a temperature of 55 °C for two hours. During this period its body mass and body temperature were monitored at half-hourly intervals. The results are summarised below.

Time (h)	**Body mass** (g)	**Body temperature** (°C)
0	58.0	20.0
½	57.3	36.5
1	51.4	40.5
1½	49.9	40.5
2	48.1	40.5

(a) Plot these results on a single sheet of graph paper.
(b) What caused the body temperature to rise during the first hour?
(c) The decrease in body mass was associated with the tortoise salivating over its fore-quarters. Explain the shape of the curve which you have drawn for the change in body mass.
(d) Suggest why the body temperature stayed at a constant 40 °C during the second hour.
(e) What general conclusions would you draw from this experiment about the way ectotherms control their body temperature?

(*Data after Cloudsley-Thompson, 1970*)

12 Two groups of fish of the same species were kept for some time at different temperatures. One group was kept at 25 °C, and the other at 35 °C. At the end of the period of time batches of fish from each group were exposed to different temperature conditions and the number of survivors counted. The results of this experiment are shown in Figure 15.9. Discuss them as fully as possible. (*SA modified*)

16 Control of Respiratory Gases

Background Summary

1 The importance of maintaining a constant level of oxygen and carbon dioxide in the blood is demonstrated by the fact that an alteration in the level of these gases results in an appropriate change in breathing (i.e. ventilation of the lungs) and the circulation.

2 It has been found that carbon dioxide is the most important stimulus initiating breathing changes, and it achieves this by increasing the **ventilation rate**.

3 Changes in the ventilation rate are coordinated by the **respiratory centre** in the medulla of the brain. This is informed of the level of carbon dioxide, and to a lesser extent oxygen, by chemoreceptors in the **aortic** and **carotid bodies**. The respiratory centre is also stimulated directly.

4 The circulation is controlled by the **cardio-vascular centre** in the medulla. It responds to, amongst other things, changes in blood pressure monitored by stretch receptors in the walls of the **carotid sinuses**.

5 The higher centres of the brain, a variety of reflexes, and the hormone adrenaline are also involved in the initiation of respiratory and cardio-vascular responses.

6 The effects of a slowly diminishing oxygen supply, such as occurs in ascending a mountain, are offset by **acclimatisation**, a series of long-range responses to low partial pressures of oxygen.

7 A more rapid response to changing conditions is seen during and after a bout of heavy muscular exercise. The respiratory, circulatory, nervous and endocrine systems all co-operate to bring about appropriate adjustments.

8 During muscular exercise the muscles respire, in part, anaerobically, incurring an **oxygen debt** which must be paid off during, or immediately after, the exercise. Lactic acid, formed during the period of anaerobiosis, is removed.

9 When facing total oxygen deprivation many animals, particularly diving mammals and birds, undergo **bradycardia:** the cardiac frequency falls and blood is redistributed to the vital organs.

Investigation 16.1
Effect of oxygen and carbon dioxide on the ventilation rate in humans

CAUTION:
Re-breathing your expired air can be dangerous and should only be done under close supervision by a teacher.

It is well known that during muscular exertion the rates of breathing and heart beat increase. Is this caused by a temporary decrease in the amount of oxygen in the blood, an increase in the level of carbon dioxide, or some other change resulting from muscular activity? The purpose of this investigation is to test whether a shortage of oxygen or an increase in carbon dioxide is the most effective stimulus initiating appropriate adjustments. The rate of gas exchange is expressed in terms of the ventilation rate, which is the total volume of air inspired per minute.

Method

A spirometer and kymograph are required. For a description of the apparatus and procedure for carrying out experiments *see* page 62. The kymograph should be set at a speed of approximately 15 mm per minute.

Work in pairs, one student acting as subject, the teacher as experimenter. Other students should observe. In this investigation the subject should sit as relaxed as possible at all times.

Procedure

EFFECT OF LACK OF OXYGEN

1 Fill the spirometer with oxygen. The carbon dioxide absorber (canister of self-indicating soda lime) should be in position, so the subject will inspire pure oxygen from the spirometer chamber.

2 Connect the subject, who should be sitting comfortably, to the spirometer.

3 Record his or her breathing movements on the kymograph drum for as long as possible. As the oxygen supply gets used up, changes will occur in the subject's breathing pattern, and he or she may begin to feel faint. *Do not go too far!* The experimenter should watch the subject carefully: as soon as there is the slightest sign of distress the experimenter should disconnect the subject immediately.

EFFECT OF REBREATHING EXPIRED AIR

1 Disconnect the subject from the spirometer allow him or her to recover from the previous experiment.

2 To investigate the effect of increasing the carbon dioxide level, remove the carbon dioxide absorber from the spirometer, so the subject will re-breathe his or her own expired air. This will become increasingly rich in carbon dioxide as the experiment progresses.

3 Having removed the carbon dioxide absorber, reconnect the subject to the spirometer and repeat the procedure which you followed for the first experiment. Record the subject's breathing for as long as possible. It is important that you should take the same precautions as before: *disconnect the subject as soon as you notice the slightest sign of stress.*

Results

1 Calculate the ventilation rate (*VR*) during each minute from the beginning to the end of each set of recordings. The *VR* is the total volume of air inspired per minute. It can be worked out from the fact that:

$$\text{Ventilation rate} = \text{frequency} \times \text{depth}$$

where frequency is the total number of inspirations carried out during the one minute period, and depth is the average volume of air inspired at each breath during the same one minute period. Express the *VR* in $dm^3\ min^{-1}$.

2 Now plot the changes in ventilation rate for *both* experiments on one sheet of graph paper, so the curves can be readily compared. The time, in minutes, should be on the horizontal axis.

3 How do the results of the two experiments compare with one another? What conclusions do you draw as to the most effective stimulus initiating changes in the ventilation rate?

For Consideration

(1) For carbon dioxide to influence the ventilation rate there must be receptors sensitive to the amount of gas in the body. Where are these receptors?

(2) You have probably found that carbon dioxide provides a very effective stimulus bringing about changes in the ventilation rate. Does this rule out the possibility that in natural circumstances, such as muscular activity, other factors besides carbon dioxide might help to bring about such adaptive changes? What might these other factors be?

Requirements
Recording spirometer with pen
Kymograph set at speed of about 15 mm min^{-1}
Eosin (or non-clogging ink)
Kymograph paper calibrated for volume
Oxygen cylinder (medical grade)

Investigation 16.2
Effect of various factors on the pulse rate

The cardiac output, that is the volume of blood pumped into the aorta per minute, is determined by the stroke volume and the cardiac frequency. The stroke volume is the volume of blood pumped into the aorta each time the heart beats, and the cardiac frequency is the number of heart beats per minute. The latter can be determined by measuring the pulse rate, which is what we shall be doing in this investigation. An interesting aspect of the pulse is that it can give us a clue as to the person's fitness.

Method

Work in pairs, one of you acting as subject, the other doing the experiments. While not taking exercise the subject should sit comfortably in a chair with an arm resting on a table at about the level of the heart.

The pulse rate is measured by placing a finger immediately over the radial artery on the median side of the wrist (Figure 16.1). Practise taking the subject's pulse rate by counting the number of throbs in a one minute period.

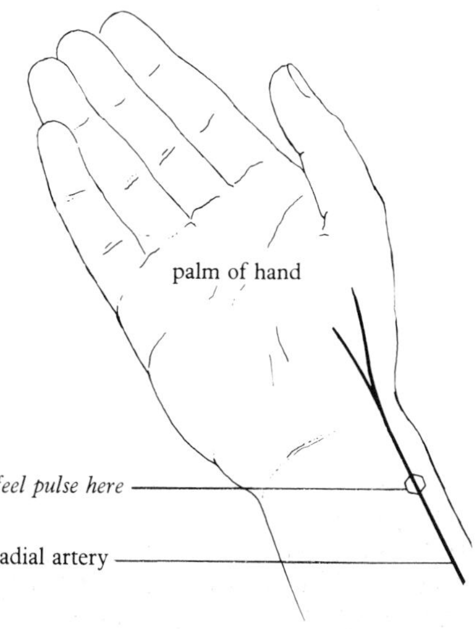

Figure 16.1 How to take a subject's pulse rate.

EFFECT OF POSTURE ON THE PULSE RATE

1 The subject should lie down quietly for five minutes after which his or her pulse rate should be determined.
2 The subject should then stand up for a further three minutes after which the pulse rate should again be taken. Explain the difference (if any) between the two readings.

EFFECT OF HYPERVENTILATION ON PULSE RATE

In this experiment it is necessary to obtain continuous readings of the subject's pulse over a period of seven minutes. This is best done by counting the number of pulses every fifteen seconds and converting these to pulses per minute afterwards.
1 With the subject seated and as relaxed as possible, the partner should take the subject's pulse rate continuously for two minutes.
2 The subject should then engage in forced breathing for 30 seconds: breathe as deeply and frequently as possible, but with the minimum of muscular effort to the body as a whole.
3 The subject now breathes normally for a further five minutes during which the partner records his pulse rate every fifteen seconds. Does the pulse rate fall below normal at any point? Explain.

EFFECT OF EXERCISE ON PULSE RATE

1 The subject should engage in a standard bout of exercise as follows: step onto a stool 45 cm high and then down again, once every three seconds, thus taking fifteen seconds in all.
2 Immediately after the exercise the partner should measure the subject's pulse rate at ten second intervals until it returns to the normal *standing* rate. Make a graph of the results, putting pulse rate on the vertical axis, time on the horizontal axis.
3 Repeat after a much heavier bout of exercise, e.g. performing a 100 metre sprint. Graph your results as before and compare with the less vigorous exercise.

Assessing fitness

The data you have obtained may be used to assess the subject's fitness. To do this, score the data as follows:

A Pulse rate lying down ('reclining pulse')

Rate	Points
50–60	3
61–70	3
71–80	2
81–90	1

B Pulse rate standing up ('standing pulse')

Rate	Points
60–70	3
71–80	3
81–90	2
91–100	1
101–110	1

C Increase in pulse rate on standing

Reclining pulse rate (**A**)	**C** Increase in pulse rate on standing		
	0–10 beats	11–18 beats	19–26 beats
50–60	3	3	2
61–70	3	2	1
71–80	3	2	0
81–90	2	1	−1

D Time taken for pulse to return to standing rate after exercise

Seconds	Points
0–30	4
31–60	3
61–90	2
91–120	1

E Increase in pulse rate immediately after exercise compared with standing rate

Standing pulse rate (**B**)	**E** Increase in pulse rate immediately after exercise		
	0–10 beats	11–20 beats	21–30 beats
60–70	3	3	2
71–80	3	2	1
81–90	3	2	1
91–100	2	1	0
101–110	1	0	−1

Calculate the total score:

Table	Points
A	
B	
C	
D	
E	
Total	

Assess fitness as follows:

Excellent	16 points
Good	12–15 "
Fair	8–11 "
Poor	less than 8 "

For consideration

(1) Do you think this is a valid way of assessing a person's fitness? Can you suggest a better method?
(2) How would you account for your result in terms of your particular life style (i.e. do you take regular exercise, do you smoke etc?).
(3) Make a list of all the factors you can think of which might cause a person's pulse rate to increase.

Requirements
Stool, 45 cm high
Facilities for taking vigorous exercise, e.g. running track or field for performing 100 metre sprint

Investigation 16.3
Effect of various factors on human blood pressure

CAUTION:
Obstructing the flow of blood to a person's arm can be dangerous. The sphygmomanometer should be used only under close supervision by a teacher.

The speed at which blood reaches the tissues is determined by the pressure. Blood in the arteries is at high pressure, which is maintained by the pumping action of the heart. However, the arterial pressure is by no means steady, but fluctuates according to the phases of the heart beat (cardiac cycle). Pressure is highest when the heart contracts (systolic pressure) and lowest when it relaxes (diastolic pressure).

In this investigation we shall confirm this, and look into several factors which may affect the systolic pressure.

Method

The blood pressure can be measured in the brachial artery by means of a sphygmomanometer, an inflatable rubber armlet enclosed within an inextensible cloth covering. The armlet is connected to a pump and mercury manometer. The pump is fitted with a release valve to allow slow deflation of the armlet.

1 The experimenter should wrap the armlet snugly (but not tightly) round the subject's upper arm well above the elbow: begin with the broad end and tuck the narrow end into the turns already made. The outlet valve should be closed to allow inflation: the milled head should be turned clockwise.

2 Feel the subject's radial pulse with your finger. Inflate the rubber armlet to a pressure of about 180 mm Hg and notice that the pulse disappears. (Why?). Now open the release valve slowly and gradually decrease the pressure until the pulse *just* reappears. This is the systolic pressure.

3 Continue to let air out of the arm band until a point is reached when the pulse gets very much weaker. This is the diastolic pressure.

4 With the subject relaxed, take several readings of the systolic and diastolic pressures until you have got used to the apparatus and are obtaining consistent results. Suitable figures for an adult would be: systolic pressure 120 mm Hg, diastolic pressure 75 mm Hg.

Experiments

EFFECT OF POSTURE ON ARTERIAL PRESSURE AND PULSE RATE

1 The subject should lie down quietly for five minutes after which his or her systolic pressure should be determined.

2 The subject should then stand up for a further five minutes after which his or her arterial pressure should again be taken. Explain the difference (if any) between the two readings.

EFFECT OF EXERCISE

1 The subject should take severe exercise for five minutes.

2 The partner should then determine the subject's systolic pressure at one minute intervals until they return to normal.

3 Plot the results, systolic pressure on the vertical axis, time on the horizontal axis. Compare with other members of your class.

Requirements
Sphygmomanometer

For Consideration

(1) Re-read the instructions on the use of the sphygmomanometer. Why does the appearance and subsequent decline in the pulse, as you deflate the arm band, indicate the systolic and diastolic pressures respectively? Explain the theory behind the phenomenon as fully as you can.
(2) Make a list of all the factors you can think of which might lead to (a) an increase and (b) a decrease in a person's blood pressure.

Questions and Problems

1 Explain as precisely as you can why:
(a) an excess of carbon dioxide if inspired is dangerous;
(b) the rate of an athlete's heart beat (cardiac frequency) increases just before he or she starts a race;
(c) violent exercise is dangerous for elderly people;
(d) carbon monoxide is poisonous.

2 It is commonly stated that the main stimulus responsible for the faster rate of breathing that occurs during muscular exercise is the increased carbon dioxide tension in the blood. However, it has been found that the ventilation rate achieved by a human subject during severe exercise is considerably greater than the maximum response shown by the same subject breathing carbon dioxide at rest. Explain.

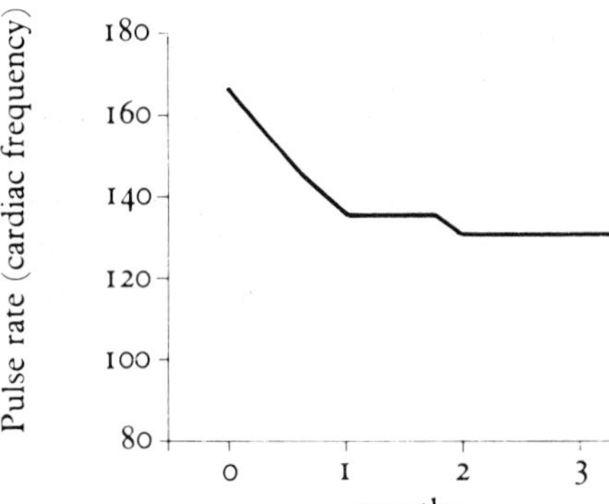

Figure 16.2 Graph showing change in pulse rate of an athlete during three and a half months regular training on a bicycle joulometer.

3 The graph in Figure 16.2 shows the pulse rate of an athlete during three-and-a-half months training on a bicycle joulometer (bicycle ergometer). The work load was kept constant throughout the training period at 14 715 watts. Comment on these measurements.

How would you expect the athlete's cardiac output (volume of blood expelled from the heart per minute), breathing frequency (inspirations per minute) and ventilation rate (volume of air inspired per minute) to change during this period? Explain fully.

4 Outline the physiological changes that take place in the human body in:
(a) performing a 100-metre sprint;
(b) a long-distance race;
(c) ascending to a height of 9000 metres in an aeroplane without oxygen apparatus;
(d) climbing a mountain 9000 metres high without oxygen apparatus.

5 The Olympic Games in 1968 were held in Mexico City and competing national teams gathered there for a much longer period in advance of the events than in previous Games. Discuss the necessity for this long period. *(O and C modified)*

6 The following table shows the blood flow in cm^3 per min to various regions of the human body while it is at rest, and also during different states of physical activity:

Region	At rest	Light exercise	Fairly strenuous exercise	Maximum exertion
Heart muscles	250	350	750	1000
Skeletal muscles	1200	4500	12 500	22 000
Kidneys	1100	900	600	250
Gut	1400	1100	600	300
Skin	500	1500	1900	600
Brain	750	750	750	750
All other regions	600	400	400	100
TOTAL	5800	9500	17 500	25 000

Explain these figures as far as you are able. *(JMB)*

7 What enables certain species of whales to remain submerged under water for as much as an hour?

8 The term hypoxia usually refers to a condition in which the availability or utilisation of oxygen is depressed. The data listed below illustrate four different types of hypoxia compared with the state of a 'normal' person breathing fresh room air. (Assume that the mass, sex, and age of all subjects are the same.)

Subject	**Haemoglobin** (g Hb per 100 cm^3 blood)	**O_2 Content of Arterial Blood** (cm^3 O_2 per 100 cm^3 blood)	**O_2 Content of Venous Blood** (cm^3 O_2 per 100 cm^3 blood)	**Cardiac Output** (litres per minute)
A Normal	15	19	15	5.0
B Hypoxia	15	15	12	6.6
C Hypoxia	8	9.5	6.5	7.0
D Hypoxia	16	20	13	3.0
E Hypoxia	15	19	18	no information

Suggest explanations of the cause of the hypoxia in subjects B to E. Subject B has an increased rate of breathing. Briefly describe the physiological mechanism that is responsible. (*SA modified*)

9 When a diver returns to the surface after being submerged at a depth of about 25 metres he or she may suffer from decompression sickness, commonly known as 'the bends'. Bubbles of nitrogen form in the blood, restricting circulation and causing partial paralysis. Great pain in the middle of the body causes the diver to bend over – hence the name given to this condition.

(a) Explain why the nitrogen bubbles are formed in the blood.

(b) What factors would be expected to increase the severity of the condition?

(c) What precautions might be taken to prevent it happening?

(d) Why is it that fat people are generally more susceptible to decompression sickness than thin people?

(e) Decompression sickness also occurs when we ascend rapidly in an aeroplane, but the height through which we can rise before suffering from 'the bends' is very much greater than for a diver (approximately 6000 metres as against 25 metres). Why the difference?

17 Defence Against Disease

Background Summary

1 The destruction of pathogenic micro-organisms, and/or the neutralization of toxic substances produced by them, is an important aspect of homeostasis.

2 The body of an organism is defended from pathogenic micro-organisms by preventing their entry and/or destroying them after they have entered. In both cases medical science has augmented the body's natural defence mechanisms with artificial ones.

3 **Preventing entry** is achieved by means of barriers, e.g. skin and clotting of blood; rejection, e.g. coughing; and destruction, e.g. lysozyme in external secretions. Artificial methods include personal hygiene, environmental health measures, antisepsis, and asepsis.

4 Destruction of micro-organisms, once they are in the bloodstream, is carried out by **phagocytosis** and the **immune response**, both functions of the white blood cells (leucocytes). The leucocytes are formed in the red bone marrow and then migrate to the **lymph nodes**.

5 The immune response involves the production of specific **antibodies** in response to **antigens** on the surface of the micro-organisms. Different types of antibodies include antitoxins, agglutinins, precipatins, lysins and opsonins.

6 **Immunity** may be conferred on an animal by active or passive means depending on whether the animal is stimulated to produce its own antibodies or receives ready-made antibodies from an external source. Active artificial immunity may be conferred by injecting antigens (**vaccine**) into the body.

7 An enhanced immunological response occurs if the body receives a second dose of antigen sufficiently soon after the first dose.

8 The currently favoured hypothesis accounting for the production of specific antibodies is the **clonal selection hypothesis**. Specific lymphocytes, already present at birth, proliferate into clones of antibody-producing **plasma cells** when required.

9 Antibodies produced by a single clone of plasma cells are called **monoclonal antibodies**. Much used in research, they have enabled the structure of specific antibody molecules to be worked out, throwing light on the nature of the association between antibody and antigen.

10 Two kinds of lymphocyte are recognised: **B lymphocytes** give rise to the **antibody-mediated immune response** as described above. **T lymphocytes** give rise to the **cell-mediated immune response**. There are several types of T lymphocyte with different functions. They migrate from the bone marrow to the lymph nodes via the **thymus gland**.

11 Sometimes an immune response is given to a harmless substance, resulting in an **allergy**. Allergic reactions are often attributable to **histamine**, and the resulting stress is combatted by the hormone **cortisol**. Cortisol also combats **inflammation**.

12 The antibody-mediated immune reaction can be seen when blood belonging to two incompatible groups is mixed, as might occur in a blood transfusion. With respect to the ABO group system, a **universal donor** (group O) can give blood to a recipient of any group without agglutination; a **universal recipient** (group AB) can receive blood from a donor of any group without agglutination.

13 An immune reaction is also seen when Rhesus positive and Rhesus negative bloods come into contact. In certain situations this occurs during pregnancy, resulting in haemolytic disease of the newborn (erythroblastosis foetalis).

14 An unfortunate aspect of the cell-mediated immune response is that foreign tissue introduced into a recipient in surgical transplantation is usually rejected. Compatibility is possible only between genetically identical (or at least very similar) individuals, otherwise the normal immune response must be prevented.

15 Our other endeavours to combat disease include the use of **chemotherapeutic agents**, e.g. penicillin and sulphonamide drugs. **Interferon**, a cell protein that prevents multiplication of viruses, may offer possibilities in the future and is claimed to be effective against certain types of cancer.

16 Plant defences against disease-causing micro-organisms include various **protective devices** (e.g. cuticle), the formation of **callus tissue**, and the production of antibiotic-like **phytoalexins**.

Investigation 17.1
Different types of white cells in human blood

CAUTION:
Because of the risk of infection you should sample only your own blood. The lancet must be sterile and used only once: throw it away afterwards in the receptacle provided.

Blood is a complex circulating tissue consisting of red and white blood cells and platelets suspended in a fluid medium, plasma. No staining is required to see the red blood cells (*see* page 104), but staining is necessary to distinguish the platelets and five types of white cells.

Procedure

We will stain a blood smear with Leishman's stain or Wright's stain which consist of a mixture of eosin and methylene blue. Proceed as follows:

1 Clean two slides thoroughly with acidified ethanol and dry them. Using a sterilised lancet, draw some of your own blood by pricking a finger or thumb. Sterilise your skin first by swabbing it with cotton wool soaked in ethanol.

2 Make a blood smear on the slide as described on page 105 (Figure 11.1). Then sterilise your skin again with ethanol.

3 Let the smeared slide dry. Now pipette onto the smear eight drops of stain and leave for about 45 seconds. Then add to the stain eight drops of distilled water and mix by rocking the slide. Leave for six to ten minutes.

4 Remove excess stain in a stream of distilled water for five seconds. Blot gently with clean, dust-free filter paper. When dry, the stained smear can be viewed without a coverslip.

5 If you wish to keep your preparation it is advisable to put on Canada balsam and a coverslip so as to protect the smear. Alternatively spray the smear with triolic spray: when this sets it forms a transparent protective covering over the smear.

IDENTIFICATION OF WHITE BLOOD CELLS

1 White blood cells can be immediately distinguished from red ones by the fact that the former have a nucleus. This will have stained purple or blue. Platelets will appear as small groups of purple dots.

2 There are five types of white cells, which can be identified by reference to Figure 17.1. Distinguish between the granulocyte (polymorph) with its granular cytoplasm and lobed nucleus (which looks like a string of sausages), and the agranulocyte with its non-granular cytoplasm and large spherical or bean-shaped nucleus.

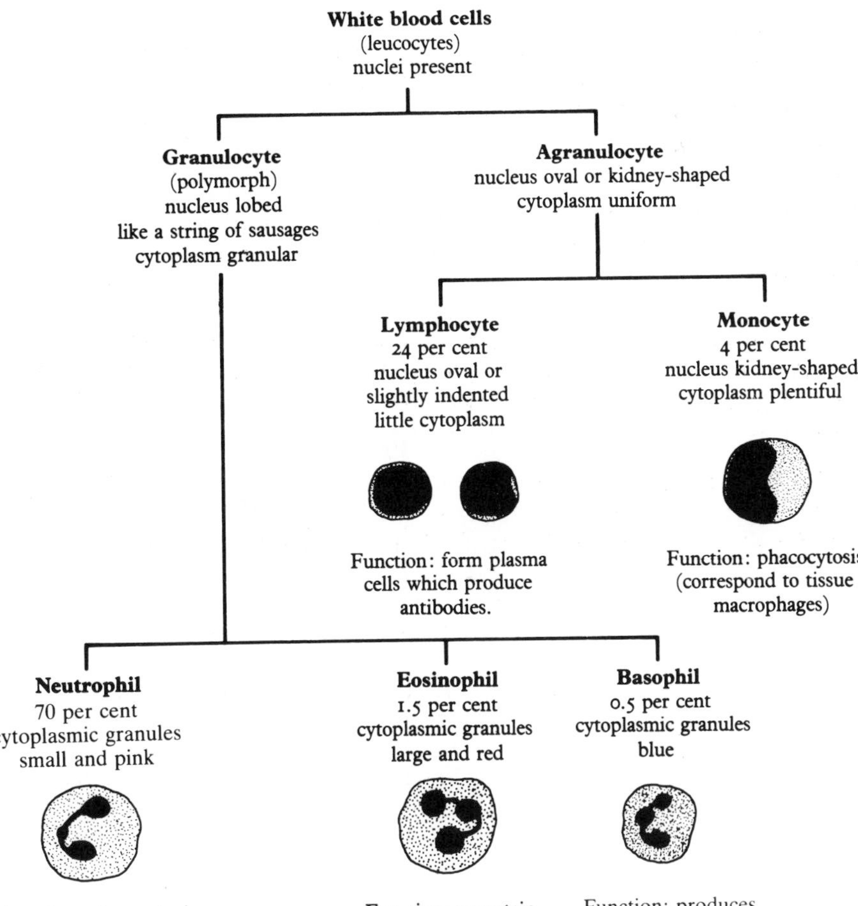

Figure 17.1 Summary of the different types of white blood cell found in human blood. The relative proportions are given as percentages of the total number of white blood cells.

Requirements
Slides ×2
Large coverslip
Sterilised lancet
Receptacle for used lancets (e.g. empty beer can)
Clean dust-free filter paper

Acidified ethanol
Ethanol and cotton wool
Leishman's or Wright's stain
Distilled water
Canada balsam and/or triolic spray

3 As can be seen from Figure 17.1, the most common type of granulocyte is the neutrophil. The most common type of agranulocyte is the lymphocyte. Make sure you can recognise these two kinds of white blood cell. What are their functions?

For Consideration

(1) Which are the most numerous of the five types of white cell in your own smear? Is any type absent altogether as far as you can see? What might be the explanation of its absence?
(2) Leishman's stain and Wright's stain consist of a mixture of acidic eosin (pink) and alkaline methylene blue (blue). Can you explain why the three types of granulocyte stain differently with these stains, and why they are given their respective names?
(3) Where in the human body, apart from the bloodstream, would you expect to find white blood cells or their derivatives? How do they get there?

Investigation 17.2
The number of white cells in human blood

CAUTION:
Because of the risk of infection you should sample only your own blood. The lancet must be sterile and used only once: throw it away afterwards in the receptacle provided.

As with red blood cells, white blood cells can be counted by employing a sampling technique using a haemocytometer. Such estimations are important clinically, for an abnormally low or high white cell count may be characteristic of certain diseases.

Apparatus

For details of the haemocytometer *see* page 106. Examine the haemocytometer slide under low power and identify the type-B squares. These are the squares you should use for your white cell count. Each type-B square has an area of $\frac{1}{25}$ mm^2, and the volume represented by a type-B square is 0.004 mm^3.

The pipette for white blood cells is the one with the mark II above the bulb. Make sure the slide and pipette are clean.

Procedure

1 Obtain a large drop of blood by pricking the end of your thumb with a sterilised lancet. Sterilise your skin first with ethanol. Do not squeeze out the blood too vigorously, this will force out a lot of tissue fluid which will dilute the cell concentration.
2 With the rubber tubing attached to the pipette, suck the blood up to the 'I' mark. Quickly dry the tip of the pipette. If the 'I' mark has been passed, touch the tip of the pipette with filter paper until the blood drops back to the 'I' mark. Then sterilise your skin again with ethanol.
3 Now suck up Turk's solution until the contents of the pipette reach the 'II' mark. If the 'II' mark is passed, the pipette must be emptied and the procedure started again. (Turk's solution renders the red blood cells invisible (how?) and stains the white cells).
4 Remove the rubber tubing from the pipette. Close the two ends of the pipette with thumb and finger and rock the pipette for at least a minute. When the blood and Turk's solution are thoroughly mixed, blow out six drops so as to expel excess Turk's solution. Your blood sample is now diluted 1 in 10.
5 Place the coverslip in the centre of the slide. Put one drop of diluted blood from the pipette onto the slide alongside the coverslip in the area between the two deep grooves. The blood should be drawn under the coverslip by capillary action. Wait five minutes to allow the cells to settle. If the blood flows into the grooves, clean the slide and put on another drop.
6 Place the slide under the microscope and adjust the illumination so the grid and cells can be clearly seen. If the cells are unevenly distributed, clean the slide and start again.
7 Count the white blood cells in at least ten type-B squares. Record your results by ruling out the appropriate number of squares on a piece of paper and writing the number of cells in each square.

Requirements
Haemocytometer (slide, coverslip, pipette, and rubber tubing)
Sterilised lancet
Receptacle for used lancets
Lens paper

Ethanol and cotton wool
Turk's solution
Distilled water
Ethanoic acid
Propanone (acetone)

Turk's solution made up as follows:
Distilled water (100 cm^3), glacial ethanoic acid (1 cm^3), gentian violet solution (1 cm^3, 1 per cent aqueous)

Note: In each square count all the cells which lie entirely within it, plus those that are touching or overlapping the top and left hand sides. Do not include those touching or overlapping the bottom and right hand sides even if they are within the square.

8 Calculate the average number of cells in a type-B square. Bearing in mind the volume represented by a type-B square, and the dilution factor, calculate the number of white cells per mm^3. A typical figure might be 6000 per mm^3. How does your result compare with this?

9 Assuming that the total volume of blood in the body is 5 dm^3, calculate the number of white cells in the entire circulation.

For Consideration

(1) In what circumstances would you expect there to be, temporarily or permanently, an abnormally large number of white blood cells in the bloodstream?
(2) In what circumstances would you expect there to be an abnormally low white cell count?

Investigation 17.3 Determination of human blood groups

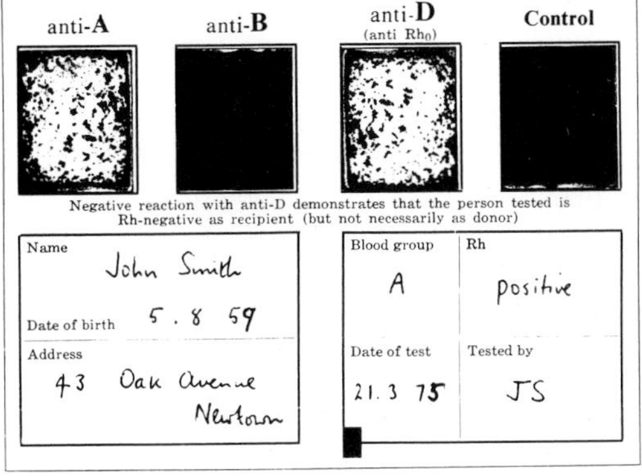

Figure 17.2 A blood grouping card. (Reproduced by permission of Nordisk Insulinlaboratorium, Gentofte, Denmark and Philip Harris Biological Limited).

The human population can be divided into four groups on the basis of the reaction between the blood of different individuals when mixed together. These groups are called **A**, **B**, **AB**, and **O**. The capital letters denote types of antigens present on the surface of the person's red blood cells. Corresponding antibodies in the plasma are designated **a**, **b**, **ab** and **o**. If a person has a particular antigen (say **A**) on their red cells, he or she cannot have the corresponding antibody (in this case **a**) in their plasma, otherwise agglutination will occur.

So the blood groups of different individuals can be summarised as follows:

Blood group	Type of antigens on red blood cells	Type of antibodies in plasma
A	**A**	**b**
B	**B**	**a**
AB	**A** and **B**	nil
O	nil	**a** and **b**

When the bloods of different individuals are mixed, as in a transfusion, no reaction takes place provided that the recipient's blood does not contain antibodies corresponding to the donor's antigens. If it does, agglutination occurs. (Normally it does not matter if the donor's antibodies are incompatible with the recipient's antigens. Why?).

In addition to the ABO system, most people's red blood cells possess an antigen called the Rhesus factor (**Rh** factor). Such people are Rh positive. People lacking this factor are Rhesus negative. The plasma of Rh negative people does not contain Rhesus antibodies but it may be induced to develop them in certain circumstances. (What circumstances?).

It is obviously of medical importance that a person's blood group should be known, so in the event of the person requiring a transfusion blood of a compatible group can be used.

Method

An individual's blood group can be determined by mixing a sample of his blood with a series of sera each containing a reagent corresponding to a specific type of antibody. The reagents contained in the sera are anti-A (corresponding to type a antibodies), anti-B (corresponding to type b antibodies), and anti-D (corresponding to Rhesus antibodies, also called anti-Rh_o).

The reagents are contained in test panels on a blood grouping card (Figure 17.2). Each panel consists of a cellulose strip on which the specific reagents have been deposited and dried.

Procedure

1 Using the standard pipette supplied, place a full drop of tap water[1] on the reagent in the anti-A test panel.

[1] Some makes of blood grouping cards require a dilute sodium chloride solution – look at the instructions.

The drop of blood on the flat end of the plastic stick should be just the right size —a hemisphere as shown below:

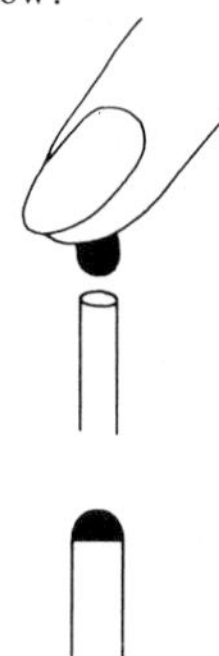

Figure 17.3 Placing a drop of blood on the plastic stick for use with the blood grouping card.

Dissolve the reagent in the water by mixing with the flat end of the plastic stick provided. Confine the mixing to a small area in the centre of the panel.

2 Clean the stick thoroughly with cotton wool and repeat the above procedure for the anti-B, anti-D and control panels. Clean the stick thoroughly with fresh cotton wool between each.

3 Sterilise a thumb or finger with ethanol. Obtain a drop of blood by pricking your thumb or finger with a sterilised lancet. Squeeze the blood onto the flat end of the plastic stick. The blood should form a hemisphere as shown in Figure 17.3.

CAUTION:
Because of the risk of infection you should sample only your own blood. Do not touch anyone else's blood. The lancet must be sterile and used only once: throw it away afterwards in the receptacle provided.

Requirements
Blood grouping card (sealed)
Dropping pipette
Plastic stick
Beaker for tap water
Cotton wool for cleaning plastic stick
Sterilised lancet
Receptacle for used lancets
Ethanol and cotton wool

Note: Blood grouping kits containing dropping pipette, plastic stick, sterile lancet and medical swab, are available from suppliers.

Blood grouping using saliva: It is possible to carry out a blood-grouping procedure using human saliva. The technique requires the student to provide a small sample of saliva rather than blood. Kits are available from suppliers.

4 Mix the blood with the dissolved reagent in the anti-A panel, and then spread it over the whole panel. Now sterilise your skin again with ethanol.

5 Clean the stick and repeat Steps 3 and 4 with the anti-B, anti-D and control panels. Clean the stick thoroughly between each.

6 Tilt the card backwards and forwards and from side to side, holding it vertically for about ten seconds in each direction. This helps to mix the test solutions, but do not let any of them run over the boundaries of the panels.

Results

If agglutination occurs the blood sample in the test panel will form red streaks and blotches. The results can be interpreted as follows:

Agglutination in the anti-A panel means you belong to group A.
Agglutination in the anti-B panel means you belong to group B.
Agglutination in both anti-A and anti-B panels means you belong to group AB.
Agglutination in neither anti-A nor anti-B panels means you belong to group O.
Agglutination in the anti-D panel means you are Rhesus positive.
No agglutination in the anti-D panel means you are Rhesus negative.

Work out the percentage of students belonging to each blood group in your class and compare with the national frequencies given in Table 17.1.

Blood group	Per cent of population
O	47
A	41
B	9
AB	3
Rh-positive	85
Rh-negative	15

Table 17.1 The percentage of the population with different blood groups in Great Britain.

For Consideration

(1) Can you account for the fact that blood groups O and A are so much more common than B and AB?
(2) Can you explain why Rh-positive individuals are so much more common than Rh-negative individuals?
(3) What is the relevance of blood groups to the mechanisms by which the body defends itself against disease?

Investigation 17.4
Action of lysozyme

Lysozyme is an enzyme which kills bacteria and is present in body fluids. It was discovered by Alexander Fleming when he shed tears into an open petri dish containing a culture of bacteria. The enzyme hydrolyses peptidoglycan, the main structural component of bacterial cell walls.

Some bacteria are more sensitive to the enzyme than others. Gram positive bacteria, those which stain readily with the gram stain of crystal violet and iodine, are particulary sensitive to lysozyme. The yellow bacterium *Micrococcus luteus* (Gram +) is particularly sensitive to the enzyme and provides a convenient assay for it. The yellow culture rapidly becomes less turbid as the cells are broken open by the lysozyme. In this investigation you can determine whether or not lysozyme is present in various body fluids, and its relative concentration therein.

Requirements
Blood lancet (sterile)
Colorimeter with filter allowing light at 600 μm to pass (1 for class)
Colorimeter tubes (or test tubes able to fit colorimeter) ×7
Cotton wool
Graph paper
Graduated pipettes (1 cm^3 and 10 cm^3, with rubber suckers)
Polythene bag
Spatula
Stopwatch or stopclock
Test tubes ×4

Ethanol (90 per cent)
Lysozyme [1 mg cm^{-3} in phosphate buffer solution (pH 8.0)]
Phosphate buffer solutions (pH 6.4 and pH 8.0, see below)

Egg white
Culture suspension of *Micrococcus luteus* [10 mg cm^{-3} in sodium chloride solution (0.85 per cent)]
Onion

To prepare the phosphate buffer solutions: This requires sodium dihydrogenphosphate solution (0.2 mol dm^{-3}) and citric acid solution (0.1 mol dm^{-3}).
(a) To make a buffer of pH 6.4: mix 70.9 cm^3 of the sodium dihydrogenphosphate solution with 29.1 cm^3 of the citric acid solution.
(b) To make a buffer of pH 8.0: mix 97.25 cm^3 of the sodium dihydrogenphosphate solution with 2.75 cm^3 of the citric acid solution.

CAUTION:
Because of the risk of infection you should sample only your own body fluids. This particularly applies to blood. For precautions to take in sampling blood see the caution note on page 162.

Procedure

1 The first task is to produce a standard curve for the action of lysozyme on *Micrococcus luteus*. Pipette 9 cm^3 of phosphate buffer solution into a colorimeter tube, or a test tube which fits into your colorimeter. Pipette 0.3 cm^3 of *M. luteus* culture into the buffer sample. Shake the mixture.
2 Place the tube in the colorimeter, and write the colorimeter reading on your recording sheet. You will be taking a reading every twenty seconds, so have a stopwatch ready.
3 Pipette 0.3 cm^3 of the lysozyme solution into the colorimeter tube and start the stopwatch. Record a colorimeter reading every twenty seconds for three minutes, and then at one minute intervals for further two minutes.
4 Plot a graph of the curve of the colorimeter reading against time.
5 Repeat in turn Steps 1 to 4, first with 0.3 cm^3 of lysozyme solution diluted to half its original strength, and then with 0.3 cm^3 of lysozyme solution diluted to a quarter the original strength. The three curves (plotted on the *same* axes) constitute your standard curves.
6 Now you can test some fluids for lysozyme activity. For example, test egg-white, blood, sweat, and tears (see below).
7 In each case collect some of the fluid in a test tube and dilute it with a known volume of distilled water (using a pipette). Following the same procedure as outlined in Steps 1 to 3, find out how rapidly the yellow colour disappears when the bacteria are treated with 0.3 cm^3 of the fluid preparation.
8 Compare your results with the standard curves. From the comparison, calculate the lysozyme content of the original fluid. To do this you must first calculate the concentration of the enzyme in the solutions which were used to determine the standard curves.

How to obtain the fluids

1 Egg white will need to be provided.
2 To obtain blood, prick a finger as explained on page 161. (Be sure you observe the necessary precautions.)
3 To obtain sweat, run up and down stairs a few times and collect some sweat from the surface of the skin.
4 To obtain tears, place your eye at the mouth of a polythene bag containing an onion and collect your tears.

For consideration

(1) A cup of egg white, if left exposed on a kitchen shelf, hardly ever goes bad. On the other hand, hard-boiled eggs rapidly go mouldy. Why?
(2) Besides the ones you have tested, which other body fluids would you expect to contain lysozyme?

Investigation 17.5
Antibiotics and bacteria

CAUTION:
Culturing bacteria is potentially hazardous. Wash your hands thoroughly before and after the experiments. Do not put your fingers near your mouth or nose while handling the bacterial cultures. Keep all test tubes and petri dishes closed except when you *must* open them, and once the lids of the petri dishes have been sealed with sellotape, keep them sealed. At the end of the practical session swab the bench with disinfectant.

Antibiotics are substances, produced by certain living organisms, which kill, or prevent the reproduction of, micro-organisms belonging to other species, including bacteria. Such substances, which include the well-known antibiotic, penicillin, are of great medical importance. This investigation is designed to demonstrate the anti-bacterial action of certain antibiotics.

Procedure

1 Obtain a stoppered bottle or test tube containing 15 cm^3 of sterile nutrient agar. Melt the agar by placing the bottle in a water bath at 100 °C.
2 Remove the bottle and cool to about 45 °C. The agar should remain in liquid form, but be cool enough to hold against your cheek. Most agars solidify at about 42 °C.
3 Obtain a test tube containing a culture of non-pathogenic bacteria on an agar slope (see list of requirements). The tube should be kept plugged with sterile cotton wood.
4 The object of the next step is to transfer a sample of bacteria from the agar slope in the test tube to the liquid agar in the bottle. To avoid contamination the whole operation should be carried out as quickly as possible under

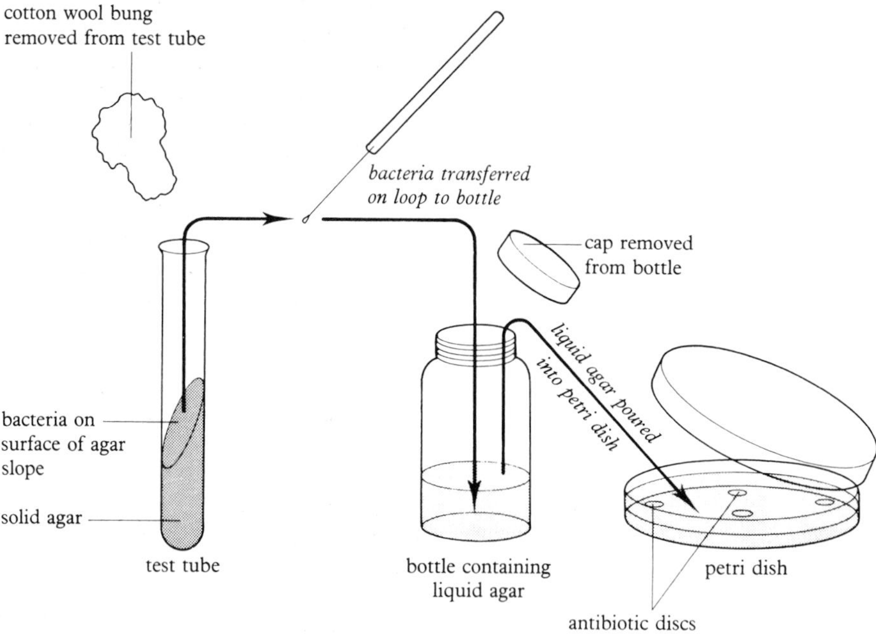

Figure 17.4 Preparation of bacterial culture in petri dish for treatment with antibiotic discs.

sterile conditions. Figure 17.4 summarises the procedure. Study the illustration and then proceed to Step 5.

5 Quickly sterilise an inoculation loop by heating it in a flame, then cooling it in sterile water.

6 Remove the cotton wool bung from the test tube containing the bacterial culture, and sterilise the mouth of the tube by passing it through a flame several times.

7 Now remove the cap from the bottle of liquid agar, flame the mouth of the bottle and with the sterilized loop transfer one loopful of bacterial culture from the agar slope to the liquid agar in the bottle. Dip the loop right into the bottle so as to thoroughly mix the bacteria with the agar.

8 Without delay pour the liquid agar containing the bacteria into a warm, sterilised petri dish. In doing this, avoid contamination by raising the lid of the petri dish only just enough to pour in the agar. (Warming the petri dish prevents water condensing on the lid as you pour in the agar.)

9 After replacing the lid, ensure even distribution of the agar by gently moving the petri dish from side to side on a flat surface.

10 After the agar has hardened, place on the surface of the agar a small disc of filter paper, which has been soaked in an antibiotic then allowed to dry. The disc should be transferred with sterile forceps. Suitable antibiotics for investigation include penicillin and aureomycin.

11 Place a control disc, i.e. one that has been soaked in water then allowed to dry, on the agar.

12 A convenient alternative to the above procedure is to use a 'multodisk'. This consists of a central control disc with side-arms leading to small discs each impregnated with a different antibiotic.

13 Fix the lid of the petri dish with sellotape. Turn the petri dish upside down to avoid condensation on the surface of the agar. Incubate at 37 °C. Examine at intervals over several days for bacterial growth.

Results

Draw a diagram of the agar surface showing the areas where bacterial growth has, or has not, occurred. How do these areas relate to the positions of the antibiotic and control discs?

The source of penicillin

1 Penicillin is obtained from the fungus *Penicillium*. With a sterile needle mix spores of *Penicillium notatum* with a drop of water on a slide.

2 Obtain a sterile petri dish of solid agar. Raise the lid and with a sterile needle make a smear of your spore suspension across the agar to one side of the dish (Figure 17.5).

3 Incubate the petri dish for 2–3 days to allow the fungus to establish itself.

4 Two or three days later, inoculate the agar with several different types of

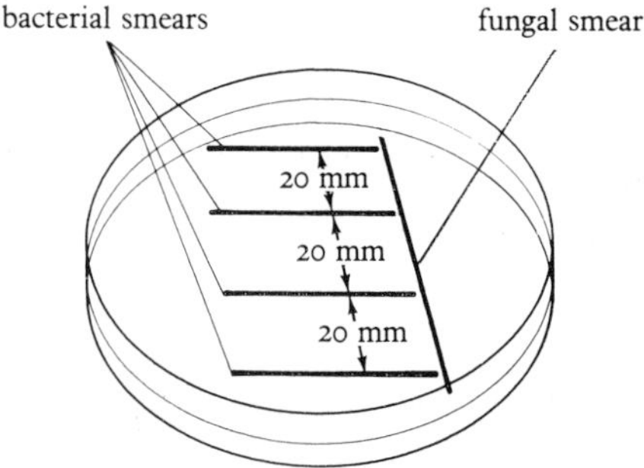

Figure 17.5 Plating of fungal and bacterial smears.

harmless bacteria. Using a sterile inoculation loop, smear the bacteria onto the agar at right angles to the fungal smear as shown in Figure 17.5. Do not inoculate more than four types of bacteria, leaving at least 20 mm between each.

5 Fix the lid of the petri dish with sellotape. Incubate upside down at 37 °C for several days and examine at intervals. Interpret your results.

For Consideration

(1) Why was it necessary to ensure sterile conditions in this investigation?
(2) When, by whom, and in what circumstances, was penicillin discovered?
(3) Suggest hypotheses to explain how antibiotics (in general) might prevent the development of bacteria.
(4) What other agents, besides those tested in this investigation, might be effective against bacteria? How would you test their efficiency?
(5) Antibiotics have been extracted from various species of fungus and soil micro-organisms. Do you think they have any use to the organisms which produce them? Explain your answer.

Requirements
Microscope
Water bath at 100 °C
Incubator at 37 °C
Bunsen burner or spirit lamp
Petri dish (diameter 88 mm) ×2
Inoculation loop
Forceps

Sterile nutrient agar (15 cm^3, in stoppered bottle)
Sterile water
Methylene blue and/or other bacterial stains
Antibiotic discs (e.g. penicillin, streptomycin) or 'multodisk'
Disinfectant for cleaning bench

Pure culture of non-pathogenic bacteria, on agar slope in test tube. (Suitable bacteria are listed in suppliers' catalogues, but make sure they are approved by your local authority.)
Spores of *Penicillium*

To make an inoculation loop: Insert the end of a 3 cm length of platinum or 'nichrome' wire into the end of a glass rod softened over a bunsen flame. The loop itself should have a diameter of approximately 2 mm.
To prepare antibiotic discs: Cut out a disc of filter paper and soak in a solution of the antibiotic. Dry and store in a sealed bottle.

Note: Sterile antibiotic discs are available from suppliers.

Questions and Problems

1 Write short explanatory notes on lysozyme, rhesus factor, interferon, and penicillin.

2 Explain the difference between: (a) antisepsis and asepsis; (b) fibrinogen and fibrin; (c) active and passive immunity; (d) homografts and heterografts.

3 Give a brief account of how antibodies are thought to be produced in the mammalian body. Bearing in mind that antibodies are too small to be seen under a microscope, how could you determine the relative amounts of a specific antibody in an individual at different times?

Figure 17.6 shows the relative amounts of a specific antibody formed in the bloodstream after (a) a first injection of an antigen, and (b) a later injection of the same antigen. Discuss the difference between the two curves.

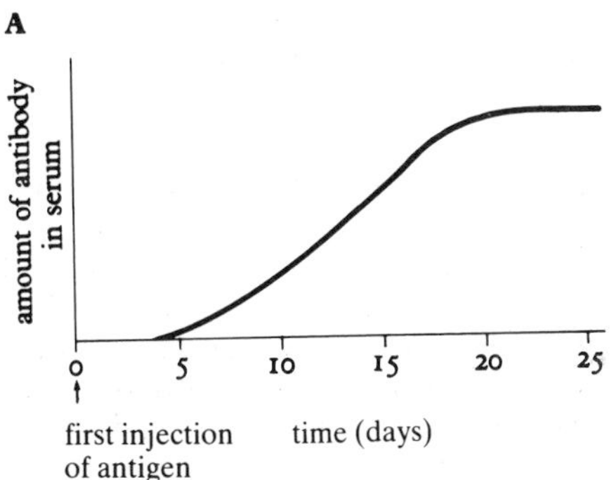

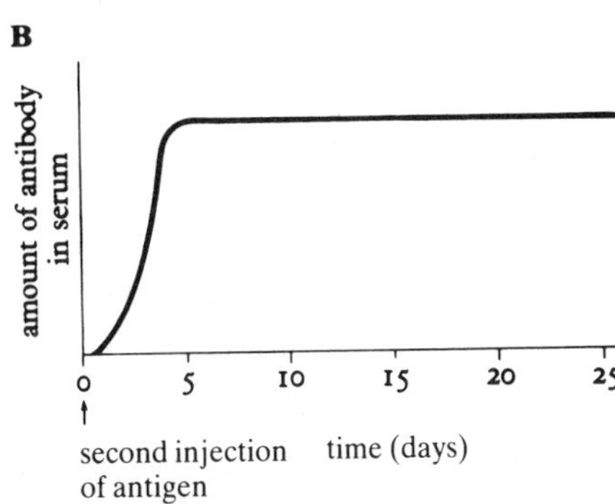

Figure 17.6 Graphs showing the amounts of an antibody formed in the bloodstream after (**A**) first injection of an antigen, and (**B**) after a second injection of the same antigen.

4 In 1952 two patients, whom we can call Mr A and Mr B, were in the same ward in University College Hospital, London. Both appeared to suffer from haemophilia, a condition in which the blood takes an abnormally long time to clot. At this time haemophilia was known to be caused by the absence of a chemical factor, anti-haemophilic globulin, necessary for the conversion of disintegrated platelets into thromboplastin.

In treating Mr A it was found that the normal clotting time could be restored by injections of anti-haemophilic globulin; however, Mr B did not respond to this treatment. It was further found that transferring plasma from Mr B into Mr A's bloodstream restored Mr A's clotting time to normal, and transferring plasma from Mr A to Mr B restored Mr B's clotting time to normal.

What conclusions could be drawn from these observations?

In transferring plasma from one patient to the other the doctors did not need to ensure that both shared the same blood group. Why was this unnecessary?

5 Whooping cough is a bacterial disease which, in humans, involves a prolonged infection of the respiratory tree. It is characterised by severe bouts of coughing interrupted by inspiratory whoops. Since the mid-1940s children have been vaccinated against the disease, though it is now widely believed that vaccination carries with it a very slight risk of brain damage.

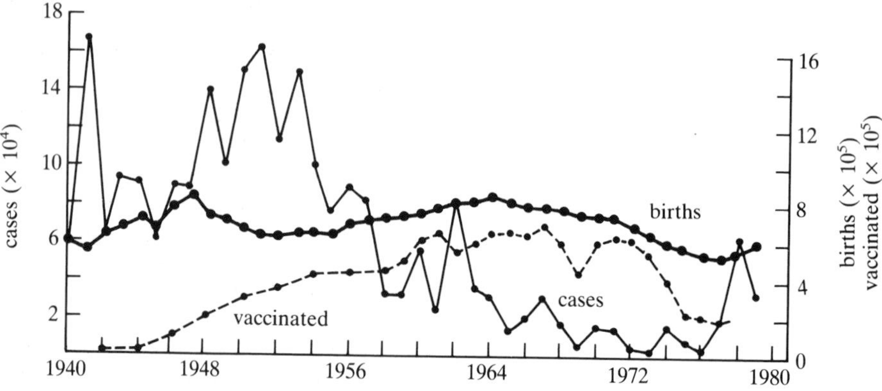

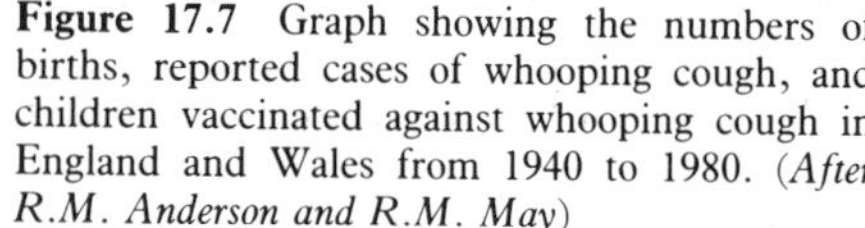
Figure 17.7 Graph showing the numbers of births, reported cases of whooping cough, and children vaccinated against whooping cough in England and Wales from 1940 to 1980. (*After R.M. Anderson and R.M. May*)

The graph in Figure 17.7 shows for the period 1940–1979 (i) the numbers of cases of whooping cough reported each year in England and Wales (ii) the numbers of children vaccinated each year and (iii) the birth rate each year.

(a) Discuss the relationship between the number of children vaccinated each year and the number who contracted the disease.

(b) During an epidemic of whooping cough in 1982, an unvaccinated child had one chance in twenty of contracting the disease in the next year. The risk of permanent brain damage as a direct result of vaccination is 1 in 40 000. The chance that a child who catches whooping cough will die of it is 1 in 3000.

What advice would you give (i) a mother with a child of twelve months, (ii) a doctor trying to promote vaccination?

(c) Whooping cough is caused by a bacterium, *Bordetella pertussis*. Suggest *in detail* one method by which a vaccine against whooping cough could be produced.

(d) Explain in detail *at the cellular and molecular level* how vaccination reduces the chance of an individual contracting the disease.

(e) Why would vaccination of babies less than six months old be ineffective?

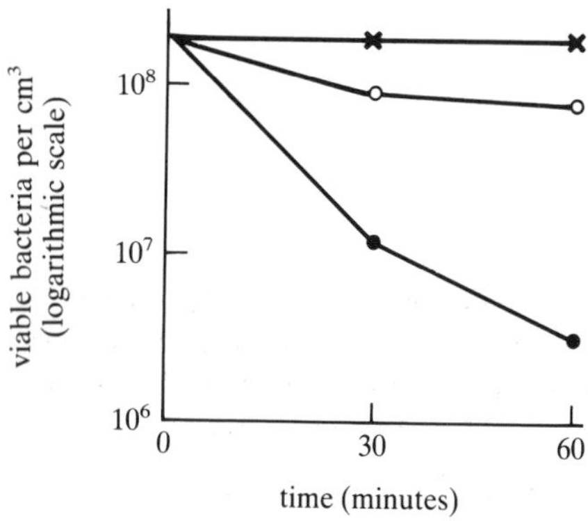

Figure 17.8 The effect on bacterial numbers of incubating about 200 million bacteria (*Staphylococcus aureus*) with 5 million human neutrophils in a total volume of 1 cm^3 of human blood serum. (*After D.L. Confer and J.W. Eaton*)
× bacteria only, no neutrophils added (control).
○ neutrophils had been treated previously with extract from *Bordetella* (whooping cough) bacteria.
● untreated (normal) neutrophils.

6 The bacterium which causes whooping cough, *Bordetella pertussis*, produces an enzyme called adenylate cyclase in large quantities. Extracts of the bacterium, when added to human phagocytic white blood cells, cause the level of cyclic AMP to rise several hundred-fold in twenty minutes. Examine the graph in Figure 17.8. (a) Explain in your own words what the graph shows. (b) Explain why secondary bacterial infections (e.g. pneumonia) are frequent during whooping cough.

7 Here are the results of three experiments on skin transplantation in mice:

Experiment 1: A piece of skin from mouse A is transplanted to mouse B. After 11 days the transplant (graft) is rejected (sloughed off).

Experiment 2: A second piece of skin from mouse A is then transplanted to mouse B. This second graft is rejected after six days.

Experiment 3: A piece of skin from mouse C is transplanted to mouse D, the latter having received injections of cellular material from mouse C before birth. The graft is not rejected.

Answer the following questions as concisely and clearly as you can:

(a) Explain the results of experiments 1 and 2.

(b) Put forward one or more hypotheses to explain the result of experiment 3.

(c) By what means, apart from the procedure outlined in experiment 3, might rejection of grafts be prevented?

(d) What would you conclude about mice A and B if no rejection had occurred?

(O and C modified)

8 Why is transplantation surgery beset with so many difficulties?

9 Write a short essay on B and T lymphocytes, explaining their respective roles in the body's defences against disease.

10 Do not be put off by the length of this question; it is not as bad as it looks!

In mammals, including man, the thymus gland is prominent at the time of birth, but gradually diminishes after birth. Removal of the thymus (thymectomy) from a four-week-old mouse produces no harmful consequences, but removal of the thymus at birth results in a wasting disease: illness with a much retarded growth rate sets in after about five weeks and death occurs by the eighth week; the lymph nodes are severely reduced in size and there is an abnormally small number of lymphocytes in the blood; the immune response does not develop, plasma cells and antibodies failing to be produced. Before reading further, suggest hypotheses to explain the results of this experiment.

In an attempt to discover the role of the thymus gland the following experiment was carried out by R.H. Levey:

Special plastic capsules were prepared. Each capsule was filled with thymus tissue obtained from a newborn mouse. The walls of the capsules contained pores too small to let cells through, but large enough to let through all chemical products of the cells.

Five groups of mice were treated as follows:

Group A: thymectomised at birth, capsules filled with thymus tissue implanted under skin.
Group B: thymectomised at birth, no capsules implanted.
Group C: thymectomised at birth, empty capsules implanted under skin.
Group D: thymectomised at birth, uncapsulated thymus tissue implanted under skin.
Group E: unthymectomised (normal mice).

The results, in summarised form, were as follows:

Group A: normal development: no wasting disease, normal lymph nodes, and lymphocyte count, normal immune response develops with full production of plasma cells and antibodies.
Group B: wasting disease.
Group C: wasting disease.
Group D: exactly like group A.
Group E: exactly like group A.

Now answer the following questions:

(a) Suggest a full explanation for these results.

(b) What is the point of setting up groups B to E?

(c) How do you think the experimenter tested the immune responses of the mice?

(d) It was known before these experiments were performed that at birth lymphocytes migrate in large numbers from the thymus gland to the lymph nodes. Is this observation compatible with the results of the experiments described above?

11 (a) Describe briefly the range of defences of a mammal against infection.

(b) State five reasons why flowering plants could not have evolved defence mechanisms identical to those of mammals.

(c) What barriers in flowering plants prevent fungus infection?

(d) In response to fungus attack, plant cells may secrete compounds known as phytoalexins. What advantage is it to the plant if the response is prompted by the *components* of a fungus cell wall instead of specific proteins produced by a fungus?

(e) Suggest five different ways in which a phytoalexin molecule might act on a fungal hypha and prevent its growth.

18 Nervous and Hormonal Communication

Background Summary

1 The **nervous system** provides the fastest means of communication within the body. In most animals the nervous system consists of a **central nervous system** (**CNS**) and **peripheral nerves**.

2 **Nerve cells** (**neurones**) vary in their structure but in general they possess a cell body (centron) from which arise a variable number of dendrites, together with one or more axons. The axon generally has a **myelin sheath**.

3 Nerve cells are broadly classified into **sensory** (**afferent**), **intermediate** (also known as **connector** and **internuncial**), and **motor** (**efferent**).

4 By recording the potential difference between the inside and outside of giant axons of the squid, it has been shown that at rest the inside is negative with respect to the outside (**resting potential**), but during passage of a nerve impulse this situation is momentarily reversed (**action potential**).

5 The resting potential is maintained by the **sodium-potassium pump**. During passage of the action potential sodium ions enter the axon whose membrane consequently becomes depolarised.

6 In the sodium-potassium pump sodium ions are expelled from the axon, and potassium ions admitted, by the same protein carrier in the membrane. When the membrane is depolarised sodium ions enter passively via specific protein channels.

7 The size of an action potential is independent of the strength of stimulation (**all-or-nothing law**). An extra-strong stimulus may generate more than one action potential but it makes no difference to their size.

8 For a brief period immediately after it has transmitted an impulse, the axon is totally inexcitable (**absolute refractory period**). This is followed by a slightly longer period during which it is partially excitable (**relative refractory period**).

9 Transmission speeds vary from 0.5 $m\ s^{-1}$ to over 100 $m\ s^{-1}$. High speeds of transmission are achieved by having a **myelin** (**medullary**) **sheath** with **nodes of Ranvier** (vertebrates), or **giant axons** (certain invertebrates).

10 Contiguous nerve cells are connected by **synapses**. Typically, a nerve cell is covered with hundreds of **synaptic knobs**. Transmission at the synapse is achieved by **chemical transmission**: a transmitter substance, **noradrenaline** or **acetylcholine**, is liberated from **synaptic vesicles** into the **synaptic cleft**, a process in which calcium ions play an essential part. In sufficient quantity the transmitter substance depolarises the membrane of the post-synaptic cell. The nerve-muscle (neuromuscular) junction operates in the same way.

11 A wide range of chemical transmitters have been found in the brain; they play an important part in many aspects of brain function.

12 Important properties of synapses include **spatial** and **temporal summation** (**facilitation**), **inhibition** and **fatigue** (**accommodation**). Synapses ensure that impulses travel in only one direction; they also account for the actions of many drugs and poisons and play a major part in control processes within the CNS.

13 Although most synapses involve chemical transmission as summarised above, some nerve junctions work by direct **electrical transmission**.

14 Nerve cells are frequently organized into **reflex arcs**. A typical reflex arc consists of receptors, sensory (afferent), intermediate, and motor (efferent) neurones, and effectors. Reflex arcs provide the anatomical basis of **reflex action**. Successive reflex arcs are interlinked by longitudinal neurones.

15 The vertebrate CNS consists of **brain** and **spinal cord**. The brain is subdivided into **forebrain**, **midbrain** and **hindbrain**, the forebrain being further divided into **endbrain** and **'tweenbrain**.

16 In lower vertebrates such as fishes integrative functions, including motor co-ordination, are carried out by the hindbrain, the forebrain and midbrain being mainly for sensory relay. In mammals integrative functions are performed by the forebrain, particularly the much expanded endbrain.

17 The **peripheral nerves** are divided into two types: **spinal** and **cranial**. The former follow a segmental pattern, the latter are less regular due to the development of specialised head structures. The basic arrangement of vertebrate cranial nerves is best seen in the dogfish.

18 Involuntary activities are controlled by the **autonomic nervous system**. This is subdivided into the **sympathetic** and **parasympathetic** systems whose actions are for the most part antagonistic.

19 Certain invertebrates, notably coelenterates, have a **nerve net** and lack any trace of a CNS. Such simple nervous systems show **interneural** and **neuromuscular facilitation**. Transmission speeds are slow.

20 The first glimpses of **through-conduction** appear in sea-anemones, but this phenomenon is more fully developed in higher invertebrates such as the earthworm where it is associated with the development of **giant axons**.

21 The brain is an integral part of the **head**. In the evolution of the animal kingdom the head becomes progressively more elaborate (**cephalisation**): starting as little more than a sensory relay centre, the brain gradually takes over the functions of integration and motor co-ordination.

22 **Hormones**, chemical messengers secreted into the bloodstream by **endocrine organs** (**ductless glands**), can be compared with nerve impulses. They provide an additional means of communication within the body.

23 The basic requirement of any endocrine organ, namely a close association between the secretory cells and bloodstream, is well illustrated by the thyroid gland. This secretes thyroxine which controls the basal metabolic rate.

24 There is a close structural and physiological connection between the endocrine and nervous systems. This is well demonstrated by the adrenal medulla and pituitary gland. The latter contains **neurosecretory cells** which, in addition to transmitting nerve impulses, produce hormones which flow along their axons.

25 Hormones affect their target cells either by influencing the action of the cell's DNA or by activating the appropriate enzymes via **cyclic AMP**.

Investigation 18.1 Microscopic structure of nervous tissue

The principal function of nerve cells is to transmit messages around the body. In order to transmit the correct messages each nerve cell must be connected with adjacent nerve cells. It must also have the means to transmit messages quickly over long distances where appropriate. Keep these functions in mind as you examine nervous tissue under the microscope.

Procedure

SPINAL CORD

1 Examine a transverse section of the spinal cord under low or medium power. Identify as many of the structures shown in Figure 18.1A as you can. Nerve cell bodies are confined to the central grey matter; longitudinal axons of ascending and descending tracts to the peripheral white matter. The small central canal is a reminder of the fact that the CNS of all chordates is hollow. This contrasts with the solid nerve cord of invertebrates such as the earthworm (*see* page 362).

2 Note the meninges surrounding and protecting the spinal cord: thick dura mater and thin pia mater, separated by the vascular arachnoid.

THE CELL BODY OF A MOTOR NEURONE

1 Look again at the transverse section of spinal cord. Locate the cell body of a motor neurone in the ventrolateral region of the grey matter (Figure 18.1B) and examine under high power.

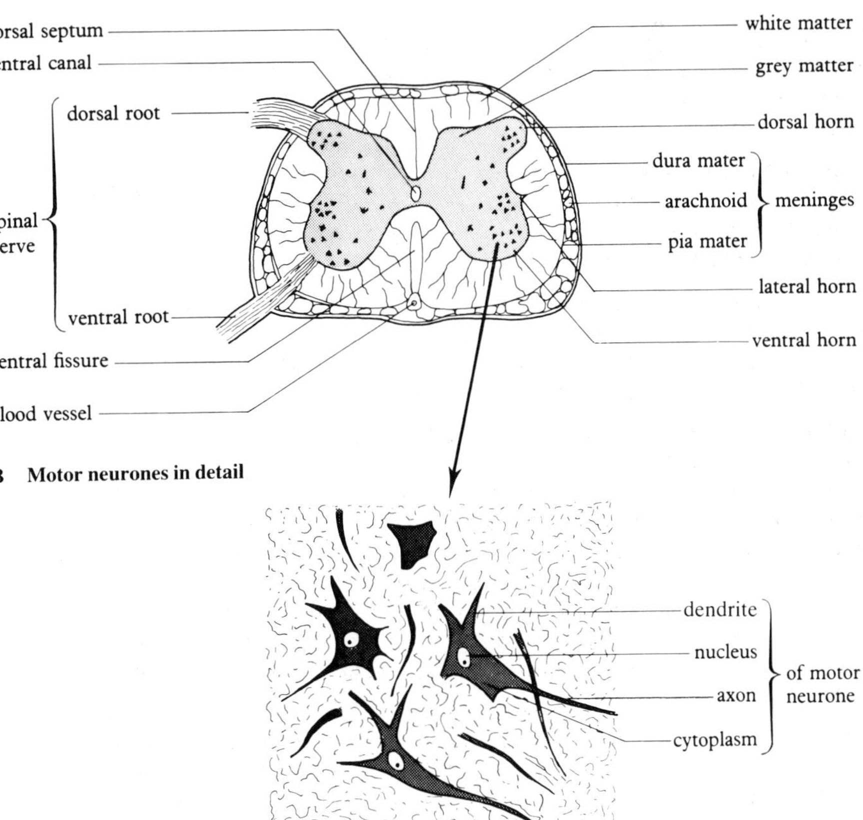

Figure 18.1 Microscopic structure of spinal cord (based on cat).

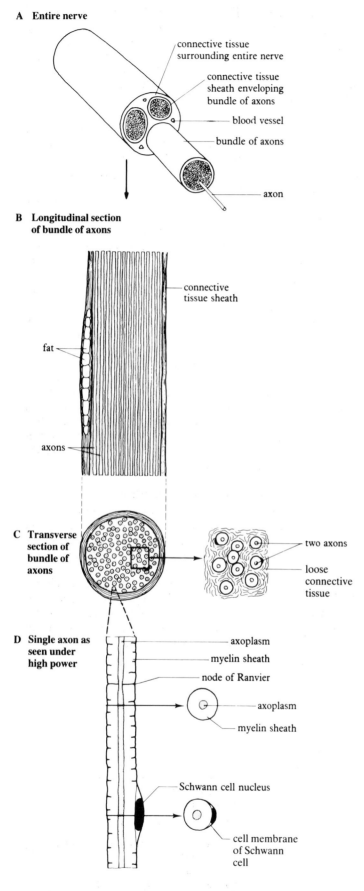

A Entire nerve

connective tissue surrounding entire nerve

connective tissue sheath enveloping bundle of axons

blood vessel

bundle of axons

axon

B Longitudinal section of bundle of axons

connective tissue sheath

fat

axons

C Transverse section of bundle of axons

two axons

loose connective tissue

D Single axon as seen under high power

axoplasm

myelin sheath

node of Ranvier

axoplasm

myelin sheath

Schwann cell nucleus

cell membrane of Schwann cell

Figure 18.2 Microscopic structure of myelinated nerve based on light microscope preparations.

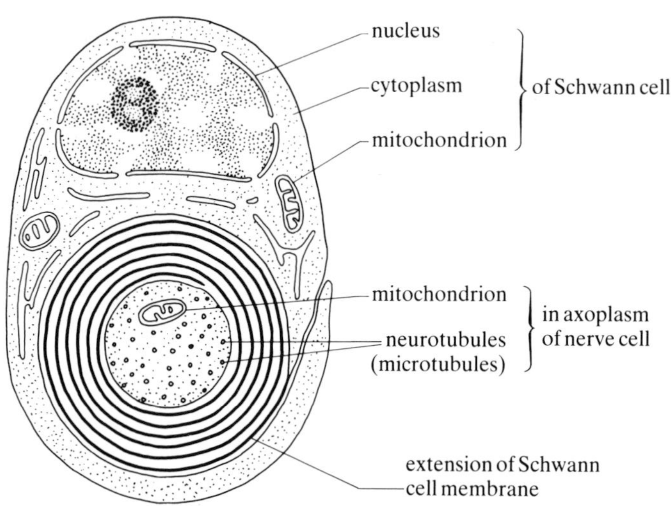

Figure 18.3 Diagram of a transverse section through an axon at the level of a Schwann cell nucleus. Note that the myelin sheath is multi-layered, the layers of lipid being formed by the Schwann cell wrapping itself round the axon as shown. In the electron microscope the axoplasm is seen to contain numerous longitudinally orientated microtubules, known as neurotubules, which are thought to assist transport of materials from the nerve cell body to the far end of the axon.

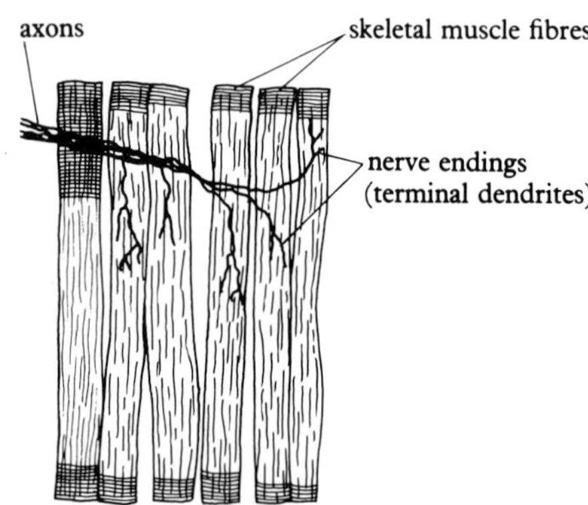

Figure 18.4 Longitudinal section of skeletal muscle showing nerve endings.

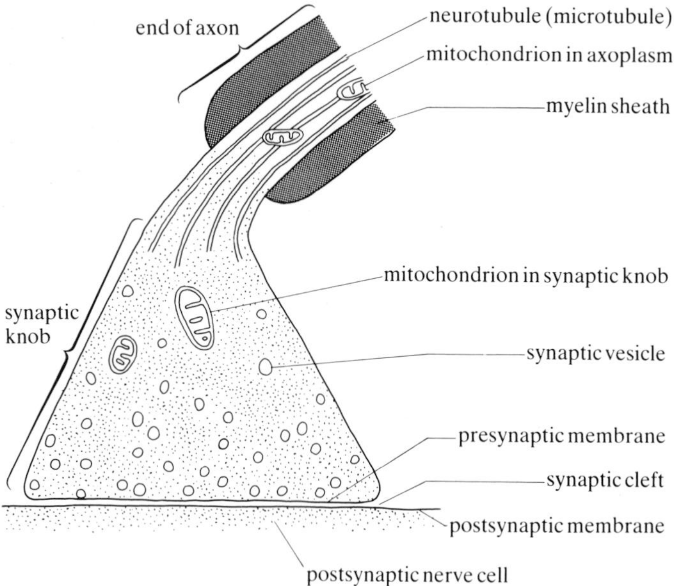

Figure 18.5 Diagram of a section through a synaptic knob, and the terminal end of the axon leading to it, as seen in a typical electron micrograph.

Note cell body (centron) with nucleus, Nissl's granules in cytoplasm, dendrites, beginning of long axon.

2 Silver preparations may show the swollen ends (terminal buttons) of dendrites of neighbouring nerve cells in contact with the membrane of the cell body: these are synapses.

MYELINATED AXON

3 Examine prepared longitudinal and transverse sections of a whole myelinated nerve, e.g. sciatic. Use Figure 18.2 to help you interpret its structure. Notice in particular myelin sheath, nodes of Ranvier and nuclei of Schwann cells.

4 Examine an electron micrograph of a transverse section of an axon which passes through a Schwann cell and its nucleus. Use Figure 18.3 to help you identify the various structures in the micrograph. Look at the myelin sheath very closely and notice that it consists of an extension of the Schwann cell membrane wrapped tightly round the axon. Since the cell membrane contains lipid, the myelin sheath itself will be made of lipid.

5 Axons often innervate effectors such as skeletal muscle. For example, what particular muscles are innervated by axons of the sciatic nerve? Examine a prepared longitudinal section of skeletal muscle showing nerve endings (Figure 18.4). Here the nerve fibres make synaptic contact with the muscle fibres.

6 Examine an electron micrograph of a section through a synapse. Identify the various structures shown in Figure 18.5, particularly the synaptic vesicles and synaptic cleft. How do nerve impulses cross the synapse?

NERVE CELLS IN THE BRAIN

1 Examine a vertical section of the cerebral cortex and notice the layer of pyramidal cells, so called because of their characteristic pyramid shape (Figure 18.6).

2 Observe a pyramidal cell under high power. Numerous dendrites towards the surface connect with other nerve cells. Its long axon extends via the lower parts of the brain to the spinal cord where it joins the descending motor tracts taking impulses to effectors.

3 Examine a vertical section of the cerebellum. Observe Purkinje cells (Figure 18.7). Note numerous dendrites ramifying towards the surface, and long axons extending downwards. The cerebellum controls fine movements, impulses in the Purkinje cells initiating or inhibiting motor activites. They receive, via their dendrities, impulses from other parts of the CNS, including the cerebral cortex.

For Consideration

(1) This investigation has been entirely about the *structure* of nerve cells and tissues. To what extent can such structural studies help us to understand how the nervous system works?

(2) Figures 18.6A and 18.7A show brain cells entire. If only small fragments of such cells are visible under the microscope, how can we be justified in making such drawings?

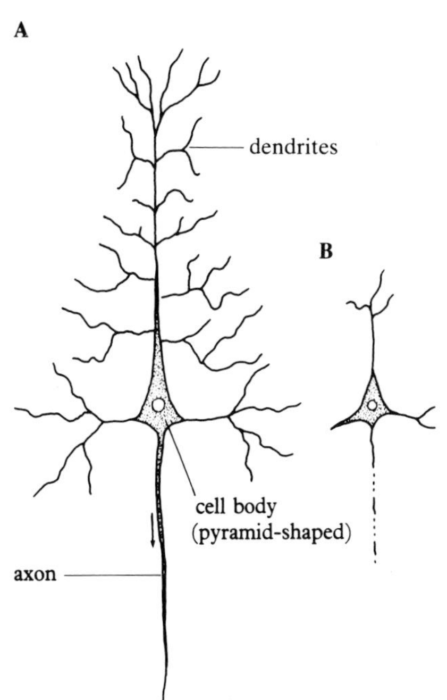

Figure 18.6 Pyramidal cell from motor area of the cerebral cortex: **A**, entire; **B**, as it appears in a microscopic section of brain.

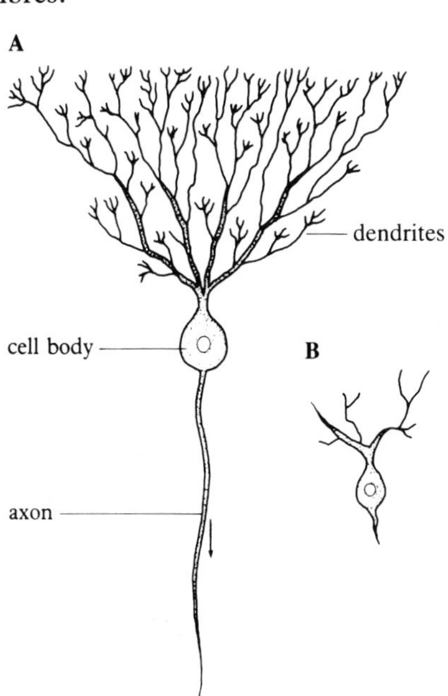

Figure 18.7 Purkinje cell from the cortex of the cerebellum: **A**, entire; **B**, as it appears in a microscopic section of brain.

Requirements
TS spinal cord
LS myelinated nerve
TS myelinated nerve
LS skeletal muscle with nerve ending
VS cerebral cortex
VS cerebellar cortex
Electron micrograph of synapse
Electron micrograph of TS axon including Schwann cell nucleus

Investigation 18.2
Nerves impulse and reflex action in the earthworm

A Opening up the worm

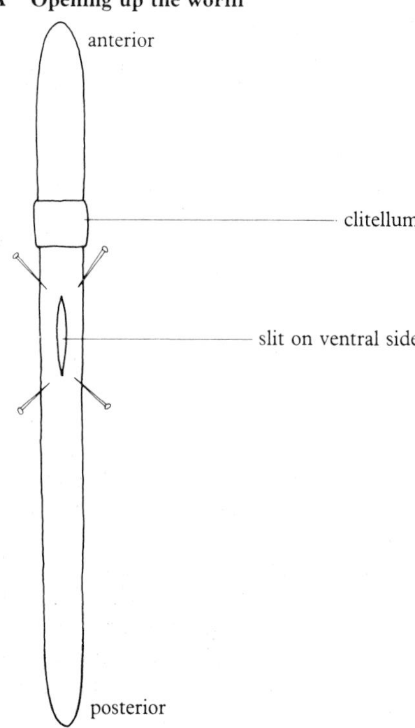

B Deflecting the body wall

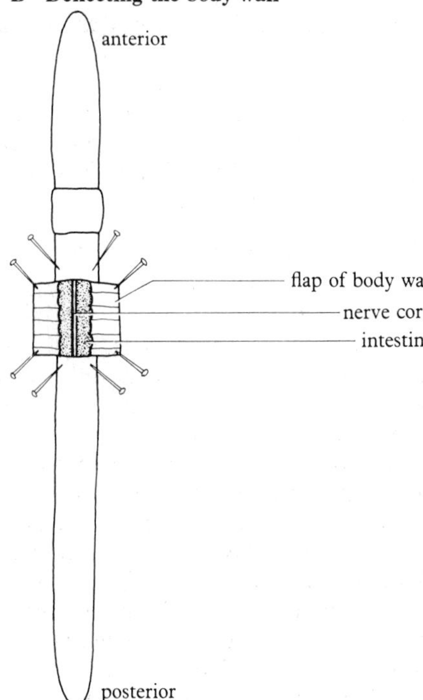

Figure 18.8 Preparing an earthworm for recording nerve impulses from the giant axons in the ventral nerve cord.

Nerve impulses can be recorded, and the properties of transmission investigated, using a cathode ray oscilloscope. In the present experiment you will record impulses from giant axons in the ventral nerve cord of the earthworm. These impulses are responsible for eliciting the earthworm's escape response, a rapid contraction of the longitudinal musculature which, in normal life, draws the worm into its burrow.

The earthworm commends itself for this purpose for two reasons. First, impulses recorded from the giant axons are unusually large and relatively little amplification is required to make them show up distinctly on the oscilloscope screen. Secondly, the giant axons are intermediate neurones in a relatively simple reflex arc, whose properties can be easily investigated.

Apparatus

OSCILLOSCOPE

The cathode ray tube contains a filament which, when heated, emits a stream of electrons. These are focused to form a narrow beam travelling towards the fluorescent screen. At the point where the beam strikes the screen a spot of light is formed. This can be moved from side to side by applying voltages to plates on either side of the beam: the 'X' deflection plates. The beam can be moved vertically up and down by plates above and below it: the 'Y' deflection plates.

To observe the small and rapid potential changes that occur during transmission of a nerve impulse, the spot is swept rapidly at constant speed from left to right forming the time base, and the action potentials, greatly amplified, are applied to the 'Y' plates. Every time this happens the spot is deflected vertically. If the spot is traversing the screen at a sufficiently high frequency, each action potential appears as a momentary stationary wave on a horizontal line of light across the screen.

The length of the wave depends on the frequency of the time base; its height depends on the amount by which the action potential is amplified before it is applied to the 'Y' plates.

The controls which you may need to alter are as follows:

Brilliance: controls the brightness of the spot on the screen.

Focus: controls the sharpness of the spot.

Y shift: moves the time base up and down; set it so the trace is set in the middle of the screen.

X shift: moves the time base from side to side; set it so the leading edge is at the extreme left of the screen.

X gain: controls the length of the time base; set it so the time base just fits onto the screen.

Variable time per cm: controls the speed and frequency of the time base. You will want to alter this in the course of your experiments: start by setting it so that separate spots are just not discernible, the time base appearing as a continuous line across the screen.

Volts per cm: controls the amplification (Y gain); set it so the action potentials are about 2 cm high.

RECORDING ELECTRODES

A pair of platinum electrodes, their ends bent upwards to form hooks, should be clamped to a stand and connected by coaxial cable to the input of the oscilloscope.

Making the preparation

You will be provided with a decerebrate earthworm, that is one whose brain has been destroyed.

1 Lightly anaesthetise the worm with, e.g. MS 222 solution. Leave it in the solution for long enough to stop it responding violently to manipulation.

2 With the worm on a piece of cork, its ventral surface towards you, hold the worm firmly about 1 cm behind the clitellum ('saddle').

3 With a pair of small scissors, make a *mid-ventral* slit through the body wall about 1.5 cm long. The front end of your slit should be about 1 cm behind the back of the clitellum. Be careful not to insert your scissors too far as the nerve cord is just under the body wall.

4 Pin the worm, ventral surface uppermost, to the cork as shown in Figure 18.8A.

5 Separate the body wall from the underlying septa (the connective tissue partitions between adjacent segments). To do this, grasp the body wall with forceps and cut the septa with small scissors or a sharp scalpel.

6 Pin back the body wall on either side, so the nerve cord can be seen lying on the ventral side of the intestine (Figure 18.8B).

7 Free the nerve cord from the underlying intestine by lifting it gently with a seeker and cutting through any connective tissue beneath it.

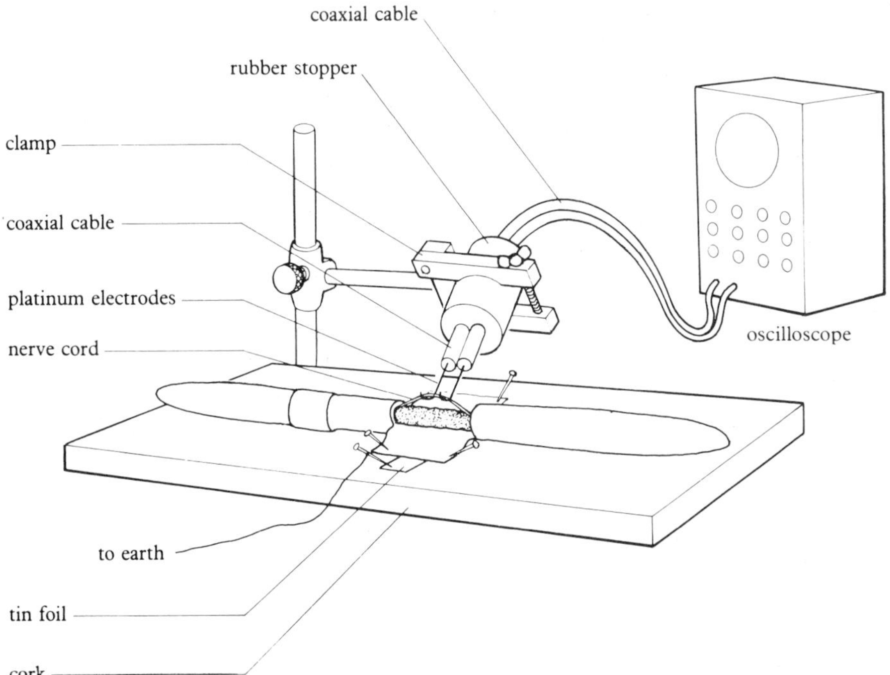

Figure 18.9 The final set-up for recording nerve impulses from the giant axons of the earthworm. The recording electrodes have been hooked under the ventral nerve cord.

8 Gently lift the nerve cord onto the hooked recording electrodes (Figure 18.9). The cord must not be stretched too much, but it should be lifted clear of the gut. There must be no film of water between the nerve cord and gut. If there is, blow it away.

Keep your preparation, particularly the nerve cord, moistened with Ringer's solution.

9 Finally, earth the preparation by sliding a piece of metal foil under the operated region of the worm and connecting this to, e.g. a gas tap.

10 Test your preparation by touching the anterior end of the worm with the point of a *wooden*-handled mounted needle. Set the gain of the oscilloscope (volts per cm) so the action potentials recorded from the giant axons are about 2 cm high. Set the time base frequency (time per cm) so the width of each impulse is approximately 1 mm.

Experiments

It is best to work in pairs, one student stimulating the worm, while the other examines the action potentials on the oscilloscope screen.

1 PROPERTIES OF THE ACTION POTENTIALS

Increase the time base frequency so as to examine the wave form of the action potentials recorded by touching (a) the anterior, and (b) the posterior end of the worm. With a pair of dividers, determine the exact height and width of the recorded action potentials. From the known amplification (gain) and time base frequency, calculate the magnitude in millivolts, and duration in milliseconds, of the action potentials.

2 RESPONSES TO TACTILE STIMULI OF DIFFERENT INTENSITIES

Re-set the time base frequency so the width of the action potentials is about 1 mm. With a needle touch the skin (a) very lightly, and (b) more sharply. How many action potentials are recorded in each case? Is there a correlation between the intensity of tactile stimulation and the number of impulses generated? Explain fully.

3 RESPONSES TO REPETITIVE TACTILE STIMULATION

Touch one end of the worm repeatedly at half-second intervals and observe the response to each stimulus: one of you should do the stimulating and the partner should watch the screen, counting and recording the number of action potentials elicited by each stimulus. Explain your results.

Clearly a 'block' develops on the afferent side of the reflex. What experiments could you perform to locate the precise point in the reflex where this block develops? What do you think might cause the development of such a block?

Allow the worm to recover and repeat the experiment noticing, this time, the muscular responses which are given to each volley of impulses. Explain your observations.

4 DIFFERENCES BETWEEN ANTERIOR AND POSTERIOR STIMULATION

Compare the action potentials recorded by stimulating the anterior end of the worm with those recorded by stimulating the posterior end. How exactly do they differ from each other? Stimulate the anterior and posterior ends of the worm simultaneously. What sort of action potentials are produced? Stimulate the middle region of the worm, e.g. just behind the clitellum. What sort of action potentials do you get now? What conclusions can you draw from your observations about the structural organisation of the earthworm's nervous system? How might you confirm them?

Requirements
Cathode ray oscilloscope
Mounted platinum electrodes connected to coaxial cable
Stand and clamp for above (*see* Figure 18.9)
Small dissecting instruments
Needle with *wooden* handle
Camel-hair brush
Pins
Sheet of cork (approx. 10 cm × 18 cm)
Piece of metal foil (approx. 1 cm × 3 cm)
Source of bright light
Pair of dividers

Earthworm Ringer's solution (*see* page 403)
Anaesthetic (MS 222, 1 g in 400 cm^3 Ringer's solution recommended)
Range of solutions of different pH

Decerebrate earthworm in dish of Ringer's solution

5 RESPONSES TO DIFFERENT TYPES OF STIMULATION

Perform experiments to find out if impulses can be elicited in the giant axons by other kinds of stimuli, e.g. gentle stroking with a camel hair brush, intense light, vibration, air currents, change in pH, chemicals. Explain your results.

As an alternative, or in addition to, the above experiment, giant axon impulses can be recorded from fanworms such as *Sabella* and *Myxicola*. The action potentials are so large that they can be recorded from electrodes placed in contact with the skin on the ventral side of the body. (For details see G.A. Shelton, 'Nerve and muscle responses in *Sabella penicillus L.*', *Journal of Biological Education*, Vol. 15, No. 1, Spring 1981)

For Consideration

What light is thrown by this investigation on (1) the nature of the nerve impulse, (2) the functioning of receptors, (3) the anatomy of the earthworm's nervous system, and (4) the behaviour of earthworms in their natural environment?

Note: Some people object on ethical grounds to experiments on decerebrate earthworms. As an alternative to carrying out this practical investigation, a film, video recording or computer simulation program of nerve impulses may be preferred.

Investigation 18.3
Spinal reflexes in humans

Many of our activities depend on reflexes. Most of these involve the brain, but some of them use only the spinal cord and will be given even when the brain is completely inactivated. If an animal's brain is destroyed whilst the spinal cord is left intact, its behaviour and reflexes can be examined in order to determine how much of the animal's activity is independent of the brain and controlled only by the spinal cord. Any reflexes observed are called spinal reflexes.

KNEE JERK

1 One of you should sit with the right thigh crossed loosely over the left knee in such a way as to slightly stretch the extensor muscle of the leg. If your partner now taps the right-knee tendon (just below the knee cap), a sharp extension of the leg results.

This is one of the simplest reflexes known in humans. An afferent neurone connects with an efferent neurone in the lumbar region of the spinal cord. There is no intermediate neurone. Reconstruct the reflex arc involved and trace the sequence of events which takes place in the course of the reflex.

2 Repeat the experiment with the subject reading a book aloud while being tested. You may find that this gives a larger jerk. How would you explain this?

3 Repeat once again but this time the subject should deliberately try *not* to give the response. What effects, if any, does this have on the reflex? Explain your observations.

ANKLE JERK

1 Kneel on a chair and let one foot dangle loosely. If your partner now taps the tendon at the back of the foot there should be a sudden extension of the foot. This reflex involves the sacral part of the spinal cord. Reconstruct the reflex arc involved.

2 Repeat stimulating at approximately two taps per second. Does the response decline or disappear on repetition? Explain.

SWALLOWING REFLEX

1 Swallow the saliva in your mouth cavity and immediately afterwards try to swallow again. You will find it difficult to swallow the second time. Why do you think this is?

2 Now drink a glass of water and note that you have no difficulty swallowing in rapid succession. Explain the difference.

PUPIL REFLEX

1 The subject, facing a bright light, should close his or her eyes for one minute and then open them. What happens to the pupils when the subject opens his or her eyes?

Requirements
Small hammer or other suitable device for obtaining knee and ankle jerks
Glass of water
Torch
Bright light

2 Shine a torch in the subject's eye and watch the pupil. What happens to the pupil? What is the function of this reflex?
3 The subject should look at an object not less than six metres away, and then at a pencil held 25 cm from his or her face. What happens to the pupils when the subject does this? What is the function of this reflex?

For consideration

(1) Which of the reflexes that you have investigated are spinal reflexes, and which ones are cerebral? Explain your answer.
(2) What other reflexes (spinal or otherwise) are shown by the human? Speculate on the part(s) of the CNS involved in each case.

Investigation 18.4 Reaction times in humans

Requirements
Reaction time recorder. Suitable systems include a pair of switches linked to a triggered cathode ray oscilloscope, microcomputer, chart recorder or stimulus-marker writing on a kymograph. If none of these is available, reaction time may be measured by timing how long it takes for the subject to catch a falling ruler. See D.G. Mackean, *Experimental Work in Biology, 8 Human Senses*, Murray, 1978.

An organism's reaction time is the period which elapses between the application of a stimulus and the performance of the response. Measuring reaction times can give us a useful insight into the speed at which our nervous system works. You will need to work in pairs, one of you serving as the subject, the other as the experimenter.

Apparatus

You will be provided with an apparatus for measuring reaction time. Basically it consists of two switches, one operated by the experimenter (switch E), the other by the subject (switch S). A recording device monitors the time interval between the operation of the two switches.

Procedure

1 *Reaction time to sight.* With the subject watching, the experimenter presses switch E. As soon as the subject sees that the experimenter's switch (E) has been pressed, the subject presses switch S. The reaction time is then measured. Repeat ten times and calculate the average reaction time. Is there any evidence that the subject improves with practice?
2 *Reaction time to touch.* The subject should close his or her eyes. The experimenter presses switch E and simultaneously treads on the subject's foot. The subject then presses his or her switch(S). Measure the subject's reaction time as before. Is the subject's reaction time longer in the second experiment than in the first? If so, why?

Analysis of results

1 With a ruler measure, as accurately as you can, the length of the nerve pathway between the point where the stimulus is received and the part of the body which responds (in this case the finger with which the subject presses the switch). Assume that visual signals are transmitted to the back of the brain and then down the spinal cord, tactile stimuli to the top of the brain and then down the cord.
2 From your measurements calculate the speed in metres per second at which impulses appear to be transmitted in the nervous system. What are the possible causes of delay as impulses traverse these particular pathways?

Further experiments

Devise a method of measuring the subject's reaction time to *sound*. Compare with the reaction time to sight, and explain any differences.

For consideration

As a means of measuring transmission speed in the nervous system, what are the sources of error in this experiment?

Investigation 18.5
Microscopic structure of adrenal medulla, thyroid and pituitary glands

Communication between different parts of the body is carried out by hormones as well as nerve impulses. The hormone is manufactured, and sometimes stored, in an endocrine organ whence it is secreted into the bloodstream. An endocrine organ would, therefore, be expected to show an intimate and extensive association between secretory cells and blood vessels. This is one of the features we shall look for in this investigation.

Procedure

ADRENAL MEDULLA

There are two adrenal glands in the mammal, one on each side of the abdomen just in front of the kidneys (*see* page 81, Figure 9.5). The medulla is the central part of the gland. It secretes the hormone adrenaline.

1 Examine the central part of a median section of adrenal gland (Figure 18.10). First notice numerous capillaries. These have a thin lining of pavement endothelium (note occasional flattened nuclei). Red blood cells may be seen in them.

2 Now look at the cells surrounding the capillaries. They are columnar in shape and elongated at right angles to the walls of the blood vessels. They are called chromaffin cells because the granules in their cytoplasm stain brown with chromium salts. A brown colour is also given if adrenaline is mixed with chromium salts or chromic acid in a test tube. This, and other evidence, suggests that these cells secrete the hormone.

3 Observe chromaffin cells under high power. Note their prominent nuclei, cytoplasmic granules (distribution within the cell?) and proximity to blood vessels.

4 What other types of cell can you see in the adrenal medulla? Account for any observations you make.

THYROID GLAND

The mammalian thyroid gland is situated in the neck close to the larynx (*see* page 109, Figure 11.5). It differs from the adrenal medulla in that the thyroid hormone (thyroxine) is stored in the gland before being shed into the bloodstream.

1 Examine a section of thyroid gland under medium power (Figure 18.11). Notice numerous follicles, each surrounded by a single layer of cuboidal cells. The cavity (lumen) of each follicle contains a colloid substance (thyroglobulin) which is usually visible in sections.

2 Consider the following information on how the thyroid works.

The follicle cells absorb iodide and other metabolites from the bloodstream; they synthesise thyroglobulin from these raw materials and shed it into the lumen of the follicle for temporary storage. When required, they absorb thyroglobulin from the lumen and convert it into thyroxine which is then secreted into the bloodstream. In addition the follicle cells respond to thyroid-stimulating hormone which reaches them in the bloodstream from the pituitary gland and causes them to increase the rate of production of thyroxine.

What predictions can you make from this information regarding the relationship between the thyroid follicles and the blood system?

3 Examine your slide again, this time under high power. Look for small blood vessels and capillaries and note their positions in relation to the follicles. Are your predictions confirmed?

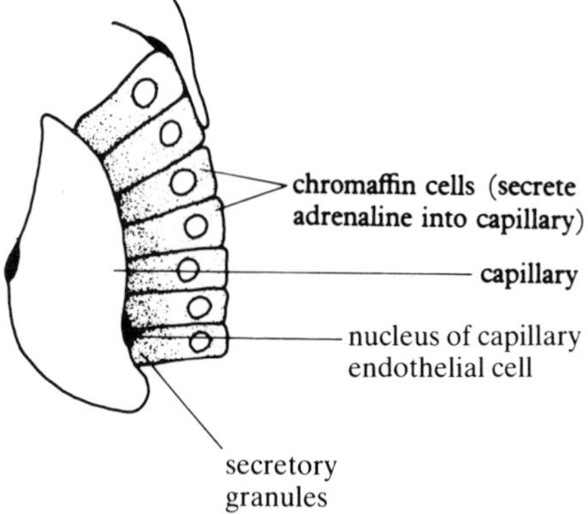

Figure 18.10 Part of the adrenal medulla as seen in section under the microscope. Note the close relationship between the secretory cells and blood system.

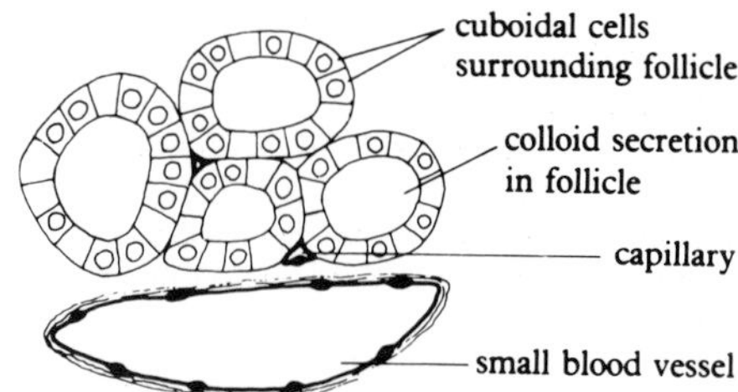

Figure 18.11 Part of the thyroid gland as seen in section under the microscope. Note the close relationship between the secretory cells and blood system.

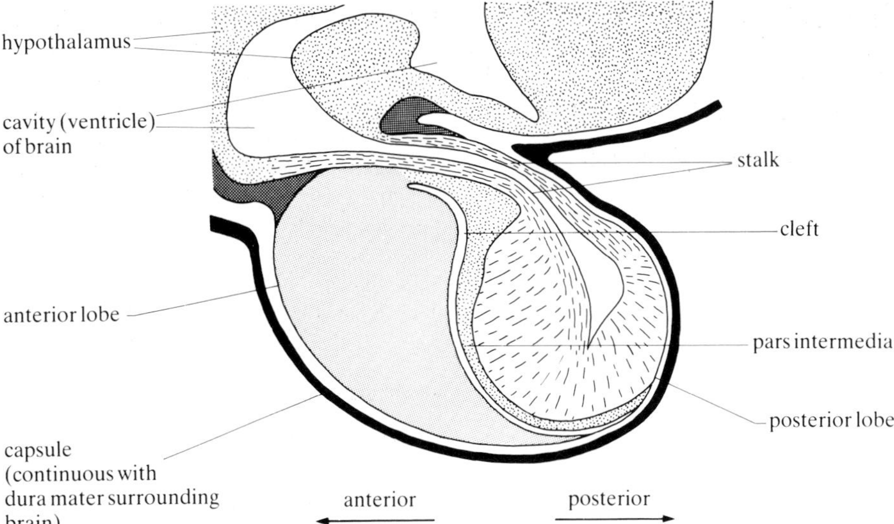

Figure 18.12 Vertical longitudinal section of pituitary gland (cat) showing its main parts.

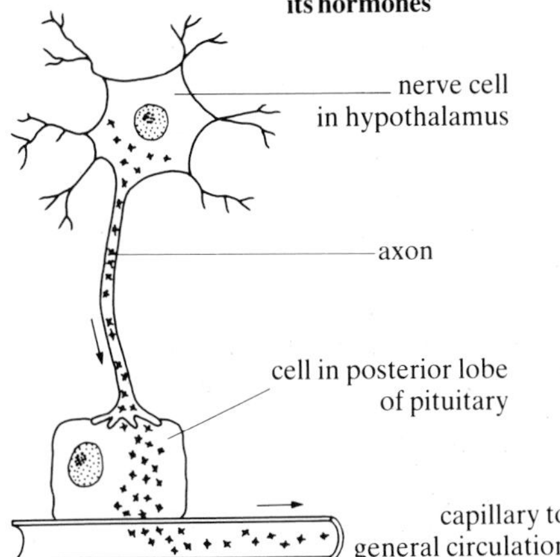

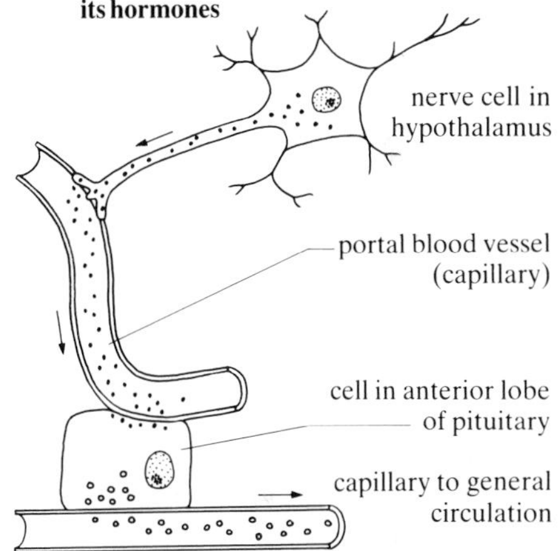

Figure 18.13 Diagram showing how the pituitary gland produces its hormones. In the case of the posterior lobe, nerve cells in the hypothalamus produce hormones (e.g. antidiuretic hormone, ADH) which pass down their axons to the posterior lobe; the hormones are then stored in the posterior pituitary cells before being released into the bloodstream in response to electrical impulses reaching the cells via the axons. In the case of the anterior lobe, nerve cells in the hypothalamus secrete releasing factors (themselves hormones) into portal blood vessels which carry them to the anterior lobe where they stimulate, or in some cases inhibit, the release of the appropriate hormones into the general bloodstream. Because they secrete hormones, the nerve cells in the hypothalamus are called neurosecretory cells. (*Based on Guillemin and Burgus*)

Requirements
Median section of adrenal gland (must include the medulla)
TS thyroid gland
VLS pituitary gland, stained to show the different parts
Sections or photomicrographs of pituitary gland to show neurosecretory pathways etc.

PITUITARY GLAND

The pituitary is the most complex of the endocrine glands, secreting numerous hormones, many of which control the activities of other glands. It is formed during embryonic development by a downgrowth from the floor of the 'tweenbrain fusing with an upgrowth from the roof of the mouth cavity.

1 Examine a longitudinal section of an entire pituitary gland under the low power. First identify the anterior and posterior lobes, using Figure 18.12 to help you. Be sure you have got the section correctly orientated and can tell the anterior end from the posterior end.

2 Figure 18.13 shows diagrammatically how the pituitary produces its hormones. Study the diagram carefully and then examine your slide under high power. Look for nerve cell bodies in the hypothalamus, portal blood vessels in the anterior lobe and axons in the posterior lobe. If available, examine specially stained sections, or photomicrographs, which show these features, particularly neurosecretory pathways leading from the hypothalamus to the posterior lobe.

For Consideration

(1) In what respects are the adrenal medulla and thyroid glands similar, and dissimilar?

(2) What tells these two glands how much hormone to secrete?

(3) Organs that respond to hormones are called target organs. They are equivalent to the effectors of the nervous system. Make a list of the target organs affected by adrenaline and thyroxine.

Questions and Problems

1 Figure 18.14 shows an oscillograph record obtained when one end of an axon is stimulated with a single shock, and electrical events are recorded from the other end. The recording electrodes, connected to an oscilloscope, are arranged as shown in the diagram: one is inserted into the axon, the other is located outside the membrane enveloping the axon.

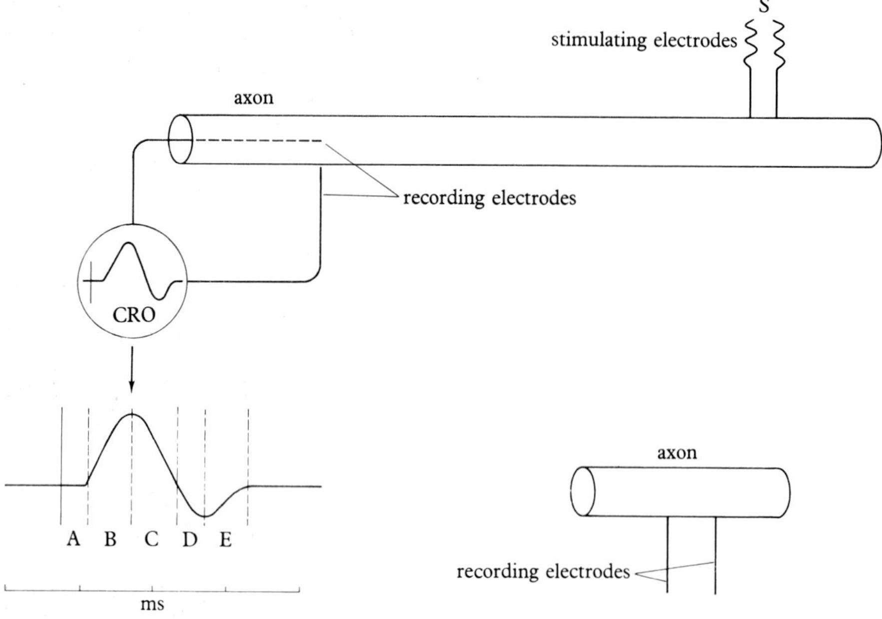

Figure 18.14 Recording electrical activity in an axon.

Explain as precisely as possible phases A to E in the oscillograph record.

What would you expect the oscillograph record to look like if both recording electrodes were placed side by side on the outside of the nerve membrane as shown at the foot of the diagram? Explain fully.

2 In view of the all-or-nothing nature of the nerve impulse, how would you explain the graded muscular responses of which our bodies are clearly capable when reacting to natural stimuli?

3 The effect of stimulating a nerve with repetitive stimuli at two different frequencies is shown in Figure 18.15. The vertical line preceding each action potential marks the moment of stimulation. Comment fully on these results.

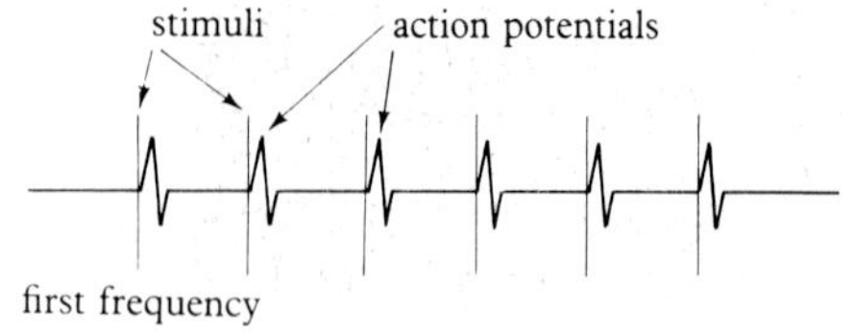

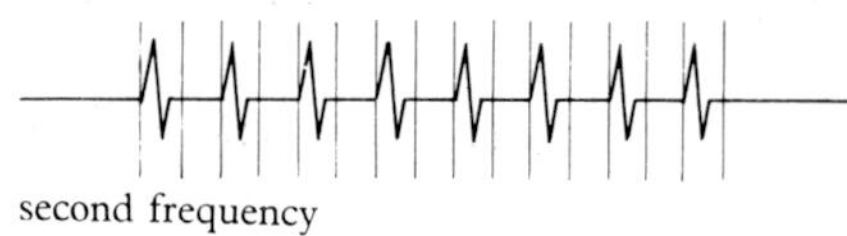

Figure 18.15 Effect of stimulating a nerve with repetitive stimuli at two different frequencies. The time scale is the same for both sets of recordings.

4 In an experiment to investigate the function of the myelin sheath, a single myelinated nerve fibre was placed on two moist glass slides separated by a short air gap. The nerve fibre was arranged so that the gap was bridged by an internodal stretch, that is a length of the nerve fibre in between two consecutive nodes of Ranvier. Each slide was covered with a film of Ringer's solution, and the gap was bridged by a moist thread as shown in Figure 18.16. After being set up, the sheath of the nerve fibre soon dried in the region of the air gap.

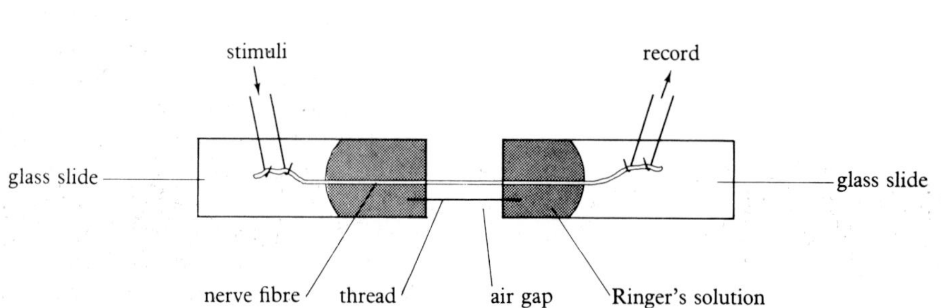

Figure 18.16 Experiment on the transmission properties of an excised myelinated nerve fibre.

A pair of fine platinum electrodes was now placed in contact with each end of the nerve fibre. Through one of the two pairs of electrodes stimuli were delivered to the nerve fibre. Through the other pair of electrodes action potentials were recorded by means of an oscillosocpe.

It was found that every time a stimulus was applied to one end of the nerve fibre, an action potential was recorded from the other end of the nerve fibre provided that the air gap was bridged by the moist thread. If the thread was removed, or allowed to dry, transmission ceased.

Explain these observations as fully as you can. What would you predict would be the result if the portion of the nerve fibre spanning the air gap included a node of Ranvier?

5 Comment on each of the following statements:
(a) Synapses prevent impulses going in the wrong direction.
(b) It is possible to suppress a reflex such as withdrawing one's hand from a hot object.
(c) Curare, the poison used by certain natives on arrow tips, produces paralysis.
(d) Certain drugs have hallucinogenic effects in which sensations are abnormal and distorted.

6 Figure 18.17 is an electron micrograph of a dendrite, synaptic knob and post-synaptic cell in the brain of a lizard.
(a) Identify structures A to E.
(b) What is the function of structure C and how does it carry out its function?
(c) In what respects is structure E unusual? Suggest reasons for your answer.
(d) Name one feature in the cytoplasm of the synaptic knob which enables it to be distinguished from the post-synaptic cell.

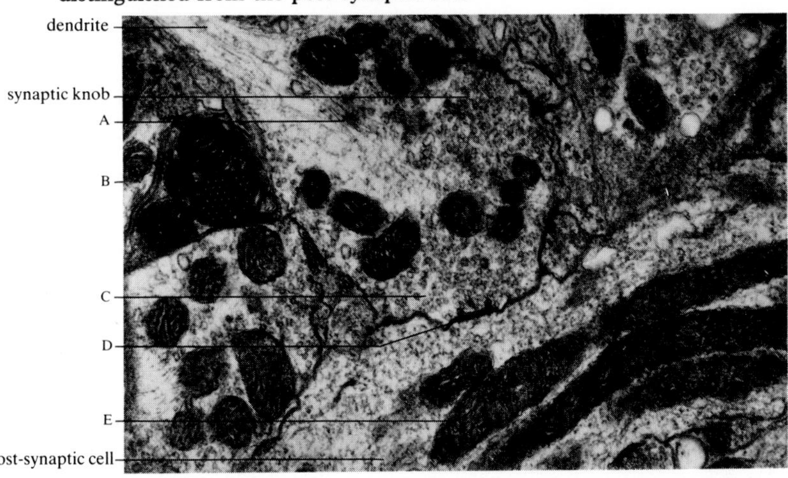

Figure 18.17 Electron micrograph of a section through a dendrite, synaptic knob and post-synaptic cell in the brain of a lizard. (*Professor E.G. Gray.*)

7 What do you understand by the term 'head'? Discuss in functional terms the sequence of evolutionary steps which you believe may have led to the development of a head of the kind seen in the vertebrates.

8 Compare concisely the nervous and endocrine system as means of communication within the body of an animal.

9 When frightened, the human body responds as follows: the face goes white, the pupils dilate, the heart beats faster, blood pressure increases, the mouth goes dry, and – in extreme cases – urination and defecation may occur. Explain these responses.

10 Answer the following questions, all of which relate to the mammalian endocrine system.
(a) Which hormones have the effect of raising the metabolic rate?
(b) Give one example of a situation where opposing effects are produced by different concentrations of one and the same hormone. Briefly discuss the survival value, if any, of your example.
(c) Which hormones control the levels of Ca^{2+} and Na^{+} in the body?
(d) Which hormones affect the retention, or otherwise, of water in the body? Briefly explain how they achieve their effects.
(e) Which hormone or hormones bring about a rise in blood pressure? Briefly explain how they achieve their effects.
(f) Name an endocrine organ which is an exocrine as well as an endocrine gland.
(g) A trophic hormone is one which stimulates another endocrine gland to secrete. Make a list of such hormones found in the mammalian body and in each case state its target organ.
(h) The pituitary is often described as the 'master gland' of the endocrine system. Briefly justify this title.

11 Give a brief illustrated account of how hormones are believed to affect their target cells.

12 Figure 18.18 shows the electrical activities in a motor neurone in response to applying three separate volleys of stimuli to an afferent nerve fibre. The first volley is small, the third large, and the second intermediate between the other two. Electrical responses are recorded from within the cell body of the motor neurone (intracellular electrodes, R_1) and from the surface of its axon (R_2). Explain the results as fully as you can.

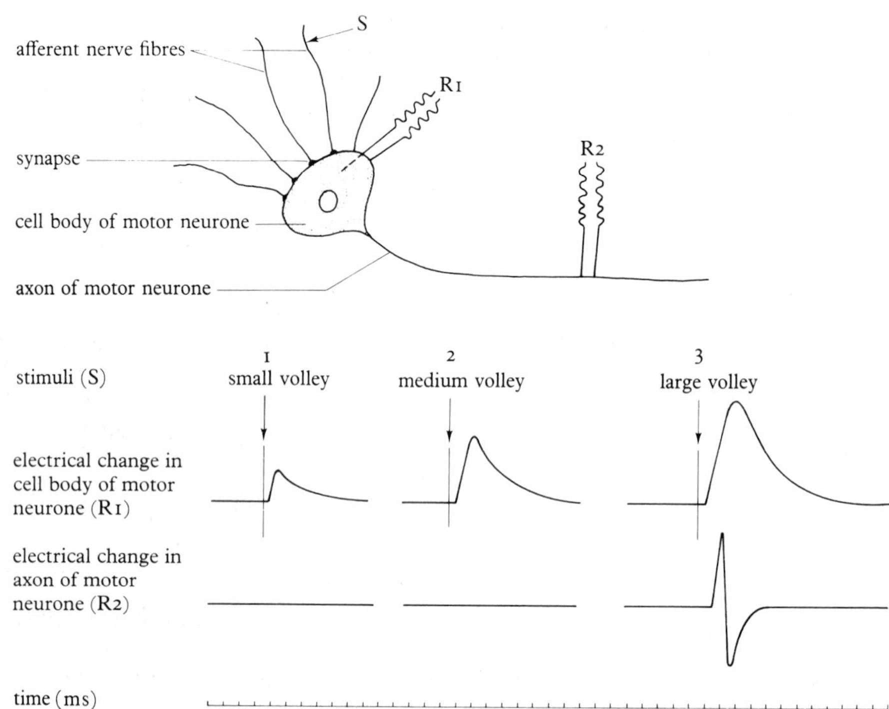

Figure 18.18 Recording electrical events in a motor neurone.

13 The responses of sea anemones can be investigated by the technique shown in Figure 18.19. A series of electrical stimuli is delivered to the base of the animal and the animal's muscular contractions are recorded by means of a thread attached to a spring lever which writes on a revolving drum (kymograph). A representative recording is shown below the diagram. Explain the results in terms of the working of the nervous system.

What other primitive features does the sea anemone's nervous system possess besides the one demonstrated by this experiment?

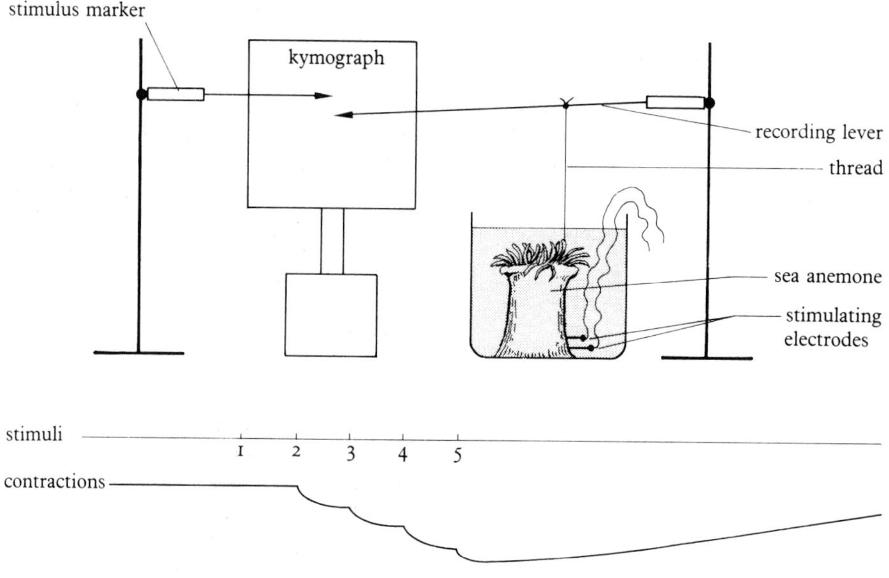

Figure 18.19 Experimental set-up for recording the muscular responses of a sea anemone to electrical stimulation.

19 Reception of Stimuli

Background Summary

1 Receptors may consist of isolated **sensory cells**, or the cells may be compacted together to form a **sense organ**. They can be classified, according to the type of stimuli to which they respond, into **chemoreceptors**, **mechanoreceptors**, **photoreceptors** and **thermoreceptors**.

2 The function of receptors is to transduce the energy associated with the stimulus into the electrical energy of nerve impulses.

3 Individual sensory cells are classified into **primary** and **secondary receptors** according to whether the sensitive device is the terminal of an afferent neurone or a specially adapted epithelial cell.

4 In general sensory cells, when stimulated, develop a local **receptor potential** (**generator potential**) which, if it builds up sufficiently, elicits **action potentials** in an afferent neurone. The frequency of discharge depends on the size of the generator potential.

5 If a stimulus is maintained, the generator potential usually declines and the action potentials decrease in frequency until they cease altogether (**adaptation**).

6 For repetitive stimuli to be detected separately the generator potential produced by each stimulus must fall below the firing threshold before the next stimulus is delivered. If the frequency is too high for this to happen, **stimulus fusion** occurs.

7 Evidence suggests that the link between the stimulus and the development of a generator potential is a chemical process. This is known to be the case in photoreceptors and may apply to other receptor cells as well.

8 Receptor cells are often inhibited either by neighbouring sensory cells, as in the case of **mutual inhibition** in the compound eye, or through efferent nerves, as in the case of the lateral line receptors of fishes.

9 Individual receptor cells are often extremely sensitive, even to the slightest stimulus. The effective sensitivity of groups of sensory cells, e.g. the rods in the eye, may be increased by **convergence** and **summation**.

10 Sensory precision, e.g. of the cones in the eye, results from the receptor units being closely packed and by having a one-to-one relationship between the sensory cells and afferent neurones.

11 The mammalian eye and ear illustrate the structure and functioning of two sense organs. In both cases the individual sensory cells are enclosed within a complex apparatus which protects them and ensures that they receive and respond to the appropriate stimulation. For example, the **pupillary reflex**, controlled by a delicate feedback mechanism, ensures that the correct amount of light enters the eye.

12 In the case of the eye the receptor cells, **rods** and **cones**, are located in the **retina** on which light rays are brought to a focus by an adjustable **lens**. The cones, which are particularly concentrated in the foveal region of the retina, are responsible for high acuity colour vision in conditions of good illumination (i.e. **daylight vision**), the rods for black-and-white vision at low levels of illumination (i.e. **night vision**). These functions of the rods and cones, resulting from their structural and physiological properties, can be related to a wide range of everyday experiences.

13 **Colour vision** depends on the differential stimulation of three types of cone, each containing a different photochemical pigment (**trichromatic theory**).

14 The **compound eye** of arthropods contrasts sharply with the vertebrate eye and illustrates how in the course of evolution the same physiological problem has been solved in two different ways.

15 The mammalian ear performs two functions: hearing and balance. Hearing is dealt with by sensory cells of the **organ of Corti** in the **cochlea**, to which sound waves are transmitted via a series of membranes, ossicles, and fluid-filled canals. The properties of the cochlea permit the ear to discriminate between sounds of different intensity and pitch.

16 **Balance** is dealt with by the **ampulla organs**, **utricle**, and **saccule** of the **vestibular apparatus**. The ampulla organs, associated with the **semicircular canals**, are sensitive to movements of the head, whilst the utricle and saccule contain **otolith organs** sensitive to the position of the head relative to the force of gravity.

Investigation 19.1
Analysis of human skin as a receptor

Requirements
Ruler
Ball-point pen with fine point
Flexible bristle mounted in wooden holder
Wooden-handled mounted pin whose sharp end has been sawn off about 0.5 cm from the tip; the cut surface must be flat and smooth
Mounted needle with sharp point
Pair of dividers
Bunsen burner
Beaker

Ice-cold water
Propanone (acetone)
Ethoxyethane (diethylether, ether)

The efficiency of a receptor in monitoring changes at the surface of the body depends on (a) the sensitivity of the individual sensory cells, (b) the variety of stimuli to which the receptor responds, (c) its ability to distinguish between, i.e. resolve, two stimuli applied simultaneously, and (d) the rapidity with which the sensory cells adapt when stimulated continuously.

Investigating (a) requires an elaborate set-up (*see* page 174), but (b), (c), and (d) can be investigated with a minimum of apparatus. In this case your own skin will be examined as a receptor. You will need to work in pairs.

Experiments

THE DIFFERENT STIMULI TO WHICH THE SKIN RESPONDS

1 With a fine ball-point pen, rule a grid of not less than 25 squares on the back of your partner's hand. The sides of the squares should be 2 mm long so the area of each one will be 4 mm^2.
2 Explore each square in turn for its sensitivity to touch, heat, cold, and pain. For touch use a flexible bristle mounted in a wooden holder. For heat and cold use a flat metal surface approximately 1 mm in diameter (a large pin with the end sawn off will do): to investigate heat reception warm the pin in hot water; to investigate cold reception cool it in propanone, ether or ice-cold water. For pain use a needle, but do not pierce the skin.
3 Draw your grid on a large scale on a sheet of paper and indicate within each square which, if any, of the four modalities listed above it is sensitive to. In this way you can map the distribution of receptors sensitive to the different kinds of stimulation in the skin.
4 The experiment can be repeated in different parts of the body so the distribution of receptors may be compared.

THE RESOLVING POWER OF THE TACTILE RECEPTORS

A receptor's resolving power is the minimum distance required between two simultaneously applied stimuli so that they can be detected as two separate stimuli rather than a single stimulus. One usually thinks of resolving power in connection with the eye, but it also applies to the sense of touch.
1 Use a pair of dividers to apply two simultaneous tactile stimuli to your partner's arm. The points should be 4 cm apart and the subject, looking in the other direction, should say when he or she feels them.
2 Vary the distance between the two points of the dividers and determine the minimum distance by which the two stimuli must be separated for the subject to feel both of them.
3 Repeat the experiment on other parts of the body including the finger tips and thigh. Record and explain your results. What is the relevance of your findings to blind people who read Braille?

ADAPTATION

1 With a needle wiggle one of the hairs on your partner's hand until the subject ceases to feel it.
2 Estimate how long it takes for the receptors at the base of the hair to adapt to continual stimulation. Is the time the same for all hairs investigated? Are there regional differences over the body surface?
3 Interpret the results of this experiment in terms of the structure and physiology of receptor cells and their connections.

For consideration

(1) What are the roles of touch, temperature and pain receptors in the overall functioning of the body?
(2) Some people claim that there are two distinct receptors in the skin, one for detecting heat and the other for detecting cold. Others say that there is only one type of receptor which responds to both heat and cold. How could we investigate which of these two hypotheses is correct?
(3) Is the skin sensitive to any other type of stimulation besides the ones investigated in this experiment? What might be the functions of these other receptors?
(4) The skin at the tips of the fingers has a greater resolving power for tactile stimulation than the skin elsewhere. What are the practical applications of this? In what other receptors, besides the skin, is resolving power important?

Investigation 19.2
Visual acuity of the human eye

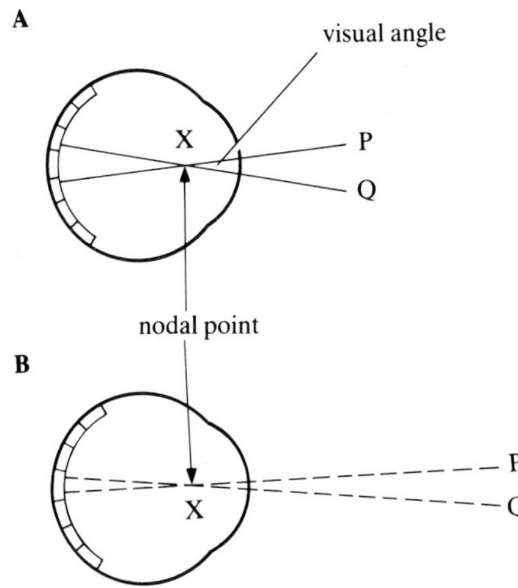

Figure 19.1 The theoretical basis of visual acuity of the eye.

Requirements
White card
Felt pen
Ruler
Tape measure
Snellen chart

The visual acuity of the eye, i.e. its efficiency at seeing things clearly, depends on its resolving power. This is the ability of the eye to distinguish between two dots on a piece of paper. In practice this depends on two factors: the distance between the two dots and their distance from the eye.

Theoretical background

In Figure 19.1 **P** and **Q** are two dots and point **X**, where the light rays from the dots cross in the eye, is called the nodal point. The angle **PXQ** is known as the visual angle. In Figure 19.1A the images of the two dots fall on two cones separated by one in between. This will give the impression of two separate dots.

Now consider what happens if the two dots are further away from the eye (Figure 19.1B). The visual angle is now smaller, and the images of the two dots fall on a single cone. Under these circumstances we get the impression of only one dot. (The same would apply if the images of the two dots fell on two next-door cones. The rule is that to be perceived separately the two images must fall on two cones that are separated by at least *one* other cone.)

Procedure

1 On a card draw two vertical lines, each 1 mm wide, and separated by 1 mm. Hang the card on the wall. At a distance of half a metre you will find no difficulty in distinguishing between the two lines, but at a distance of five metres they appear completely fused.

2 Now approach the card and note the maximum distance from the card at which you can see two distinct lines. Measure this distance. We shall take this as the distance between the card and the nodal point in the eye.

3 Assuming that the distance between the nodal point and the retina is 15 mm, calculate the distance between the two images on the retina. Do this by constructing a scale diagram similar to the ones in Figure 19.1.

4 Find the value in degrees of the visual angle. In this case, where the two stimuli can *just* be perceived separately, we call it the minimum visual angle or angle of distinctiveness.

5 Examine a Snellen chart. This is used to determine people's visual acuity. On the chart you will see that each letter, or set of letters, has a number underneath: this is the maximum distance, in metres, at which a person with normal vision can see the letters distinctly.

Visual acuity is given by the following equation:

$$V = \frac{d}{D}$$

where V is the visual acuity, d is the maximum distance at which a given letter can be read by the subject, and D is the distance at which the same letter can be read by a 'normal' eye.

6 Using the Snellen chart, determine the visual acuity of each of your eyes separately, and of both eyes together. If you wear glasses, determine your visual acuity with and without glasses. How good is your eyesight compared with other members of your class?

For consideration

(1) Explain your ability to see a given letter on the Snellen chart in terms of the visual angle and the size of the retinal image.

(2) What is the relationship between visual acuity and the resolving power of the eye?

(3) How does the resolving power of the eye compare with two-point discrimination by the skin as measured in Investigation 19.1?

(4) The width of a cone is approximately 5 μm. How does this relate to the distance between the two images on the retina which you have calculated in this experiment? Account for any discrepancies.

Investigation 19.3
Structure of the mammalian eye

The eye is an elaborate sense organ consisting of a layer of light-sensitive cells, the retina, in front of which is a transparent cornea and adjustable lens for focusing the light.

Procedure

DISSECTION OF THE EYE

1 Use the eye of, e.g. sheep or ox. The posterior part of the eye will probably have fat clinging to it. Note the transparent cornea continuous with the tough, white sclera (sclerotic layer). The cornea is devoid of blood vessels: what are the consequences of this?

2 Notice the conjunctiva covering the surface of the cornea; it is continuous with the mucous membrane of the eyelids.

3 Remove the fat from the eyeball so as to expose the optic nerve and extrinsic eye muscles (function?).

4 Make an *almost* complete circular cut round the edge of the cornea, in front of where it joins the sclera (dotted line 1, Figure 19.2A). The watery fluid which emerges is aqueous humour (function?). Deflect the cornea forwards like a lid. Note the iris (brown), pupil, front of lens. With a blunt needle push the lens backwards and forwards and from side to side. What restricts its movement?

5 Make a circular cut all round the eyeball so as to cut the eye into anterior and posterior halves (dotted line 2, Figure 19.2A). Remove the gelatinous vitreous humour with large forceps. What is its function?

6 Now examine the interior of the eye (Figure 19.2B). In the posterior half observe the retina (grey), choroid (black) and sclera (white). Notice blood vessels radiating from the point where the optic nerve is attached to the retina (blind spot). To one side of the blind spot the fovea centralis (yellow spot) should be visible.

7 Now look at the front half of the eyeball. The retina is continuous with the ciliary body which forms a circular black band round the lens. With a blunt needle gently move the lens and observe that it is attached to the ciliary body by a delicate suspensory ligament.

8 Make two radial cuts in the wall of the anterior half of the eye and remove the portion of the wall in between (dotted line 3, Figure 19.2A). Leave the lens attached to the rest of the wall. This should enable you to see more clearly the relationship between the lens, ciliary body and iris. Use a hand lens or binocular microscope if necessary. Compare with the diagram in Figure 19.3A.

9 How would you describe the appearance of the lens and how does it feel to the touch? Explain.

MICROSCOPIC STRUCTURE OF THE CILIARY BODY AND IRIS

1 Examine the ciliary body and iris in a median section of the eye (Figure 19.3B).

2 Examine the ciliary body in detail. It contains circular, radial, and meridional muscle fibres (the ciliary muscle) responsible for changing the shape of the lens during accommodation to near or far objects. When the circular

A Mammalian eye: exterior

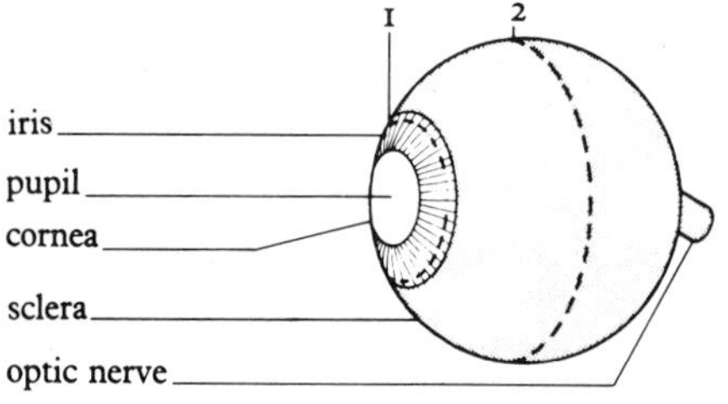

anterior half: exterior

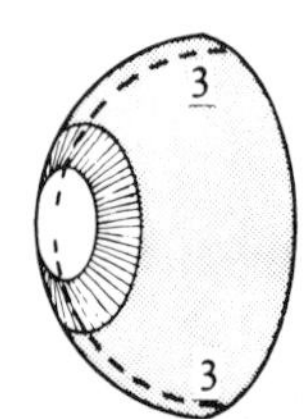

B Interior view

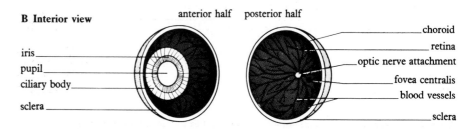

anterior half

iris
pupil
ciliary body
sclera

posterior half

choroid
retina
optic nerve attachment
fovea centralis
blood vessels
sclera

Figure 19.2 Dissection of mammalian eye.

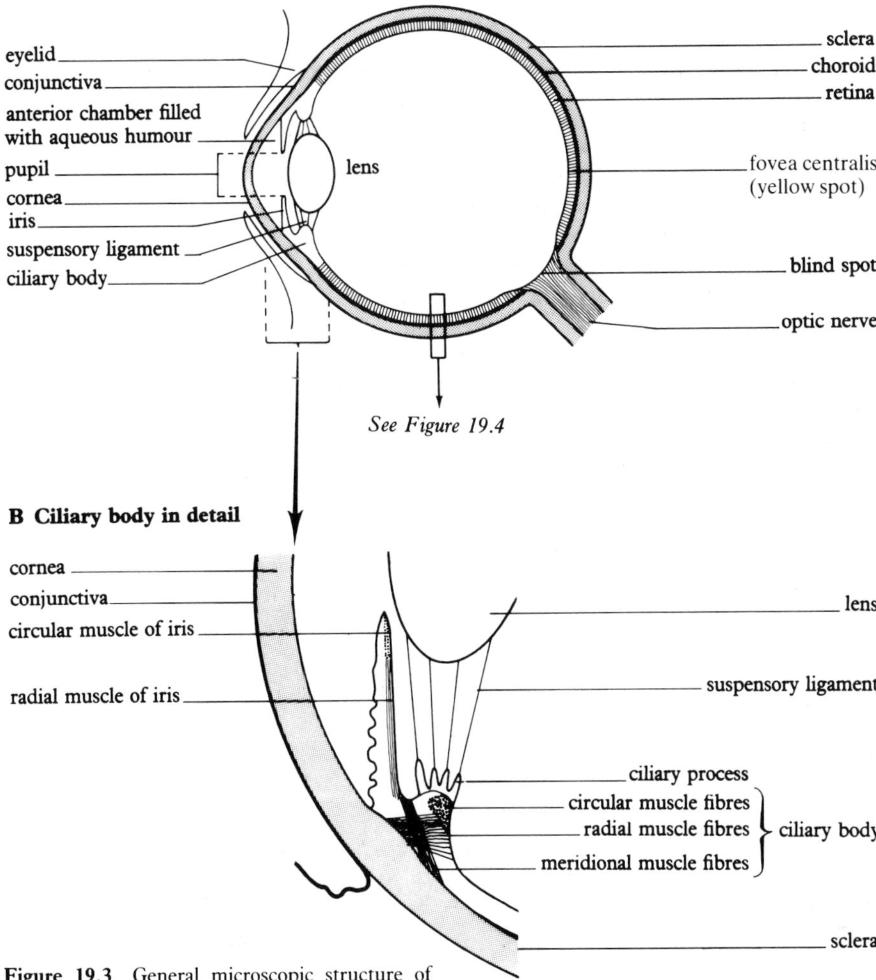

Figure 19.3 General microscopic structure of mammalian eye.

and radial muscles contract the tension on the lens is relaxed: the lens assumes a more rounded shape and its front bulges forwards.

When the circular and radial muscles relax the reverse happens and the lens is pulled out into a more flattened shape. This is further aided by contraction of the meridional muscles. What triggers these various muscles to contract and relax?

3 Now turn your attention to the iris. This contains circular and radial muscle fibres which constrict and dilate the pupil respectively. Under what circumstances do these muscles contract and relax?

MICROSCOPIC STRUCTURE OF THE RETINA

1 Examine a vertical section of the retina (not the foveal region) under high power. Observe the various layers shown in Figure 19.4A, using Figure 19.4B to help you interpret them. Note the choroid and sclera (sclerotic layer) outside the retina. The choroid is vascular, its outer membrane being pigmented. The sclera is composed of connective tissue: mainly collagen fibres with some elastic fibres.

2 Examine a vertical section of the fovea. How does it differ from the non-foveal part of the retina?

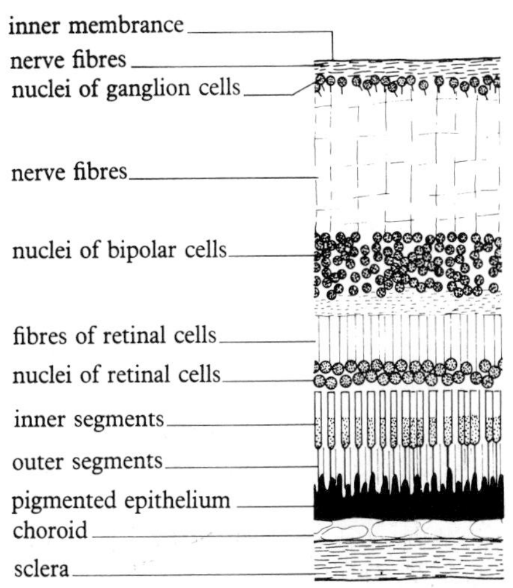

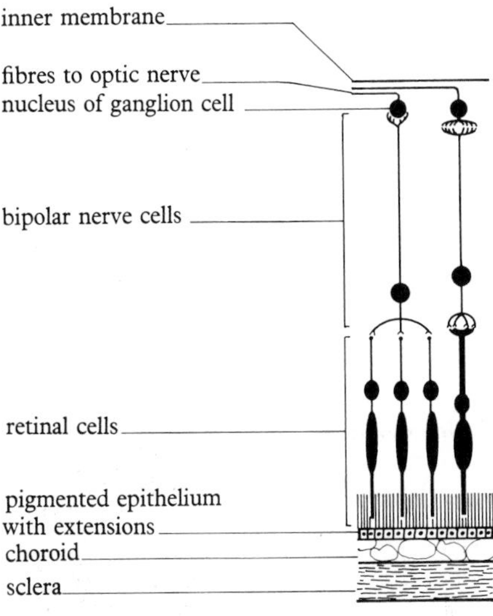

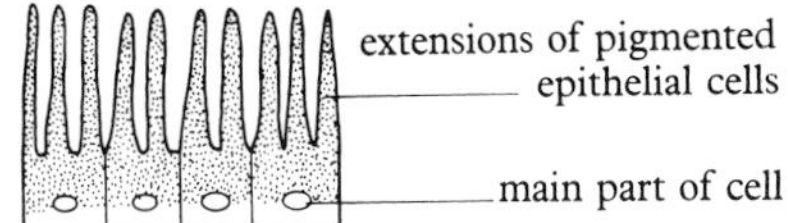

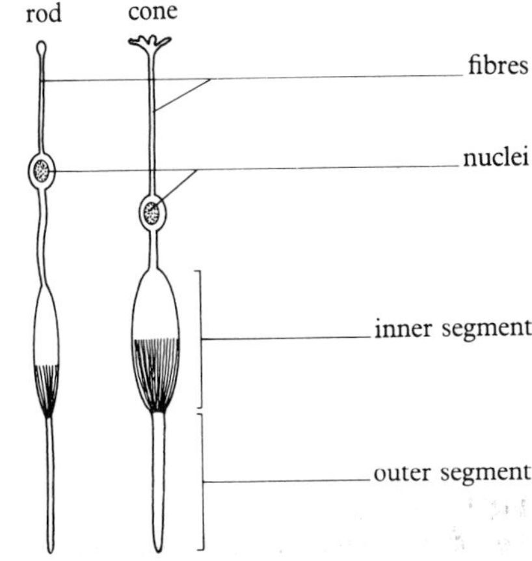

Figure 19.4 Microscopic structure of the mammalian retina and associated structures.

Requirements
Binocular microscope or hand lens
Dissecting instruments

Eye of, e.g. sheep or ox
HS or VS eye (for ciliary body and iris)
VS non-foveal part of retina, light and dark adapted
VS foveal part of retina

3 Can you tell the difference between the two types of retinal cells: the rods and cones? This may be difficult because they are densely packed and in certain parts of the retina they look alike. In general cones are fatter than rods (Figure 19.4D). The centre of the fovea (fovea centralis) contains only cones, densely packed and unusually slender. Moving outwards from the fovea centralis, the cones become fatter, and rods are present in ever increasing proportions. The extreme periphery of the retina contains only rods. What is the functional significance of these facts?

4 Examine an individual retinal cell (rod or cone) in as much detail as you can using Figure 19.4D to help you. The dark part of the inner segment contains numerous densely packed mitochondria.

5 Compare the retina of a light adapted and dark adapted eye. How do they differ with regard to the distribution of pigment in the pigmented epithelium at the base of the retina? Explain the reason for the difference.

For consideration

(1) Summarise the ways in which the following parts of the eye are adapted to perform their functions: (a) lens, (b) ciliary body, (c) iris, (d) retina.

(2) List the parts of the eye in Figure 19.3A which carry out each of the following functions in the human: (a) focusing light rays, (b) protecting the interior of the eye from physical damage, (c) protecting the retina from over-stimulation, (d) seeing things clearly in colour, (e) enhancing sex appeal.

Investigation 19.4
Structure of the mammalian ear

The ear is a complex sense organ responsible for hearing and balance. In this investigation we shall confine our attention to the ear's auditory function. Bear in mind that essentially the ear consists of a series of tubes and canals through which sound waves are transmitted to mechanoreceptors in the head.

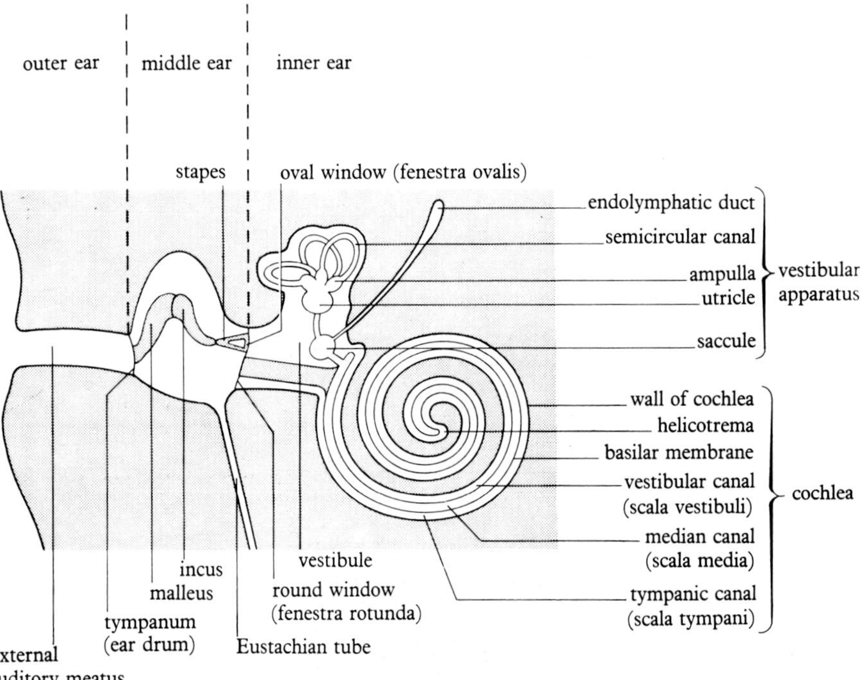

Figure 19.5 Diagrammatic vertical section through the mammalian ear.

Procedure

1 First study Figure 19.5 or a model of the ear. Note that the ear is subdivided into an air-filled outer and middle ear, and a fluid-filled inner ear.

2 Examine the outer ear in detail. Notice the flap-like pinna (function?), and the external auditory meatus leading to the tympanum (ear drum).

3 Examine the middle ear in detail. It contains three ear ossicles (malleus, incus, and stapes) which are held in position by delicate muscles. Why muscles rather than ligaments?

4 Examine the inner ear in detail. It contains the membranous labyrinth which consists of the vestibular apparatus (semicircular canals, ampullae, utricle, and saccule) together with the median canal of the cochlea. The whole of the membranous labyrinth is filled with fluid (endolymph) and surrounded by fluid (perilymph). The perilymph is enclosed within the bony labyrinth which includes the vestibular and tympanic canals of the cochlea.

5 Examine a vertical section of the cochlea under low power. Refer to Figure 19.6A and B to see how your section relates to the ear as a whole.

6 Notice that the cochlea is subdivided by membranes into three fluid-filled canals:

(a) **Vestibular canal** (scala vestibuli)

(b) **Middle canal** (scala media, cochlear duct)

(c) **Tympanic canal** (scala tympani).

What parts of the inner ear does each of these canals connect with?

7 In addition to the canals observe the other structures shown in Figure 19.6. What do you make of the helicotrema, the small orifice linking the vestibular and tympanic canals at the apex of the cochlea? Is it likely to be more of a hindrance than a help?

8 Examine the organ of Corti under high power. Note in particular the sensory cells between the tectorial and basilar membranes (Figure 19.6C). How are these sensory cells stimulated? What function is performed by the pillars?

9 Use Figure 19.6 to trace the pathway taken by sound waves as they are transmitted through the ear to the organ of Corti.

For Consideration

(1) In what ways is the structure of the ear related to its auditory function?

(2) Deafness is caused by the organ of Corti failing, for some reason, to respond to sound waves entering the external auditory meatus. There are several kinds of deafness, each having a different cause. Speculate on the possible causes of deafness and suggest how they might be remedied.

(3) Why is it an advantage to have two ears rather than only one?

Requirements
Diagram or model of ear
VS cochlea

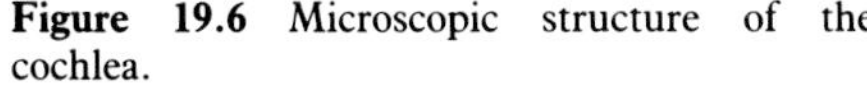

Figure 19.6 Microscopic structure of the cochlea.

A Cochlea from the side

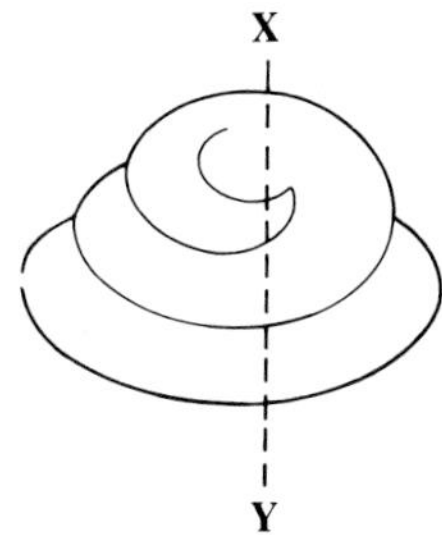

B Vertical section of cochlea X – Y

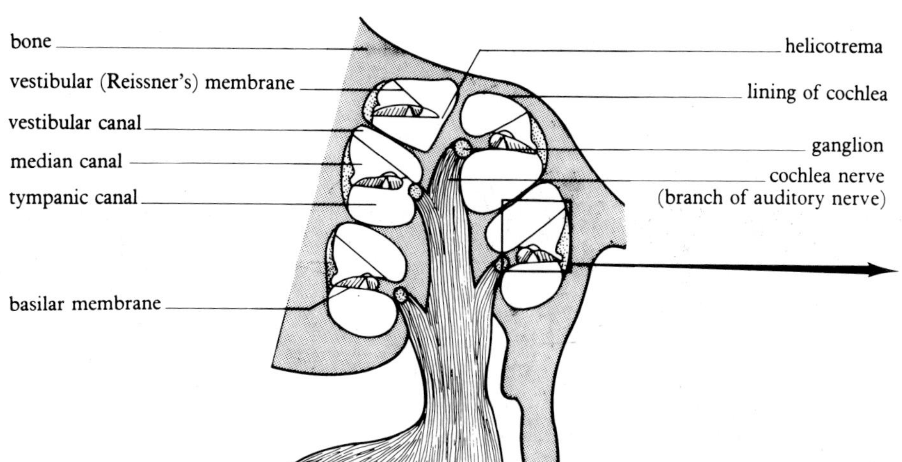

C Organ of Corti in detail

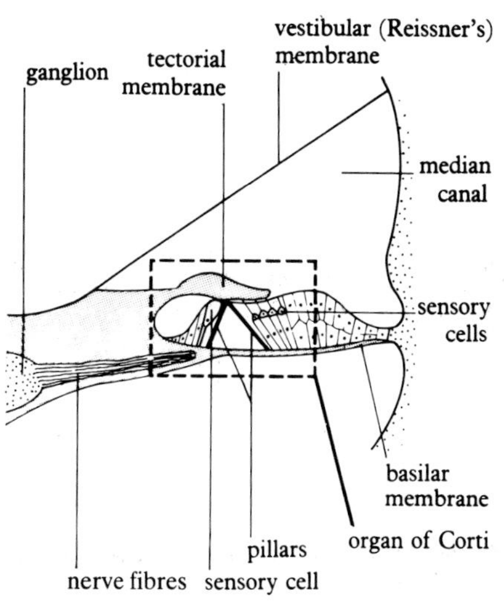

Questions and Problems

1 Describe the electrical and ionic events that occur in a sensory cell when the latter is stimulated. What is the evidence that such events occur, and how do they compare with what happens in a nerve fibre when it transmits an impulse?

2 Explain each of the following phenomena as concisely as you can:
(a) Wearing a coarse shirt produces a tickling sensation at first but after a period of time this sensation ceases.
(b) Treating sensory cells with an ATP inhibitor results in the receptor failing to respond to stimulation.
(c) When reading a book the words you are looking at directly are sharply defined whereas surrounding words are blurred.
(d) It is impossible to see a very faint star by looking directly at it, but it is possible to do so if you look slightly to one side of it.
(e) The flicker on a cinema screen can be detected if one looks at the screen out of the corner of one's eye, but not if one looks directly at it.
(f) If you go into a dimly lit room from bright daylight, it is at first difficult to see anything, but gradually objects become visible.
(g) In very dim light it is impossible to distinguish between different colours, everything appearing as black, white, or various shades of grey.
(h) When pipetted into the eye, atropine causes the pupil to dilate.
(i) A person who is continually subjected to very loud high-pitched sounds may eventually become permanently deaf to such sounds.
(j) After a few minutes on the rotor in a fairground a person suffers from temporary dizziness.

3 In myopia parallel rays of light are brought to a focus in front of the retina; in hypermetropia the rays are focused behind the retina. What are the symptoms and possible causes of these two conditions? Astigmatism is another refractive abnormality in which there is a difference of curvature in the various meridians of the eye. What will be the consequences of this condition?

4 Look at Figure 19.7 from a distance of at least 30 cm. Close your left eye and focus on A with your right eye. Now slowly move the book towards you. What happens to B as you do this? Explain fully.

Repeat the process, but this time focus on B and see what happens to A. What conclusions can be drawn?

Figure 19.7

5 Figure 19.8 shows the different types of cell in the retina of a vertebrate.
(a) In which direction do light rays enter the retina in the diagram?
(b) (i) Name the layer indicated by A.
(ii) Name the cells labelled B, C, D, E and F.
(iii) State the functions of cells D and E.
(c) What is the significance of the fact that
(i) cells E1, E2 and E3 all connect with cell C2, and
(ii) cell C3 has four synaptic contacts with cell D?
(d) What happens to the long extension of cell B after it leaves the retina?
(*CL modified*)

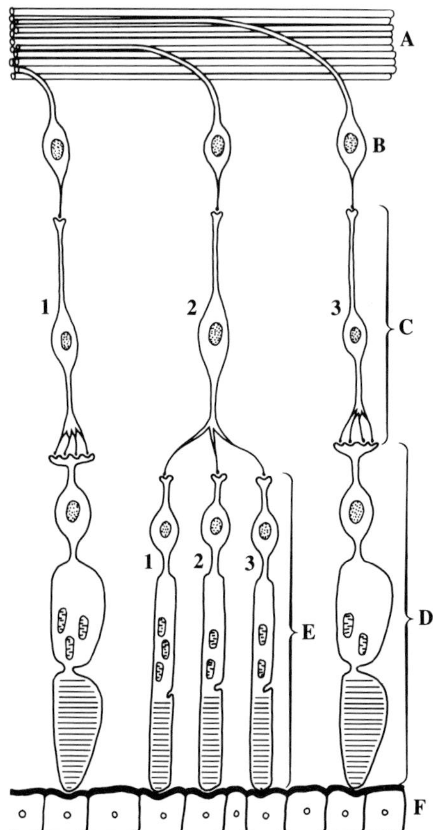

Figure 19.8 Diagram through the retina of a vertebrate eye.

6 Receptors have been described as 'biological transducers'. Explain what this means with special reference to the mammalian eye.

7 Give a brief description of the following sensory functions in humans, relating each to the structure of the organ involved:
(a) detection of angular acceleration of the head;
(b) detection of sound waves by the inner ear;
(c) reception of visual images of different light intensity. (*JMB*)

8 (a) Which parts of the human eye (i) reflect, (ii) refract, and (iii) absorb light?
(b) Which parts of the human ear (i) gather, (ii) transmit, and (iii) transduce sound?

9 It is claimed that bees can distinguish between yellow and blue. How would you test whether or not this is true? Describe experiments you would carry out, paying attention to any special considerations you would need to take into account in designing them.

10 Outline how you would assess the sensory capacity of a newly discovered animal. *(CCJE)*

11 Very few humans make full use of their sensory receptors. Discuss.

12 The following letter (slightly abridged) was published by the Times newspaper on 3rd January 1986:

Sleepers awake
From the Reverend Kevin M. Pelham
Sir, Although never having had the privilege of a British Rail sleeper, I have travelled extensively by rail in all parts of Australia.

Whenever the bunk lay across the direction of travel (usually in double sleepers) I have been hard put to get any rest at all. When, however, in single cabins whose beds lie along the route of the train, sleep was both easy and blissful.
Yours faithfully,
KEVIN M. PELHAM,
St. Margaret's Presbytery, Carshalton Beeches.

Write a brief letter to the Times offering a possible explanation of the Reverend Pelham's experience.

20 Effectors

Background Summary

1 Effectors are structures which respond directly or indirectly to stimuli. The body's principal effectors are **muscles** and **glands**.

2 Vertebrate muscles are classified into **skeletal** (voluntary, striated), **visceral** (involuntary, non-striated, 'smooth'), and **cardiac** (heart) muscle. Each possesses certain characteristic properties.

3 Generally muscles contract when impulses reach them through the nervous system but sometimes, as in the case of cardiac muscle, contractions are **myogenic**, i.e. they arise within the muscle tissue itself.

4 Vertebrates have two kinds of skeletal muscle: **fast twitch** and **slow twitch**. The former is for short bursts of activity, the latter for prolonged activity.

5 When a skeletal muscle is excited, either directly with a single electrical stimulus or by a single impulse through the nerve that innervates it, it responds – after a brief latent period – by **contracting**.

6 When it contracts, the muscle may shorten without developing tension (**isotonic contraction**) or it may develop tension without shortening (**isometric contraction**).

7 On repetition at sufficiently high frequencies muscle twitches can **summate** to produce a **tetanus**. By varying the duration of a train of high-frequency stimuli, graded contractions can be produced. Graded contractions are also produced by different numbers of motor units being activated (see below).

8 In contrast to visceral and cardiac muscle, skeletal muscle contracts rapidly but fatigues comparatively quickly.

9 Contraction of a muscle fibre is initiated by an electrical impulse (**action potential**) which has the same ionic basis as the nerve impulse. The muscle action potential obeys the **all-or-nothing law** and is followed by an absolute and relative **refractory period**.

10 A skeletal muscle is subdivided into bundles of fibres, each bundle being innervated by a single axon: this comprises a **motor unit**. Each fibre contains numerous **myofibrils** which are made up of alternating sets of thick myosin and thin action **filaments**. The orderly arrangement of the filaments gives skeletal muscle its striated appearance.

11 Studies on the fine structure of muscle indicate that when skeletal muscle contracts the thick and thin filaments slide between one another, possibly propelled by **cross bridges** acting as ratchets. Energy is supplied by ATP from mitochondria situated between adjacent myofibrils.

12 The muscle action potential is linked with contraction by a mechanism which involves the **sarcoplasmic reticulum**. Calcium ions, released by the reticulum, initiate the hydrolysis of ATP.

13 Studies on the molecular structure of actin and myosin have clarified the role of the filaments, cross bridges and calcium ions in muscle contraction.

14 In the intact body skeletal muscles are caused to contract by impulses reaching them from the central nervous system. Often the correct degree of contraction is achieved by reflexes arising from stretch receptors within the muscles themselves (muscle spindles) or in the tendons (tendon organs).

15 Other effectors, besides muscle, include **chromatophores** (pigment cells), **electric organs**, **light-producing organs**, and **nematoblasts** (stinging cells). The last is an example of an **independent effector**.

Investigation 20.1
Action of skeletal muscle

The physiological properties of skeletal muscle can be investigated by applying electrical stimuli either to the muscle direct or to the nerve that supplies it. In the latter case the muscle and its nerve are removed from a leg to give a nerve-muscle preparation. A convenient preparation is the sciatic nerve and gastrocnemius (calf) muscle of frog or toad. The nerve is placed in contact with a pair of electrodes through which electrical shocks can be delivered; the muscle is attached to a lever which records its contractions on a revolving drum (kymograph).

Apparatus

This consists of (1) the stimulating equipment, (2) the muscle bath, and (3) the kymograph.
For details of the kymograph *see* page 384. As with other experiments involving the kymograph, it is necessary to know the speed at which the drum rotates. If this is not already known, a time tracing should be made with a tuning fork or electronic time marker.

For stimulating, use an electronic stimulator. The stimulator should have a marker output which is connected to

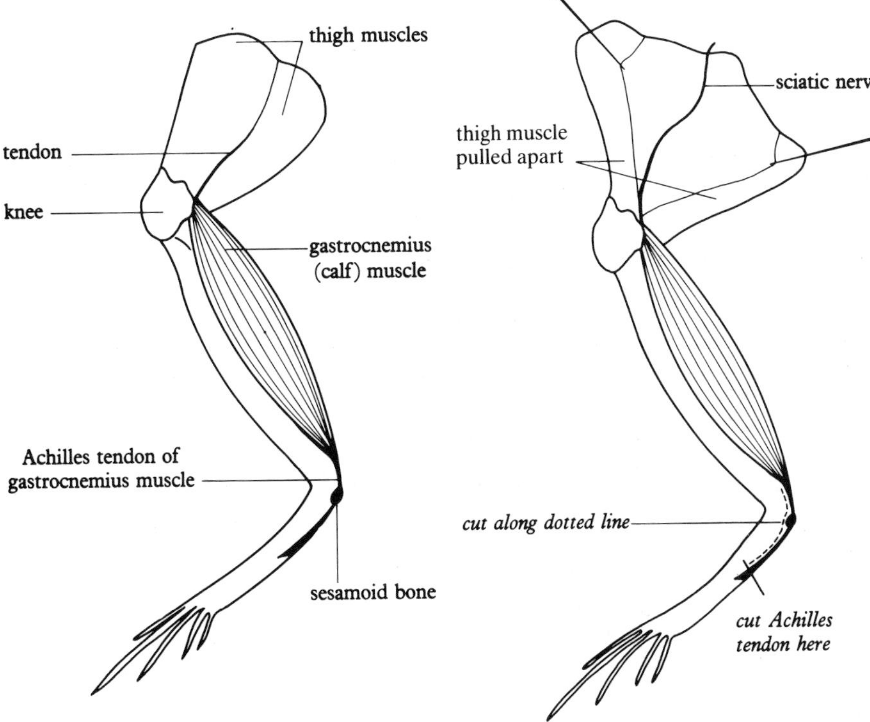

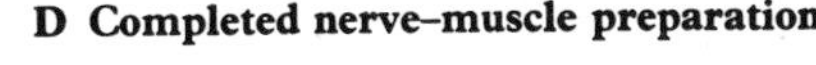

C Detachment of nerve–muscle preparation from rest of leg
D Completed nerve–muscle preparation

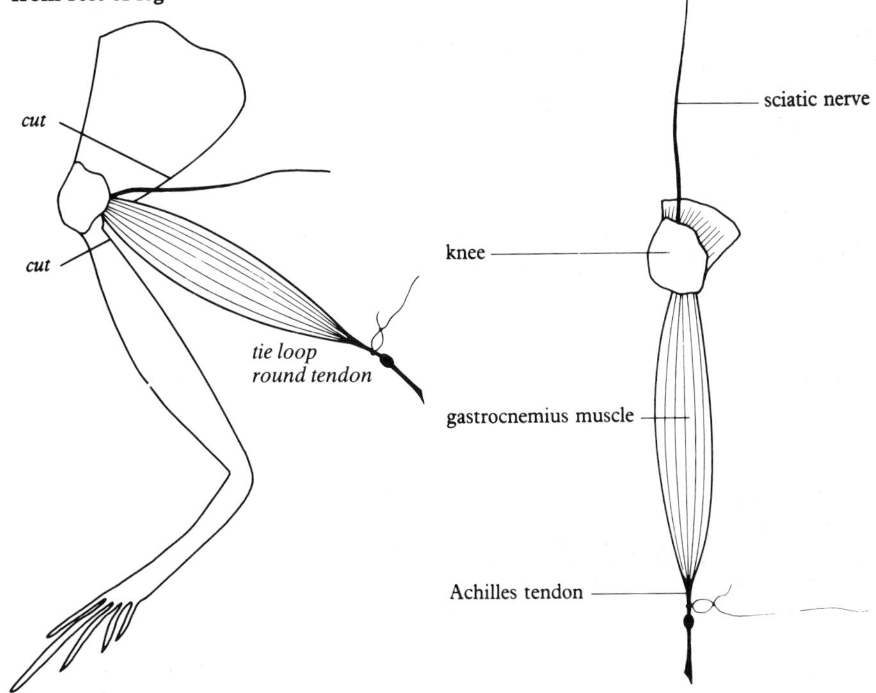

Figure 20.1 The making and setting up of a nerve-muscle preparation using the sciatic nerve and gastrocnemius muscle of frog.

a stimulus marker. This makes a mark on the kymograph drum every time a stimulus is delivered.

Making the Nerve-Muscle Preparation

You will be provided with the hind leg of a frog or toad. To keep the tissues alive keep the leg well moistened with Ringer's solution. Remember this is no ordinary dissection; it is more like an operation performed by a surgeon – the tissue has got to function properly afterwards. Proceed as follows:

1 Skin the leg. This can be done by grasping the skin at the top of the leg with a pair of forceps and stripping off the skin like pulling off a stocking.

2 Place the leg, posterior surface uppermost, on a piece of cork, and identify the structures shown in Figure 20.1A. (The posterior surface can be easily recognised by the glistening white tendon just above the knee).

3 With your thumbs, pull apart the two muscles in the thigh. This will expose the ribbon-like sciatic nerve which lies between them. Pin the muscles down on either side. (Figure 20.1B.)

4 Follow the nerve up as far as you can, i.e. to the cut end of the leg. Lift up the cut end of the nerve with small forceps and carefully separate the nerve from surrounding tissue down to the knee. Be careful not to nick the nerve.

5 With a scalpel blade, free the Achilles tendon from the foot and cut it *below* the sesamoid bone (Figure 20.1B).

6 Take hold of the tendon with forceps and gently free the gastrocnemius muscle from the rest of the leg all the way up to the knee.

7 With thread, tie a double knot round the Achilles tendon just *above* the sesamoid bone; then make a small loop by tying a second double knot approximately 2 mm from the first as shown in Figure 20.1C. Cut one of the two loose ends of the thread but leave the other about 4 cm long. (It will be used for lifting the preparation later.)

8 Lay the nerve and the muscle to one side of the leg as shown in Figure 20.1C. Now cut through the leg immediately above and below the knee, making sure you do not damage either the gastrocnemius muscle or the sciatic nerve.

9 You have now completed making your nerve-muscle preparation which should look like Figure 20.1D.

10 Fix your preparation to the floor of the muscle bath as shown in Figure 20.2. When you lift up the preparation to put it in the muscle bath, lift it by the thread, *not* by the nerve! Push a pin first through the edge of the knee and then into the hole in the floor of the bath. Pour enough Ringer's solution into the bath to *just* cover the preparation.

11 Drape the sciatic nerve over the stimulating electrodes. Adjust the position of the electrodes so that the nerve, though firmly in contact with the electrodes, is not unduly stretched.

12 By means of the loop at the other end of the preparation, hook the Achilles tendon onto the recording lever. The position of the lever can be adjusted so that the muscle, though somewhat stretched, is not under too great a tension. The recording arm of the lever should be approximately horizontal.

13 Finally make sure that the kymograph drum is as high as it can be on its spindle. Adjust the height of the muscle bath so the point of the recording lever is approximately one centimetre from the bottom of the recording paper.

EXPERIMENT 1 THE SINGLE TWITCH

1 Set the kymograph at about 10 mm s^{-1}. Bring the tip of the recording lever into contact with the paper about one centimetre from the base of the drum. Record a base line by allowing the drum to make one complete revolution.

2 Place the recording tip of the stimulus marker immediately beneath the tip of the recording lever.

3 Record the responses of the muscle to a series of single shocks of graded intensity. Start with the stimuli so weak that no response is given (i.e. the shocks are below threshold). Then gradually increase the strength until a full (i.e. maximal) response is given. Note that the response is a rapid twitch. Let the muscle relax completely after each twitch. Do you get any twitches of intermediate size?

4 Set the kymograph at a much faster speed – about 400 mm s^{-1}. Make sure the tips of the recording lever and stimulus marker are exactly aligned: give each a little flick with your finger to make sure that they are.

5 Now record a single maximal twitch in response to a strong stimulus. Notice that there is a discernible delay between the moment of stimulation (as registered by the stimulus marker) and the onset of the muscular response. This is called the latent period.

EXPERIMENT 2 SUMMATION

1 With the kymograph set at about 100 mm s^{-1}, record the response to two shocks in quick succession. The interval between the two shocks should be such that the response to the second shock starts well after the muscle has begun to relax following the first contraction.

2 Repeat the procedure, gradually decreasing the interval between the two shocks until there is no distinction between the two responses: they should become smoothly summated to give a single contraction larger than the twitch obtained in the first experiment.

EXPERIMENT 3 TETANUS

1 Set the kymograph at about 20 mm s^{-1}. Make a base line round the drum.

2 Now record the response of the muscle to approximately three seconds of repetitive stimulation. The frequency of the stimuli should be sufficiently high for the individual twitches to fuse together into a smooth prolonged response. This is called a tetanus. After three seconds, stop stimulating and let the muscle relax until the point of the lever returns to the base line. (There is no need to record for the full duration of the muscle relaxation, but note how long it takes to return to the base line).

3 Repeat at lower frequencies. Try to find the minimum frequency required

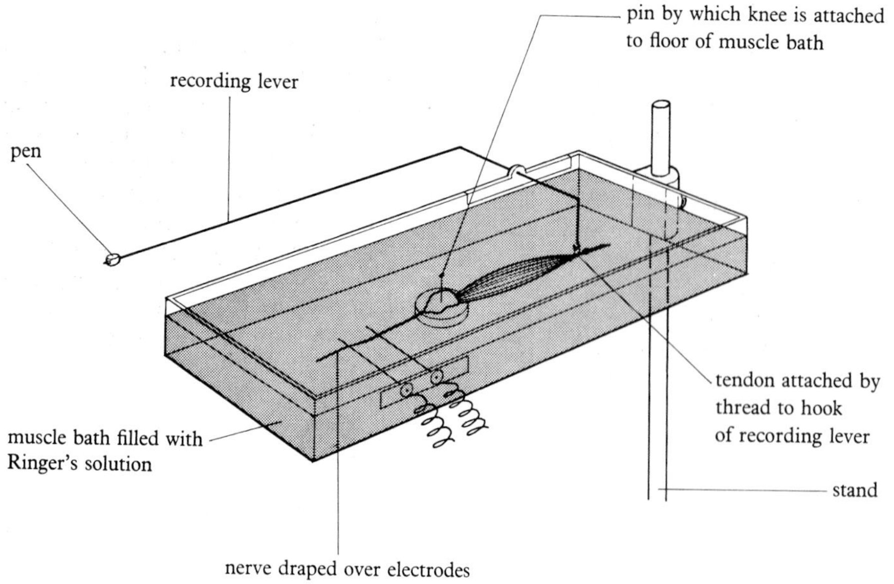

Figure 20.2 Muscle bath showing nerve-muscle preparation in position.

to fuse the individual twitches into a smooth tetanus. (A response in which the individual twitches can be seen is called a clonus.)

EXPERIMENT 4 FATIGUE

1 Slow the drum to about 0.5 mm s^{-1} and make a new base line.
2 Now stimulate the nerve repeatedly at two stimuli per second until no recordable response is given by the muscle.
3 When the preparation is thus fatigued shift the electrodes to that they are in contact with the muscle, one on each side of it.
4 Now stimulate the muscle at two stimuli per second. Record the responses.

Presentation of Results

1 Remove the paper from the kymograph drum.
2 Cut out your recordings and stick them in your laboratory notebook. In the case of Experiment 2 (summation of contractions) display the recordings in sequence *one above the other* showing the way the second contraction fuses with the first as the interval between the two stimuli is gradually decreased.
3 Beneath each recording, or set of recordings, give a time scale. For Experiments 1–3 draw a horizontal line corresponding to 0.5 seconds; for Experiment 4 (fatigue) a line corresponding to five seconds would be more appropriate.
4 For a single twitch (Experiment 1) measure the following:
(a) Latent period (time delay between the moment of stimulation and the onset of the muscular response) in milliseconds.
(b) Contraction time in seconds.
(c) Relaxation time in seconds.
(d) Duration of twitch, i.e. (b) + (c).
(e) Contraction height in mm.
5 Measure the height of the largest completely summated response obtained in Experiment 2, and of the tetanus obtained in Experiment 3.
6 Finally measure the time taken for no recordable contractions to be given in Experiment 4 (a) when the nerve is stimulated, and (b) when the muscle is stimulated.

For Consideration

(1) What is the latent period due to? Make a list of *all* the factors which may contribute to it.
(2) What light is shed by the results of Experiments 2 and 3 on the normal functioning of nerves and muscles in the intact animal?
(3) Do the results of Experiment 4 enable you to say whereabouts in a nerve-muscle preparation fatigue occurs in the course of repetitive stimulation?
(4) What may fatigue be due to?
(5) When you stimulated your nerve-muscle preparation with shocks of graded intensity, you may have found that with shocks just above threshold one or more twitches of intermediate size were given. Explain this phenomenon. Does it contradict the all-or-nothing law of nerve and muscle?

Note

1. If a stimulus marker is not available, the moment of stimulation can be recorded by using the contact key at the base of the kymograph as the stimulator switch. The key is operated by an arm that projects from the spindle of the kymograph, so a stimulus is delivered each time the drum revolves. When you have recorded the response of the muscle, mark the moment of stimulation by slowly revolving the drum by hand until the shock is just sent in to the nerve and a single twitch is recorded on a stationary drum.
2. If available, a chart recorder may be used instead of a kymograph. If used with a data memory system, multiple copies of the recordings can be obtained so that each student has a complete set of results.
3. Most of the experiments described in this investigation can also be carried out using a strip of body wall, 2 to 3 cm long, obtained from an earthworm or from a tube-dwelling polychaete such as *Sabella* or *Myxicola*. The nerve cord should be excluded or the results may be complicated by rhythmical locomotory movements. The longitudinal muscle is stimulated direct by placing the electrodes in contact with it.

Requirements
Kymograph
Muscle bath with recording lever and electrodes
Stimulus marker
Time marker or tuning fork
Stimulator
Stand for muscle bath
Pipettes ×2
Pins
Thread
Dissecting instruments
Piece of cork approximately 12 × 12 cm

Eosin
Amphibian Ringer's solution (500 cm^3)

Hind limb of frog or toad (*Xenopus*), cut from the body as high up as possible, and kept in Ringer's solution. The animal should be pithed beforehand (*see* page 115)

Investigation 20.2
Structure of skeletal muscle

Vertebrate muscle is classified into visceral (non-striated, smooth), skeletal, and cardiac muscle. In each case the cells are adapted for contraction. The close relationship between structure and function is particularly apparent in the case of skeletal muscle.

Figure 20.3 Structure of skeletal muscle. The detail of the striations shown in **B** is visible in good light microscope preparations.

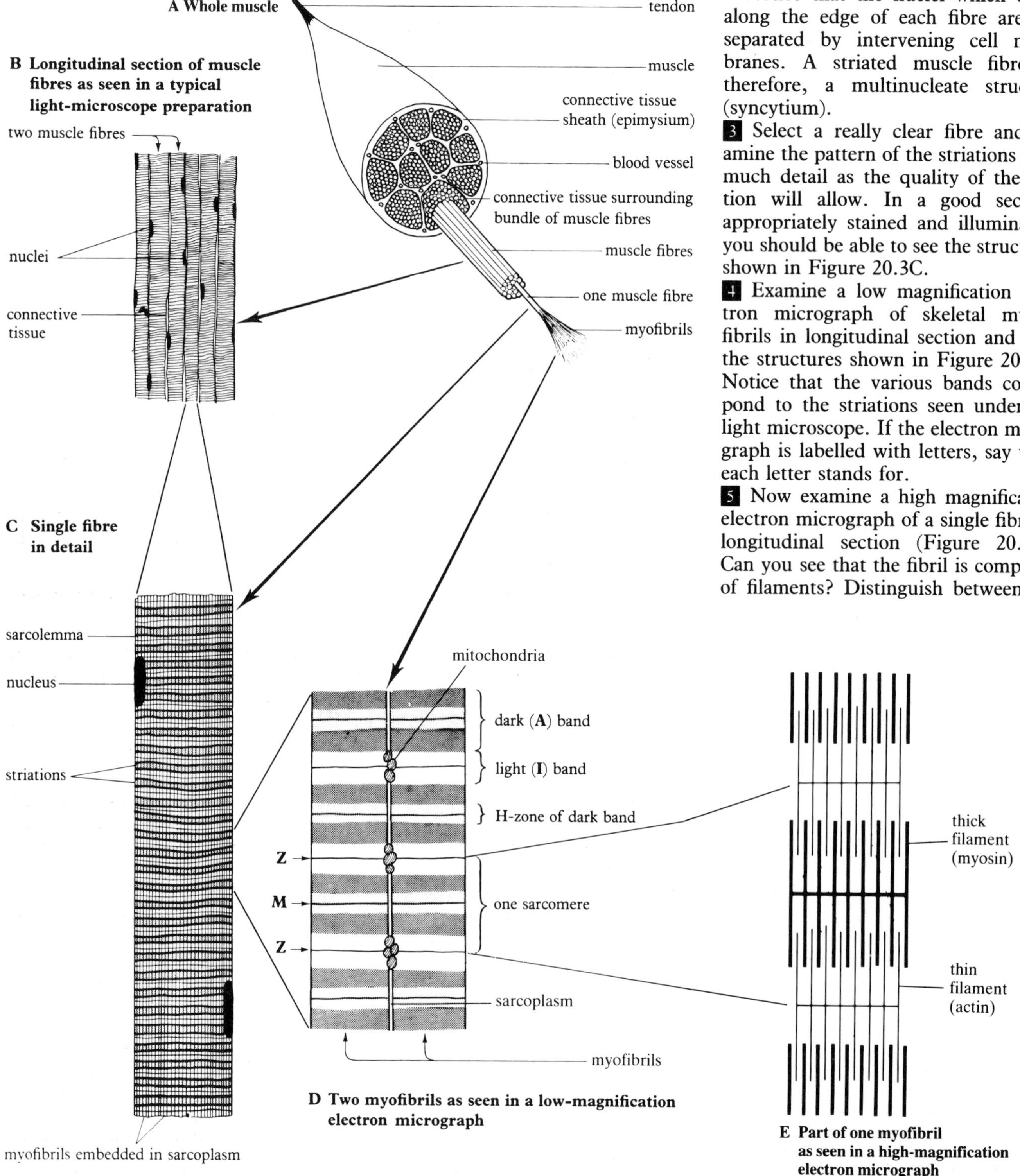

Procedure

1 Refer to Figure 20.3A to see how the muscle fibres are arranged within the muscle. Note that they are surrounded by a connective tissue sheath, the epimysium.

2 Examine a longitudinal section of skeletal muscle under high power. You should be able to see the structures shown in Figure 20.3B.

Notice that the nuclei which occur along the edge of each fibre are not separated by intervening cell membranes. A striated muscle fibre is, therefore, a multinucleate structure (syncytium).

3 Select a really clear fibre and examine the pattern of the striations in as much detail as the quality of the section will allow. In a good section, appropriately stained and illuminated, you should be able to see the structures shown in Figure 20.3C.

4 Examine a low magnification electron micrograph of skeletal muscle fibrils in longitudinal section and note the structures shown in Figure 20.3D. Notice that the various bands correspond to the striations seen under the light microscope. If the electron micrograph is labelled with letters, say what each letter stands for.

5 Now examine a high magnification electron micrograph of a single fibril in longitudinal section (Figure 20.3E). Can you see that the fibril is composed of filaments? Distinguish between the thick (myosin) and thin (actin) filaments. Can you see how they are arranged? Does their arrangement agree with Figure 20.3E?

6 Look carefully at the thick and thin filaments in the region where they overlap. Can you see bridges interconnecting them. What is the function of the bridges?

7 Now look for the endoplasmic (sarcoplasmic) reticulum in both the low and high magnification electron micrographs. You should be able to see traces of it beneath the sarcolemma and between adjacent myofibrils. What can you say about its function?

For Consideration

(1) What contribution has the electron microscope made to our understanding of how skeletal muscle contracts?

(2) What would you expect Figure 20.3E to look like if the muscle was fully contracted? Explain in as much detail as you can how the change from the relaxed to the contracted state is brought about.

Requirements
Microscope

LS skeletal muscle
Electron micrograph of skeletal muscle fibrils (low magnification, LS)
Electron micrograph of skeletal muscle fibril(s) (high magnification, LS)

Questions and problems

1 Explain the circumstances in which an isolated muscle may
(a) develop tension without shortening,
(b) shorten without developing tension,
(c) shorten *and* develop tension.

2 A cathode ray oscilloscope was used for recording, simultaneously, the action potential and the tension from an isolated muscle fibre of the frog at 20 °C. Comment on the results which are shown in Figure 20.4.

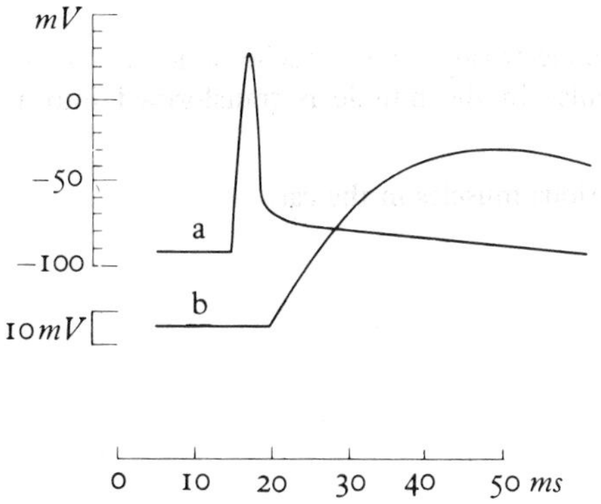

Figure 20.4 Simultaneous recording of (a) action potential and (b) tension in an isolated muscle fibre of frog. (*After Hodgkin and Horowicz*)

3 Draw up a table in which skeletal, visceral and cardiac muscle are compared from both a structural and functional point of view.

4 In suitable conditions isolated segments of mammalian intestine will contract spontaneously and rhythmically even after all their nerve plexuses have been inactivated by drugs such as nicotine or cocaine. How would you account for this?

It has been found that spontaneous movements of the mammalian intestine are enhanced (i.e. increased in frequency and amplitude) by acetylcholine, but suppressed by adrenaline. Explain.

5 (a) What is the all-or-nothing law? The nerve of a nerve-muscle preparation (*see* page 193) was stimulated with a series of single shocks of gradually increasing intensity. The responses of the muscle, recorded on a slowly revolving drum, are shown in Figure 20.5.
(b) How would you reconcile these results with the all-or-nothing law?
(c) What would you expect the results to be if the same series of stimuli were delivered to (i) the whole muscle and (ii) a single muscle fibre?

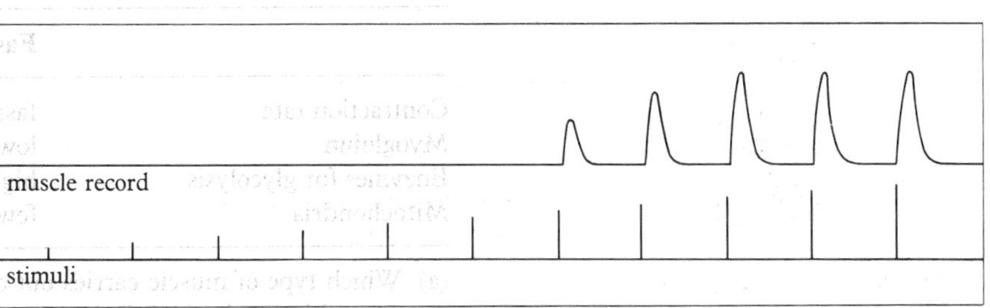

Figure 20.5 Kymograph recording of responses of the muscle of a nerve-muscle preparation to stimulation of the nerve with a series of shocks of gradually increasing intensity. The relative intensity of the stimuli is indicated by the heights of the vertical lines in the lower record.

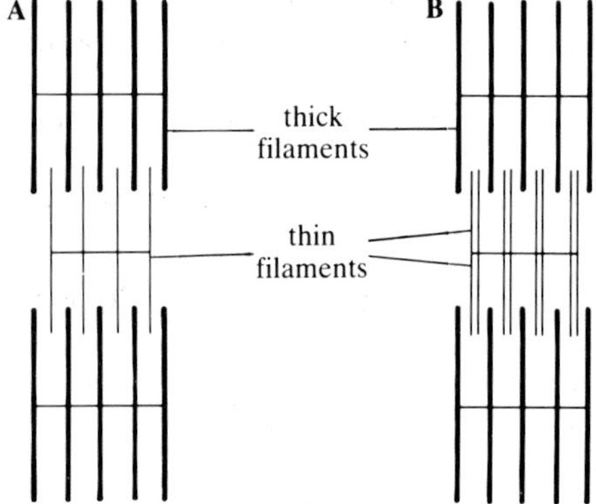

Figure 20.6 The thick and thin filaments of a skeletal muscle fibril as they appear in the electron microscope.

6 Figure 20.6 shows the arrangement of the thick and thin filaments in longitudinal sections of a muscle fibril as seen in the electron microscope. Why is it that in some longitudinal sections the filaments are arranged as in Figure 20.6A whereas in other sections taken from the same muscle they are arranged as in Figure 20.6B? Illustrate your explanation with a diagram.

7 Figure 20.7 is an electron micrograph of striated muscle tissue taken from a highly active muscle.
(a) Name the regions labelled A and B.
(b) Name structure C. What is its function in the muscle?
(c) Is the muscle in the micrograph contracted or relaxed? How do you know?
(d) Name the structures labelled D. What special features do they show in this particular micrograph? Speculate on why they should show these features.

Figure 20.7 Electron micrograph of a longitudinal section of striated muscle tissue. (*Dr. M.J. Cullen*)

8 Explain the role of calcium ions (a) when an electrical impulse reaches a nerve-muscle junction, and (b) when the electrical impulse in the muscle is transformed into a mechanical contraction.

9 The table shows the contraction times of various muscles in the cat:

Muscle	**Contraction time**
Internal rectus	7.5 ms
Inferior oblique	18.7 ms
Gastrocnemius	39 ms
Diaphragm	480 ms
Stomach	2.2 s

Discuss these figures in relation to the functions of these particular muscles.

10 Humans possess two types of skeletal muscle fibres, fast twitch and slow twitch. The following table shows how they differ:

	Fast twitch (white)	**Slow twitch** (red)
Contraction rate	fast	slow
Myoglobin	low concentration	high concentration
Enzymes for glycolysis	high	low
Mitochondria	few	many

(a) Which type of muscle carries out aerobic respiration, and which type specialises in anaerobic respiration? Relate your answer to the information given in the table.

Duration of exercise	Relative contribution (per cent) from: Anaerobic respiration	Aerobic respiration
10 s	83	17
2 min	40	60
10 min	9	91
60 min	1	99

The table in the margin shows the relative contributions of aerobic and anaerobic respiration to the total energy output in athletes who are running races of various distances:

(b) What will happen to the products of anaerobic respiration during and after a short distance race?

(c) What proportion of fast-twitch and slow-twitch muscles might suit a potential long-distance athlete?

Different sports require different degrees of stamina. The following results were obtained from a group of highly trained athletes:

	Percentage of slow twitch muscle (the rest is fast twitch muscle)	**Maximum oxygen uptake** ($cm^3\ min^{-1}\ kg^{-1}$)
Cross country skiers	77	83
Long distance runners	63	80
Canoeists	60	69
Swimmers	50	65
Weight lifters	47	50
100/200 m runners	44	57

(d) Plot these data on graph paper. Discuss whether athletes good at a particular event are born or made.

(e) When a dogfish swims slowly for a long time its fat reserves become exhausted but its glycogen reserves do not. Is this consistent with the above data for humans?

Data from: T. Reilly (1981) *Sports Fitness and Sports Injuries* Faber, 1981; U. Bergh *et al, Medicine and Science in Sports*, Vol. 10, 1978.

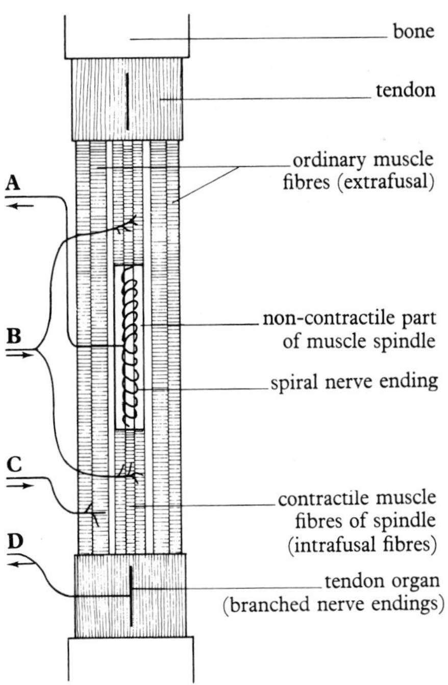

Figure 20.8 Schematic diagram of muscle spindle and tendon organ. **A**, **B**, **C** and **D** are nerve fibres, and the arrows indicate the direction in which impulses are transmitted.

11 Muscle spindles and tendon organs are associated with skeletal muscles. Figure 20.8 is a highly schematic diagram of these two types of stretch receptor and their nerve supply. The following are the results of experiments carried out to investigate their physiology:

(a) The whole muscle is stretched. *Result*: a train of nervous impulses is discharged in nerve fibre **A**, the frequency of impulses being proportional to the stretching force. Only very slight stretching is required to elicit this response.

(b) If **B** is stimulated the same result is produced as in (a).

(c) **C** is stimulated while impulses are being discharged in **A**. *Result*: the frequency of impulses in **A** decreases.

(d) The tendon is stretched. *Result:* impulses are discharged in **D**, but this only occurs if the stretching is fairly severe.

(e) If the nervous system is intact, stretching the tendon may result in a decrease in the frequency of impulses in **C**.

(f) With prolonged stretching of the muscle and tendon, discharge of impulses in **A** and **D** continues for a long time without any diminution in frequency.

What conclusions would you draw from these experiments as to the role and mode of functioning of the muscle spindle and tendon organ in the living animal?

12 Comment briefly on each of the following statements:

(a) The flatfish *Paralichthys albiguttus* can change the colour and pattern of its markings to suit its background.

(b) If a tentacle of the sea anemone *Anemonia* is stroked repeatedly with a fine glass rod the withdrawal response spreads to neighbouring tentacles, but the discharge of nematoblasts is confined to the tentacle which is stimulated.

(c) Swamp-dwelling fishes have to find their way about in the dark.

(d) The electric eel, *Electrophorus*, can kill prey without touching it.

21 Locomotion

Background Summary

1 Locomotion is generally brought about by a system of **muscles** in conjunction with a **skeleton**. The skeleton may be an **endoskeleton**, **exoskeleton**, or **hydrostatic skeleton**.

2 The skeleton is operated by sets of **antagonistic muscles** whose actions, controlled by **reciprocal innervation**, bring about movement and maintain posture.

3 In considering the locomotion of any animal three things must be taken into account: **propulsion**, **support**, and **stability**. These can be conveniently dealt with in relation to the medium in or on which the organism moves: **water** (e.g. fishes), **land** (e.g. tetrapods), or **air** (e.g. birds).

4 In fishes propulsion is generally achieved by side-to-side movement of the tail (or sometimes the whole body), achieved by differential contraction of the **myotomes**. The mechanical principles involved in this kind of propulsion also apply to spermatozoa, many aquatic invertebrates, and flagella.

5 In cartilaginous fishes (elasmobranchs) support is achieved by the large **pectoral fins** and the **heterocercal tail fin**. In bony fishes (teleosts) support is achieved by the buoyant effect of the **swim bladder**, the tail fin being **homocercal**.

6 Stability in fishes is achieved by the various fins collectively counteracting **yawing**, **pitching**, and **rolling**.

7 Some aquatic animals propel themselves by a mechanism akin to that of the breaststroke of a swimmer. This also applies to the action of cilia.

8 Although terrestrial locomotion can be achieved by undulatory movements, it generally involves the use of **limbs** acting as **levers**. For effective action the limbs must be operated by appropriate muscles acting across well lubricated **joints**.

9 The various muscles are conveniently classified, according to the effects they produce, into **protractors** and **retractors**, **abductors** and **adductors**, **flexors** and **extensors**, and **rotators**.

10 In tetrapods support is achieved by the limbs acting as **struts** and the **vertebral column** as the span of a **cantilever bridge**.

11 Stability in a moving tetrapod is maintained by its **diagonal locomotory pattern** aided by **vestibular reflexes** and reflexes arising from various **proprioceptors**, notably muscle spindles.

12 Locomotion in air depends on the possession of wings. In a gliding bird the wing acts as an **aerofoil**. Similar aerodynamic principles apply to all flying animals, but the structural and physiological basis of flight varies from one group to another. This can be appreciated by comparing the flight mechanisms of birds and insects.

13 At the cellular level movement is less well understood. In the case of **amoeboid movement** it involves changes in the physical properties of the cytoplasm. Amoeboid movement and the bending of cilia and flagella may involve sliding of filaments similar to that which occurs in muscle.

Investigation 21.1
Types of musculo-skeletal system

Skeletons may be conveniently classified, on the basis of their topographical relationship to the muscles that operate them, into endoskeletons where the skeleton is internal to the muscles, and exoskeletons where the skeleton is external to the muscles. The endoskeleton is typical of vertebrates, the exoskeleton of arthropods. To these two types of skeleton may be added a third, the hydrostatic skeleton, where the muscles surround a fluid-filled cavity. This is found in various soft-bodied invertebrates.

Procedure

ENDOSKELETON

1 As an example of an endoskeleton, examine the tail of a dogfish. Cut a hand-section a short distance behind the pelvic fins and remove the skin from one side.

2 View the cut surface end-on. Notice that the vertebral column is completely enveloped by blocks of muscle, the myotomes (Figure 21.1). The individual muscle fibres have been cut in cross section.

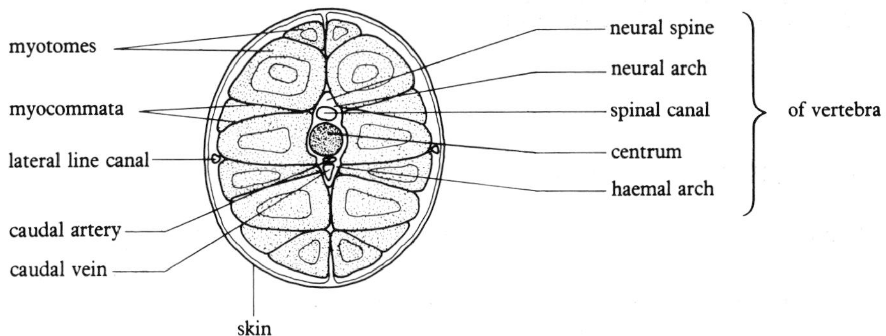

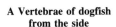

Figure 21.1 Transverse section through the tail of a dogfish. The haemal arch is formed by the union of the left and right transverse processes. It envelopes and protects the caudal artery and vein.

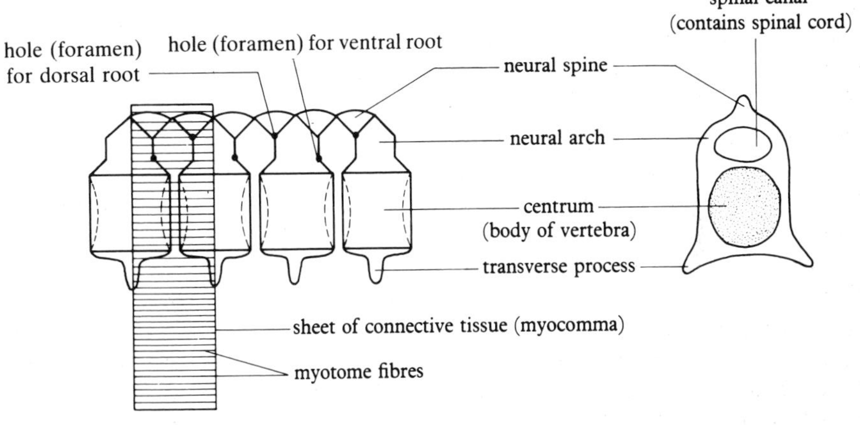

Figure 21.2 Vertebral column of dogfish.

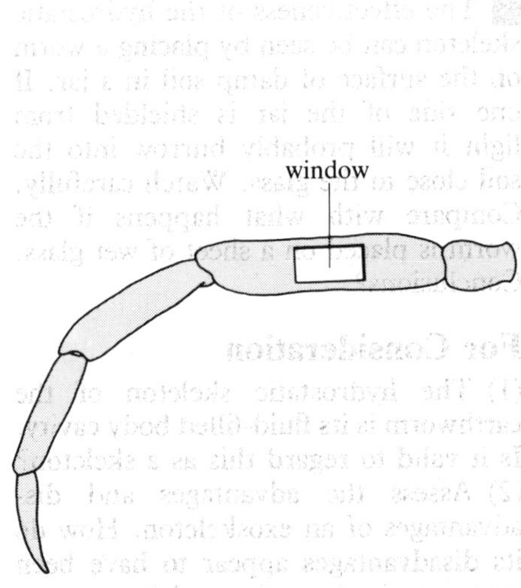

Figure 21.3 Leg of the shore crab *Carcinus* showing a window cut in the side of the largest segment.

3 In side-view notice connective tissue sheets, the myocommata, between successive myotomes. Tease out some of the muscle fibres and confirm that they are orientated longitudinally.

4 The fibres of each myotome run longitudinally from one vertebra and myocomma to the next. The vertebrae, myotomes and myocommata are all serially repeated along the body, i.e. they are metamerically segmented. What is the significance of this? Notice that the myotomes are ≷-shaped when viewed from the side.

The effectiveness of the myotomes in generating propulsive movements can be appreciated by watching fish in an aquarium tank.

5 Examine the vertebral column in side-view, noting its segmented pattern and the structures shown in Figure 21.2. Why are the neural spines so small? (Compare with mammal, page 204.)

6 Examine a transverse section of an embryo dogfish (tail region) under the microscope. Observe details of the vertebra, myotomes and myocommata. Notice that the muscle fibres are oriented longitudinally.

EXOSKELETON

1 Remove one of the largest legs from a freshly killed crab (the shore crab *Carcinus* is recommended on account of its large size).

2 With a scalpel blade, cut a rectangular window in the side of the largest segment of the limb (Figure 21.3). Be careful not to damage the structures inside.

3 When you have cut your window, you will see the white flexor and extensor muscles inside the limb. Note that the muscles are enclosed *within* the hard cuticle (exoskeleton).

4 Remove the muscles (which are soft), leaving the tendon-like apodemes to which they are attached.

5 With small forceps grasp each of the two main apodemes in turn and pull gently. Note that one of the apodemes flexes the leg, the other extends it.

6 Investigate the joint, as fully as you can, using a hand lens or binocular microscope. How do you think it works?

7 The crab's leg may seem a clumsy affair but it is by no means ineffective, as a cursory examination of a living

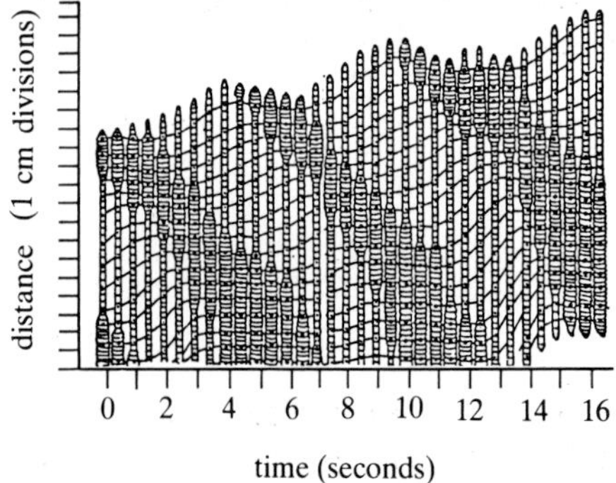

Figure 21.4 Diagram showing the sequence of events in the passage of three successive peristaltic bulges along an earthworm. The bulges are moving from the anterior to the posterior end. The wavy lines link the same relative points (marked by dots) on the worm and show the distance moved forward by them at one second intervals. (*After Sir James Gray*)

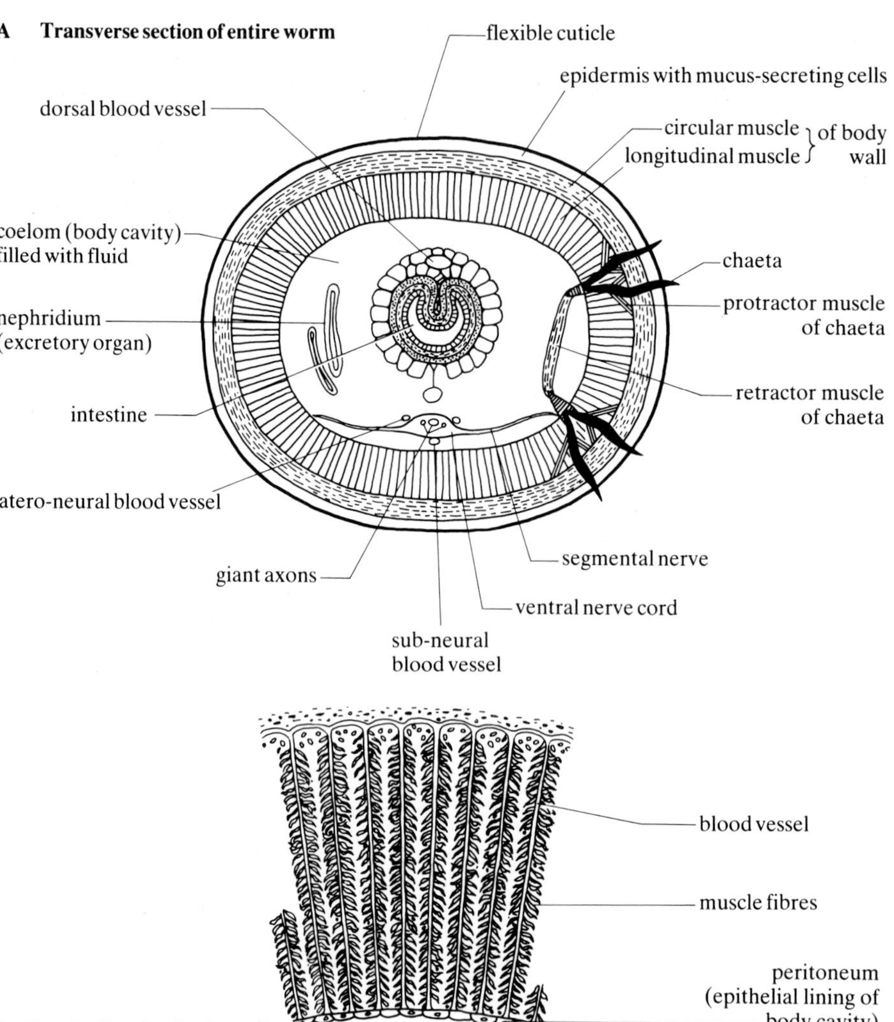

Figure 21.5 Transverse section of earthworm showing the structures involved in locomation and movement. Contractions of the body wall muscles are coordinated by the ventral nerve cord. The giant axons transmit impulses which bring about rapid contraction of the longitudinal muscle and simultaneous protraction of the chaetae: this is the animal's escape reaction.

Requirements
Microscope
Hand lens or binocular microscope
Dissecting instruments
Jar of damp soil
Sheet of glass

Dogfish tail (several students can share)
Vertebral column of dogfish
TS and LS earthworm (preferably intestinal region)
TS dogfish embryo (tail region)

Fish (any kind that uses tail propulsion) in tank
Largest leg of crab (e.g. *Carcinus*)
Live crabs in dish
Cockroaches in cage
Earthworm on damp filter paper in dish

specimen will show. For a more efficient example of an exoskeleton in action observe a cockroach running across the floor of a cage.

HYDROSTATIC SKELETON

1 Watch an earthworm crawling forwards on damp filter paper in a dish. Observe a 'peristaltic' bulge travelling from the head backwards. It is accompanied by protraction of the chaetae (bristles). The combined effect results in effective propulsion.

2 Observe successive bulges as they pass backwards along the body. Does the sequence of events agree with the diagrams in Figure 21.4?

3 Examine a transverse and longitudinal section of the earthworm under low power (Figure 21.5). Notice the large body cavity, thick muscular body wall and (if the section has gone through one) a chaeta.

4 Look carefully at the body wall. The body wall muscles are in two layers: an outer layer of circular muscles and an inner layer of longitudinal muscles whose fibres are neatly arranged in bundles. Which is the thickest layer, and why? Will these muscles account for your earlier observations on the live worm?

5 The effectiveness of the hydrostatic skeleton can be seen by placing a worm on the surface of damp soil in a jar. If one side of the jar is shielded from light it will probably burrow into the soil close to the glass. Watch carefully. Compare with what happens if the worm is placed on a sheet of wet glass. Conclusions?

For Consideration

(1) The hydrostatic skeleton of the earthworm is its fluid-filled body cavity. Is it valid to regard this as a skeleton?

(2) Assess the advantages and disadvantages of an exoskeleton. How do its disadvantages appear to have been overcome in the arthropods?

Investigation 21.2
Functional analysis of the muscles in the hind leg of the rat

CAUTION:
Several serious diseases can be caught from rats. Wear a laboratory coat and thin rubber gloves while you are dissecting, and wash your hands thoroughly afterwards.

Requirements
Dissecting instruments

Rat, freshly killed for dissection
Rat, preserved in e.g. formalin

Note: As an alternative to the rat, a pig's trotter may be used. Trotters are readily available from the butcher. Though slightly atypical because of the specialised nature of the digits, the muscles are easy to dissect and their actions can be readily investigated by pulling.

The purpose of this exercise is to investigate the functions performed by the muscles in the hind limb of a vertebrate. At one time such an analysis would have been strictly anatomical, each muscle being carefully dissected away from the skeleton and named according to its position. We shall adopt a more functional approach, the muscles being described in terms of their functions.

Procedure

1 Skin one of the hind legs of a freshly killed or deep frozen rat. Note the muscles, packed tightly together, under the skin.

2 Systematically separate the superficial muscles from one another. Each muscle is enveloped by a thin connective tissue sheath (*see* page 196). Remove the connective tissue so as to free the muscle. Follow the muscle upwards to its origin and downwards to its insertion. The origin and insertion are usually on bones, but in some cases they may be on the connective tissue sheath surrounding other muscles.

3 When you have freed a muscle from its neighbours, pull it so as to determine its action. Then, and only then, cut it at its origin and/or insertion and either deflect it or remove it. This will enable you to see, and dissect, the deeper muscles beneath.

4 One of the problems in dissecting a freshly killed rat is that it is difficult to see the precise demarcation between one muscle and the next. However, it is much easier to see the individual muscles in a preserved rat. So have a preserved rat alongside you, and systematically dissect its muscles as you proceed with your analysis. This will help you to be certain that your reconstruction of the muscles is anatomically, as well as functionally, correct. (Unfortunately you will not be able to investigate the action of the muscles in the preserved rat as the leg will be stiff and the joints immoveable.)

5 At the appropriate stages of your investigation, make diagrams of the leg showing the various muscles. Label the muscles according to the following classification, adding in each case any necessary qualifications:

Protractor: draws femur forwards
Retractor: draws femur backwards
Abductor: draws femur outwards
Adductor: draws femur inwards
Knee flexor: draws femur and tibia-fibula towards each other, i.e. closes knee joint
Knee extensor: draws femur and tibia-fibula away from each other, i.e. opens knee joint
Ankle flexor: draws foot towards tibia-fibula, i.e. closes ankle joint
Ankle extensor: draws foot away from tibia-fibula, i.e. opens ankle joint
Inward thigh rotator: rotates femur inwards
Outward thigh rotator: rotates femur outwards.

Make clear which muscles are antagonistic to each other.

For Consideration

(1) How many muscles have you accounted for in the hind leg of the rat?
(2) How many of the muscles belong to each of the groups listed above?
(3) Which of the muscles do you consider to be the most important in normal locomotion of the rat?
(4) Although numerous muscles are responsible for operating the hind leg, there is only one nerve (the sciatic nerve) in the leg. How is it that this one nerve can co-ordinate the actions of all the muscles?

Investigation 21.3
The mammalian skeleton

Naming, and learning how to recognise, the individual bones in the mammalian skeleton (which is what the authors of this book had to do when they were at school) can be a time-consuming and tedious exercise. In this investigation we shall be more concerned with the functions of the bones and their relationships with each other.

Procedure

1 Examine a mounted rabbit skeleton and identify the various parts (Figure 21.6). It is composed almost entirely of bone, with cartilage only at the articular surfaces. (The microscopic structure of bone and cartilage are dealt with on page 24–5.) What functions are performed by the skeleton as a whole?

2 For convenience the skeleton is subdivided into the following parts:

(1) **Axial**
- (a) Skull
- (b) Vertebral column (backbone)
- (c) Ribs
- (d) Sternum (breastbone)

(2) **Appendicular**
- (a) Limbs
  - (i) Forelimb (arm)
  - (ii) Hindlimb (leg)
- (b) Girdles
  - (i) Pectoral (shoulder) girdle
  - (ii) Pelvic (hip) girdle

Re-examine the rabbit skeleton and note how these parts relate to each other spatially. What do the terms axial and appendicular mean?

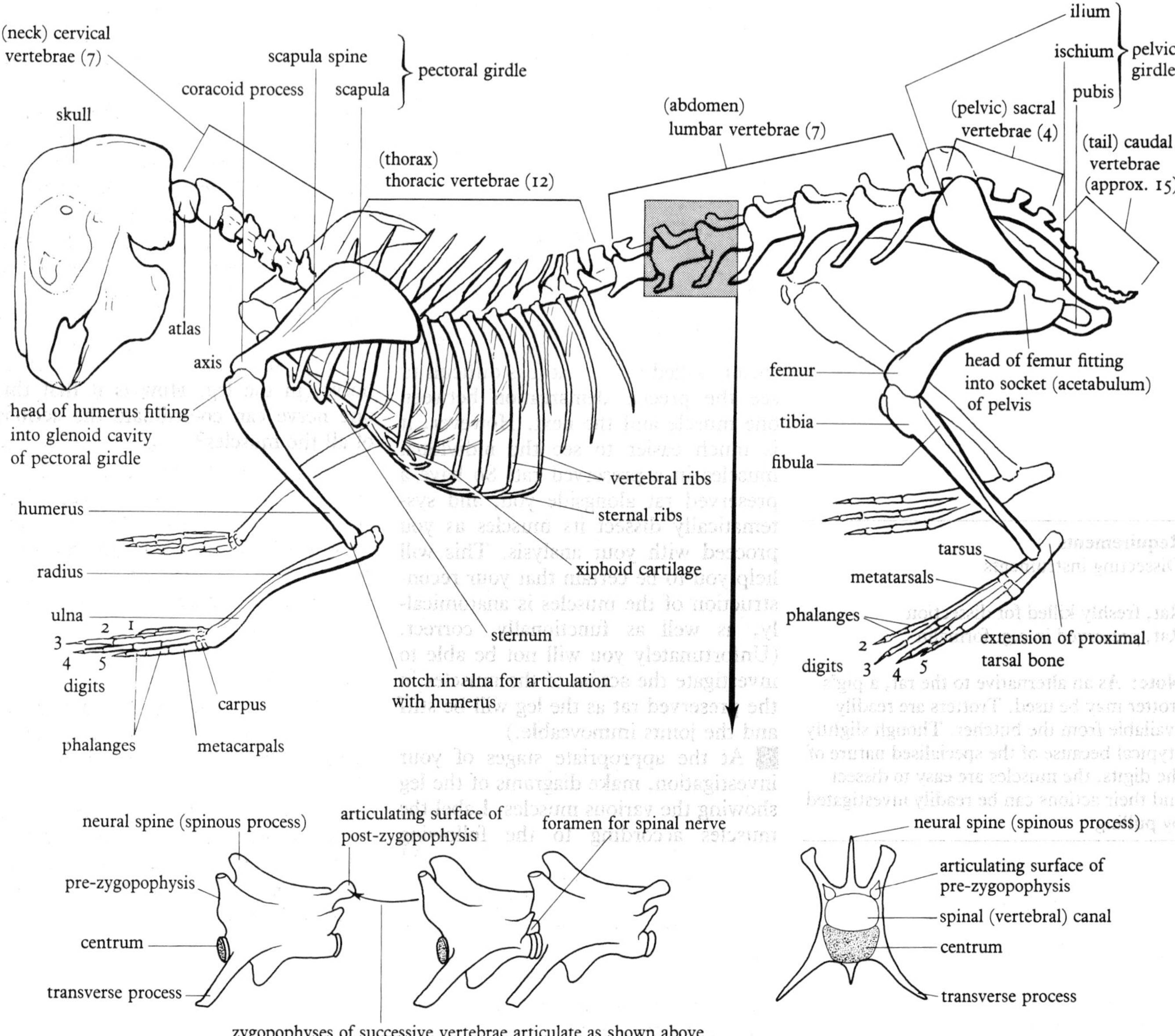

Figure 21.6 Diagram of the skeleton of rabbit. Below the complete skeleton are four lumbar vertebrae, in side view (left) and anterior view (right).

3 Examine individual bones and relate them to the mounted skeleton. Pay particular attention to

(i) **articulating surfaces:** try fitting bones together, estimating how much freedom of movement they have;

(ii) **projections:** these are usually for the attachment of tendons and ligaments for which they are often adapted by being flattened.

4 Examine the vertebrae. Start with a lumbar vertebra and then compare it with the others.

Questions to answer

In studying the skeleton see if you can answer the following questions:

(1) For what functional reason do the lumbar vertebrae have particularly large centra?

(2) What function might be performed by the prominent lateral processes which project from the sides of the lumbar vertebrae, but are not found elsewhere in the vertebral column?

(3) Why are the neural spines of the lumbar and thoracic vertebrae relatively long compared with most of the cervical vertebrae?

(4) Why are the transverse processes of the atlas vertebra, and the neural spine of the axis vertebra, relatively large and flat?

(5) You will notice that the ribs are double-headed. With what specific parts of the thoracic vertebrae do the heads articulate? What is the point of this double articulation?

(6) Why are the four sacral vertebrae fused together?

(7) In life the ilium is firmly, but not immoveably, attached by ligaments to the first sacral vertebra. Functional significance?

(8) On the other hand the scapula is more loosely attached to the vertebral column. Why?

(9) What function(s) would you ascribe to the pubis and why are the two halves of the pelvic girdle fused together?

(10) Why are the ilium and scapula flattened?

(11) What is the scapula spine for?

(12) What function(s) would you ascribe to the sternum?

(13) Some of the limb bones possess bumps, crests and grooves. What are these for?

(14) How does the articulation of the forelimb with its girdle compare with that of the hindlimb?

(15) How does the hip joint compare with the other joints of the hindlimb? Functional significance? What about the forelimb?

(16) What explanation would you suggest for the lower part of each limb consisting of *two* parallel bones?

(17) What function do you think is performed by the backward extension of the tarsus in the hindlimb? Is there a functional equivalent in the forelimb? If so, where?

(18) Any suggestion as to why the hindlimb has only four digits?

(19) Compare the relative sizes of the different components of the forelimb and hindlimb. What significance would you attach to the differences?

(20) How do the caudal vertebrae differ from the more anterior vertebrae, and why?

Other verebrate skeletons

1 Examine a human skeleton or model thereof. Compare it with the rabbit skeleton, particularly with reference to the structure of the vertebral column. To what extent is the structure of the human skeleton related to the fact that the human is bipedal?

2 Examine the skeleton of a frog. Compare it with the rabbit skeleton, particularly with reference to the sacral vertebrae, pelvic girdle and hindlimbs. How is the structure of the frog's skeleton related to its method of locomotion?

3 Examine the skeleton of a bird, e.g. pigeon. Compare it with the rabbit skeleton particularly with reference to the pectoral girdle and sternum. Notice that the sternum has a deep keel. This is for attachment of the flight muscles. Describe in detail the origin and insertion of the flight muscles and explain how their contractions result in lowering and raising the wings.

For consideration

(1) To what extent is the skeleton of the rabbit like a cantilever bridge? What is the functional significance of the analogy?

(2) To what extent does the human skeleton depart from a cantilever construction, and why? Can you think of a more appropriate analogy for the human skeleton?

Requirements

Mounted skeleton of rabbit
Individual bones of rabbit
Mounted skeleton of human, or model thereof
Mounted skeleton of frog
Mounted skeleton of bird

Investigation 21.4
Formation and structure of a limb bone

Bone is formed as a result of the activities of embryonic mesenchyme cells. Mesenchyme cells may develop directly into membrane (dermal) bones (e.g. scapula, skull roof, etc.), or into cartilage which is then turned into bone (ossified). Limb bones are always preformed in cartilage.

Procedure

1 Examine a longitudinal section of a limb bone of a mammalian embryo. The main body of the limb bone is called the shaft, the ends are known as the epiphyses. Identify the different parts of the shaft and epiphysis, using Figure 21.7A to help you.

2 Now look in detail at the base of the epiphysis where cartilage is being replaced by bone. (Figure 21.7B). Here the cartilage cells (chondrocytes) enlarge to form hypertrophic cartilage. The innermost hypertrophic cartilage cells secrete an enzyme which causes the cartilage to calcify. This isolates the cells from their source of nourishment, so they die and disrupt. As this happens they are invaded by osteoblasts which proceed to secrete bone matrix. The bone formed at this stage is permeated by numerous cavities containing blood vessels, and the osteocytes (as the bone cells are now called) are somewhat irregularly arranged. This

Figure 21.7 Microscopic structure of a developing limb bone.

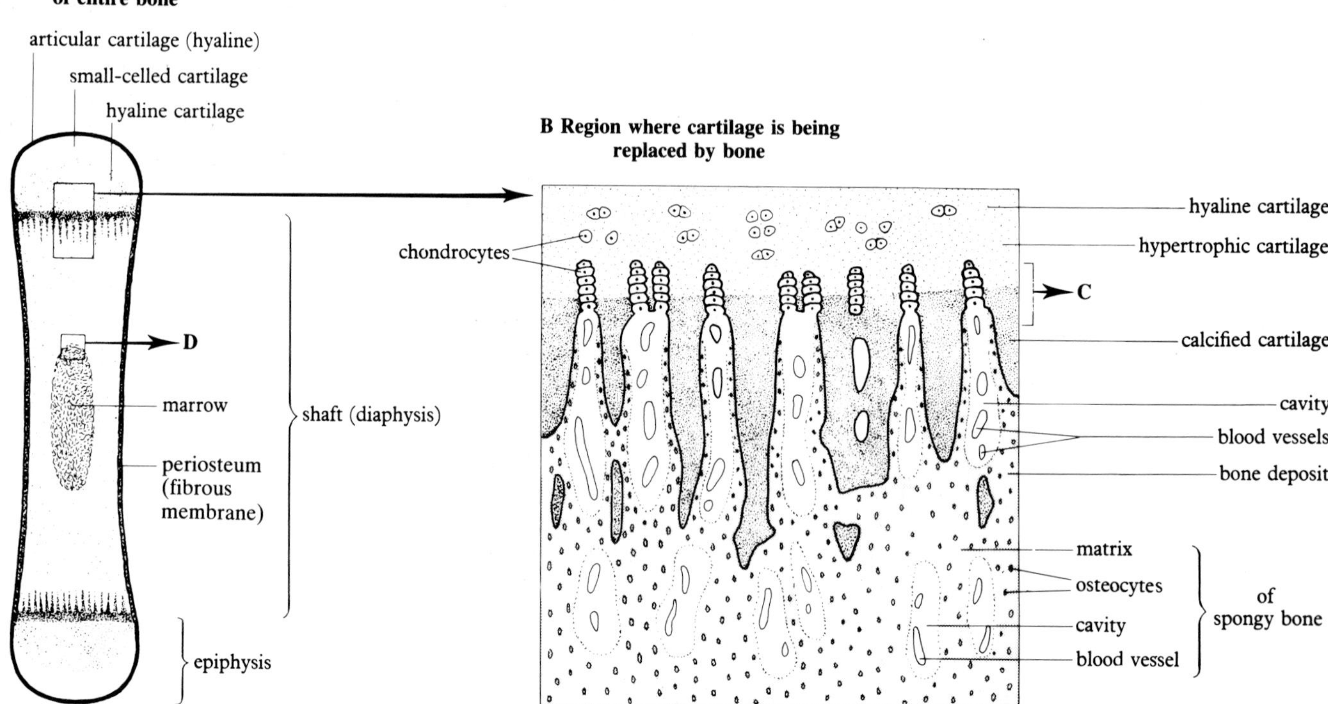

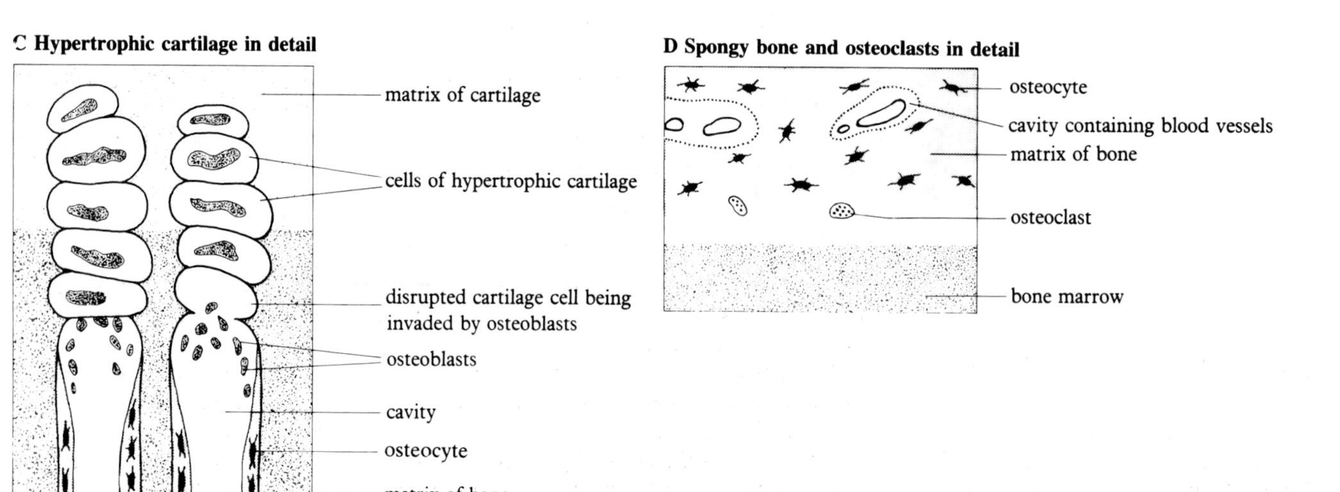

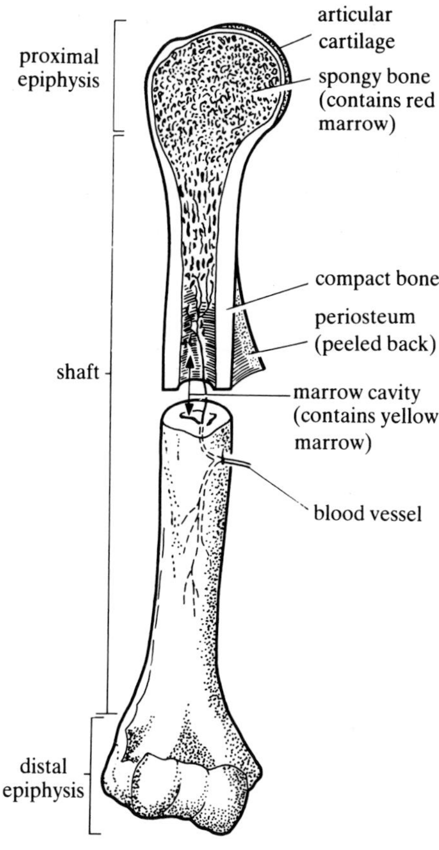

Figure 21.8 A limb bone (humerus), the top half of which has been sectioned longitudinally to show the inside. (*After G.J. Tortora*)

Requirements
LS developing limb bone
TS and LS compact bone
Limb bone of e.g. cow, sawn longitudinally

type of bone is called spongy or cancellous bone.

3 Find a cartilage cell which is being invaded by osteoblasts and examine it in as much detail as you can (Figure 21.7C).

4 Examine spongy bone under high power (Figure 21.7D). Notice the numerous cavities and the stellate form of the osteocytes.

5 At birth the cartilage in the epiphyses becomes ossified. However, the bands of hypertrophic cartilage persist, thus allowing the bone to continue growing in length. Increase in girth of the shaft takes place by the addition of new bone by osteoblasts just beneath the periosteum.

As new bone is laid down, old bone is resorbed at the centre. This is achieved by osteoclasts, large multinucleate cells formed by the fusion of certain osteoblasts. Normally resorption of old bone keeps pace with the formation of new bone, with the result that an expanding cavity develops in the centre of the shaft, the marrow cavity. This contains soft fatty tissue and, in some bones, numerous blood sinuses where blood cells are formed. This is the bone marrow. Examine spongy bone in the immediate vicinity of the marrow cavity. Can you see any osteoclasts? (Figure 21.7D).

6 Osteoclasts are important throughout the time the bone is developing. Their eroding activities enable the bone to be continually changed and remodelled to meet the stresses and strains to which the limb is subjected. They are also responsible for cutting channels into new bone thereby enabling the invasion of blood vessels. These channels become the Haversian canals of mature compact bone (*see* page 24–5).

7 The sides of the shaft of a fully formed limb bone are composed of compact bone (Figure 21.8). The epiphyses consist of a superficial layer of compact bone with spongy bone beneath. Confirm this by looking at a fully formed limb bone (of e.g. cow) which has been sawn in two longitudinally so as to expose the inside (Figure 21.8).

For Consideration

(1) How is the formation and structure of a limb bone related to the functions that it has to perform?

(2) The topographical positions of compact and spongy bone in a limb bone such as the femur is ideally suited for carrying heavy loads. Explain.

Questions and Problems

1 (a) An animal propels itself forward by pushing backwards against its surroundings.' Discuss.

(b) A science-fiction film depicted an organism from another planet as moving by means of a rotating propeller. Do you think this is feasible?

2 Devise a method for measuring the force exerted by an earthworm moving forward on a horizontal surface? How is its movement achieved?

3 An eel swims forward by throwing its body into waves of undulation which pass from head to tail. What mechanical forces are set up during this process and what is their musculo-skeletal basis?

The marine ragworm *Nereis* swims forward by the same method as the eel, but the waves, instead of passing from head to tail, travel from tail to head. The only external structural difference between an eel and *Nereis* is that the latter has paddles projecting from the sides of the body (Figure 21.9). Why should the possession of these paddles make it necessary for the propulsive wave to travel from tail to head?

Figure 21.9 The ragworm Nereis swims by waves of undulation which pass forward along the body from tail to head. (*After Sir James Gray*)

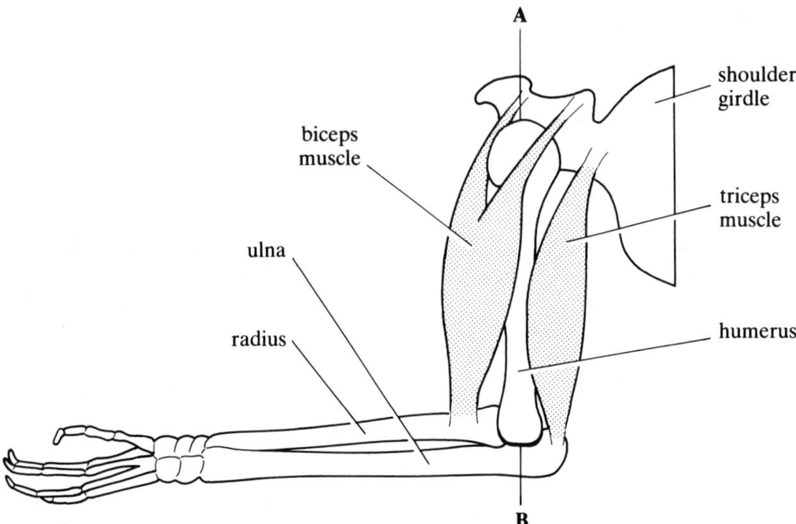

Figure 21.10 The human arm showing the biceps and triceps muscles.

4 Figure 21.10 shows the biceps and triceps muscles and their attachments in the human arm.
(a) What effect on the arm does each muscle have when it contracts?
(b) What sort of joints are present at positions A and B?
(c) When a person lifts something up, the muscles contract in such a way as to produce the correct movement of the arm. Explain, in as much detail as you can, the neural mechanism by which this is achieved.

5 'The great fish moved silently through the night water, propelled by short sweeps of its crescent tail. The mouth was open just enough to permit a rush of water over the gills. . . . Lacking the flotation bladder common to other fish and the fluttering flaps to push oxygen-bearing water through its gills, it survived only by moving. Once stopped, it would sink to the bottom and die of anoxia.'
(From '*Jaws*' by Peter Benchley, Andre Deutsch, 1974)
Explain how, by actively moving, Jaws managed to keep himself up in the water.

6 Give an example, with brief explanatory notes, of each of the following:
(a) an animal which has a hydrostatic skeleton as well as an exoskeleton;
(b) an animal which swims by a 'jet-propulsion' mechanism;
(c) an animal which moves sideways;
(d) a fish that walks;
(e) an animal which uses its hind legs for jumping and swimming;
(f) a mammal that flies;
(g) a fish that glides.

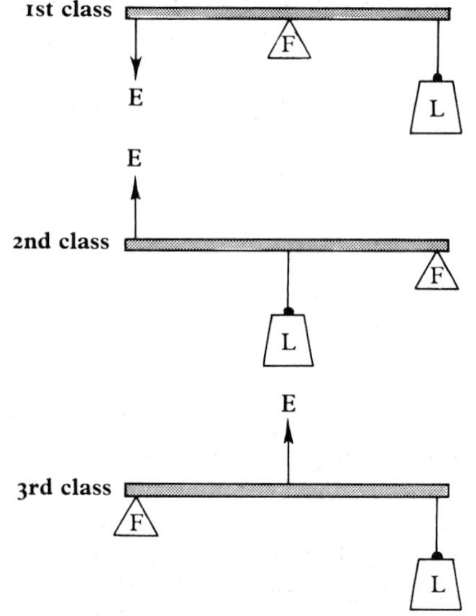

Figure 21.11 Three classes of lever. **E**, effort; **F**, fulcrum; **L**, load.

7 Figure 21.11 shows three different types of lever. Give examples, with diagrams, of specific situations in the human musculo-skeletal system where each type of lever occurs.

8 'A cow has four legs, the milking stool has only three.' Discuss. (*OCJE*)

9 Discuss in physiological terms the problem of learning to ride a bicycle.

10 Compare the flight mechanism of birds and insects.

11 How has modern research on cells thrown light on amoeboid movement and on the bending of flagella and cilia?

22 Behaviour

Background Summary

1 Techniques for investigating animal behaviour include kymographs, slow-motion cinematography, video recording, time-lapse and multiple-flash photography, various types of activity recorder, and direct observation.

2 Behaviour can be broadly divided into **species-characteristic** and **individual-characteristic** behaviour. Both involve certain fundamental processes, e.g. reflex action, orientation and learning.

3 **Reflex action** includes the escape responses of many invertebrates, which, because of their comparative simplicity, lend themselves readily to experimental analysis. Such is the case with the giant-axon reflexes of the earthworm and squid.

4 **Orientation behaviour**, commonly divided into **kinesis** and **taxis**, is well illustrated by the responses of small organisms such as flatworms to food and light. It can be investigated in terrestrial animals such as woodlice by means of a **choice chamber**.

5 Given that the animal is appropriately motivated, species-characteristic behaviour is initiated by **releasing stimuli** and ended by **terminating stimuli**. This is seen in numerous cases of territorial behaviour, threat and appeasement displays. It is apparent that in many instances a **stimulus-filtering mechanism** must be involved.

6 In many cases of species-specific behaviour, particularly those involving sexual activity, synchronisation between the participating individuals is essential. This is illustrated by the stickleback in whose **chain behaviour** the importance of reciprocal **sign stimuli** has been demonstrated. In other animals external chemical stimuli (**pheromones**), and **hormones**, may influence the animal's motivational state. A vertebrate's motivational state is closely associated with the hypothalamus.

7 Under certain circumstances species-characteristic behaviour may entail aberrant behaviour, as is illustrated by **displacement** and **vacuum activity**.

8 **Learning** can be conveniently, if somewhat artificially, divided into **habituation**, **associative learning**, **imprinting**, **exploratory learning** and **insight learning**. Associative learning can be distinguished into the **conditioned reflex** (classical conditioning) and **trial and error learning** (operant conditioning).

9 At the physiological level learning can be interpreted on a purely neural basis, or (more controversially) in biochemical terms as a change in the nucleic acid content of the brain cells. The two theories, which are by no means incompatible, are both supported by experimental evidence.

10 Insight learning can provide a clue as to the meaning of the term **intelligence**, a difficult concept to define and even more difficult to analyse at the physiological level.

11 Research on birds and mammals suggests that early experiences associated with the environment may play a crucial part in the development of behaviour.

Investigation 22.1 Behaviour of the earthworm

In lower animals like the earthworm comparatively simple acts of behaviour can be analysed in terms of the workings of receptors, nerves and effectors. Much can be learned by direct observation with minimum manipulation of the animal.

Procedure

1 Observe a worm crawling on damp absorptive paper. Note that forward locomotion is achieved by peristaltic swellings passing from front to rear.

2 Allow the worm to crawl forward. Stimulate the head by stroking it gently with a camel-hair brush. What happens to the peristaltic swellings? Stimulate more strongly until anti-peristalsis occurs. What happens if and when a peristaltic wave meets an anti-peristaltic wave? What sort of nervous system might be involved in these responses?

3 Tap the head with a blunt seeker and note that this results in rapid shortening followed by anti-peristalsis. This constitutes the animal's escape reaction and is particularly important when the worm comes out on to the surface of the soil on warm, wet nights. The effectiveness of this reaction is increased by the chaetae. Notice what happens to the chaetae when (a) the head, and (b) the posterior end are stimulated.

4 Confirm that rapid shortening of the whole body is evoked by a tap applied to *either* end. This escape response is mediated by impulses which are quickly transmitted along the length of the body by giant axons in the ventral nerve cord (*see* Figure 21.5, page 202).

5 Tap the head again and watch the extreme posterior end carefully. Describe what happens and explain its adaptive significance.

6 Devise, and if time allows carry out, experiments (a) to test the reactions of earthworms to different kinds of stimuli, e.g. light and/or sound of varying intensity, temperature, chemicals, pH etc., and (b) to investigate the extent to which earthworms discriminate between different kinds of potential food.

Requirements
Microscope
Large sheet of absorptive paper
Glass plate
Jar of damp soil
Dissecting dish or piece of cork
Dissecting instruments
Camel-hair brush
Live earthworms in Ringer's solution
TS and LS earthworm

For Consideration

(1) Reconstruct the reflex arc involved in the earthworm's escape response, including the receptors and effectors.
(2) To what extent do the results of your experiments relate to the behaviour of earthworms in their natural habitat?

Investigation 22.2
Orientation and feeding behaviour of flatworms

Requirements
Binocular microscope or hand lens
Microscope
Slide and coverslip
Dish (approx. 20 × 25 cm)
Lamp
Opaque cardboard
Squared paper
Protractor

Flatworms (up to 10, starved)
Fresh liver

Although reflex action plays an important part in the behaviour of lower animals, more elaborate behaviour patterns also exist. Comparatively simple behaviour patterns are seen in the way free-living flatworms orientate themselves in relation to environmental stimuli, notably light and food. Different species of flatworm differ markedly in their responses, so be sure to use the same species in each experiment.

Experiments

1 Watch the activities of up to ten flatworms in a dish in semi-darkness. Then switch on a lamp placed 60 cm above the dish. Observe their behaviour carefully and note any changes.

2 Now bring the lamp closer to the dish by 15 cm and repeat your observations. Continue to do this until the lamp is only 15 cm from the dish. Now switch the lamp off and observe what happens. Interpret your observations.

3 Place your lamp 20 cm above the dish and cover half the dish with a piece of opaque cardboard. Record what happens and interpret your results.

4 Place a single flatworm in a glass dish which has a sheet of squared paper underneath. Repeat step 1, but this time plot the position of the flatworm every 30 seconds on squared paper. Afterwards join up the points. Compare the speed of movement and angle of turning in the light and dark. If time allows, do the same thing with other individuals.

5 Look at a specimen under a hand lens or binocular microscope. Can you find any possible light receptors?

6 Gently push the flatworms to one end of the dish and place a small piece of fresh liver at the other end. Observe what happens and make notes on the behaviour of the animals. Does the type of behaviour change as the animals get closer to the food? Describe fully and explain. What sort of receptors are involved and where are they?

7 Induce a specimen to feed on a piece of fresh liver. Record its behaviour and observe the actions of the pharynx.

8 Remove the pharynx from one of your larger light-coloured specimens. This can be done by placing the specimen on a slide and pressing down on it with a coverslip. The pressure usually causes the eversible pharynx to pop out and come adrift.

9 Place the isolated pharynx in a watchglass of water and put some food in contact with it. Watch under the lowest power of the microscope. Explain what happens in terms of muscle action and nervous control.

For Consideration

(1) In this investigation you have been observing the behaviour of a simple animal. You should now try to put forward a physiological explanation of your observations. Your explanation will be incomplete if it does not include reference to receptors (eyes, chemoreceptors, etc.), nervous coordination (brain, peripheral nerves, etc.) and locomotory equipment (muscles, cilia, etc.).
(2) What is the difference between orientation responses of the kind that you have observed in this investigation, and reflex actions?

Reference: For identifying flatworms, see H. Mellanby, *Animal Life in Fresh Water*, Methuen.

Investigation 22.3
Habituation in fanworms

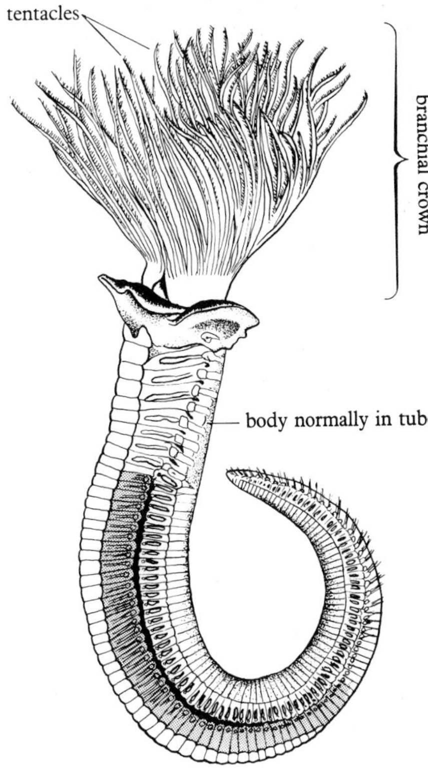

Figure 22.1 A tube-dwelling fanworm.

Fanworms are polychaetes, a group of marine annelids. At the anterior end is an array of delicate tentacles, called the branchial crown (Figure 22.1). This is used for gas exchange and also for filter feeding: the tentacles possess numerous cilia whose beating carries food particles towards the mouth. In normal circumstances the branchial crown projects from the opening of a protective tube. The tentacles are very sensitive, responding to touch and in some cases to shadows falling on them.

Procedure

1 Very gently brush the branchial crown with a mounted needle until the worm withdraws slowly. What sort of response is this, and through what kind of nerves is it mediated?

2 Touch the branchial crown more strongly until the worm jerks back rapidly into its tube.

3 This rapid response is mediated through a giant-axon system. If available, examine a transverse section of a fanworm and note the giant axon(s) in the ventral nerve cord. Also notice the extensive longitudinal musculature in the body wall.

4 Connect a pair of electrodes of the kind illustrated in Figure 22.2 to the output of a stimulator.

5 Stimulate the branchial crown with repetitive stimuli at a frequency of approximately two per second. Your stimuli should be sufficiently strong to elicit the rapid response. What happens to the rapid responses? Are slow responses still given after the rapid responses have ceased?

6 Repeat Step 3 by stimulating a single tentacle with a needle in exactly the same place each time. After the responses have declined, shift the point of stimulation to either another part of the tentacle or a different tentacle. Record what happens. Conclusions?

7 If stimulation of a single tentacle fails to evoke a rapid response, what happens if you stimulate two, three, or more tentacles simultaneously? Conclusions?

For Consideration

(1) List the possible sites in the giant-axon reflex pathway where transmission failure might be occurring in the decline of the rapid response.
(2) What further experiments might be done to locate the site exactly?
(3) What might be the adaptive value of the rapid response?
(4) What information do these experiments provide on the structural organization of the nervous system of this animal?
(5) Do you think it is valid to regard habituation as a type of learning?

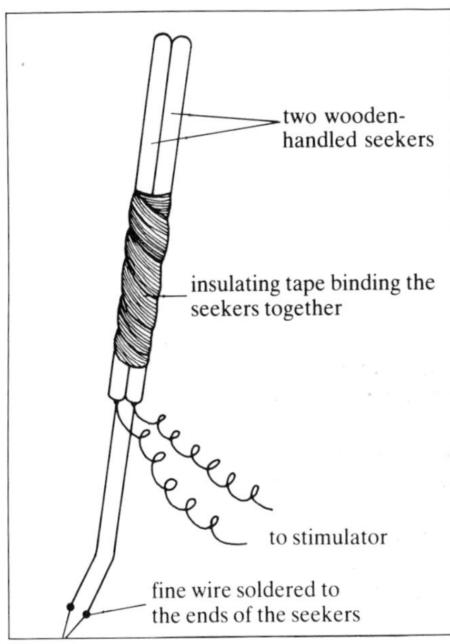

Figure 22.2 The stimulating electrodes for Investigation 22.3.

Requirements
Microscope
Apparatus for delivering single electrical stimuli
Stimulating electrodes (*see* Figure 22.2)

Fanworm (e.g. *Sabella*, *Myxicola*, *Branchiomma*, *Eudistylia*). The worm should be in its tube in *cold* sea water.
TS fanworm (if available)

Investigation 22.4
Orientation responses of woodlice to humidity

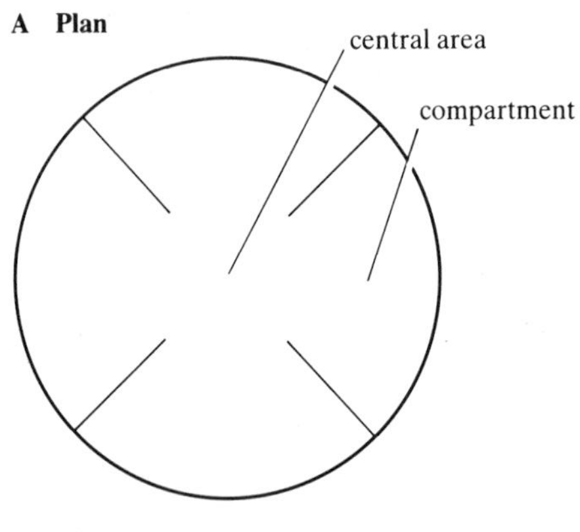

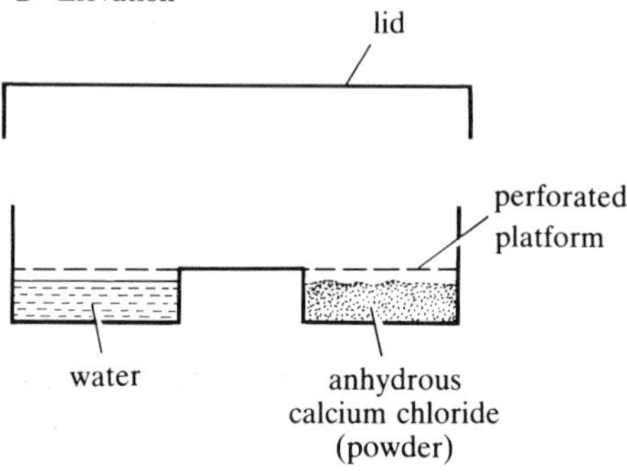

Figure 22.3 A choice chamber.

Requirements
Choice-chamber (*see* above)
Cardboard box with observation slit
Silica gel or anhydrous calcium chloride
Woodlice (up to 20)

Orientation behaviour enables animals to discriminate between different types of environment and select the one in which they are most likely to survive. This does not of course imply that there is any conscious choice by the animal; it can take place by simple neural mechanisms that lead to an involuntary response. This aspect of behaviour can be investigated by means of a choice chamber.

Apparatus

There are several kinds of choice chamber but they all work on the same principle. A plastic or perspex box is subdivided into two or more compartments which are in open communication with each other. The conditions in each compartment can be varied with respect to such conditions as humidity, light, food, temperature etc. If a single variable is being investigated, e.g. humidity, only two compartments need be used (one humid, the other dry). If two variables are being investigated simultaneously, the other compartments need to be used. Figure 22.3 shows a choice chamber set up for investigating humidity.

Procedure

1 Assemble a humidity choice-chamber as in Figure 22.3. Put water under one compartment and anhydrous calcium chloride or silica gel under the opposite one.
2 Put up to 20 woodlice in the central area of the choice chamber. Cover the choice chamber with a lid or sheet of glass. After allowing the woodlice to settle down, record how many are above the water and how many above the calcium chloride.
3 Now cover the whole assemblage with a cardboard box perforated by an observation slit. There should be only just enough light for you to see the woodlice.
4 Examine at intervals and, noting the time, record the percentage of woodlice over the water.
5 Plot your results as a graph, putting the percentage of individuals on the vertical axis and time on the horizontal axis.

Further Experiments

1 In their natural environment woodlice may not be faced with a simple 'choice' of the kind that you have presented them with in the above experiment. It is possible that they may in reality have to choose between, say, a region with a favourable temperature but unfavourable humidity and a region with a favourable humidity but unfavourable temperature.

Devise, and if possible carry out, experiments to investigate the preferential behaviour of woodlice in relation to various combinations of the following conditions: humidity, temperature, illumination and contact with solid objects.
2 Devise an apparatus in which woodlice are presented with a humidity or temperature *gradient*. By means of such an apparatus investigate the range of humidity or temperature for which they show a preference.

For Consideration

(1) In their natural environment woodlice tend to congregate under logs, stones, etc. What particular feature (or features) of this situation do you think they find attractive?
(2) From watching woodlice in the choice-chamber, did you get any clues as to *how* they find their way into the most agreeable situation?

Investigation 22.5
Orientation responses of blowfly larvae to light

Blowflies lay their eggs on dung. When the eggs hatch the larvae burrow into, and feed on, the dung. The larvae show a rapid orientation response to light which is clearly related to their environment and way of life.

Procedure

1 Obtain a large sheet of non-white paper and draw on it a circle of diameter 24 cm. Divide this circle into 30° sectors.
2 With as little surrounding light as possible, position two lamps at approximately 90° to each other on each side of the circle (Figure 22.4).
3 Place up to 10 blowfly larvae in the centre of the circle and switch one of the lights on. Record the number of blowflies in the sector of the circle leading directly to the light.
4 When all the larvae are moving in a definite direction relative to the light, switch that lamp off and the other one on. Record what happens.

5 Try different variations on this experiment. In all cases record the responses of the larvae, if possible quantitatively, in relation to light.
6 Place a few blowfly larvae on the surface of, e.g. damp sawdust or bran, in a beaker. What relevance does their observed behaviour have to the above experiments?
7 Devise, and if time allows carry out, an experiment to find out if the speed of the larva's response is related to the intensity of the light.

For Consideration

(1) Relate these experiments to blowfly larvae in their natural habitat.
(2) Find out as much as you can about the larva's sense organs and nervous system. Put forward a hypothesis explaining the mechanism by which the larva is directed away from light.

Requirements
Sheet of non-white paper (at least 25 cm square, *see* above)
Lamps ×2
Beaker of damp sawdust or bran

Blowfly larvae (up to 10)

A Plan

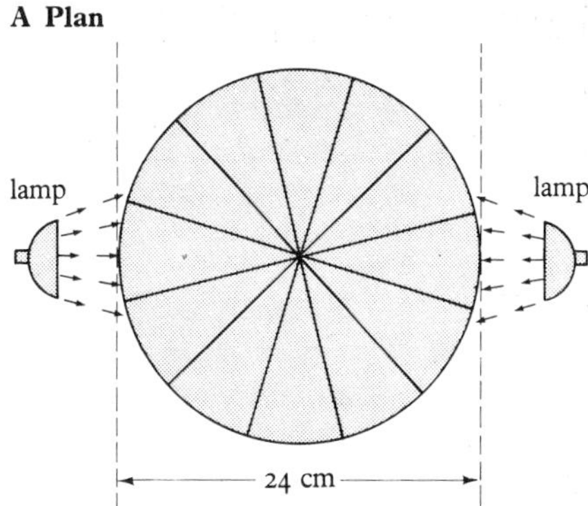

B Elevation

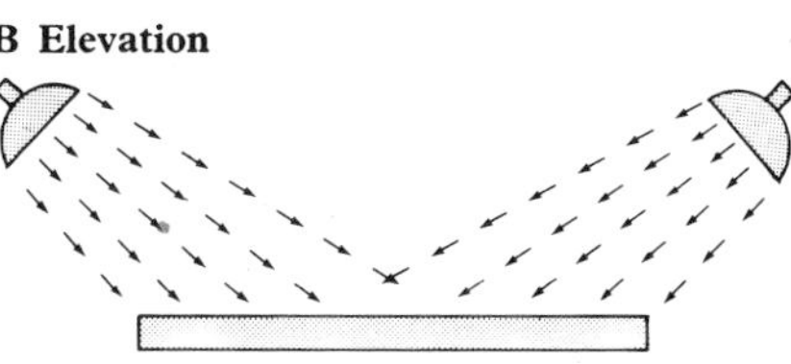

Figure 22.4 Arrangement for Investigation 22.5 on the responses of blowfly larvae to light.

Investigation 22.6
Behaviour of snails

The common garden snail, *Helix aspersa*, is in many ways an ideal animal on which to carry out simple behaviour experiments: it is large, moves slowly and is reasonably responsive to stimuli.

This investigation is more open-ended than the preceding ones. It is up to you to decide which particular phenomena you would like to investigate, and then to design and carry out appropriate observations and experiments. Here are some questions which might form the basis of one or more investigations.

Questions

(1) Do snails respond to directional illumination, and if so do they move towards or away from light?
(2) Do snails show a preference for humid rather than dry situations?
(3) Do snails respond to gravity, and if so do they move towards or away from it?
(4) Can snails detect the presence of food situated close to them, and if so what particular food materials attract them?
(5) Is there any evidence that snails respond to the presence of other individuals in their vicinity?
(6) Do snails respond to different environmental temperatures, and if so in what way do they respond?
(7) What sort of stimuli cause a snail to retract into its shell?

A useful technique

Snails have mucous glands on the foot and they leave a trail of slime behind them as they move along. If you allow a specimen to move around on a sheet of glass, you can follow where it has been by sprinkling a little powder onto the glass and then removing it from the non-slimy areas by holding the glass in a vertical position and tapping it gently. Alternatively place the glass under a gentle stream of water from a tap.

For consideration

Relate your observations to the kinds of habitats where snails occur.

Requirements
Sheet of glass (approx. 20 cm × 30 cm)
Powder
Other materials and apparatus as requested by individual students

Snails, *Helix aspera*

Investigation 22.7
Learning in lower animals

It is claimed by many observers that lower animals such as flatworms and earthworms show associative learning. In this type of behaviour the animal learns to associate a specific stimulus with a particular situation. In this investigation you are invited to test this claim for yourself.

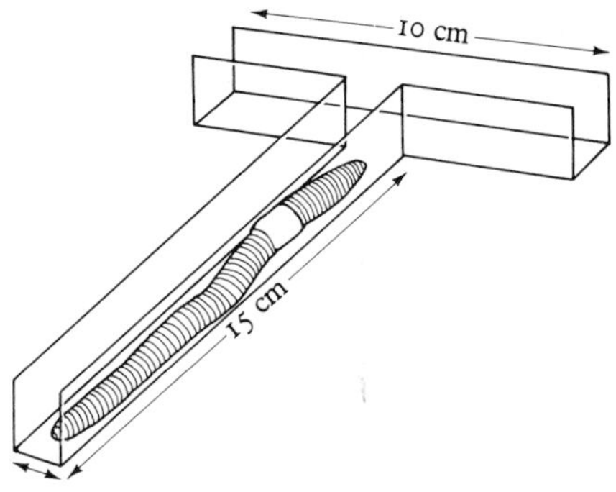

Figure 22.5 A simple T-maze for training experiments with the earthworm. The maze can be conveniently constructed out of perspex. The passages should be sufficiently wide for the animal to fit comfortably and snugly into them, and the walls should be sufficiently high to prevent the worm climbing out.

Method

It is suggested that you should try to teach the animal to associate a particular situation with an unpleasant stimulus, which in this case is a weak electric shock. For this you require an apparatus capable of delivering repetitive stimuli at a high frequency.

The output of the stimulator should be connected to a pair of electrodes. The electrodes illustrated in Figure 22.2, page 211 will do nicely.

When stimulating the animal, switch on the stimulator and then touch the animal briefly with the electrodes. The intensity of the stimuli should be just sufficient to evoke an observable response.

Before you start training the animal you must determine the correct intensity of stimulation. To do this, start by stimulating with weak shocks, then gradually increase the intensity of the stimuli until a clear response is given. Don't over-stimulate: the object of this experiment is to train the animal, not to electrocute it.

Procedure

FLATWORMS

Try training a flatworm (e.g. *Planaria* sp.) to associate a light stimulus with an electric shock.

1 Place the flatworm in a dish of water in semi-darkness.

2 When it has settled down, shine a bright light on it and then, about one second later, give it a brief electric shock. The animal should give no visible response to the light, but it should respond to the electric shock.

3 Repeat at regular intervals to see if eventually the animal responds as soon as the light is shone on it, i.e. *before* the shock is administered.

4 Record your results and if possible present them in the form of a graph.

EARTHWORMS

Try training an earthworm to turn left in a simple T-shaped maze.

1 Place the worm in the stem of the 'T' (Figure 22.5). Encourage it to move forwards by gently stroking the posterior end.

2 When it comes to the junction the worm should turn left or right. If it turns left and reaches the end of the cross-piece of the 'T', return it to the beginning and start again. If it turns right, stimulate it with a brief electric shock when it reaches the end, then return it to the beginning and start again.

3 Repeat the procedure to see if eventually the animal learns always to turn left so as to avoid the electric shock. The animal should be kept moist at all times.

4 Record your results and, if possible, present them in the form of a graph.

For Consideration

(1) What difficulties have you encountered in this investigation? How might they be overcome?

(2) Assuming you have been successful, the flatworm and the earthworm both show associative learning in these two experiments. However, the *type* of associative learning differs in the two cases. How do they differ?

(3) Can you think of any situations in their natural habitats where associative learning might be useful to these two animals?

(4) What further experiments might be carried out on learning in these animals?

Requirements
Stimulating equipment
Electrodes (*see* Figure 22.2)
Dish
Lamp capable of producing bright light
'T' maze (*see* Figure 22.5)

Flatworm (e.g. *Planaria* sp.)
Earthworm

Investigation 22.8
Learning in rats and gerbils

Many animals can learn to find their way through mazes of varying degrees of complexity, particularly if encouraged by a reward. This experiment involves training rats and/or gerbils to master a comparatively simple maze.

Procedure

1 Use a maze of the type shown in Figure 22.6. This can be constructed from a cardboard or wooden box fitted with hardboard or polystyrene partitions. The whole maze should have a transparent cover.

2 Put non-odorous food in the food box at the end of the maze and place an uninitiated gerbil or rat at the starting point. The animals should be deprived of food for up to 24 hours before the start of the experiment.

3 Now run a trial. This consists of letting the animal find its way to the food box. Time how long it takes and score the number of errors it makes in doing so. You must decide what constitutes an error: for practical purposes the animal may be considered to have made an error if its head passes a correct opening.

4 When the animal reaches the food box reward it with food and give it three-quarters of a minute to eat it. Then transfer it to the starting point and run another trial, recording the time taken to complete the maze, and the number of errors, as before.

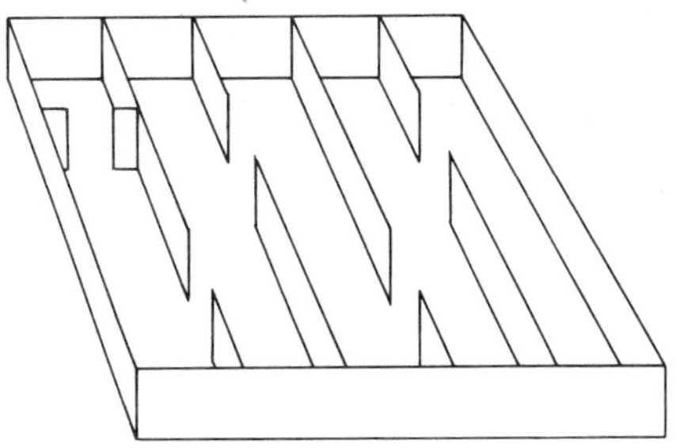

Figure 22.6 Plan of maze suitable for use with rats and gerbils. The maze should be of approximately 50 cm side and at least 10 cm high.

5 If time permits continue the experiment until the animal completes the maze without making any errors.

Results

Plot (a) the time taken to complete the maze, and (b) the number of errors (vertical axis), against the trials. Can any conclusions be drawn regarding the ability of rats or gerbils to learn?

For Consideration

(1) What bearing do your results have on the behaviour of these animals in their natural habitats?

(2) Can you suggest any factors that might speed up the process by which these animals learn to master the maze?

(3) What experiments might be carried out to compare the maze-learning abilities of small mammals with, e.g. cockroaches and toads?

Requirements

Maze of the type shown in Figure 22.6
Processed rat or gerbil food (available from supplier)
Rat or gerbil, starved for 24 hours before experiment

Investigation 22.9
Learning in humans

Memory is one of the most important human attributes and is the basis of much of our behaviour. In this investigation you will construct a trial and error graph illustrating your ability to recall a list of words, and then consider some of its implications.

Procedure

1 A list of 20 words will be read to you. Listen carefully, and immediately afterwards write down as many of them as you can. They need not be in the right order. Head your list *Trial 1* and fold the paper so that you cannot see what you have written.

2 The list will now be read again. Write down the words again, head the list *Trial 2* and fold the paper as before.

3 Repeat the above procedure until you can remember all 20 words. Head your lists *Trial 3*, *4*, *5* etc.

4 You will now be given a copy of the list of words. Score the result of each trial as the number of *errors*. An error is a word left out or a wrong one included. Write the number of errors at the bottom of each of your lists.

5 Make a *trial and error graph* of your results. Put the number of errors on the vertical axis and the numbers of the trials on the horizontal axis. Join the points with straight lines.

6 Divide the words in the teacher's list into 5 groups: group A is the first 4 words, group B the second 4 words, group C the third 4, group D the fourth 4, and group E the fifth 4.

7 Take the first trial and score how many words *in each group* you included in your list. It does not matter whereabouts in your list the words occur as long as they occur somewhere. Write the five scores at the end of your list.

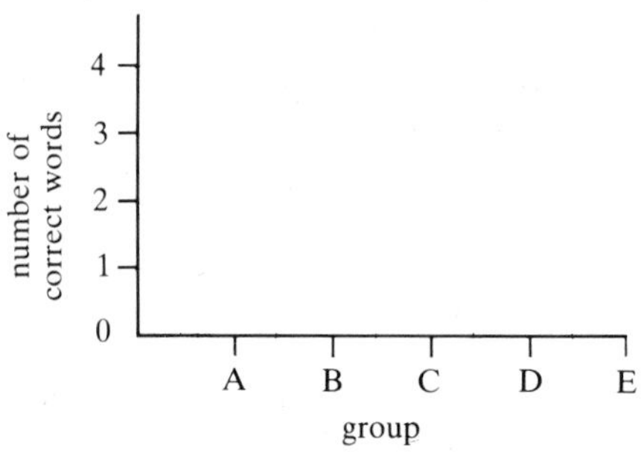

Figure 22.7 Axes of the graph for analysing the results of your trial and error experiment.

Requirements
Squared paper
Coloured crayons or felt pens
List of 20 words to be read out by the teacher

Note: Aspects of human learning and memory are dealt with in a computer program in NELCAL Biology, *Pack 4, Behaviour* by R. Fisher.

8 Plot the results as a bar chart, putting the number of correct words in each group on the vertical axis and the letters designating the groups on the horizontal axis (Figure 22.7).

9 Repeat Step 7 for the rest of the trials. Plot all the results on the same sheet of graph paper so that they can be readily compared.

For consideration

(1) What features of your trial and error graph are common to all members of your class? What features are unique to you personally?

(2) What factors might cause you to learn the list of words more slowly? How could you investigate such factors?

(3) It has been suggested that when you try to learn a list of words you tend to remember the ones at the beginning and end of the list more quickly than the ones in the middle. This is known to psychologists as *primacy* and *recency*. Do your results support this suggestion? Of what value might it be in everyday life?

(4) It could be argued that the test carried out in this investigation is a measure of concentration and intelligence as well as memory. How could you modify the test so that it is a measure of memory only?

Questions and Problems

1 To what extent can an animal's behaviour be explained by the capabilities of its receptors?

2 How far can the behaviour of animals be explained in terms of reflex action?

3 In an experiment on woodlouse behaviour a perspex-walled chamber 40 centimetres long with a constantly maintained humidity gradient from one end to the other was prepared. The chamber was kept under conditions of constant temperature and illumination for 48 hours. One hundred adult woodlice were placed in the centre of the chamber at 10 a.m. (Time 0). Observations were made at intervals and the distribution of woodlice was found to be as shown in the Table.

Relative humidity %	**Number of woodlice** 3 h	14 h	24 h	48 h
0–10	0	2	0	8
10–20	0	15	0	12
20–30	0	16	0	9
30–40	2	6	0	11
40–50	0	20	1	7
50–60	3	17	5	14
60–70	10	8	9	8
70–80	25	6	35	10
80–90	35	4	30	11
90–100	25	6	20	10

(a) Comment on these results.
(b) Suggest an hypothesis to explain them.
(c) What experiments would you carry out to attempt to confirm your hypothesis?

(OCJE)

4 Discuss the meaning and usage of the terms 'instinct' and 'intelligence' in the context of animal behaviour.

5 Hermit crabs live inside the shells of dead molluscs. When a hermit crab is selecting a shell, it touches, rolls and probes it before choosing it for a home. The intertidal hermit crab *Pagurus hirsutiusculus* prefers whelk shells of the genus *Nucella*.

(a) Suggest some features of whelk shells which would allow *Pagurus* to distinguish between the shells of different species.

(b) Suggest three reasons why it is necessary for *Pagurus* to probe inside the shell.

(c) The crabs were exposed to various minerals. When the crabs touched some of these minerals they exhibited 'exploratory behaviour'. They rolled the lumps and probed them. The other minerals were ignored.

All the crabs explored $CaCO_3$ (calcite), $CaCO_3$ (aragonite), and $CaSO_4$ (gypsum). They ignored $SrSO_4$ (celestite), $MnCO_3$ (rhodochrosite), $FeCO_3$ (siderite) and SiO_2 (quartz). On this basis what stimulus does the crab respond to? Suggest another experiment to test your hypothesis.

(d) If the crab was presented with the choice between a natural $CaCO_3$ shell and an iron replica, which would it choose and why?

(e) Explain why it is valuable to the crab to have its exploratory behaviour triggered in this way.

6 The graphs in Figure 22.8 show habituation to touch as seen in the tube worm *Branchiomma*. In each the responses of a group containing 17–21 worms were tested by brushing the protruding branchial crown. Two separate experiments were carried out. In the first experiment the worms were stimulated so gently that they only responded by withdrawing slowly into their tubes. In the second experiment the stimuli were sufficiently strong to evoke a rapid response from the worms. In Figure 22.8 Graph A shows the results of the first experiment (slow withdrawals), and Graph B shows the results of the second experiment (rapid responses). Comment fully on these results.

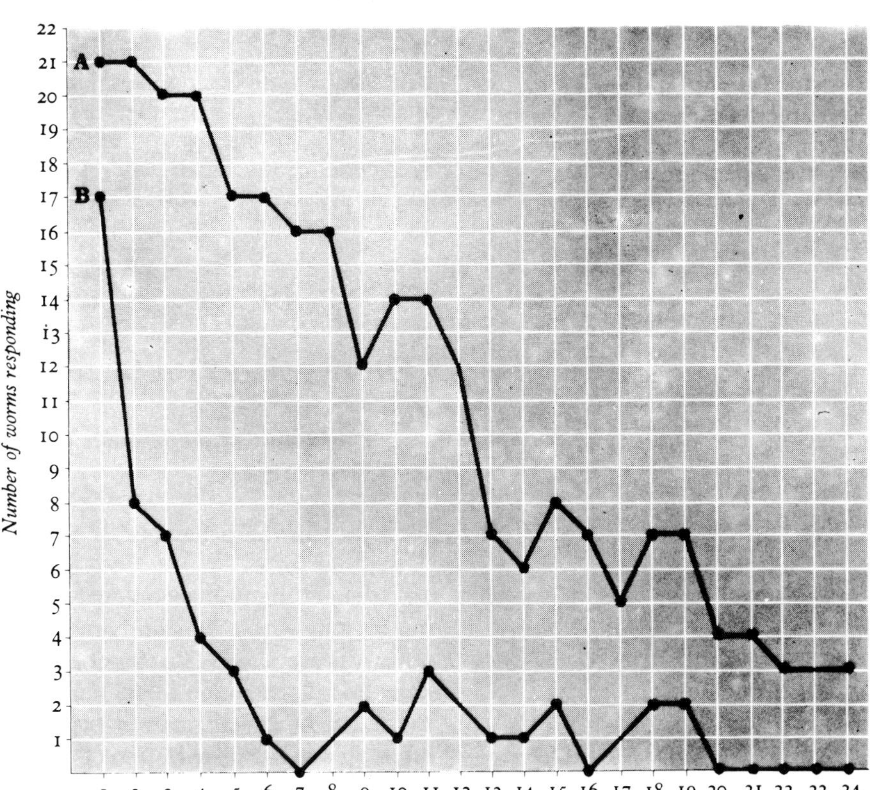

Figure 22.8 Habituation to touch by the tube worm *Branchiomma*. **A**, slow withdrawals; **B**, rapid responses. (*After Krasne*)

7 Biologists are not agreed as to the precise meaning of the word 'intelligence', but it is generally held to represent the degree to which an animal can respond adaptively to new environmental situations. Bearing this in mind, outline the tests which you would make to investigate the intelligence of an animal.

8 In the behaviour of the British newt *Triturus* there is an elaborate and sustained encounter (lasting about 20 minutes) involving courtship display in which the female stimulates the male by prodding him. He responds by depositing a spermatophore which she then picks up with her cloaca. In the newt *Euproctus* which lives in fast-flowing streams in the Pyrenees, the male waits in hiding and pounces on the female as she passes. He then wraps his tail round her and transfers sperm to her.

Comment on these behaviour patterns. Discuss how each is adapted to its respective environment. Which do you think is the more primitive?

9 Devise an experiment involving associative learning which could show whether (a) a monkey was colour blind, or (b) a dog could differentiate between two high-pitched sounds.

10 The passage below is the first part of an article which appeared in the Sunday Times on 31st March, 1985.

A flock of brain waves

The cattle grid has defeated and confined sheep for decades. So it is a source of intense interest to Rupert Sheldrake that flocks near Blaenau Ffestiniog in north Wales have learned to traverse cattle grids by tucking up their little legs and rolling. In ovine terms, this represents a giant leap in reasoning power.

Naturally, the authorities are anxious to contain this flamboyant behaviour. They have taken steps to isolate the Welsh sheep so that they don't go to market and boast about their grid-rolling activities to other sheep.

Dr Sheldrake, however, believes that their efforts will be to no avail. It is at the core of his hypothesis of Causative Formation that sheep all over the country will sooner or later spontaneously do likewise. Put simply, Sheldrake's hypothesis holds that an animal will find a task easier to learn if others of the species have already mastered it.

The blue tit is a case in point. The first incidence of this bird pecking at the top of a milk bottle and drinking from it was recorded in Southampton in 1921. The habit spread quickly; by 1947 nearly all blue tits in the UK were practised milk thieves.

The crucial point is that the new behaviour did not emanate from Southampton, but popped up all over the country. This cannot be explained by blue-tit traffic, since the bird dislikes travelling.

(a) How might Sheldrake's hypothesis of 'causative formation' be tested experimentally either on humans or on some other species?
(b) Are you satisfied that the blue-tit's habit of opening milk bottles did not spread by learning? What could be done to investigate this matter?
(c) Do you believe that in general paranormal phenomena are amenable to scientific investigation?
(d) Critically review the above passage as an example of *scientific* writing.

23 Cell Division

Background Summary

1 Cell division is responsible for **reproduction** and **growth**. In both cases the chromosomes must be correctly distributed between the daughter cells. The sequence of events which takes place from one cell division to the next constitutes the **cell cycle**.

2 Two main types of cell division are recognised: **mitosis** and **meiosis**. The latter is involved principally in the formation of **gametes**, or – in certain plants – **spores**.

3 Mitosis can be observed, and filmed, in plant endosperm tissue. Meiosis may be seen in developing spores, pollen grains, embryo sacs, eggs or sperms.

4 A cell normally contains two of each type of chromosome, the **diploid state**. Mitosis preserves this condition. Meiosis, however, results in the daughter cells containing only one of each type of chromosome, the **haploid state**.

5 Both types of cell division involve the orderly movement of chromosomes on a **spindle apparatus**. The process can be conveniently, if artificially, divided into five stages.

6 In **interphase** the cell prepares for division and the genetic material (DNA) replicates; in **prophase** the chromosomes make their appearance as distinct bodies; in **metaphase** they arrange themselves on the equator of the spindle; in **anaphase** they separate and move towards opposite poles of the spindle; and in **telophase** the cell divides into two.

7 In mitosis homologous chromosomes do not associate with one another. At metaphase they arrange themselves independently on the spindle, and at anaphase the sister chromatids of each chromosome part company independently of its homologue. Thus the daughter cells have the same chromosome and genotype constitution as the original cell.

8 In meiosis there are two successive divisions. In the first, homologous chromosomes come together (associate) and subsequently segregate into the daughter cells. In the second division, the sister chromatids of each chromosome segregate into the daughter cells. The overall effect is to reduce the number of chromosomes from the diploid to the haploid state. The four cells produced usually differ in genotype.

9 When homologous chromosomes come together in prophase of the first meiotic division, the different pairs do so independently. This has important genetic consequences (*see* Chapters 28 and 29).

10 During prophase of the first meiotic division the chromatids of homologous chromosomes usually become attached at certain points called **chiasmata** where breakage and rejoining may occur. This permits **crossing over** to take place, a process with important genetic consequences (*see* Chapters 28 and 29).

11 Modern research has thrown light on the role of the spindle apparatus in cell division. The chromosomes (or chromatids) are moved apart by a sliding filament mechanism similar to that which occurs in muscle.

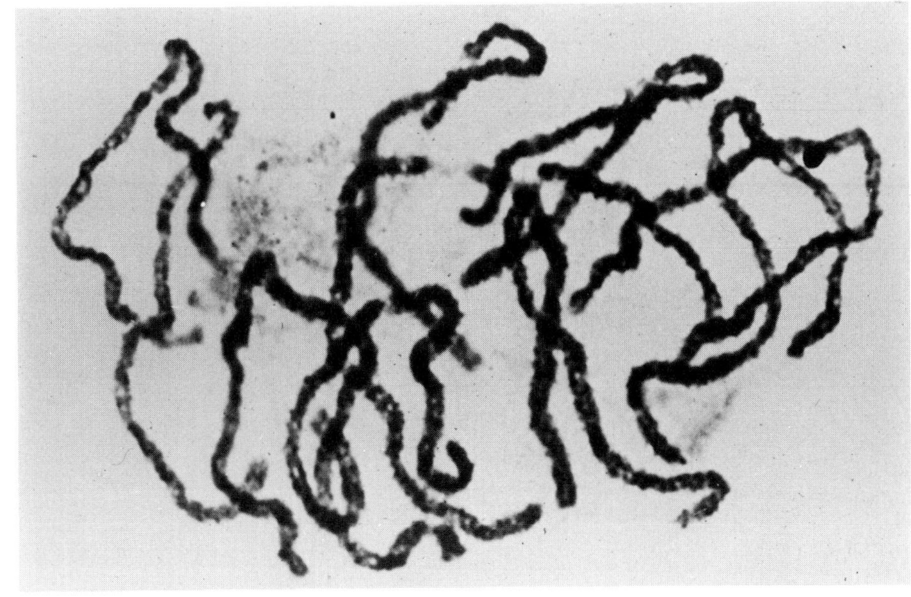

Before you start

Look at the illustration on the left. It is a photomicrograph of the chromosomes in a cell which is about to divide. The cell is at mid prophase, an early stage in both mitosis and meiosis. The chromosomes, though still thread-like, have become distinct. How many are there? It must be an even number – why? What is the diploid number of this cell? What would be its haploid number?

In the next three investigations we shall see what happens to the chromosomes when a cell like this divides, first by mitosis and then by meiosis.

A) Interphase

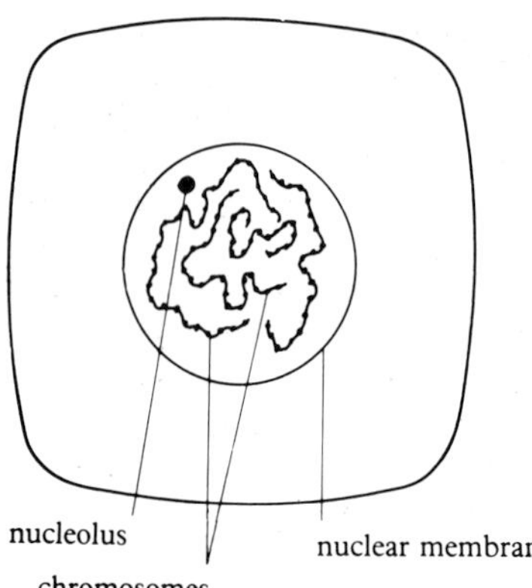

B) Early prophase

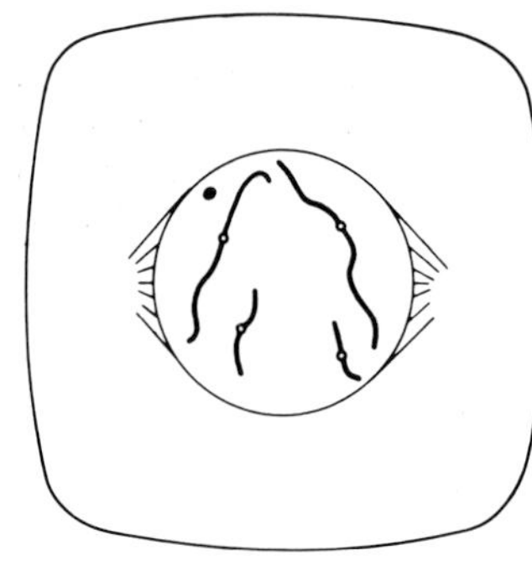

C) Late prophase

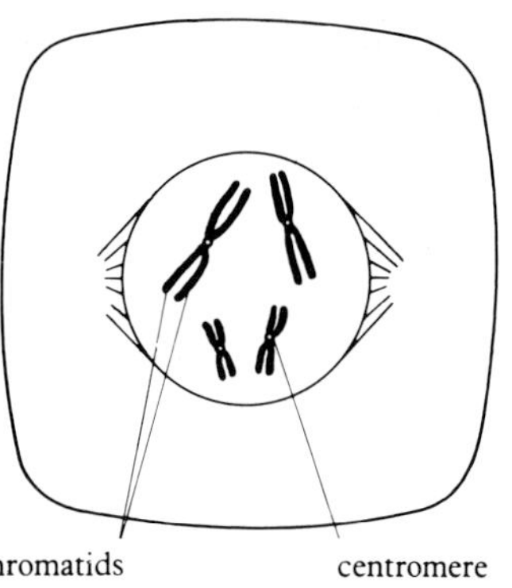

D) Early metaphase

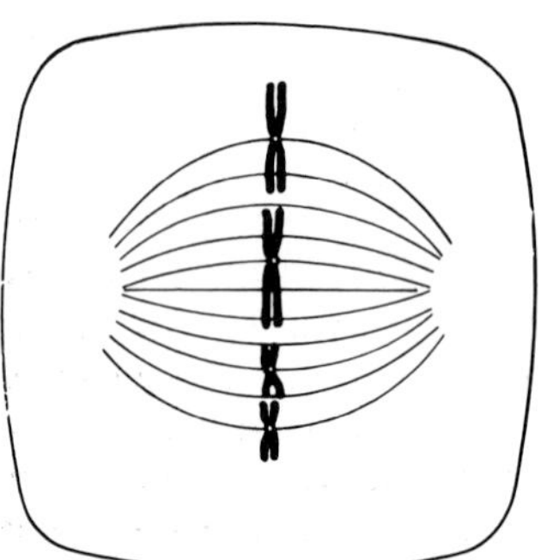

E) Late metaphase

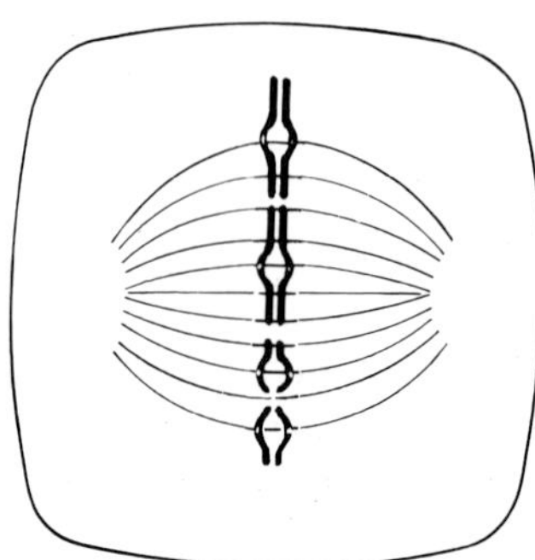

F) Early anaphase

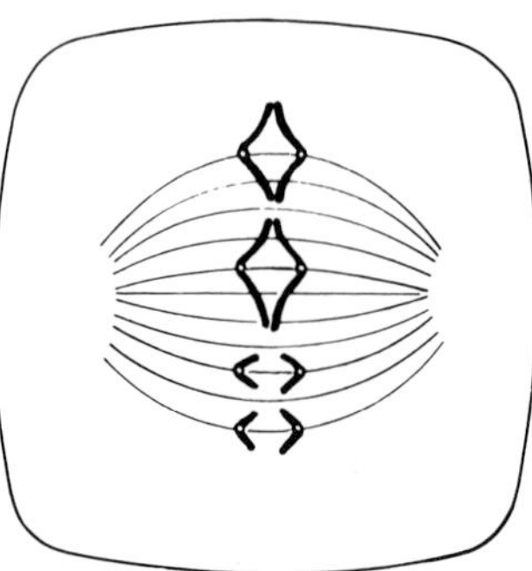

G) Late anaphase

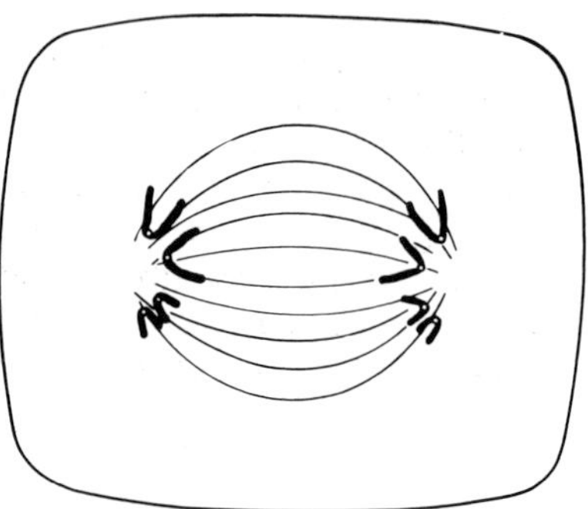

H) Early telophase

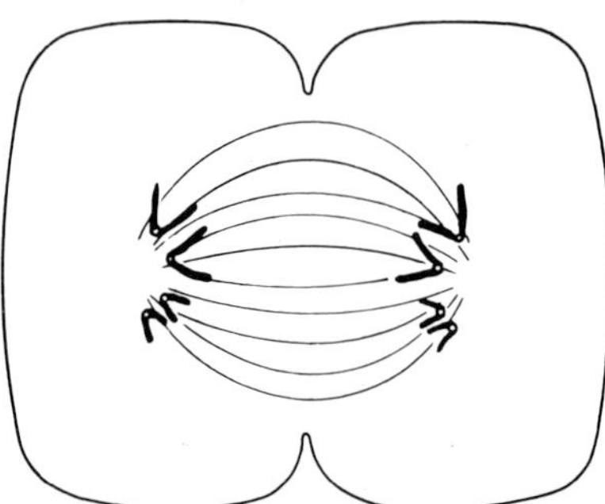

I) Late telophase

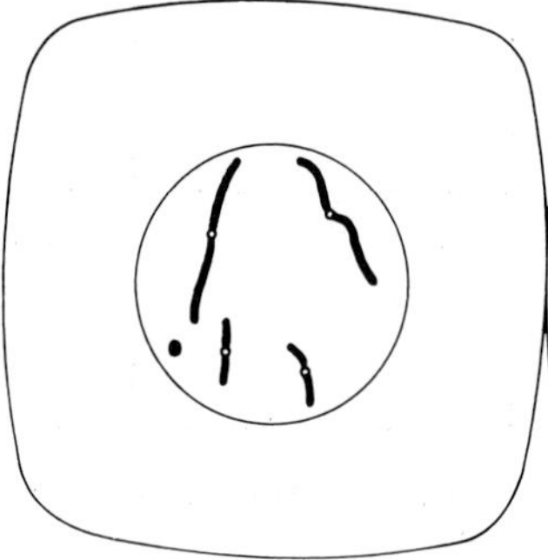

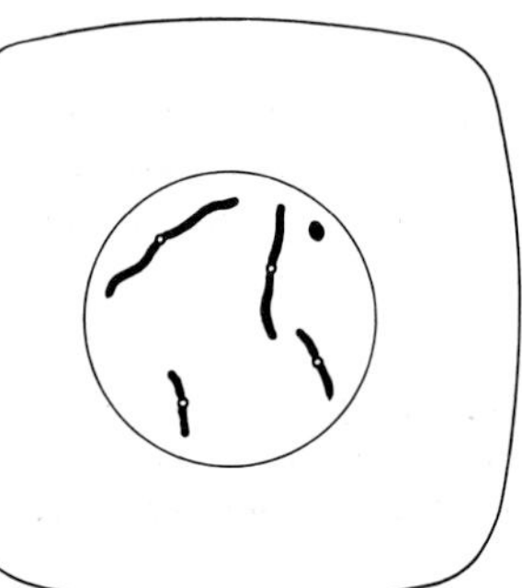

Figure 23.1 Diagram illustrating the behaviour of chromosomes during mitosis. For simplicity only two pairs of chromosomes are shown, one short pair and one long pair. In metaphase (D and E above) the chromatids will be orientated on the spindle at all sorts of angles.

Investigation 23.1
Observation of stages of mitosis in root tip

If the chromosomes are selectively stained with a dye such as acetic orcein, stages in mitosis can be observed in tissues where cell division occurs. An example of such a tissue is the meristematic tissue located in the apical meristem, or zone of cell division, in the tip of a growing root.

Procedure

1 Cut off the apical 5 mm from the tip of a growing lateral root of, e.g. broad bean.
2 Place the root tip in a watch glass containing acetic orcein stain and 1.0 mol dm^{-3} hydrochloric acid in the approximate proportions of ten parts of stain to one part of acid.
3 Warm, but *do not boil*, for five minutes on a hotplate. The acid helps to macerate the tissue (why is that desirable?)
4 Place the stained root tip on a clean microscope slide. Cut it in half transversely and discard the half furthest from the apex.
5 Add two or three drops of acetic orcein to the root tip on the slide.
6 Without interfering too much with the arrangement of the cells, break the root tip up with a needle so as to spread it out as thinly as possible.
7 Put on a coverslip, cover it with filter paper and squash gently. If necessary, irrigate with more stain.
8 Warm the slide on a hotplate for about ten seconds to intensify the staining. (The slide should be very warm, but not too hot to touch).
9 Examine for stages in mitosis.
10 Supplement the information obtained from your own slide by observing mitotic figures in a prepared longitudinal section of the root tip of, e.g. onion (*Allium* sp.). Compare with mitosis in an animal, e.g. *Ascaris*.
11 Watch a film or video recording of mitosis. Notice in particular that it is a dynamic and continuous process. Dividing it up into a series of static stages is a purely arbitrary convention.

Recording your Observations

Divide a page of your laboratory notebook into eight boxes, labelled as shown in Figure 23.2. Using Figure 23.1 to help you, identify as many stages of mitosis as you can. Bear in mind that Figure 23.1 is diagrammatic; the chromosomes will not be as neatly arranged in your preparation, and there will be more of them. Make annotated sketches in the appropriate boxes, showing the arrangement of the chromosomes. What can you say about the chromosome number of the plant from which the root was obtained?

For Consideration

(1) In what situations apart from those studied here would you expect to find mitosis taking place in animals and plants?
(2) Mitosis preserves the diploid state. Which particular events in mitosis ensure that this is so?
(3) Sometimes, search as one may, no dividing cells are visible in a root squash. Suggest possible reasons for this. (The authors hope that you have not been unlucky today!)

Mitosis in root tip of	
1. Interphase	**2.** Early prophase
3. Late prophase	**4.** Metaphase
5. Early anaphase	**6.** Late anaphase
7. Early telophase	**8.** Late telophase

Figure 23.2 How to present your observations of mitosis.

Requirements
Microscope
Slide and coverslip
Hotplate
Filter paper
Mounted needle
Razor blade
Watch glass

Acetic orcein
Hydrochloric acid (1.0 mol dm^{-3})

Lateral root of, e.g. broad bean
LS root tip of, e.g. *Allium*
Slides of *Ascaris* for mitosis

Broad bean seeds should be germinated in damp peat 10 days before the laboratory session. When the radicle is approximately 12 mm long, cut off the tip to stimulate growth of lateral roots.

Note: Suitable alternatives to broad bean include sunflower, hyacinth and garlic. Roots growing out from bulbs often give good results.

A) Interphase

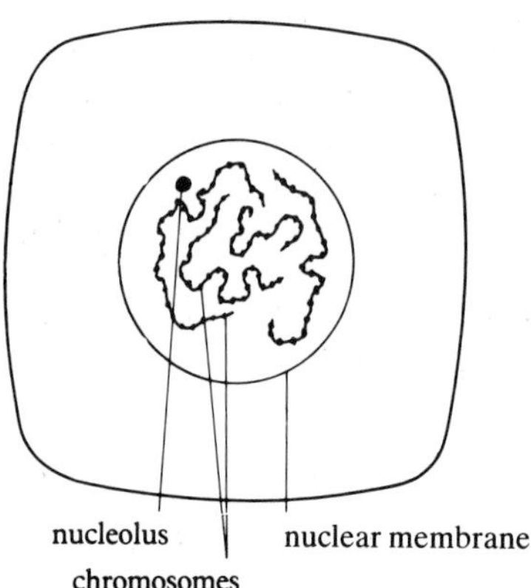

B) Early prophase I

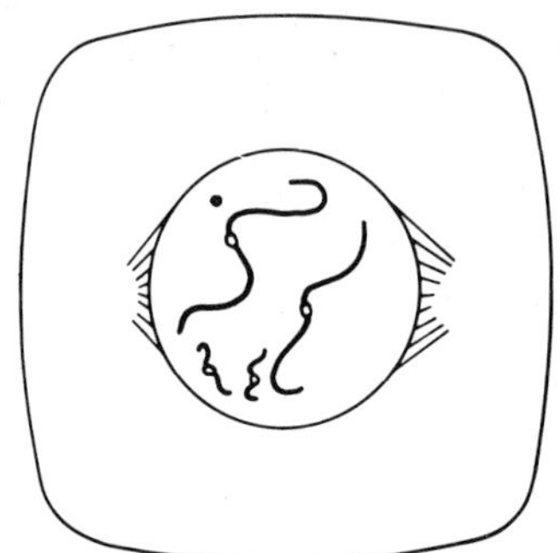

C) Mid prophase I

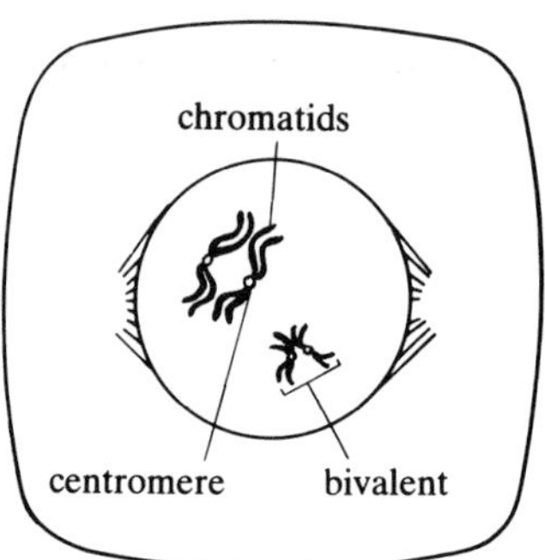

D) Late prophase I

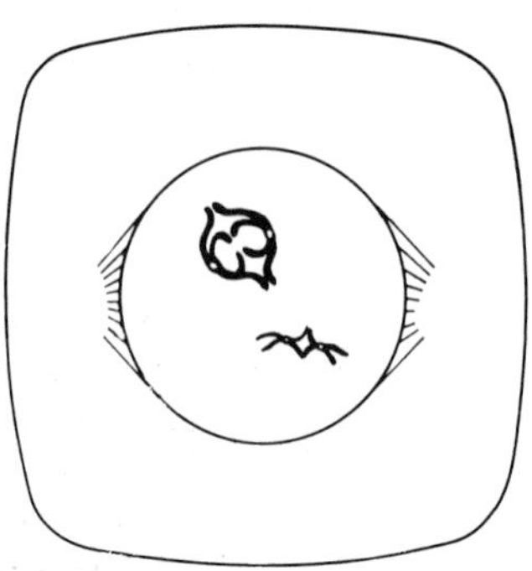

E) Metaphase I

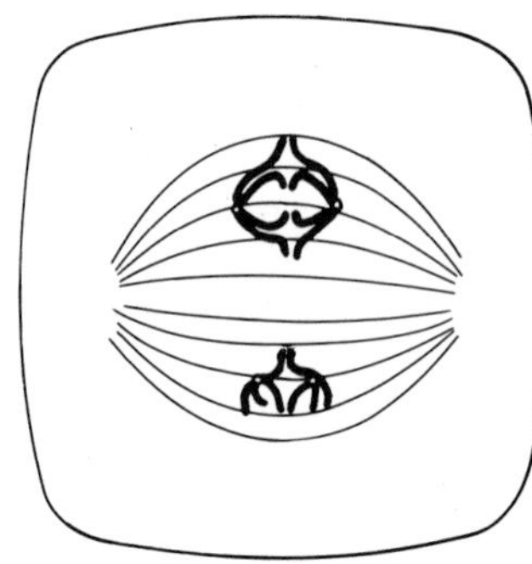

F) Anaphase I

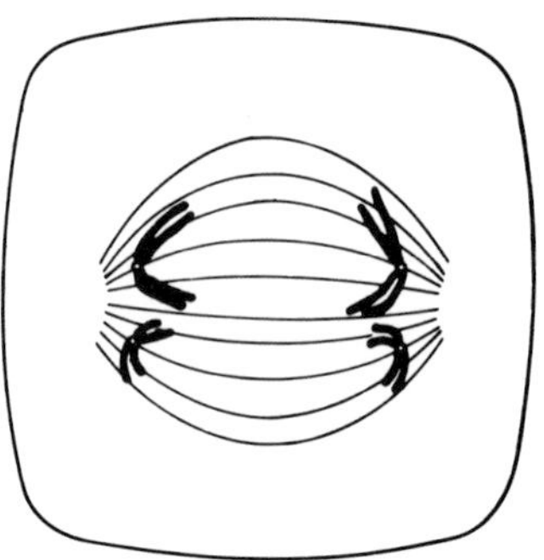

G) Telophase I

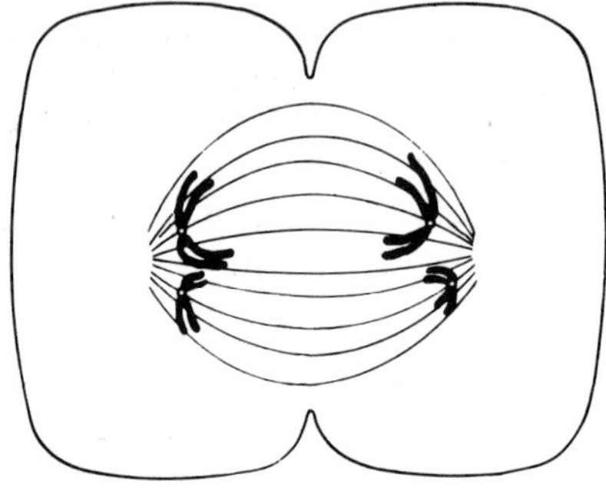

H) Prophase II

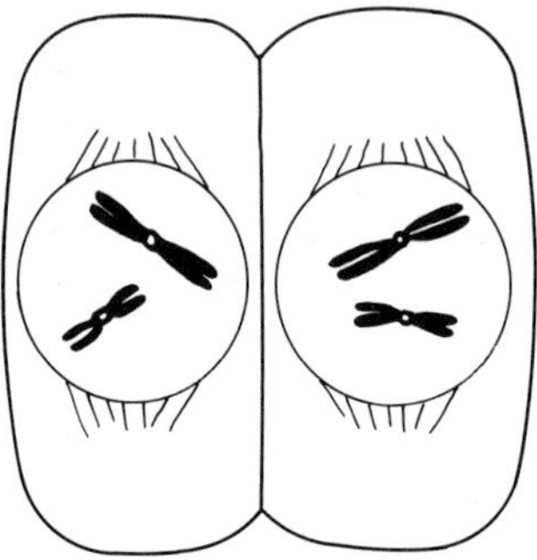

I) Metaphase II

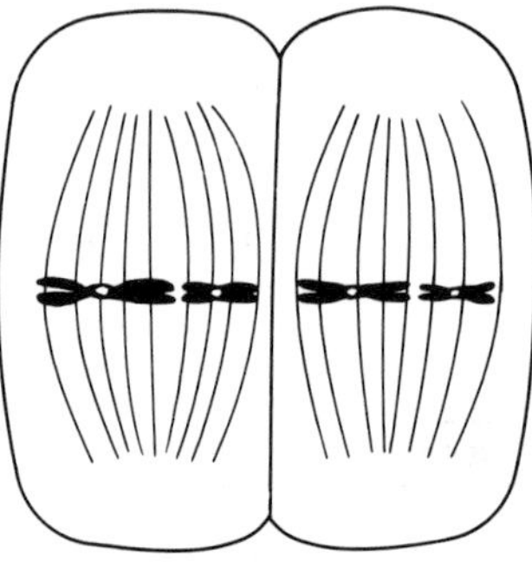

J) Anaphase II

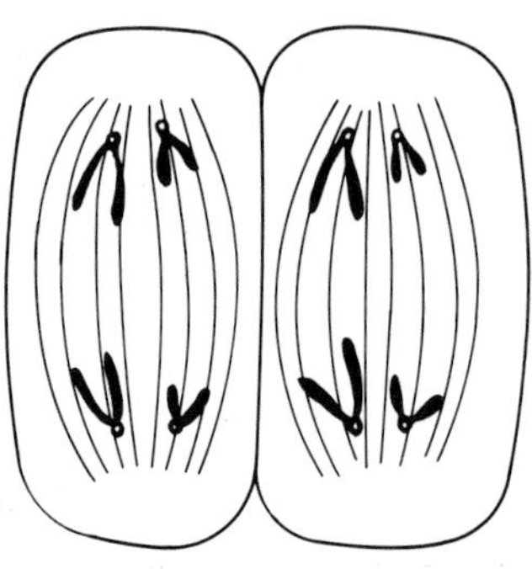

K) Telophase II

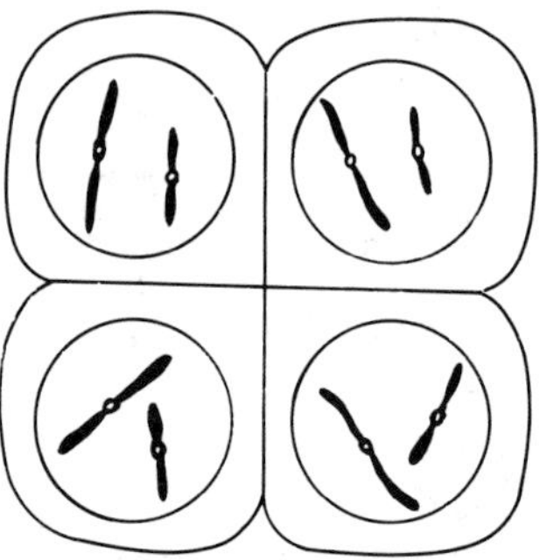

four daughter cells
(tetrad)

Figure 23.3 Diagrams illustrating the behaviour of chromosomes during meiosis. As in Figure 23.1, only two pairs of chromosomes are shown, one short pair and one long pair.

Investigation 23.2
Observation of stages of meiosis in anther

Requirements
Microscope with oil immersion
Hand lens or binocular microscope
Slides and coverslips
White tile
Hotplate
Filter paper
Mounted needle
Forceps
Glass rod

Acetic orcein
Hydrochloric acid (1.0 mol dm^{-3})

Hyacinth bulb
TS or LS anthers of, e.g. lily
TS mammalian testis

Meiosis can be observed in immature anthers that are still enclosed inside the flower bud. Within such anthers diploid pollen mother cells may be found dividing meiotically to form haploid pollen grains. Anthers displaying a pale creamy colour generally have meiotic stages in them.

Hyacinth is recommended. A hyacinth bulb contains a dormant inflorescence of flower buds. Each flower bud contains six stamens. The technique involves squashing an anther and staining it with acetic orcein.

Procedure

1 Take a hyacinth bulb and remove the enveloping leaves so as to expose the inflorescence. The flower buds at the base of the inflorescence are the most advanced, those at the apex are the youngest. Make slides of both, and of intermediate buds between the two extremes.
2 With a needle and forceps open up a bud on a white tile. Using a hand lens or binocular microscope, identify the anthers. In the more advanced flowers at the base of the inflorescence, the anthers will probably be distinctly yellow.
3 Remove an anther and place it on a clean microscope slide. Add two drops of acidified acetic orcein (ten parts stain to one part 1.0 mol dm^{-3} hydrochloric acid.)
4 Squash with a glass rod and leave for one minute to allow the stain to penetrate the tissue.
5 Put on a coverslip, cover it with filter paper and squash gently. If necessary, irrigate with more stain.
6 Warm the slide on a hotplate for about ten seconds to intensify the staining. (The slide should be very warm, but not too hot to touch).
7 Examine for stages in meiosis.
8 Supplement the information gained from your own preparation by observing stages of meiosis in prepared sections of the anthers of, e.g. lily. Compare with prepared sections of mammalian testis.

Recording your Observations

Using the same technique as for Investigation 23.1, and using Figure 23.3 to help you, identify as many stages of meiosis as you can. Bear in mind that Figure 23.3 is diagrammatic; The chromosomes will not be as neatly arranged in your preparation, and there will be more of them.

CHIASMATA

Use oil immersion to look at cells in late prophase. Examine in detail pairs of homologous chromosomes (bivalents). Use figure 23.4 to help you interpret them in both this Investigation and the next one. Look for chiasmata and note the position of the centromere.

For Consideration

(1) In what situations apart from the ones studied here would you expect to find meiosis taking place?
(2) Meiosis reduces the chromosome number from diploid to haploid. Which particular events, in meiosis ensure that this is so?
(3) What events in meiosis are similar to those that occur in mitosis?

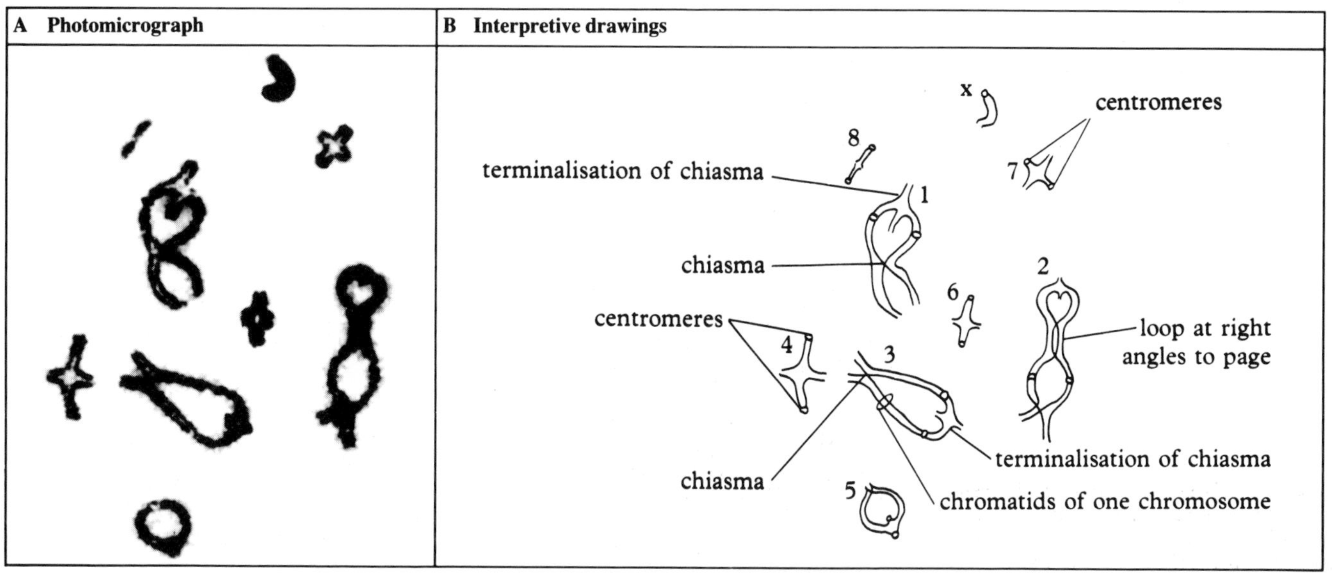

Figure 23.4 Chromosomes at late prophase I in a meiotically dividing cell from grasshopper testis. **A** Photomicrograph. **B** Interpretive drawings. Note pairing of homologous chromosomes. In bivalents 1, 2, and 3, each chromosome can be seen to consist of a pair of chromatids. Individual chromatids cannot be detected in bivalents 4, 5, 7, and 8, and only with difficulty in 6. The **X** chromosome has no partner. *(Bernard John, Australian National University)*

Investigation 23.3
Observation of stages of meiosis in testis of locust

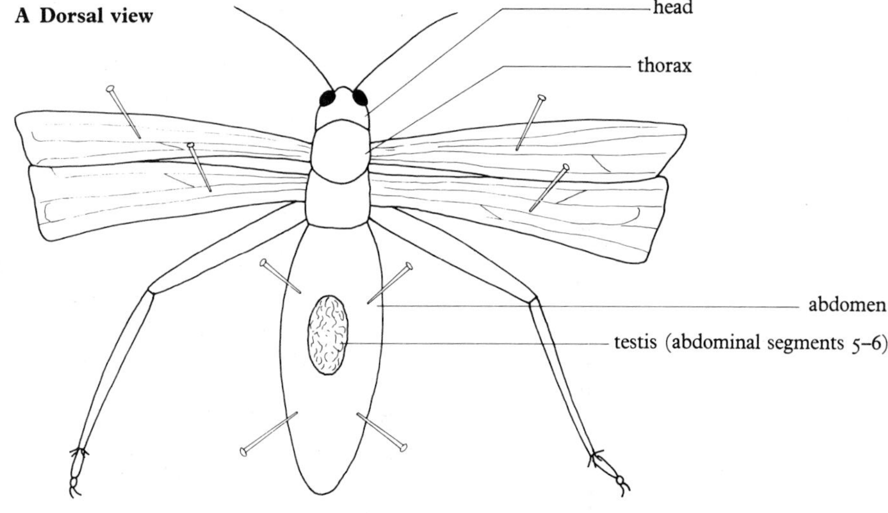

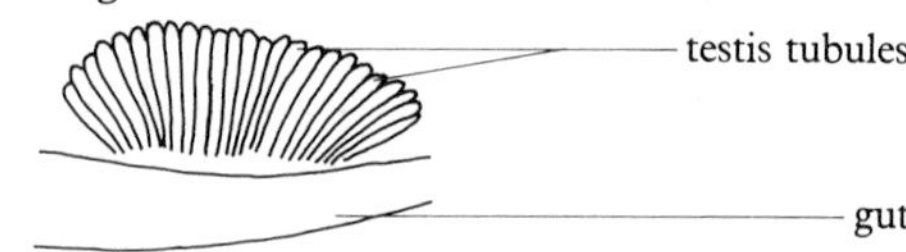

Figure 23.5 Diagrams showing the testis in the abdominal cavity of the locust.

In animals meiosis always takes place in the gonads. A convenient place where meiotic figures can be seen is the testis of the locust. It is necessary to use adult males that are within 7–14 days of their last moult, or fifth instar males that are almost ready to moult into adults.

You can use either the desert locust (*Schistocerca gregaria*), or the migratory locust (*Locusta migratoria*). In the former the testes are easier to dissect out, because there is less fat.

Procedure

1 Pin out a freshly killed male locust, dorsal side uppermost, under water in a dish. Pin out the wings on each side.
2 Open up the abdomen by a mid-dorsal longitudinal cut. Pin back the body wall.
3 Using a hand lens or binocular microscope, identify the testes. Together with fat, these make up an oval body lying above the gut in abdominal segments 5 and 6 (Figure 23.5). Transfer the testes to a microscope slide.
4 Remove as much of the fat (yellow) as you can, leaving only the white tubules of the testes. Two or three tubules are sufficient.
5 Gently squash the tubules with a glass rod so as to spread out the tissue. Remove excess water from the slide with filter paper.
6 Add several drops of acetic orcein stain and put on a coverslip. Cover with filter paper and squash gently, tapping the coverslip with a blunt instrument. This helps to spread the chromosomes.
7 Warm the slide on a hotplate for about ten seconds to intensify the staining. (The slide should be very warm, but not too hot to touch).
8 Examine for stages in meiosis and compare with the results of Investigation 23.2. Again use Figure 23.4 to help you interpret the chromosomes.

For Consideration

(1) Where and when would you expect to find meiosis taking place in a *female* locust?
(2) Where and when would you expect to find *mitosis* taking place in a male or female locust?

Requirements
Microscope
Hand lens or binocular microscope
Slide and coverslip
Small dissecting dish
Dissecting instruments
Glass rod
Filter paper

Acetic orcein

Male locust (either young adult or fifth instar nymph that is about to moult), killed with chloroform (trichloromethane)

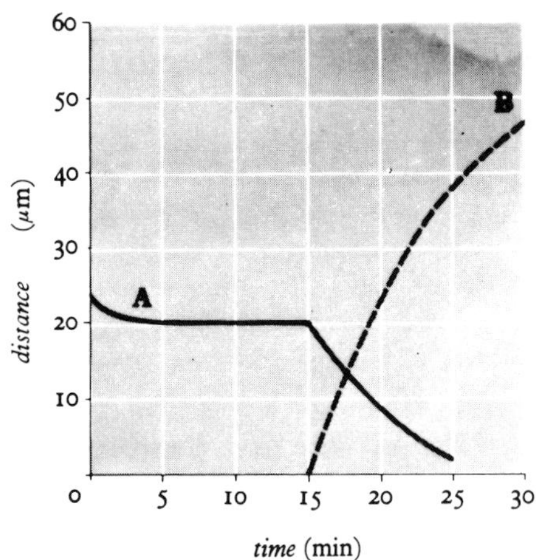

Figure 23.6 Graph illustrating the movement of chromosomes in a cell during mitosis.

Questions and Problems

1 Make clear the difference between (a) chromosome and chromatid; (b) homologous chromosomes and sister chromatids; (c) diploid and haploid; (d) centriole and centromere.

2 What functions are performed by mitosis? Briefly summarise the *principles* behind each of the stages in mitosis.

3 Speculate on the following:
(a) What factors might trigger the onset of mitosis?
(b) What might cause the nuclear membrane to disappear when it does?
(c) What might cause simultaneous movement of the chromatids during anaphase?
(d) What initiates the formation of a new cell membrane at the end of mitosis?

4 The graph in Figure 23.6 illustrates the movement of chromosomes within a cell during mitosis. Curve A shows the changes in the distance between the centromeres of the chromosomes and the poles of the spindle. Curve B shows changes in the distance between the centromeres of sister chromatids. On the time scale, zero (0) marks the beginning of the time when the chromosomes line up on the equator.

Describe what is happening to the chromosomes 15 to 20 minutes after time 0. Why does curve A fall slightly during the first 5 minutes? *(NSW modified)*

5 Sketch the arrangement of the chromosomes of a plant cell with a diploid number of 6 (a) at early anaphase of mitosis, and (b) at early anaphase of a first meiotic division. What is the significance of the differences between them?

6 Without going into the mechanisms of either in detail, outline the essential differences between mitosis and meiosis. Summarise the importance of these two types of cell division in the lives of organisms.

7 To what extent do you consider (a) mitosis to be a homeostatic process, and (b) meiosis to be random?

8 Figure 23.7 shows the chromosomes of three dividing cells. In each case say whether the cell is undergoing mitosis or meiosis and what stage it has reached. Give reasons for your answers.

Figure 23.7 The chromosomes of three dividing cells.

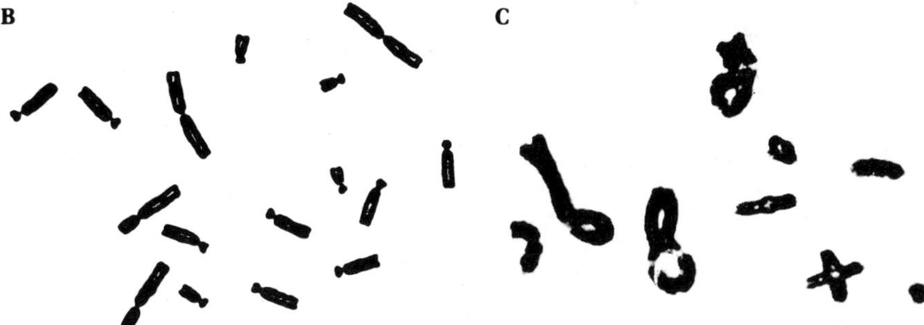

9 Figure 23.8 is a photomicrograph of chromosomes at a certain stage of cell division.
(a) Name the type of cell division, and stage, as precisely as possible.
(b) Name the structures labelled A, B and C.
(c) Make line drawings of the chromosomes, interpreting them as fully as you can.

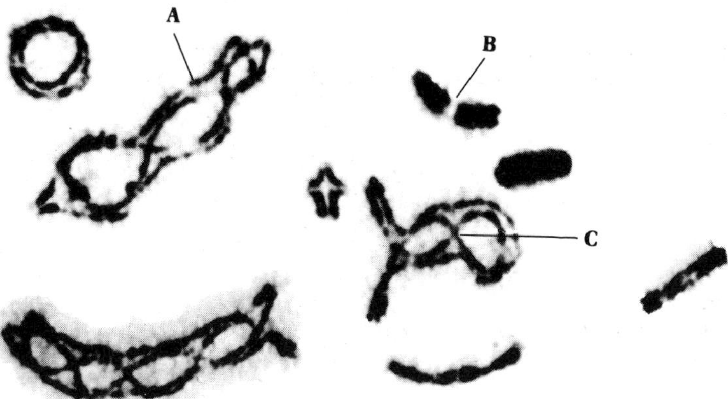

Figure 23.8 Photomicrograph of chromosomes at a certain stage of cell division.

24 Reproduction

Background Summary

1 Reproduction can be **asexual** or **sexual**. Asexual reproduction produces offspring which are genetically identical to one another and the parent. Sexual reproduction, in contrast, often less prolific, confers genetic variation.

2 Reproduction is often associated with survival over unfavourable periods.

3 The simplest kind of sexual reproduction is demonstrated by bacterial conjugation in which transfer of genetic material occurs without the use of gametes.

4 Most organisms employ **gametes**. These may be **isogametes**, **anisogametes** or **heterogametes**. Organisms with isogametes are generally distinguishable into **plus** and **minus strains**, foreshadowing the development of eggs and sperm in higher forms. Gametes are haploid, the diploid condition being restored when they fuse to form a zygote.

5 The structure of **eggs** and **spermatozoa** is related to their functions: the spermatozoon is a motile vehicle for the male's genetic material, the egg receives genetic material from the sperm and provides nourishment for the embryo.

6 In the process of **fertilisation** the spermatozoon, aided by its **acrosome reaction**, penetrates the egg membrane, its haploid set of chromosomes (**paternal chromosomes**) uniting with those of the egg (**maternal chromosomes**).

7 Many aquatic animals show **external fertilisation**. Most terrestrial animals have **internal fertilisation** with oviparity, ovoviparity or viviparity. In mammals nourishment of the embryo is provided by a placenta, and there is extensive **care of the young**.

8 In humans sexual reproduction starts with **gametogenesis: spermatogenesis** in the testes of the male, **oögenesis** in the ovaries of the female. In both cases the sequence of events, involving meiosis, is essentially the same.

9 The microscopic structure of the **testis** and **ovary** is directly related to their functions of producing large numbers of sperm and eggs respectively.

10 The anatomy of the male and female **reproductive systems** is geared towards bringing sperm into contact with an egg and subsequently protecting and nourishing the developing embryo into which the zygote develops.

11 In the human female, the **sexual cycle** follows a monthly pattern, **ovulation** alternating with **menstruation**. The sequence of events is controlled by complex interactions between **gonadotrophic hormones** from the pituitary gland and **ovarian hormones** from the gonads themselves.

12 In the event of fertilisation and successful implantation, the hormonal balance is altered in such a way that menstruation is temporarily suspended and the woman becomes **pregnant**. The **placenta** takes over the function of secreting the ovarian hormones which, together with other hormones produced by the pituitary, ensure that **parturition** (birth) and **lactation** occur at the appropriate time.

13 Some mammals, like the human, can reproduce at any time of the year; others have specific **breeding seasons** the timing of which is controlled by a combination of environmental and hormonal factors.

14 In the human male there is no sexual cycle as such but sexual activities are controlled by hormones comparable to those found in the female.

15 In flowering plants the reproductive apparatus is embodied in the **flowers**. From a functional standpoint the male gamete nuclei in the **pollen grains** produced in the anthers are equivalent to sperm, and the **egg cell** contained in the embryosac within the ovule is equivalent to the ovum.

16 **Pollination**, the process by which pollen is transferred from the male to the female parts of flowers, is equivalent to copulation and is achieved in a variety of ways. Fertilisation is achieved by the formation and growth of a **pollen tube** which conveys the male nuclei to those of the egg cell.

17 In flowering plants a **double fertilisation** takes place, one male nucleus fusing with the egg cell to form a zygote, the other with the polar nuclei to form the primary endosperm nucleus.

18 After fertilisation the zygote develops into the **embryo**, the primary endosperm nucleus into the **endosperm tissue**, the ovule into the **seed**, the integuments into the **seed coat**, and the ovary into the **fruit**.

19 Sometimes an organism develops from an unfertilised egg, a phenomenon called **parthenogenesis**. Two types of parthenogenesis are recognised, diploid and haploid, and – if occurring naturally, as they do in certain animals – they can be used to achieve rapid proliferation without males.

20 Most animals have separate sexes (**dioecious**), but some animals and the majority of plants are hermaphroditic (**monoecious**). On account of its genetic disadvantages, most monoecious organisms have mechanisms for reducing the chances of self-fertilisation, though exceptions occur.

21 Many organisms, particularly plants and lower animals, can reproduce **asexually**. In most cases asexual reproduction occurs in addition to sexual reproduction. The offspring are all genetically identical and constitute a **clone**.

22 Asexual methods of reproduction include binary and multiple **fission**, **spore-formation**, **budding**, **fragmentation** and **vegetative propagation**.

23 Although asexual reproduction has certain disadvantages, it is used commercially to propagate organisms, particularly plants, which possess certain desirable features that one wishes to perpetuate.

24 An essential part of the reproductive processes of many organisms is **dispersal**. An organism may be dispersed in the form of **spores**, **seeds**, **fruits** or **larvae**, according to the species in question. Agents of dispersal include animals, wind, and water.

Investigation 24.1
Observing fertilisation

Requirements
Microscope
Slides and coverslips
Cavity slides
Mounted needle
Pipette
Petri dishes
Watchglasses
Syringe

Potassium chloride solution, (0.5 mol dm^{-3})

*Sea urchin, e.g. *Echinus* or *Arbacia*
*Tube worm, *Pomatoceros triqueter*
African clawed toad, *Xenopus laevis*, mating (*see* Appendix 7, page 400)

* Available from Marine Biological Laboratories.

Note: If the African clawed toad is used, it is advisable to combine this investigation with Investigation 26.1 (*see* page 258).

It is not easy to study fertilisation, but by using suitable material in the right conditions the process can sometimes be observed. For obvious reasons it is best to use organisms which have external fertilisation. Such organisms include sea urchins, marine worms and toads.

Sea Urchin

Male and female sea urchins produce sperms and eggs in March or April. In some species spawning can be induced by injecting them with 0.5 mol dm^{-3} potassium chloride solution (1 cm^3) close to the mouth. Eggs and sperm are shed through pores close to the mouth. Eggs form an orange fluid, sperms a white fluid.

1 With separate pipettes collect eggs and sperm, and place them in two different petri dishes.

2 Transfer some eggs to a drop of sea water on a clean *cavity* slide. Gently lower a coverslip onto the drop of fluid.

3 Locate eggs under low power. With a fine pipette transfer a drop of the milky sperm suspension to the edge of the coverslip.

4 Look down the microscope for sperm to swim into the field of view. Observe as much as possible of fertilisation. Look particularly for the lifting of the fertilisation membrane.

Marine Worm

The marine worm *Pomatoceros* produces eggs and sperm at any time of the year. The animal lives in a calcareous tube attached to rocks and stones. It is commonly found on rocky shores between the tide marks.

1 With a scalpel chip away the narrow tail end of the tube, and do the same with the broader head end. Then push the worm out of the tube from the rear with a blunt needle. Place the worm in a watchglass of sea water.

2 Repeat for several worms, placing males in one watchglass and females in another. The sexes can be distinguished by the fact that the males are yellow or orange and females purple.

3 The worms release their eggs and sperms as soon as they are removed from their tubes. With a pipette transfer a drop of sea water from the watchglass containing female worms to a cavity slide. Observe eggs, if present, under low power.

4 Add a drop of sea water from the watchglass containing males, quickly put on a coverslip and observe under the microscope. Alternatively, put on the coverslip *before* adding the sperms and then introduce the sperms at the edge of the coverslip as in the sea urchin technique described above. Observe fertilisation.

Toad

The normal breeding season of the African clawed toad, *Xenopus laevis*, is July, but mating and spawning may be induced at any time of the year by injecting them with gonadotrophic hormone. So readily do they respond to this treatment that for many years they were used for testing pregnancy: if the urine of a woman, suspected of being pregnant, was injected into a female toad, subsequent spawning could be taken as unequivocal evidence that the woman was pregnant.

1 With a wide pipette, transfer eggs and sperm from a pair of mating toads to a clean cavity slide, along with some of the water that they were in.

2 Observe under the low power of the microscope and watch for fertilisation. Does the appearance of the egg change in any way after fertilisation? Explain fully.

For Consideration

(1) What events, too small to see down your microscope, take place during the process of fertilisation?
(2) What important functions are fulfilled by fertilisation?

Investigation 24.2
Dissection of the reproductive system of the rat

CAUTION:
Several serious diseases can be caught from rats. Wear a laboratory coat and thin rubber gloves while you are dissecting, and wash your hands thoroughly afterwards.

Despite its apparent complexity, the mammalian reproductive system is essentially quite simple. In both sexes there are two gonads (testes and ovaries) from which tubes lead to the midline where they join a single tube to the exterior. In the male this latter tube is shared by the urinary system.

Note: This dissection can be carried out on a rat which has been deep-frozen or preserved following a dissection of other systems.

Procedure

1 Before commencing the dissection identify the urinary and genital openings on the ventral side (Figure 9.1, page 79). Note that in the male there is just one urino-genital opening at the end of the penis, whereas in the female there are separate urinary and genital openings, the former being located just anterior to the latter.

2 In the male, notice also the scrotal sacs which contain the testes, and in the female identify the nipples.

3 Open up the abdominal cavity as instructed on p. 79, cutting *round* the urinary and genital openings (dotted line in Figure 9.1). Pin back the skin and cut back the body wall in the usual way. In the female notice the mammary glands adhering to the inside of the skin.

4 Ligature the hepatic portal vein and remove the gut as instructed on page 80.

You are now in a position to proceed with your dissection of the reproductive apparatus.

5 First notice that in both sexes the tubes leading to the urino-genital openings are covered by a layer of muscle beneath which lies the pubis, part of the pelvic girdle (Figure 24.1A for male; 24.1B for female).

MALE

1 With scissors cut open one of the scrotal sacs (dotted line on left-hand side of Figure 24.2A).

2 With forceps grasp hold of the testis, or the fat attached to it, and draw it forwards. Note that this pulls up the bottom of the scrotal sac: this is because the cauda epididymis is attached to it by the gubernaculum, a strand of muscle whose contraction was responsible for the descent of the testis during development.

3 Identify the structures seen in Figure 24.2B, if necessary using a hand lens or binocular microscope to help you.

4 Remove the muscle overlying the pubis of the pelvic girdle. With large scissors cut through the pelvic girdle on either side of the mid-line and remove the pubis (dotted lines in Figure 24.1A). This will expose the urethra which leads into the penis.

5 Identify the epididymis and vas deferens leading from the testis. Follow the vas deferens to the mid-line and ascertain that it, along with its fellow from the other side, opens into the anterior end of the urethra.

6 Also opening into the urethra at this point is the duct of the bladder, which receives the ureters from the kidneys. Check that these structures and their connections are visible in your dissection.

7 Now identify the glands associated with the reproductive tract: a gland associated with the inner end of each vas deferens; a pair of large seminal vesicles and coagulating glands at the inner end of each vas deferens; prostate glands lying ventral to the urethra just behind the bladder; a pair of Cowper's glands at the base of the penis, and a pair of preputial glands towards the tip of the penis. What is the general function of these glands?

A Male

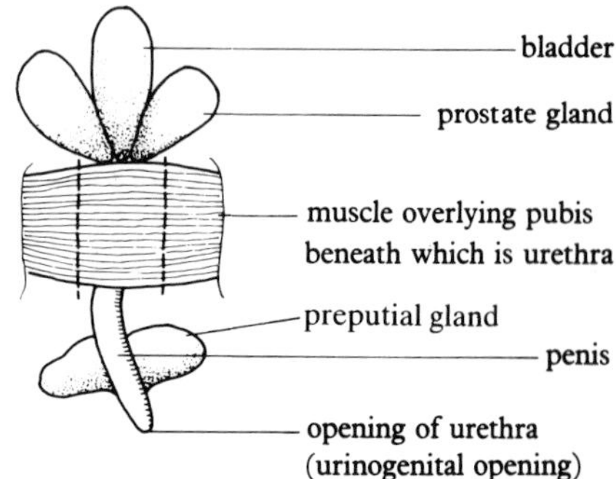

B Female

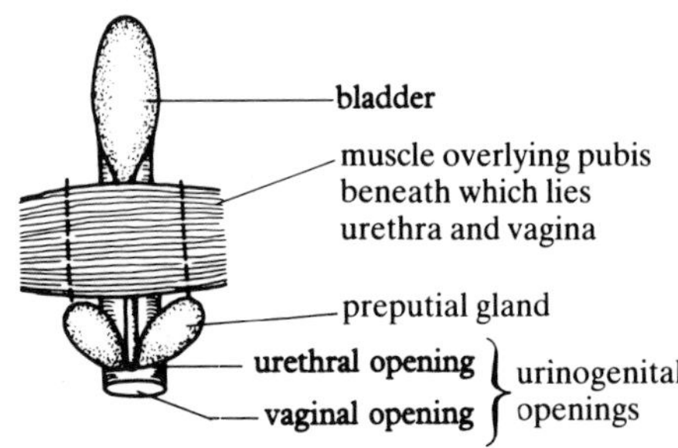

Figure 24.1 The urinogenital openings and associated structures in the rat.

8 Note that in the male the urethra serves as a common urino-genital duct.
9 Finally, investigate the blood vessels serving the reproductive organs, particularly the spermatic artery and vein, derived (usually) from the dorsal aorta and posterior vena cava respectively. Together the spermatic artery and vein constitute the spermatic cord.

10 Cut open the scrotal sac of a fresh-killed male rat and expose the testis. Cut into the testis and release some of the milky fluid onto a slide. Add a drop of 0.9 per cent sodium chloride solution and put on a coverslip. Observe sperm under low and high power.

Figure 24.2 Dissection of reproductive system of male rat.

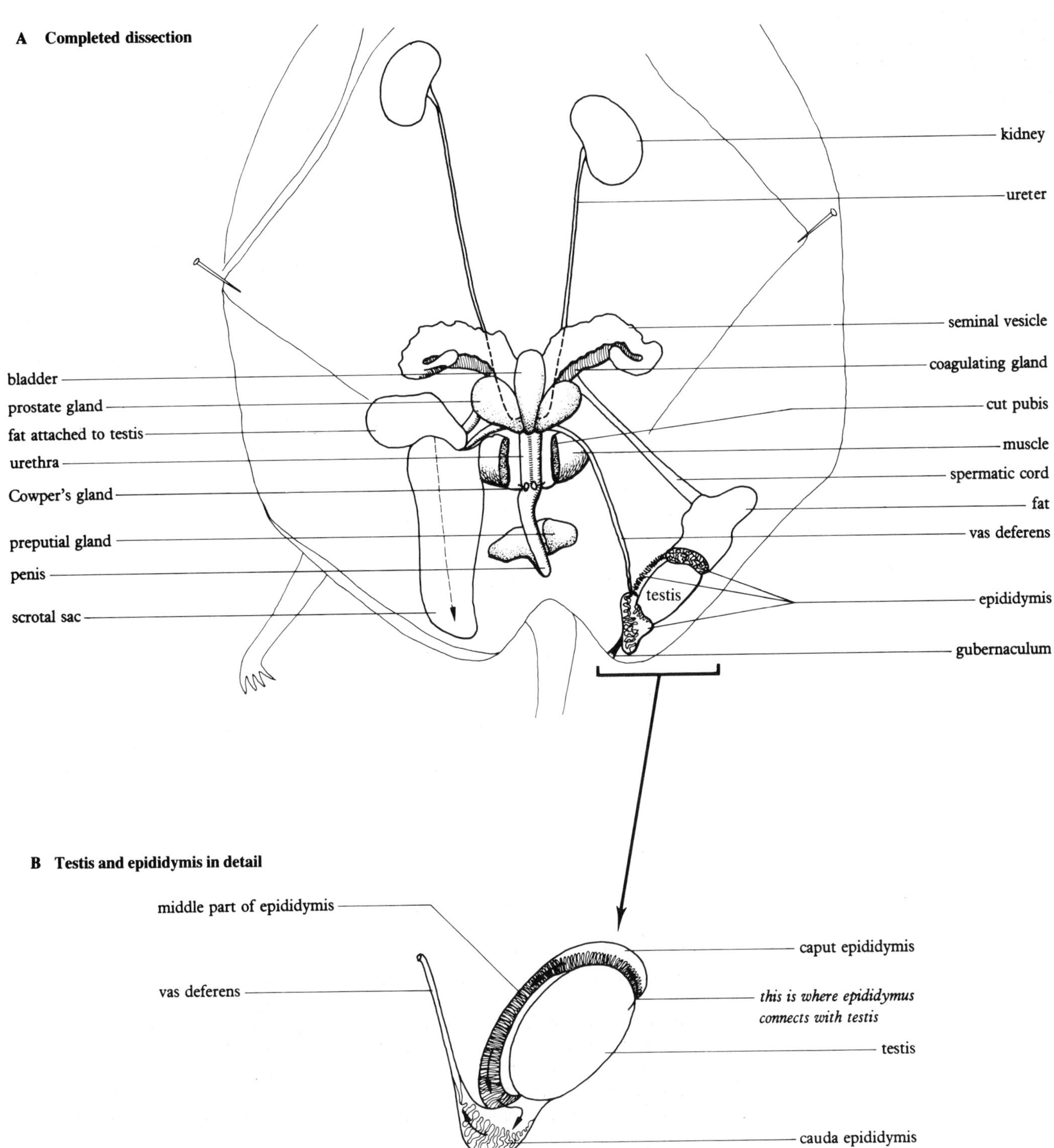

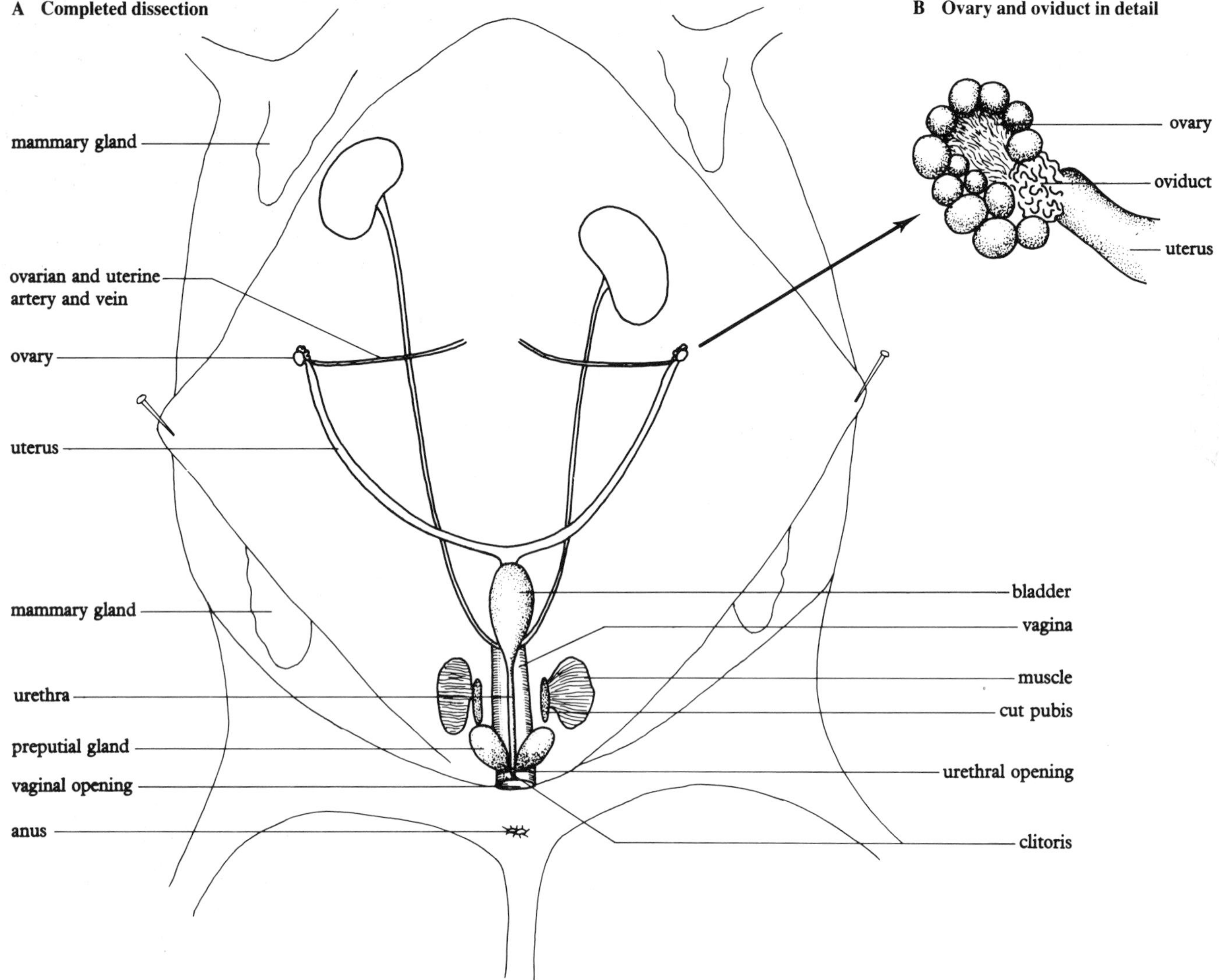

Figure 24.3 Dissection of reproductive system of female rat. If the rat is pregnant, the uterus is larger and the uterine artery and vein more extensive.

Requirements
Microscope
Hand lens or binocular microscope
Dissecting instruments
Thread
Cotton wool
Slide
Coverslip
Rubber gloves

Sodium chloride solution (0.9 per cent)

Male and female rats for dissection

FEMALE

1 Remove the pubis as in the male (dotted lines in Figure 24.1B). This will exposed the narrow urethra beneath which is the more bulbous vagina (Figure 23.4A).

2 Identify the small ovaries and – with the aid of a lens or binocular microscope – the short, coiled oviduct (Figure 24.3B).

3 The oviducts on each side lead to a long V-shaped uterus, the two horns of which unite in the mid-line to form the vagina (Figure 24.3A).

4 As in the male the bladder receives the ureters from the kidney, and opens into the anterior end of the urethra. Confirm this in your dissection. A pair of preputial glands will be seen at the posterior end of the urethra.

5 Note that in the female the urethra (urinary duct) and vagina (genital duct) are separate.

6 Identify the ovarian and uterine arteries and veins. With which major blood vessels do these connect? The uterine blood vessels are especially large and prominent during pregnancy.

7 If the rat is pregnant the much expanded uterus will be seen to contain a variable number of embryos which can be removed and examined. In removing an embryo notice the umbilical cord and placenta.

For Consideration

(1) What are the principal similarities and differences between the male and female reproductive systems?

(2) You will have observed that in the male the urethra serves as a common urinogenital duct conveying both urine and sperm to the exterior, whereas in the female the urinary and genital systems have separate openings to the exterior. How would you explain this difference between the two sexes and what are its physiological consequences?

Investigation 24.3
Microscopic structure of mammalian testis and ovary

The testis and ovary contain developing sperm and eggs respectively. In both cases diploid primordial germ cells, associated with the germinal epithelium, divide mitotically to form spermatogonia and oögonia which grow and then undergo meiosis to form, ultimately, spermatozoa and ova respectively.

Testis

1 Examine a prepared section of mammalian testis under low power (Figure 24.4A). Observe numerous seminiferous tubules cut in various planes.

2 Examine the wall of a seminiferous tubule under high power. Can you identify the structures shown in Figure 24.4B? Trace the sequence of developmental stages: spermatogonia → spermatocytes → spermatids → spermatozoa. Can you see any stages in meiosis?

3 Observe that the tails of the spermatozoa hang into the lumen of the seminiferous tubule. Their heads are buried in large Sertoli cells. Can you detect Sertoli cells? What is their function?

4 Now examine the tissue between adjacent seminiferous tubules under high power (Figure 24.4C), noting interstitial (Leydig) cells and capillaries embedded in connective tissue. What is the function of the Leydig cells and why are they located close to capillaries?

Figure 24.4 Microscopic structure of mammalian testis. Secondary spermatocytes are short-lived and do not normally appear in microscopic preparations.

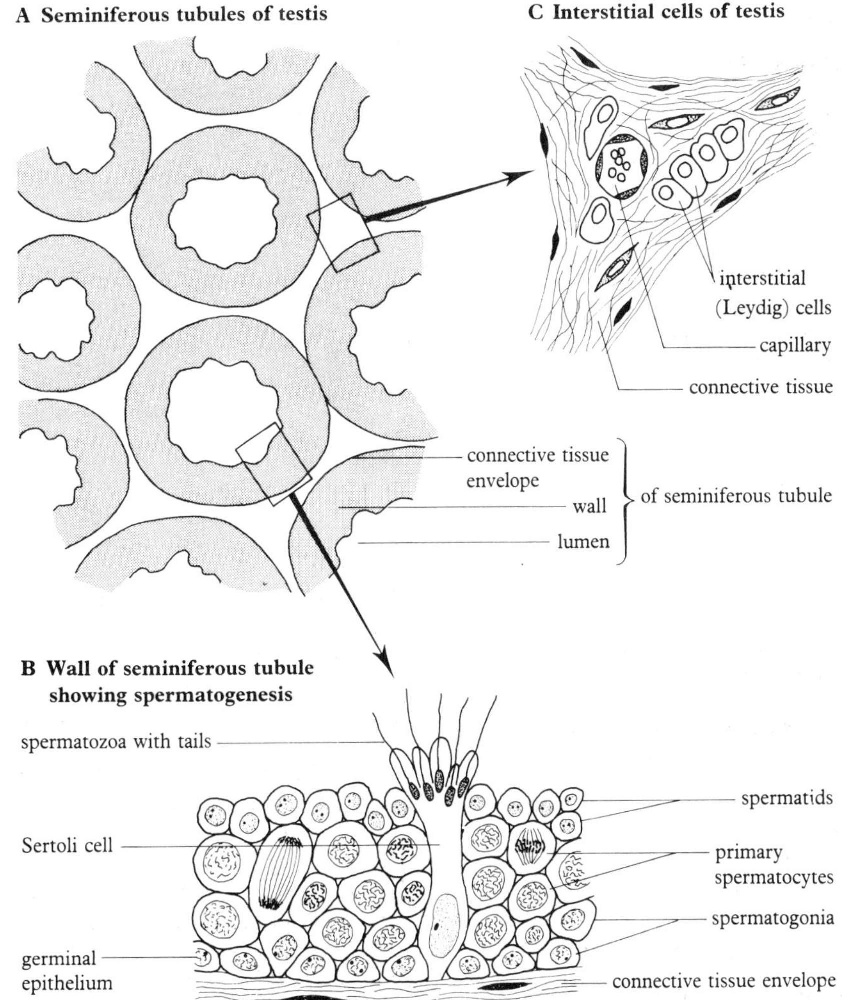

Requirements
Microscope

Section of mammalian testis
Section of mammalian ovary showing developing Graafian follicles
Section of mammalian ovary showing corpus luteum

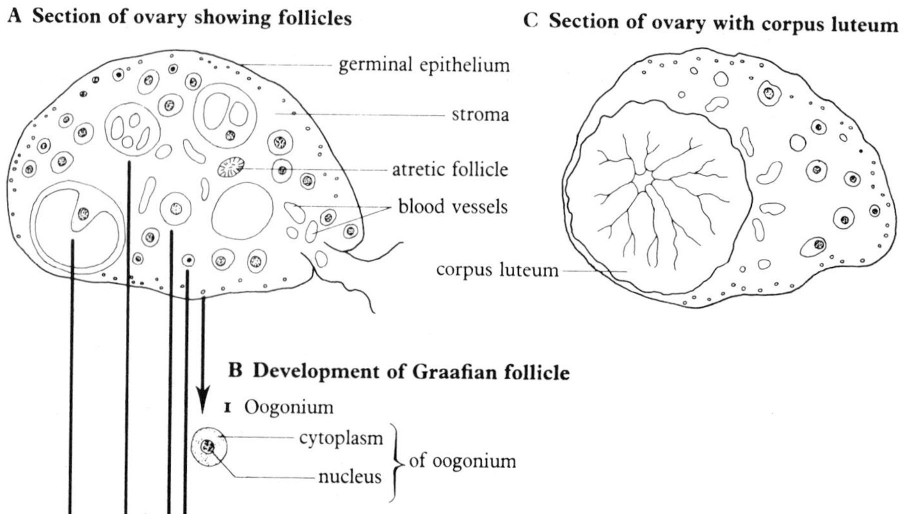

A Section of ovary showing follicles

germinal epithelium
stroma
atretic follicle
blood vessels
corpus luteum

C Section of ovary with corpus luteum

B Development of Graafian follicle

1 Oogonium
cytoplasm
nucleus
of oogonium

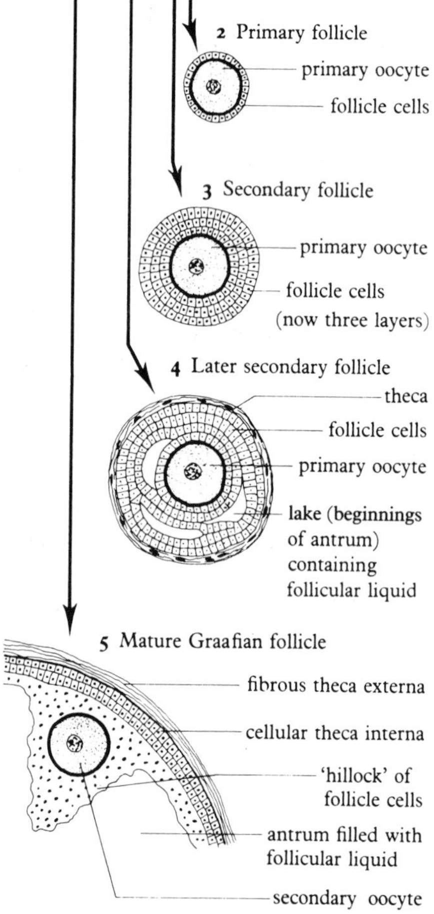

2 Primary follicle
primary oocyte
follicle cells

3 Secondary follicle
primary oocyte
follicle cells (now three layers)

4 Later secondary follicle
theca
follicle cells
primary oocyte
lake (beginnings of antrum) containing follicular liquid

5 Mature Graafian follicle
fibrous theca externa
cellular theca interna
'hillock' of follicle cells
antrum filled with follicular liquid
secondary oocyte

Figure 24.5 Microscopic structure of mammalian ovary. In **B**, the first meiotic division occurs just before ovulation, the second meiotic division occurs just after fertilisation.

Ovary

1 Look at a section of mammalian ovary under low power and identify the structures shown in Figure 24.5A.

2 Now turn over to high power and examine as many stages in the development of a Graafian follicle as you can find. Use Figure 24.5B to help you to interpret the stages.

3 How does ovulation take place? If available, examine a slide which shows this.

4 As many as 400 000 primary follicles may be present at birth, but normally only about 400 develop into mature Graafian follicles. The rest degenerate into atretic follicles. How often are Graafian follicles formed?

5 After ovulation the hollow Graafian follicle develops into a solid corpus luteum. Examine a prepared section of an ovary containing a corpus luteum (Figure 24.5C).

For Consideration

(1) What are the essential similarities and differences between the development of sperm and eggs in the mammal?

(2) How are the developmental events, which you have observed to occur in the testis and ovary, controlled?

Investigation 24.4
Arrangement of flowers on a plant

The flowers are the part of the plant resonsible for sexual reproduction and they must be in the best possible positions for carrying out their functions. These functions include pollination and producing seeds for effective dispersal. Bear these two functions in mind as you look at the way flowers are arranged on plants.

Procedure

1 First examine the flowering shoot of a plant such as bluebell, foxglove, lupin or willowherb and notice the relationship between the flowers and the stem (Figure 24.6). The flowers together constitute the inflorescence. Note that the flower stalk (pedicel) is borne in the angle between a small leaf (bract) and the main stalk of the inflorescence (peduncle).

2 If the plant is at a sufficiently advanced stage of development, notice the developmental transition from apex to base of the inflorescence. Towards apex: unopened flower buds. Further back: open flowers with stamens and carpels in various states of maturity. Further back still: fruits. Below this level you will see little else but foliage leaves.

3 Many other types of inflorescence are found in nature. They can readily be seen by examining a range of different species of flowering plants. How do the variations arise? They do so mainly by the peduncle branching in various ways, and by the pedicels varying in length (they may indeed be absent altogether, the flowers arising directly from the peduncle).

Examine the plants provided and sketch the arrangement of the flowers in each case. Compare your sketches with the diagrams in Figure 24.7. What can you say about the possible functional significance of each pattern?

4 One particularly specialised inflorescence is found in the Compositae, the family which includes the dandelion. Here the apex of the peduncle is expanded and flattened and bears numerous small flowers. This type of inflorescence is called a capitulum (Figure 24.7H).

For consideration

(1) What are the possible advantages to the plant of having an inflorescence instead of just a single flower?

(2) What can you say about the possible functional significance of each type of inflorescence illustrated in Figure 24.7?

Requirements
A variety of flowering plants, some with single flowers and others displaying the different kinds of inflorescence illustrated in Figure 24.7.

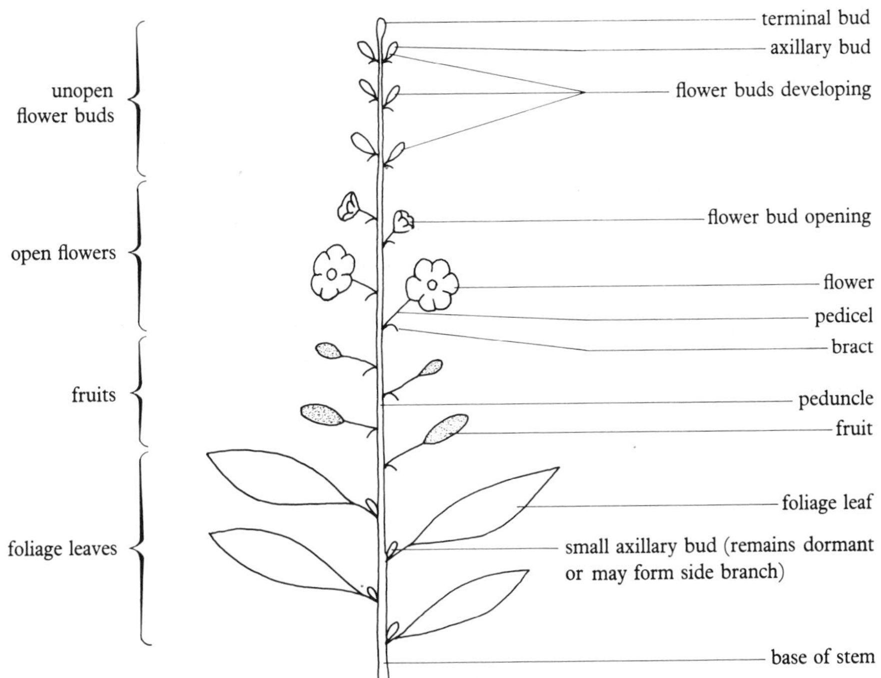

Figure 24.6 Diagram of a generalised plant to show the arrangement of the flowers and related structures.

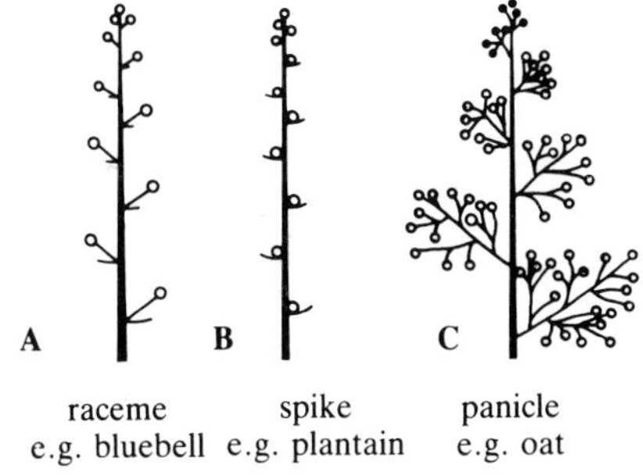

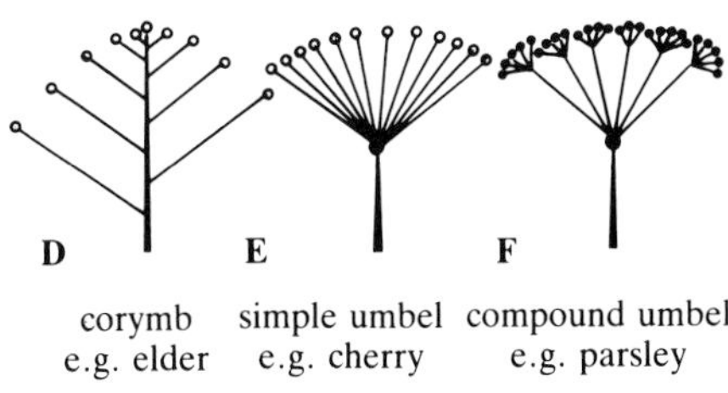

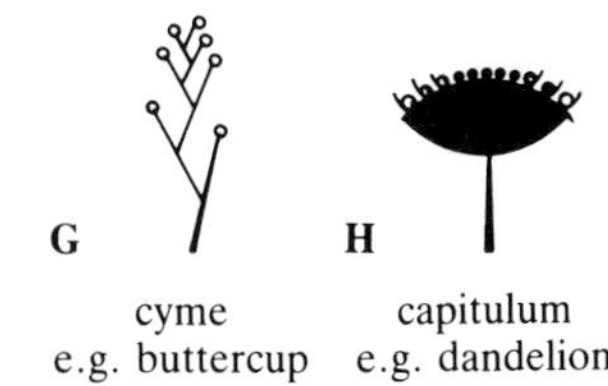

Figure 24.7 The main types of inflorescence found in nature. Further variations on these themes occur, and intermediate conditions are also found.

Investigation 24.5
Structure of flowers

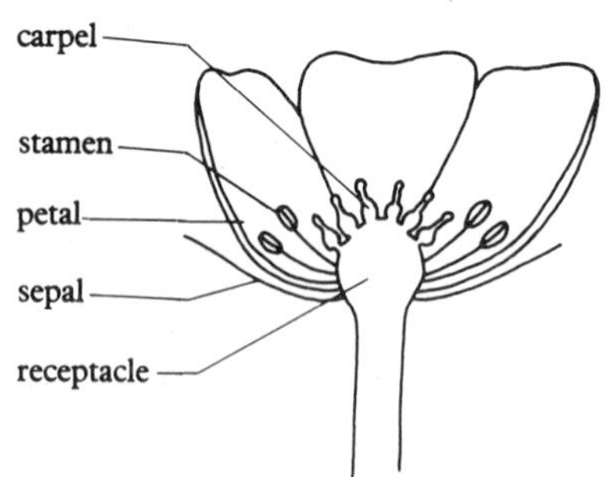

Figure 24.8 Structure of a generalised flower. Flowers of the buttercup family (*Ranunculaceae*) conform closely to the organisation illustrated here.

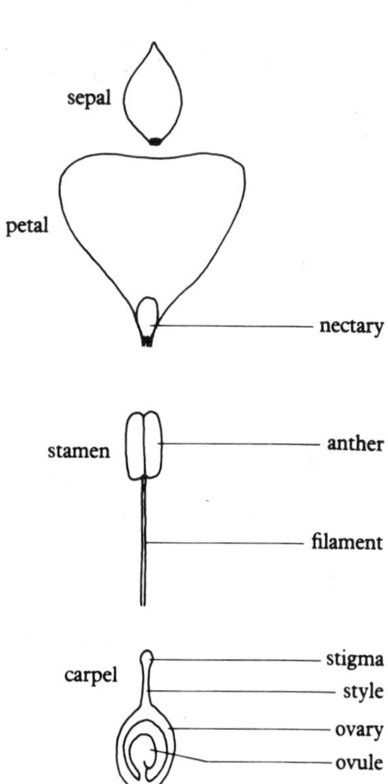

Figure 24.9 Detail of component parts of flower, based on buttercup.

The flower consists of a series of whorls of modified leaves which collectively produce, protect, and ensure the union of, the gametes. The whorls of structures are attached to a receptacle, the expanded end of the flower stalk.

Structure of a Typical Flower

1 Examine a flower of e.g. buttercup, and note the four whorls of structures (Figure 24.8). The whorls are, from the outside inwards:

Calyx (sepals): usually small, green and leaf-like.

Corolla (petals): often coloured and scented for attracting insects, and with nectaries (sacs which secrete a sugary solution) towards the base for rewarding them.

Androecium (stamens): each stamen consists of an anther and filament. Each anther contains four pollen sacs in which the pollen grains develop.

Gynaecium (carpels): each carpel consists of stigma, style and ovary. The ovary contains one or more ovules in each of which is an egg cell.

2 Remove a representative component of each whorl and examine its parts under a hand lens or binocular microscope (Figure 24.9).

Variations in flower structure

1 Flowers of different species may vary in the numbers, arrangement, and degree of fusion of the component parts. Examine the flowers of a range of species so as to appreciate the extent to which the component parts may vary. These are some of the main variations that may be observed:

Sepals: number variable; show varying degrees of fusion; may be green and leaf-like, or coloured and petal-like (petaloid).

Petals: number variable; like sepals, show varying degrees of fusion, in some cases forming tube (corolla tube); nectaries may be absent; colour and scent varies widely; sepals and petals may be fused or indistinguishable from one another, in which case they form, together, the perianth.

Stamens: number may be large and variable or smaller and fixed; anthers vary in size; filaments may vary in length and in their mode of attachment to the anther; base of filaments may be attached to the petals or perianth rather than the receptacle; show varying degrees of fusion, in extreme cases forming a tube round the carpels.

Carpels: number may be large and variable or smaller and fixed; styles vary in length; may be separate or joined; if joined there is much variation in the method of fusion; the ovary may stand proud upon the receptacle (superior ovary) or be sunk down into the receptacle (inferior ovary).

2 Flowers also vary in their symmetry. The flower may be radially symmetrical (actinomorphic) or bilaterally symmetrical (zygomorphic) (Figure 24.10). Examine one or more representatives of each type.

Examples of actinomorphic flowers include buttercup, lily, tulip and bindweed (*Convolvulus*). Zygomorphic flowers include sweet pea, deadnettle, snapdragon and orchids.

A zygomorphic flower can be cut in only one plane to give two equal and opposite halves; an actinomorphic flower, however, may be cut in more than one plane to give two equal and opposite halves. Do you agree with this distinction from looking at the two types of flower?

3 Flowers are usually hermaphrodite, but sometimes they are unisexual. In the latter either the stamens or carpels are absent. Examine unisexual flowers (male and female) of e.g. hazel, sycamore, oak, beech, maize, poplar or willow.

4 Much of the variation in flower parts can be attributed to their modes of pollination. Insect-pollinated flowers such as the buttercup tend to have showy petals, with lines (honey-guides) pointing towards a source of nectar, nectaries, scent and large sticky spiny pollen grains. Wind-pollinated flowers such as grasses (Figure 24.11) tend to lack showy petals, nectar-guides, nectar, nectaries and scent. They

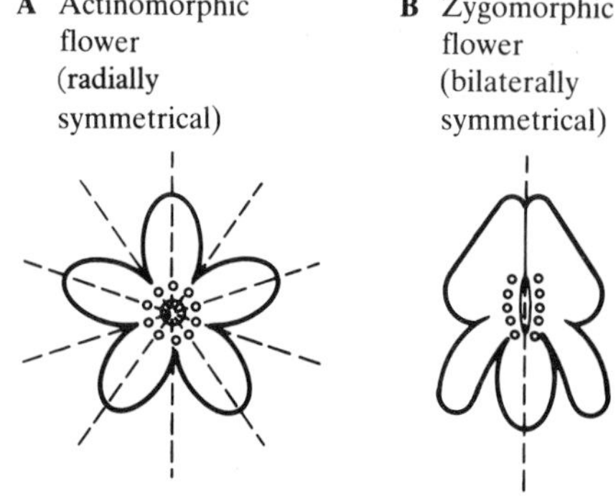

Figure 24.10 The two types of symmetry found in flowers. In both diagrams the flower is being viewed from above. The dotted lines indicate the planes through which the flowers can be cut so as to give two equal and opposite halves.

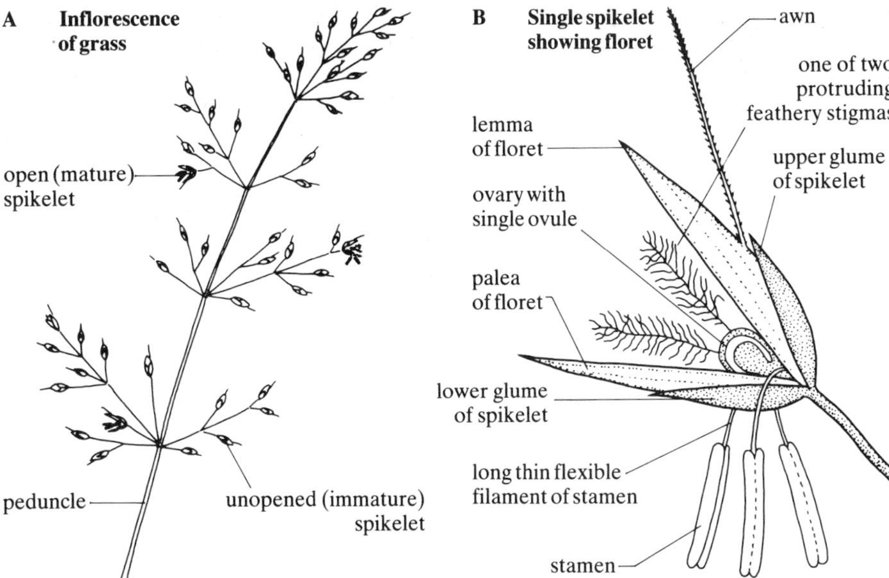

Figure 24.11 Inflorescence and flower of a grass. This type of inflorescence is a panicle (*see* Figure 24.7, page 233).

Requirements
Binocular microscope or hand lens
Needles
Small forceps
Razor blade
White tile

Actinomorphic flower, e.g. buttercup
Flowers showing variation in the numbers, arrangement and degree of fusion of the component parts
Zygomorphic flower, e.g. sweet pea
Unisexual flowers, male and female, e.g. hazel
Grass, inflorescence

usually have stamens which hang outside the flower and which produce large quantities of small, smooth, dry, light pollen grains. The stigmas are exposed to the wind and have a large surface area.

Examine the inflorescence of a grass (Figure 24.11A). The individual flowers are known as florets. They are aggregated into groups called spikelets. Different groups of grasses differ in the number of florets per spikelet. The species illustrated in Figure 24.11A has one floret per spikelet. Examine a spikelet and notice that at its base there is a pair of leaves (glumes). Now examine an individual floret under a binocular microscope (Figure 24.11B). The floret consists of two leaves, the lemma (larger) and the palea, surrounding one ovary and three stamens. The ovary supports two feathery stigmas and contains one ovule.

For Consideration

(1) From your observations what basic features do virtually all flowers have in common?
(2) Which flowers of the ones that you yourself have examined conform most closely to the basic pattern, and which ones deviate most widely from it?
(3) How would you explain *functionally* the main differences between a grass flower and the flower of e.g. a buttercup?

Investigation 24.6 Recording floral structure

With so much variation in flower structure between different species of plant, it is important to have a convenient and standardised way of recording their structure. In this practical three methods of recording flower structure are explained, and you are invited to apply them to a range of different flowers.

Method 1

DRAWING THE HALF-FLOWER

This provides an elevation of the flower. You should cut the flower along the median plane, i.e. the plane in line with the main stem (Figure 24.12). In zygomorphic flowers cutting along this plane will give two equal and opposite

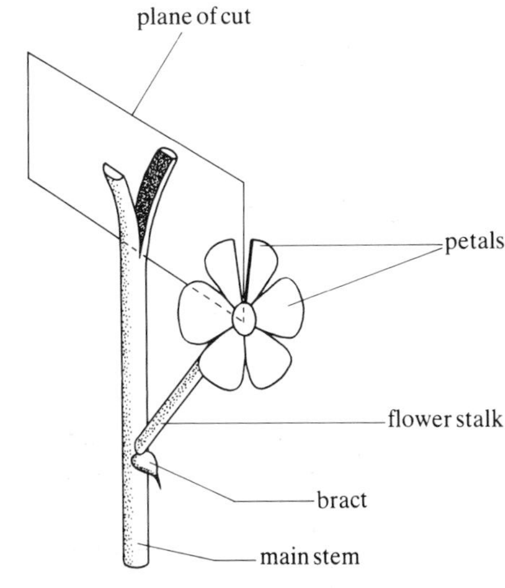

Figure 24.12 To prepare a half-flower cut the floral structures along the median plane as shown in this diagram.

halves. Draw a half-flower (Figure 24.13A) and/or construct a simple diagram of the cut surface, i.e. a vertical section (Figure 24.13B).

Method 2

FLORAL DIAGRAM

This provides a plan of the flower as viewed from above, and should look like a diagrammatic transverse section (Figure 24.13C). In constructing a floral diagram hold the flower so the bract, if present, faces you and the peduncle is furthest away.

If the petals, sepals or stamens are joined, link them with simple brackets; if the stamens arise from the petals link them with radial lines.

Method 3

FLORAL FORMULA

This is the simplest and quickest way of representing the structure of a flower. Written in coded form, it enables a person to work out the structure of the flower.

The floral formula is given by writing capital letters corresponding to the whorls as follows: **K** for **calyx**; **C** for **corolla**; **A** for **androecium** and **G** for **gynaecium**. Each letter is followed by a figure denoting the number of units in the whorl. If the number is large and variable it is expressed as infinity (∞). A floral formula is given in Figure 24.13D.

Actinomorphy is designated by writing ⊕ at the beginning of the formula.
Zygomorphy is designated by writing ↑ at the beginning of the formula.
A **superior ovary** is designated by putting a line below the gynaecium number, e.g. **G**$\underline{\mathbf{5}}$.
An **inferior ovary** is designated by putting a line above the gynaecium number, e.g. **G**$\overline{\mathbf{5}}$.
If units are joined, put their number in brackets, e.g. **K(5)**.
If some units are joined but others free, the former only are put in brackets, e.g. **A(4) + 2**.
If one whorl is united with another, their symbols should be tied, e.g. $\overset{\frown}{\text{C5A5}}$.
If the sepals and petals are replaced by a **perianth**, the symbol used is **P**.

Note: It is sometimes difficult to see how many carpels there are in the gynaecium. The number of carpels usually equals
(a) the number of stigmas,
(b) the number of chambers in the ovary,
(c) the number of lines down which the fruit wall splits to release the seeds (*see* Investigation 24.10, page 240).

Procedure

Examine the flowers of different plants. In each case sketch the half-flower and floral diagram and give the floral formula. Start with a simple actinomorphic flower which lacks any special complications. Then examine other flowers, both actinomorphic and zygomorphic, displaying the normal range of variations. In each case consider the possible functional significance of the floral pattern, particularly in relation to its pollination mechanism.

For consideration

(1) Of the three methods of recording flower structure, which one provides the most information about the flower? In describing a flower, is this method sufficient on its own, or should the other methods be used as well?
(2) Of what use are floral formulae, and to whom?

Requirements
Binocular microscope or hand lens
Needles
Small forceps
Razor blade
White tile

A range of actinomorphic and zygomorphic flowers, with pedicels and bracts

Figure 24.13 Representation of floral structure.

A Half-flower

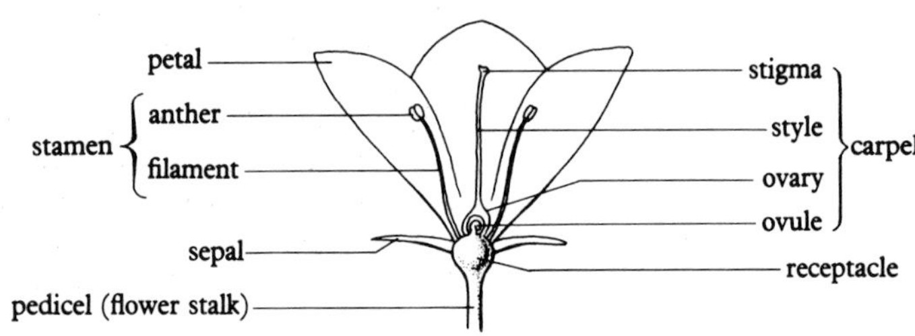

B Vertical section

C Transverse section (floral diagram)

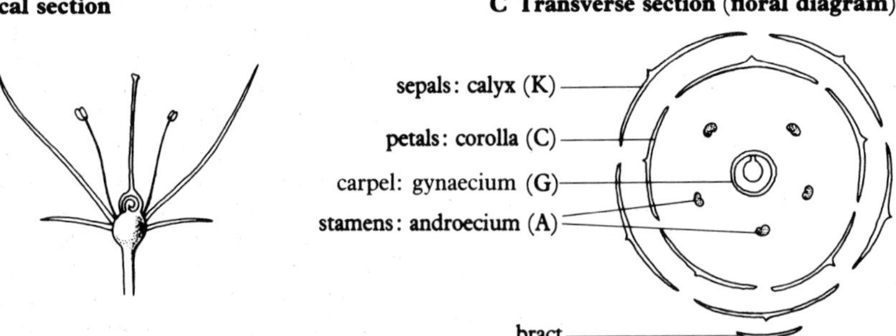

D Floral formula ⊕ K5 C5 A5 G$\underline{1}$

Investigation 24.7
Microscopic structure of stamen and carpel

In a flower the stamens and carpels contain pollen grains and egg cells respectively. The pollen-containing part of the stamen is the anther. The egg-containing part of the carpel is the ovule: the ovary contains one or more ovules, each of which contains an embryo sac with an egg cell inside. In this investigation we shall look at the microscopic structure of the anther and ovule. Both can be seen clearly in a transverse section of an unopened flower – a flower bud.

Figure 24.14 Microscopic structure of the flower of the lily.

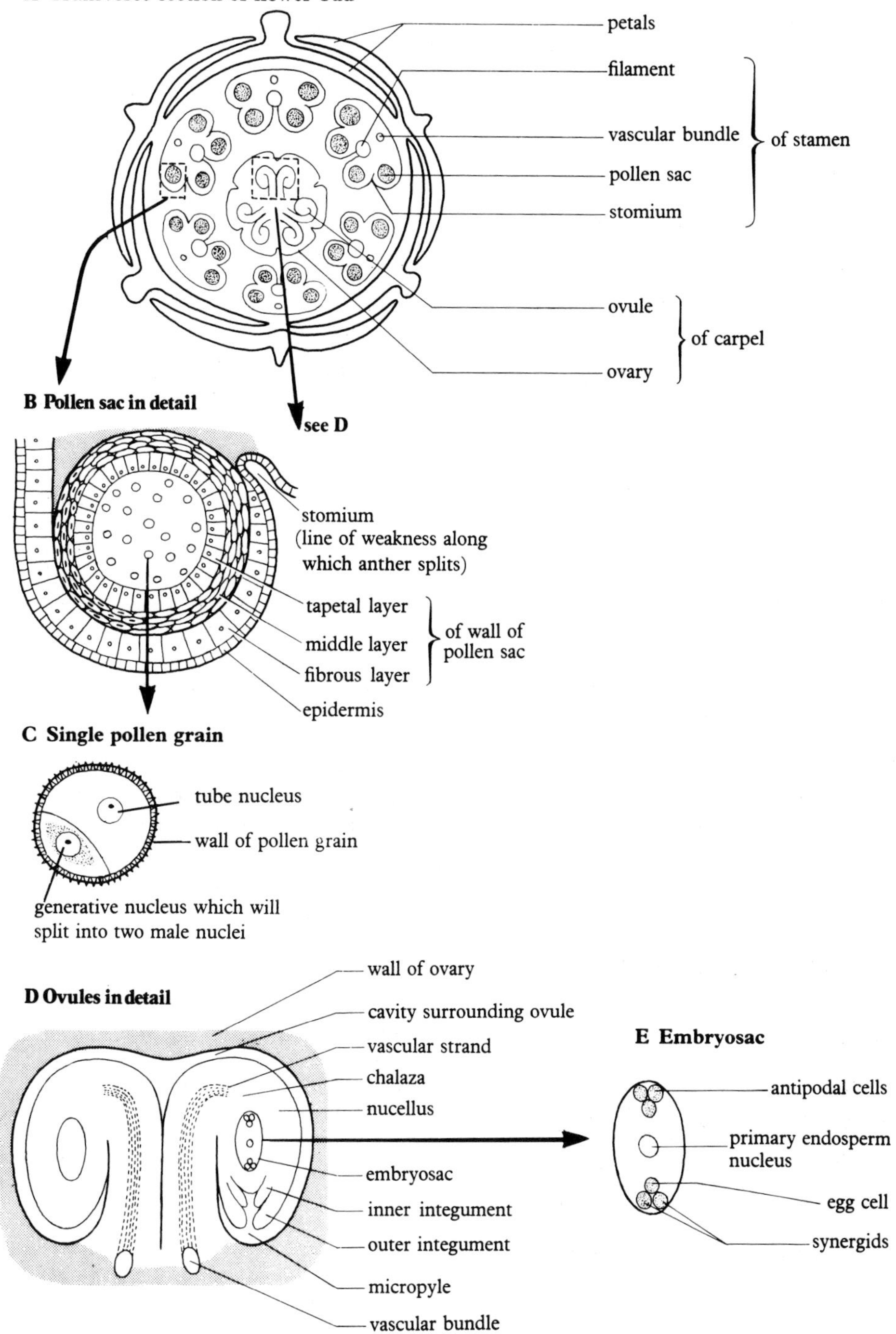

ANTHER

1 Examine a transverse section of a flower bud of lily and identify the anthers (Figure 24.14A).

2 Examine an anther under high power (Figure 24.14B). Note the four pollen sacs and examine their contents.

The contents depend on the state of maturity of the anther:

(1) If immature, the pollen sacs will be full of closely packed pollen mother cells.

(2) If more mature they will contain pairs or tetrads of cells (pollen tetrads) resulting from meiotic division of the pollen mother cells. Chromosomes may be observed, telling you at what stage of meiosis the cells have been fixed.

(3) If completely mature they will contain fully formed pollen grains. The pollen grain has a single haploid nucleus to start with, but this soon divides mitotically into a generative and tube nucleus (Figure 24.14C). The former divides again to form the two male gamete nuclei.

3 Observe the wall of the pollen sac, noting the inner tapetal layer which nourishes the developing pollen grains, and the middle and fibrous layers. Drying out of the cells of the fibrous layer creates tension which causes the anther to split open at the stomium, a line of weakness running longitudinally along each side of the anther from top to bottom.

OVARY

1 Return to low power and locate the ovary in the centre of the flower bud.

2 Examine an ovary under high power and observe the structures shown in Figure 24.14D, particularly the ovule.

3 Focus onto the contents of the embryo sac in the centre of the ovule. How many nuclei can you see in the embryosac? The answer will depend on its state of maturity and the level of the section.

The embryo sac starts by having a single haploid nucleus which is formed by meiosis from an embryo sac mother cell. The haploid nucleus of the embryo sac then undergoes successive mitotic divisions to give a total of eight nuclei, two of which (the polar nuclei) will fuse to form a central fusion nucleus. Each of the seven resulting nuclei becomes surrounded by membranes to give the cells shown in Figure 24.14E. The antipodal cells at the chalazal end of the embryo sac are thought to provide nourishment for the embryosac, the synergids at the micropyle end are nonfunctional eggs and degenerate. In the act of fertilisation the egg cell (ovum) fuses with one male

Requirements
Microscope
TS flower bud of lily

nucleus to give the zygote, and the diploid fusion nucleus fuses with the other male nucleus to form the triploid primary endosperm nucleus. The latter gives rise to the endosperm tissue which envelops and nourishes the embryo.

4 Examine the rest of the ovary noting the structures in Figure 24.14D.

For Consideration

(1) Where and when does meiosis take place in a flowering plant?
(2) Compare the gametes, and the way they develop, in the flowering plant and mammal.

Investigation 24.8
Pollination mechanisms

In the course of evolution various structural and physiological mechanisms have arisen which tend, with varying degrees of efficiency, to promote cross-pollination and prevent (or at least reduce the chances of) self-pollination.

Procedure

Examine the flowers of a wide range of species out-of-doors and in the laboratory, and find out as much as you can about their pollination mechanisms. Answer these questions for each species:
(1) Is it pollinated by wind or animals?
(2) If by animals, is it pollinated by flies, bees, butterflies, birds, or what?
(3) In what ways is the flower adapted to promote cross-pollination?
In answering this last question the following general summary may help:

FEATURES FAVOURING CROSS-POLLINATION

1. The anthers may be situated below the level of the stigma(s) so there is no possibility of pollen falling onto the stigma of the same flower, e.g. yellow toadflax *Linaria vulgaris* and many other plants.
2. The anthers may be borne on long flexible filaments favouring wide scattering of pollen grains, e.g. grasses.
3. Brightly coloured sepals, petals, perianth or bracts may attract insects. Flowers are often grouped together into a dense inflorescence which makes a bright splash of colour. Experiments on insect vision have shown that blue and yellow are the most effective colours for attracting insects.
4. Production of scent to attract insects. Some insects have a sensitive sense of smell. Scent production is particularly marked in flowers pollinated at night by moths, e.g. honey-suckle, night-scented stock, butterfly orchid.
5. Nectar as a bait. This is a sugary solution secreted by nectaries, sac-like glands at the bases of the petals. (N.B. Some bee-pollinated flowers have only pollen as bait).
6. The nectaries are often located deep down, often at the base of a corolla tube, so the insect has to probe right into the flower.
7. The petals may be so arranged as to make it easy for the insect to alight on the flower and insert its proboscis into it. For example, one or more of the petals may be adapted as a landing platform, e.g. orchids, deadnettle, snapdragon.
8. Nectar-guides, spots or markings on one or more of the petals, may direct the insect to the nectaries, e.g. orchids, yellow toadflax, wild pansy.
9. When an insect alights on the flower and inserts its proboscis the stamens are jerked in such a way that pollen is deposited on the insect's body, e.g. sage.
10. A variety of mechanisms, some involving flap-like valves, ensure that the stigma is exposed when the insect enters, but is covered when it withdraws, e.g. violet, iris, orchids.
11. The pollen may be placed on the insect's body (e.g. proboscis, head, etc.) in such a position as to ensure that it is deposited on the stigma when the insect visits another flower, e.g. orchids, deadnettle, yellow toadflax, sage.
12. A specific application of (11) is seen in heterostyly, the condition in which the styles of different flowers may differ in length, e.g. primrose, purple loosestrife.
13. The pollen grains may be sticky or sculptured, thus enabling them to cling to the body of the insect, or light and dry, enabling them to be carried by wind.
14. The stamens and carpels within a given flower may mature at different times (dichogamy). Stamens ripen before carpels in, e.g. ivy, geranium, and sage (protandrous condition). Carpels ripen before stamens in, e.g. plantain, horsechestnut, arum lily (protogynous condition).

Requirements
Binocular microscope or hand lens
Needles
Small forceps
Razor blade
White tile

A range of flowering plants illustrating different methods of pollination

15. The stamens and carpels may be located in different flowers, i.e. the flowers are unisexual. This comparatively unusual situation is found mainly amongst wind-pollinated plants.
(a) Monoecious condition: male and female flowers on same plant, e.g. hazel, beech, oak, sycamore.
(b) Dioecious condition: the male and female flowers on separate plants, e.g. holly, willow, poplar.
16. Self-sterility. In many flowering plants pollen will not develop on, and indeed may poison, a stigma of the same plant, e.g. certain orchids.
17. A variety of highly specialised mechanisms which vary according to the plant in question – e.g. arum lily. Other examples may be found in textbooks of botany.

For Consideration

(1) Consider each of the flowers that you have examined and try to decide how efficient it is at securing cross-pollination and preventing self-pollination.
(2) Although cross-pollination is genetically desirable, it is not necessary that it should happen invariably. For this reason the various mechanisms listed above are by no means fool-proof. Indeed, some plants have mechanisms which specifically encourage self-pollination. Can you suggest what these mechanisms might be?
(3) Do any animals show structural features or mechanisms comparable to those that promote cross-pollination in plants?

Investigation 24.9 Pollen and pollen germination

Requirements
Microscope
Cavity slide and coverslip
Paintbrush
Needle

Sucrose (0.4 mol dm^{-3})
Chloral hydrate
Phenol
Iodine solution
Methyl green in ethanoic acid
Acetocarmine
Neutral red

Flowers of a variety of insect- and wind-pollinated plants (with ripe stamens)
Flowers of nasturtium, deadnettle, chickweed or shepherd's purse (with ripe stamens)
LS pollinated carpel
Scanning electron micrographs of pollen grains

Pollen grains are conveyed from one flower to another, adhere to a stigma and send out pollen tubes which grow towards the egg cell. In this instance we shall look at the structure of pollen grains, and look into one of the factors that may influence the growth and development of the pollen tube.

Structure of Pollen Grains

1 Collect pollen grains from the anthers of the plants provided. Mount them in water and examine under high power. Can you deduce from the structure of the pollen grains whether the plant is insect or wind-pollinated? Are your deductions supported by the structure of the flower from which the pollen grains were obtained?
2 The external structure of pollen grains can be seen in much more detail with the scanning electron microscope. Look at scanning electron micrographs of pollen grains of different species of flowering plant. What do you infer from your observations?
3 Clear some pollen grains in a drop of chloral hydrate or phenol and mount in iodine solution or methyl green in ethanoic acid. Examine under high power noting two-layered wall and two nuclei. What functions are fulfilled by the nuclei?

Germination of Pollen

1 With a paint-brush transfer a few pollen grains of, e.g. nasturtium, deadnettle, chickweed or shepherd's purse, into a drop of sucrose solution (0.4 mol dm^{-3}) in the central depression of a cavity slide. Put on a coverslip.
2 Place your slide in a dark place at 20°–30 °C and examine at intervals for one-to-two hours. Observe pollen tubes.
3 Stain by irrigating your slide with a drop of acetocarmine or neutral red. Look for tube nucleus and two male nuclei. What is the fate of the two male nuclei in normal circumstances?
4 Examine prepared longitudinal sections of carpels which have been pollinated. Make sketches to illustrate the growth of the pollen tube into the stigma and down the style to the ovary.

For Consideration

(1) How could your experiment on pollen germination be extended to investigate the effect of temperature on pollen germination?
(2) It is said that when a pollen grain lands on a suitable stigma, the latter produces a sugary secretion, varying in concentration from about 2 to 4 per cent, which holds the pollen grains and facilitates their germination. How would you test the claim that the sugary secretion facilitates pollen germination? How would you find out the optimum concentration of the solution?
(3) What events in a mammal are equivalent to these events in a flowering plant
(a) the deposition of pollen grains on the stigma?
(b) the growth of the pollen tube?

Investigation 24.10
Structure and dispersal of fruits and seeds

A fruit in the strict sense of the word is formed from the ovary. Generally after fertilisation the ovary expands, enclosing and protecting the seed(s) which are formed from the ovules. The wall of the fruit, known as the pericarp, is derived from the wall of the ovary. As well as protecting the seeds, the fruit is adapted in various ways to promote dispersal.

In practice a number of other floral structures besides the ovary may contribute to the formation and dispersal of the fruits. These include the style, receptacle, sepals, and bracts.

Procedure

Look at Figure 24.15. This shows diagrammatically the various parts of the flower which may contribute to the formation and dispersal of the fruits. Bear this diagram in mind as you examine various fruits.

1 Examine a fruit of buttercup or one of its close relatives (*Ranunculus* species). Notice that the fruit is really nothing more than an expanded carpel containing a single seed (Figure 24.16A). Such fruits are called achenes. How do you think they are dispersed?

2 Examine a fruit of wood avens (*Geum urbanum*). This is an achene too, but in this case the style becomes woody and its tip is hooked for clinging to the fur of animals etc. Test its ability to cling to your clothes.

3 Examine a cleaver (*Galium aparine*). In this case the pericarp of the fruit bears hooked hairs for attachment to animal fur. Look carefully at the hairy pericarp and test its ability to cling to your clothes.

4 Imagine a capitulum (*see* page 233) in which the compact inflorescence is surrounded by a ring of overlapping bracts. After fertilisation, the bracts become woody and each develops a hooked tip. The result is a bur which is very efficient at clinging to the fur of animals.

Examine a bur of burdock and test its ability to cling to your clothes. Cut it vertically and observe the single-seeded fruits each of which is crowned with a tuft of hairs developed from the sepals.

5 Cut open a plum or cherry and examine its contents. This fleshy, succulent fruit develops from a single carpel containing a single seed (Figure 24.16B).

Pericarp three-layered: outer epicarp ('skin') is protective (against what?), middle mesocarp is fleshy and tasty, inner endocarp ('stone') protects the seed (against what?) How are these seeds dispersed?

6 Examine a raspberry, loganberry or blackberry. The fruit consists of a group of small drupes (an aggregate of drupelets) on the receptacle. Remove the drupes and note the receptacle: anything interesting about it? Examine an individual drupe in detail and note that it contains a single seed.

7 Cut a tomato in half vertically, and another one horizontally. This kind of fruit (technically called a berry) consists of several multi-seeded carpels fused together. The mesocarp and endocarp are soft, fleshy and juicy, the epicarp forming an outer covering of variable thickness (Figure 24.16C).

The seeds have hard protective seed coats. How many carpels does the fruit consist of? How can you tell? Can you think of other examples of this kind of fruit? How do they differ, and how are the seeds dispersed?

8 Examine the external features of a strawberry. In this case the fleshy, edible part of the fruit is formed from a swollen receptacle. This is called a false fleshy fruit (Figure 24.16D): the receptacle bears on its surface numerous small dry fruits (achenes) each of which contains a single seed.

Cut the strawberry vertically and note the relationship between the achenes and the receptacle.

9 The apple is another example of a false fleshy fruit (Figure 24.16E). The pericarp of the true fruit is the 'core', which contains the seeds ('pips'). Since the ovary of the flower is inferior, the fruit comes to be enveloped by the swollen receptacle. Pear is similar. Such fruits are known as pomes.

Cut an apple (or pear) vertically and horizontally through the centre. How

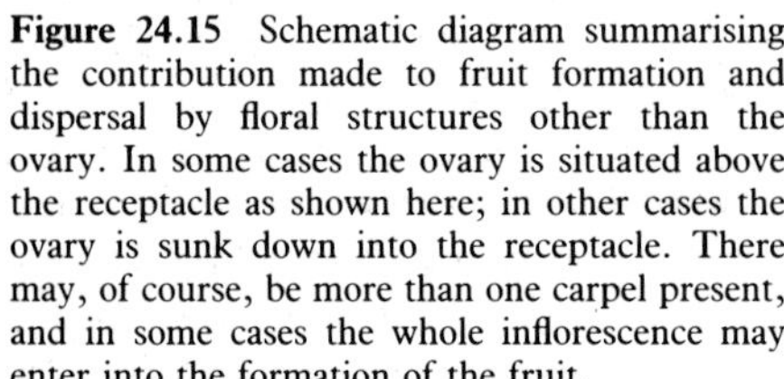

Figure 24.15 Schematic diagram summarising the contribution made to fruit formation and dispersal by floral structures other than the ovary. In some cases the ovary is situated above the receptacle as shown here; in other cases the ovary is sunk down into the receptacle. There may, of course, be more than one carpel present, and in some cases the whole inflorescence may enter into the formation of the fruit.

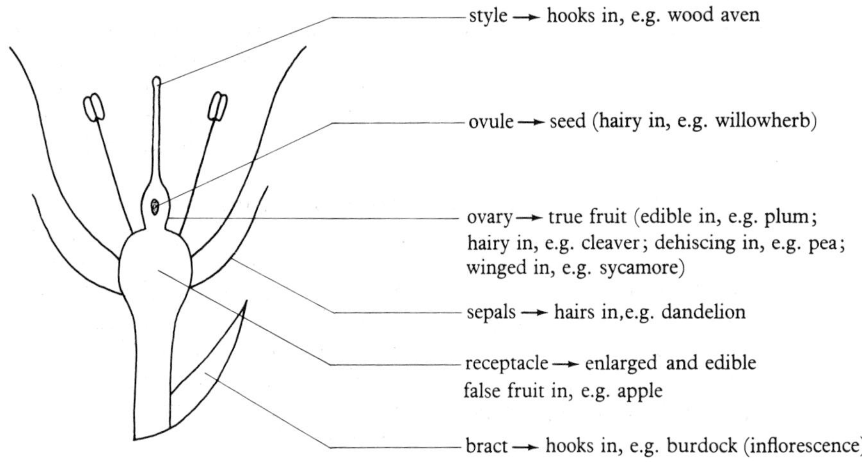

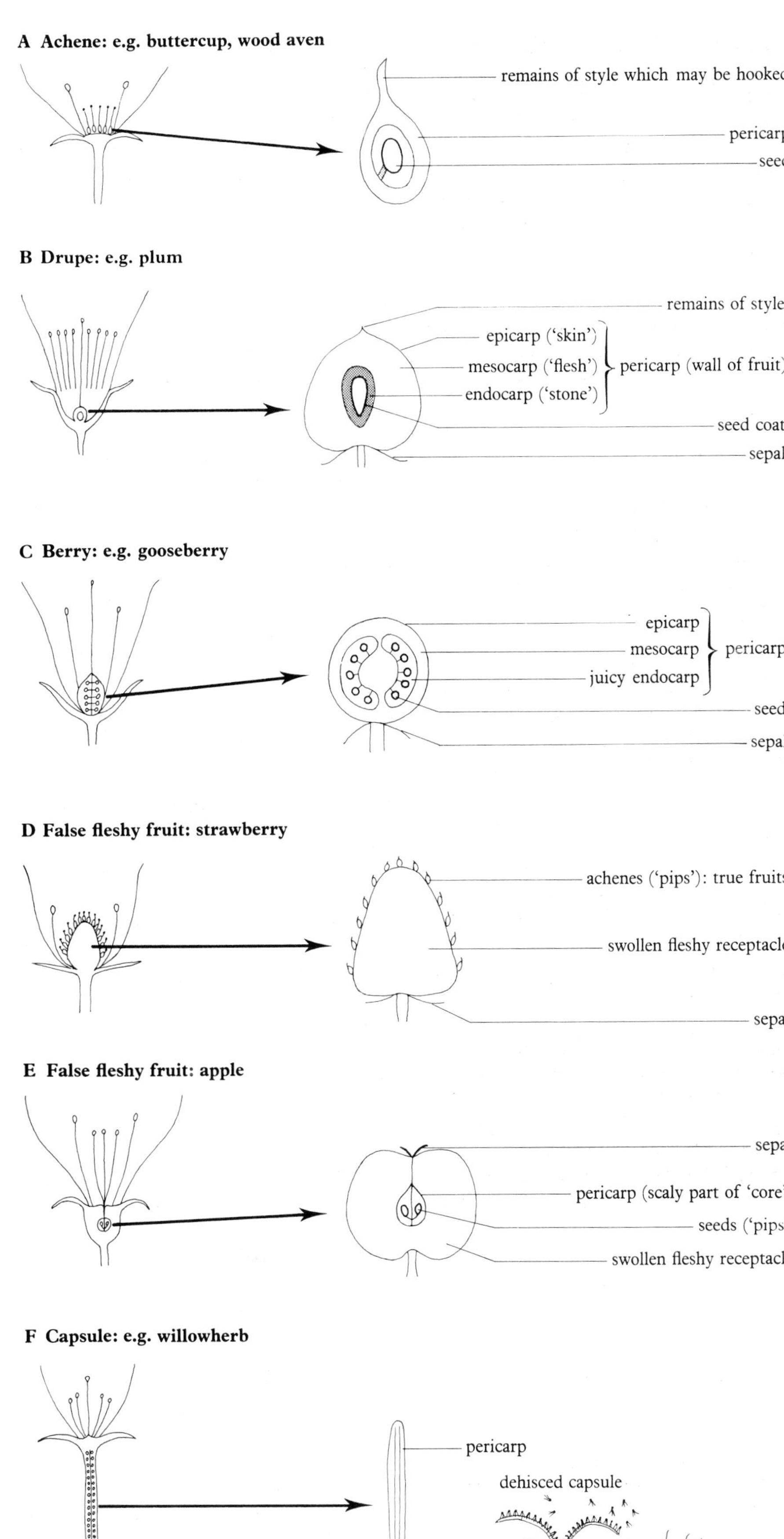

Figure 24.16 Diagrams of a selection of fruits showing how, in all cases, the fruit is formed from the ovary and the seeds from the ovules.

many carpels are there? How many seeds in each carpel?

10 Examine a pod of pea or bean. The pod is a fruit formed from a single carpel whose 'leathery' pericarp splits (dehisces) along one or both sides. Examine representative pods and follicles before and after dehiscence.

11 Examine the fruit of rosebay willowherb. This type of fruit is called a capsule. It is formed from several carpels joined together (Figure 24.16F). Slice the capsule longitudinally. Can you see seeds inside? Cut another capsule transversely. How many carpels does it consist of?

12 Investigate the mechanism by which the seeds of rosebay willowherb are released. Place the unopened capsules on a hotplate and observe the dispersal mechanism in action. What happens if you breathe on the open capsule, or place it in a drop of water? Explain.

13 Remove one of the seeds of rosebay willowherb from the dehisced capsule and examine it under a binocular microscope or hand lens. Note that the seed is hairy. Test the ability of the seed to float through the air. This illustrates the fact that it isn't only fruits that are adapted for dispersal; sometimes the seeds are too.

14 Examine the fruit of a sycamore tree. The wall of the carpel is expanded to form two (or in some species three) wings. Note the twirling parachute effect when thrown into the air. How many wings must the released fruit have for effective dispersal? Explain.

15 Some fruits are very small and light, and have hairs which serve as a parachute. Release some of the hairy fruits of groundsel or dandelion and note how long they take to reach the ground. What is the effect of a slight gust of air?

16 Examine the hairy fruits of groundsel and dandelion under a binocular microscope. In both cases the hairs are derived from the sepals of the original flower. How would you explain the fact that in the dandelion the 'pappus' of hairs is borne on the end of a long stalk. What is the functional significance of this?

17 Many fruits may be spread incidentally by water. However, relatively few are specifically adapted for water dispersal. An exception is the coconut. Examine a half-coconut. It is a drupe but the mesocarp, instead of being fleshy, is fibrous and contains air spaces to aid floating.

Requirements
Binocular microscope or hand lens
Hotplate
Needles
Small forceps
Razor blade
White tile

Fruits: buttercup; wood avens; cleaver; burdock; plum or cherry; raspberry, loganberry or blackberry; tomatoes ×2; strawberry; apples ×2; pea or bean (before and after dehiscence); rosebay willowherb; sycamore; groundsel; dandelion; coconut (half).

For consideration

(1) Classify the fruits which you have examined into the following categories:
(a) Fruits dispersed by clinging to animals.
(b) Fruits dispersed by being eaten by animals.
(c) Fruits dispersed by splitting open.
(d) Fruits dispersed by wind.
(e) Fruits dispersed by water.
Do you think this is a useful way of classifying fruits? Can you think of a better way?

(2) Can you think of any types of fruit, or methods of dispersal, *not* mentioned in this investigation?

(3) Dispersal is not only important to plants, it is important to animals too. How is dispersal achieved in animals generally and to what extent can animal mechanisms be compared with those of plants?

Investigation 24.11
The value of the pappus in the dispersal of fruits of dandelion

Many members of the family Compositae, to which the dandelion and thistles belong, have their calyx in the form of a group of hairs called a pappus. These hairy tufts persist on the ovaries until the ovaries become fruits and are dispersed. They then serve as parachutes, aiding dispersal by wind. Do the pappuses really increase the distance to which the fruits are carried? We shall study the dandelion *Taraxacum* spp.

Requirements
Stand, boss and clamp
Large sheets of plain paper or card
Pencils
Ruler
Cardboard screen
Safety razor blade

Fruits with pappi of dandelion, thistle or other Composite. Dry fruits can be stored in polythene bags until required.

Procedure

1 Place a clamp stand on a large sheet of paper or card on the laboratory bench. Fix a clamp to the top of the stand. Arrange it so that the tip of the clamp is directly above the centre of the sheet of paper, and the base of the clamp stand faces away from the centre. Mark with a cross on the paper the position of the centre.

2 Close all windows, and if necessary erect a cardboard screen around your experiment, so that the air is as still as possible.

3 Select twenty dandelion fruits with undamaged pappuses. Holding them with the pappus at the top, drop them in turn from the tip of the clamp stand onto the paper. Mark with a pencil the position at which each fruit lands.

4 To simulate the effects of wind on fruit dispersal, create a draught. Open a window, take the experiment outside, or blow air from a hair dryer or a blow heater onto the clamp stand. You may need to extend your sheets of paper in a 'downwind' direction.

5 Drop the same twenty fruits as before, and record on the paper in a different colour the positions where the fruits first land. Make sure that you collect up each fruit afterwards (sometimes difficult!).

6 Record the air speed with an anemometer (*see* Appendix 4).

7 Using a razor blade, cut the pappus from each of the twenty fruits. Repeat both the previous experiments in exactly the same way as before, the windy treatment first. Use different colours or symbols to record the landing positions of the de-pappused fruits.

8 Measure and record the distance in mm of each landing position from the central marked point.

9 Using a t-test or a Mann-Whitney U-test (*see* Appendix 6), find out if the pappus significantly increases the distance to which fruits are carried (a) under still conditions or (b) in faster air speeds.

For consideration

(1) In what ways is wide seed dispersal likely to be valuable to dandelions?

(2) Under what environmental conditions do you think that dandelion fruits are usually released?

(3) The dandelion plant expends much energy in producing pappuses on its fruits. It also invests energy in producing a tall fruiting stalk (peduncle or scape) on which the fruits are exposed to the faster air away from the ground. Do you think this investment of energy is worthwhile? Explain your answer.

(4) If pappuses are valuable in fruit dispersal, why have they not evolved in forest trees to disperse their fruits.?

Investigation 24.12
Vegetative reproduction in plants

A Swollen taproot

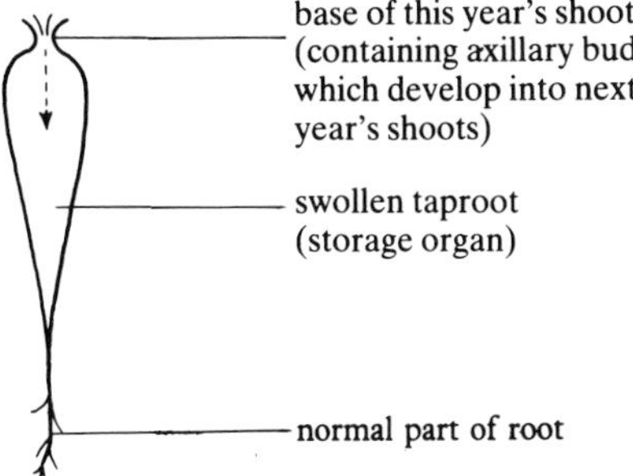

B Root tubers

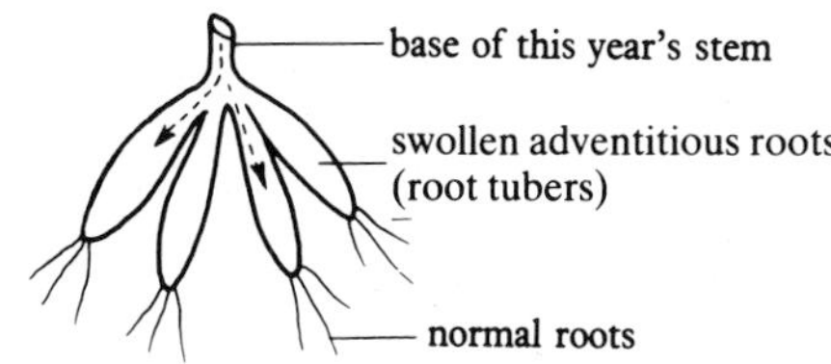

Figure 24.17 Two types of perennating organs formed from roots. Broken arrows indicate movement of food materials from the foliage leaves of this year's plant into the perennating organ.

Figure 24.18 Two types of perennating organs formed from stems. Solid arrows indicate movement of food materials from perennating organ to new plant or new perennating organ. Broken arrows indicate movement of food materials from the foliage leaves of this year's plant into the perennating organ.

Many herbaceous plants survive the winter by means of a perennating organ which lies dormant in the soil over the winter and develops into one or more new plants the following year. The perennating organ may be a modified stem, root, leaves or bud, depending on the plant in question. But whatever structure the perennating organ develops from, the fundamental cycle of events is the same: food materials are translocated from the leaves of the plant to the developing organ, and the following year these food reserves are mobilised and moved to the growing regions of the new plant.

Perennation is often associated with asexual reproduction (vegetative propagation). Perennation and vegetative reproduction take place by different means depending on which plant is under consideration. In this investigation we shall look at some of the main methods.

1 SWOLLEN TAPROOT

As the name implies, the perennating organ is formed from the taproot, i.e. the main root (Figure 24.17A). The taproot expands and fills up with food. The above-ground parts of the plant die except for the axillary buds at the base of the stem from which new shoots develop the following year.

Examine a swollen taproot of e.g. radish or carrot. How could you ascertain that this is a modified root and not some other part of the plant? Carry out tests to find out in what chemical form the food is stored (*see* page 42).

2 ROOT TUBERS

Storage organs may be formed not from a taproot but from adventitious roots. They are called root tubers (Figure 24.17B). The latter expand, store food and survive the winter, new plants being formed from axillary buds the following year. Examine root tubers of e.g. dahlia, lesser celandine, and test them for their reserves.

3 STEM TUBERS

A stem tuber is a swollen underground stem which stores food, survives the winter, and gives rise to new plants from axillary buds the following year (Figure 24.18A).

Examine a potato plant showing new tubers and (if possible) the remains of the old tuber. Now look at a single tuber. Being a modified stem, it possesses axillary buds and leaves in the usual way. These are the so-called 'eyes' of the potato. The 'pupil' represents the axillary bud and the 'eyebrow' the tiny scale leaf. New plants sprout from the axillary buds. What is the food reserve in the potato tuber?

4 RHIZOME

A rhizome is a horizontally growing underground stem which continues to live for many years (Figure 24.18B). Each year the terminal bud at the end of the stem turns up and produces leaves and flowers above the ground, whilst contractile adventitious roots are formed below ground. The lateral bud closest to the terminal bud continues the growth of the rhizome, food materials for this being supplied by the aerial shoot. Other lateral buds may produce new rhizomes which branch off the parent stem. In some species the rhizome is short, thick, and slowly growing (like the one in Figure 24.18B), whilst in others it is long, thin and quickly-growing.

Examples: iris, water lily, Solomon's seal (short, thick type); fern, Michaelmas daisy, couchgrass, marram grass, mint, ground elder, thistle, bracken (long, thin type).

Examine representative rhizomes of the short-thick and/or long-thin type. Test for food reserves. Cut transverse sections and stain in acidified phloroglucinol or FABIL. Conclusions?

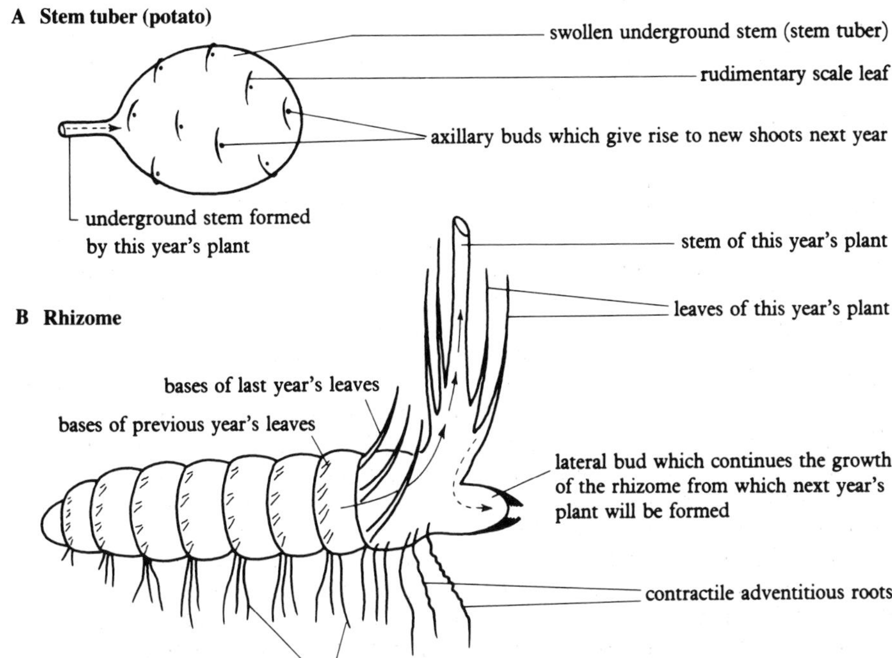

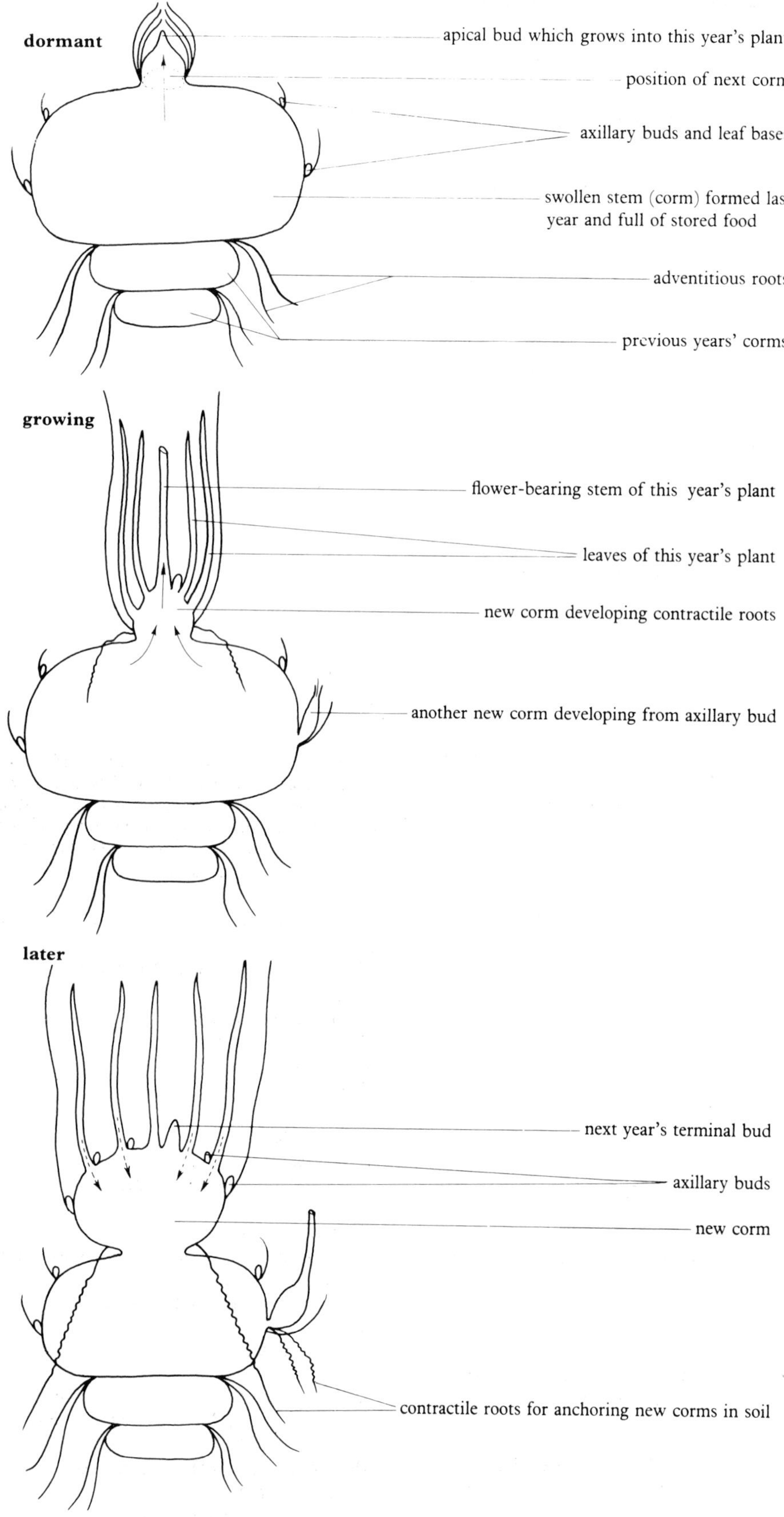

Figure 24.19 Diagrams of a corm. Solid arrows indicate movement of food materials from perennating organ to new plant or new perennating organ. Broken arrows indicate movement of food materials from the foliage leaves of this year's plant into the perennating organ.

5 CORM

A corm is a short, swollen, vertically growing underground stem (Figure 24.19). It stores food and survives the winter, giving rise to new plants and corms the following year. The terminal bud gives rise to the new plant, axillary buds developing into either new plants or new corms. Contractile adventitious roots keep the corm anchored to the soil.

Examine a corm of e.g. crocus. Cut it in half vertically. Note the solid stem with a central vascular strand. Stain with acidified phloroglucinol. If available, examine corms at various stages of development.

6 BULB

A bulb consists of a short vertical stem bearing adventitious roots, thick fleshy leaves (or leaf bases), and a variable number of axillary buds (Figure 24.20). In the centre is the terminal bud which develops into a new plant after the winter is over. The axillary buds develop into new bulbs.

Examine a bulb of e.g. onion or daffodil. Cut it in half vertically from below upwards. Identify the features noted above, particularly the terminal bud and the thick fleshy leaves. Is each fleshy structure a complete leaf or just the leaf base? How do the outermost leaves differ from those further in and what do they represent? Test a leaf for food reserves. If available examine bulbs at different stages of development.

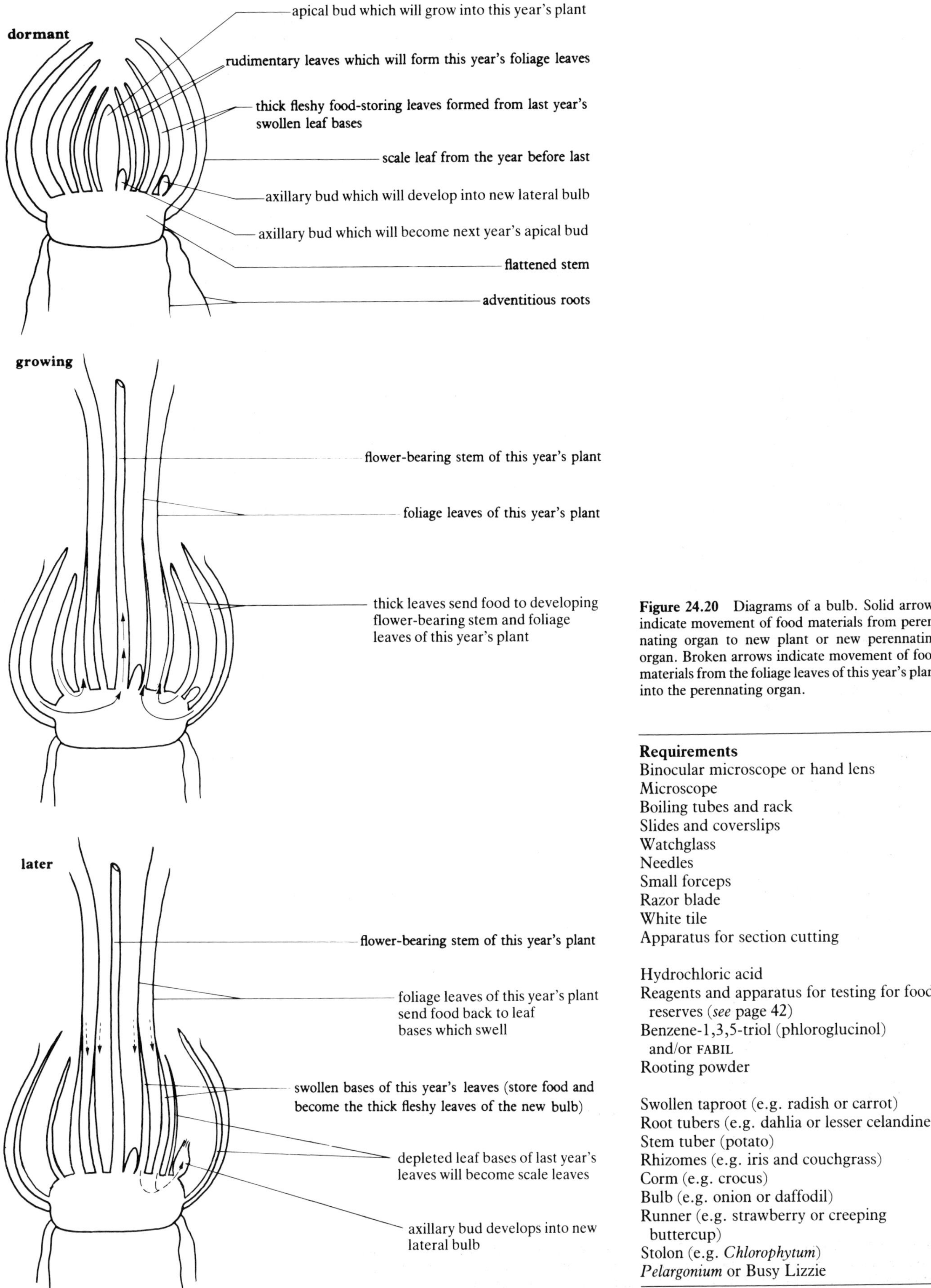

Figure 24.20 Diagrams of a bulb. Solid arrows indicate movement of food materials from perennating organ to new plant or new perennating organ. Broken arrows indicate movement of food materials from the foliage leaves of this year's plant into the perennating organ.

Requirements

Binocular microscope or hand lens
Microscope
Boiling tubes and rack
Slides and coverslips
Watchglass
Needles
Small forceps
Razor blade
White tile
Apparatus for section cutting

Hydrochloric acid
Reagents and apparatus for testing for food reserves (*see* page 42)
Benzene-1,3,5-triol (phloroglucinol) and/or FABIL
Rooting powder

Swollen taproot (e.g. radish or carrot)
Root tubers (e.g. dahlia or lesser celandine)
Stem tuber (potato)
Rhizomes (e.g. iris and couchgrass)
Corm (e.g. crocus)
Bulb (e.g. onion or daffodil)
Runner (e.g. strawberry or creeping buttercup)
Stolon (e.g. *Chlorophytum*)
Pelargonium or Busy Lizzie

7 RUNNER

Vegetative reproduction does not necessarily involve the formation of a perennating organ. Some plants reproduce vegetatively by sending out side-branches which develop into new plants. Such is the case with runners Figure 24.21A. A runner is a horizontally growing, above-ground stem which grows from one of the lower axillary buds on the main stem. At regular intervals along the length of the runner are small axillary buds which give rise to new plants. Once the new plants are self-supporting the internodal sections of the runner have no further function.

Examine a strawberry plant or creeping buttercup with one or more runners and note the above features.

8 STOLON

Some stems grow so long that their mass causes them to bend over. Where a node touches the soil the axillary bud at that node develops into a new plant (Figure 24.21B).

Examine a spider plant (*Chlorophytum*) with stolons. Gardeners often encourage plants to reproduce vegetatively by fixing the stolon to the soil with a staple, a procedure called layering. This can be done with e.g. blackcurrant and gooseberry bushes.

9 CUTTINGS

Though not a natural method of vegetative reproduction, this is widely used by gardeners. A stem is cut and pushed into the soil or some other suitable medium. Adventitious roots grow out from the submerged part of the stem, particularly if the cut end is treated with a growth substance (*see* page 275).

Try taking cuttings of e.g. geranium or Busy Lizzie: Cut off the end of a branch just below a node. Place the cut end in a boiling tube of water so that you can watch the adventitious roots developing. Take several cuttings; dip the cut ends of some of them in 'rooting powder', leave the others untreated and compare the speed with which they develop adventitious roots.

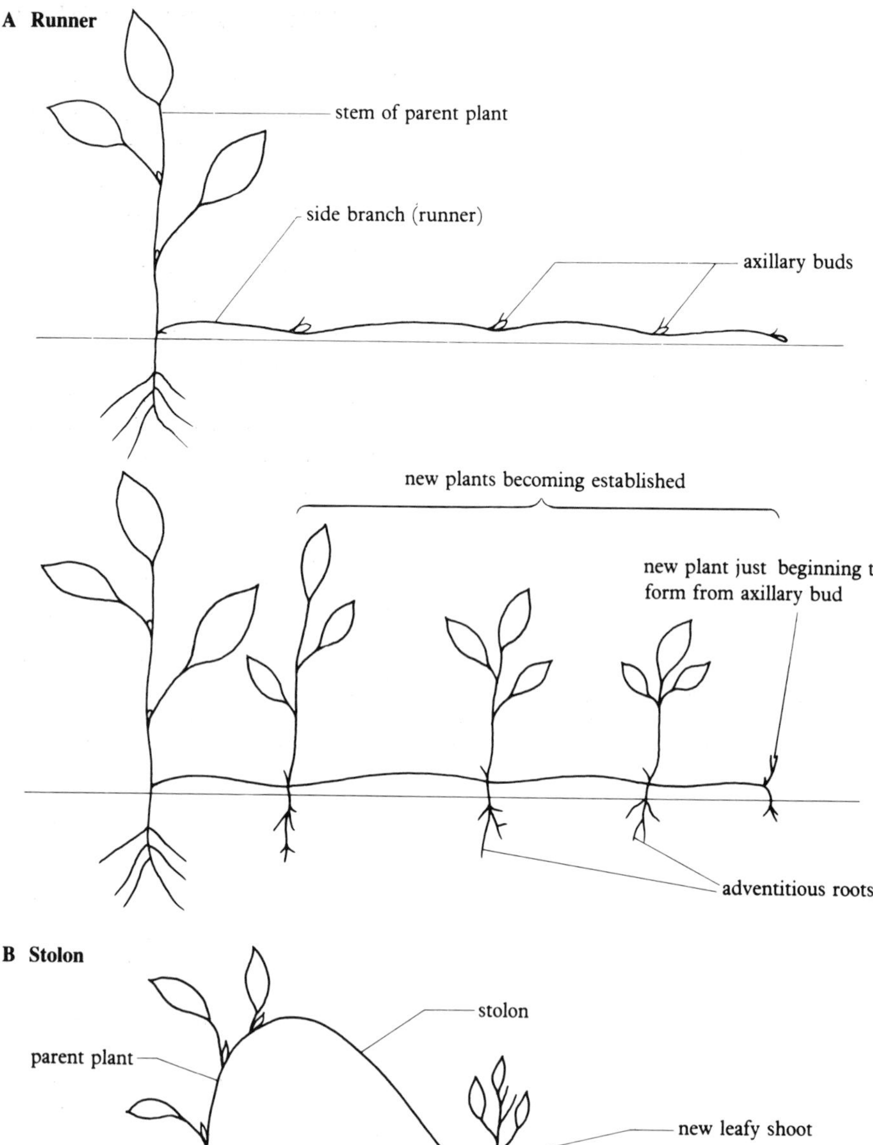

Figure 24.21 Vegetation reproduction by means of runner and stolon.

For consideration

(1) Which structure or structures mentioned in this investigation involve:
(a) perennation *and* reproduction,
(b) perennation *without* reproduction,
(c) reproduction *without* perennation,
(d) perennation by means of a swollen stem,
(e) perennation by means of swollen leaves?

(2) The products of asexual propagation of an individual constitute a clone. Why is it useful for a market gardener to be able to produce a clone of strawberries? What problems might be encountered in doing this?

(3) Do animals show any processes that can be considered as equivalent to vegetative reproduction in plants?

Questions and Problems

1 Spermatozoa have been kept in a deep-frozen state for as much as ten years without losing their viability. Eggs, however, will only survive such treatment for a few hours at the most. Speculate on this difference.

2 What do you anticipate would be the effect on the reproductive future of a human female if, during the prepubertal period, the following took place:
(a) a course of FSH (follicle-stimulating hormone) was administered;
(b) one ovary was surgically removed;
(c) both ovaries were surgically removed;
(d) both fallopian tubes (oviducts) were ligatured?
Give reasons for your prognostications. *(O and C)*

3 The graph in Figure 24.22 shows how the body temperature of a human female changes in the course of the menstrual cycle.
(a) Comment on the shape of the graph.
(b) What use can be made of this graph in advising people on how to avoid conception?

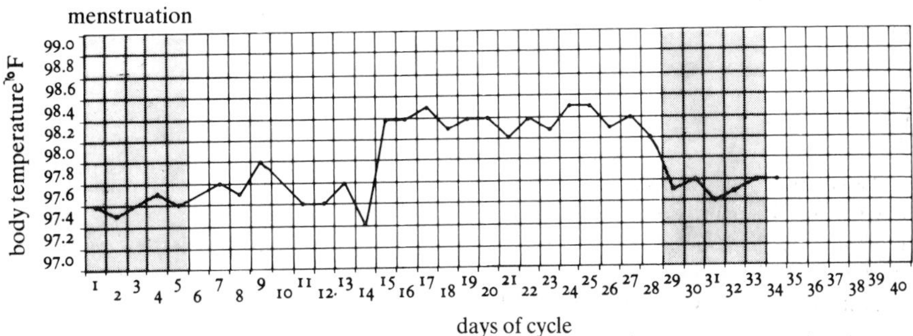

Figure 24.22 Graph showing fluctuations in the basal body temperature of a human female in the course of the oestrous cycle. *(After R.J. Demarest and J.J. Sciarra)*

(c) Copy the graph (or stick a photocopy of it) onto a sheet of paper. Beneath it, on the same horizontal scale, draw in curves showing the relative concentrations of (i) the gonadotrophic hormones FSH (follicle stimulating hormone) and LH (luteinising hormone), and (ii) the gonadial hormones oestrogen and progesterone.
(d) State where the above hormones are produced and the effects which follow when their concentrations (i) increase, and (ii) decrease.
(e) What happens to the concentration of progesterone if a fertilised egg becomes implanted in the uterine wall, and what are the consequences? What is the relevance of this to the contraceptive pill?

4 In each of the months January, March, July and October, five adult male specimens of a particular species of mammal were collected in the wild. Their bodies were weighed and after dissection, paired testis and paired epididymis masses were also obtained. The data were as follows:

January			March			July			October		
B (kg)	T (g)	E (g)	B (kg)	T (g)	E (g)	B (kg)	T (g)	E (g)	B (kg)	T (g)	E (g)
5.2	12.4	2.4	6.5	4.7	1.5	6.8	2.6	0.8	5.4	4.7	1.4
6.4	13.8	2.5	5.7	6.0	1.8	6.3	1.8	1.1	6.6	4.3	1.3
6.9	16.6	3.6	6.8	5.0	1.3	6.3	2.5	0.8	7.4	3.9	1.0
7.5	12.0	2.9	7.5	5.6	1.9	5.2	1.6	0.3	6.3	6.6	1.5
8.0	10.7	2.6	8.5	5.7	1.5	8.4	2.5	1.0	6.8	9.5	1.8

B = Body mass T = Paired testis mass E = Paired epididymis mass
(a) Present these data in graphical form in order to show variation in the mass of the testis in the months concerned.
(b) On graph paper plot testis mass against epididymis mass.
(c) Discuss the possible reproductive pattern of the species concerned.
(d) What additional evidence, if any, would you need to confirm your ideas on this pattern? *(O and C)*

5 In rabbits it has been found that ovulation occurs only after copulation has taken place. It has been shown that it is the act of copulation which is the stimulating factor rather than any chemical stimulus from semen or spermatozoa. Describe what must be the experimental evidence for this last statement.

Partial pressure of oxygen ($kN\ m^{-2}$)	**Percentage saturation of blood with oxygen**	
	Mother	Foetus
1.3	8	10
2.7	20	30
3.9	40	60
5.3	65	77
6.6	77	85
8.0	84	90
9.3	90	92
10.6	92	92

6 The data given in the margin show the difference between the blood of a pregnant woman and that of the foetus developing in her uterus. Plot the data on a graph and comment on the differences between the two curves.

7 Your biological interests have led you to a position where it is essential to establish the reproductive pattern of a particular species of mammal which is well represented and successful in the wild. You have been supplied with sufficient, healthy, sexually mature individuals of both sexes for normal breeding, but despite your having arranged optimum conditions for their captive existence, they have failed to breed. This failure is not because you have kept them for insufficient time. Assuming that you have adequate facilities and funds, how would you now proceed in your aim to discover the normal reproductive activity of this species? *(O and C)*

8 Comment on the following statements:
(a) Bacteria show sex in its simplest and most rudimentary form.
(b) The greater the degree of parental care, the fewer the offspring produced.
(c) Asexual reproduction is commonest amongst animals that also show marked powers of regeneration.
(d) In animals the sexes are usually in separate individuals whereas in plants they are usually on the same individual.
(e) Some mammals have young which are born at a more advanced stage than others.

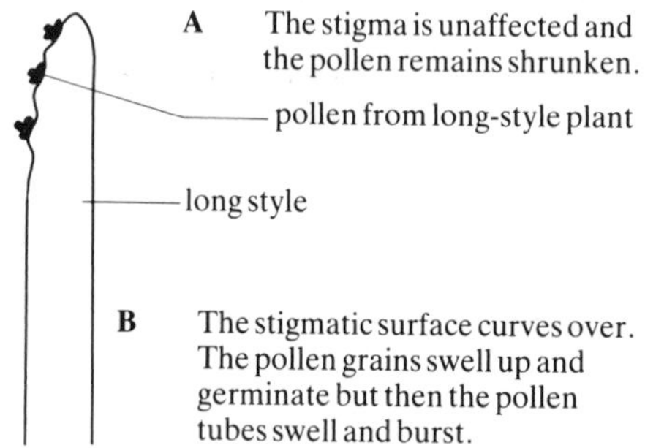
A
The stigma is unaffected and the pollen remains shrunken.
pollen from long-style plant
long style
B
The stigmatic surface curves over. The pollen grains swell up and germinate but then the pollen tubes swell and burst.

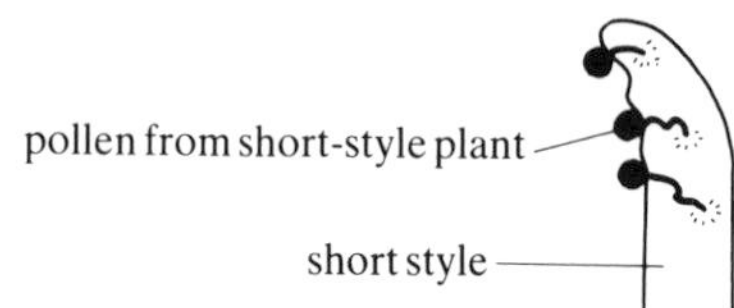
pollen from short-style plant
short style

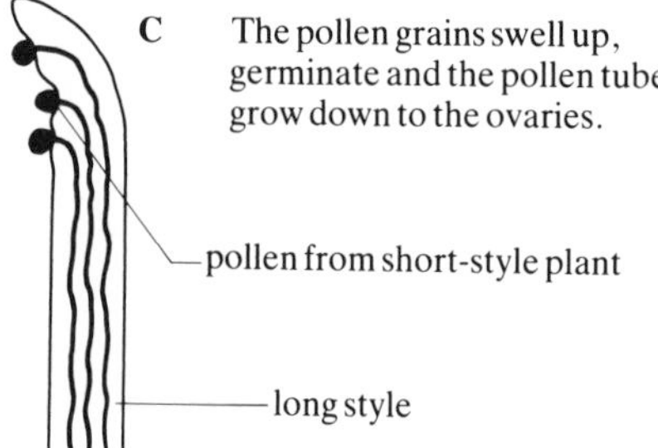
C
The pollen grains swell up, germinate and the pollen tubes grow down to the ovaries.
pollen from short-style plant
long style

Figure 24.23 Events following three different pollinations in *Linum grandiflorum*.

9 *Linum grandiflorum* (a species of flax) is an example of a plant which has two types of flower, distinguishable by length of style. Due to physiological mechanisms successful fertilisation is only possible between flowers with long styles and flowers with short styles.

Events which follow three different pollinations are shown as A, B and C in Figure 24.23.

It has been found that the solute concentration of the pollen contents and the solute concentration of the cells of the stigma and style are in the following ratios:

	pollen	:	stigma and style
pollination A	5	:	4
pollination B	7	:	1
pollination C	4	:	1

(a) Explain the mechanism which is causing the stigmatic surface to curve in B and C.
(b) Explain how fertilisation is being prevented in pollination A.
(c) Explain how fertilisation is being prevented in pollination B.
(d) Copy the diagram of pollination C onto your answer page and beside it make a fully labelled diagram to show the effect of pollen from a long-style plant being deposited on the stigmatic surface of a short-style plant, given that the concentration ratio is 4:1 as in C.
(e) Describe the role of the pollen tube in a typical flowering plant. *(AEB)*

10 What do you consider to have been the major evolutionary trends in the animal kingdom as far as reproduction is concerned? Illustrate your answer with examples. Are the same trends also seen in the plant kingdom?

11 'The evolution of flowering plants has been closely bound up with the evolution of insects.' Discuss.

12 'By means of various adaptions, living organisms have been able to exploit terrestrial environments.' Discuss this statement with reference to adaptation for reproduction. *(O and C)*

13 What are the advantages of asexual reproduction compared with sexual? What commercial use do humans make of asexual reproduction?

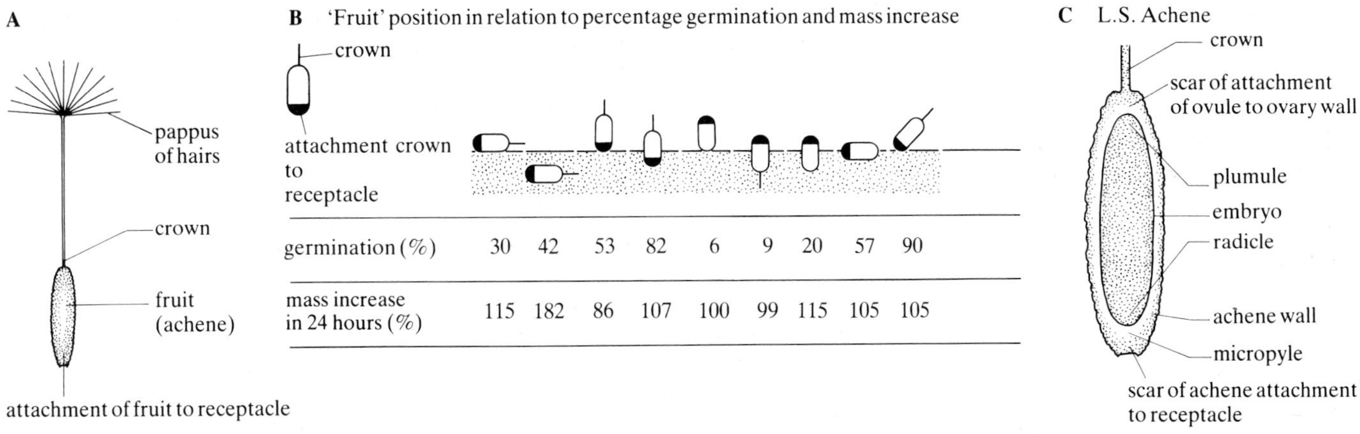

Figure 24.24 Fruit of the dandelion *Taraxacum officinale*. **A** External structure of the fruit and associated structures. **B** Percentage germination and increase in mass in relation to the positions of the fruits. **C** Longitudinal section of the fruit (*achene*). (*Data after J.C. Sheldon*)

14 The fruits of dandelion (*Taraxacum officinale*) are usually released with the parachute (a pappus of hairs) attached (Figure 24.24A). These fruits may be blown a long way by the wind.

The pappi were removed and the fruits were sown in soil of constant water content in different positions. The percentage germination and increase in mass were then measured. The results are shown in Figure 24.24B.

Experiments in which the fruits were immersed in methylene blue for 4, 16 and 24 hours and then sectioned showed that water did not enter the fruit through the thick achene wall. It entered mainly through the scar where the fruit was attached to the receptacle (Figure 24.24C).

(a) Under natural conditions, with the pappus attached, in which positions is the fruit most likely to fall, and why?

(b) Discuss these results.

(c) Construct an hypothesis to explain them.

25 The Life Cycle

Background Summary

1 In all organisms with sexual reproduction **meiosis** (halving of the chromosome number) and **syngamy** (union of gametes) divide the life cycle into **haploid** and **diploid** phases.

2 In all animals and in most lower plants, the haploid phase is represented only by the gametes. However, in mosses, ferns and many other plants, the life cycle shows an alternation between a haploid gamete-producing **gametophyte** and a diploid **sporophyte**, which produces haploid **spores**. This is called **alternation of generations**.

3 In mosses the gametophyte is the more prominent generation, the sporophyte being attached to, and dependent upon, the gametophyte. For successful reproduction the gametophyte requires wet conditions, the sporophyte, dry.

4 In ferns the sporophyte is the more prominent generation, the gametophyte being variously reduced. As in mosses, wet conditions are essential for reproduction of the gametophyte and dry conditions for the sporophyte.

5 In certain ferns the sporophyte produces two kinds of spores (**heterospory**): **microspores** give rise to male sperm-producing gametophytes, whilst large **megaspores** give rise to female egg-producing gametophytes.

6 In some primitive plants, e.g. certain green algae, there is no sporophyte: the diploid zygote undergoes meiosis, giving rise to a haploid adult which produces gametes. In some cases motile haploid **zoospores** may be interpolated into the life cycle between the zygote and adult.

7 Conifers and flowering plants continue the tendency seen in ferns to reduce the gametophyte. In both groups the gametophyte is incorporated into the body of the sporophyte, being represented in the male by the protoplasmic contents of the **pollen grain** (microspore) and its derivative, the pollen tube; and in the female by the protoplasmic contents of the **embryo sac** (megaspore).

8 The rise of the sporophyte, and decline of the gametophyte, can be seen as an adaptation to life on dry land. It is associated with the evolution of reproductive mechanisms involving transfer of pollen, and the seed habit, typical of higher plants.

9 Certain animals have an asexually reproducing stage in their life cycle, but, as far as is known, there is no true alternation of generations in the genetic sense in the animal kingdom.

Investigation 25.1
Life cycle of moss

Mosses show alternation of generations between a small leafy haploid gametophyte and a diploid spore-producing sporophyte which grows out of, and is dependent upon, the gametophyte.

Gametophyte

1 Examine a whole gametophyte plant, noting simple stem, leaves, and rhizoids (Figure 25.1A). Mount a leaf in water and examine. What can you say about its structure? Observe a rhizoid under the microscope. How does it compare with a true root? How capable do you think this plant is of surviving dry conditions?

2 Examine transverse sections of the leaf and stem under high power. In the leaf note the lamina and, if present, midrib. In the stem note the epidermis, cortex and conducting tissue (if present). There is no vascular tissue like that of higher plants.

3 Examine gametophytes under a lens or binocular microscope and look for male rosettes at the top of certain branches, and female rosettes lower down. Why are the male rosettes generally higher up the plant than the female rosettes? The male rosette consists of a group of antheridia enveloped by a 'cup' of leaves; the female rosette consists of a group of archegonia enveloped by a 'cup' of leaves.

4 Tease out the contents of a male rosette in a drop of water on a slide and examine under high power. Observe antheridia, paraphyses (sterile hairs) and, if possible, sperm cells (antherozooids). If sperm are present irrigate the slide with iodine or Noland's solution to see their flagella.

5 Tease out the contents of a female rosette in a drop of water and observe under high power. Note archegonia, each with egg cell and neck.

Figure 25.1 Structure of gametophyte of moss. These diagrams, and those in Fig. 25.2 are based on the moss *Mnium*.

6 Examine a prepared vertical section of a male rosette under low power. Note enveloping leaves, paraphyses, antheridia, sperm cells (Figure 25.1B). The paraphyses absorb water and are said to help hold water in the rosette. (Why should this be necessary?).

7 Examine a prepared vertical section of a female rosette under low power. Note enveloping leaves, paraphyses, archegonia with neck and egg-cell (Figure 25.1C). How is fertilisation brought about?

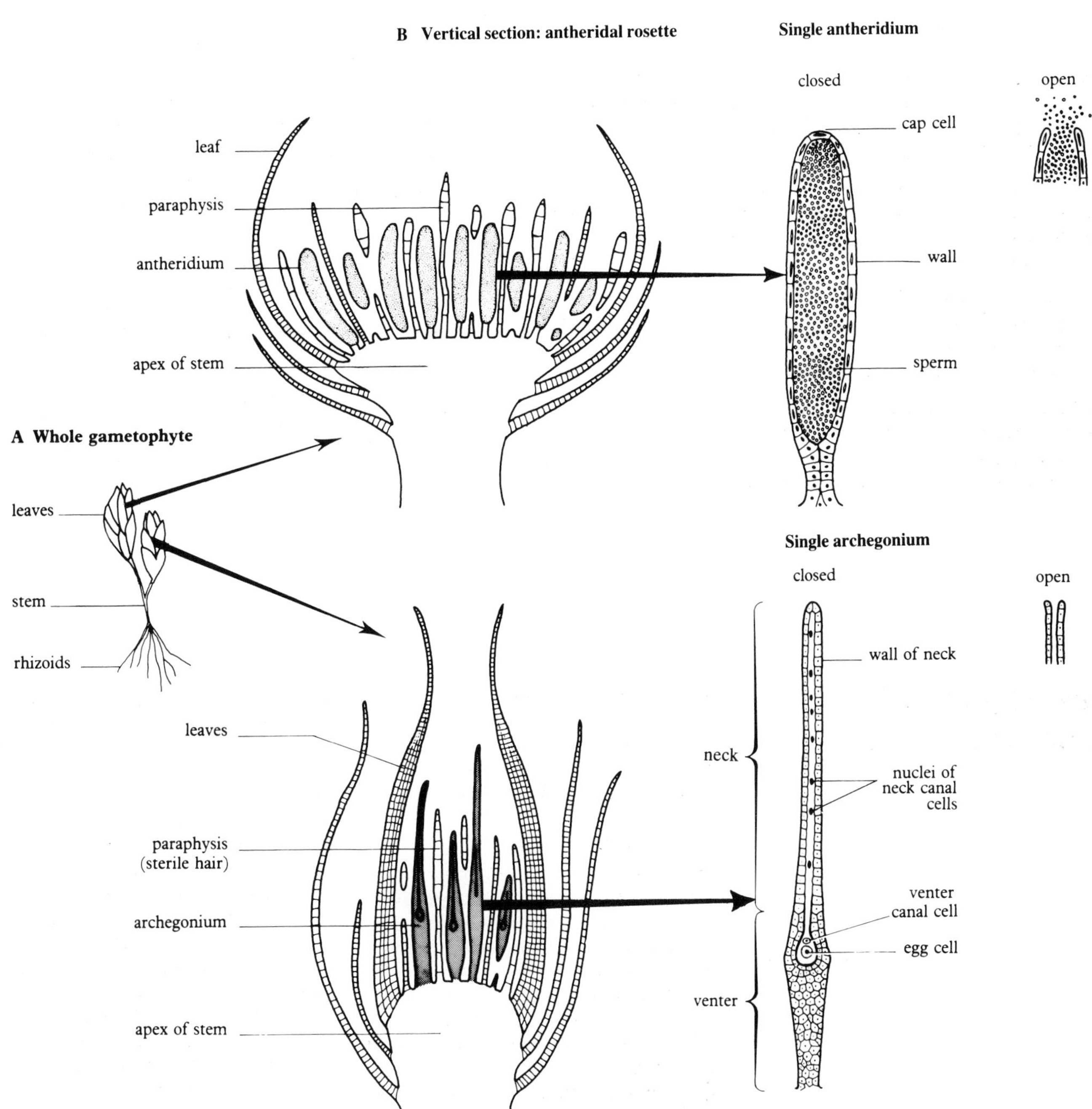

Requirements
Microscope
Hand lens or binocular microscope
Slides and coverslips
Plasticine (modelling clay)
Mounted needle

Iodine solution
Noland's solution

Moss gametophytes and sporophytes (entire)
TS stem of moss
TS leaf of moss
VS male rosette (antheridial rosette) of moss
VS female rosette (archegonial rosette) of moss
LS and TS moss capsule
WM protonema

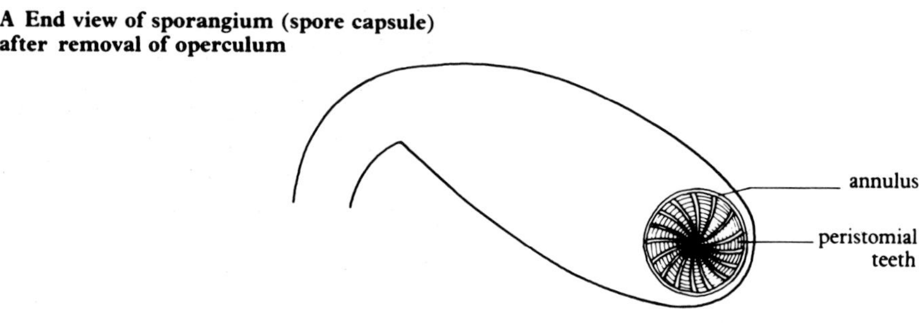

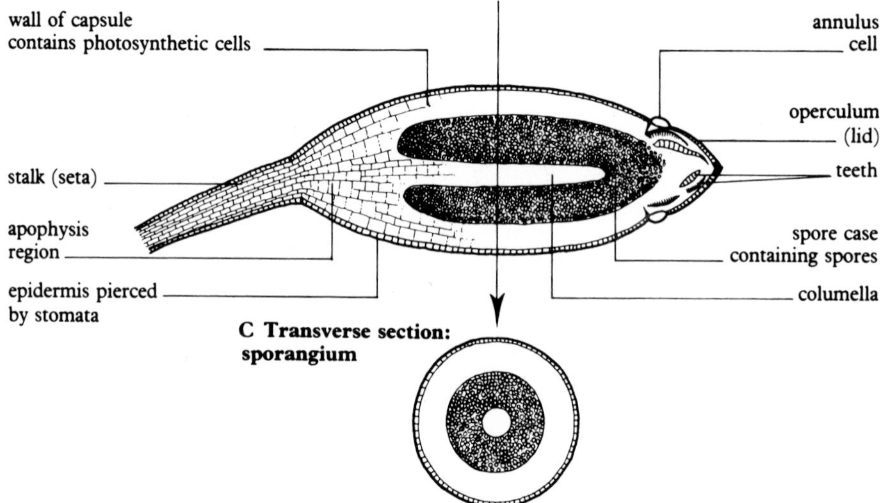

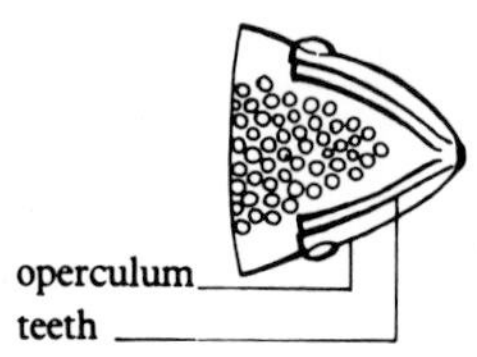

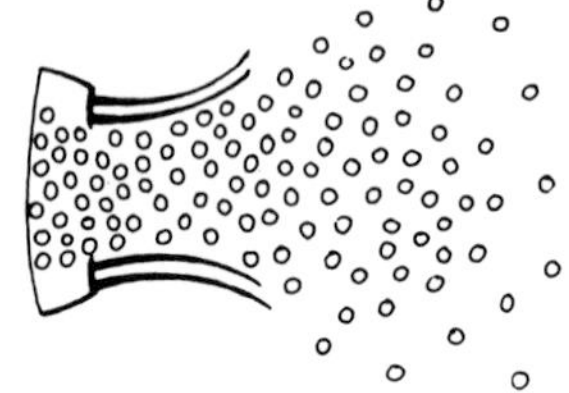

Figure 25.2 Structure of sporangium of moss.

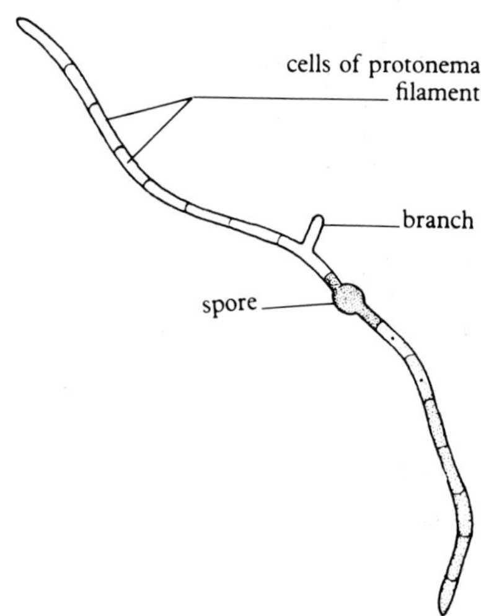

Figure 25.3 Young protonema of moss.

Sporophyte

1 After fertilisation the zygote develops into the young sporophyte. This grows out of the female rosette carrying with it the upper part of the archegonium which eventually falls off.

Examine sporophytes in various stages of development. Note spore capsule located at the upper end of a stalk whose foot is embedded in a female rosette. The stalk contains vascular strands continuous with those in the gametophyte.

2 Remove a capsule and a short length of its stalk. With a needle take off the operculum. Insert the stalk into a piece of plasticine on a slide in such a way that you can look down a microscope at the peristomial teeth (Figure 25.2A). Now breathe on the capsule and observe down the microscope. What happens? Explain your observations.

3 Examine a median longitudinal section of a capsule. Notice the spore sac, spores (or spore mother cells), annulus cells, teeth, operculum, and other features shown in Figure 25.2B. What is the three-dimensional shape of the spore sac? This can be deduced by examining a transverse section of the capsule (Figure 25.2C). What is the function of the annulus? How are the spores released and dispersed (*see* Figure 25.2D)?

Protonema

1 The spores do not develop into a new gametophyte direct, but first give rise to a filamentous alga-like protonema. This produces buds which, in turn, give rise to gametophytes. Look at the diagram of a protonema in Figure 25.3.

2 Examine a protonema under high power (Figure 25.3). Note the branched filament whose cells have chloroplasts; also formative spore. Buds with rhizoids may be seen.

For Consideration

(1) Mosses have been described as the amphibians of the plant kingdom. Do you think this is justified?

(2) Which do you consider to be the dominant generation, the gametophyte or sporophyte?

(3) To what extent is the sporophyte (a) self-supporting; (b) dependent on the gametophyte?

(4) What function is fulfilled by the protonema stage in the life cycle? Do you think it is more of a liability than a help?

Investigation 25.2
Life cycle of fern

In ferns the sporophyte is the dominant generation and the gametophyte is reduced to a small alga-like prothallus. The two generations are independent of each other.

Sporophyte

1 Examine an entire plant (Figure 25.4) and note the horizontal rhizome (*see* page 243) with old leaf bases and roots; leaves (fronds) subdivided into pinnae and pinnules.

2 Examine prepared sections of rhizome, roots, leaves and a leaf stalk (rachis), noting the vascular tissues. The vascular tissues have xylem and phloem like those of higher plants. How does the fern sporophyte compare with that of mosses? And how does it compare with the flowering plant?

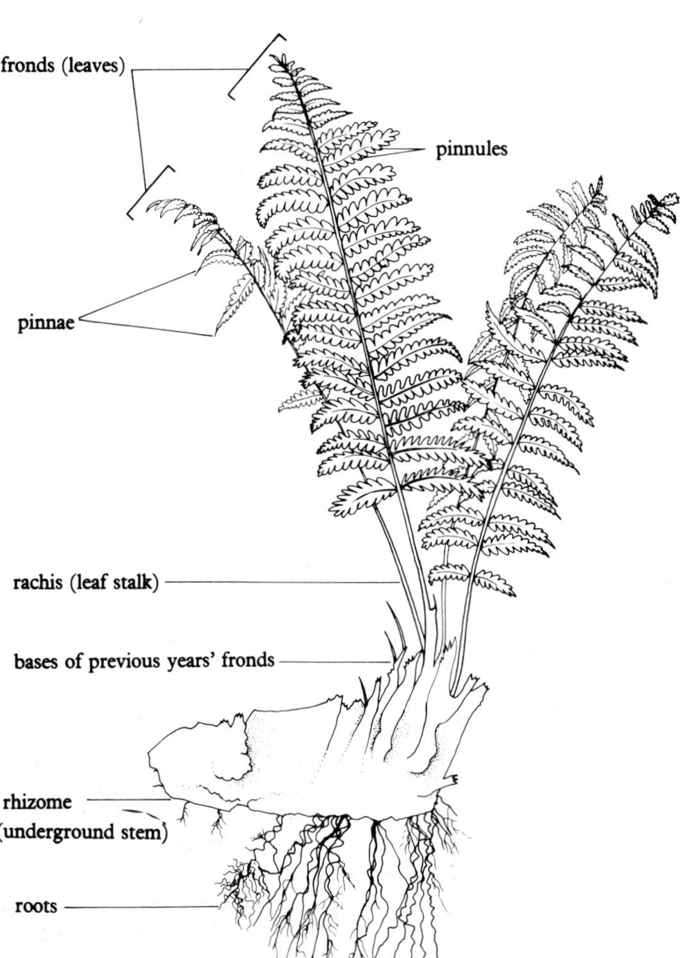

Figure 25.4 The sporophyte of the fern *Dryopteris* has a creeping underground rhizome. This represents the stem. The above-ground parts of the plant are the leaves (fronds) whose structure is illustrated here.

3 Certain pinnules, known as sporophylls, produce spores. The latter are formed in sori on the undersides of the sporophylls (Figure 25.5A). In some species each sorus is protected by an umbrella-like indusium (Figure 25.5B). With a needle remove an indusium from one of the sporophylls so as to reveal sporangia (spore capsules) beneath. Mount a mature sporangium in water and notice the annulus cells and other features shown in Figure 25.5C.

4 Place a few mature sporangia on a dry slide and either mount them in glycerine or leave them under a hot lamp to dry out. Examine under low power. Watch the capsule dehiscing. Whereabouts in the wall of the capsule does splitting occur? Compare with Figure 25.5C. Can you explain the mechanism of dehiscence?

5 Examine a transverse section of a sporophyll, noting the structures shown in Figure 25.5B. In particular observe the sporangia cut in various planes.

Gametophyte (Prothallus)

1 Each spore is potentially capable of developing into a prothallus. This is small and reduced, living on the surface of damp soil.

Examine a mature prothallus, noting its simple structure and shape. Mount it in water, lower surface uppermost, and examine under low and high powers. In what ways is it adapted to lead an independent existence? Note that there is no vascular tissue. In its structure the prothallus is on about the same level as a simple multicellular alga – very different from the much more elaborate sporophyte.

2 Examine a prepared whole mount and/or horizontal section of a prothallus. Observe antheridia and archegonia in surface view. Both are located on the underside of the prothallus, as are the rhizoids. Archegonia are closer to the apical notch than the antheridia (Figure 25.6A). In good preparations coiled sperm may be visible in the antheridia, and an egg cell in some of the archegonia (Figure 25.6B).

3 Examine a vertical section of a prothallus to see antheridia and archegonia in side view (Figure 25.6C, D). How are the sperms released from the antheridia and how do they enter the archegonia? How do the antheridia and archegonia of ferns compare with those of mosses?

4 After fertilisation the zygote develops into the sporophyte. At first this is small and rudimentary, with its foot embedded in the lower side of the prothallus. Later, when the sporophyte's roots and leaves develop, the prothallus – no longer required – withers and dies.

Examine a prothallus with young sporophyte attached and note the young leaves, roots, and foot embedded in the prothallus (Figure 25.7).

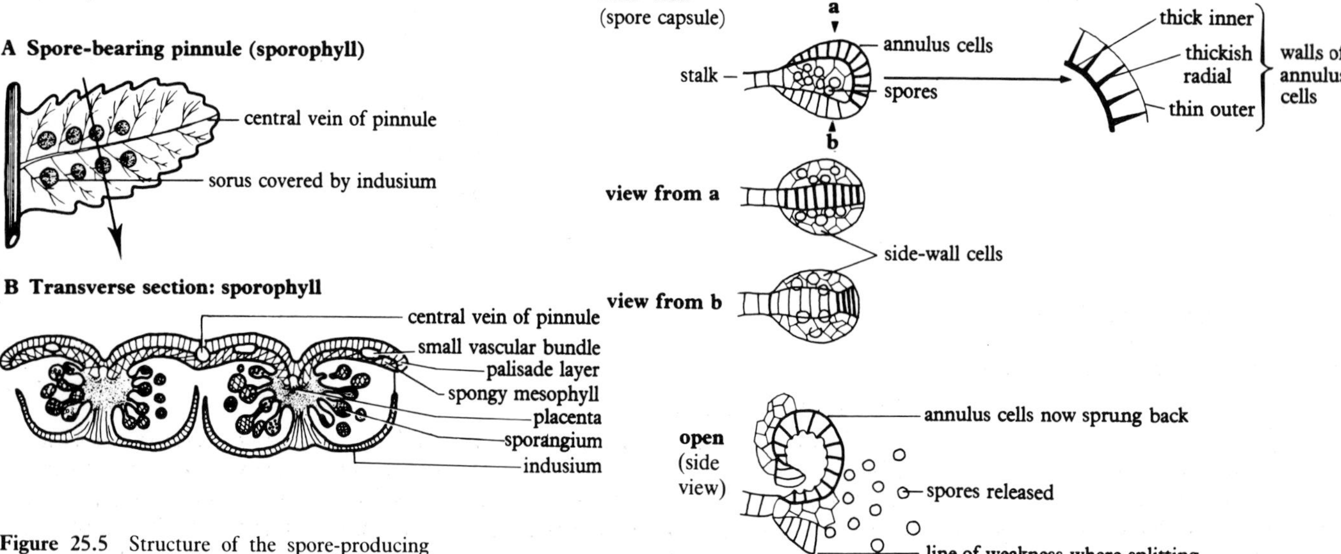

Figure 25.5 Structure of the spore-producing apparatus of the sporophyte of a fern. These diagrams, and those in Figure 25.6, are based on the common fern *Dryopteris*.

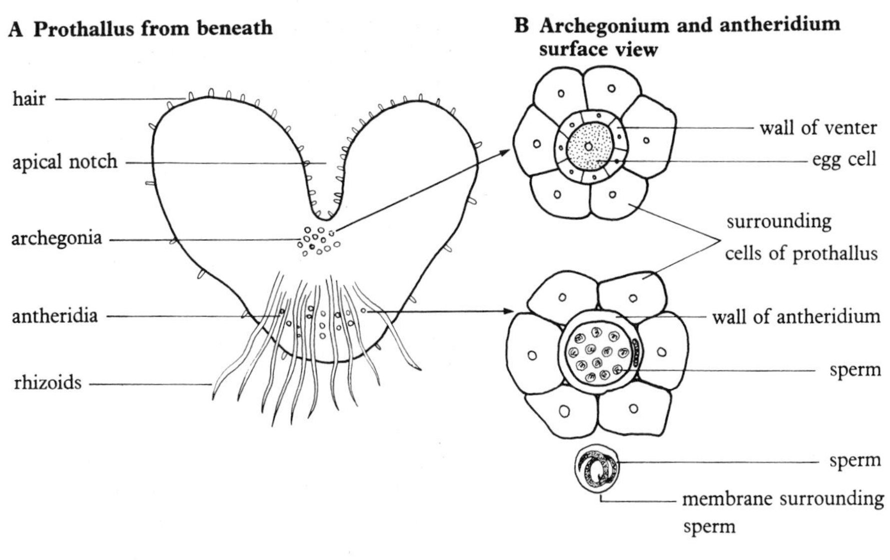

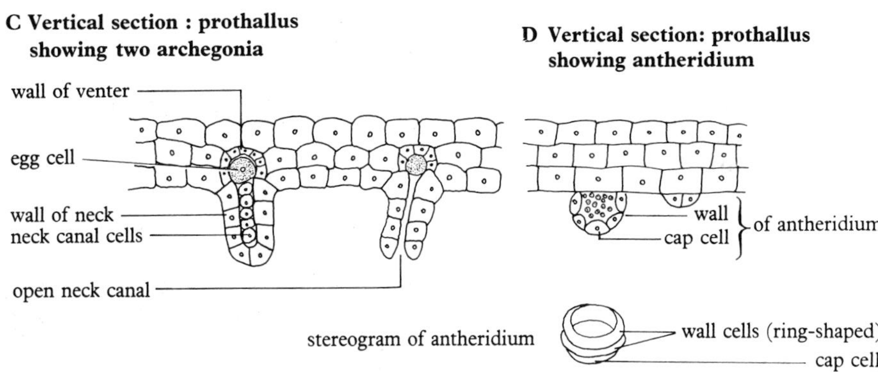

Figure 25.7 Young sporophyte growing out of the prothallus.

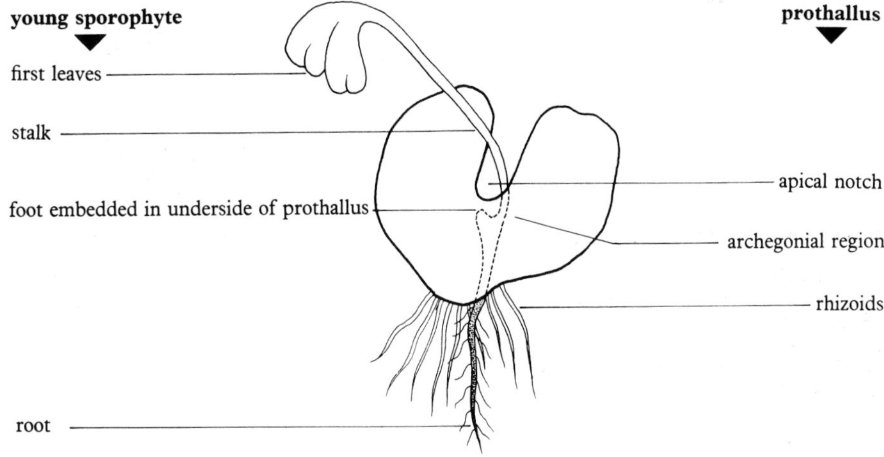

Figure 25.6 Structure of the gametophyte of fern.

Requirements
Microscope
Hand lens or binocular microscope
Slides and coverslips
Mounted needle
Lamp

Glycerine

Fern sporophytes entire
Fronds with sori
Fern gametophytes (prothalli) with antheridia and archegonia
Fern gametophytes with young sporophytes attached
TS rhizome
TS rachis
TS sporophyll showing sporangia
WM and HS gametophyte
VS gametophyte showing antheridia and/or archegonia
WM gametophyte with young sporophyte attached

For Consideration

(1) To what extent are ferns adapted to life on land?
(2) What are the weak points in the life cycle, i.e. the stages at which the plant is most vulnerable?
(3) Is the sporophyte entirely self-supporting?
(4) How does the mechanism of spore-dispersal compare with that of mosses?
(5) What are the major differences between mosses and ferns with respect to their structure and life cycle? (Make a table to compare them.)

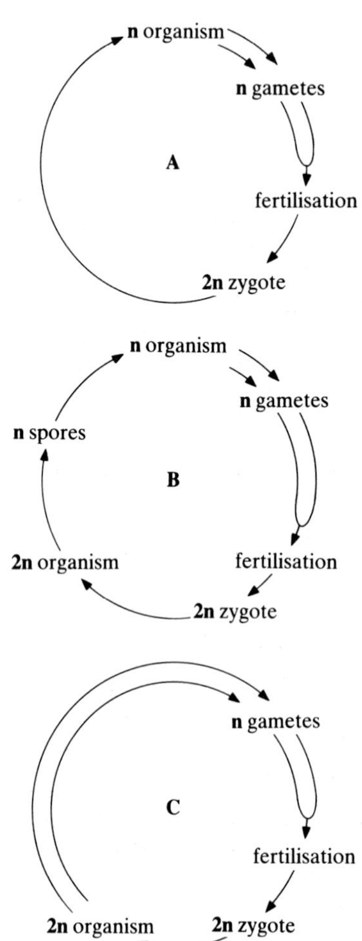

Figure 25.8 Three types of life cycle. **n**, haploid; **2n** diploid.

Questions and Problems

1 Make a list of features of their anatomy and physiology which equip mosses and ferns to live on land. In what respects are they poorly equipped for life on land? How do your answers fit in with the range of habitats which they occupy?

2 Figure 25.8 shows three types of life cycle.
(a) Whereabouts does meiosis occur in each life cycle?
(b) Give one example of an organism which shows each type of life cycle, and give brief details of its cycle.
(c) Suggest two advantages of having a type C life cycle. (*AEB modified*)

3 (a) (i) Distinguish between the diploid and haploid condition in cells.
(ii) What genetic advantages have diploid organisms over haploid organisms?
(b) Give a concise account of the roles of mitotic and meiotic divisions in the life histories of:
(i) a named plant which shows a dominant haploid phase,
(ii) a named animal which shows a dominant diploid phase,
(iii) any named organism which shows a regular alternation between a clearly distinguishable haploid phase and diploid phase. (*JMB*)

4 It is generally agreed that flowering plants have evolved from (ultimately) ferns.
(a) What changes would have to take place in the structure and life cycle of the fern *Dryopteris* for it to evolve into a flowering plant?
(b) Do any present-day plants provide information as to the intermediate steps that may have occurred in the above transition?

5 What advantages are gained by mosses and ferns in having alternation of generations in the life cycle? To what extent do flowering plants show such an alternation, and why is it less obvious?

6 'A flower is not an organ of sexual reproduction; it produces spores, not gametes.' How far is this true?

7 'There is not a single case of true alternation of generation in the animal kingdom.' Discuss.

8 Write an essay on the colonisation of dry land by plants.

9 Write an essay entitled 'Alternation of Generations'.

10 Explain the differences between:
(a) haploid and diploid,
(b) sporophyte and gametophyte,
(c) microspore and megaspore,
(d) sporophyll and sporangium,
(e) spore and seed.

11 'Life cycles can generally be divided into diploid and haploid phases, but organisms differ in the relative emphasis given to each phase.' Discuss this statement.

LEARNING RESOURCE CENTRE
FILTON COLLEGE
FILTON AVENUE
BRISTOL
BS34 7AT

0117 9092228

26 Patterns of Growth and Development

Background Summary

1 **Growth**, the permanent increase in size undergone by an organism, results from **cell division**, **assimilation**, and **cell expansion**.

2 Growth may be measured by estimating increase in a chosen linear dimension (e.g. height), by estimating the increase in the number of cells, or by estimating increase in volume, total mass or dry mass. Each has its snags and a source of inaccuracy common to them all is that growth may be **allometric**, different parts of the body growing at different rates.

3 Growth may be illustrated by a **growth curve** from which the growth rate and percentage growth can be derived. For many purposes this last is the most meaningful way of expressing growth.

4 In most organisms growth takes place in a smooth and regular pattern. An exception is provided by the arthropods in which growth is **intermittent**. This is because arthropods possess a hard cuticle which must be shed (**moulting, ecdysis**) before growth can take place.

5 Starting with fertilisation, the development of form (**embryology**) can be divided into cleavage, gastrulation, and organogeny.

6 **Cleavage** may be equal or unequal, depending on the yolk content of the egg. It results in the formation of a hollow **blastula**.

7 At its simplest, **gastrulation** occurs by invagination of the blastula. It results in the formation of two layers of cells, the inner layer lining the **archenteron**. In most animals, particularly where much yolk is present, gastrulation involves cell migration as well as, or instead of, invagination.

8 Gastrulation in vertebrates is followed by development of the **notochord** and **neural tube** from the mid-dorsal region of the inner and outer layer of cells respectively.

9 Meanwhile the **mesoderm** develops either by evagination of the archenteron wall or by inward migration of cells from the lips of the blastopore. Either way, the mesoderm lies between the outer layer of cells (**ectoderm**) and lining of the gut (**endoderm**).

10 In most animals the mesoderm surrounds a cavity, the **coelom**. This expands, giving rise to the general body cavity.

11 In vertebrates the mesoderm becomes subdivided into **somitic**, **nephrogenic** and **lateral plate** mesoderm. The first two are metamerically segmented, the last unsegmented. The somites give rise to the axial skeleton and muscles, the nephrogenic mesoderm to the kidney, and the lateral plate mesoderm to the muscles of the gut wall and body wall and to the heart.

12 Various organs are now moulded out of the different parts of the ectoderm, endoderm, and mesoderm.

13 In **amniotes** (reptiles, birds, and mammals) the embryo is situated above a **yolk sac** from which nourishment may be gained. Also, extra-embryonic membranes are formed.

14 The **extra-embryonic membranes** protect, provide a means of excretion for, and in mammals nourish the embryo. Their evolutionary development is associated with the cleidoic ('closed') egg, or with internal (uterine) development, and may be seen as an adaptation to life on dry land.

15 The extra-embryonic membranes are the **chorion** and **amnion** (enclosing the amniotic cavity), and the **allantois** (enclosing the allantoic cavity). Part of the allantois fuses with the chorion to form the highly vascularised **allanto-chorion**.

16 In all amniotes the chorion, amnion, and amniotic cavity are protective. In reptiles and birds the allantoic cavity is an excretory chamber, and the allanto-chorion, a respiratory gas exchange surface. In eutherian mammals the allanto-chorion becomes the **placenta**, and the stalk of the allantoic cavity becomes the **umbilical cord**.

17 In mammals, at birth, fundamental changes occur in the respiratory and circulatory systems as a result of the respiratory gas exchange function of the placenta being taken over by the lungs.

18 In some animals one or more **larval stages** are interpolated between egg and adult. In general, larvae are important in dispersal, feeding and (in certain specialised cases) asexual reproduction.

19 Larvae develop into the adult by **metamorphosis** which may involve a total reorganisation of larval structures. In insects and amphibians metamorphosis is brought about by a combination of external (environmental) and internal (hormonal) factors.

20 In insects a distinction is made between **hemimetabolous** insects with incomplete or gradual metamorphosis, and **holometabolous** insects with complete metamorphosis.

21 In flowering plants development starts with the growth of the zygote into the embryo within the seed. The developing embryo is nourished by the neighbouring **endosperm tissue** (see page 262).

22 Seeds remain dormant for varied periods of time. Development continues only when the seed **germinates** and a young shoot (**plumule**) and root (**radicle**) grow out.

23 Until it can photosynthesise for itself, the developing seedling is nourished by food reserves within the seed. In **endospermic seeds** (e.g. wheat) some of the endosperm remains for use when the seed germinates. In **non-endospermic seeds** (e.g. pea and bean) the endosperm is entirely used up by the time the seed germinates and nourishment is provided by food stored in the **cotyledons**.

24 Two types of germination are recognised: **hypogeal** and **epigeal**. In hypogeal germination the epicotyl elongates, in epigeal germination the hypocotyl elongates. These two types of germination are related to whether nourishment is provided by the cotyledons or endosperm tissue.

25 Conditions required for successful germination include water, correct illumination, suitable temperature, and presence of oxygen. Internally a rapid mobilisation of food reserves takes place: insoluble substances are hydrolysed into soluble ones which are translocated to the growing points of the seedling.

26 Growth and development of the shoot and root take place by cell division in apical (primary) meristems followed by cell expansion and differentiation. This **primary growth** results in the formation of **primary tissues**.

27 Increase in girth takes place by **secondary growth** which results in the laying down of **secondary tissues**, formed from secondary meristems (**cambium cells**).

28 There are two cambium layers in a typical woody perennial: a **vascular cambium** gives rise annually to secondary xylem and phloem, a **cork cambium** forms protective corky cells (**periderm**) and secondary cortex. **Lenticels** in the periderm permit respiratory gas exchange.

Investigation 26.1 Observations of live amphibian embryos

A Vertical section: 2-cell stage

animal pole

pigment

vitelline membrane

cleavage furrow

vegetal pole

B Horizontal section: 4-cell stage

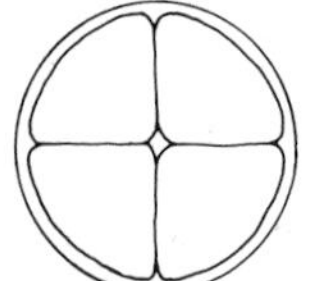

C Vertical section: 8-cell stage

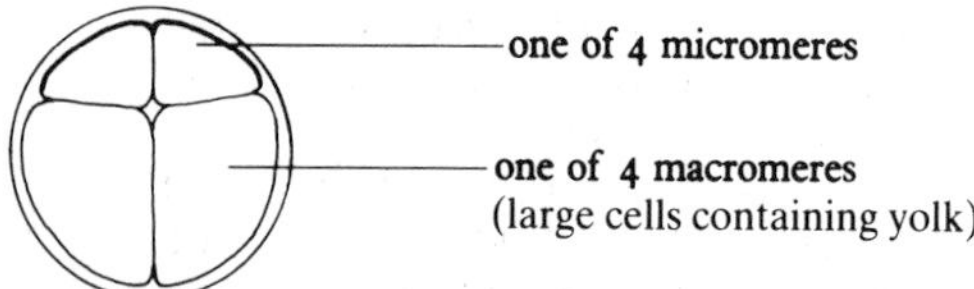

D Vertical section of blastula

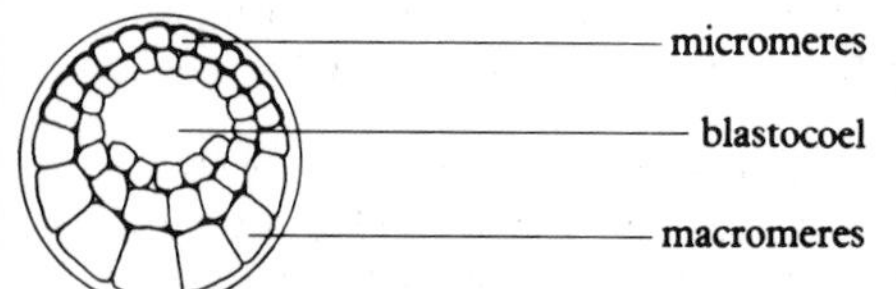

Figure 26.1 Cleavage in the frog or toad as seen in section. The yolk provides nourishment for the developing embryo.

Amphibians are much used by embryologists because they are tolerably easy to handle and their development is relatively uncomplicated. Furthermore, they demonstrate the fundamental sequence of changes which occurs during the development of a typical chordate. True, the tadpole is unique to amphibians and the details of gastrulation are more complex than in primitive chordates, but the broad picture of development is typically chordate.

Observations can be carried out on any amphibian at the appropriate time of the year. A species much used by embryologists is the African clawed toad, *Xenopus laevis*, which can be induced to mate and spawn at any time of the year by treatment with gonadotrophic hormone (*see* page 401).

Procedure

1 With a wide pipette, transfer a recently laid fertilised egg to a watch glass. Cover with the same water that the egg came from. Examine it under a hand lens or binocular microscope.

2 Watch for cleavage. In *Xenopus* the first cleavage division normally occurs one-to-two hours after laying. In what plane are the first three cleavage divisions? Note the many-celled blastula. This remains enclosed inside the transparent vitelline membrane.

3 Try to relate the cleavage stages which you can see to the vertical sections in Figure 26.1.

4 Continue to watch the developing embryos at intervals over the next few days. Gastrulation normally occurs about eight hours after laying: it involves an inward migration of cells to form the gut. The blastopore, where the cell migration occurs, eventually closes (Figure 26.2). Notice the yolk plug – what does it represent? Neurulation occurs about 24 hours after laying: notice the formation of the neural folds which eventually fuse to form the neural tube. Which end of the neural tube is going to form the brain?

5 The larva (tadpole) hatches (i.e. breaks out of the vitelline membrane) on about the third day. If you are lucky enough to be around when this happens, watch carefully. By this stage the gut has acquired an opening to the exterior at the posterior end (the anus), but as yet there is no opening at the anterior end, only a pouch-like depression called the stomadaeum.

Note: The exact rate of development depends on various factors including temperature, and also on the species. The figures given above are based on *Xenopus laevis* at normal room temperature. Further development of the larva is dealt with in the next investigation.

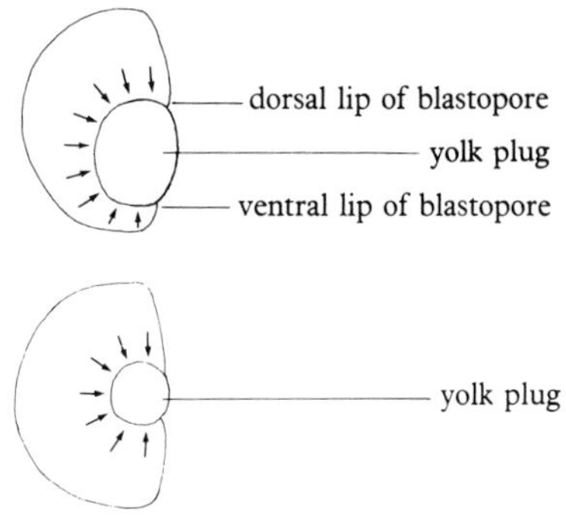

Figure 26.2 Closing of the blastopore in a frog or toad. This marks the end of gastrulation.

Requirements
Binocular microscope or hand lens
Watch glass
Wide pipette

Newly laid fertilised eggs of amphibian, e.g. *Xenopus laevis* (*see* Appendix 7, page 400)

For Consideration

(1) How would you investigate the influence of environmental factors on the rate of development of an amphibian?
(2) How would you investigate the amphibian embryo's source of energy during cleavage?
(3) What factors might cause the egg of *Xenopus* to start cleaving?
(4) What factor or factors might control the plane of successive cleavage divisions?
(5) Does the development of an amphibian entail changes in bulk as well as form? Explain your observations on this point.

Investigation 26.2 Development of tadpole

The development of the tadpole can be followed by observing live tadpoles of *Xenopus*, or some other amphibian such as the common frog at the appropriate time of the year, and also by studying preserved specimens.

Observations of external features may be supplemented by an examination of transverse and/or longitudinal sections of the various stages.

Procedure

THE YOUNG TADPOLE

1 Examine a newly hatched tadpole. To what extent does it look like Figure 26.3A which is based on the tadpole of the common frog?

In general tadpoles at this stage possess the following features:
(a) A short tail which gradually lengthens.
(b) On the ventral side of the head, a group of mucus glands, together forming a temporary attachment organ, by which the tadpole fixes itself to weeds, etc. The tadpole is, therefore, sessile at this stage and remains so until the tail is long enough to serve as an effective locomotory device.
(c) Three pairs of external gills, vascularised outgrowths of the skin, which are not connected with the pharynx.
(d) A straight gut with, as yet, no mouth. The stomadaeum is visible externally but does not yet open to the pharynx. How does the tadpole gain nourishment at this stage?
(e) An S-shaped tubular heart which, though simple at this stage, soon starts to sub-divide into atrium and ventricle.
(f) Four pairs of pharyngeal pouches which do not yet connect with the exterior. They are destined to develop into the internal gill pouches.

Observe the above features in live and/or preserved tadpoles.

FROM HATCHING TO METAMORPHOSIS

2 During the ensuing three months the tadpole undergoes a series of changes which you can see for yourself by examining tadpoles at different stages of development. Transfer the tadpole to a watch glass of water with a wide pipette. Add ether from a pipette, one drop at a time, until the tadpole stops moving.

The developmental changes, in approximate sequence, are as follows:
(a) The attachment organ degenerates and the tail elongates so the tadpole ceases to be sessile and becomes motile. The tail acquires a fully functional series of segmental myotomes whose contractions permit lateral movements of the tail similar to those displayed by the tail of a fish.
(b) Special sense organs develop (nasal sacs, eyes and inner ears).
(c) The gut becomes long and coiled, suitable for a herbivorous diet.
(d) A mouth develops, the stomadaeum breaking through to the pharynx. The mouth develops horny jaws with small rasping teeth for feeding on algae, encrusting vegetation, and such like.
(e) The external gills are replaced by internal gills associated with four pairs of gill pouches leading from pharynx to exterior.
(f) An operculum, a ventro-lateral fold of skin, grows back to cover the gill openings. The resulting opercular chamber connects with the exterior by an opercular opening on the left hand side of the head (Figure 26.3B).
(g) Limb buds appear which gradually develop into paired limbs. The hind limbs are fully visible in the later stages of development, but the forelimbs are concealed beneath the operculum (Figure 26.3C).
(h) A pair of lungs develops as pouches from the ventral side of the pharynx, but the lungs are not yet functional.

Observe the above features in live or preserved tadpoles. In particular note the gill pouches and gills.

METAMORPHOSIS

3 Towards the end of the third month the tadpole undergoes a comparatively sudden and dramatic metamorphosis into the adult, as a result of which it becomes terrestrial. Many of the adult structures are already present in rudimentary form, but at metamorphosis they complete their development and become functional.

Here is a summary of the important changes that occur, some of which can be seen in Figure 26.3D.

(a) The nasal sacs acquire internal openings into the bucco-pharynx.
(b) Eyelids characteristic of the adult develop.
(c) The middle ear develops and a functional tympanic membrane forms.
(d) The mouth widens, the horny jaws and teeth being replaced by true jaws and teeth; jaw muscles and tongue develop.
(e) Skull bones develop, resulting in the head changing shape.
(f) The hyoid pump develops and becomes functional.
(g) The limbs increase in size: the left fore-limb protrudes through the opercular opening, the right one breaks through the skin.
(h) The pelvic girdle develops, resulting in the characteristic humped-back appearance of the adult.
(i) The tail shortens, its cells being broken down and resorbed by the digestive action of lysosomes.
(j) The colour pattern characteristic of the adult develops.
(k) The gut shortens, this being associated with the change from a herbivorous to carnivorous diet.
(l) The gill pouches close up, the first pair forming the Eustachian tubes. The gill arches go to form the laryngeal cartilages.
(m) The heart completes its development, an inter-atrial septum developing.
(n) Changes occur in the pattern of arterial arches, a double circulation becoming established.
(o) The lungs, already present, become functional.

Observe as many of the above changes as you can in live and/or preserved specimens. Metamorphosis is initiated and controlled by the release of thyroxine from the thyroid gland (*see* Investigation 27.5).

Figure 26.3 Diagrams summarising the major external changes that occur during the development of the frog tadpole. Based on the common frog *Rana temporaria*.

A Immediately after hatching

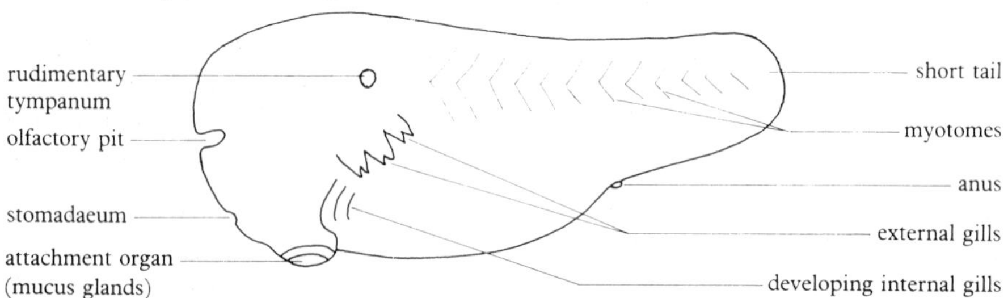

B Later

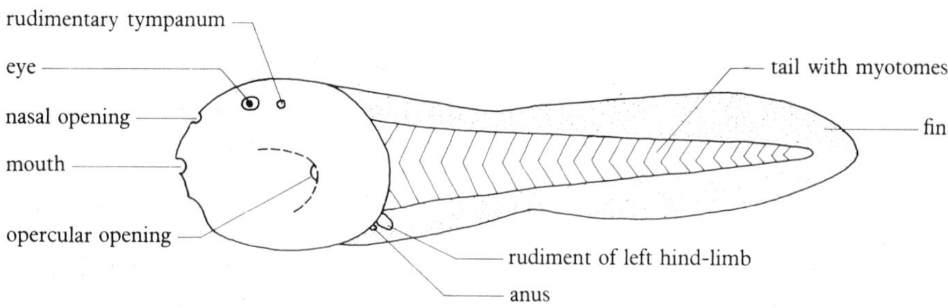

C Immediately before metamorphosis

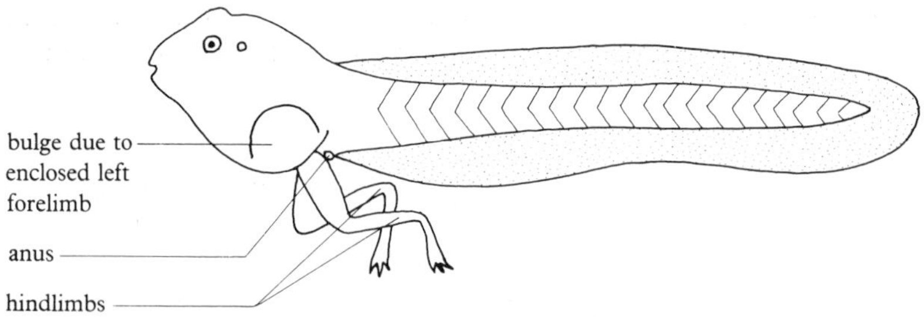

D Immediately after metamorphosis

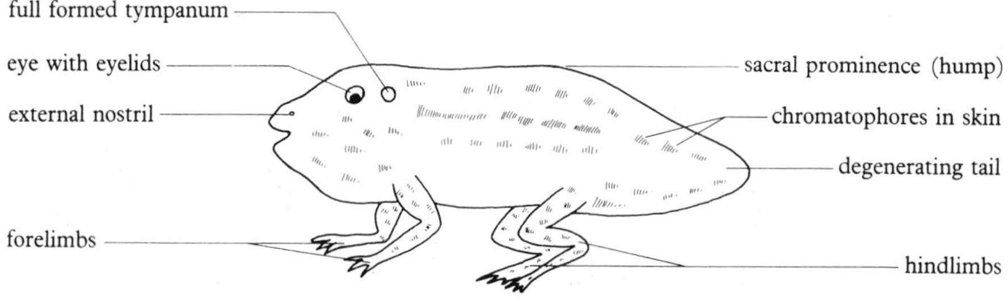

For Consideration

(1) Can the adult frog be regarded as fully terrestrial? (Find out as much as you can about the adult).
(2) What are the natural hazards in the life cycle of amphibians? Plainly these hazards are not so acute as to have caused the group to become extinct. How have they managed to survive?
(3) The change from gill breathing to lung breathing is associated with structural changes in the arterial arches. Find out as much as you can about these changes, and summarise them.

Requirements
Binocular microscope or hand lens
Microscope
Watch glass
Wide pipette

Live tadpoles of common frog or *Xenopus laevis*
Preserved tadpoles (various stages)

Investigation 26.3
Development of chick

Hen's eggs hatch after three weeks' incubation following laying. During the first week it is possible to see organ-formation and the extra-embryonic membranes. What are the extra-embryonic membranes and which vertebrates possess them?

Examination of Live Embryo

1 Construct a plasticine cradle to hold an egg in the sideways position.
2 Now take a three-to-five day egg from the incubator and, without rotating it or changing its orientation, place it in the cradle.
3 Let the egg stand for several minutes so the embryo floats to the top of the yolk.
4 Without removing the egg from the cradle, cut away the shell from the upper side of the egg. Use only the *tips* of a pair of scissors. When you have removed the shell you should see the embryo lying on top of the yolk.
5 Draw off the albumen with a pipette until the surface of the yolk is uncovered.
6 Examine the embryo under a binocular microscope or lens. Using Figure 26.4 as a guide, note brain (fore-, mid-, and hind-brain vesicles), developing eye, limb buds and tail. Can the heart be seen, and is it beating?
7 Observe the lining of the yolk sac containing the vitelline arteries and veins. Note red blood cells circulating outwards in the main vitelline artery, and back in the vein. What is the function of this circulation?
8 Next find the allantois: at this stage it is a small balloon-like sac, but later it will expand until it makes contact with most of the lining of the shell. What is the function of the allantois?
9 Now look for the amnion and chorion, the membranes surrounding the embryo. What are their functions?
10 Using forceps and small scissors carefully remove these membranes from above the embryo. With a blunt needle gently deflect the embryo to one side and notice its connection with the yolk sac.

Observation of Live Embryo over Several Days

1 Take a three-day egg and mark out an 18 mm square on the shell in pencil immediately above the embryo.
2 Carefully cut out the square with a hack-saw blade, taking care not to rupture the underlying white shell-membrane. Wear a sterile face mask from now on.
3 With a sterile blade and small forceps, remove the exposed shell membrane.
4 Now place a 22 mm cover-slip over the aperture and seal it in position with molten paraffin wax.
5 Mark the egg with your name and return it to the incubator.
6 Observe the embryo at intervals during the next few days. Trace the development of organs, particularly the eye, heart and limb buds.

Making a Permanent Preparation of Embryo

The embryo from the first experiment can be used for this.
1 Break open the yolk sac and carefully cut away the embryo plus the surrounding yolk sac wall containing the vitelline arteries and veins.
2 Float the embryo in a dish of warm sodium chloride solution (0.9 per cent). Flush away any yolk or albumen clinging to the embryo or to the yolk sac wall.

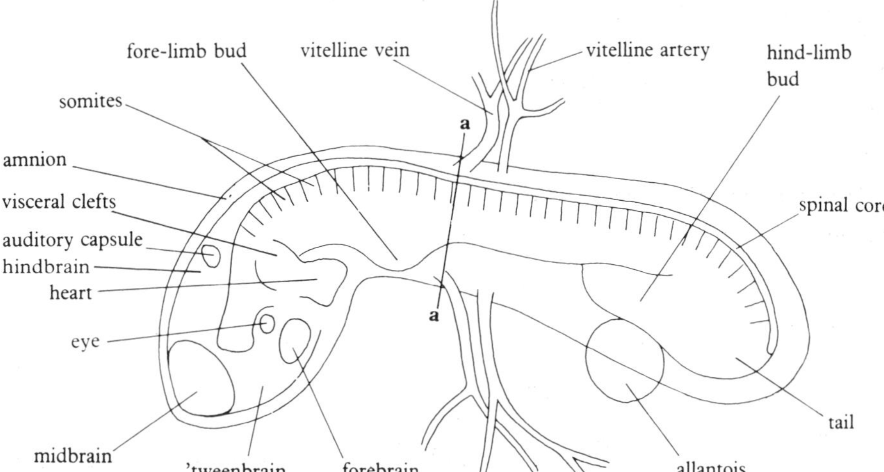

Figure 26.4 Diagram of whole mount of chick embryo showing the various structures which are visible at the 3–4 day stage.

Requirements
Binocular microscope or hand lens
Sterile face mask
Hacksaw blade
Cardboard for coverslip support
Plasticine
Large petri dish
Small petri dish
22 mm coverslips ×2
Slide
Hot plate
Wide pipette

Beaker of molten paraffin wax with small paintbrush and spatula
Sodium chloride solution (25 cm^3, 0.9 per cent)
Bouin's fluid (10 cm^3)
Acidified ethanol (4 drops of strong HCl in 100 cm^3 of 70 per cent ethanol)
50 per cent ethanol (10 cm^3)
70 per cent ethanol (10 cm^3)
90 per cent ethanol (10 cm^3)
Absolute ethanol (20 cm^3)
Xylene (10 cm^3)
Canada balsam

Three-day fertilised eggs of chick (×2) in incubator

Note: Some people object on ethical grounds to experiments on live chick embryos. As an alternative to carrying out this practical investigation a film and/or prepared slides may be preferred.

3 Using a wide pipette transfer the specimen to a small petri dish. Gently spread it out on the floor of the dish, so the embryo is lying in the centre of the yolk sac wall.
4 Now cover the specimen with Bouin's fixative and leave for at least an hour.
5 After fixation, replace the Bouin's fluid with several changes of tap water to wash the specimen. This should be done for at least 30 minutes.
6 Stain in borax carmine for up to 24 hours.
7 Differentiate in acidified ethanol until the specimen is semi-transparent. Observe in the petri dish under low power until internal structures become plainly visible. This may take as much as an hour.
8 Dehydrate in 70 per cent ethanol (10 minutes), 90 per cent ethanol (10 minutes), and two lots of absolute ethanol (total of at least 30 minutes).
9 Clear in xylene for at least 15 minutes.
10 Mount in Canada balsam under a large coverslip supported round the edge by a cardboard frame.
Note: The times for staining and differentiation are by no means absolute; both processes may be accelerated by warming on a hotplate.
11 Examine your preparation under low power noting: neural tube expanded anteriorly into fore-, mid- and hind-brain vesicles, eye, heart, somites, vitelline blood vessels. Are the extra-embryonic membranes visible? Compare with Figure 26.4.

For Consideration

(1) What are the salient differences between the development of amphibians and birds?
(2) In what way is the embryo of birds adapted for terrestrial development? How does the bird embryo compare with that of other terrestrial vertebrates in this respect?
(3) From where does the developing chick embryo receive its oxygen and food supply? How does this compare with amphibians?
(4) How does the developing chick embryo dispose of its nitrogenous waste?
(5) Draw and label a transverse section of a chick embryo cut at level a–a in Figure 26.4.

Investigation 26.4
Development of embryo of flowering plant

After fertilisation the following changes take place in the flower: the zygote develops into the embryo; the primary endosperm nucleus divides to form the endosperm tissue, which surrounds and nourishes the embryo; the ovule develops into the seed, the integuments forming the seed coat; and the ovary forms the fruit.

The developmental changes listed above can be seen in *Capsella bursa-pastoris*, shepherd's purse.

Procedure

1 First examine a whole plant of shepherd's purse. The youngest part of the plant is the apex where unopened flower buds may be seen; further back open flowers are visible, and further back still heart-shaped fruits, developed from the ovaries of post-fertilisation flowers, will be seen. Trace the developmental sequence from apex to base. Two stages are illustrated in Figure 26.5.

A Fruit soon after fertilisation
(side wall of fruit removed)

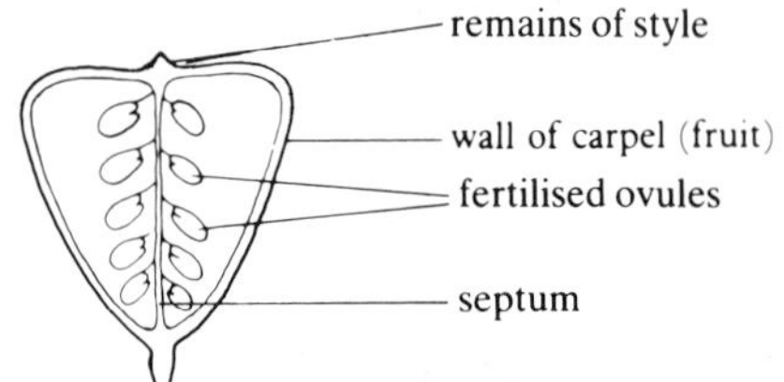

B Mature fruit after dehiscence

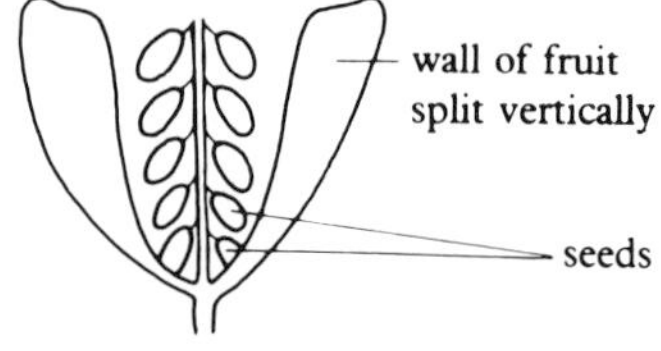

Figure 26.5 Fruit and seeds of shepherd's purse, *Capsella bursa-pastoris*.

Figure 26.6 (*far right*) Diagrams illustrating development of the embryo and associated structures in shepherd's purse *Capsella bursa-pastoris*. The diagrams are not all drawn to the same scale: in fact the carpel and its contents grow steadily larger after fertilisation.

2 Open one of the youngest fruits (towards the apex) and note two rows of ovules (Figure 26.5A). Remove a few of them and mount in chloral hydrate or acetocarmine. Note stalk of ovule, integuments and embryosac containing embryo which is attached by a suspensor to the end of the embryosac nearest the micropyle (Figure 26.6B).

3 Mount ovules of different ages in chloral hydrate. Start with ovules from fruits towards the apex of the plant, and then work your way down the stem towards the base. In each case observe intact ovules first, then gently press the coverslip with a needle so as to burst the ovule and release the embryo. If the embryo is too transparent try mounting another one in acetocarmine.

4 Using Figure 26.6 to help you, reconstruct the sequence of stages in the development of the embryo and the formation of the seed. In the fully formed embryo note the plumule, radicle, and cotyledons. What happens to the endosperm and suspensor as development proceeds?

5 Supplement this investigation by examining prepared longitudinal sections of the fruit of shepherd's purse.

For Consideration

(1) What useful function is formed by the suspensor?

(2) During development the embryo bends over so the cotyledons point downwards. Significance?

(3) What is the function of the cotyledons?

(4) The final event in the formation of the seed is the drying out of the inside with the result that the water content is reduced from approximately 80 to 10 per cent. How might this be achieved and what is its purpose?

Requirements
Microscope
Slides and coverslips
Mounted needle

Chloral hydrate
Acetocarmine

Shepherd's purse plant bearing flowers and fruits
LS fruit of shepherd's purse

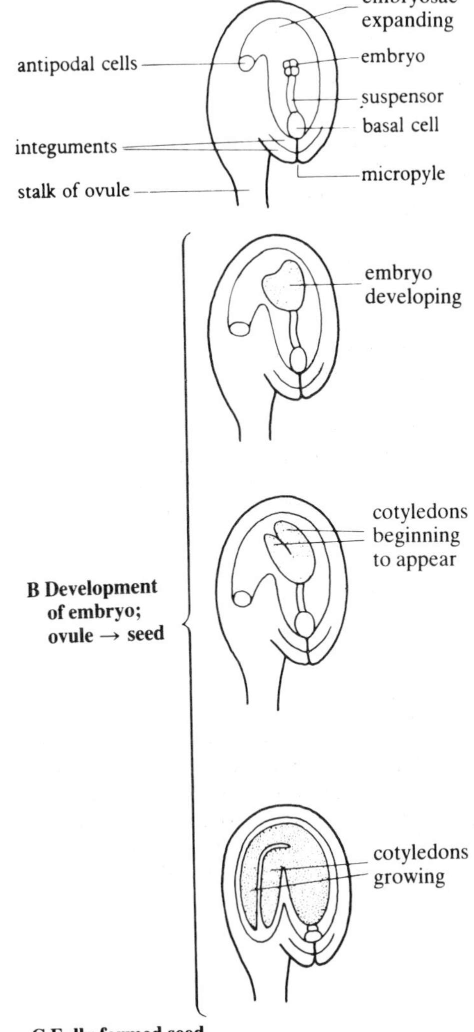

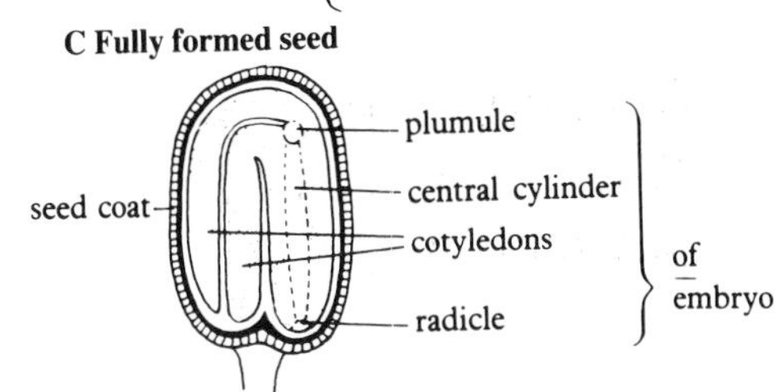

Investigation 26.5 Structure of seeds

In the seeds of most plants the embryo is surrounded by a variable amount of endosperm tissue which serves as a food supply during germination. In other seeds there is little or no endosperm tissue, food being supplied by the enlarged cotyledons. Flowering plants are divided into monocotyledons and dicotyledons: the former possess seeds with only one cotyledon, the latter have two cotyledons.

Whatever other factors are required for germination, one essential factor is water: the first clearly observable event in germination is the imbibing of water. As a result of this the embryonic tissues swell and rupture the seed coat.

Broad Bean

1 Examine a dry broad-bean seed (the so-called 'bean') and notice the seed coat, micropyle and hilum (Figure 26.7A). The hilum is the scar of the seed stalk, originally the stalk of the

A End-on view

seed coat (testa)
micropyle
hilum

B Cut open

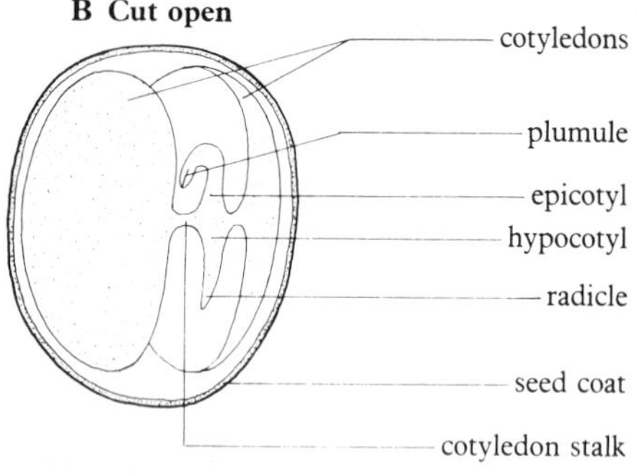

Figure 26.7 Structure of broad bean seed, a non-endospermic seed.

ovule. Split open a bean pod: the pod is the fruit – detach one of the seeds and confirm that the hilum is the scar of the seed stalk.

2 Compare the dry seed with one which has been soaked in water for 24–48 hours. Note the large increase in size. By weighing the two seeds, estimate the percentage increase in mass: does this represent the percentage increase in water content?

How, and by what route, might water be taken up by the seed? How could you investigate this by experiment?

3 Remove the seed coat of the soaked seed and note that it consists of two layers, an outer testa and inner tegmen. From what structures in the unfertilised ovule are these two layers derived?

4 The broad bean is a non-endospermic dicotyledon. Remove one of the two cotyledons. Note plumule, radicle, cotyledon and cotyledon stalk (Figure 26.7B). Note absence of endosperm tissue.

5 Stain the whole of the embryo (including a cotyledon) in iodine solution. Conclusion? Carry out tests for other food reserves (*see* page 42).

6 With a sharp razor blade cut thin sections of a cotyledon. Mount the sections in iodine solution and examine them under the microscope. Starch grains should be visible.

Castor Oil

1 Compare the dry seed with one that has been soaked for 48 hours. The seed stalk has an outgrowth (the caruncle) which covers the hilum and micropyle (Figure 26.8A). The caruncle is said to play some part in imbibition of water. How could you test this suggestion?

2 Slice the soaked seed horizontally down the centre of its flattened side and examine the cut surface. Note the very small plumule and radicle at one end of the seed. Being a dicotyledon, the embryo has two cotyledons; they are thin and delicate and flattened against the endosperm (Figure 26.8B). The endosperm is plentiful.

3 Slice another soaked seed vertically, i.e. in a plane at right angles to the previous section. What does this tell you?

4 Treat the cut surface of the seed with Sudan III. Conclusions? Test for other food reserves.

Wheat

1 Examine a dry wheat grain. The grain is in fact a *fruit*, the seed itself being inside. Note the groove down one side (Figure 26.9A). At the base is a scar where the fruit was attached to the stem.

2 Slice a soaked seed longitudinally parallel with the groove. Treat the cut surface of one half-seed with iodine solution. The tissue which stains blue is the starchy endosperm (Figure 26.9B). Notice how bulky it is compared with other parts of the seed.

3 Wheat is a monocotyledon and therefore has only one cotyledon. It is a small shield-like structure called the scutellum and lies between the endosperm and the main part of the embryo. Treat the cut surface of your second half-seed with Sudan III. Does this help you to see the embryo? What does it tell you about the embryo?

4 The peripheral region of the endosperm is called the aleurone layer and is rich in protein. Outside this is the

A End-on view

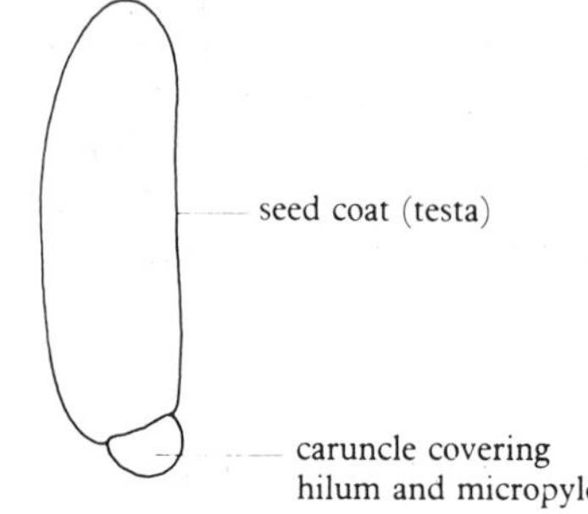

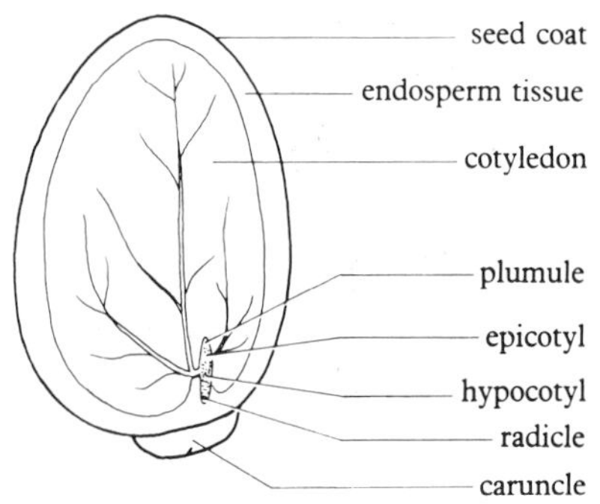

Figure 26.8 Structure of the seed of the castor oil plant, an endospermic seed.

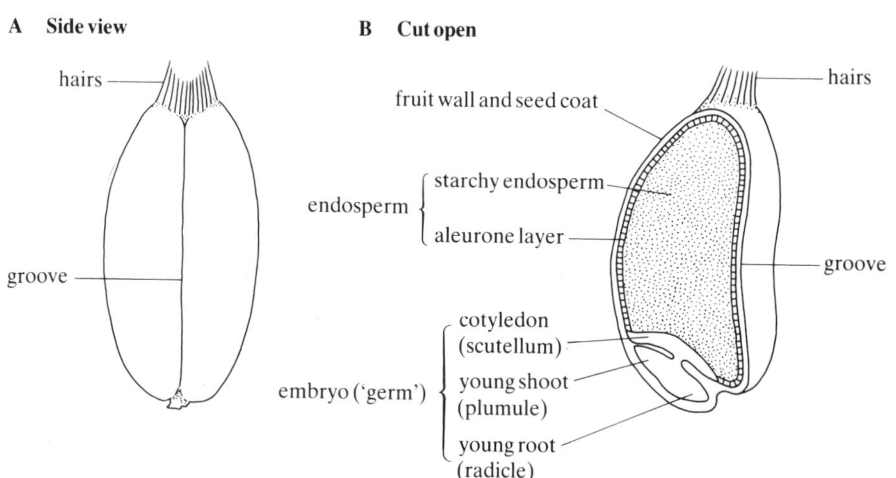

Figure 26.9 Structure of a wheat grain. The seed is endospermic.

Requirements
Balance
Dish
Razor blade

Iodine solution
Sudan III
Reagents for other food tests (*see* page 42)

Broad bean seed (dry)
Broad bean seed soaked for 24–48 hours
Castor oil seed (dry)
Castor oil seed soaked for 48 hours
Wheat grain (dry)
Wheat grain soaked for 24 hours
Other seeds as required

seed coat and fruit wall (pericarp), fused together. The bran of wheat, containing much cellulose (fibre), includes all these layers.

Other Seeds

1 Using the same techniques as above, examine other seeds. In each case either remove the seed coat or split the seed lengthways in order to examine the embryo. Note the relative extents of the cotyledons and endosperm.

2 Test the soaked seeds for their food reserves. Present your results in the form of a table.

For Consideration

(1) What are the advantages of seeds being in a dried-out state while they are lying in the soil?
(2) Why is it necessary for a seed to absorb water before it can germinate?
(3) Describe in detail how you could investigate factors affecting the rate at which the seeds of a particular species absorb water prior to germination.
(4) What is the commercial importance of each of the seeds that you have studied in this investigation?

Investigation 26.6
Hypogeal and epigeal germination

These two types of germination are related to the different sources of nourishment available to the germinating seed. In hypogeal germination the epicotyl elongates, in epigeal germination the hypocotyl elongates.

Hypogeal Germination

1 Observe your broad bean embryo from Investigation 26.5. Imagine the epicotyl elongating rapidly: what will happen?

In hypogeal germination the epicotyl elongates, with the result that the plumule is thrust upwards through the soil, but the cotyledons remain below ground (hence *hypo*geal). Until the shoot develops its first green leaves, nourishment comes from the large cotyledons which contain stored food reserves. There is little or no endosperm tissue.

2 Examine seedlings of a hypogeal plant (e.g. broad bean) which have been caused to germinate at different times so the developmental sequence can be followed. Compare with Figure 26.10A.

3 Observe the germination of other hypogeal plants, e.g. runner bean, pea, wheat or maize, and compare with the broad bean. Notice that in the broad bean and its relatives the plumule is bent back (forming a 'plumular hook') as the shoot emerges. This is to protect it as it is pushed through the soil. In wheat, maize and other grasses the shoot points straight up, the plumule being protected by a sheath-like cover, the coleoptile. The coleoptile ruptures when the first leaves emerge.

Figure 26.10A Stages in germination of broad bean, to illustrate hypogeal germination. The times, which are given as the number of days after the beginning of soaking, are very approximate and assume good growing conditions. E, epicotyl; H, hypocotyl. **Figure 26.10B** *Overleaf.*

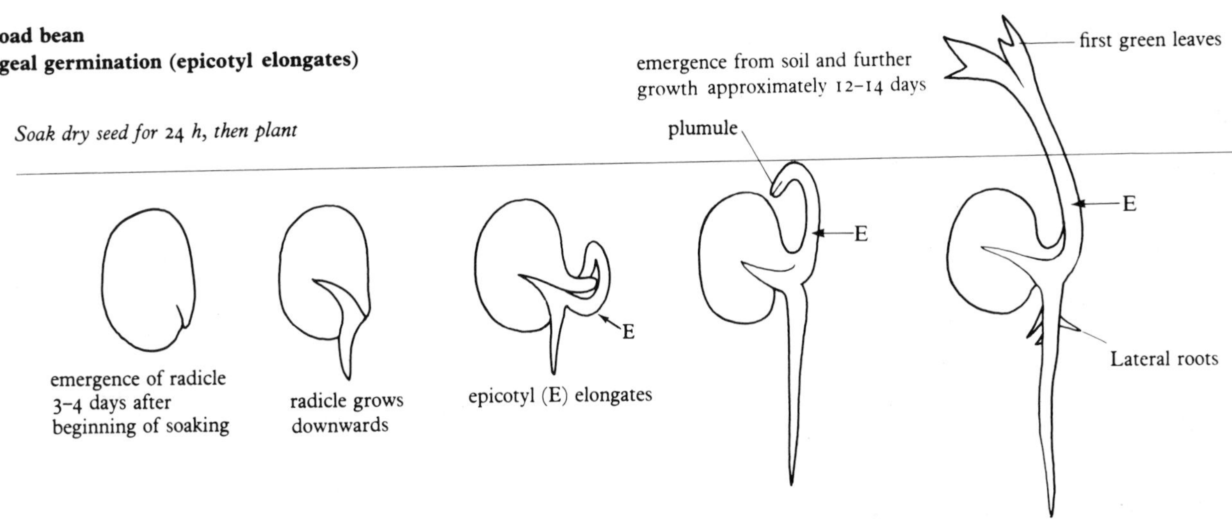

B Sunflower
Epigeal germination (hypocotyl elongates)

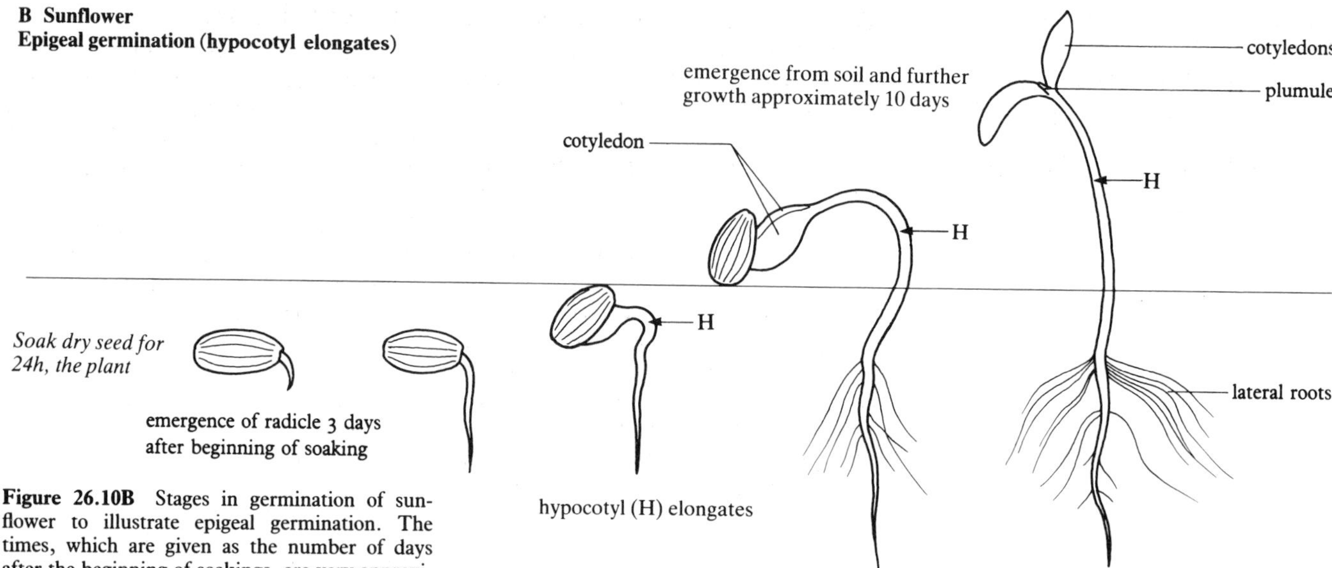

Figure 26.10B Stages in germination of sunflower to illustrate epigeal germination. The times, which are given as the number of days after the beginning of soakings, are very approximate and assume good growing conditions. **E**, epicotyl; **H**, hypocotyl. (**A** *On previous page*).

Requirements
Dish
Razor blade

Broad bean seeds
Castor oil seeds (from Investigation 26.5)

Seedlings showing different stages of hypogeal germination (e.g. bean)
Seedlings showing different stages of epigeal germination (e.g. sunflower)

Epigeal Germination

1 Observe the sliced castor oil seed from Investigation 26.5. Imagine the hypocotyl elongating rapidly. What will happen?

In epigeal germination the hypocotyl elongates with the result that the delicate cotyledon(s), protected by the ruptured seed coat, are thrust up above the soil surface where, exposed to light, they turn green and photosynthesise. During germination nourishment comes from the endosperm tissue which is usually, but not invariably, extensive.

2 Examine a series of seedlings of an epigeal plant (e.g. sunflower) resulting from staggered germination, and note the developmental sequence. Compare with the sequence in Figure 26.10B.

3 Observe the germination of other epigeal plants, e.g. mustard, cress, marrow, French bean or castor oil.

For Consideration

(1) Compare hypogeal and epigeal germination from a structural and physiological point of view.
(2) The seeds of epigeal plants usually contain abundant endosperm tissue – why is this?
(3) The seeds of hypogeal plants usually contain large, fleshy cotyledons – why?
(4) Although the seeds of epigeal plants usually contain abundant endosperm tissue, there are some that do not, e.g. sunflower, marrow and sycamore. How do you think such plants obtain nourishment during germination?

Investigation 26.7
Effect of an impermeable testa on seed germination

Requirements
Petri dish ×2
Whatman No. 4 filter paper ×4
Binocular (dissection) microscope
Forceps
Mounted needle

Seeds of rockrose (*Helianthemum* spp.).

Procedure

1 Count out forty seeds of rockrose (e.g. *Helianthemum chamaecistus*).
2 Chip the testas of 20 seeds in turn: hold each seed with forceps under a dissecting microscope and chip off a small part of the testa with a mounted needle.
3 Place this batch of chipped seeds on two layers of moistened filter paper in a petri-dish.
4 Place twenty untreated seeds on two layers of moist filter paper in a petri-dish, as a control.
5 Keep the petri-dishes on a laboratory bench and moisten the filter paper from time to time to replace water lost by evaporation.
6 Examine the seeds after a week and record the percentage germination in each dish.

For consideration

(1) Are you satisfied that you have evidence that chipping the testa of the seeds promotes germination?
(2) Why do you think that unchipped seeds do not germinate? Devise an experiment to test your hypothesis.
(3) Suggest ways in which the testa of a seed in soil might be broken down.
(4) What effect will an impermeable testa have on the timing of germination under natural conditions? In what circumstances might this be favourable to the species?

Investigation 26.8
Localisation and activity of enzymes at various stages of maize grain germination

When a cereal grain germinates, its reserves of starch are broken down under the influence of the enzyme starch phosphorylase. Eventually glucose is formed. This is absorbed from the endosperm by the growing embryo which then uses it to synthesise new compounds and to provide the energy needed for such syntheses. Stages in this process can be followed in maize (*Zea mays*) by using stains to detect starch, phosphorylase and glucose. The procedure which follows provides instructions for staining a single seedling. However, if seeds at different stages of germination are available, the events which occur during germination can be followed in sequence.

1 Cut two maize seedlings carefully down their longitudinal axis to produce two half seedlings.

2 Using forceps, place a single half seedling into each of the three solutions provided so that the cut surface is immersed in the liquid. The three solutions contain iodine, silver nitrate and phenolphthalein diphosphate respectively. Do not get silver nitrate on your fingers, since it is toxic and it stains.

3 Leave your half-seedlings in the solutions for at least half an hour.

4 Remove the seedling from the iodine. Draw a diagram to show the intensity of the blue staining on the cut surface of the seedling. Ignore the brown colour of the iodine itself.

5 Remove the seedling from the silver nitrate. This stains reducing sugars (such as glucose) a black colour. Draw a diagram with a soft pencil to show the intensity of the black staining.

6 Remove the seedling from the phenolphthalein diphosphate solution. In the presence of phosphatase enzymes the solution will have been hydrolysed to phenolphthalein which will give a red colour in alkaline solution. Place the seedling in the 'alkali' solution for two minutes. Examine it and draw a diagram showing the intensity of the red colour.

For consideration

(1) Assume that the phosphatase activity is proportional to the metabolic rate of the tissues. Account for the distribution of colour on your diagrams in terms of the biochemistry of seed germination.

(2) Which parts of the embryo are most metabolically active, and why?

(3) To what purposes will glucose be put in the embryo?

Requirements

Razor blade or scalpel
Forceps
Binocular microscope or hand lens
Pencil, red crayon and blue crayon
Watch glasses ×3
Shallow dishes

Solutions of iodine, silver nitrate, phenolphthalein diphosphate and 1 mol dm^{-3} sodium carbonate (labelled 'alkali'), prepared as follows:
Iodine – dissolve 4 g potassium iodide in 600 cm^3 distilled water, add 2.5 g iodine crystals and make up to 1 dm^3.
Silver nitrate – make up a small volume with a concentration of 1.7 g per 100 cm^3 distilled water
Phenolphthalein diphosphate – dissolve 0.5 g of the calcium salt in 100 cm^3 of distilled water. Store in a refrigerator until needed and filter before use.

Petri-dish containing two germinating maize grains and one germinating French bean seed in water
Maize seedlings: use a large-seeded variety which has been treated with a fungicide. Sow in cool, well-lit conditions about two weeks before the practical session. The maize should have germinated to the point where the plumules and radicles have emerged, but the plumules have not broken through the cotyledons and the radicles have not started branching. Before use, wash the seedlings thoroughly to remove soil. After handling the seedlings, wash your hands so as to remove any fungicide which may have got on them.

Investigation 26.9
Primary growth of flowering plant

Primary growth takes place at the apex of the stem and root. It involves division of primary meristematic cells (apical meristem) and it results in the formation of primary tissues.

To investigate primary growth it is necessary to study sections and/or cleared whole mounts of young stem and root apices.

Root Apex

1 Obtain a germinating seed of maize or some other comparable grass (Figure 26.11). Instead of having a main root the seedling develops a bundle of adventitious (fibrous) roots, typical of grasses. The plumule is protected by a sheath-like coleoptile.

2 Cut one of the roots about 15 mm from the tip and mount in chloral hydrate which clears the tissue.

3 Examine under medium power, reducing the illumination as much as possible. Start with the extreme tip, where the cells are youngest, and work back to the older parts of the root. Note successively:

(a) Root cap cells (protective)

(b) Zone of cell division (cells cube-shaped, dividing mitotically)

(c) Zone of cell expansion (cells progressively more elongated as one passes back along the root).

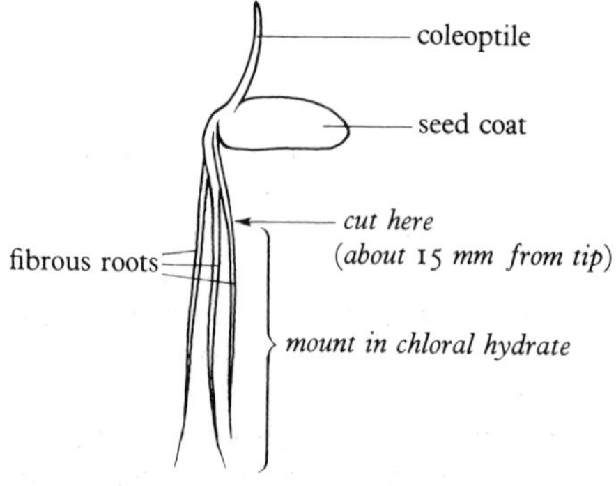

Figure 26.11 Preparation of young maize roots for viewing under the microscope.

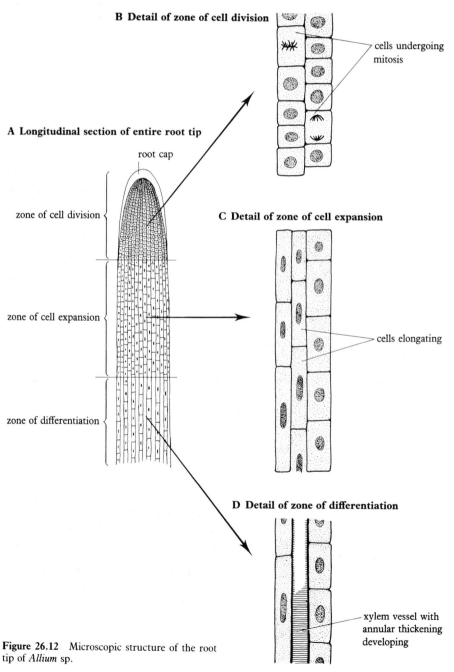

Figure 26.12 Microscopic structure of the root tip of *Allium* sp.

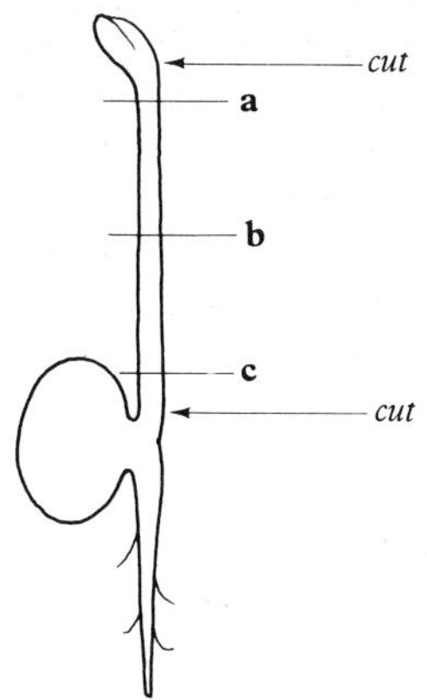

Figure 26.13 Young seedling of broad bean. Cut the shoot at the two points indicated. Section at levels a, b, and c.

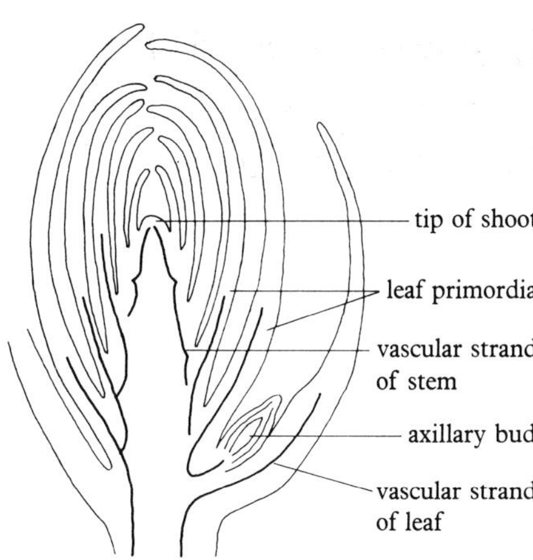

Figure 26.14 Longitudinal section of the stem apex of lilac.

Requirements
Microscope
Slides and coverslips
Razor blade
Watch glasses
Pith

Chloral hydrate
Phloroglucin (benzene-1,2,3-triol)
Phloroglucin
Hydrochloric acid (concentrated)
FABIL
Dilute glycerol

Germinating maize seed (Figure 26.14)
Germinating pea or bean with radicle 10–20 mm long (Figure 26.16)
LS root tip of onion (*Allium* sp.)
LS stem apex of lilac

(d) Zone of differentiation (cells acquire features, particularly of their walls, characteristic of specific tissues, e.g. xylem, phloem, etc. Xylem vessels with annular or spiral thickening should be evident).

4 Take a germinating pea or bean with a radicle 10–20 mm long and examine it under a hand lens or binocular microscope. Describe what you see.

5 With a sharp razor blade cut thin longitudinal sections and mount them in water or dilute glycerine. Examine under microscope. Note zones of cell division, expansion and differentiation. How do these relate to the root hair zone?

6 Examine a prepared longitudinal section of the root tip of, e.g. onion (*Allium* sp.) under low and high powers (Figure 26.12). Start at the tip and work back noting in particular mitotic figures in the zone of cell division. The root cap and zone of expansion will also be clearly visible and possibly the zone of differentiation showing spiral or annular thickening in developing xylem elements.

Shoot Apex

1 Remove the tip of the plumule of a germinating broad bean, and cut it close to its attachment to the seed.

2 Holding the isolated shoot in a piece of moistened pith (*see* page 124), cut transverse sections at levels **a**, **b**, and **c** in Figure 26.13 and place them in water in separate watch glasses.

3 Stain a thin section from each watch glass in either acidified phloroglucin or FABIL, then mount in dilute glycerol.

4 Compare your sections. What conclusions can you draw regarding the development of primary tissues in the shoot?

5 Examine a longitudinal section through the shoot apex of, e.g. lilac (Figure 26.14). Start at the tip and work back. How does the section compare with that of the root apex? In addition to the zones of cell division, expansion and differentiation, note the developing vascular strands, leaf primordia with vascular tissue going to them, and axillary buds.

6 On the upper surface of the shoot meristem there are one to three layers of cells called the tunica. The cells below form the corpus. How many tunica layers can you see in your shoot apex? What layers of cells do the tunica layer(s) form in the leaf primordia?

For Consideration

(1) Compare the development of a primary shoot and root. Explain the differences between them in terms of the functions which these two parts of the plant ultimately have to carry out in a herbaceous plant such as lupin.

(2) In the apical meristem of a root or shoot the cell divisions do not all occur in the same plane. Describe the planes in which they occur, and explain the contribution which each makes to the finished product.

Investigation 26.11
Secondary growth of flowering plant

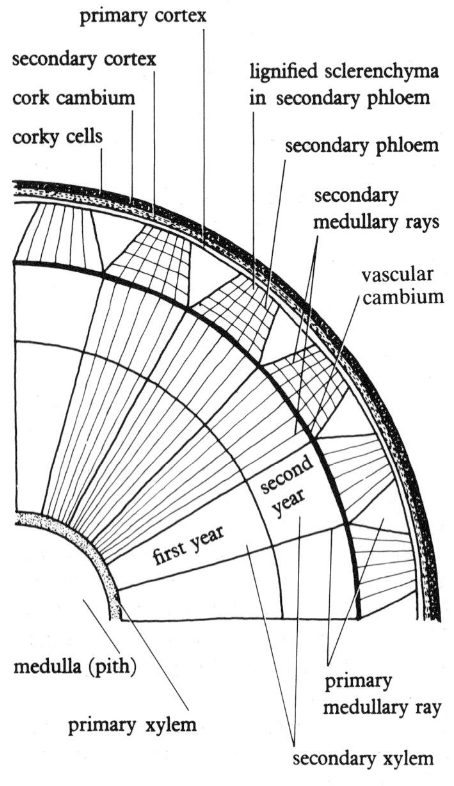

Figure 26.15 Transverse section of lime twig *Tilia* sp., autumn of the second year.

Primary growth is mainly concerned with growth of the plant in a longitudinal direction. In contrast, secondary growth is responsible for increasing the girth of the stem and root. It occurs by division of secondary meristematic cells (cambium) within the primary tissues, and it results in the formation of secondary tissues.

Procedure

COMPARISON OF SUCCESSIVE YEAR'S GROWTH

1 Cut transverse sections of a woody twig of lime tree (*Tilia* sp.), dated autumn of second year. From your knowledge of how secondary tissues are formed, what would you *expect* the appearance of such a section to be?

2 Stain some sections in iodine, others in acidified phloroglucin, then mount in dilute glycerine. Note the general appearance of your sections under low power. Are your predictions confirmed?

3 Now examine the detailed distribution of tissues (Figure 26.15). Note primary and secondary xylem, vascular cambium, secondary phloem. The secondary phloem contains blocks of lignified sclerenchyma in between the sieve tubes, which – though unusual – makes it easier to see. Little or no primary phloem will be visible (why?). Observe the primary and secondary medullary rays: what are their functions?

4 Distinguish between first- and second-year wood, and between spring and autumn wood. What is the functional significance of the difference between spring and autumn wood?

5 At the periphery note corky tissue. What functions are performed by this tissue?

6 What would you expect a lime twig to look like in transverse section in the autumn of its *first* year? Cut sections and stain. Are your predictions correct?

7 What would you expect a lime twig to look like in the *spring* of its first year? Test your predictions by cutting sections, staining them and examining.

8 Cut transverse sections of woody twigs of other plants, e.g. beech, oak, etc. Stain and mount. Report on differences and similarities between them.

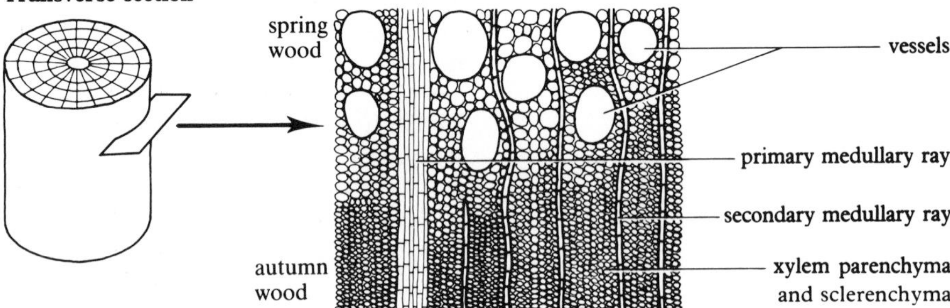

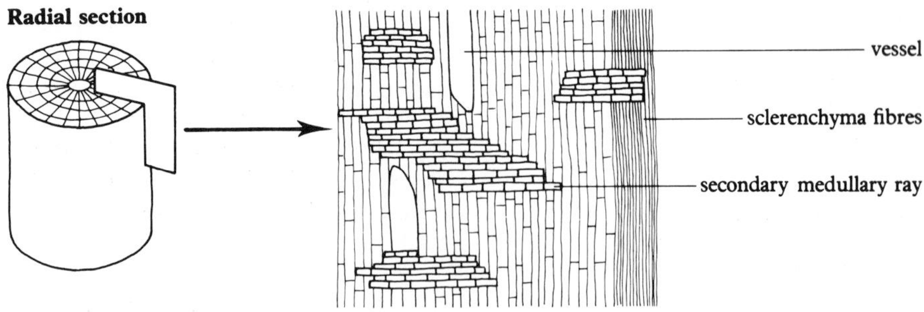

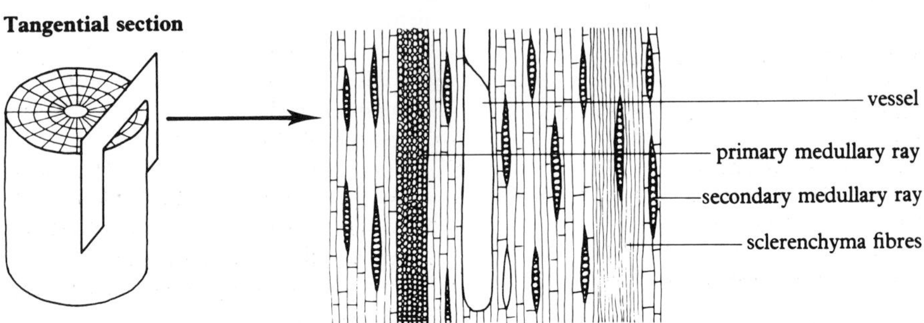

Figure 26.16 Section of secondary xylem (wood).

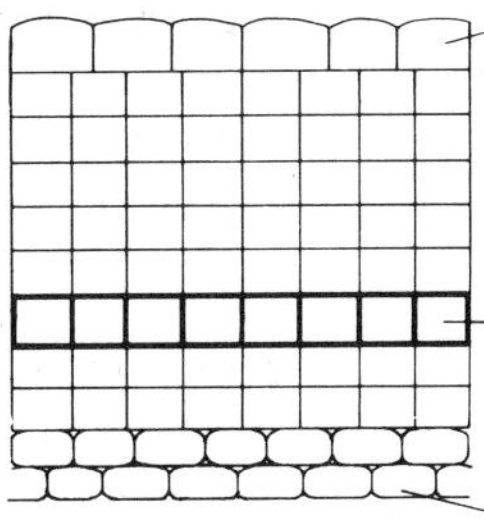

epidermis
cells cut off from the cork cambium in this direction form corky cells
corky cells (phellem)
periderm
cork cambium (phellogen)
cells cut off from the cork cambium in this direction form secondary cortex
secondary cortex (phelloderm)
primary cortex

Figure 26.17 Diagram showing the corky cells and associated structures found at the surface of a secondarily thickened stem.

WOOD

1 The main structure formed in secondary growth is wood. This, more than any other tissue, is responsible for increasing the girth of the stem. Whereabouts is the wood in your sections?

2 Reconstruct the three-dimensional anatomy of wood by cutting transverse, radial, and tangential sections of a woody twig (Figure 26.16). Stain some sections in iodine, and others in acidified phloroglucin.

3 Note the relationship between lignified (woody) xylem elements, constituting the secondary xylem tissue, and non-lignified medullary rays. Do the medullary ray cells always contain starch?

4 Describe the different types of element that make up the wood. What functions do you think they perform?

Supplement the information gained from your own sections by examining prepared sections.

5 Examine the cut surface of the felled trunk of a small tree. Notice, and count, the annual rings. What do they represent? How old was the tree when it was felled? Can you distinguish between the spring and autumn wood in each annual ring?

6 If available, examine the cut surface of the felled trunk of an older tree. Distinguish between the heartwood in the centre, and the sapwood further out. How do they differ structurally and functionally? What is the relevance of this to the timber industry?

CORK

1 Examine the cells towards the surface of a secondarily thickened stem. A layer of corky cells, of variable thickness, is formed beneath the original epidermis from a cork cambium which also forms a limited amount of secondary cortex (Figure 26.17).

2 Periodically the layer of corky cells is interrupted by a mass of loosely packed cells which constitute a lenticel. Examine a prepared slide showing the detailed structure of the corky cells and lenticel (Figure 26.18).

ROOT

1 Examine transverse sections of secondarily thickened roots of different ages, noting the form and distribution of the primary and secondary tissues.

2 How do the sections differ from those of stem? How would you explain the differences?

For Consideration

(1) Make a sketch showing the distribution of tissues in a two-year-old stem and root. Explain to yourself (or, better, to someone else!) how this pattern is arrived at during development.

(2) Make a sketch of the trunk, branches and twigs of an oak tree. Assuming that the tree is 80 years old, write onto the diagram the numbers of annual rings which you would expect to find at various levels.

(3) To what extent can the properties of wood be explained by the structure of its cellular elements?

(4) Discuss the commercial importance of wood in terms of its cellular and chemical composition.

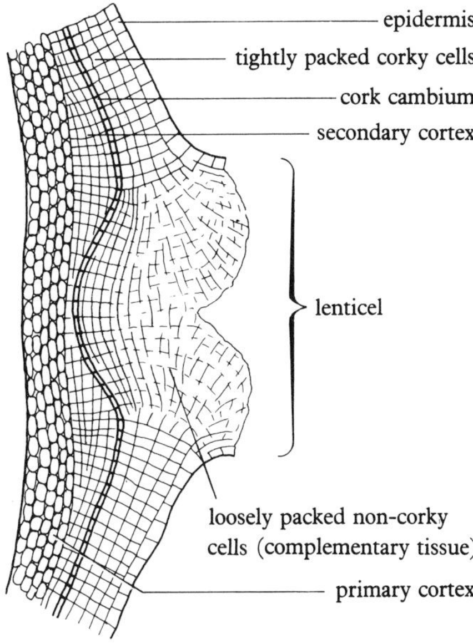

Figure 26.18 Diagram of a lenticel seen in section. Based on elder.

Requirements
Microscope
Slides and coverslips
Watch glasses
Razor blade

Iodine solution
Benzene-1, 3, 5-triol (phloroglucin)
Hydrochloric acid (concentrated)
Dilute glycerol

Twigs of lime (*Tilia* sp.): spring and autumn of 1st year, and autumn of 2nd year
Twigs of other woody perennials, e.g. beech, oak, etc.
Transverse, radial, and tangential sections of wood
TS cork showing lenticel
Transversely cut trunk of young tree showing annual rings
Transversely cut trunk of older tree showing heartwood and sapwood

Questions and Problems

1 Write a short essay on the problem of measuring growth.

2 The female sheep, the ewe, may have one, two or three lambs per pregnancy. At first the lambs feed only on milk, but after about five weeks they begin to eat solid food.

A research worker was interested in the effect of the number of lambs per ewe on the growth of lambs. To investigate this problem she weighed lambs of different classes every four weeks. The classes were as follows:
Singles (single lambs reared by their own mother);
Twins (twins reared by their own mother);
Triplets (triplets reared by their own mother);
Twins reared as singles (lambs born as twins, but shortly after birth one was transferred to another ewe, and both lambs were reared as singles).

Her data are summarised in the Table in the margin where each number is the mean for a large number of lambs:

Age (weeks)	**Mass** (kg)			
	Singles	Twins	Triplets	Twins reared as singles
2	10.0	7.2	6.5	7.9
6	19.5	13.7	13.1	16.8
10	28.5	20.9	20.2	25.0
14	37.0	28.6	27.0	33.6
18	43.7	35.1	33.1	41.0
22	48.5	40.0	37.9	46.1
26	51.8	44.3	42.4	49.3

(a) For each period of four weeks, calculate the growth rate (as kg per four-week period) for each class and tabulate your results.
(b) Present your calculated data in the form of a graph of growth rate against age of lamb.
(c) Comment upon the differences in growth rate of the different classes.
(d) Do you consider that food supply is the only factor which affects the growth rate of the different classes?

In your answers to parts (c) and (d) you should refer to the appropriate parts of the graph and give quantitative data to amplify your statements. *(CL)*

3 The following data are the results of making daily growth measurements on a locust over a period of 24 days during its development:

Day	**Total body mass** (mg)	**Width of head** (mm)	**Length of hind femur** (mm)
1	100	3.0	7.0
2	100	3.5	7.5
3	100	4.0	8.0
4	140	4.0	8.0
5	160	4.0	8.0
6	200	4.0	8.0
7	230	4.0	8.0
8	230	4.4	9.2
9	230	4.7	10.5
10	230	5.0	12.0
11	280	5.0	12.0
12	350	5.0	12.0
13	410	5.0	12.0
14	470	5.0	12.0
15	530	5.0	12.0
16	600	5.0	12.0
17	600	5.6	13.3
18	600	6.4	14.8
19	600	7.0	16.4
20	600	7.6	18.0
21	760	7.6	18.0
22	900	7.6	18.0
23	1050	7.6	18.0
24	1200	7.6	18.0

(a) Plot these three sets of data on a single sheet of graph paper so that they can be readily compared.
(b) Interpret each of the graphs and account for any differences between them.
(c) Draw the form of graph you would expect to obtain if you plotted, for the human, body mass against time, from birth to maturity. Compare and contrast this with the results obtained for the locust.

4 Write short explanatory notes on cleavage, gastrulation, neurulation and organogeny.

5 Compare the structure and functions of the extra-embryonic membranes in mammals and birds.

Part of grain	**Dry mass** (per cent)	**Chemical constituents**
Starchy endosperm	82–86%	Starch, gluten
Aleurone layer	3–4%	Protein, cellulose
Germ (embryo)	6%	Protein, oil, vitamins, minerals
Pericarp	5%	Cellulose

6 The relative dry mass and the main chemical constituents of the different parts of wheat grain are given in the table in the margin.

When the grain is milled into white flour the pericarp, aleurone layer and germ are discarded and only the starchy endosperm remains. Use the information given here to discuss the nutritional aspects of bread-making.

7 The tip of a bean root was marked with Indian ink. Each mark was 2 mm from the next. After several days it was noticed that some of the marks were no longer the same distance apart. Here are two hypotheses to account for this result:

(a) Cells have divided in the regions between adjacent marks; more divisions have occurred in the region where the marks have moved furthest apart.

(b) Cells between certain marks have elongated more than others.

How would you investigate which hypothesis is correct?

8 In the 1930s Howard C. Dittmer carefully separated the soil from the root system of a single rye plant (*Secale cereale*). He had grown it for 120 days in a box of soil 30.5 cm wide, 30.5 cm broad and 56 cm deep. He carefully measured the extent of the root system. The total area of root surface (excluding root hairs) was 639 m^2 and the combined length of the roots was 623 km!

(a) What surface area of root lies beneath each square metre of soil surface?

(b) (i) In the root meristem the dividing cells are in rows about 30 cells long (*see* Figure 26.12, page 268). Each cell in a row divides once a day. At maturity, each cell produced by cell division is about 50 μm long.
Estimate from these figures how far a root tip grows in a day.

(ii) How many roots would have to grow at this rate to provide a root system 623 km long in 120 days?

(b) (i) Suppose an average root is 0.5 mm (500 μm) in diameter at the tip. Calculate the cross-sectional area of such a root, assuming that it is circular.

(ii) How many such roots could fit within a hole 1 mm square?

(iii) How many such roots could fit into a hole 1 cm square?

(iv) How many such roots could grow down at once through the cross-sectional area of the soil in the pot (930 cm^2)?

(c) Critically discuss the results of your calculations. How do you think that Dittmer calculated the total length and surface area of the roots?

(d) List the environmental factors which might influence the rate at which roots grow. In each case, explain why the factor might influence growth rate.

9 The following results were obtained from a study of the germination and early growth of a cereal. The grains were sown in soil in a greenhouse and at two-day intervals samples were taken and separated into the two components, endosperm and embryo (or young plant), which were then oven-dried and weighed:

Time after sowing (days)	**Total dry mass** (g)	**Dry mass of endosperm** (g)	**Dry mass of embryo** (g)
0	0.045	0.043	0.002
2	0.043	0.041	0.002
4	0.040	0.032	0.008
6	0.036	0.020	0.016
8	0.035	0.009	0.024
10	0.040	0.006	0.034

Plot the results graphically and describe in words what they show. (*O and C*)

10 Germination starts with the uptake of water by the seed. (a) What factors may trigger this process to start taking place? (b) Make a list of the subsequent events which this makes possible.

11 Summarise the changes which occur in the circulation of the human foetus at, or soon after, birth.

12 Compare the growth of a flowering plant with that of a vertebrate animal.

13 Describe in detail the ontogeny (development) of (a) a sieve tube, and (b) a xylem vessel. (From your knowledge of the finished product in each case try to *work out* the sequence of events rather than look them up in a book).

14 Figure 26.19 is a transverse section through part of a secondarily thickened stem showing three annual rings (labelled **A**, **B** and **C**).

(a) Name structures 1 and 2, and state their functions.
(b) Which is the oldest annual ring: **A**, **B** or **C**? How do you know?
(c) Describe three *visible* ways in which the autumn wood differs from the spring wood.
(d) Suggest why (i) ring **A** is wider than ring **B**, and (ii) the autumn wood in ring C is subdivided into two parts.

15 In one of the Californian National Parks there is a redwood tree (*Sequoia* sp.) which, having leaned over to one side, appears to have produced a wedge to support itself as shown in Figure 26.20.

(a) What would you expect a transverse section cut at level A to look like? (Do not show individual cells.)
(b) Explain how this situation may have come about.

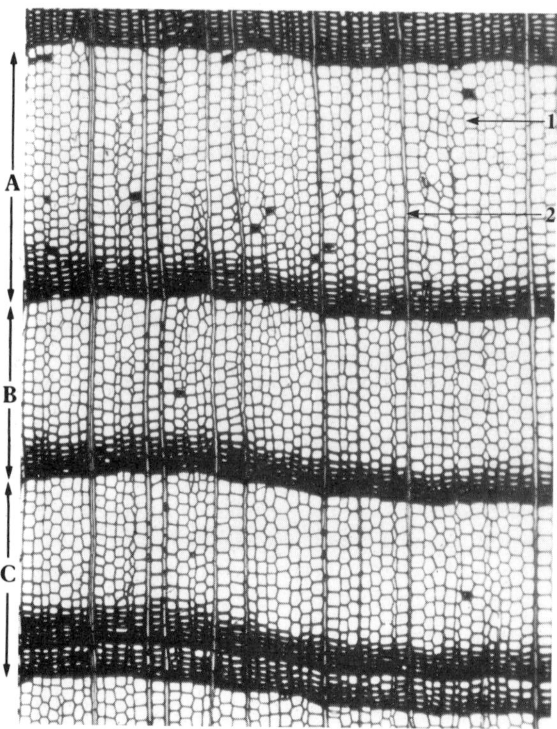

Figure 26.19 Transverse section through part of a secondarily thickened stem.

Figure 26.20 The redwood tree (*Sequoia sempervirens*) referred to in question 17. T, trunk; W, wedge.

27 The Control of Growth

Background Summary

1 Growth is influenced by a combination of external and internal factors. The internal factors are affected by the external ones.

2 In flowering plants experiments indicate that a hormone (**auxin**, **indole-acetic acid**, **IAA**) promotes growth of the shoot. Auxin achieves its effect by influencing cell elongation. A variety of synthetic **growth substances** have the same effect.

3 Plants often respond to directional stimuli by means of growth movements (**tropisms**). Experiments suggest that the tropic responses of shoots to gravity and light (**geotropism** and **phototropism**, respectively) can be explained by an unequal distribution of auxin within the plant.

4 Further experiments indicate that a shoot's positive phototropic response results from auxin moving to the dark side of the shoot, rather than being destroyed on the illuminated side.

5 In geotropism the stimulus of gravity is detected by the falling of **starch statoliths**, and in the root the response is brought about by a growth-inhibitor produced by the root cap.

6 Other growth responses shown by plants include **chemotropism** and **thigmotropism**. Plants also respond to diffuse stimuli that do not come from a particular direction (**nastic responses**).

7 Although it normally exerts its effects on cell elongation, auxin can also promote cell division. Its other functions include maintenance of **apical dominance** by suppression of lateral buds; growth of adventitious roots; initiation of secondary growth and ripening of fruit; inhibition of leaf-fall and termination of dormancy of buds. Synthetic auxins are of considerable commercial importance, for example as herbicides.

8 A second category of plant growth substances are **gibberellins**. These are responsible for bolting, promoting internodal growth, and side-branching of stems, inhibiting root growth, and bringing about parthenocarpy. They achieve their growth-promoting effects by initiating both cell division and elongation.

9 **Cytokinins** (**kinins**) are a further group of plant growth substances. They promote cell division and, in conjunction with other growth substances, including auxins, they control cell differentiation and break dormancy.

10 Another plant hormone is **abscisic acid**. This promotes fruit-fall and possibly leaf-fall, brings on the dormancy of buds, inhibits seed germination, and may be the root growth inhibitor mentioned in point 5.

11 **Ethene** (ethylene) is also involved in a number of plant responses. For example, it promotes ripening of fruit, triggers leaf-fall, and releases buds and seeds from dormancy.

12 Of all external factors, **light** and **temperature** have the most pronounced effects on plant growth and development. Each influences a variety of important developmental processes. Lack of light results in **etiolation**.

13 Experiments on Grand Rapids lettuce seeds indicate that germination is promoted by red light and inhibited by far-red, a phenomenon with important ecological implications.

14 Further experiments have shown that light is perceived by a photochemical substance, **phytochrome**, which exists in two inter-convertible forms, one sensitive to red light, the other to far-red. A plant's response to light is determined by the balance between these two forms of phytochrome.

15 In addition to germination the phytochrome system is involved in stem elongation, leaf expansion, chlorophyll-synthesis, growth of side-roots, leaf fall and flowering.

16 Phytochrome probably exerts its action through the intermediacy of a hormone. There is particularly strong evidence for this in the photoperiodic control of flowering.

17 **Photoperiodism** is the response of an organism to day-length. Photoperiodic responses are shown by animals as well as plants, and may involve behaviour and other responses as well as growth.

18 In photoperiodic control of flowering, plants can be divided into **long-day**, **short-day**, and **day-neutral plants**. The category to which a plant belongs is related to its ecological situation. As in other phenomena involving the phytochrome system, the plant's response depends on a balance between the two forms of phytochrome. The link between the perception of the stimulus and the flowering response appears to be hormonal.

19 The influence of temperature on plant growth is most obvious in the case of flowering. Sometimes flowering will only take place if the seeds or plants have been subjected to a period of chilling (**vernalisation**).

20 Growth in animals is also controlled by hormones, e.g. the **pituitary growth hormone** of mammals, and the **moulting** and **juvenile hormones** of insects. The latter are involved in the control of metamorphosis, in which respect they are equivalent to **thyroxine** in amphibians.

21 There is mounting evidence that in both plants and animals hormones controlling growth exert their action by activating the appropriate genes.

22 Growth and development may be temporarily interrupted by **dormancy**. Important in distribution and survival over unfavourable periods, dormancy is found in seeds, buds, spores (including zygospores), eggs, perennating organs, and adult organisms.

23 There is much variation in the length of time a dormant structure can survive, and the severity of the conditions which it can endure.

24 Dormancy is initiated and terminated by a combination of external and internal factors. The external factors include day-length (photoperiodism) and temperature. The dormant seeds of some plants require an obligatory period of chilling before germination can take place (**stratification**).

25 Internally chemical substances (hormones) appear to be involved in dormancy. This is established in the case of seeds and buds, and also in the initiation of leaf fall, a prerequisite to winter dormancy in deciduous trees.

26 In insects **diapause** is comparable to dormancy in plants. **Hibernation** and **aestivation** are also types of dormancy found in certain animal groups. As in plants, animal dormancy is controlled by hormones.

Investigation 27.1

Effect of indoleacetic acid on the growth of coleoptiles and roots

It has been known for many years that indoleacetic acid (IAA) affects the growth of shoots and roots. In this experiment these effects are investigated in relation to specific concentrations of IAA.

Procedure

In this experiment it is convenient to work in groups of five.

1 Prepare five labelled petri dishes, with lids, containing the following:

(a) 2 per cent sucrose plus 100 mg dm^{-3} IAA
(b) 2 per cent sucrose plus 1.0 mg dm^{-3} IAA
(c) 2 per cent sucrose plus 10^{-3} mg dm^{-3} IAA
(d) 2 per cent sucrose plus 10^{-5} mg dm^{-3} IAA
(e) 2 per cent sucrose alone.

Other dilutions can also be used if desired.

2 Take 25 germinating wheat seeds which have been kept in the dark. Work in as dark a place as possible, or in red light in a darkroom.

With a razor blade cut off the distal 2 mm of the coleoptiles. Then sever each coleoptile exactly 10 mm further back, thereby isolating a 10 mm length of coleoptile. Do this for all 25 seeds, so you have 25 lengths of coleoptile, all 10 mm in length. Place five coleoptiles in each petri dish.

3 Repeat with the radicles, placing five in each petri dish.

4 Put lids on the five petri dishes and place them in darkness in an incubator at 25 °C.

5 After approximately 48 hours, remove the petri dishes and measure the length of (a) the coleoptiles, (b) the portion of leaf which was enclosed within each coleoptile when it was cut, and (c) the radicle. Record your measurements and for each treatment calculate the *average* lengths of the coleoptile, leaf, and radicle.

6 Express your results as change in length of coleoptile, leaf, and radicle in mm. Plot changes in length for all three on a single sheet of graph paper: length on the vertical axis, auxin concentrations equally spaced on the horizontal axis.

For Consideration

(1) Why was it necessary to remove the tips of the coleoptiles and radicles before performing this experiment?
(2) For what reason were the auxin solutions made up with sucrose?
(3) What general conclusions would you draw from your results?
(4) How do your results relate to the normal growth of the coleoptile, leaves and radicle?

Requirements

Incubator at 25 °C
Ruler with mm divisions
Petri dishes with lids ×5
Wax pencil
Razor blade
White tile

2 per cent sucrose solution (see below)
Indoleacetic acid (IAA) solutions in sucrose (see below)

Germinating wheat seeds grown in the dark at 25 °C for at least five days. (The coleoptiles must be about 15 mm long)

Make up 1 dm^3 of stock IAA solution: dissolve 200 mg IAA in 2 cm^3 ethanol (absolute). Add 900 cm^3 distilled water and heat for 5 minutes at 80 °C to evaporate the ethanol. Cool, and make up to 1.0 dm^3 with distilled water. Store in refrigerator.

Prepare the five solutions thus:

(a) **100 mg dm^{-3} IAA + 2 per cent sucrose**: to 100 cm^3 of stock IAA add 100 cm^3 of 4 per cent sucrose solution in a stoppered flask.
(b) **1.0 mg dm^{-3} IAA + 2 per cent sucrose**: take 10 cm^3 of stock IAA and make up to 1.0 dm^3 with water; to 100 cm^3 of this solution add 100 cm^3 of 4 per cent sucrose.
(c) **10^{-3} mg dm^{-3} IAA + 2 per cent sucrose**: take 1.0 cm^3 of (b) and make up to 1.0 dm^3 with water. To 100 cm^3 of this solution add 100 cm^3 of 4 per cent sucrose.
(d) **10^{-5} mg dm^{-3} IAA + 2 per cent sucrose**: take 10 cm^3 of (c) and make up to 1.0 dm^3 with water. To 100 cm^3 of this solution add 100 cm^3 of 4 per cent sucrose.
(e) **2 per cent sucrose**: to 100 cm^3 of 4 per cent sucrose solution add 100 cm^3 of water.

Investigation 27.2
Measurement of tropic responses of coleoptiles and radicles

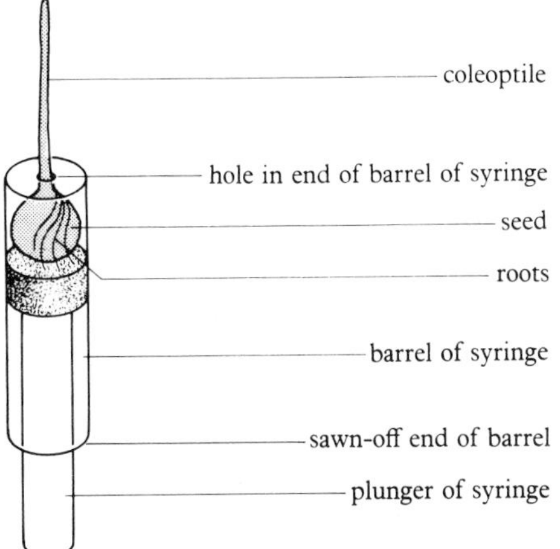

Figure 27.1 Moist chamber, constructed from plastic syringe, for mounting a germinating seed for observations on phototropism.

Requirements
Microscope
Eyepiece with micrometer scale
Moist chamber (*see* Figure 27.1)
Slide
Elastic band

Germinating seed of oat, barley or wheat grown in the dark at 25 °C

It is well known that stems normally grow towards light, i.e. they are positively phototropic. In this experiment the phototropic response of a coleoptile is observed and measured. The same technique can then be used to measure other responses of coleoptiles and radicles.

Procedure

For this experiment you require a microscope whose eyepiece has been fitted with a micrometer scale (*see* page 378).

1 Bend the microscope downwards towards you, so the tube is horizontal and the stage vertical. Darken the room and arrange for a source of light to strike the microscope stage from one side.

2 Take a germinating oat, barley, or wheat seed, which has a straight coleoptile. Mount the seed in a moist chamber constructed from a plastic syringe (Figure 27.1). The coleoptile should protrude from the chamber as shown.

3 With an elastic band, attach the moist chamber to a slide. Clip the slide to the microscope stage so the coleoptile is pointing directly upwards. Position it so that the tip of the coleoptile, when viewed down the microscope, corresponds exactly with the mid-point of the micrometer scale.

4 With the coleoptile illuminated from one side, observe the tip of the coleoptile for 5–10 minutes until it starts moving in a definite direction. Then rotate the moist chamber through 180° on its vertical axis so the other side of the coleoptile now receives the strongest illumination. Re-adjust the position of the moist chamber so the coleoptile tip corresponds to the centre of the micrometer scale, as before.

5 Take readings of the position of the coleoptile tip at regular intervals for up to an hour.

6 Plot position of coleoptile tip (vertical axis) against time. What conclusions can you draw?

Further experiments

Using the same technique of mounting a germinating seed in a moist chamber and viewing under the microscope, investigate one or more of the following:

1 The response to directional illumination of a coleoptile whose tip has been removed.

2 The response of a coleoptile to gravity.

3 The response of a radicle to directional illumination.

4 The response of a radicle to gravity.

5 The response to gravity of a radicle whose root cap has been removed.

For Consideration

(1) Have you obtained any inconsistent or anomalous results in the course of your experiments? If so, how would you attempt to explain them?

(2) What was the reason for rotating the coleoptile through 180° at Step 4 in the phototropism experiment?

(3) What is the relevance of your results to the normal life of the plant?

Investigation 27.3
Effect of auxin on leaf abscission

Many deciduous trees lose their leaves in autumn. This seems in many cases to be a response to the increasing night length as autumn wears on. The changes in night length, monitored by phytochrome, probably exert their effects by altering the concentrations of hormones in the leaves. One theory is that auxin, produced in the tip of a leaf, diffuses down the petiole during the summer and prevents leaf abscission. Leaves fall off when the auxin production ceases. In this experiment we test this idea on geraniums (*Pelargonium* spp.).

Procedure

1 Select a mature *Pelargonium* plant with at least twelve leaves, and count the exact number of leaves.

2 By drawing numbers out of a hat or otherwise, assign each leaf on the plant randomly to one of three treatments. Treatment one (the control) consists of leaves in which no special treatment is applied. In treatment two the leaf blades or laminas are carefully removed but the stalks (petioles) are left intact. In treatment three the leaves are treated in the same way as in treatment two, except that a blob of lanolin containing 1 per cent auxin is placed on the cut end of each petiole.

3 Set up the treatments as indicated. Attach a numbered label to each petiole indicating the treatment to which it has been subjected.

4 Examine the plant after three weeks, and again after six weeks. Record on the second occasion exactly what has happened to each leaf.

Requirements
String tags

Indole-acetic acid in lanolin (1 per cent). Dissolve the auxin in a little ethanol before mixing it into the lanolin.

Healthy leafy plant of geranium (*Pelargonium* sp.)

For consideration

(1) How could you test experimentally that an increase in night length triggers leaf abscission?
(2) If a herbivore eats a leaf blade, what will happen to the petiole?
(3) What are the functions of the abscission layer?
(4) Which other plant hormones besides auxin are involved in leaf abscission and in what way?
(5) Suggest four possible advantages to deciduous trees of losing their leaves in winter.

Investigation 27.4
Gibberellic acid and the production of amylase in germinating barley grains

When a cereal grain germinates, the insoluble storage compounds in the endosperm are hydrolysed. This produces soluble sugars such as maltose, which are absorbed by the growing embryo. What stimulates the digestion of the starch in the endosperm? One hypothesis suggests that the stimulus is provided by the hormone gibberellic acid (GA_3) released from the embryo.

Procedure

1 You are provided with eight petri-dishes containing blue starch-iodine agar. If amylase enzymes are released into this agar, they will digest the starch and the blue colour will disappear.

2 Four of your petri dishes have had gibberellic acid (GA_3) incorporated in the agar, and four have not. Label the bases of the dishes which have received GA_3 with G END L, G EMB L, G END D, and G EMB D respectively. Mark the remaining dishes END L, EMB L, END D and EMB D. In this code G stands for gibberellic acid, END for the endosperm end of the grain, EMB for the embryo end of the grain, L for living and D for dead.

3 Place twenty barley grains in a beaker of boiling water for ten minutes. Then lift them out carefully with forceps and place them on a ceramic tile.

4 Using a razor blade, cut each boiled grain transversely about half way down (Figure 27.2). After each grain has been cut, transfer its endosperm and embryo halves to the appropriate petri dishes with the cut side of the grain exposed to the agar. The two END D dishes should each receive ten boiled endosperm halves. The two EMB D dishes should each receive ten boiled embryo halves. Space the grains on the agar as far apart as you can.

5 Repeat Step 4 with 20 unboiled grains. In this case the two END L dishes will each receive ten unboiled endosperm halves, and the two EMB L dishes will each gain ten unboiled embryo halves.

6 Incubate the petri dishes in an oven for 48 hours at 30 °C.

7 When incubation is complete, examine the dishes. For each grain in each treatment, record the diameter in mm of any clear region in the agar beneath the grain.

8 Examine the insides of the grains themselves. In which grains have the contents been liquefied? Test the contents of the grains for reducing sugars with Benedict's reagent or for glucose with Clinistix. Record your results.

9 Calculate the area of the clear region surrounding each grain (area of a circle $= \pi r^2$). Work out the average area of the clear region in each treatment and tabulate the results. If you consider it appropriate, carry out statistical tests to determine whether the grains in each treatment produced significantly different quantities of amylase (*see* Appendix 6, page 393).

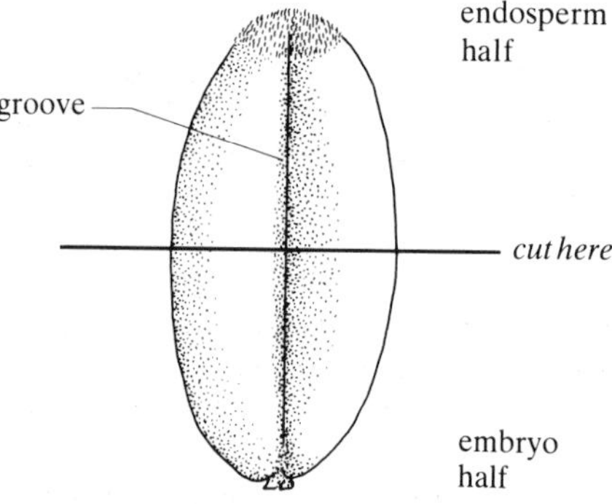

Figure 27.2 Diagram of cereal grain to show where to make the transverse cut in Investigation 27.4.

For consideration

(1) Does gibberellic acid affect the production of amylase by barley grains?
(2) Suggest reasons for the differences in amylase production between boiled and unboiled grains.
(3) Did your embryo halves produce some amylase? If so, how?
(4) Is it fair to assume that the area of the clear region around each grain is directly proportional to the number of amylase molecules secreted?
(5) Gibberellic acid might cause the release by the aleurone layer of enzymes stored there. Alternatively, it might trigger the synthesis of enzymes as well as their release. Suggest two experiments which would distinguish between these hypotheses.

References: M. Black, *Control Processes in Germination and Dormancy*, Oxford Biology Reader no.20, Oxford University Press, 1972.
P.W. Freeland, 'Gibberellic acid enhanced α-amylase synthesis in halved grains of barley (*Hordeum vulgare*): a simple laboratory demonstration', *Journal of Biological Education*, no.6, pages 369–375, 1972.
J. Coppage & T.A. Hill, 'Further experiments on gibberellin-stimulated amylase production in cereal grains', *Journal of Biological Education*, no.7, pages 11–18, 1973.

Requirements
Bunsen burner, tripod, gauze
Beaker
Forceps
Razor blade
Ceramic tile
Oven
Refrigerator
Ruler

Clinistix strip
Benedict's reagent
Petri dishes containing starch-iodine agar ×8 (four containing gibberellic acid and four not see below)

Barley grains ×40 (soaked in water for four hours before the experiment)

Prepare petri dishes as follows: Dissolve 200 mg soluble starch in a little water and make up to 100 cm^3. Heat until boiling then add 1.5 g Oxoid no.1 agar powder. Stir vigorously until the agar is dissolved then split the hot agar into two halves (50 cm^3 each). To one half of the agar add 0.5 cm^3 of 100 ppm (0.01 per cent) gibberellic acid in ethanol and stir. To the other half of the agar add 0.5 cm^3 of ethanol as the control. When agar cools to 60 °C, pour 10 cm^3 into each of the eight petri dishes. Immediately add two drops of iodine solution to each dish; stir vigorously distributing the iodine to form a uniformly coloured gel. Store in fridge at 2 °C until required.

Investigation 27.5
Control of metamorphosis in amphibians

In animals, as in plants, growth and development are controlled by hormones. In vertebrates a hormone directly involved in growth is thyroxine, secreted by the thyroid gland. Thyroxine is an amino acid derivative which contains iodine derived from the diet.

A developmental event in which thyroxine has been implicated is metamorphosis in amphibians. This is the development of the larva (tadpole) into the adult (*see* Investigation 26.2, page 259. In this investigation certain aspects of this event are explored.

The African clawed toad, *Xenopus laevis*, is suitable for this investigation. Instructions on the rearing of *Xenopus* tadpoles are given on page 401. Alternatively tadpoles of the common frog or toad may be used.

In the experimental part of this investigation it is conventient to work in pairs, one student investigating thyroxine, the other iodine.

Thyroxine and Metamorphosis

1 Obtain seven dishes 10 cm in diameter. Label them **A** to **G**.
2 In **A** place natural pond water, or Holtfreter's solution, to a depth of 5 cm. In **B** place a solution containing 0.1 mg dm^{-3} of thyroxine; into **C** a solution containing 0.05 mg dm^{-3} thyroxine; into **D** a solution containing 0.01 mg dm^{-3} thyroxine; into **E** a solution containing 0.1 mg dm^{-3} iodine; into **F** a solution containing 0.05 mg dm^{-3} iodine and into **G** a solution containing 0.01 mg dm^{-3} iodine.
3 Into each dish place at least five, and not more than ten, pre-metamorphosis tadpoles. There should be the same number of tadpoles in each dish.
4 Examine the tadpoles at regular intervals during the course of their subsequent development. Record their relative sizes and state of maturity. Note when metamorphosis occurs.

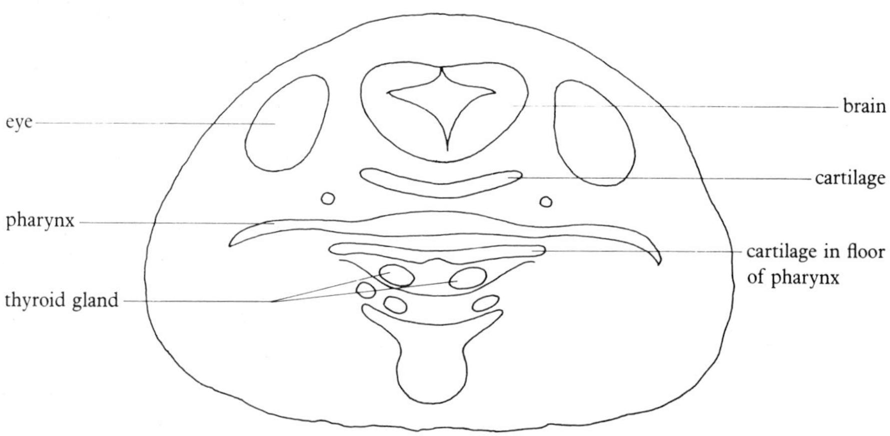

Figure 27.3 Diagram of transverse section of post-hind limb tadpole (*Rana*) to show position of the thyroid gland beneath the pharynx.

5 What conclusions would you draw from your results?

Changes in the Thyroid Gland during Development

1 First be sure that you can recognise the thyroid gland when you see it in a microscopic section, and that you understand its histology. If you have not already done so, examine a section of mammalian thyroid gland (*see* Investigation 18.5, page 178).
2 Now examine a transverse section of a tadpole whose hind limbs have developed (post-hind limb tadpole). The thyroid gland will be seen immediately beneath the floor of the pharynx. Can you recognise it? If necessary refer to Figure 27.3 to help you locate it.
3 Now examine a transverse section of a tadpole whose hind limbs have not yet developed (pre-hind limb tadpole). Can you find the thyroid gland? How does its appearance compare with what you observed in the previous section?
4 What conclusions do you draw from your observations? Do they fit in with the results of your experiment on thyroxine?

For Consideration

(1) In the control of amphibian metamorphosis thyroxine is an *internal* factor. What *external* factors might be involved in controlling metamorphosis?
(2) How could you investigate whether or not each of the external factors listed in your answer to (1) *actually* controls metamorphosis?
(3) What are the consequences if (a) a child and (b) an adult human fail to receive sufficient iodine in their diets?
(4) Thiourea is said to block the incorporation of iodine into thyroxine in the thyroid gland. How would you investigate the effect of this thyroid inhibitor on metamorphosis?

Requirements
Microscope
Dishes (10 cm diameter, 6 cm high) ×7
Wax pencil

Pond water or Holtfreter's solution
Thyroxine solutions (*see* below)
Iodine solutions (*see* below)

Pre-metamorphosis tadpoles of, e.g. *Xenopus laevis*
TS pre-hind limb tadpole
TS post-hind limb tadpole

Make up stock solution of thyroxine: dissolve 0.1 g thyroxine in 10 cm^3 of 0.1 mol dm^{-3} sodium hydroxide. Add 90 cm^3 of water.
Add 1.0 cm3 of this solution to 1.0 dm^3 of pond water or Holtfreter's solution. This gives a solution of 1.0 mg dm^{-3} thyroxine.
Prepare the three solutions thus:
(a) **0.1 mg dm^{-3} thyroxine**: add 100 cm^3 of stock thyroxine to 900 cm^3 of pond water or Holtfreter's solution.
(b) **0.05 mg dm^{-3} thyroxine**: add 50 cm^3 of stock thyroxine to 950 cm^3 of pond water or Holtfreter's solution.
(c) **0.01 mg dm^{-3} thyroxine**: add 10 cm^3 of stock thyroxine to 990 cm^3 of pond water or Holtfreter's solution.

Make up stock solution of iodine: dissolve 0.1 g of iodine crystals in 10 cm^3 of ethanol. Add 90 cm^3 of water. Add 1.0 cm^3 of this solution to 1.0 dm^3 of pond water or Holtfreter's solution.
Prepare the three solutions thus:
(a) **0.1 mg dm^{-3} iodine**: add 100 cm^3 of stock iodine to 900 cm^3 of pond water or Holtfreter's solution.
(b) **0.05 mg dm^{-3} iodine**: add 50 cm^3 of stock iodine to 950 cm^3 of pond water or Holtfreter's solution.
(c) **0.01 mg dm^{-3} thyroxine**: add 10 cm^3 of stock iodine to 990 cm^3 of pond water or Holtfreter's solution.

Holtfreter's solution made up as follows: To 1.0 dm^3 of distilled water add 3.5 g sodium chloride, 0.05 g potassium chloride, 0.10 g calcium chloride, 0.02 g sodium hydrogencarbonate, and dissolve.

Questions and Problems

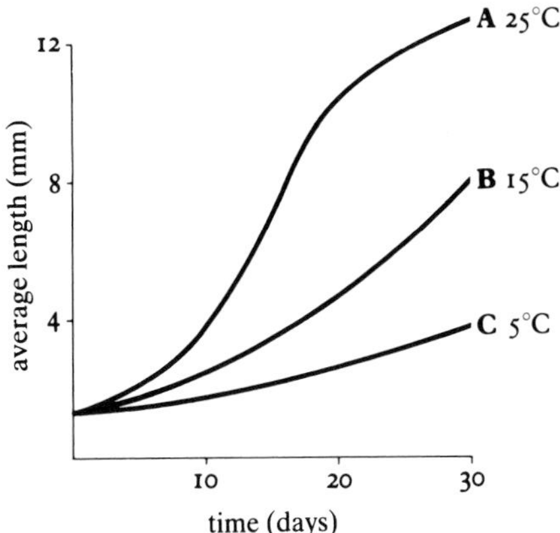

Figure 27.4 Graph showing the growth rate in three populations of the fairy shrimp *Chirocephalus* at different temperatures.

1 The graph in Fig. 27.4 shows the rate of growth in three populations of the fairy shrimp *Chirocephalus*, an aquatic crustacean, over a period of 30 days under different temperature conditions. Population **A** is kept at 25 °C, population **B** at 15 °C and population **C** at 5 °C. Suggest an explanation for the different growth rates and discuss the implications of the data. (*VUS*)

2 (a) List the essential conditions that are required for seeds to germinate successfully.
(b) How would you show that these conditions are required for germination?
(c) Suppose a seed failed to germinate even when provided with these conditions, what measures might you take in order to end its dormancy thereby allowing it to germinate?

3 The effects of the application of the same quantity of various concentrations of auxin on the rate of elongation of the roots and shoots of oat seedlings was determined. The results (given below) were expressed as percentage stimulation of growth compared with untreated controls; thus a minus sign indicates relative inhibition. Suggest explanations for the results and discuss their relevance in relation to the opposite geotropic responses of typical roots and shoots:

	Percentage stimulation of growth								
	Concentration of applied auxin (parts per million)								
	10^{-6}	10^{-5}	10^{-4}	10^{-3}	10^{-2}	10^{-1}	1.0	10.0	100.0
Root	+5	+20	+20	+10	−18	−55	−90	−95	−98
Shoot	0	0	0	+5	+20	+100	+180	+150	+10

(*O and C*)

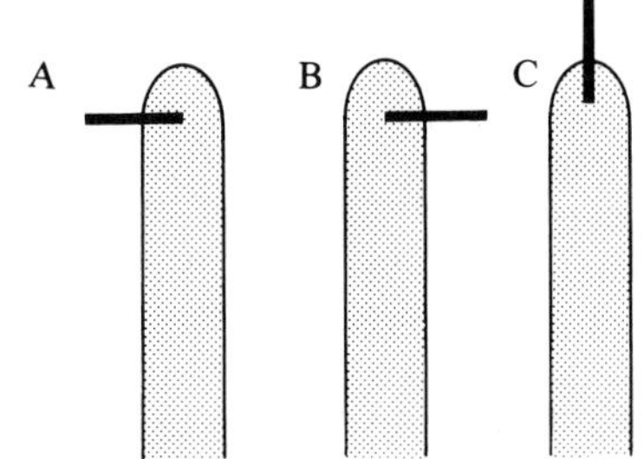

Figure 27.5 Three experiments in which thin pieces of mica are inserted into the tip of a coleoptile.

4 (a) What evidence is there to support the view that a stem is (i) negatively geotropic, (ii) positively phototropic?
(b) In the light of the auxin theory predict, with a full explanation, the results of experiments A, B and C in Figure 27.5.
(c) Describe how you would show the presence of a growth substance in a stem or coleoptile. (*AEB modified*)

5 Define and illustrate 'apical dominance'. Explain briefly how you believe the dominance of the apex is maintained.

6 Three similar groups of shoots were treated in the dark as follows:
Group **A**: the shoots were laid horizontal (*horizontal throughout*).
Group **B**: the shoots were laid horizontal for 1 hour only and then returned to the vertical position (*horizontal 1 hour only*).
Group **C**: the shoots were laid horizontal but their apices were removed (*decapitated horizontal throughout*).

One-half, one, two, three and four hours after the beginning of the experiment the curvature of the shoots was measured. A positive (+) curvature indicates upward bending and a negative (−) curvature downward bending. The results were:

Time (hours)	Group **A** Horizontal throughout	Group **B** Horizontal 1 hour only	Group **C** Decapitated horizontal throughout
$\frac{1}{2}$	−5	−5	−4
1	0	0	−2
2	+25	+23	+4
3	+40	+16	+5
4	+70	+3	+7

All results are given in degrees.
Plot the results and outline the main conclusions you can draw from the experiment. (*O and C*)

7 Discuss the commercial importance of plant growth substances.

8 In a carefully designed and executed experiment, groups of pea plants were subjected to the following treatments:
A Apical bud removed
B Apical bud removed and auxin placed on cut stump
C Apical bud removed and gibberellic acid placed on cut stump
D Apical bud removed and kinetin placed on cut stump
E Plants left intact.
At intervals after treatment the lengths of the axillary shoots were determined and the results are given below.

Days after start of treatment	**Mean total axillary shoot lengths per plant** (mm)				
	A	**B**	**C**	**D**	**E**
2	3	3	3	3	3
4	10	4	12	9	3
6	30	4	45	32	3
8	50	5	90	47	3
10	78	6	116	80	3
13	118	30	150	119	3

N.B. Assume that the environmental conditions were the same for all treatments throughout.
(a) Plot the results graphically. (b) Discuss the results.

(O and C)

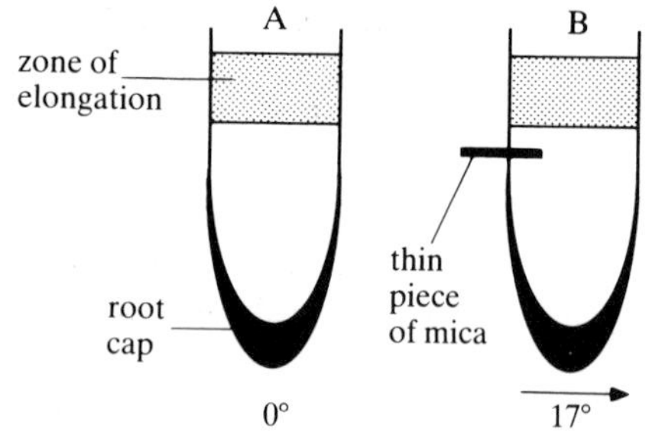

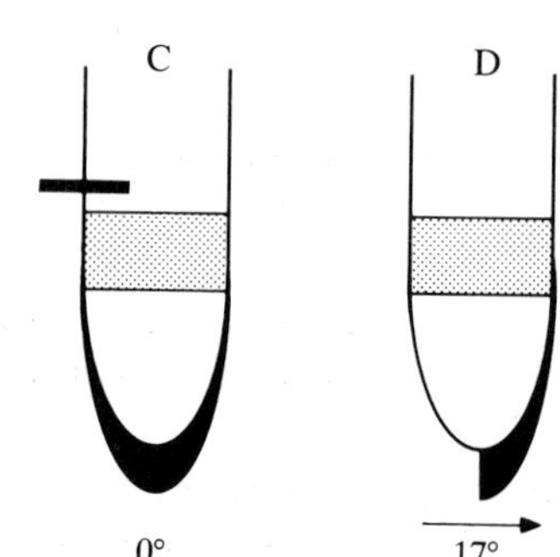

Figure 27.6 Experiments on the control of growth of the roots of pea seedlings. The angle, and direction, of bending are given beneath each diagram.

9 The control of root growth in pea seedlings was investigated by a series of experiments, four of which are illustrated in Figure 27.6. In each case the root was subjected to a particular treatment and orientated vertically; the angle through which the root subsequently bent was measured, and the direction of bending noted.
(a) What do you conclude from experiments A to D about
(i) the role of the root cap in the growth of the root, and
(ii) the mechanism by which the root cap exerts its influence?
(b) Predict the effect of
(i) removing the whole of the root cap from a vertically orientated root, and
(ii) repeating experiment B on a *horizontally* orientated root with the mica on the lower side.

10 Three species of the genus *Lolium* and a hybrid between two of them were tested for their vernalisation requirements. All the strains were grown under controlled conditions (23 °C day temperature; 17 °C night temperature; long photoperiods). Sample plants of each strain were then subjected to different periods of time at 4 °C before being returned to the original conditions. In the table below are recorded the number of days which elapsed between the end of the cold treatment and the onset of flowering:

	Number of days between end of cold treatment and onset of flowering			
	Strains of *Lolium*			
Weeks at 4 °C	**A**	**B**	**C**	**A × B** (hybrid)
0	(did not flower)	40	25	75
1	160	38	25	62
2	110	36	25	50
4	90	34	25	40
8	35	32	25	32
16	24	28	25	24

(a) Plot the results graphically. (b) Discuss the results. *(O and C)*

11 The data below show the effect of controlled periods of light and dark on the subsequent flowering behaviour of the cocklebur (*Xanthium strumarium*), an American weed in the daisy family.

Hours of alternating light and dark periods		**Response**
Light	Dark	
8	16	flowering
8	16 with light flash in middle of dark period	no flowering
16	16	flowering
16	8	no flowering
16	8 with dark flash in middle of light period	no flowering
8	8	no flowering
12	12	no flowering

(a) Is cocklebur a short day plant, a long day plant, or a day-neutral plant?

(b) Examine these data and discuss whether flowering is triggered by the length of the day or the length of the night.

(c) How long does the inductive period have to be?

(d) Explain in terms of P_r and P_{fr} how phytochrome enables the leaf to measure time. Assume that during the day red light predominates so that the phytochrome exists mainly in the P_{fr} form.

(e) Use your hypothesis to explain in terms of P_r and P_{fr} why a light flash in the middle of the dark period interrupts flowering, but a dark flash in the middle of the light has no effect.

(f) Would the effect of the light flash in the middle of the dark period depend on the wavelength? What would be the effect of a flash of red light? A flash of blue light? Sketch an action spectrum for the response.

(g) How could the effect of a light flash in the middle of the dark period be immediately reversed?

(*Data from*: D. Vince-Price, *Photoperiodism in Plants*, McGraw-Hill, 1975.)

12 The relation between moisture content and respiration of wheat grains (milligrams of CO_2 produced per 100 grams dry mass per day) was determined with the following results:

Moisture content %	13.0	14.0	15.0	16.0	16.5	17.0
Respiration rate	0.6	0.7	1.0	2.9	6.0	11.0

(a) Suggest possible explanations for these results. (b) What bearing do they have on the problems of seed dormancy and the storage of grain in large quantities by farmers? *(O and C)*

13 Dormancy is controlled by an interaction between a hormone which induces it and another hormone which terminates it. Illustrate this statement by reference to the dormancy of buds. Does the same principle apply to animals?

14 Figure 27.7 summarises the sizes of the testes and length of the antlers of roebuck deer in Australia in relation to the seasons of the year. What does this information suggest to you about the way the growth of the antlers is controlled? *(SA)*

Figure 27.7 Graphs showing the seasonal growth of the antlers in roebuck deer in relation to testis size and day length.

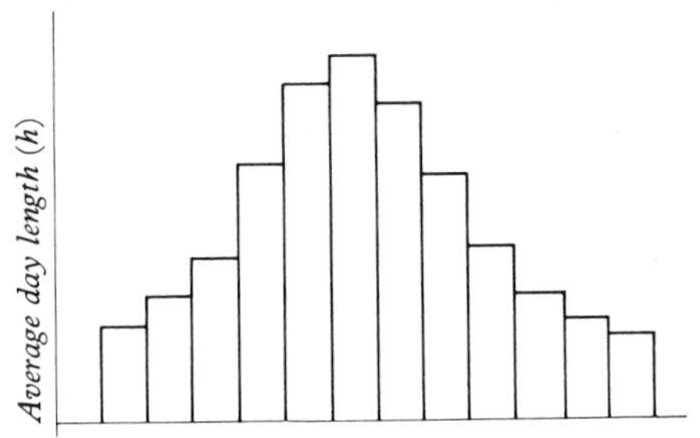

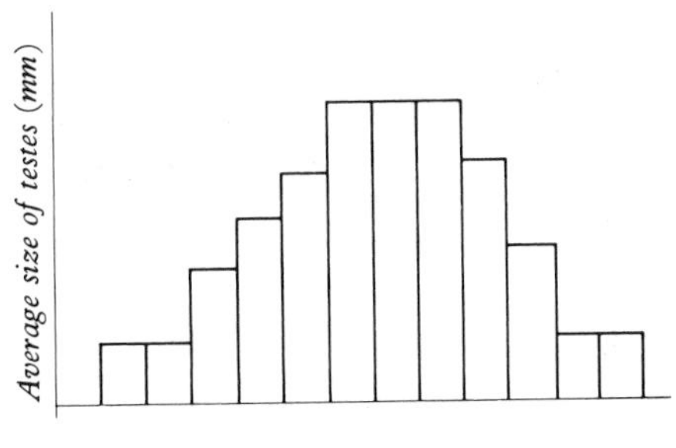

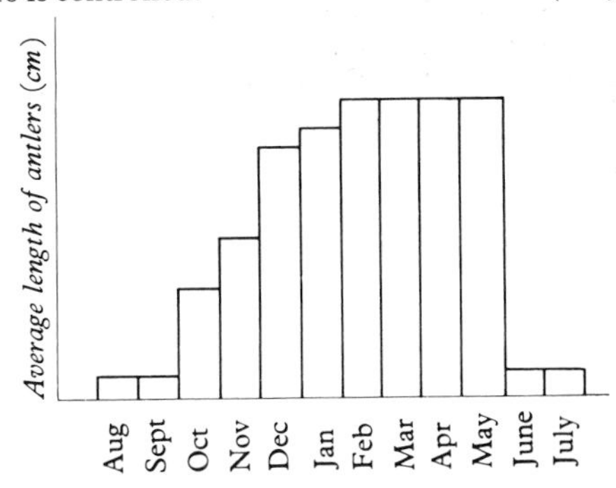

28 Mendel and the Laws of Heredity

Background Summary

1 The first quantitative experiments on heredity of any significance were carried out in the middle of the nineteenth century by Mendel on the garden pea.

2 In his first investigations Mendel studied the inheritance of a single pair of contrasting characteristics (**monohybrid inheritance**).

3 From the monohybrid cross it can be concluded that (i) inheritance is particulate (it is now realised that the 'particles' are the genes), (ii) that genes occur in pairs (alleles) which may be **dominant** or **recessive** with respect to one another (from which the concept of **heterozygosity** and **homozygosity** emerge), and (iii) that only one allele of a gene may be carried in a single gamete. These conclusions are embodied in Mendel's First Law, the **Law of Segregation**.

4 The transmission of genes depends on chance and can be expressed in terms of probability. In interpreting the results of genetic experiments one must beware of sampling error.

5 The conclusions drawn from the monohybrid cross can be interpreted in terms of **meiosis**.

6 If identical homozygotes are crossed, nothing but homozygotes will be produced and a **pure line** is established. This is called **true breeding**.

7 An organism's characteristics (**phenotype**) are determined, at least in part, by its genetic constitution (**genotype**). A single phenotype may be produced by more than one genotype.

8 To establish whether an organism is homozygous or heterozygous a **back cross** (**test cross**) can be carried out.

9 Examples of monohybrid inheritance in humans include albinism, cystic fibrosis, and chondrodystrophic dwarfism (achondroplasia).

10 In later experiments on the garden pea Mendel studied the inheritance of two pairs of characteristics (**dihybrid inheritance**).

11 From the dihybrid cross it can be concluded that each allele of one gene may combine randomly with either allele of the other gene. This is embodied in Mendel's Second Law, which is called the **Law of Independent Assortment**.

12 As with monohybrid inheritance, the transmission and assortment of alleles depends on chance and can be expressed in terms of probability.

13 As with monohybrid inheritance, a single phenotype may be produced by more than one genotype. A **back cross** (**test cross**) can be carried out to establish an organism's genotype.

14 The conclusion drawn from the dihybrid cross can be interpreted in terms of **meiosis**.

15 Although it forms the foundation of modern genetics, Mendel's work was carried out without any knowledge of chromosomes, genes, or meiosis. Its significance was not realised until 1900.

Investigation 28.1
Monohybrid inheritance in maize, tobacco and tomato seedlings

Procedure

1 You are provided with samples of maize (corn) seeds. All the seeds were obtained from one plant.

2 Plant out 60 seeds in a tray of soil that measures approximately 40 × 20 cm. Keep in a warm, light place and water frequently.

3 When the seedlings have grown sufficiently (about 28 days after sowing), examine each tray for observable differences. Are all the seedlings alike, or are there visible differences? If there are differences, count each type. What is the ratio between them? What conclusions can you draw?

4 Sprinkle tobacco seeds on a petri dish of fine damp soil or agar jelly (1.5 per cent). To ensure that the distribution of seeds is not too dense, first mix the tobacco seeds with fine sand in the proportion of about two-thirds sand to one-third seeds.

5 When the seedlings have grown sufficiently (10–14 days after sowing), examine them for any observable differences. Count the different types, and calculate the ratio between them. Conclusions?

6 Place tomato seeds on the surface of some compost in a series of small pots, approximately three seeds per pot. Once the seedlings are established remove the less robust ones, so that there is one seedling per pot.

7 Observe, and describe, any differences between the tomato seedlings with respect to the colour of the cotyledons, the colour and/or hairiness of the stems, and the shape of the leaves.

8 Choose a particular pair of contrasting features (e.g. purple and green stems) and count the number of tomato seedlings showing each feature. Calculate the ratio between them and draw such conclusions as you can.

Requirements
Trays of soil approx. 40 × 20 cm
Petri dish containing fine damp soil or 1.5 per cent agar
Small pots of compost

Seeds of corn (maize)
Seeds of tobacco plant (*Nicotiana tabacum*)
Seeds of tomato plant

Note: The seedlings will need to be grown in advance of the practical session.

For Consideration

(1) How close are your ratios to the expected ones? If they are not very close, use the chi-squared test to analyse them statistically. (*See* Appendix 6, page 394).
(2) Have you obtained any anomalous results, i.e. results that appear to contradict Mendel's Laws? If you have, try to explain them.

Investigation 28.2 Monohybrid and dihybrid inheritance in maize (corn) seeds

Requirements
Maize (corn) cobs showing segregation for the following kernel characters:
Cob **A**: purple, yellow, 3:1
Cob **B**: purple, yellow, 1:1
Cob **C**: non-shiny (starchy), shiny (waxy), 3:1 or 1:1
Cob **D**: purple, yellow, wrinkled, smooth, 9:3:3:1
Cob **E**: purple, yellow, wrinkled, smooth, 1:1:1:1
(The above cobs are all available from suppliers.)

In maize (corn) a single cob (ear) is covered with several hundred kernels which represent the fruits. Each kernel contains a single seed and is similar in its internal structure to a grain of wheat (*see* Figure 26.9, page 264). Each seed contains an embryo formed as a result of a single fertilisation. It is, therefore, diploid. The fertilizations are independent of each other, and each gamete-forming cell underwent meiosis independently of all the others. In human terms what is the relationship between two embryos belonging to the same cob?

The kernels display a number of easily recognized characteristics such as colour and shape: thus they may be purple or yellow, smooth or shrunken, etc.

Procedure

MONOHYBRID INHERITANCE

1 Examine cob **A**. This was produced by self-pollinating a flower of the parent plant. Count the purple and yellow kernels and determine the ratio between them. Do you think it is sufficient to count the kernels in one (or several) rows, or should all the kernels in the cob be counted?
2 Which is the genetically dominant colour, purple or yellow?
3 Letting **P** be the symbol for purple kernel, and **p** for yellow, what can you say about the genetic constitution (genotype) of the purple and yellow kernels?
4 What was the genotype for kernel-colour of the plant on which this cob developed?
5 Construct a genetic diagram to illustrate the cross involved in the production of cob **A**.
6 How would you determine the genotype of one of the purple kernels in cob **A**?
7 Examine cob **B**. Determine the ratio of purple to yellow kernels.
8 Construct a genetic diagram to illustrate the cross involved in the production of this cob.
9 Examine cob **C**. Can you see that some kernels are more shiny than others? Count the shiny and non-shiny kernels and determine the ratio between them.
10 The shiny and non-shiny kernels in cob **C** differ in their starch content. Shave off the top of a kernel of each type and stain the cut surface with iodine solution. Notice that the non-shiny kernel stains blue-black, whereas the shiny kernel stains red. The blue-black colour indicates starch, the red colour dextrin. Dextrin is a polysaccharide like starch but simpler – an intermediate between starch and maltose.

DIHYBRID INHERITANCE

1 Examine cobs **D** and **E**. The kernels differ from each other with respect to *two* pairs of characteristics; each is purple or yellow, and smooth or wrinkled. Make sure that you can recognise each type of kernel.
2 In each of the cobs **D** and **E**, estimate the number of kernels that are:
(a) purple and smooth;
(b) purple and wrinkled;
(c) yellow and smooth;
(d) yellow and wrinkled.
3 Construct a genetic diagram illustrating the crosses involved in the production of cobs **D** and **E**.

For Consideration

(1) Can you state Mendel's first and second laws? How precisely do the results of your analysis of maize cobs support these two laws?
(2) What tentative conclusions can you draw from your experiments on cob **C** about the way genes work?

Investigation 28.3
Genetic constitution of maize pollen

Requirements
Microscope
Slide and coverslip
Needles
Iodine solution

Maize floret (available from supplier)

It follows from the result of monohybrid crosses that the gametes formed by a heterozygous organism differ in their genetic constitution: approximately half contain the dominant allele, the other half the recessive allele. Although this is an inevitable theoretical conclusion, it is difficult to prove because genetic differences seldom reveal themselves in the gametes. Usually gametes look identical. However, an exception to this is provided by maize.

Theoretical background

In maize a distinction can be made between starchy and non-starchy plants. Starchy plants have cells containing normal starch which stains blue-black with iodine; non-starchy plants contain an abnormal form of starch, which gives a reddish-brown reaction with iodine. The same distinction is seen in the kernels (*see* Investigation 28.2). Starchy is dominant to non-starchy.

Consider a heterozygous maize plant resulting from a cross between starchy and non-starchy parents. Since starchy is dominant to non-starchy, the heterozygous plant will be starchy. Now the alleles responsible for this condition determine the presence or absence of starch in the pollen grains as well as in the adult. So pollen grains produced by this plant will be expected to be starchy and non-starchy in approximately equal numbers. In this investigation we shall test this prediction.

Procedure

1 You are provided with a floret of a heterozygous maize plant. With needles, tear off the enveloping bracts and remove one of the anthers.

2 Place the anther in a drop of iodine solution on a microscope slide. With needles break the anther open and tease out the pollen grains. Put on a coverslip and wait for the stain to take effect.

3 View the pollen grains under medium power. If they appear uniform, alter the illumination by changing the angle of the substage mirror. *Don't illuminate too brightly*. The most common reason why people find it difficult to see the difference between the two types of pollen is that they have too much light coming through the microscope.

4 Count the number of dark and light pollen grains in a total of up to 100. Do your results confirm the prediction that the heterozygous plant produces two types of gametes in approximately equal numbers?

For Consideration

(1) Which of Mendel's laws is given considerable support by the results of this experiment? Explain fully.

(2) Do you consider that a *failure* to demonstrate the existence of genetically different types of gamete would seriously undermine Mendel's theory?

Investigation 28.4
Handling *Drosophila*

Drosophila, the fruit fly, is an ideal animal for experimental genetics. It can be kept easily in the laboratory, and at 25 °C the complete life cycle takes only 10–14 days. Moreover, a single female lays between 80 and 200 eggs, so it does not take long to produce a large population.

Before you can do genetic experiments with *Drosophila* you must learn to handle the flies, recognise the different strains, and identify the sexes. That is the purpose of this investigation.

Rearing the flies

Fruit flies used in experimental work are descendants of wild species that feed on yeasts and plant sugars such as are found on damaged fruits. In the laboratory they can be cultured in bottles containing a nutrient medium. This consists of syrup, raisins, banana, yeast, etc., set into a jelly with agar. A chemical agent is added to prevent unwelcome growths from developing on the agar.

The life cycle

The life cycle is summarised in Figure 28.1. Following impregnation, the female stores sperm in her spermotheca from which a large number of eggs are fertilised. Once laid, the eggs develop into larvae which burrow into the medium. After two moults, the larvae leave the medium and crawl into drier parts of the bottle, usually up a roll of filter paper provided for the purpose. They then pupate and after a few days the adults emerge, mate, and the cycle starts again.

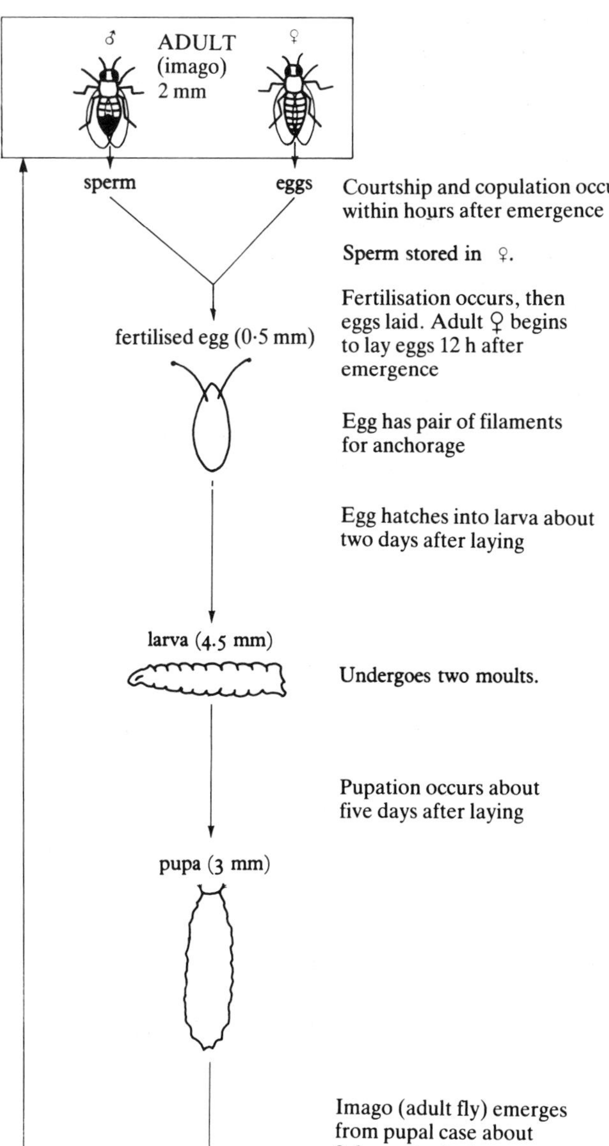
♂ ADULT ♀
(imago)
2 mm
sperm
eggs
Courtship and copulation occur within hours after emergence
Sperm stored in ♀.
Fertilisation occurs, then eggs laid. Adult ♀ begins to lay eggs 12 h after emergence
fertilised egg (0·5 mm)
Egg has pair of filaments for anchorage
Egg hatches into larva about two days after laying
larva (4.5 mm)
Undergoes two moults.
Pupation occurs about five days after laying
pupa (3 mm)
Imago (adult fly) emerges from pupal case about 9 days after laying

Figure 28.1 Life cycle of the fruit fly, *Drosophila melanogaster*. The times apply to fruit flies kept at 25 °C. (*Based on* Haskell).

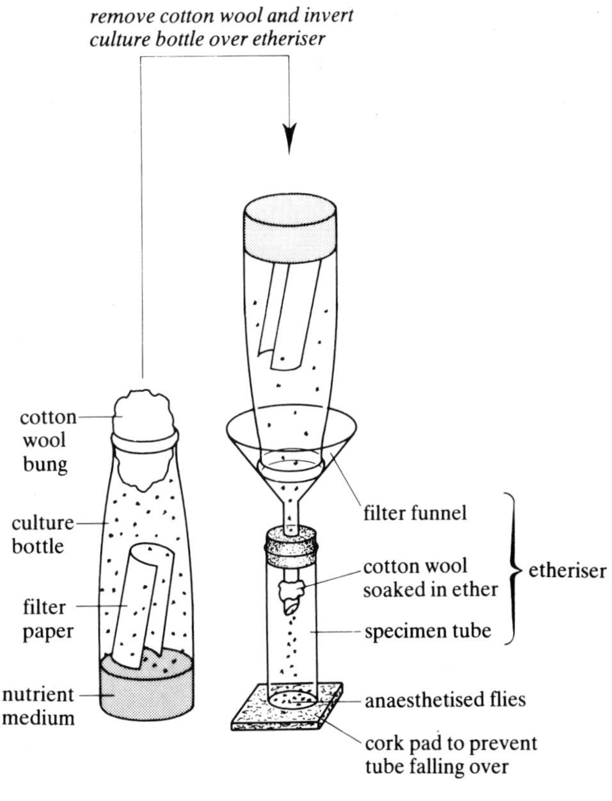
remove cotton wool and invert culture bottle over etheriser
cotton wool bung
culture bottle
filter paper
nutrient medium
filter funnel
cotton wool soaked in ether
specimen tube
etheriser
anaesthetised flies
cork pad to prevent tube falling over

Figure 28.2 Method of anaesthetising *Drosophila*.

Examination of Live Flies

Examine a culture bottle containing a pure line (what's that?). Adult flies of both sexes should be present, also larvae burrowing in the culture medium and, possibly, pupae on the glass or filter paper.

Now examine several pure-line flies from the bottle marked 'wild-type'. Being active animals, they must be anaesthetised first. This is done as follows (Figure 28.2):

1 Pipette a few drops of ether on the cotton-wool of an etheriser. Return unwanted ether to the bottle and replace the stopper immediately: ether fumes are dangerous.

2 Tap the culture bottle so the flies are dislodged from the mouth of the bottle and the cotton-wool bung.

3 Quickly remove the cotton-wool bung and place the funnel of the etheriser over the open mouth of the culture bottle. Turn the etheriser and culture bottle the other way up and tap the latter gently until at least ten flies have entered the etheriser. Then replace the stopper of the culture bottle.

4 As soon as the flies in the etheriser stop moving, remove the funnel of the etheriser and tip the flies onto a white tile.

5 Examine the flies under a lens or binocular microscope.

Anaesthetised *Drosophila* usually remain unconscious for about ten minutes. Avoid giving them too much ether; a fly with arched abdomen, legs bunched together and wings deflected upwards, is probably dead.

Recognising and sexing the Wild Type

The wild type is the normal (non-mutant) fly. It is designated by the symbol +. Its characteristics include the following: eyes round and red, body grey, wings approximately the same length as (or slightly longer than) the abdomen. A fly may of course be normal for some characteristics but mutant for others.

1 Examine wild type flies and notice the above features. The wild type bottle contains both males and females (*see* below). Young flies are pale coloured with incompletely expanded wings.

2 With a paintbrush separate the wild type flies into males and females. Male and female specimens of *Drosophila* can be distinguished as shown in Figure 28.3.

Recognising the Mutants

Having examined the wild type it is now necessary to identify some of the mutant strains of *Drosophila*.

1 Examine one or more mutants from the culture bottles provided. Use a hand lens or binocular microscope as required.

2 Table 28.1 gives a list of five of the more easily recognised mutants which may be available to you. Be sure you can recognise them all.

	Male	Female
	tarsus	
1	Rounded abdomen	Pointed abdomen
2	Black transverse stripes at posterior end of abdomen so close together they appear as a single dark blob	Black transverse stripes at posterior end of abdomen narrow and clearly separated
3	Pair of chitinous claspers on ventral side of abdomen at posterior end	Claspers absent
4	Row of small bristles (sex comb) on first tarsal joint of forelegs	Sex combs absent

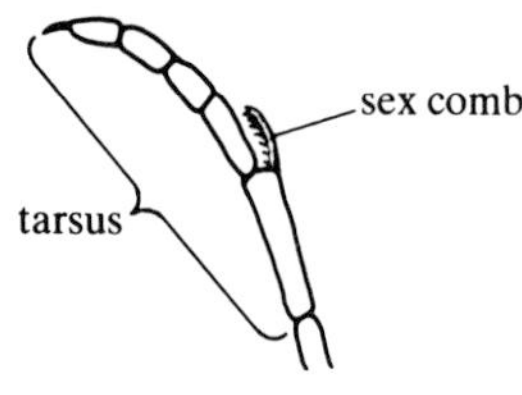

Figure 28.3 *Drosophila melanogaster*. How to tell the difference between the wild-type male and female.

Table 28.1 Summary of the five mutants of *Drosophila melanogaster* featuring in the investigations outlined in Chapters 28 and 29.

Name of mutant	Symbol	No. of chromosome on which gene is located	Phenotypic Characteristics
White	w	1 (X chromosome)	White eyes
Yellow	y	1 (X chromosome)	Yellow body
Brown	bw	2	Brown eyes
Vestigial	vg	2	Reduced wings
Ebony	e	3	Black body

Requirements
Hand lens or binocular microscope
White tile
Paintbrush
Etheriser (Figure 28.2)

Wild-type flies
Mutant flies (*see* Table 28.1)

All flies should be pure-breeding (homozygous) in labelled culture bottles.

For Consideration

(1) Speculate on the possible functional significance of the differences between male and female *Drosophila*.
(2) How do you think the mutant strains have arisen? Do you think they have advantages over the wild type?
(3) Before proceeding to Investigations 28.5 and 28.6, plan in detail a series of breeding experiments which you yourself would carry out to investigate heredity in *Drosophila*. Base your programme on the flies examined in this laboratory session.

Reference: B. Shorrocks, *Invertebrate Types: Drosophila*, Ginn, 1972.

Investigation 28.5 Monohybrid inheritance in *Drosophila*

If you have done Investigation 28.4, you should now be ready to set up some crosses with *Drosophila*. Start by performing a simple monohybrid cross between the wild type and one of the mutant strains, e.g. vestigial wing. You will require pure-breeding flies of each sex. The females must be virgins. To ensure this they must be isolated from males within eight hours of hatching from the pupae. This has been done: you will be provided with female wild type flies and male mutant flies in separate culture bottles.

Setting up a parental cross

1 Anaesthetise up to 10 wild type virgin females and 15 vestigial-winged males, and transfer them to a new bottle containing culture medium. To do this, place the anaesthetised flies on a white tile, then with a paintbrush push them gently one by one into the new culture bottle.
2 Leave the bottle on its side until the flies recover so they do not stick to the medium. Use only mature adults for crossing, and make sure you do not over-anaesthetise them (*see* Investigation 28.4, page 287).
3 Label your bottle with your name, indicating the cross which you have set up, as follows:

P ♀+ × ♂vg (date:)

4 When you are sure that at least one female and two male flies have recovered, put your bottle in an incubator at 25 °C.
5 *One week later*, when the eggs have hatched into larvae, remove the parent flies. The $\mathbf{F_1}$ flies should emerge over a period of several days approximately 10–14 days after the cross was set up.
6 Do you think you should set up the reciprocal cross, i.e. ♂+ × ♀vg? If you think it does not matter, explain your reasoning.

Setting up an F_1 Cross

1 Anaesthetise all the $\mathbf{F_1}$ flies from your first cross and tip them onto a white tile. How would you describe them phenotypically? What is the ratio of males to females? Explain your observations.
2 Now cross $\mathbf{F_1}$ flies amongst themselves. In this case the females need not be virgins. (Note why.) Label the bottle as follow:

P ♀+ × ♂vg (date:)
$\mathbf{F_1}$ all +
$\mathbf{F_1}$? × ? (date:)

Incubate at 25 °C.
3 After one week remove the parents from the culture bottles. Allow a further week to elapse and then examine the $\mathbf{F_2}$ offspring.

Examination of F_2 Flies

Ideally, analysis of the $\mathbf{F_2}$ flies should be started the day after the first flies emerge and continued daily until all the flies have emerged. Counted flies should be killed each time. Alternatively, wait until sufficient flies have emerged to provide an adequate sample.
1 Anaesthetise in the usual way and tip all the $\mathbf{F_2}$ flies onto a white tile. With a paintbrush separate them into groups according to wing-length. Then subdivide each of these groups into males and females.
2 Count the numbers in each group. How many of each type? What is the ratio between them? Within each group how many are males and how many females?

Requirements
Hand lens or binocular microscope
White tile
Paintbrush
Etheriser
Culture bottles

Virgin ♀ wild type flies
♂ vestigial-winged flies
(Other types of fly if required)

Note: All flies should be pure-breeding (homozygous) in labelled culture bottles.

Other Monohybrid Crosses

1 Cross $\mathbf{F_1}$ flies with vestigial wing (homozygous recessive). Predict the outcome and see if it agrees with your result.
2 Try crossing the wild type with other mutants, e.g:
Wild type with brown eye (+ × bw)
Wild type with ebony body (+ × e)

Results

Write a full account of your experiments and the results obtained.

For Consideration

(1) Why was it necessary to use pure-breeding flies for the parental cross?
(2) Why did you have to use *virgin* females when you set up your parental cross but not when you crossed the $\mathbf{F_1}$ flies amongst themselves?
(3) Why was it necessary to remove the parent flies before the $\mathbf{F_1}$ flies emerged from their pupae?
(4) On the basis of genetic theory, what ratios of phenotypes were you expecting in the $\mathbf{F_2}$? How closely do your actual results match the expected ratios? Use the chi-squared test to compare them statistically (*see* Appendix 6, page 394).

Investigation 28.6 Dihybrid inheritance in *Drosophila*

Requirements
Hand lens or binocular microscope
White tile
Paintbrush
Etheriser
Culture bottles

Virgin ♀ wild type flies
♂ ebony vestigial flies
(Other types of fly if required)

Note: All flies should be pure-breeding (homozygous) in labelled culture bottles.

Having set up, and analysed, monohybrid crosses in the previous investigation, we will now move on to a more complex situation and try setting up some dihybrid crosses. The principle is exactly the same as before but this time we shall be considering *two* pairs of characters.

Procedure

1 Using exactly the same technique as that described in Investigation 28.5, set up a dihybrid cross between pure-breeding wild type virgin females and ebony vestigial males, i.e. ♀++ × ♂e vg, and/or a reciprocal cross.
2 Label the bottle. Remove the parent flies one week after you have set up the cross. After two weeks examine the $\mathbf{F_1}$ offspring.
3 Now cross $\mathbf{F_1}$ flies amongst themselves and carry the investigation through to the $\mathbf{F_2}$. After one week remove the adults in the usual way.
4 In analysing the $\mathbf{F_2}$ flies record the numbers of each type, i.e. grey-bodied, normal wing; grey-bodied, vestigial wing; ebony-bodied, normal wing; and ebony-bodied, vestigial wing. Calculate the ratio between them. Explain your results.
5 Cross $\mathbf{F_1}$ flies with ebony vestigial (homozygous recessive for both characters). Predict the outcome and see if it agrees with your result.
6 Try setting up other dihybrid crosses, e.g. between the wild-type and ebony bodied, brown-eyed flies (++ × e bw).

Results

Write a full account of your experiments and the results obtained.

For Consideration

(1) What are the possible genotypes of the $\mathbf{F_2}$ wild type flies from the first cross above? How could you determine the genotype of a particular $\mathbf{F_2}$ fly?
(2) On the basis of genetic theory, what ratios of phenotypes were you expecting in the $\mathbf{F_2}$? How closely do your actual results match the expected ratios? Use the chi-quared test to compare them statistically (*see* Appendix 6, page 394).

Note: (i) As an alternative to the procedure described in Investigations 28.5 and 28.6, crosses may be set up by putting unhatched pupae together in culture bottles. This eliminates the necessity to anaesthetise and sex flies and collect virgin females. For details see E.L. Oxlade, 'A short-cut with *Drosophila*', *School Science Review*, vol. 64, no. 227, 1982
(ii) Various computer simulations of genetics are available, for example NELCAL Biology, Pack 1 Genetics by R. Fisher.

Questions and Problems

1 In *Drosophila* straight wing is dominant over curved wing. What would be the result in the F_1 generation of crossing a homozygous straight-winged fly with a curved-winged fly? What would be the result in the F_2 generation of crossing two of the F_1 flies? How would you determine the genotype of one of the F_2 straight-winged flies?

2 In *Drosophila*, black body colour is recessive to grey body colour. A geneticist had three pairs of flies with grey bodies designated **A**, **B**, and **C**. He crossed **A** × **B** and obtained 109 grey-bodied flies; **A** × **C** gave 80 grey-bodied and 28 black-bodied; whilst **B** × **C** gave 76 grey-bodied flies. Explain, giving reasons, the expected genotypic and phenotypic ratio when the flies **A**, **B**, and **C** are crossed with flies having black bodies. *(UL)*

3 Cystic fibrosis is caused by a recessive gene. Affected individuals are homozygous for the defective allele. Heterozygous individuals are normal. A pair of normal parents produce a defective child, their first. What is the probability that their next child will be defective? These particular parents know no biology, but they are intelligent and want to know the reasoning on which your conclusion is based. Explain it to them simply, but thoroughly.

4 Albinism in humans is caused by a recessive gene which is transmitted in a normal Mendelian fashion. A phenotypically normal (non-albino) couple have four children: the first three are normal, the fourth is an albino:
(a) What can you say about the genotypes of the parents?
(b) What is the probability that their next child will be an albino?
(c) One of the normal children marries a normal woman. What predictions can be made concerning their first child?
(d) The albino child marries a normal woman. What predictions can be made regarding their first child?
Where there are several possibilities, state them. Show your reasoning.

5 Four flowers were chosen on a tall sweet-pea plant. The unripe anthers were carefully removed, and the receptive stigmas dusted with pollen from a short sweet-pea plant. The pollinated flowers were covered with paper bags, and at the end of the season 26 seeds were collected from the four pods. Sixteen of these seeds grew into tall plants and ten into short plants. Suggest explanations of this result and state what further experiments you might carry out to test the truth of your suggestions. *(O and C)*

6 In human beings the ability to taste phenylthiourea depends upon the presence of a dominant gene.
(a) Construct diagrams showing
(i) the genotype and phenotype of the parental generation and the F_1 generation, and the gametes of the cross between a homozygous 'taster' and a homozygous 'non-taster';
(ii) the genotype and phenotype of the progeny of a cross between two genotypes of the F_1 type in (i).
(b) Study Figure 28.4. State, with reasons, the possible genotype of persons **A**, **B**, **C**, **D**, and **E**. *(CL modified)*

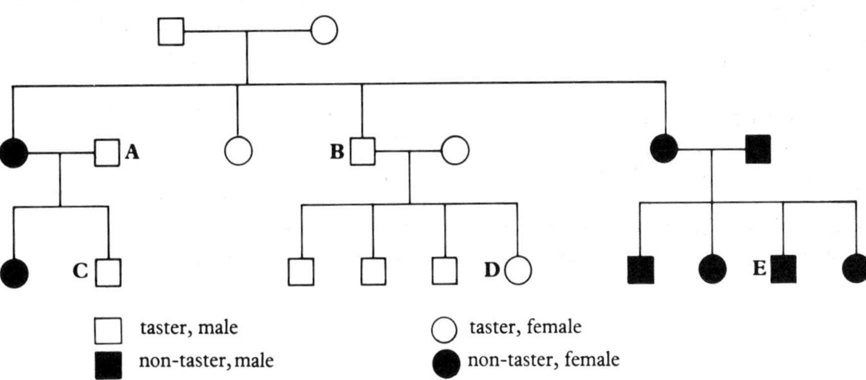

Figure 28.4 The occurrence of phenylthiourea tasters in a family.

7 Tongue-rolling is due to a dominant gene. If a man, whose parents are both non-rollers, marries a rolling girl, whose mother and grandparents are rollers and whose father and sister are non-rollers, what are the chances that their first child will be a roller? Show your reasoning.

In fact their first child, a boy, turns out to be a roller. He eventually marries another roller and between them they produce two sons, neither of whom can roll, and three daughters, two of whom can roll, whilst the third cannot. Express the transmission of tongue-rolling in this family, through all four generations, in the form of a pedigree chart like the one given in Figure 28.4.

8 Discuss the genetic implications of the following experiment:

(a) An inbred plant of barley, susceptible to mildew, was pollinated by hand using pollen from an inbred plant showing resistance to mildew, precautions being taken to prevent self-pollination.

(b) Eleven F_1 plants, which were all resistant to mildew, were grown and were allowed to self-pollinate naturally. All the seeds were collected and later sown to produce the F_2 generation.

(c) Five hundred and twelve F_2 plants were grown, but as there was no attack by mildew no observations could be made. The plants were allowed to self-pollinate and all the seeds were collected.

(d) A sample of the seed was sown and the F_3 plants were found to consist of 586 which were infected with mildew and 1014 which were resistant to mildew.

(O and C)

9 Tall, cut-leaved tomato plants are crossed with dwarf, potato-leaved plants giving in the F_1 generation nothing but tall, cut-leaved plants. These are allowed to cross with each other producing in the F_2 generation 926 tall, cut-leaved; 288 tall, potato-leaved; 293 dwarf, cut-leaved; and 104 dwarf, potato-leaved. What explanation can be offered for these results? *(O and C)*

10 In the summer squash plant white fruit is dominant over yellow, and the disc fruit shape is dominant over sphere. A cross between a plant with white disc fruits and one with yellow sphere fruits gave:
25 plants with white disc fruits; 26 plants with white sphere fruits;
24 plants with yellow disc fruits; 25 plants with yellow sphere fruits.
If the white disc parent is self-fertilised, what proportion of its offspring will have yellow sphere fruits? Show how you arrive at your answer. *(O and C)*

11 In a species of plant petal colour is determined by one pair of alleles and stem length by another. The following experimental crosses were carried out.

Experiment 1: A purple-flowered plant was crossed with several red-flowered plants. The progeny were all purple-flowered plants.

Experiment 2: A short-stemmed plant was crossed with several long-stemmed plants. The progeny were all short-stemmed.

Experiment 3: A different purple-flowered, short-stemmed plant of the same species was crossed with several red-flowered long-stemmed plants. The following progeny were obtained:
37 purple-flowered short-stemmed; 34 red-flowered short-stemmed;
41 red-flowered long-stemmed; 35 purple-flowered long-stemmed.

(a) What are the dominant alleles?

(b) What are the probable genotypes of the purple-flowered and short-stemmed plants used in experiments 1 and 2?

(c) With the aid of diagrams, explain the results obtained in experiments 1 and 2.

(d) With the aid of a diagram, explain the results of experiment 3.

(e) If the purple-flowered, short-stemmed plant used in experiment 3 had been self-fertilised, what proportion of the progeny would you have expected to be red-flowered and what proportion would you have expected to be short-stemmed?

(f) From your knowledge of reproduction in flowering plants explain
 (i) how the crosses required in experiment 3 could be ensured,
 (ii) how self-fertilisation could be ensured. *(AEB)*

12 In guinea pigs, black coat colour is dominant to brown and short hair is dominant to long hair. These characters are not linked. A breeder has only stocks of pure breeding, long-haired brown and pure breeding, short-haired black guinea pigs. Explain clearly the breeding programme to be followed to obtain pure breeding, long-haired black guinea pigs. *(UL)*

13 Normal (wild-type) strains of the fruit fly *Drosophila melanogaster* have greyish-brown bodies if developed on food media free of silver salts, but have yellow bodies if certain silver salts are added to the food on which the larvae develop. Strains homozygous for the recessive allele yellow (**y**) have yellow body-colour regardless of whether their food contains silver salts or not.

You have a single living yellow fruit fly, and the food on which it has developed is unknown; you also have a stock of normal (wild-type) fruit flies. Describe how you would proceed to find out whether or not the yellow body-colour of the single yellow individual was genetically or environmentally produced. *(HK)*

14 Haldane and Poole examined the incidence of a family's susceptibility to the development of blisters on feet in hot weather. The pedigree shown in Figure 28.5 was obtained over 5 generations; circles indicate females and squares indicate males while black symbols indicate that the individual is affected by foot blistering. Marriages are shown by horizontal lines directly connecting symbols and the children of a marriage are shown connected by a line above the symbols. From the evidence given here, deduce as much as you can about the genetics of the condition and its source. *(OCJE)*

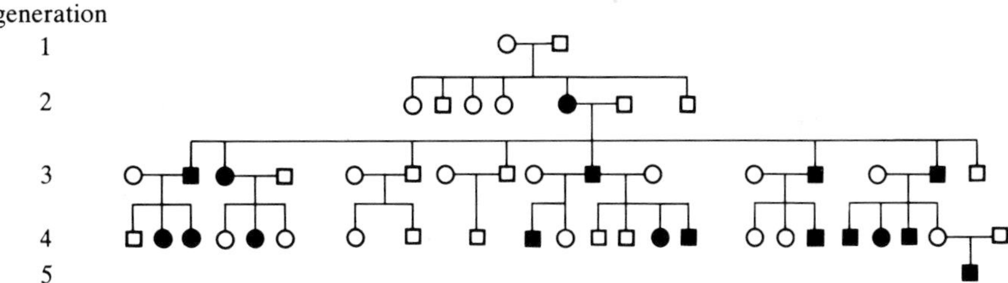

Figure 28.5 Human pedigree showing susceptibility to the development of blisters.

29 Chromosomes and Genes

Background Summary

1 In dihybrid crosses genes sometimes appear to contradict Mendel's Second Law and fail to assort independently. This can be explained by postulating that such genes are carried on the same chromosome (**linkage**).

2 Genes linked together on the same chromosome constitute a **linkage group**. In *Drosophila* the number of linkage groups equals the haploid number of chromosomes, and the sizes of the linkage groups correspond to the sizes of the chromosomes. This was one of the earliest pieces of evidence that genes are carried on the chromosomes.

3 Homologous chromosomes are normally identical in appearance (**autosomes**). An exception is provided by the **sex chromosomes** which are **heterosomes**. Sex is generally determined by the **X** and **Y** chromosomes. In humans the female is **homogametic** (**XX**), the male **heterogametic** (**XY**). In certain other organisms the reverse is the case.

4 Experiments indicate that genes controlling observable characteristics other than sex, are carried on the **X** chromosome (**sex linkage**). Though open to question, it is generally thought that few, if any, such genes are carried on the **Y** chromosome, at least not in the human.

5 In humans sex linkage is seen in the inheritance of colour-blindness and haemophilia, the latter being of historic interest in the royal families of Europe.

6 Usually crosses involving linked genes produce a small proportion of offspring with new combinations (**recombinations**) in addition to the **parental combinations**. This can be explained by **chiasmata-formation** and **crossing-over** during meiosis.

7 Crossing-over enables geneticists to work out the relative positions of genes on a chromosome. In general the distance between two genes is proportional to their **cross-over value** (**cross-over frequency**). In this way **chromosome maps** can be established.

8 **Gene loci** in chromosome maps of *Drosophila* can be correlated with the **bands** seen in the **giant chromosomes** of the larval salivary glands. This, and much other information, suggests that genes are located in a linear sequence on the chromosomes. In recent years the technique of cell fusion has been used to map human chromosomes.

9 Certain characteristics, e.g. blood groups, are controlled by **multiple alleles**. In the case of the **ABO** blood-group system, three alleles are involved, only two of which can be present in any one individual. The blood group alleles are inherited in a normal Mendelian manner. Knowledge of the inheritance of blood groups is sometimes used in legal questions of paternity.

10 The inheritance of blood groups, together with data from a wide range of breeding experiments, indicate that between the two extremes of complete dominance and no dominance there are all degrees of **partial dominance**.

11 A medically important example of partial dominance is provided by the inheritance of **sickle-cell anaemia**. Studies on the cause of this condition have also thrown light on the way genes express themselves.

12 Many situations are known where a particular combination of genes is lethal (**lethal genes**). Sometimes a lethal gene is rendered relatively, but not completely, harmless in the heterozygous state, another example of partial dominance.

13 A particular characteristic is sometimes controlled by two or more pairs of alleles interacting with one another, e.g. the comb condition of poultry. Gene interaction is also seen in the phenomenon of **epistasis** in which the presence of one gene suppresses the action of another.

Investigation 29.1
Relationship between genes and chromosomes in *Drosophila*

Unfortunately it is not possible to look at an organism's chromosomes under the microscope and say which particular genes occur on each one. However, it is possible to draw certain conclusions about the relationship between genes and chromosomes by carrying out breeding experiments. Once again we shall use our old friend *Drosophila*. Use the same technique as that described in Investigation 28.5, (*see* page 289).

Experiment 1

1 Set up a cross between wild-type virgin females and brown-eyed, vestigial-winged males, i.e. ♀++ × ♂ bw vg. Label the bottle. After one week remove the parent flies, and after two weeks examine the $\mathbf{F_1}$ offspring.

2 Now cross $\mathbf{F_1}$ flies amongst themselves and carry the investigation through to the $\mathbf{F_2}$. Do not forget to remove the $\mathbf{F_1}$ flies.

3 Analyse the F_2 flies, recording the numbers of individuals showing each combination of characteristics. Calculate the ratio between them.
4 Explain your results. What do they tell you about the relationship between the genes responsible for the brown eye and vestigial wing conditions, and the chromosomes that carry them?

Experiment 2

1 Set up a cross between wild-type male flies and white-eyed, yellow-bodied virgin females, i.e. ♂++ × ♀ w y. Label the bottle. After one week remove the parent flies and after two weeks examine the F_1 offspring.
2 Analyse the F_1 flies, recording the numbers and sexes of each type.
3 Explain your results. What results would you expect to get if you crossed the F_1 flies amongst themselves?
4 Now cross F_1 flies amongst themselves and carry the investigation through to the F_2. As before, do not forget to remove the F_1 flies.
5 Analyse the F_2 flies, recording the numbers and sexes of each type. Are your predictions confirmed? What conclusions would you draw regarding the relationship between the genes controlling white eye, yellow body, and sex?

Experiment 3

1 Set up a cross between wild-type virgin females and white-eyed, yellow-bodied males, i.e. ♀ + + × ♂ w y. Proceed exactly as in Experiment 2.
2 Record, and explain the results obtained in both the F_1 and F_2 generations.

Results

Write a full account of your experiments and the results obtained.

For Consideration

(1) What conclusions would you draw from Investigations 28.6 and 29.1 regarding the relationship between genes and chromosomes in *Drosophila*?
(2) Are your conclusions supported by the information in Table 28.1?
(3) What further experiments would need to be done to build up a complete picture of *Drosophila's* chromosomes and the genes they carry?

Requirements
Hand lens or binocular microscope
White tile
Paintbrush
Etheriser
Culture bottles

Virgin ♀ wild-type flies
♂ brown-eyed, vestigial-winged flies
♂ wild-type flies
Virgin ♀ white-eyed, yellow-bodied files
♂ white-eyed, yellow-bodied flies

Note: All flies should be pure-breeding (homozygous) in labelled culture bottles.

Investigation 29.2
Genetic analysis of the products of meiosis in *Sordaria fimicola*

The way characteristics are passed on from parents to offspring depends on, amongst other things, how the alleles of a given gene segregate during meiosis. This in turn depends on how the chromosomes are orientated on the spindle at metaphase of the first meiotic division and whether or not crossing over takes place between particular chromatids. In the fungus *Sordaria* meiosis results in the formation of spores which are distinguishable into two types, black and white. The sequence in which the spores are arranged in the spore case can give us important information on how the alleles responsible for spore-colour have segregated during meiosis.

The organism

Sordaria belongs to a group of fungi called the Ascomycetes. It consists of branched filaments (hyphae) which are haploid. The life cycle is summarised in Figure 29.1. Sexual reproduction takes place between neighbouring hyphae. Nuclei migrate from one hypha into the other and fuse in pairs. Each diploid nucleus resulting from this fusion gives rise to a perithecium which consists of a group of spore-producing structures called asci (singular ascus).

Initially each ascus has a single diploid nucleus. This undergoes three successive divisions: the first two are meiotic (meiosis I and II respectively) and the third is mitotic. The result is that each ascus contains eight haploid spores (known as ascospores). Within each ascus the eight ascospores are arranged in a linear séquence corresponding to the order in which they are formed. In other words the spores containing the two nuclei resulting from any particular nuclear division are next door to one another.

The colour of the ascospores varies: some are white, others black. The colour of a particular spore is determined by its genetic constitution. White spores contain an allele which we can designate **W**, black spores contain a corresponding allele which can be designated **B**.

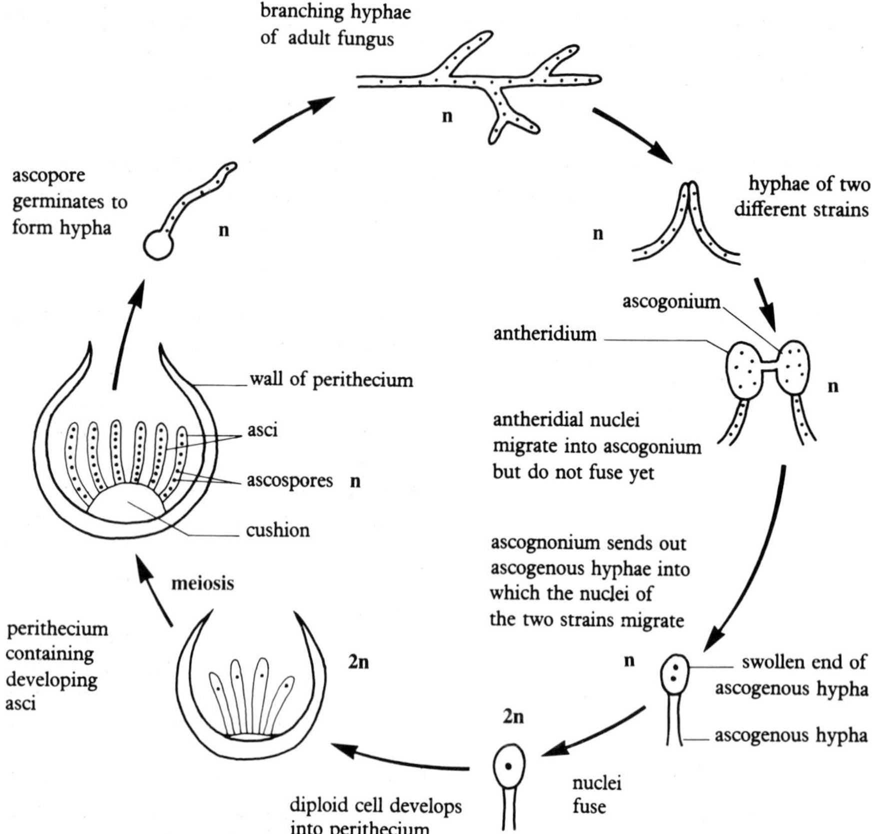

Figure 29.1 Simplified life cycle of an ascomycete fungus of the Sordaria type. The eight ascospores inside each ascus are formed by three successive nuclear divisions, meiosis I and II followed by mitosis. The ascospores are therefore haploid, as are the hyphae to which they give rise. **n**, haploid; **2n**, diploid.

Requirements
Microscope
Slides and coverslips
Inoculating needle
Incubator at 25 °C
Slides and coverslips

Cornmeal agar in petri dish

White-spored and black-spored strains of Sordaria (available from supplier)

Procedure

1 With a sterile needle inoculate a plate of cornmeal agar with about 1 mm^3 of white-strain and 1 mm^3 of black-strain *Sordaria*, separated by a distance of approximately 30 mm. Incubate at 25 °C in darkness for ten days.

2 *Ten days later* small dark perithecia will be observed resting on the agar. With a needle pick off several of the largest ones from the area where the two cultures have met, and also from the area close to where you inoculated.

3 Mount each perithecium separately in water on a slide. Put on a coverslip and tap it *gently* to squash the perithecium and spread out the asci. Do not tap too hard or the asci may burst.

4 Examine perithecia under high power and look for three types of asci: those with only black spores, those with only white, and those with both. Does an individual perithecium contain only one type, or more than one? Explain.

5 Now carefully examine asci containing black and white spores. How many of each are there within a single ascus? Is the number fixed or variable? Explain.

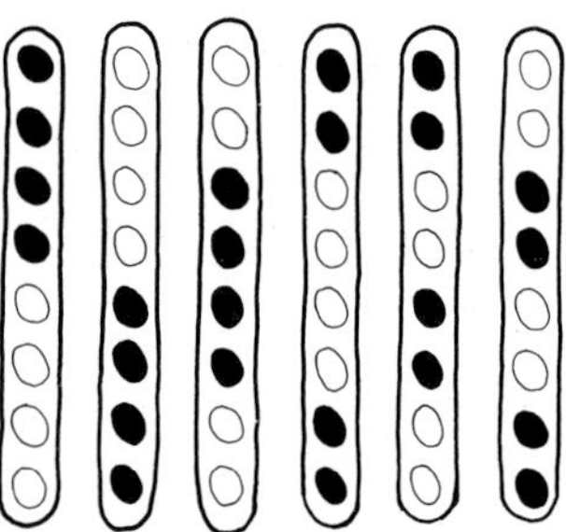

Figure 29.2 Diagram showing the possible arrangements of spores in the asci of *Sordaria*.

6 Make diagrams illustrating all the different arrangements of black and white spores which you can observe in your asci. Do they agree with Figure 29.2? Which arrangements are most common?

7 Using the symbol **W** for the allele controlling white spore colour, and **B** for the allele controlling black spore colour, and assuming that the two alleles occur at the same locus, construct diagrams to show how the behaviour of chromosomes during cell division produces the various arrangements observed. What conclusions do you draw from the relative frequency of each arrangement?

For Consideration

(1) Figure 29.2 shows the types of asci produced by a hybrid between a white spored and black spored strain of the ascomycete *Sordaria fimicola*. How would you account for the various spore arrangements? What would you expect the frequency of each type to be?

(2) Your observations in investigation 29.2 will have revealed certain important genetic principles. What are these principles and what is their general significance?

(3) The bread mould *Neurospora* is an Ascomycete with a life cycle similar to that of *Sordaria*. In a laboratory experiment an albino strain of *Neurospora* was crossed with the normal pink wild-type strain. Ascospores formed by the offspring were isolated at random and allowed to germinate. The resulting cultures were 2018 albino and 1996 pink. Explain this result.

Investigation 29.3
Preparation of giant chromosomes from the salivary glands of *Drosophila* larvae

Certain insect chromosomes, notably those in the salivary glands of *Drosophila* larvae, are unusually large and if appropriately stained can be seen to be banded. Correlations between cross-over data and the positions of the bands suggest that the bands correspond to specific gene loci, including those responsible for the mutants listed in Table 28.1. Giant chromosomes can be prepared for observations under the light microscope as follows:

A Intact larva

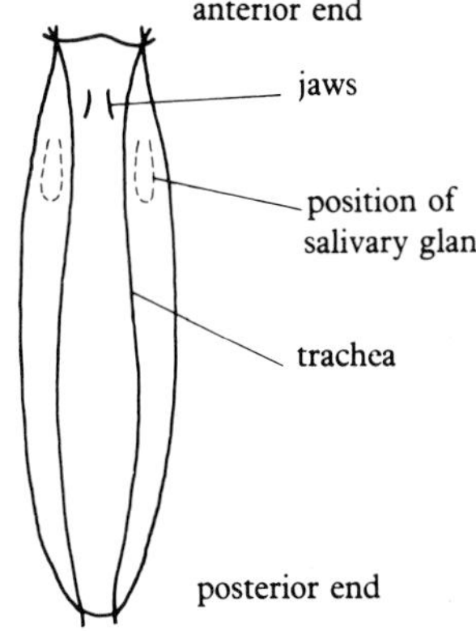

B After decapitation

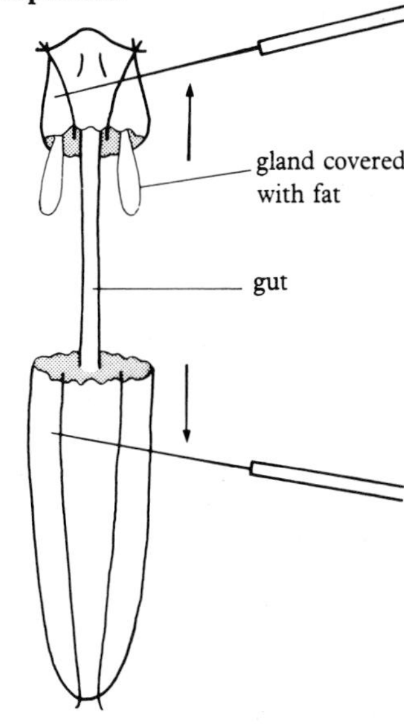

Figure 29.3 Technique for exposing the salivary glands of *Drosophila* larva.

Requirements
Microscope
Binocular microscope or hand lens
Slide
Coverslip
Fine forceps
Mounted needles
Filter paper

Acetic orcein stain
0.7 per cent sodium chloride in hydrochloric acid (1.0 mol dm^{-3})

Drosophila larvae
Prepared slide of giant chromosomes

Additional Requirements for Permanent Preparation
Siliconised coverslip*
Albumen
Hotplate
Ethanol (96 per cent)
Canada balsam

* To siliconise coverslip, dip coverslip quickly into silicon fluid.

Note: As an alternative to *Drosophila* larvae, the larvae of the blowfly (*Calliphora* sp.) may be used. They have the advantage of being comparatively large, which makes removal of the salivary glands much easier and avoids the need for a binocular microscope.

Temporary Preparation

1 Obtain a *Drosophila* larva from a culture bottle and place it in a drop of acidified sodium chloride on a microscope slide. Examine the larva under a binocular microscope (a hand lens is less satisfactory) and identify the structures shown in Figure 29.3A. Be sure you can tell the anterior from the posterior end.
2 Hold the posterior end down with a needle or grasp it with fine forceps; place a needle on the head and pull the head from the body as shown in Figure 29.3B. Identify the two elongated transparent salivary glands on either side of the gut. Detach them, and remove everything else from the slide.
3 Cover the glands with a drop of acetic orcein stain. Leave for 10–15 minutes, preferably on a warm hotplate. Make sure the tissue does not dry up; if necessary add more stain.
4 Put on a coverslip. Press down on the coverslip and tap it with the handle of your mounted needle. Remove surplus stain with filter paper. The cells should rupture and the chromosomes spread out. Locate giant chromosomes under low power and examine them in detail under high power.
5 If your preparation has been unsuccessful, observe giant chromosomes in a prepared slide.

Permanent Preparation

1 Dissect out the salivary glands as for the temporary preparation.
2 Place a small drop of acetic orcein onto a thick siliconised coverslip and transfer the glands to it. Leave for 15–20 minutes.
3 At the end of the 15–20 minute period, remove most of the stain from the coverslip with the edge of a piece of filter paper so the glands stick to the coverslip.
4 Cover a slide with a thin layer of albumen by placing a very small drop of albumen in the centre of the slide and rubbing it all over the surface with a *clean* finger.
5 Place a drop of stain onto the albuminised slide and invert your coverslip, plus the glands, onto it.
6 Press down on the coverslip and tap it. Remove surplus stain with filter paper.
7 Dip your slide in a jar of ethanol (96 per cent) and wait until the coverslip falls off. The stained squashed chromosomes should remain spread out on the slide.
8 Remove the slide from the ethanol, allow it to dry, and then mount it in Canada balsam under a thin coverslip. Leave on hotplate to dry.

For Consideration

(1) Why is it necessary in the making of a permanent preparation for the coverslip to be siliconised and the slide albuminised?
(2) Can you suggest why the chromosomes in the salivary glands of *Drosophila* larvae should be abnormally large?
(3) How would you investigate what the bands in the giant chromosomes represent?

Questions and Problems

1 In *Drosophila* red eye is dominant over brown eye and yellow body is dominant over dark body. In an experiment a red eyed, yellow-bodied fly is crossed to a brown eyed, dark-bodied fly. The F_1 flies are all red eyed with yellow bodies. Two of the F_1 flies are crossed, with the following results in the F_2:

Red eyed, yellow body	126;	Brown eyed, dark body	39;
Red eyed, dark body	5;	Brown eyed, yellow body	3.

(a) What is the approximate ratio between the F_2 offspring?
(b) Give, with brief reasons, two possible theoretical results which you might have expected.
(c) How would you explain the ratio which was actually obtained? *(O & C modified)*

2 In the fruit fly *Drosophila* normal antennae and grey body are linked and are dominant to twisted antennae and black body.

When a normal fly was crossed with one carrying the recessive alleles the offspring were all of the normal type. One of these latter was then crossed with a fly homozygous for the recessive alleles and the following numbers of offspring were obtained:

Normal antenae and grey body	90;	Twisted antennae and grey body	11;
Normal antennae and black body	9;	Twisted antennae and black body	86.

(a) Explain this result.
(b) Make an annotated diagram of the bivalent which produced the recombinant classes. *(AEB)*

3 Figure 29.4 represents a pair of homologous chromosomes during prophase of meiosis, showing the positions of two pairs of alleles, **Rr** and **Qq**.
(a) During which anaphase(s) of the two meiotic divisions do alleles **R** and **r** and alleles **Q** and **q** subsequently separate?

	alleles **R** *and* **r**	*alleles* **Q** *and* **q**
A	at anaphase I	at anaphase I
B	at anaphase I	at anaphase II
C	at anaphase II	at anaphase I
D	at anaphase II	at anaphase II
E	at anaphase I and again at anaphase II	at anaphase I and again at anaphase II

(b) Draw a diagram showing the chromosomes and alleles present in the cells resulting from the second meiotic division.
(c) Draw a diagram showing the chromosomes and alleles present in the meiotic products assuming that a chiasma had *not* been formed between the two homologous chromosomes.
(d) Briefly explain the genetic significance of the phenomenon featured in this question. *(CL modified)*

Figure 29.4 A pair of homologous chromosomes during prophase of meiosis showing the positions of two pairs of alleles, Rr and Qq.

4 Explain the term 'cross-over frequency'. In a certain organism, genes **A, B, C,** and **D** were studied and it was found that the cross-over frequency between **A** and **B** was 20 per cent, **A** and **C** 5 per cent, **B** and **D** 5 per cent, and **C** and **D** 30 per cent.
(a) What is the probable sequence of these genes on the chromosome?
(b) What would you expect the cross-over frequency between genes **A** and **D** to be?
(c) Discuss the significance of crossing over. *(O and C)*

5 The following crosses, involving four genes (P, Q, R and S) on a pair of homologous chromosomes, produced the following cross-over values shown in the margin.
Which of the linkage maps shown below best represents the arrangement of the genes on the chromosome? Give reasons for your choice. *(NI modified)*

Parents	Cross-over value (%)
PpQq × ppqq	6
RrSs × rrss	8
QqSs × qqss	28
PpRr × pprr	30

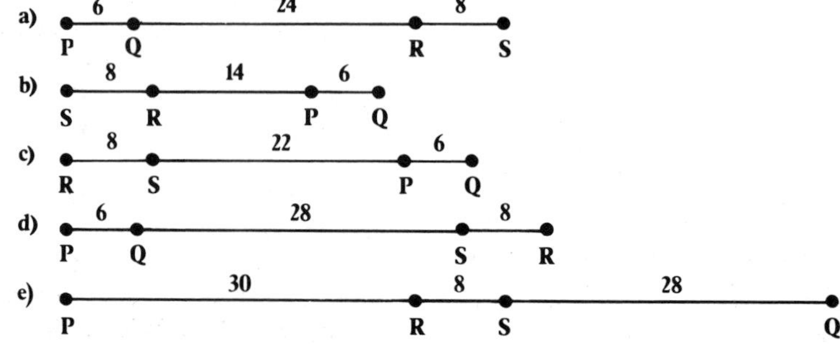

6 **A, a** and **B, b** are two pairs of *alleles* located in different *linkage groups*, and showing *independent assortment*. They are, therefore, due to genes located on different chromosomes. In fact the genes for **A, a** are on a pair of *autosomes*, and those for **B, b** on the **sex-chromosomes**. The male is the *heterogametic sex*, and the **Y** chromosome is genetically empty.

A female *homozygous* for the *dominant* alleles, **A** and **B**, is mated to a male which *phenotypically* shows both in the recessive condition.

(a) What is his *genotypic constitution* in respect of these factors?
(b) What will be the genotypes of the F_1 generation?
(c) Explain the meanings of the words in italics. (*O and C*)

7 Figure 29.5 shows a human pedigree for red-green colour-blindness. Circles indicate females, squares males. Filled-in circles and squares indicate red-green colour-blind individuals; open circles and squares indicate normal vision.

(a) State, as far as possible, the genotypes of each individual in the pedigree.
(b) What conclusions can you draw as to the inheritance of colour-blindness?
(c) (i) Which individuals in the pedigree are carriers?
(ii) What is meant by the term 'carrier' in this context?
(iii) Normal-sighted male carriers do not exist. Why?
(d) By means of a diagram show one way by which individuals 11 and 12 in the pedigree could have a colour-blind grand-daughter.

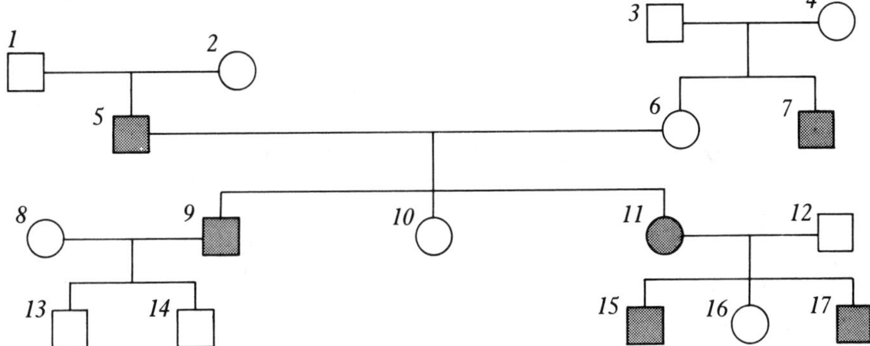

Figure 29.5 Human pedigree showing the inheritance of red-green colour-blindness.

8 Imagine you are a genetic counsellor. You are visited by a boy called John and his sister Susan. Both are normal, as are their parents, but they have a haemophiliac brother. John and Susan are worried that their children, when they have them, might turn out to be haemophiliacs. What would your advice be to each?

9 A farmer had two sons. The first, born when he was young, grew into a handsome, healthy youth in whom he took great pride. The second, born much later, was always a sickly child, and neighbours' 'talk' induced the farmer to bring his wife to court disputing its paternity. The grounds of the dispute were that the farmer, having produced so fit a first son, would not be the father of the weakling. The blood groups involved are shown below[1].

	Group	*Type*
Farmer	**O**	**M**
Mother	**AB**	**N**
First son	**A**	**N**
Second son	**B**	**MN**

What advice would you give the court?

10 After eight years of married life, during which time she had failed to become pregnant, Mrs X met and fell in love with Mr Y. During the ensuing five years three children were born. In the meantime the persons involved had tried to come to an understanding and wished to determine which of the two men was the father of each child. The blood types of those involved were determined, the results are shown in the margin.

	Group	*Type*
Mr X	**O**	**MN**
Mrs X	**O**	**MN**
Mr Y	**A**	**N**
First child	**O**	**MN**
Second child	**O**	**M**
Third child	**A**	**N**

What do you conclude as to the paternity of each child? Give your reasoning. (Case history from A. S. Wiener, *Blood Groups and Transfusion*, Thomas, 1943)

[1] The blood groups A, B, AB and O are controlled by three alleles, **A, B,** and **O,** any two of which may be combined together in a heterozygous individual. Homozygous individuals possess two identical alleles, viz. **AA, BB** or **OO**. **A** and **B** are both dominant to **O**. The blood types M, N and MN are controlled by two alleles, **M** and **N**, the heterozygote being **MN**.

11 Thalassaemia is a type of human anaemia rather common in the Mediterranean population, but relatively rare in other populations. The disease occurs in two forms, minor and major; the latter is much more severe, in fact usually lethal. The severely affected individuals are homozygous for a defective dominant gene whereas the mildly affected are heterozygous for the same gene. Persons free of the anaemia are homozygous for the normal allele. It can be assumed that the disease is inherited in a normal Mendelian manner.

(a) Letting **T** be the allele for thalassaemia, and **t** the normal allele: a man with minor thalassaemia marries a normal woman. What types of children with respect to thalassaemia may they expect and in what proportions? Diagram the germ cell unions producing children in this marriage.

(b) In another family both father and mother have thalassaemia minor. What are the chances that their children will be affected? Diagram the unions as before.

(c) A child has thalassaemia major. From the information given so far, what might you expect the genotypes of the parents to be? Diagram the possible genotypes and germ cells as before. *(OCJE)*

12 A recessive mutant of the gene which is responsible for chlorophyll synthesis in the tomato plant causes the plant to be colourless when present in the homozygous condition. Such a plant dies as a seedling after it has used up its supplies of food. In the heterozygous state the mutant produces a pale plant but one that does survive.

A normal green tomato plant was crossed with a pale heterozygote and the seeds formed from the cross were collected. These seeds were subsequently planted and a number of tomato plants reared which were self-pollinated. Once again the seeds were collected and a further generation of plants grown.

The ratio of normal green to pale plants in this generation was found to be 5:2. How can these results be explained? *(AEB)*

13 In shorthorn cattle the coat colour can be red (allele **W**), white (allele **w**), or in the heterozygous condition, roan. In addition, the polled (without horns) condition is dominant to the horned condition. What will the genotypes and phenotypes of the F_1 and F_2 generations be if homozygous polled red cattle are crossed with white horned cattle? How would you establish a pure breeding strain of red polled shorthorns from your F_2 generation? *(O and C)*

14 A broad leaved, red flowered snapdragon was crossed with a narrow leaved, white-flowered plant and the offspring were all broad leaved and had pink flowers. One of these F_1 plants was crossed with a broad leaved, white-flowered plant of unknown breeding behaviour, and the following offspring were obtained:

100 broad leaved, pink; 35 narrow leaved, pink;
95 broad leaved, white; 30 narrow leaved, white.

How would you explain these results? *(CCFE)*

15 In poultry the genes for rose comb (R) and pea comb (P), if present together, produce walnut comb. The recessive alleles of both, when present together in the homozygous condition, produce single-comb. What are the possible results that might be obtained by crossing a rose-combed fowl with pea comb? Explain your reasoning in full. What general principle is demonstrated here? *(CCJE)*

16 The following data (*from* Sinnott, Dunn, and Dobzhansky) show the results of a large number of matings carried out with a yellow variety of house mouse:

Parents	**Offspring**	
	Yellow	Non-yellow
yellow × non-yellow	2 378	2 398
yellow × yellow	2 396	1 235

How would you explain these data?

30 The Nature of the Gene

Background Summary

1 Experiments first carried out by Griffith and later by Avery on *Pneumococcus*, and since repeated on other bacteria, point to **nucleic acid** as being the carrier of genetic information.

2 Two principal types of nucleic acid exist in cells: **deoxyribonucleic acid** (**DNA**) and **ribonucleic** acid (**RNA**). Both consist of chains of **nucleotides**, each nucleotide consisting of a **pentose sugar, phosphate group** and one of five **organic bases** (**A, G, C, T,** and **U**). DNA contains **A, G, C,** and **T**; in RNA **T** is replaced by **U**.

3 According to the **Watson-Crick hypothesis**, based on X-ray crystallography and chemical analysis, DNA is a double helix consisting of two coiled chains of alternating phosphate and sugar groups, the latter being interconnected by pairs of bases linked in a specific way: **A** with **T** and **C** with **G**. This is known as 'complementary base pairing'.

4 Evidence suggests that DNA undergoes accurate **replication**, the mechanism being **semi-conservative**. In the intact cell this occurs during interphase, prior to cell division.

5 There is good reason to believe that DNA exerts its influence by controlling **protein synthesis**. A **gene** can be looked upon as a segment of the DNA chain; in general a single gene is responsible for the synthesis of one protein, or part of it (the **one gene-one protein hypothesis**).

6 Protein synthesis takes place on the **ribosomes** in the cytoplasm. DNA, confined mainly to the nucleus, controls protein synthesis by determining the order in which amino acids are linked together on the ribosomes. Each amino acid is coded for by a triplet of bases in the DNA. The sequence of amino acids in the protein is determined by the sequence of base triplets in the DNA.

7 In controlling protein synthesis the DNA is first transcribed into **messenger RNA** which is then, through the intermediacy of **transfer RNA**, translated into protein structure.

8 Ribosomes occur in groups or chains (**polyribosomes, polysomes**) and it is thought that during protein synthesis they move in convoy along the messenger RNA strand, thereby speeding up the assembly of amino acids into polypeptide chains. The formation of ribosomes is controlled by the **nucleolus**; ribosomes contain **ribosomal RNA** conjugated with protein.

9 It has been found that different triplets of bases can code for the same amino acid. The code is, therefore, **degenerate**. Triplets corresponding to all the known amino acids have now been characterised. Other triplets are involved in stopping and starting the message. The code is believed to be of universal occurrence in organisms.

10 The code is almost invariably **non-overlapping**, i.e. a given triplet codes for one amino acid, and none of its constituent bases codes for any other amino acid.

11 Generally only part of the DNA within a gene is expressed, i.e. used for protein synthesis. The parts that are expressed are called **exons**, the unused parts are called **introns**.

12 The potency of DNA in controlling protein synthesis can be seen in **viruses**, notably bacteriophage, whose nucleic acid has been shown to take over the metabolic machinery of the host cell.

13 Other ways in which DNA (and/or RNA) show their influence in cells include **cancer** (cancer-causing DNA segments called **oncogenes** have been discovered), **bacterial transduction**, and **recombinant DNA technology** (*see* page 307).

Investigation 30.1 Making models of DNA, RNA, and protein synthesis

If you think that research necessarily means using sophisticated techniques and complicated apparatus, it is sobering to reflect that Watson and Crick found that building models, using little more than stands, clamps and pieces of wire, was an essential step in unravelling the structure of DNA and understanding how it works (Figure 30.1). In this session you will have an opportunity to follow in their footsteps.

Procedure

Using match sticks, plasticine of different colours, and any other suitable materials, construct flat models (i.e. models which lie flat on a table) illustrating the following:

1 *The molecular structure of DNA*. Show the relationship between the sugar, phosphate and organic bases, the molecular basis of the helical con-

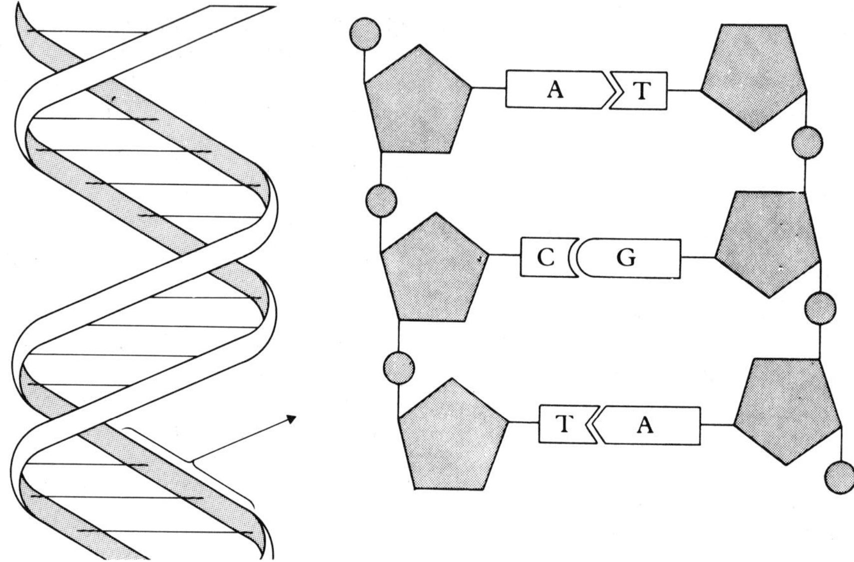

Figure 30.1 The Watson-Crick model of DNA.

figuration and the complementary relationship between the bases.

2 *How DNA replicates.* Build a short length of DNA, made up of, say, five pairs of nucleotides. Construct ten further nucleotides of the same type as those in your DNA molecule. Now make your DNA replicate.

3 *Formation of messenger RNA.* Show how DNA is transcribed into messenger RNA, one of the two strands of the DNA serving as the template for the synthesis of the RNA.

4 *How messenger RNA controls the assembly of a protein.* Make models of amino acids, transfer RNA molecules and a short length of messenger RNA. Show how the sequence of bases in the messenger RNA is translated into protein structure.

5 *The action of polyribosomes.* Make models of two ribosomes (more if you wish). Move the ribosomes in convoy along a strand of messenger RNA and show how each one results in the formation of a polypeptide chain.

6 *The three-dimensional structure of DNA.* If time and opportunity allow, try building a three-dimensional (stereo) model of DNA similar to the one in Figure 30.1. Represent the individual nucleotides as accurately as possible, and show how they relate to each other spatially.

Requirements
Eight different colours of plasticine (modelling clay)
Match sticks
Other materials as available

For Consideration

(1) What is the evidence for each of the structures and processes which you have represented as a model?
(2) Why do you think Watson and Crick found it necessary to build models of the DNA molecule?
(3) When Watson and Crick built their model of DNA they paid particular attention to the shape (stereochemistry) of the four bases. Why?

Investigation 30.2
Distribution of DNA and RNA in root-tip cells

One piece of evidence supporting the DNA-RNA theory is that RNA is found in the cytoplasm as well as in the nucleus, but DNA is mainly confined to the nucleus. In this experiment the distribution of DNA and RNA in undifferentiated cells will be investigated by staining with chemicals specific for each nucleic acid. Two techniques will be tried: the Feulgen technique stains only the DNA; the methyl green-pyronin technique, however, stains the RNA and DNA with different colours. Root-tip cells of bean provide suitable material.

Testing for DNA with Feulgen Stain

The technique involves hydrolysing the DNA with acid. This liberates aldehydes which restores the red colour of bleached Feulgen solution. The roots should be fixed in acetic ethanol for two hours before you begin.

1 Transfer the fixed material to *either* 1.0 mol dm^{-3} HCl at 60 °C for six minutes in an oven, *or* 50 per cent HCl at room temperature for fifteen minutes. This treatment hydrolyses the DNA and macerates the tissue.

Requirements
Microscope
Oven at 60 °C
Slides and coverslips
Watch glasses
Razor blade
Filter paper

Hydrochloric acid (1.0 mol dm^{-3})
Feulgen solution
Acetocarmine
Methyl green-pyronin stain
Distilled water
Ethanol: 70, 90 per cent and absolute
Xylene
Canada balsam

Bean roots fixed in acetic ethanol
Bean roots fixed in absolute ethanol

To obtain roots:
Germinate broad bean seeds 10 days previously. When radicle is 1.5 cm long, cut off tip to stimulate growth of lateral roots. Fix lateral roots in acetic ethanol for Feulgen, and absolute ethanol for methyl green-pyronin.

Feulgen's reagent prepared as follows:
Dissolve 1.0 g basic fuchsin in 200 cm^3 boiling distilled water. Filter. Add 30 cm^3 hydrochloric acid (1.0 mol dm^{-3}) and 3.0 g potassium metabisulphite to the filtrate. Allow to bleach for 24 h in the dark. If solution is still coloured the residual colour should be adsorbed on carbon. Filter. Store in tightly stoppered bottle in dark.

Methyl green-pyronin stain prepared as follows:
Methyl green 0.15, pyronin 0.25, ethanol 2.5, glycerine 20 vols. Make up to 100 vols. with 0.5 per cent carbolic acid.

2 Transfer the root to a watch glass of colourless Feulgen solution for one to two hours. If time is short the reaction can be accelerated by placing the watch glass on a warm surface.
3 Cut off the terminal 3 mm of the root and transfer it to a microscope slide, discarding the rest. Add acetocarmine which intensifies the Feulgen stain.
4 Tease out the stained root tip and put on a coverslip. Place a piece of filter paper on the coverslip and press gently so as to spread out the tissue and soak up surplus stain.
5 Examine under low and high power. What is the distribution of DNA in the cells?

Testing for DNA and RNA with Methyl Green-Pyronin Stain

The stain is a mixture of methyl green and pyronin. DNA takes up the methyl green, and RNA the pyronin. This enables the two types of nucleic acid to be distinguished, at least in good preparations. The roots should be fixed in absolute ethanol for 30 minutes before you begin.
1 With a clean sharp razor blade cut thin longitudinal sections of the terminal 3 mm of a root. Place the sections on a slide and cover with aqueous methyl green-pyronin stain for 30 minutes.
2 Draw off the stain with a pipette and replace with distilled water. Change the water several times so as to thoroughly wash the sections.
3 Mount the sections in distilled water and view under low and high powers. DNA should be stained blue-green, RNA red.
If your preparation is successful and you wish to make it permanent, continue as follows:
4 Remove the coverslip and cover the sections with successively 70 per cent, 90 per cent and two changes of absolute ethanol, spending one to two minutes in each. Do not spend too long in the ethanol or you will wash out the red stain.
5 Cover with xylene for one minute.
6 Mount in Canada balsam.

For Consideration

(1) From your observations in this investigation what predictions can you make about the way the nucleus communicates with the cytoplasm in controlling the development of the cell?
(2) DNA is not entirely confined to the nucleus; small amounts occur in the cytoplasm. Whereabouts in the cytoplasm does it occur and what is it doing there?

Questions and Problems

1 Trace, as concisely as you can, what happens to the DNA in a piece of meat from the moment it enters a person's mouth to the moment it becomes incorporated into his or her genes.

2 Briefly, and without resorting to chemical formulae, explain the structure of DNA. How does it differ from RNA?
The following is the sequence of bases in one of the two strands of part of a DNA molecule:

CAGGTACTG

What will be the sequence of bases in the other strand?
What evidence supports the sequence you suggest?

3 Bacterial cells were fed with labelled nitrogen-containing food. On division the DNA strands of the daughter cells were found to contain labelled nitrogen. These daughter cells were then fed on normal food and when they, in turn, divided, it was found that the cells produced contained DNA in which only half the strand contained labelled nitrogen atoms. How can this be explained? *(AEB modified)*

4 Let the amount of DNA present in the nucleus of a cell at the beginning of interphase be x. What will be the amount present at (a) the end of interphase, (b) the end of mitosis, (c) the end of a first meiotic division, and (d) the end of a second meiotic division? Give reasons for your answers.

5 (a) Francis Crick put forward the hypothesis that each amino acid is coded for by a triplet of bases in DNA. Why a triplet?
(b) The following sequence of bases in DNA codes for the formation of a polypeptide consisting of ten amino acids:
GTTAACCGAACGGTTAGATGTACATTTAAG
(i) Give the initial letters of the messenger RNA bases responsible for transcribing the above sequence.
(ii) What will be the sequence of amino acids in the resulting polypeptide?

6 Briefly explain how it is believed that the DNA in the nucleus of a cell controls the synthesis of proteins in the cytoplasm. Mention some of the more important evidence supporting your suggestions.

7 The amino acid sequence of part of the enzyme lysozyme from normal (wild type) T4 bacteriophage and a mutant bacteriophage are given below. The part of the sequence involved in the mutation is tinted.

Normal (wild type) Thr – Lys – Ser – Pro – Ser – Leu – Asn – Ala – Ala – Lys

Mutant Thr – Lys – Val – His – His – Leu – Met – Ala – Ala – Lys

(a) Could this mutant have arisen by a change in a single base pair in T4 DNA? If not, how might this mutant have been produced?
(b) What is the base sequence of the messenger RNA which codes for the five amino acids in the wild type?

8 Describe the properties of DNA that allow self-replication to take place, together with one piece of experimental evidence that indicates how this process occurs.
In sickle-cell anaemia one of the DNA codons for glutamic acid is changed to that for valine, so the haemoglobin formed does not function in the normal way. From your knowledge of the sequence of events involved in protein synthesis explain why the mutant haemoglobin would be synthesised. *(O & C)*

9 What do you understand by the one gene-one enzyme hypothesis? What evidence supports it? This hypothesis was first postulated in the 1940s. Do you consider that it should be modified in the light of more recent research?

10 In the bread mould *Neurospora crassa*, a biosynthetic pathway can be interrupted by three mutations. Mutant **X** will grow if provided with cystathionine, homocystine, or cysteine; mutant **R** will grow only on homocysteine but accumulates cystathionine; mutant **W** will grow if provided with homocysteine or cystathionine, but not on cysteine.
(a) Sketch the sequence of biosynthesis of these three chemicals and indicate the positions of the metabolic blocks imposed by mutants **X**, **R**, and **W**.
(b) (i) What do you predict would be the result of crossing the mutants in pairs **X** with **R**, **X** with **W**, and **W** with **R**.
(ii) What conclusion would you draw if your predictions turned out to be correct? *(SA modified)*

11 The following metabolic pathway in humans was discovered by A. E. Garrod in the early 1900s:
dietary and/or tissue protein → tyrosine → hydroxyphenylpyruvic acid →
→ homogentisic acid → fumaric and acetoacetic acids → Krebs' citric acid cycle
This pathway ensures that in normal circumstances the amino acid tyrosine, derived from excess protein, is disposed of metabolically. However, in certain individuals large quantities of homogentisic acid are excreted in the urine, which consequently turns black on standing. This condition is known as alkaptonuria and Garrod showed that, though rare, it runs in families. Suggest explanations of this condition in terms of modern genetic and biochemical theory.

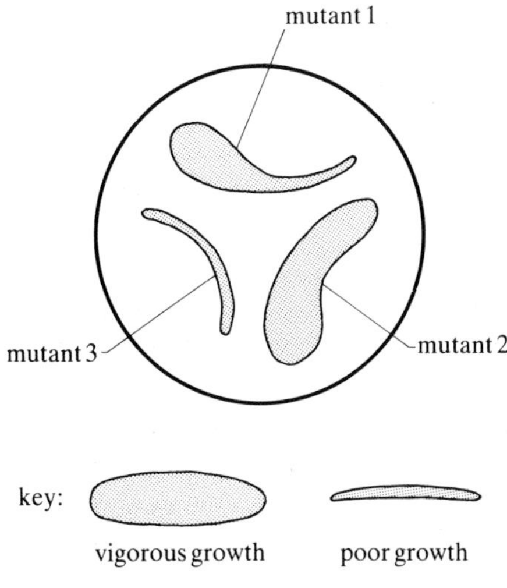

Figure 30.2 Bacterial mutants on an agar plate.

12 Three bacterial mutants are unable to grow on a medium lacking substance Z. The normal wild type of bacterium synthesises Z from inorganic materials in three stages, each of which requires a specific enzyme. The normal biochemical sequence leading to the production of Z is shown below.

Inorganic materials and energy source $\xrightarrow[\text{enzyme A}]{}$ substance X $\xrightarrow[\text{enzyme B}]{}$ substance Y $\xrightarrow[\text{enzyme C}]{}$ substance Z

Pure strains of the mutants were streaked on to an agar plate containing inorganic materials and a substance which provided an energy source. After incubation the plate had the appearance shown in Figure 30.2.

Breeding tests showed that each mutant strain lacked the ability to produce Z because it lacked one of the three necessary enzymes in the biochemical sequence, a different one in each case. Any substance which could be made, but not used, accumulated and diffused into the agar around the bacterial colonies. Mutant 2 was unable to produce enzyme A. Other tests showed that none of these strains produced an inhibiting substance which could stop the growth of the others.

(a) Mutant 2 lacked enzyme A and could not make substance X from raw materials.
   (i) From which two substances could mutant 2 make Z?
   (ii) What could be the origin of these two substances?

(b) Explain the following:
   (i) Mutant 1 had little growth next to mutant 2;
   (ii) Mutant 1 had vigorous growth next to mutant 3.

(c) Which enzyme was lacking in mutant 3?

(d) How would you test your answer to (c)? *(JMB-N)*

13 The gene for the β chain of haemoglobin is carried in humans on chromosome number 11. It contains three sequences of sense (expressons = exons) which are separated by two intervening sequences (interruptons = introns). The introns do not code for any part of the final amino acid chain. When a messenger RNA molecule is made along the whole sequence, the RNA sequences which represent the introns are cut out by enzymes. The sequences complementary to the exons are spliced together again by enzymes. This forms a functional messenger RNA which leaves the nucleus. Its message is translated into protein at the ribosomes.

(a) Suggest as many functions for introns as you can.

(b) How do the cutting enzymes know exactly where to cut the messenger RNA?

(c) What use can be made by humans of the cutting and splicing enzymes?

(d) In the sequence for haemoglobin β chain, a change of one base (codon UAG to codon UAU) stimulates a mutant form of the haemoglobin (haemoglobin Constant Spring) in which the β chains are 29 amino acids longer than usual. What has happened?

14 What experiments would you perform to test whether DNA is the hereditary material of organisms? *(CCJE)*

15 'The relation between DNA and protein is rather like that between the hen and the egg in the well-known question of which came first.' Discuss this statement. *(CCJE)*

16 In what ways has research on (a) bacterial genetics, (b) nutrition of Fungi, and (c) reproduction of viruses helped scientists to elucidate the genetic code?

17 Nucleic acids can code for each other and for proteins, but proteins cannot code for nucleic acids. Why? *(OCJE)*

18 Figure 30.3 is an electron micrograph of a stage in the life cycle of the bacteriophage virus.

(a) Name the structures labelled **A** and **B**.

(b) Briefly describe, without diagrams, the sequence of events preceding the stage illustrated in the micrograph.

(c) Some viruses contain RNA instead of DNA. Describe two methods by which such viruses can direct the synthesis of viral protein by the host cell.

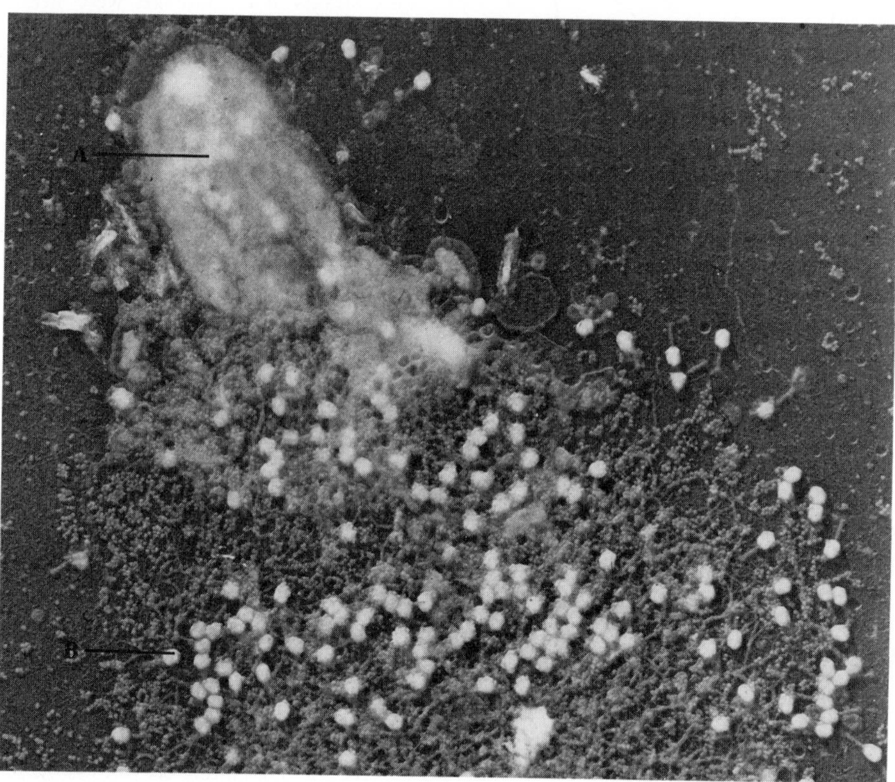

Figure 30.3 A stage in the life cycle of bacteriophage.

31 Genes and Development

Background Summary

1 Development involves a highly ordered sequence of events, elaborately controlled in space and time.

2 Experiments on unicellular organisms indicate that the nucleus is not only necessary for development to proceed, but that it also determines what sort of structure the cell develops into.

3 It is also apparent that the cytoplasm can play an important part in controlling development. In some multicellular organisms the fate of a particular cell is determined by which part of the original egg cytoplasm it comes to contain.

4 In chordate embryos the origin of certain structures can be traced back to specific **presumptive areas** in the blastula.

5 Although the destiny of most tissues is determined as early as the blastula stage, some tissues show considerable plasticity in what they can develop into. The fate of such tissues is determined by neighbouring tissues (**organisers**) which induce them to develop in a particular way.

6 An example of a powerful organiser is **chorda-mesoderm** whose inductive capacity has been demonstrated by transplantation experiments in amphibian embryos.

7 Development is controlled by the action of a *sequence* of organizers. This can be seen in the development of the vertebrate eye which has been analysed in some detail, but little is known about the chemical nature of the organisers involved.

8 Returning to the role of the nucleus, does the DNA content of the nucleus of a particular cell change during the course of development, or does it remain unaltered? Evidence, principally from nuclear-cloning experiments in amphibians and culturing of carrot tuber cells, suggests that the latter is the case.

9 How, then, does cell differentiation take place? Evidence suggests that different parts of the genetic code operate at different times during development. It would seem that at any given moment a proportion of the genes are in some way masked or 'switched off'. This concept can be illustrated by the formation of different types of haemoglobin during development and is supported by Jacob and Monod's work on the synthesis of sugar-splitting enzymes in colon bacteria, *Escherichia coli*.

10 In eukaryotic organisms, general masking of genes is carried out by basic proteins (**histones**) which are associated with the chromosomes. Selective masking is carried out by acidic proteins.

11 Cell fusion experiments have confirmed that the masking of genes is reversible, i.e. the genes can become de-repressed when circumstances permit.

12 Masking of genes may occur at the level of transcription by repressing the DNA, or at the level of translation by repressing the messenger RNA.

13 A variety of external environmental influences can affect development. Generally these tend to be cruder, more all-or-nothing, than the subtler internal influences.

14 **Senescence**, a natural process of decline culminating in death, is caused by somatic mutation, mistakes in protein synthesis, cell degeneration, faults in homeostasis, and autoimmunity.

15 DNA fragments from mammals, transferred to bacteria in plasmids, can cause the bacteria and their progeny to synthesise mammalian proteins, e.g. insulin, for human use. The replication of genes in this way is called **gene cloning** and it is the basis of **recombinant DNA technology** or **genetic engineering**.

Investigation 31.1
Organising ability of the dorsal lip of the amphibian gastrula

During development certain cells exert a powerful influence over other cells. This was originally demonstrated by the classical experiments of Spemann and Mangold: they showed that in amphibians a secondary embryo could be produced by transplanting a piece of dorsal lip of the blastopore from one embryo to the ventral surface of another. You can test this for yourself by a slightly different method. It has been found that secondary embryonic tissues can be produced by implanting a small piece of the dorsal lip into the blastocoel of an early gastrula. If the implantation is carried out on the dorsal side of the gastrula, subsequent movements of the endodermal cells during gastrulation will carry the implant round to the ventral side where, lodged between the ectoderm and endoderm it should, with luck, induce the formation of a secondary embryo.

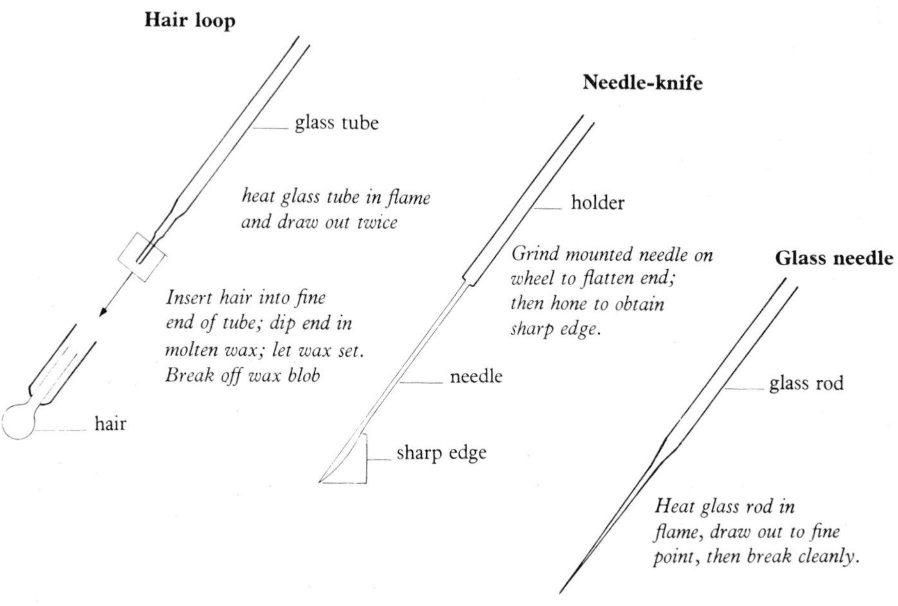
Hair loop
glass tube
heat glass tube in flame and draw out twice
Insert hair into fine end of tube; dip end in molten wax; let wax set. Break off wax blob
hair
Needle-knife
holder
Grind mounted needle on wheel to flatten end; then hone to obtain sharp edge.
needle
sharp edge
Glass needle
glass rod
Heat glass rod in flame, draw out to fine point, then break cleanly.

Figure 31.1 Micro-dissection instruments for embryonic surgery.

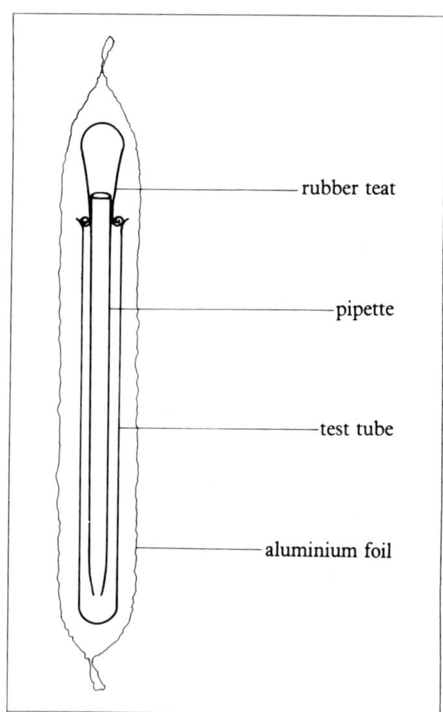
rubber teat
pipette
test tube
aluminium foil

Figure 31.2 Sterile pipette for use in experimental embryology. The whole assemblage should be autoclaved before use.

Equipment

This experiment involves carrying out an operation under a binocular microscope. Micro-dissection instruments should be used: fine forceps for decapsulation of embryo, a hair loop for holding the embryo in position, and a needle-knife and glass needle for embryonic surgery. These are illustrated in Figure 31.1.

You are also provided with operating dishes (solid watch glasses containing agar), and culture dishes (petri dishes containing agar). The purpose of the agar is to provide a soft bed for the embryo. Niu-Twitty solution is also provided: this has been found to be an ideal medium for amphibian development.

Precaution

As you will see below, the first step in the experiment is to decapsulate the gastrulae. Once they are decapsulated be careful to ensure that in their dishes and pipettes the *naked embryos do not come into contact with the air-liquid interface*. If they do they will burst.

Procedure

1 Decapsulate two gastrulae using fine forceps. Do this in a small petri dish containing Niu-Twitty solution. First remove the jelly coat (quite easy) and then remove the vitelline membrane (difficult).

2 Transfer the gastrulae with a sterile pipette to an operating dish containing Niu-Twitty solution.

3 Excise a small piece of the dorsal lip of the blastopore from one of the gastrulae (the donor). Use the hair loop to hold the gastrula steady and use a needle-knife for cutting. Do not apply too much pressure or you will burst the embryo.

4 Make a slit in the roof of the blastocoel of the other gastrula (the recipient) and push in the piece of dorsal lip using the glass needle as shown in Figure 31.3.

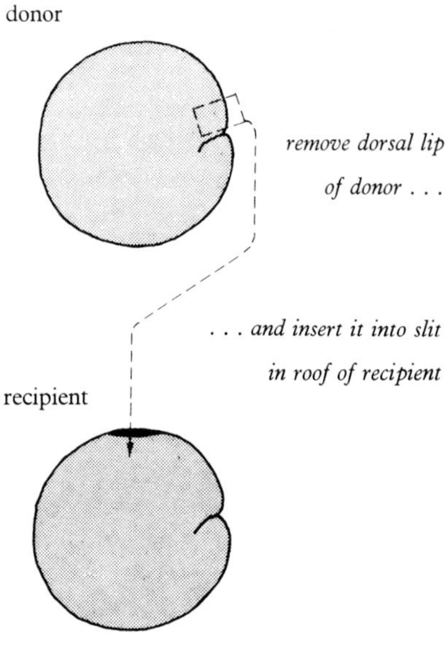

donor

remove dorsal lip of donor . . .

. . . and insert it into slit in roof of recipient

recipient

Figure 31.3 Procedure for transplanting the dorsal lip of amphibian gastrulae. (×12)

Requirements
Operating instruments all of which must be sterilised by flaming or ethanol before use:

Fine forceps (2 pairs)
Glass needle (*see* Figure 31.1)
Needle knife (*see* Figure 31.1)
Hair loop (*see* Figure 31.1)

Sterile pipette (*see* Figure 31.2)
Binocular microscope
Operating dish (solid watch glass containing 2 per cent agar)
Culture dish (5 cm petri dish containing 2 per cent agar)

Niu-Twitty solution (*see* right)

Early gastrulae of *Xenopus*

5 Leave the recipient for 30–60 minutes in the operating dish for healing, and then transfer it to a separate culture dish containing Niu-Twitty solution. Label the lid with a wax pencil.
6 Set up a control: dacapsulate a gastrula, make a slit in the roof of the blastocoel but do not implant anything into it. Treat as step 5.
7 Observe at regular intervals during the next week. If your embryos survive make comparative drawings of the recipient and control.

For Consideration

(1) Build up an hypothesis to explain the mechanism by which the dorsal lip causes the production of a complete secondary embryo on the ventral side of the recipient.
(2) Why do you think the recipient does not reject the dorsal lip of the donor by an immune response?

Niu-Twitty solution made up as follows:
A 3.4 g sodium chloride
50 mg potassium chloride
80 mg hydrated calcium nitrate (V)
100 mg manganese sulphate (VI)
500 cm^3 distilled water
B 110 mg sodium hydrogenphosphate
20 mg potassium hydrogenphosphate
250 cm^3 distilled water
C 200 mg sodium hydrogencarbonate
250 cm^3 distilled water
Dissolve **A**, **B**, and **C** in warm water, then mix. To prevent bacterial growth add 1.0 g sulphadiazene sodium per 500 cm^3.

Investigation 31.2
Growth and differentiation of isolated cells *in vitro*

The growth and differentiation of cells is controlled by a complex system of interacting factors, some derived from the cells themselves and some from the environment. In recent years much information about these factors has come from tissue culture experiments in which isolated groups of cells obtained from embryos and adults have been grown in a nutrient medium outside the body, i.e. *in vitro*. In the present experiment you will attempt to grow isolated heart cells of the chick in tissue culture.

Precaution

One of the main reasons for failure in tissue culture work is infection of the tissue. For this reason you should wear a sterile face mask throughout the procedure and you should touch living material only with sterile instruments. Forceps and scissors must be absolutely clean and either flamed or dipped in ethanol before use. Sterile pipettes should be returned to a sterile test tube when not in use.

Procedure

1 Obtain a fertilised hen's egg (8–10 days old). Support it in a cradle of plasticine. Wipe the egg with ethanol and allow it to dry.
2 Crack the shell over the air space (blunt end). Remove the shell at the blunt end with forceps and then the white opaque membrane beneath it.
3 Using sterilised forceps remove the embryo and place it in sterile saline in a petri dish.
4 Dissect out the heart and transfer it to another petri dish of saline. Cut the heart into small pieces of 0.5 mm diameter using a sterilised blade.
5 Sterilise a large coverslip in ethanol and dry it by rubbing it between two sheets of sterile filter paper. With a 1 cm^3 disposable syringe without needle place a piece of the chopped tissue in the centre of the coverslip. The tissue is now known as the explant.
6 Blot around the explant with sterile filter paper till almost dry. Then, using a 1 cm^3 syringe, add one drop of nutrient medium. Spread out the medium round the tissue to cover a circular area not more than ¾ of the diameter of the depression of a large cavity slide or watch glass.
7 Sterilise a large cavity slide or watch glass in ethanol and dry it with sterile filter paper. Spot it with four spots of vaseline at the corners of where the coverslip will lie. Now invert it and bring it down onto the top of the coverslip.

Requirements
Microscope (phase-contrast if possible)
Incubator at 37 °C
Sterile face mask
Dissecting instruments
Large cavity slide, or watch glass
Large coverslip
Sterile 1-cm^3 syringe without needle
Petri dishes ×2
Glass rods ×2
Paintbrush
Sterile filter paper
Cotton wool
Plasticine (modelling clay)
Vaseline
Molten wax-vaseline mixture

Ethanol for sterilisation
Chick saline
Nutrient medium

Fertilised hen's egg 8–10 days (*see* page 401)

Nutrient medium prepared as follows:
A medium 199
B chick serum
C chick embryo extract
(All obtainable from supplier)
Mix immediately before laboratory work commences in the proportions: **A**, 80 per cent; **B**, 10 per cent; **C**, 10 per cent. Each of the above ingredients can be stored indefinitely, the medium 199 in the ordinary part of a refrigerator, the serum and embryo extract in the freezer compartment.

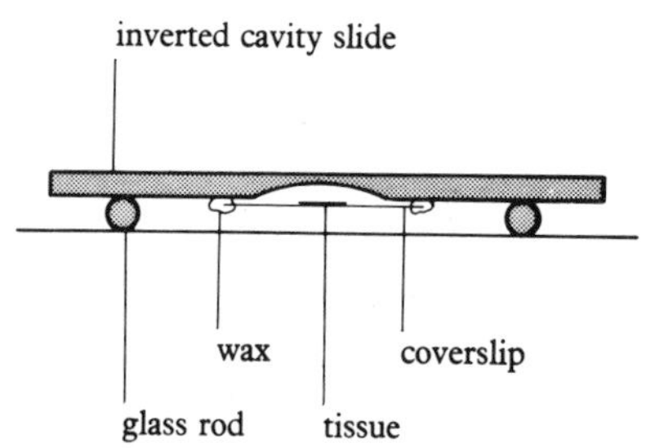

Figure 31.4 Set-up for tissue culture. A watch glass can be used in place of the cavity slide.

8 While still inverted seal around the edge of the coverslip with molten wax-vaseline mixture using a paintbrush. Make sure that the seal is good.
9 Incubate upside down on glass rods at 37 °C for two days (Figure 31.4). (N.B. the slide should be upside down and the coverslip beneath it).

TWO DAYS LATER

10 Turn the slide and coverslip over so that the coverslip is now on top of the slide and the explant is enclosed in a hanging drop of culture solution.
11 Observe under the high-power of, preferably, a phase-contrast microscope. You should be able to see fibroblasts and possibly epitheliocytes and amoebocytes growing out from the original explant.

For Consideration

(1) To what possible uses might tissue culture be put?
(2) To what extent are the cells which have grown out from your explant similar to, and different from, those of the original heart tissue?
(3) What light does rearing tissues *in vitro* throw on the normal development of tissues in the intact embryo, i.e. *in vivo*?

Note: Some people object on ethical grounds to experiments involving the use of chick embryos. As an alternative to the above investigation, plant and/or amphibian tissues may be cultured. Kits, with instructions, are available from suppliers.

Investigation 31.3 Development of the vertebrate eye

Requirements
TS head of embryo (amphibian or chick) through eyes at various stages of development

The development of the eye is worth studying in detail because it illustrates the organised sequence of events involved in the differentiation of a complex organ.

Procedure

Using prepared slides reconstruct the sequence of changes that takes place as the eye develops. You will need to examine a large number of slides to piece together all the stages.

First the neural tube is formed by invagination of the mid-dorsal ectoderm, then the anterior end of the neural tube swells up to form the brain. The eye then develops as follows (Figure 31.5):
1 An optic vesicle is formed on each side of the head as an outgrowth from the side of the brain.
2 A lens is formed by thickening and invagination of the ectoderm adjacent to the optic vesicle.
3 The optic vesicle invaginates to form an optic cup.
4 The inner wall of the double-walled optic cup gives rise to the sensory and nervous layers of the retina; the outer wall gives rise to the pigment layer.
5 The ectoderm adjacent to the lens forms the cornea.

For Consideration

(1) Suggest what induces the formation of the neural tube, optic vesicle, lens, optic cup, and cornea. How would you test your suggestions experimentally?
(2) What other organs or systems in a vertebrate might develop under the influence of a hierarchy of organisers?
(3) What are the advantages of development being controlled in this kind of way?

Figure 31.5 Development of the vertebrate eye as seen in sections of the head of vertebrate embryos.

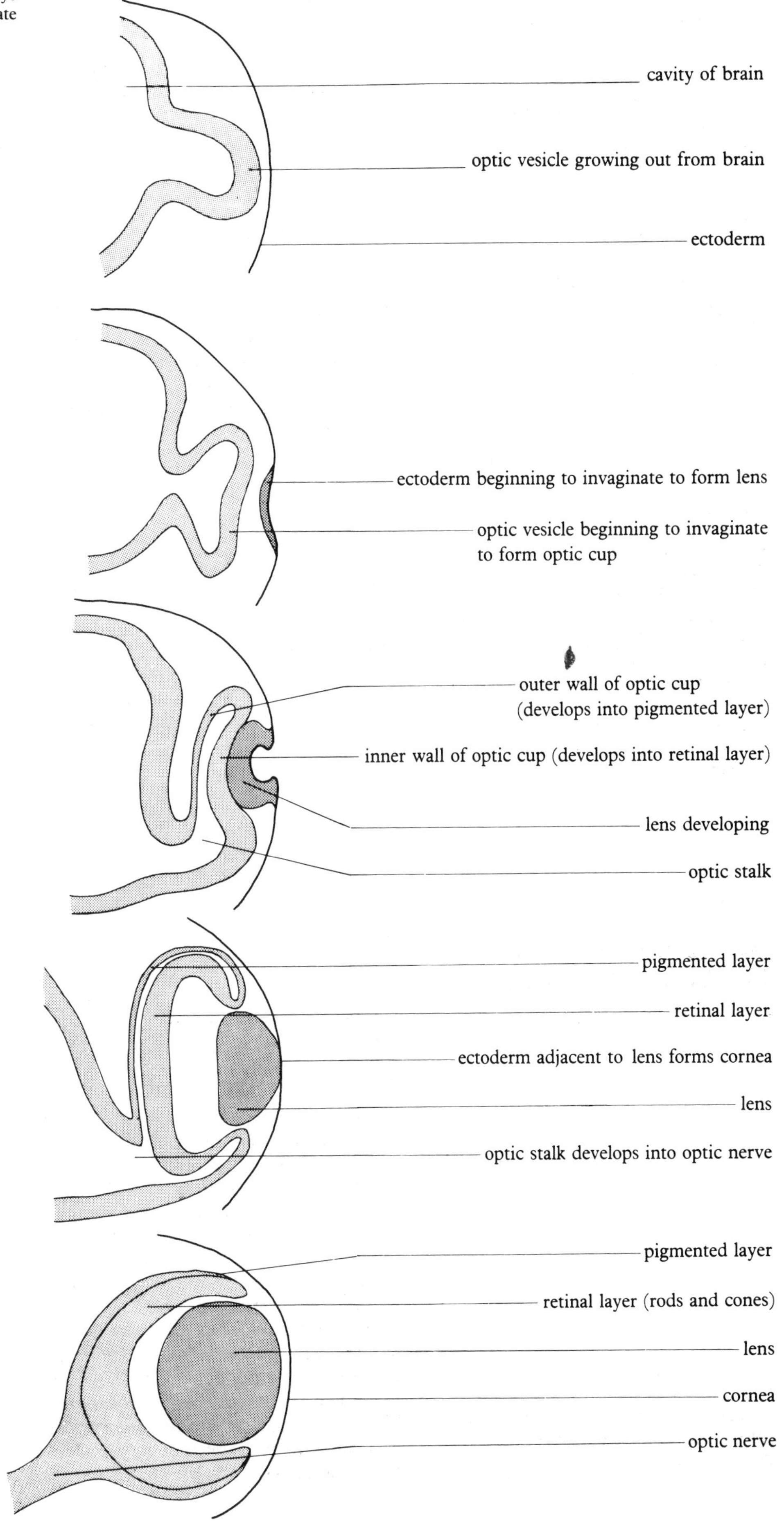

Questions and Problems

1 Explain what is meant by the term *organiser*, illustrating your answer by reference to the development of the vertebrate eye. Describe experiments which you would carry out (a) to demonstrate the validity of the organiser concept, and (b) to discover the chemical nature of the organiser.

2 The haemoglobin synthesised by an adult human contains two types of polypeptide called *alpha* and *beta* respectively. Each consists of a long chain of amino acids in the usual way.

The kind of haemoglobin synthesized in the foetus differs from that produced by the adult in that it contains *alpha* and *gamma* polypeptide chains.

It is known that the synthesis of the two kinds of haemoglobin, foetal and adult, is under genetic control.

(a) Explain, as precisely as you can, the *replacement* of foetal by adult haemoglobin at birth in terms of the action of genes.

(b) Why is it necessary for the foetus and adult to have different kinds of haemoglobin?

3 Figure 31.8 shows the system of organisers which is believed to control cell differentiation in the newt. Examine the diagram carefully and then answer the following questions:

(a) What do the second line of structures (head endoderm, head mesoderm, etc.) *develop* into?

(b) What is the spatial relationship between an organiser and the structure it induces?

(c) What cell layers in a late gastrula appear to play little or no part as organisers?

(d) What do you understand by the primary organiser in Holtfreter's scheme?

(e) What sort of experiments do you think the scheme is based on?

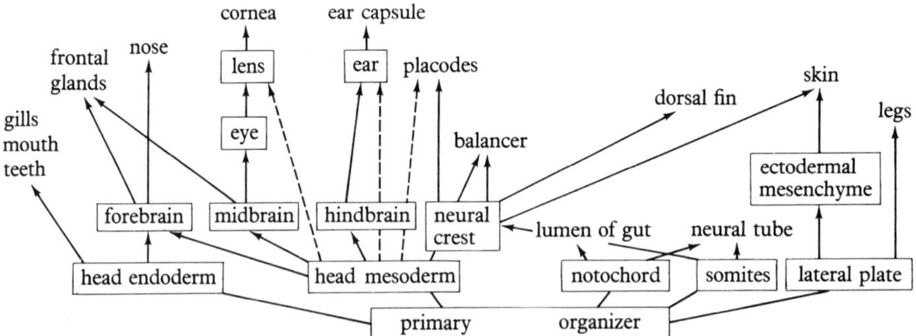

Figure 31.6 Diagram of secondary organisers in the newt (*after* Holtfreter, from *Cell Biology*, A.J. Ambrose and D.M. Easty, Van Nostrand Reinhold, 2nd ed, 1977).

4 Describe experiments which have been carried out to investigate the role of the nucleus in cell differentiation. What conclusions would you draw from the experiments you describe?

5 Consider the following information:

(a) When a small piece of tissue from the secondary phloem of a carrot taproot is cultured in a liquid medium containing salts, sugar and vitamins, the tissue grows slowly mainly by cell division.

(b) In contrast, when similar tissues are exposed to the same medium supplemented by coconut milk (the liquid endosperm of the coconut) the tissues grow rapidly by cell division and turn green.

(c) Single cells which break off from the dividing carrot tissue in (b) divide actively, and some develop roots, leaves and eventually flowers.

(d) Single cells removed from a carrot *embryo* and grown in a nutrient medium with coconut milk pass through a sequence of developmental stages similar to those gone through by a fertilised egg when it develops into an embryo. They eventually develop into carrot plants.

Now answer the following questions:

(i) What can you infer from these experiments about the genetic content of mature carrot cells?

(ii) Speculate on the role of coconut milk.

(iii) Put forward reasons for the different results in (b) compared with (c), and in (c) compared with (d).

(iv) Suggest ways in which these results could be put to practical use.

6 Several instances are known (see question 5, for example) where differentiated plant cells from an established tissue can be shown to be totipotent, i.e. capable of developing into a complete new organism. In contrast, attempts to demonstrate the totipotency of differentiated animal cells have only been successful when the nucleus of the differentiated cell is transferred to the cytoplasm of an enucleated fertilised egg. Can you explain this difference?

7 Write an essay on nucleo-cytoplasmic interactions. *(CCJE)*

8 The disaccharide sugar lactose is made up of glucose and galactose joined by β-galactoside linkages. The experiment described below was made to investigate the induction of the enzyme β-galactosidase in the bacterium *Escherichia coli.*

E. coli cells were added to four separate test tubes, A-D. Each test tube contained a basal nutrient medium consisting of inorganic salts, amino-acids and nitrogenous bases, together with the additional compounds indicated in the following table:

Additions	Tube **A**	Tube **B**	Tube **C**	Tube **D**
10% galactose	+	−	−	−
10% glucose	+	+	+	+
10% lactose	−	+	+	+
protein synthesis inhibitor	−	−	+	−
aza-guanine	−	−	−	+

\+ indicates presence, and — absence, of the additional compound.
Samples were removed from each tube at 0, 1, 2, 3 and 4 hours. Cells from each sample were disrupted and the amount of enzyme present in the sample determined. The results are shown below.

Time of removal of the sample (hours)	**Enzyme activity** (arbitrary units)			
	Tube A	Tube B	Tube C	Tube D
0	0.35	0.34	0.30	0.35
1	0.35	0.63	0.28	0.60
2	0.40	1.08	0.30	0.90
3	0.40	1.78	0.25	1.15
4	0.50	2.30	0.20	1.22

(a) Plot these results graphically.
(b) What conclusions would you draw as to how the enzyme β-galactosidase is induced? *(JMB-N modified)*

9 Explain the terms gene splicing, gene cloning and genetic engineering. What are the potential advantages and dangers of advances in this area of biology? *(CCJE)*

32 The Organism and its Environment

Background Summary

1 The study of organisms in relation to their environment is the science of **ecology**.

2 For convenience the ecological system can be divided into units of decreasing size: the **biosphere, biogeographical regions, biomes, zones, habitats** and **microhabitats**.

3 Within a given habitat, or range of habitats, each organism occupies a specific **ecological niche**. This is its role in the ecosystem. Its niche in the presence of competitors and predators (its **realised niche**) is more restricted than its niche in their absence (its **fundamental niche**).

4 The various conditions in which organisms live constitute their **environment**. A distinction may be made between **biotic** and **abiotic** (**physical**) **factors** of the environment. Those connected exclusively with the soil are called **edaphic factors**.

5 **Abiotic factors** include temperature, water, light, humidity, wind and air currents, pH, mineral salts and trace elements, water currents, salinity, wave action, topography, and background.

6 Biotic factors include predation, competition, and other interrelationships between organisms including one using another as a habitat or for other purposes.

7 Competition can be divided into **interspecific** and **intraspecific**. Coexistence is impossible between two species which occupy exactly the same ecological niche (**competitive exclusion principle**).

8 Organisms generally live in **communities** which, together with the non-living components of the environment, make up an **ecosystem**. The study of communities and ecosystems is known as **synecology**.

9 Communities do not happen suddenly; they grow gradually by a natural process in which one species is succeeded or replaced by another. This **succession** results eventually in the establishment of a stable **climax community**. The colonisation of a previously unoccupied area is known as a **primary succession**, in contrast to a **secondary succession** which is the recolonisation of an area whose previous occupants have been partially or completely destroyed. The destruction of an existing community may result in a succession which is different from the previous one (**deflected succession**).

10 An important aspect of ecosystems is **population growth**. Populations, if unchecked, grow exponentially. Growth is limited by various factors which together constitute **environmental resistance**. Some of the factors are **density-dependent**, others **density-independent**.

11 Fluctuating about a set-point, populations are generally held reasonably constant by a homeostatic mechanism involving negative feedback (*see* Chapter 13). However, sudden changes may occur in a population if some factor of the environment is suddenly changed. This can be seen in the growth of the human population over the last 200 years.

12 In an individual community the size of the population will be determined by the **birth rate**, **death rate**, **immigration** and **emigration**.

13 An ecosystem is composed of **producers**, **consumers**, and **decomposers** whose activities result in matter being cycled. The **carbon** and **nitrogen cycles** are applications of this general principle.

14 The nutritional relationships between producers and consumers can be seen in **food chains** and **food webs**. Whilst matter is cycled, energy is transferred through the system, a proportion being lost as heat at each level.

15 Estimations can be made of the numbers and total mass of individuals at each **trophic level** of a food chain or web. The mass is known as the **biomass**. The decrease in numbers and biomass at each level gives the **pyramid of numbers** and **pyramid of biomass** respectively.

16 Pyramids of numbers and biomass often contain anomalies which can be resolved by constructing **pyramids of energy**. Energy flow through food chains or webs invariably decreases at successive trophic levels.

17 The net rates at which producers and consumers accumulate energy are known as the net **primary production** and **secondary production** respectively. Measurements of productivity in these terms are particularly useful in ecosystems which yield harvests of animals or plants for use by humans.

18 The study of the individual species in a community is called **autecology**. Autecological studies aim to analyse the relationship between the organism and its environment in the broadest sense.

19 One of the most powerful influences in the environment is the human. Pollution, the indiscriminate use of pesticides and herbicides, radioactive contamination, urbanisation and the exploitation of our natural resources, aggravated by the population explosion, are some of the more obvious ways in which we have affected our environment.

Investigation 32.1
Investigating the distribution patterns of organisms (Part I)

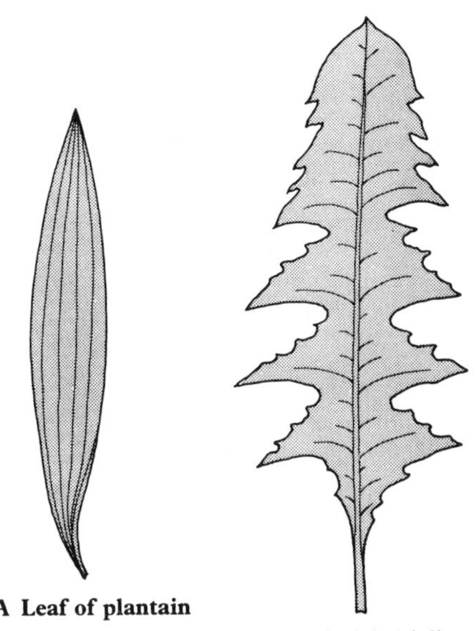

Figure 32.1 Leaves of plantain and dandelion.

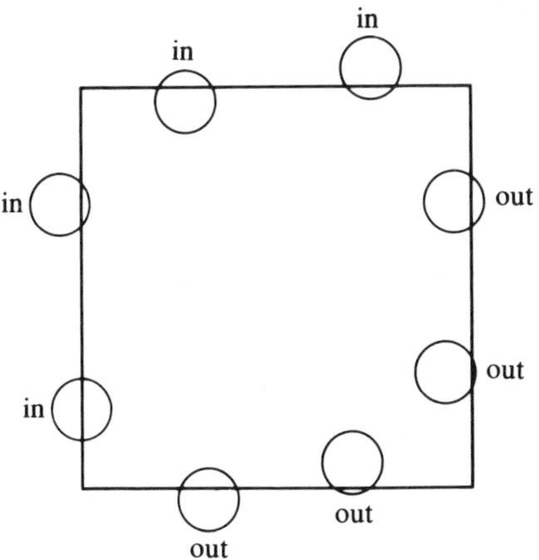

Figure 32.2 Procedure for counting plants that are partly inside, and partly outside, a quadrat. For the top and left hand sides of the quadrat regard a plant as *inside* if any part of it, however small, falls inside the frame. For the bottom and right hand sides of the quadrat, regard a plant as *outside* if any part of it, however small, falls outside the frame.

One aim of autecological studies is to assess why a given species should abound in one locality and be sparse in another. Obviously to answer this question it is necessary to investigate the distribution of the species as accurately as possible. In this exercise we shall examine the distribution of species where each individual organism can be seen.

Method

As it is rarely possible to count all the individuals present in a given locality, one resorts to sampling. Sampling methods take many different forms, but one commonly used involves the use of a quadrat frame. A metal or wooden frame of suitable area is laid on the ground and the number of individuals within it are counted. Quadrats are placed, either regularly or randomly, over as large an area within the locality as is feasible, so an accurate assessment can be made of the numbers of individuals per unit area. This is called the **density**.

Alternatively you can use a grid consisting of a quadrat which has been subdivided into 100 small squares. You then count up the total number of squares in which the organism occurs. The figure you get is called the **percentage frequency**.

Procedure

Which particular organisms you choose to investigate must depend on where you live. The following examples illustrate the principles.

PLANTAINS AND DANDELIONS

Plantains and dandelions are common in fields and lawns. In both cases a single plant consists of a main flower-bearing stem surrounded by a ring of six to twelve leaves at ground level. If not in flower, dandelions and plantains can be distinguished by the shapes of their leaves (Figure 32.1).

1 Select an area, and decide what particular species you wish to investigate.

2 Lay a one-metre quadrat frame on the ground, and count the number of plants inside it. If some of the plants are partly inside the quadrat and partly outside it, follow the procedure explained in Figure 32.2.

3 Repeat Step 2 with the quadrat in at least five different places, chosen at random. Before you proceed, think carefully about how best to ensure that the placing of the quadrat is *random*. There are many ways of achieving this.

4 Work out the average number of plants per square metre in the field.

5 Repeat Steps 2 to 4 in another contrasting area. Compare the density of the plants in the two areas.

EARTHWORMS

Assess the relative population densities of earthworms in the soil in two different undisturbed localities. A simple, though not entirely satisfactory, method is to extract the worms by chemical means.

1 Choose a day when the ground is neither frozen nor dry. Lay a series of one-metre quadrat frames systematically on the surface of the ground in each of two localities. Alternatively mark out a series of one-metre squares with string.

2 Using a watering can with a rose, spray each square metre with one gallon of water containing potassium permanganate (7–9 g). Within 30 minutes most or all of the worms in the top metre or so should come to the surface. Some may not quite reach the surface but they can be exposed by digging.

3 Count and record the number of worms in each square metre.

Alternative method:

1 Choose a day which is relatively warm and wet. Before nightfall lay a series of one-metre quadrat frames on the ground, or mark out with string as above.

2 After nightfall examine the ground with a flash-lamp. Look for earthworms lying on the surface. Tread softly, for the worms will jerk back into their burrows if the ground is vibrated.

3 Count and record the number of worms in each square. Do you think this is an adequate method of estimating the worm population in the soil?

PLANARIANS

Planarians are flatworms which live under stones in streams.

1 Choose two different streams, or two stretches of the same stream, both of which contain stones of approximately the same size.

2 Examine the underside of one or more stones and identify any planarians present. Initially, they will appear as small blobs 2-3 mm across, varying in colour from grey to black.

3 When you have learned to identify planarians, lay a *metal* quadrat frame on the floor of the stream and examine the underside of all the stones within the frame. Count and record the number of planarians in one square metre.
4 Repeat with the quadrat in a different position. Take as many samples as possible in the first locality, and then go on to the second.
5 Other animals that live under stones might also be investigated including the freshwater shrimp (*Gammarus*), leeches, limpets and other molluscs, caddis fly larvae.

Processing your results

You now have a series of population samples from two different localities. Calculate the average number of organisms per square metre in each locality. This is the arithmetic mean.

Is the arithmetical mean the same for both localities? By how much do they differ? Do you think the difference is simply the result of chance? What do you understand by the term sampling error? Do you think this may be responsible for the difference?

Is it sufficient only to compare the arithmetical means of the two populations? What further information do you need to make a more meaningful comparison of the two populations?

Now consult Appendix 6.4 (page 398). Calculate the standard deviation for each of the two localities, and then work out the standard error. Do you consider the difference in size between the two populations to be significant?

If you do consider the difference to be significant, suggest hypotheses to explain the difference. How would you test your hypotheses?

For Consideration

(1) Do you have any criticisms of the methods used in this investigation for estimating the sizes of populations? Can you suggest any improvements?
(2) Were the statistical tests necessary? If you feel they were unnecessary justify your reasoning.
(3) If you have obtained a significant difference between the sizes of two populations, suggest a reason for the difference. What further investigations should be carried out to test your suggestion?
(4) What sort of quadrat would you use for studying the distribution of oak trees in a mixed woodland?
(5) In what circumstances is it better to express an organism's abundance as percentage frequency rather than density?

Note: Some of the problems of sampling with quadrats are explored in a computer simulation in NELCAL Biology, Pack 3 Sampling by R. Fisher.

Requirements
Quadrat frame (1 m^2, metal if counting aquatic animals)
Watering can with rose
Spade or trowel
Flash-lamp
Clipboard and paper for recording data
Top pan balance (for measuring 5-9 g quantities of potassium permanganate)

Potassium permanganate (solid)

Investigation 32.2
Investigating the distribution patterns of organisms (Part II)

In the previous investigation each individual organism could be seen. However, there are some species – many mosses for example – where the organisms merge together and cannot be distinguished individually. The distribution pattern of such species is best expressed in terms of percentage cover. This is the proportion of a given area, expressed as a percentage, occupied by the organism.

Estimating percentage cover by means of a grid.

A grid is simply a quadrat which has been subdivided into smaller squares. In the following exercise use a one-metre quadrat subdivided into 100 squares (Figure 32.3). Proceed as follows:

1 Find a suitable area of ground that has patches of a plant species whose distribution pattern you wish to investigate.
2 Lay the grid on the ground, and estimate the number of squares which contain the plant. If a square is only partly filled with the plant, take this into account in making your estimate. For example, four squares that are each a quarter full count as one square. The final figure you arrive at is the percentage cover.
3 Repeat the above procedure with the grid in at least five different places, chosen at random.
4 Calculate the average percentage cover of the plant species in the area.
5 Repeat Steps 2 to 4 in another contrasting area. Compare the percentage

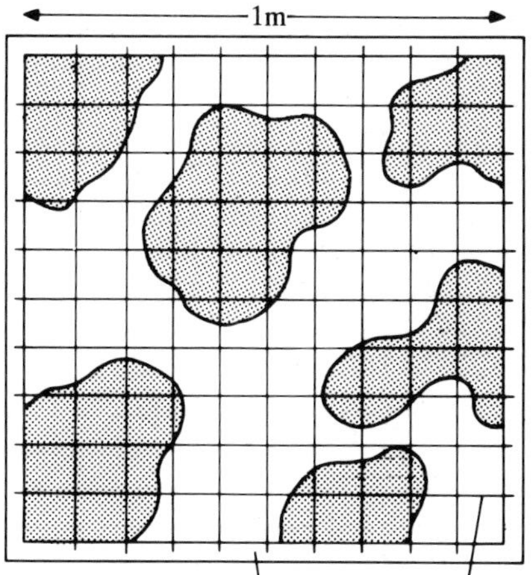

1m

wooden frame string or wire

Figure 32.3 A grid for estimating percentage cover. The stippled areas represent patches of the species being investigated. In this case the percentage cover is approximately 42%. Grids can be made any size to suit the particular habitat being investigated.

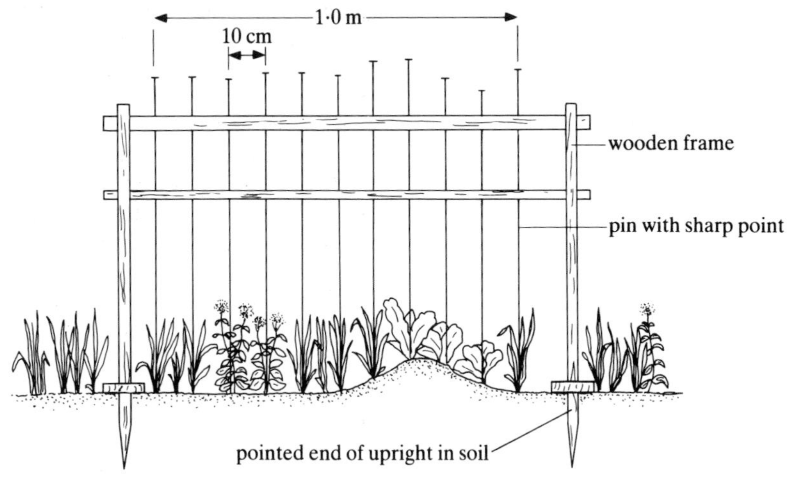

Figure 32.4 A point frame. The dimensions can be varied to suit the particular habitat being investigated. (*After* W. H. Dowdeswell, *Ecology, Principles and Practice*, Heinemann, 1984)

Requirements
Grid (*see* Figure 32.3)
Point frame (*see* Figure 32.4)
Clip board and paper for recording data

cover of the plant in the two areas.

Do you think this is a valid method of estimating the abundance of a plant species in an area. If not, why not? What are the main reasons for any inaccuracies in the results? What could be done to improve the method?

Estimating percentage cover by means of a point frame

A point frame consists of a horizontal bar from which hangs a row of sliding pins (Figure 32.4). Proceed as follows:

1 Obtain a point frame with the same dimensions as the one in Figure 32.4.

2 Visit the same area of ground, and investigate the same plant species, that you analysed with your grid.

3 Insert the frame into the ground. Carefully lower each point in turn through the frame, and count the number of pins which touch the plant.

4 Repeat with the frame in as many different places, chosen randomly, as you have time for.

5 Work out the average percentage cover of the plant as follows:

$$\text{percentage cover} = \frac{\text{hits}}{\text{hits} + \text{misses}} \times 100$$

6 Use the point frame to compare the distribution patterns of the plant in different areas, as in the previous experiment with the grid.

For consideration

(1) Which do you think the most accurate apparatus for measuring percentage cover, a grid or a point frame? Give reasons for your choice.

(2) How could you determine the relative accuracy of the two methods? How could their accuracy be increased?

(3) If you have obtained a significant difference between the population sizes of the species in two habitats, suggest possible reasons for the difference. How could you test your suggestions experimentally?

Reference: Revised Nuffield Advanced Level Biology, *Practical Guide 7, Ecology, (Investigation 27F), Longman, 1986.*

Investigation 32.3
Changes across a habitat

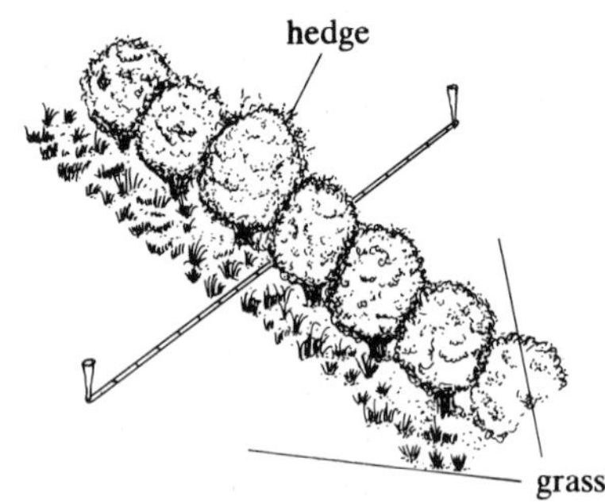

Figure 32.5 Making a line transect.

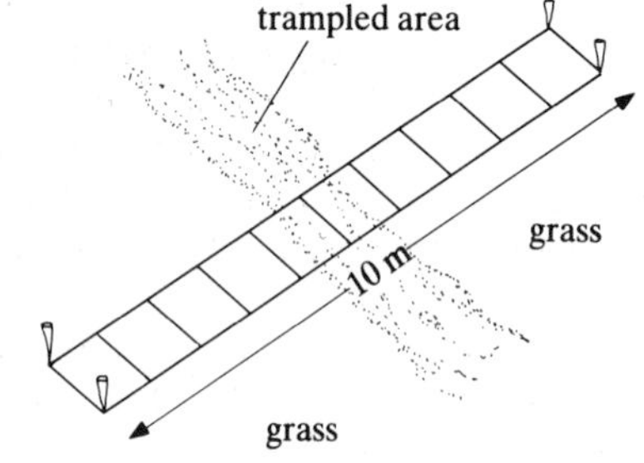

Figure 32.6 Making a belt transect.

Requirements
Plastic-covered clothes line (10 m long and marked at 5 cm intervals with stake at each end)
Plastic-covered clothes lines (10 m long and marked at 1 m intervals with stake at each end) × 2
Bamboo canes, (1 m long) × 10
Squared paper and clip board for recording data

In some situations one notices that there may be a gradual change in the species composition of a community from one part of a habitat to another. This is particularly noticeable at the edge of a pond where the water gives way to the land, and on a rocky sea-shore between the high and low tide marks. Such changes can be described, and related to environmental gradients, by making a transect. There are two kinds of transect, a line transect and a belt transect.

Making a line transect

1 Obtain a plastic-covered clothes line, ten metres long, which has been marked 5 cm intervals. There should be a stake at each end.
2 Select a community in which there appears to be a gradual change in the species composition across a gradient, e.g. a hedgerow which is not too thick but where there is plenty of ground vegetation.
3 Stretch the line across the ground at right angles to the hedge (Figure 32.5).
4 On a sheet of squared paper, draw a line to represent the transect line.
5 Starting at one end of the transect, identify the plants whose leaves touch or cross the line, either above or below it. If you don't know the name of a plant, invent a name or call it by a letter. Record the position of each epecies on the squared paper, indicating the length in millimetres of the transect line that is occupied by its leaves.
6 Construct a histogram for each species showing the length of the transect line *within successive 25 cm stretches* that it occupies. The transect line lengths should be on the vertical axis. Draw the histograms for each species separately, one above the other so that they can be readily compared.

Are any plants present on one side of the hedge but not on the other? Suggest reasons for any differences which you have observed. How could you test your hypotheses experimentally?

Making a belt transect

1 Select an area of mixed vegetation which has a trampled path running across it.
2 Stretch two lines across the area at right angles to the path. The lines should be one metre apart. This is your belt transect.
3 With bamboo canes divide the transect into one metre squares as shown in Figure 32.6.
4 Estimate the density, percentage frequency or percentage cover of specific plant species within each square. (The density is the number of individual plants per unit area. The frequency is the proportion of small squares within each larger square which contain the species in question. The percentage cover is the percentage of the ground area covered by the species.)

Which particular plant species appear to be most affected by trampling? Which species, if any, appear to thrive in the trampled area? Can you recognise any differences between these two groups of species in their growth form or leaf structure which might account for their distribution patterns?

Further observations

Make line or belt transects across other habitats as instructed by your teacher. In each case, try to correlate any observed changes in the abundance of different species with environmental differences. For example, it should be possible, using the techniques outlined in Appendix 4 (*see* pages 386–88), to sample in each quadrat the light intensity, soil water percentage, soil organic matter percentage or soil nutrient levels.

For consideration

(1) Which provides the greater amount of information about changes in the species composition in an area, a line transect or a belt transect?
(2) How could you adapt the belt transect technique to map the vegetation in the vicinity of the path?

Investigation 32.4
Using a Lincoln index to estimate the number of flour beetles in a culture

Requirements:
Wooden tray (50 × 50 cm × 10 cm deep, filled with wholemeal flour to 5 cm depth).
Cellulose or oil paint (any bright colour)
Paint brushes (sizes 00 and 1) × 2
Petridishes (one with a moist filter paper base, one with dry paper)
Refrigerator
Ice in a sandwich box
Empty sandwich boxes × 2
Ten pill boxes (about 5 cm across)
Card (5 × 10 cm)

Adult beetles (at least 100)

One simple way to estimate the number of individuals in a population of an animal species is to capture, mark and release back into the population a certain number of individuals. When they have had time to mix randomly with the rest of the population, some more individuals are captured. The proportion of marked individuals amongst these should be the same as the proportion of marked individuals in the whole population. The *number* of marked individuals in the population is known and so it is possible to estimate the total population size. The experiment can be carried out in the laboratory with flour beetles or mealworm beetles, or in the field with woodlice, pond skaters, grasshoppers, dragonflies or snails.

Procedure

1 You are provided with a wooden tray containing wholemeal flour. Into it release a known number of beetles from the stock supply. Your tray should receive at least fifty beetles, preferably as many as possible.

2 Using a large paint brush, take out at least twenty-five beetles from the culture and place them in the petridish which contains moist filter paper.

3 Replace the lid and put the dish in the ice compartment of a refrigerator. Leave for two minutes, or until the beetles have stopped moving. Take out the dish and place it in a bed of ice in a sandwich box.

4 Use the large paint brush to turn the beetles the correct way up if necessary. Then with a small paint brush place a small dot of paint on one of the beetles' wingcases (elytras). Resist the temptation to paint any other part of the body!

5 When the paint is nearly dry, transfer the beetles to the dry dish, using the large paint brush. Then mark more beetles if necessary.

6 When you have marked a number of beetles equivalent to 10 per cent of those which you have already added to the flour tray, place them in the flour. Write on the tray the number of marked individuals added.

7 Record *elsewhere* the total number of beetles in the box.

8 Keep the trays at a temperature above 15 °C. At the next convenient time, 12–48 hours after setting up the cultures, sample the trays for flour beetles:

9 Place into the trays, at random, ten small pill-boxes each about 5 × 5 cm. Take the top off each pill-box, invert it and press it into the flour until it reaches the bottom of the box. Press all the boxes in position as quickly as possible.

10 Count the beetles in each pill box. Slide a piece of card beneath the mouth of a pill box and lift the card and the pill-box together. Tip the contents into an empty sandwich box, record the number of marked and unmarked beetles, and transfer them to a second sandwich box.

11 Estimate the size of the beetle population in the tray from the relationship (the 'Lincoln Index'):

$$P = \frac{n_1 \times n_2}{n_3}$$

where P = total population size
n_1 = number of marked individuals released
n_2 = total number of individuals recaptured
n_3 = number of marked individuals recaptured

For consideration

(1) Compare your estimate of the number of beetles in a tray with the actual number which you added in the first place. Account for any discrepancies.
(2) Is it likely that during your experiment there was no reproduction of the flour beetles? Did the marked individuals live as long as the unmarked ones?
(3) State three other assumptions which you are making in calculating the population size in this way.
(4) Suggest the sorts of species with population sizes which are easy or difficult to determine in this way.
(5) In what ways might this technique be valuble in ecological research?

Reference: S.D. Wratten and G.L.A. Fry, *Field and laboratory exercises in ecology*, Arnold, 1980.

Investigation 32.5
Population growth: multiplication of yeast cells

Requirements
Microscope
Haemocytometer (*see* page 106)
Graduated cylinder (50 cm^3)
Conical flask (250 cm^3)
Cotton wool
Pipette
Linear (arithmetical) graph paper
Semi-logarithmic graph paper

Nutrient medium for yeast (e.g. cider or 2 per cent sucrose solution)

Suspension of brewer's yeast

The principles involved in population growth and its checks can be seen clearly in the growth of unicellular organisms such as yeast. Such organisms have a comparatively high rate of reproduction and, therefore, lend themselves well to studies over a short period of time. Yeast cells reproduce rapidly by budding.

In this investigation a small group of yeast cells is allowed to multiply in a nutrient medium for about a week, and the concentration of yeast cells present is estimated at regular intervals.

Method
Yeast cells can be counted by means of a haemocytometer (*see* page 106).

Procedure
1 Using a clean graduated cylinder, measure 50 cm^3 of nutrient solution (e.g. cider) and pour it into a 250 cm^3 conical flask.
2 Swirl the flask containing a suspension of yeast cells and, once they are well mixed, add one drop to the flask of nutrient medium.
3 Plug the latter flask with cotton wool and place it in a warm cupboard.
4 Using a haemocytometer, take cell counts twice daily over a minimum of three days. Swirl the flask before withdrawing a sample onto the haemocytometer slide. There is no need to dilute the sample. It is essential that the cells should be evenly distributed before they are counted. On each occasion carry out at least two independent cell counts keeping the results separate. Yeast cells multiply by budding: to ensure comparability, count as a cell every bud you can clearly see, even if the bud is distinctly smaller than the parent cell.

Procedure for counting
Choose an appropriately sized square on your haemocytometer grid. Count in as many squares as possible and record the numbers systematically. From this information calculate the number of cells per cubic centimetre.
5 Plot your results on linear (arithmetical) graph paper, time on the horizontal axis, number of cells per cubic centimetre on the vertical axis.
6 Plot a second graph of the results with time on the horizontal axis and the *logarithm* of the number of cells on the vertical axis. The quickest way of doing this is to use semi-logarithmic graph paper. In this kind of graph paper the marks on the vertical axis have already been calibrated on a logarithmic scale, but labelled on a direct scale. In other words the figure 5, for instance, is located at the logarithm of 5.
7 Compare the semi-logarithmic and linear plots. Allowing for the difference in scale, is there any difference in the appearance of the two curves? Explain the difference. What is the point of the semi-logarithmic plot?

For Consideration
(1) How would you describe the shape of the curve in your linear graph? Explain the reason for each phase in the curve. The period during which the population is growing at its fastest is the exponential phase. Explain this term.
(2) From your semi-logarithmic plot determine the doubling time during the exponential phase, that is the time it takes for the population to double. From this work out the division rate, that is the number of cell divisions per unit time.
(3) Below are given figures for the world human population since 1800:

Year	Population size
1800	8.1×10^8
1850	1.1×10^9
1900	1.6×10^9
1950	2.5×10^9
1960	2.9×10^9
1970	3.5×10^9
1986	5.0×10^9

Plot these data on semi-logarithmic graph paper, putting population on the vertical (semi-logarithmic) axis and years on the horizontal axis.

How does the curve compare with that for yeast? What factors may affect the world population in the future?

Investigation 32.6
Analysis of an ecosystem

Individual organisms within a community interact to produce an ecosystem. Ecosystems are generally very complex and it is as well to start with a comparatively simple system. Such is illustrated by a community of freshwater organisms in a laboratory aquarium tank. If there is a large number of students the organisms can be conveniently divided into a series of glass jars.

In studying any ecosystem a number of fundamental questions need to be answered. These include the following:
(1) What organisms are present?
(2) Where do they live?
(3) How do they relate to each other nutritionally, etc.?
(4) How do they relate to each other in other ways, e.g. does one organism provide protection for another, etc.?
(5) What physical factors are important in maintaining the ecosystem?

Procedure

Present the results of your observations in a table with the following headings:

Name of organism	Location	Food	Eaten by	Other relation-ships	Abiotic factors

NAME OF ORGANISM

1 Using a key (*see* page 407), identify all the organisms, both animal and plant, present in your aquarium tank or jar. Include microscopic as well as macroscopic organisms. In the case of microscopic organisms, pipette a drop of water from a series of different levels (surface, middle, bottom) onto a slide, put on a coverslip and examine under the microscope.

LOCATION

2 Where does the organism occur within the habitat? Does it move from place to place, and if so, how? Or is it sessile? Draw a diagrammatic vertical section of the aquarium showing the positions of the various organisms. Do any of them occupy specific microhabitats?

FOOD

3 If possible observe each organism feeding, and/or examine its feeding apparatus and draw such conclusions as you can about the nature of its food. If necessary, examine the contents of its gut. With small animals like the water flea, *Daphnia*, this can be done by placing the specimen in the cavity of a depression slide and viewing it as a transparent object under the low power of the microscope. Which animals are predators?

EATEN BY

4 What organisms, if any, is each animal and plant consumed by?

OTHER RELATIONSHIPS

5 The following are the kinds of questions to answer here:
(a) What is the spatial relationship between members of the same species, and different species? Do the organisms live temporarily or permanently in groups? If so, why?
(b) Does the organism, either individually or collectively, provide protection for another organism? This might be achieved by its providing cover from predators or physical factors, camouflage, etc.
(c) Does the organism reside temporarily or permanently on the body of another organism? An animal which lives attached to another animal without being parasitic on it is known as an epizoite. A plant which lives attached to another plant without being parasitic on it is known as an epiphyte.
(d) Is the association between animals or plants which live in or on one another parasitic, mutualistic or commensal?

ABIOTIC FACTORS

6 Abiotic factors are those which are not directly related to the presence of other organisms. The most obvious abiotic factor affecting aquatic organisms is water, but are all the organisms completely dependent on it? Can any of them survive on land? What is the relevance of this to a real pond?

Other abiotic factors to consider include light, temperature, oxygen content, water movement. Can you think of others?

To what extent do each of the organisms appear to be dependent on these factors? Is there evidence that their distribution within the aquarium is influenced by any of these factors? How would you test your suggestions experimentally?

For Consideration

(1) Construct a food web to show the nutritional inter-relationships between the various organisms in your aquarium.

Requirements
Binocular microscope or hand lens
Microscope
Slides and coverslips
Cavity slide
Pipette (capable of reaching bottom of aquarium)
Watch glasses

Freshwater aquarium divided, if necessary, into a series of glass jars.

(2) An aquatic ecosystem, such as a pond or river, usually contains one or more animals which can be called top carnivores. What does this term imply? What do you predict would happen in your aquarium ecosystem if a top carnivore was introduced? Suggest examples of such top carnivores.
(3) Draw a diagram to show how carbon circulates in the aquarium. Do not simply produce a generalised carbon cycle, but show how it occurs in *your* particular ecosystem.
(4) Do the same for the nitrogen cycle.

Investigation 32.7
Relationship between predator and prey

Requirements
Jars of approximately equal shape and capacity × 6
Pipette

Rich culture of *Daphnia*
Damsel fly nymphs × 6
Short twigs × 6

In a natural community one species of animal may prey upon another. The feeding relationship between these two species will determine their relative abundance.

In this investigation the predator–prey relationship between two common pond animals is analysed. The two animals are the damsel fly nymph (predator) and the water flea, *Daphnia* (prey).

Procedure

1 Obtain six jars, all of approximately the same shape and capacity, and place an equal volume of pond water in each. Label them **A-F**. They should not be more than about two-thirds full.
2 Place one damsel fly nymph in each jar, providing it with a short twig on which to cling. Leave the larva for about ten minutes to settle down.
3 With a pipette transfer a specific number of *Daphnia* specimens from a rich culture to each jar. To jar **A** add five *Daphnia*, to **B** add ten *Daphnia*, to **C** add 15 *Daphnia*, to **D** add 20 *Daphnia*, to **E** add 30 *Daphnia*, and to **F** add 50 *Daphnia*.
4 Leave each jar for 40 minutes after you have added the *Daphnia*.
5 At the end of the 40 minutes for each jar, remove the damsel fly nymph, and count the number of *Daphnia* still remaining.
6 Record your results, and pool them with those of the rest of the class. From the class results, calculate the average number of *Daphnia* remaining in each jar at the end of the 40 minutes.
7 Plot the average number of *Daphnia* eaten (vertical axis) against the number of *Daphnia* in each jar before predation started (horizontal axis).

For Consideration

(1) What can you say about the relationship between the rate of predation and prey-density?
(2) What conclusions can be drawn regarding the control of an animal population by predation?

Investigation 32.8
The energetics of a stick insect (*Carausius morosus*)

The energy budget of a primary consumer can be determined in the laboratory for the Indian stick insect (*Carausius morosus*). The individuals in normal laboratory populations are all females. The energy in the food they eat is egested (in faeces and uric acid), released in metabolism as heat energy, or devoted to eggs and growth in body mass.

Procedure

1 Select a healthy shoot of privet (*Ligustrum ovalifolium*) with four to ten leaves. Without detaching them from the shoot, trace the outlines of all the leaves onto squared paper. Make sure that you record the position on the shoot which each leaf occupied.
2 Weigh the shoot and record its mass (P1).

3 Use parafilm to cover the top of a McCartney bottle or small beaker containing water. Push the base of the privet shoot through the parafilm into the water. Place the bottle in the centre of half a petri dish and stabilise it with plasticine.
4 Weigh a stick insect (to at least two decimal places) and record its mass (I1). Put it onto the privet.
5 Add to the petri dish base a humidifier consisting of a McCartney bottle containing water with pieces of paper towelling stuck into it. Stabilise it with plasticine.
6 Cover the privet, stick insect and humidifier with a bell-jar or coffee-jar. Leave the apparatus for a week.
7 After a week you will need to collect the stick insect, its eggs, its egesta and the uneaten leaves. You will also have to measure the respiration rate of the insect.
8 Remove the insect and determine its mass to at least two decimal places. Record its mass (I2).
9 Place the insect in a respirometer (*see* page 67) and determine its metabolic rate as volume of oxygen absorbed per unit time at room temperature.
10 Weigh a cavity microscope slide (E1). Carefully collect all the egesta you can find, place them in the cavity of the slide and reweigh (E2).
11 Weight another cavity microscope slide (EGGS1). Carefully collect all the eggs you can find, place them in the cavity of the slide and reweigh (EGGS2).
12 Extract the remains of the privet shoot from its water. Blot it dry. Reweigh it (P2).
13 Remove each leaf from the shoot in turn. Place it on its original outline on the graph paper. Draw round the edge of the leaf.
14 The masses determined so far are all *fresh* masses. If you have time, determine the *dry* masses of stick insect, leaf blades, egesta and eggs. Reweigh them after they have been heated in an oven at 105 °C for at least 48 hours.

Requirements
Bell jar or coffee jar
Petri dish base
McCartney bottles or small beakers
Parafilm or clingfilm
Paper towel or cotton wool
Plasticine
Graph paper
Balance (weighing to two or three figures)
Drying oven
Cavity microscope slides
Respirometer (*see* page 67)

Privet (*Ligustrum ovalifolium*) shoots
Indian stick insect (*Carausius morosus*)

Processing the results

The masses you have determined (in grams) can be converted into energy contents (in kJ) by applying simply conversion factors. For the stick insect, FE = E + R + P. FE is the energy in the food eaten, E is the energy in egesta, R is the heat lost in metabolism and P is the energy content diverted to eggs and the body of the insect.

1 The fresh mass of privet eaten is P2 − P1. Calculate its energy content, assuming that 1 g fresh privet contains 6 kJ.
2 As a check, count squares on the graph paper to estimate the area of leaves eaten by the insect. Weigh leaves of known area to calculate the mass per cm^2 of leaf. Then convert the area of leaf eaten to the equivalent mass, and calculate its energy content, assuming that 1 g of fresh privet contains 10 kJ.
3 The fresh mass of egesta produced is E2-E1. Calculate its energy content, assuming that 1 g fresh egesta contains 10 kJ.
4 Calculate the heat lost in metabolism in a week by assuming that as a consequence of the uptake of 1 cm^3 of oxygen, 0.02 kJ of heat are released.
5 To calculate the secondary production of the insect (P in the equation) add the fresh mass of eggs (EGGS2 − EGGS1) to the increase in fresh mass of the insect (I2 − I1). Calculate their energy content by assuming that 1 g of eggs or insect contains 10 kJ.
6 Put together your energy budget equation. Does it balance?

For consideration

(1) What was the value of the parafilm over the bottle which held the privet stem in water?
(2) List the sources of error in the experiment.
(3) What effect would a change in mean temperature have on the energy budget?
(4) If you have used in the experiment insects of a variety of sizes, can you find any trends in the energy budgets with size? Speculate on the reasons for these trends.
(5) How might you expect the energy budget to differ in a carnivorous insect of the same size?

References: R.J. Slatter 'The energy budget of the stick insect,' *School Science Review* vol. 62, no. 219, 1980. Revised Nuffield A-level Biology, *Practical Guide* 7, Investigation 29B, Longman, 1986.

Investigation 32.9
Effect of eutrophication upon the growth of duckweed

Requirements
Beakers ($250cm^3$ or large) × 20
Glasshouse
Colorimeter and tubes
Measuring cylinder
Marker for writing on glass
Balance

Sodium nitrate(v)
Calcium monohydrogen phosphate

Duckweed plants (*Lemna* spp.)

Many waterways, lakes and ponds are polluted with nitrates and phosphates. The nitrates are mainly derived from fertiliser run-off, the phosphates from sewage and detergents. What effects do these pollutants have on plant growth both separately and together?

Procedure

1 Place 250 cm^3 of water from the same pond into each of 20 beakers.
2 There are eight nutrient addition treatments, each applied to two beakers. Label each beaker with its appropriate treatment symbol: P_1, P_2, N_1, N_2, N_1P_1, N_1P_2 N_2P_1 or N_2P_2. Four control beakers (labelled C) have no nutrient additions.
3 In this code N_1 is a small addition of nitrate (as 1 g sodium nitrate), N_2 is a large nitrate addition (5 g sodium nitrate), P_1 is a small phosphate addition (0.1 g $CaHPO_4$) and P_2 is a large addition of phosphate (0.5 g $CaHPO_4$). To each beaker add the appropriate mass of salt(s) and stir thoroughly.
4 To each beaker add ten plants of a *Lemna* species, e.g. *L. gibba*. Count and record the total number of leaves on the plants in each treatment.
5 Arrange the beakers in a glasshouse in a 4 × 5 pattern. Their positions should be randomised and recorded on a plan.
6 At intervals of two weeks, examine the beakers. Count and record the total numbers of leaves on the plants in each beaker. Then randomise the beakers again.
7 After four weeks the growth of algae in some beakers may become obvious. At each sampling date record by eye the relative densities of algae in each beaker. Pour some of the water from each beaker into a clean test tube or colorimeter tube and determine with a colorimeter how much light the chlorophyll in the sample has absorbed.
8 Draw graphs of the numbers of leaves per treatment and the chlorophyll absorption in each treatment with time.

For consideration

(1) What were the effects of eutrophication on the duckweed and the algae?
(2) Which was more effective at promoting growth, the nitrate or the phosphate?
(3) Often the addition of nitrate and phosphate together increases growth far more than might be expected from the effects of the nitrates or phosphates alone. Did such an interaction occur in your experiment? If so, explain it.
(4) The salts were added as *sodium* nitrate and *calcium* phosphate. Can you be sure that the effects you observed are not due to the sodium and calcium rather than the nitrate and phosphate? Design an experiment to eliminate this possibility (not so easy!).
(5) How did the growth conditions in your beakers differ from those which duckweed might encounter in a eutrophicated waterway?
(6) What are the implications of your results for freshwater habitats? Apart from the changes in algal and duckweed numbers, what other organisms might be affected, and how?

Questions and Problems

Source of variety	Relative increase in leaf area at 5°C	% survival after freezing at −5°C
Israel	27.9	0
Portugal	24.2	0
Denmark	16.4	14
Norway	9.3	88

1 (a) How do plants survive periods of low temperature?
(b) How would you expect plants living in a Mediterranean climate, where the main limiting factor is summer drought, to differ from those in Northern Europe, where winter cold is critical?
(c) Commercial varieties of the perennial grass, *Dactylis glomerata* (cocksfoot), from different geographical areas were studied with regard to growth and survival at low temperatures with the results given in the margin.
Comment on these results. *(OCJE)*

2 A quadrat frame with 25 divisions, each of 10 cm side, was thrown at random ten times in each of two near-by areas of chalk grassland, one heavily, the other lightly, trampled. A species was awarded one point for each of the smaller divisions of the frame in which it occurred, irrespective of the number of individuals by which it was represented in those divisions. The results for five species are given below.

Species	Trampling	
	Heavy	Light
Sheep's fescue (*Festuca ovina*)	205	241
Mouse-ear hawkweed (*Hieraceum pilosella*)	2	60
Bulbous buttercup (*Ranunculus bulbosus*)	10	25
Hoary plantain (*Plantago media*)	55	10
Ribwort plantain (*Plantago lancelolata*)	27	29

(a) Apply an appropriate statistical test to see if the results are significant or not.
(b) Comment on the results.
(c) Describe how you would investigate further the differences observed.
(O & C modified)

3 Suggest explanations of the following and in each case indicate how you might test your hypotheses:
(a) Mosses are usually more abundant on north-facing than south-facing walls.
(b) Certain species of lichen are totally absent from most industrial areas, though common elsewhere.
(c) The ground flora is comparatively sparse in a beech wood.
(d) Rosebay willowherb (*Epilobium* sp.) is generally one of the first plants to become established in a desolate area such as a bomb site.
(e) In a freshwater stream planarian flatworms are found only under stones.

4 Yeast is a unicellular fungus. The table shows the number of yeast cells counted through a microscope after the establishment at 0 hours of a yeast culture.

Hours	0	4	8	12	16	20	24	28	32	36	40	44	48
Number of yeast cells	2	5	8	15	29	52	86	116	134	142	143	142	130

(a) How would you establish a yeast culture in order to obtain such data?
(b) What method would you use to obtain reliable yeast-cell counts?
(c) Assuming yeast divides by binary fission once every four hours, construct a table similar to that above to show the *theoretical* population growth over a period of 36 hours starting with one cell at 0 hours.
(d) Graph on a single set of axes the actual data in the table above and the theoretical data in your own table.
(e) Compare the actual and theoretical growth curves up to 36 hours. Explain the differences between them.
(f) How do you explain the shape of the actual growth curve after 36 hours? *(AEB)*

5 Suppose a population of a single species of bacterium is grown in a nutrient broth at 37 °C under favourable conditions. We can simulate the increase in population size by a simple model in which, neglecting bacterial death, the population size doubles every 20 minutes, like this:

Time (min)	0	20	40	60	80	100
Population size	1	2	4	8	16	32

(a) Outline a practical method you might use to determine the increase in population size in a bacterial population.
(b) Using a scientific calculator, calculate the logarithm (base ten) of each of the population sizes in the lower row of the table above, and tabulate them.
(c) Plot a graph of the logarithm of the population size against the time in minutes. What do you notice?
(d) Read off the horizontal axis of the graph the time in minutes which it takes for the logarithm of the population size to double.

In the table below there are some real data for the increase in numbers of the bacterium *Lactobacillus bulgaricus* with time.

Time (min)	0	20	40	60	80	100
Population size	1	2	5	12	30	56

(e) In *L. bulgaricus*, is the doubling time longer or shorter than in the hypothetical population in the first Table?
(f) Using a scientific calculator, calculate the logarithm (base ten) of each of the population sizes of *L. bulgaricus* in the lower row of the table above, and tabulate them.
(g) Plot a graph of the logarithm of the population size against the time in minutes.
(h) Read off the horizontal axis of the graph the time in minutes which it takes the logarithm of the population size to double.
(i) What does the doubling time mean in terms of the way bacterial cells reproduce?

6 The graphs in Figure 32.7 show the changes in populations of two species of *Paramecium* (*P. caudatum* and *P. aurelia*) grown in culture either singly or together in a mixed culture. Discuss these results. (*JMB*)

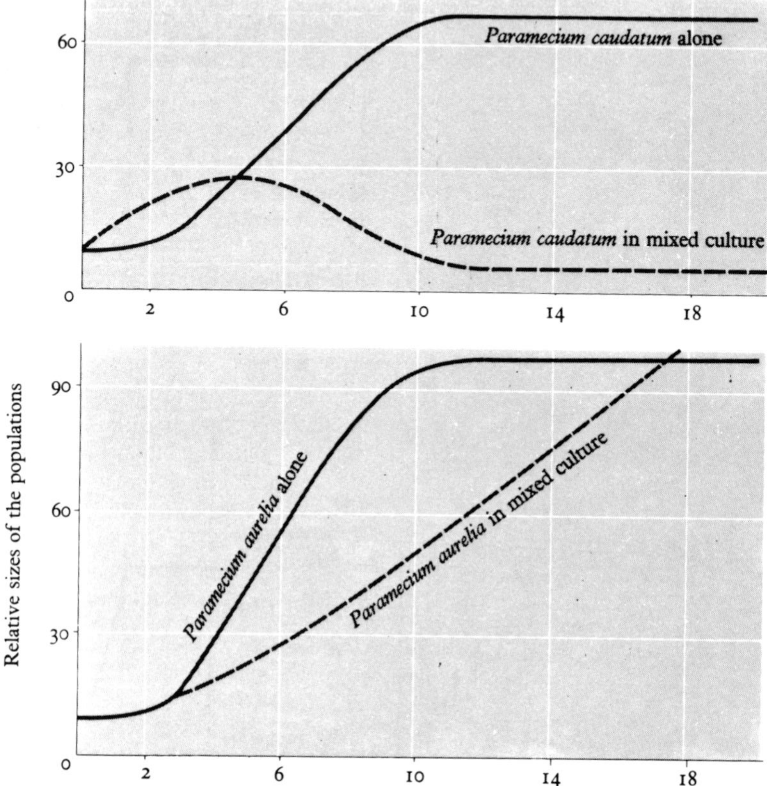

Figure 32.7 Graphs showing changes in populations of two species of *Paramecium* grown in culture either singly or together in mixed culture.

7 Show, by describing named examples, how:
(a) plants may affect the distribution patterns of other plants;
(b) plants may affect the distribution patterns of animals;
(c) animals may affect the distribution patterns of plants;
(d) animals may affect the distribution patterns of other animals. (*JMB*)

8 Investigations have been made of competition between two species of flour beetles of the genus *Tribolium*. These small beetles can live out their entire life cycles in a jar of flour, provided fresh flour is added from time to time.

If individuals of the species *Tribolium castaneum* and *Tribolium confusum* are introduced into the same jar of flour, one species is always eventually eliminated while the other continues to thrive. Sometimes one species 'wins' the competition, sometimes the other. The relative numbers of individuals of each species originally introduced into the jar do not seem to affect the outcome.

One series of investigations involved the effect of temperature and relative humidity on the outcome of the competition between the two species. The results of these investigations are shown in the table below. Twenty to thirty different jars of flour containing individuals of both species were maintained at each of the six different 'climates' and the eventual 'winner' of the competition in each jar was noted. The percentage of 'wins' for each species at each climate is shown in the table. (Each species can survive alone in any of the climates.)

Climate	**Temperature** (°C)	**Relative humidity** (%)	**Results of competition** % wins for *T. castaneum*	% wins for *T. confusum*
Hot-wet	34	70	100	0
Hot-dry	34	30	10	90
Warm-wet	29	70	86	14
Warm-dry	29	30	13	87
Cool-wet	24	70	31	69
Cool-dry	24	30	0	100

Comment on the above data. (*VUS*)

9 A population of grasshoppers in a meadow was sampled by sweep netting on two successive occasions. All of the grasshoppers captured in the first sampling were marked with a spot of harmless quick-drying paint on the dorsal surface of the thorax. Twenty of these marked grasshoppers were kept inside a net cage which was left out in the meadow. All of the remaining individuals were released. Two days later, the population of grasshoppers was sampled again in exactly the same way as before. Details of the animals captured are given in the table.

Grasshoppers captured on Day 1	Marked grasshoppers released on Day 1	Marked grasshoppers captured on Day 3	Unmarked grasshoppers captured on Day 3
200	180	30	120

(a) Calculate the estimated population size for the grasshoppers in the meadow.
(b) Suggest a reason why some of the original marked grasshoppers were kept enclosed in a cage and not released.
(c) List the circumstances in which population estimates using marking-recapture methods might be inaccurate. (*JMB–N modified*)

10 The data below show the results of experiments on the cycling of various plant nutrients in two ecosystems. Ecosystem A is dominated by gorse, whilst ecosystem B is dominated by beech trees. Compare the two ecosystems in terms of their nutrient cycles and comment on the differences you observe.

	Ecosystem	**Chemical Nutrient** (kg/ha)		
		N	P	K
Total plant uptake	A	245.0	7.6	95.0
	B	40.4	3.4	36.0
Retained in plants	A	86.0	3.5	36.0
	B	3.4	0.7	5.0
Content in litterfall	A	158.0	4.0	13.0
	B	37.0	2.5	8.0
Leached from canopy	A	1.0	0.1	46.0
	B	0.0	0.2	23.0

(OCJE)

11 Figure 32.8 summarises the feeding relationships between certain plants and animals, and between one animal and another, in a wood. Using this information, and other examples known to you, explain what is meant by (a) a food chain, (b) a food web, (c) an ecosystem. *(AEB)*

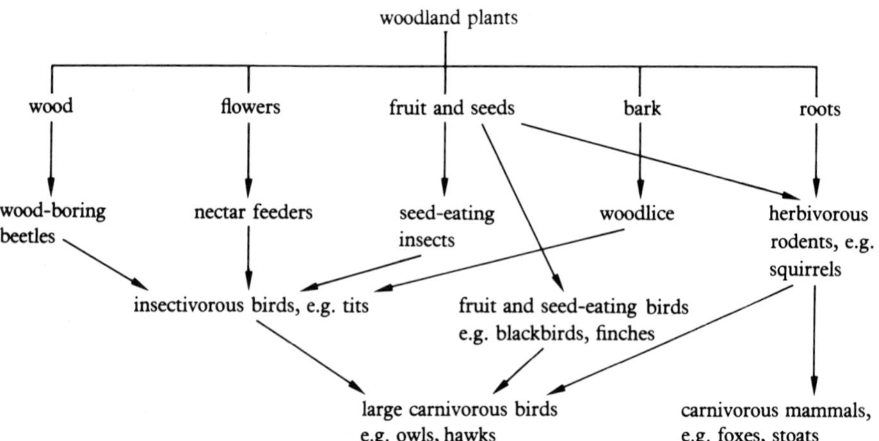

Figure 32.8 Diagram showing the feeding relationships between organisms in a wood.

12 Comment on the following figures for the United Kingdom:

Total solar radiation incident	610 000 M J	$\times 10^9$ year^{-1}
Gross primary production harvested from plants	1116 M J	$\times 10^9$ year^{-1}
Imports of foodstuffs	104 M J	$\times 10^9$ year^{-1}
Edible food from all crops (plants and animals)	137 M J	$\times 10^9$ year^{-1}
Energy required by population (as food)	241 M J	$\times 10^9$ year^{-1}
Energy put into agriculture as fuel	145 M J	$\times 10^9$ year^{-1}
Energy put into agriculture as fertilisers and lime	128 M J	$\times 10^9$ year^{-1}
Energy put into agriculture as machinery	49 M J	$\times 10^9$ year^{-1}
Energy put into agriculture as other	18 M J	$\times 10^9$ year^{-1}

(OCJE)

13 The seasonal changes in the concentration of inorganic nitrogen in the water of an overgrown canal were determined at monthly intervals over a period of one year. Comment on the results given in the margin. *(O and C)*

Month	**Inorganic nitrogen** (parts per million)
Jan.	0.101
Feb.	0.105
Mar.	0.115
Apr.	0.153
May	0.172
June	0.128
July	0.103
Aug.	0.090
Sept.	0.085
Oct.	0.094
Nov.	0.097
Dec.	0.098

14 Figure 32.9 shows the productivity in relation to certain environmental factors in a marine ecosystem in the North Sea.

(a) What environmental factor has most influence on producer increases during February?

(b) Account for the smaller outburst in productivity that takes place in late summer.

(c) Draw on the graph the curve that would best indicate the biomass of the secondary consumers.

(d) An inspection of the areas under the curves indicates that the biomass ratio between producers and primary consumers is of the order of 1.4 to 1.

(i) In what way does this ratio differ from that which would be expected from a terrestrial ecosystem such as a field or a wood?

(ii) Suggest two reasons for the difference.

(e) If the above data had been collected for a sea area in the tropics where light and temperature do not change significantly, predict two effects on the standing biomass of producers throughout the year. *(O & C)*

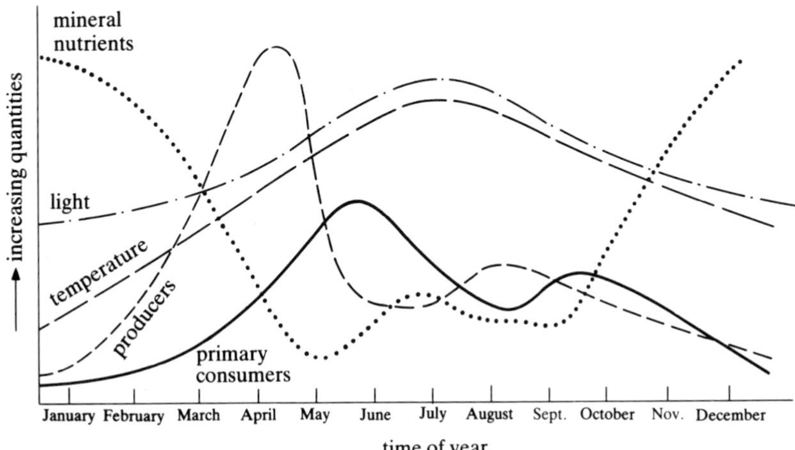

Figure 32.9 Graph showing fluctuations in productivity and environmental conditions in a marine ecosystem in the North Sea during one year.

15 The crown of thorns starfish, *Acanthaster planci*, inhabits tropical waters where it feeds on coral polyps. Observations by underwater divers have shown that in certain coral areas large numbers of starfish gather together to form large aggregations of hundreds, even thousands, of individuals. When the food supply in one area has been used up the starfish move to another neighbouring reef.

(a) Suggest hypotheses to explain what causes the starfish to congregate together.

(b) Describe experiments you might carry out to test your hypotheses.

(c) What are the possible advantages and disadvantages of *Acanthaster's* aggregation behaviour?

Off the north-east coast of Australia, *Acanthaster* has caused very severe damage to the coral of the Great Barrier Reef. Before 1959 the starfish population was kept in check by the giant triton, a large carnivorous mollusc; but since then the number of tritons has decreased with a corresponding increase in the starfish population.

(d) Suggest hypotheses to explain why the triton population has declined since 1959.

(e) Put forward suggestions as to how the starfish might be kept under control by humans. Consider the relative merits and demerits of each method.

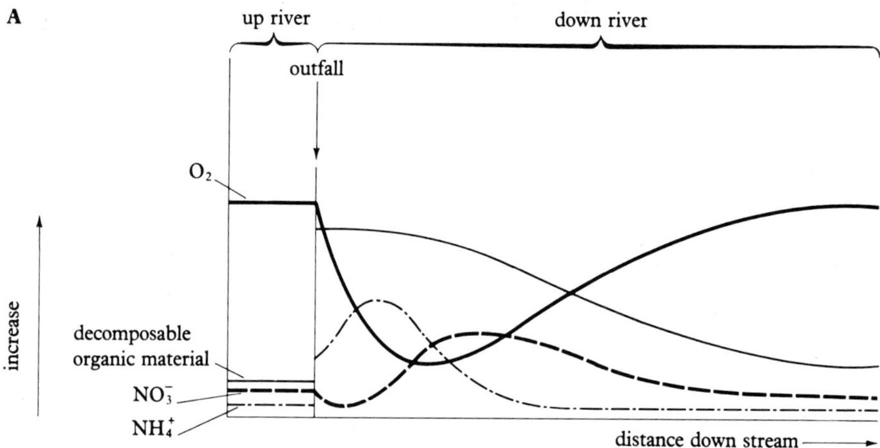

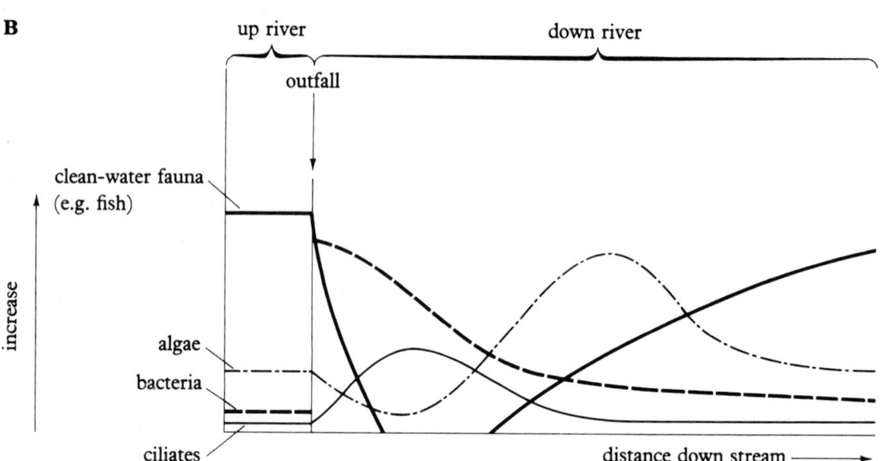

Figure 32.10 (**A**) Chemical and (**B**) biotic changes in a river into which sewage flows. (*Data from* Hynes, 1960.)

16 Domestic sewage is rich in saprotrophic bacteria and in organic material which is readily decomposed. When such sewage is discharged into a river it causes a number of chemical and biotic changes for some distance downstream from the 'outfall', i.e. the point at which it enters the river.

Typical changes have been summarised by Hynes (1960) and are shown graphically in Figure 32.10.

Figure 32.10A deals with chemical changes, indicating the amounts of various materials present in the river above the outfall and at various distances downstream from the outfall.

Figure 32.10B shows the changes in abundance of some of the biotic components over the same stretch of river as that covered by Figure 32.10A.

Give reasoned explanations for the changes expressed by the curves, relating them to each other where possible. (*JMB*)

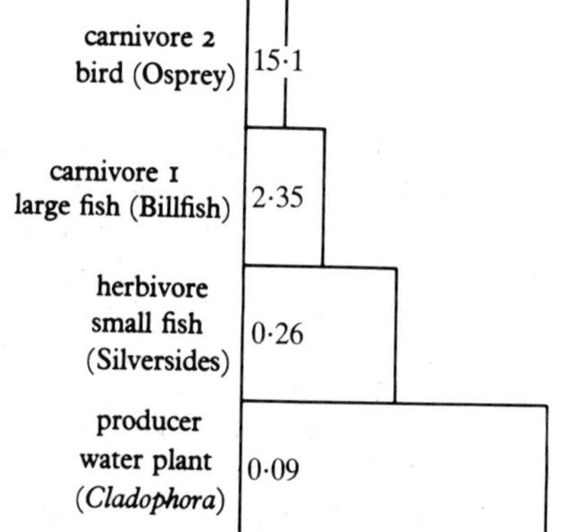

Figure 32.11 The amounts of DDT at various levels in a food chain. The figures denote the total mass of DDT in kilograms per hectare (kg ha^{-1}) occupied by the species. The width of each bar is an approximate measure of the biomass at each level of the chain.

17 One of the problems we have created for ourselves is pollution of the environment with injurious chemicals such as DDT. The data shown in Figure 32.11 have been collected in the U.S.A. The area of each rectangle represents the total mass of organisms of the species involved in the food chain. This mass is called the biomass. The number in each rectangle indicates the amount of DDT at each level of the chain,

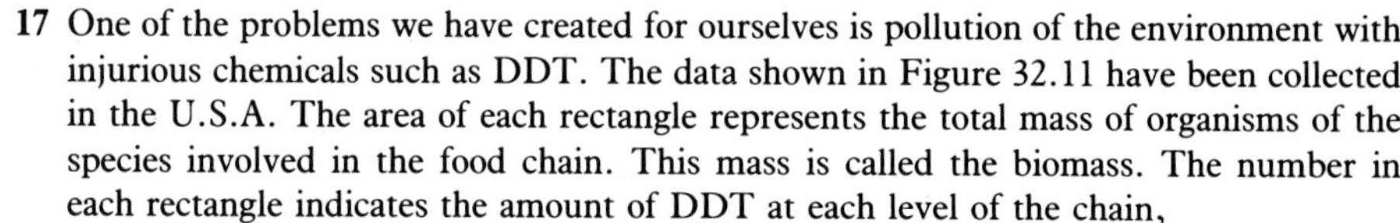

(a) What conclusions would you draw from the data?
(b) Attempt to explain the data in physiological terms.
(c) In parts of the U.S.A. it has been found that the death rate from DDT poisoning is higher among carnivorous birds than other organisms. Why do you think this is?
(d) Suggest ways of overcoming the problem of DDT pollution. (*VUS*)

18 Write a short essay on the ecological aspects of one of the following: (a) Conservation; (b) Deforestation; (c) Famine relief; (d) Intensive farming.

33 Associations between Organisms

Background Summary

1 Associations between organisms may be **interaspecific** or **interspecific**. Both are widespread, and often the association is very close.

2 Three types of interspecific association are recognised: **parasitism, commensalism** and **mutualism**. There is no sharp distinction between them. Increasingly the term **symbiosis**, once used synonymously with mutualism, is used to cover all three types of association.

3 In parasitic associations the parasite lives temporarily or permanently in or on the host, deriving benefit from it and causing harm to it. To qualify as a *bona fide* parasite an organism must fulfil the criteria embodied in this definition.

4 Parasites fall into two groups: **ectoparasites** and **endoparasites**. Endoparasites in turn may be either **intercellular** or **intracellular**.

5 A so-called parasite need not be totally dependent on parasitism for its existence. Certain parasites can feed on dead as well as living material. Others depend on parasitism for some, but not all, constituents of their diet.

6 Parasites generally have clearly observable effects on their hosts. The harm caused varies with the parasite. Those that kill their hosts are considered to be poorly adjusted and less highly evolved than those which cause relatively little harm.

7 Parasites show a number of **adaptations** to the parasitic way of life. These adaptations relate to their structure, physiology, immune system and life cycle; they are shown particularly clearly by the malarial parasite and liver fluke.

8 A full knowledge of the parasite's life cycle can enable effective **control measures** to be devised, as can be seen in the case of schistosomiasis (bilharzia).

9 In commensalism the commensal benefits but the host neither loses nor gains. This rather loose relationship can be considered as midway between parasitism and mutualism.

10 In mutualism both organisms benefit. The association may be obligatory, neither partner being able to survive without the other, or facultative in which either or both can, if necessary, exist alone. In some cases the association is so intimate that the two form what may be regarded as a single organism.

11 Intraspecific associations can be seen in **social organisation**, which is particularly well developed in insects and mammals. In social insects **pheromones** play an important part in holding the colony together and controlling the development and behaviour of the individuals within it.

12 Amongst insects social organisation, though efficient, is, in the main, rigid and stereotyped. This contrasts with primates, particularly humans, where flexibility is a noticeable feature.

13 In social species, whether mammalian or insect, **communication** between individuals is of paramount importance. Only in this way can the integrity and efficiency of the colony or society be maintained.

Investigation 33.1
Examination of the liver fluke *Fasciola hepatica*

The liver fluke *Fasciola hepatica* inhabits the liver and bile passages of sheep where it causes much damage culminating in 'liver rot'. In its adult structure and life cycle the fluke shows many adaptations for parasitism. Pay special attention to these adaptive features as you examine it.

Procedure

ADULT

1 Examine a whole mount of the adult, first under a hand lens or binocular microscope, then under the low power of an ordinary microscope. Note in particular those features which enable it to live in the host's liver. Observe its size and shape, anterior and ventral suckers, mouth, pharynx, gut with two main branches and numerous side branches. Why is the gut branched?

2 Using Figure 33.1 to help you, identify the various components of the genital system. Flukes are hermaphroditic. The genital system is geared to producing large numbers of eggs. During copulation the penis of one individual protrudes through the genital pore and is inserted into either the genital atrium or Laurer's canal of the other fluke. Fertilisation takes place at x in the diagram, the point where the oviduct, yolk ducts and Laurer's canal converge upon the uterus. After fertilisation the egg, surrounded by a few yolk cells, is enclosed in a capsule hardened by the shell gland and then stored in the uterus. As well as serving as a tube for the entry of sperm, Laurer's canal is said to allow surplus eggs to escape.

3 In ripe specimens note numerous eggs in the uterus. Almost certainly self-fertilisation occurs on a fairly large scale. Does this matter?

4 Next examine sections of *Fasciola* to obtain a full picture of the spatial relationship between the various structures seen in the whole mount. First determine the level of the body at which the section was cut and decide whether it is a transverse, longitudinal or oblique section: what you will see depends on the level and plane of the section. Looking at Figure 33.1, what structures would you *expect* to see in sections cut in the planes a-a, b-b, c-c, and d-d?

5 In addition to the structures listed for the whole mount, observe thick cuticle with spines; mesenchyme; circular, longitudinal and dorso-ventral muscles. What do the muscles achieve?

6 Make a list of the ways in which the adult fluke is adapted to a parasitic mode of life.

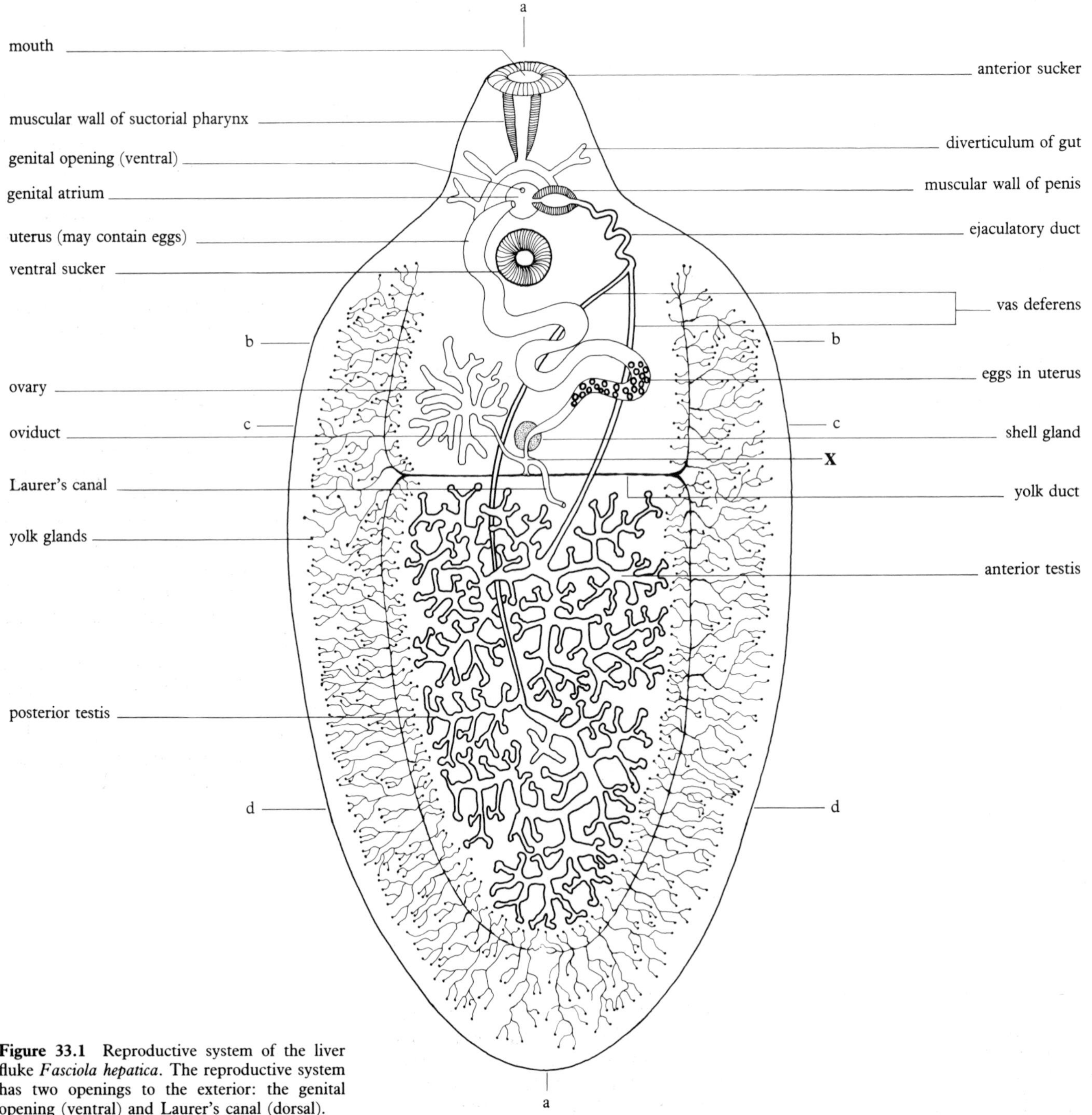

Figure 33.1 Reproductive system of the liver fluke *Fasciola hepatica*. The reproductive system has two openings to the exterior: the genital opening (ventral) and Laurer's canal (dorsal).

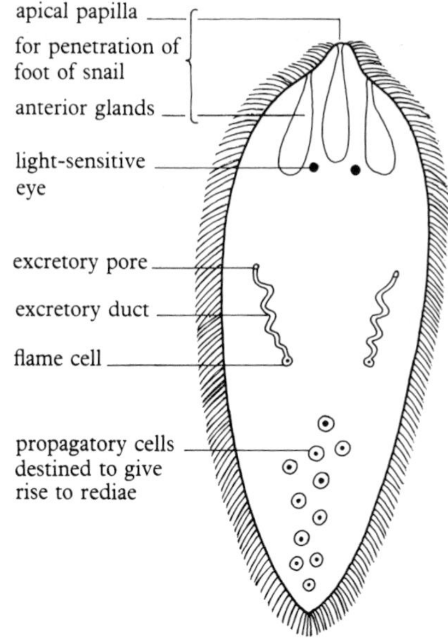

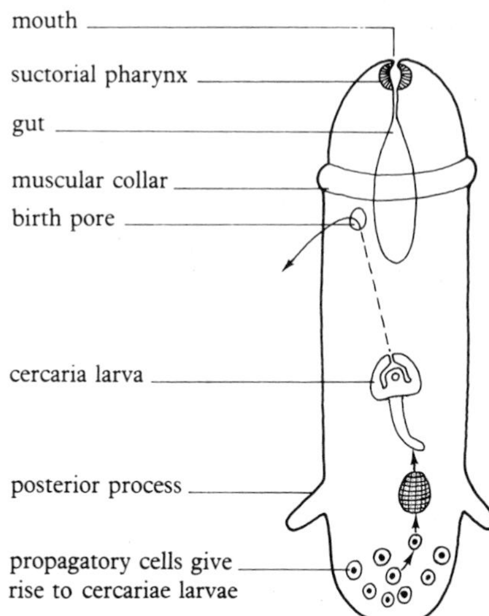

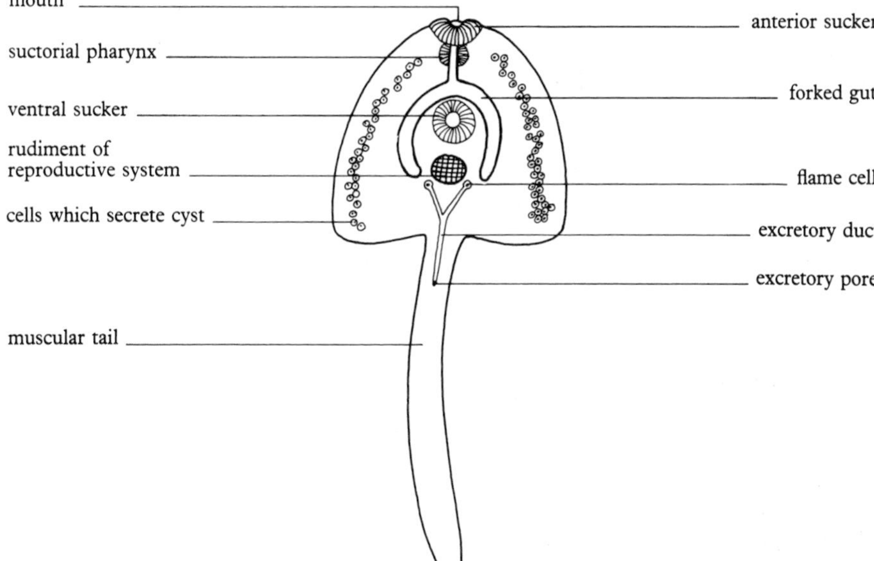

Figure 33.2 The three larval stages of the liver fluke *Fasciola hepatica*.

Requirements
Binocular microscope or hand lens
Microscope
Slide and coverslip
Watchglass
Glass rod

Ethanol (10 per cent)

Limnaea truncatula (live specimens)
WM *Fasciola*
TS and LS *Fasciola*
WM miracidium
WM redia
WM cercaria

LARVAE

1 Examine a prepared slide of a miracidium larva under high power (Figure 32.2A). Note the cilia, anterior glands, eye spots (if visible), and propagatory cells which will give rise asexually to the next generation of larvae. Longitudinal and circular muscles are also present in the wall of the miracidium.

2 In what respects does the miracidium differ from the adult? How would you explain the differences in terms of the roles of the miracidium larva and adult in the life cycle?

3 Obtain live specimens of the snail *Limnaea truncatula* or closely related species. Species of snail other than *L. truncatula* harbour liver flukes similar to *Fasciola*. With a glass rod crush the shell in a watchglass with a little water. Examine the contents of the watchglass under low power for rediae and/or cercariae larvae (Figure 33.2 B and C).

4 Study the behaviour of live cercaria larvae in the watchglass. How do they move? Test their response to various kinds of stimulation.

5 Mount cercariae in water on a slide. Immobilise them by irrigating with ten per cent ethanol. Observe the muscular tail and general resemblance to adult. The flickering of flame cells may also be seen.

6 If rediae are available note the posterior processes, muscular collar and birth pore. Can you see cercariae or further rediae larvae developing inside them?

7 Augment your study of rediae and cercariae larvae by examining prepared whole mounts.

8 What are the most obvious observable differences between the redia and cercaria? How would you explain the differences?

For Consideration

(1) The main purpose of this investigation has been to observe the liver fluke's adaptations for a parasitic mode of life. Make a list of all the adaptations you can think of? How many of them have you yourself been able to observe?
(2) Where, when and how are the three types of larva (miracidium, redia and cercaria) formed in the course of the life cycle?
(3) What are the natural hazards in the liver fluke's life cycle and how are they overcome?
(4) From your knowledge of the life cycle suggest methods by which the liver fluke might be controlled.

Investigation 33.2
Examination of three parasitic fungi

A fungus characteristically consists of a branching system of thread-like hyphae. The whole network is known as a mycelium. There is no chlorophyll present, feeding taking place by saprotrophic or parasitic means. Reproduction generally takes place sexually and asexually.

Parasitic fungi are of considerable economic importance. They include the downy and powdery mildews, potato blight fungus, and the rusts of wheat and other cereals. In general, hyphae enter the leaves and feed on the contents of the cells, destroying them in the process. Parasitic fungi display many adaptations for parasitism which can be well seen in the following cases.

Downy Mildew

Peronospora is parasitic on various plants including onion, beet, clover, cabbage, wallflower, and shepherd's purse. Its principal method of reproduction is by means of spores (conidia). When a conidium lands on the surface of a leaf, if moisture is present it germinates to produce a hypha which enters the leaf through a stoma and then branches into an extensive mycelium. Short side branches called haustoria penetrate into, and absorb the contents of, the host's cells. Eventually hyphae grow out through the stomata and form tree-like condiophores which produce conidia at the tips of their branches. On being released, the conidia are dispersed by wind to other host plants. Although asexual conidia-formation is the more prolific method of reproduction, the fungus can also reproduce sexually within the host plant.

1 Observe the fungus on the leaves of a plant. Examine under a hand lens or binocular microscope. Note conidiophores bearing conidia.

2 With needles tease out part of the mycelium, mount it in lactophenol on a slide and examine under high power. How would you describe its appearance? The hyphae are multinucleate and aseptate, i.e. the mycelium is a coenocyte.

3 Examine the mycelium in a prepared section of an infected plant. Notice the hyphae *between* the host's cells, and haustoria devouring the contents. Stages in sexual reproduction may also be seen: antheridia and oogonia in various stages of development; zygotes and zygospores.

Figure 33.3 Life cycle of the potato-blight fungus *Phytophthora infestans*.

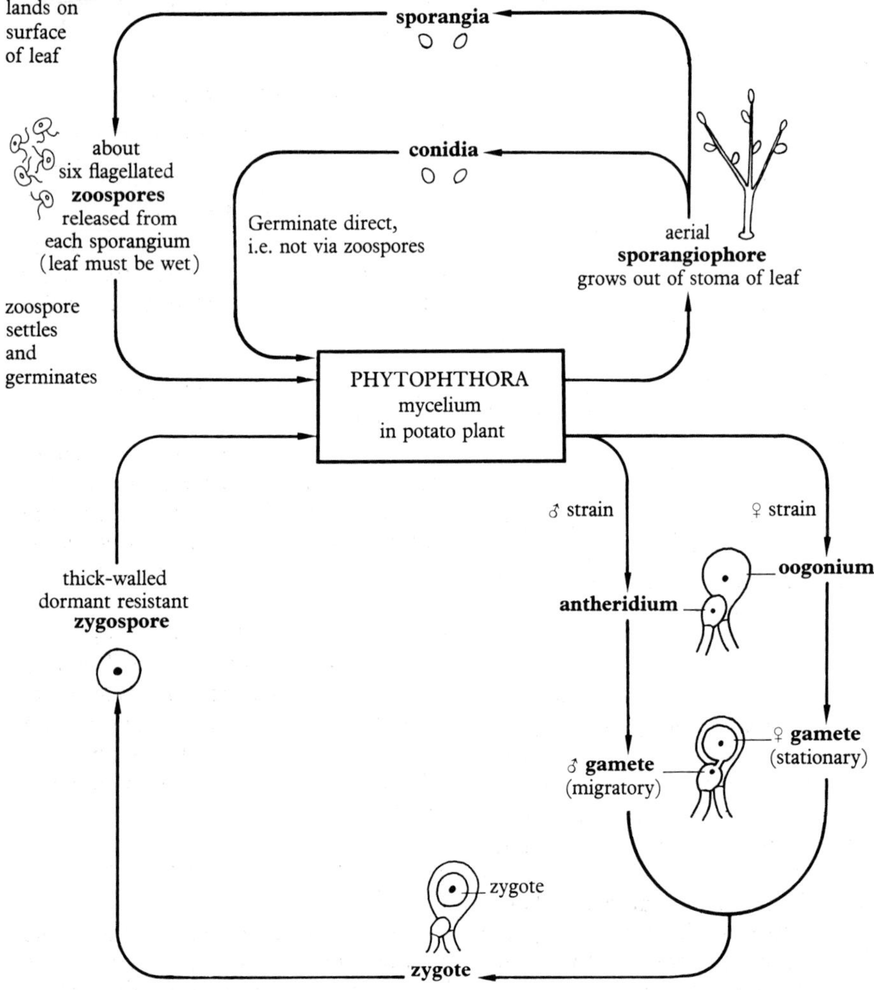

Potato-Blight Fungus

The life cycle of *Phytophthora infestans* is shown in Figure 33.3. This important fungus is similar to *Peronospora* but differs from it in that the hyphae may penetrate through the epidermis as an alternative to entering the leaf via the stomata, the mycelium eventually grows through the entire plant including the tubers, and asexual reproduction takes place not only by the formation of conidia like *Peronospora*, but also by sporangia which, when they land on a wet leaf, give rise to motile zoospores.

1 If available, examine an infected potato plant and compare it with a healthy one. What are the symptoms of the disease?

2 Examine the mycelium in a section of an infected leaf and note its general similarity to *Peronospora*.

Damping-off Fungus

Pythium attacks seedlings, particularly of mustard, cress, cucumber and grasses. The stems of infected plants lose their rigidity. In its structure and

Requirements
Microscope
Binocular microscope or hand lens
Slide and coverslip

Lactophenol

Section of plant infected with *Peronospora*
Section of plant infected with *Phytophthora*
Section of plant infected with *Pythium*
Live plants infected with fungi

life cycle *Pythium* is basically similar to *Phytophthora*. The principal difference is that, instead of growing *between* the cells, the hyphae grow *through* them, feeding on their contents as they do so. The host is, therefore, damaged quickly and extensively. After the host has died the fungus continues feeding on it saprotrophically.

1 If available, examine, e.g. cress seedlings infected with *Pythium*. How do they differ from healthy plants? What is the cause of the symptoms?

2 Examine a section of infected plant and observe the hyphae in the cells.

For Consideration

(1) For successful growth these three fungi depend on being able to penetrate into the host's cells. How do you think they achieve this?
(2) Make a list of the ways these three fungi are adapted to a parasitic mode of life. Which particular adaptations do they share with the liver fluke?
(3) Now that you have studied the life cycle of *Phytophthora* suggest methods by which it can be controlled.
(4) Which of these three parasites do you consider to be least well adjusted to its host, and why?

Investigation 33.3 Observations of various interspecific associations

Interspecific associations show all gradations from situations where one species benefits and the other is demonstrably harmed (parasitism), through cases where one gains and the other neither loses nor gains (commensalism), to cases where both species derive benefit (mutualism).

Partnerships may be facultative, each of the two species being capable of leading an independent existence if necessary, or obligatory, where one or other partner cannot survive without the other. In extreme cases a mutualistic association may be so intimate that the two partners form what can be regarded as a single organism.

There are also varying degrees of spatial intimacy between the species. Least intimate are associations where one species lives on the surface of the other. Such associations include the epiphytic and epizoic ones referred to on page 321. At the other extreme are associations where one of the two species may live inside the cells of the other.

This investigation provides you with an opportunity of examining a selection of associations. Try to decide into which category each one fits.

GREEN HYDRA AND CHLORELLA

Examine a green hydra (*Chlorohydra viridissima*) under low and high powers. Observe the unicellular green organism *Chlorella* (in this case called *Zoochlorella*) in its endodermal cells. (*see* Figure 3.16, page 30). This well known association is a case of mutualism. What precisely does each organism gain? Could each survive without the other? How would you test this?

NEMATODES AND EARTHWORM

Examine an active nephridium of an earthworm in saline under low power and observe roundworms (*Rhabditis* sp). Where exactly are they in relation to the nephridium? What do they appear to feed on?

Examine a small piece of tissue from a decaying earthworm under low power. Are live roundworms visible? Conclusions?

APHID AND GREEN PLANT

Examine a leaf of, e.g. sycamore or rose, under a hand lens or binocular microscope. Observe aphids. Can you see them feeding? What can you say about this association? How does the association between aphid and plant compare with that between mosquito and humans?

MALARIAL PARASITE AND HUMANS

Examine a human blood smear showing the malarial parasite. Note that some of the red blood cells contain the parasite (darkly stained). What kind of parasite are we dealing with here?

TRYPANOSOME AND MAMMAL

Examine a mammalian blood smear showing trypanosomes, the causative agent of African sleeping sickness. The parasites are small elongated organisms. Where are they in relation to the red blood cells?

GALL WASP AND FLOWERING PLANT

Gall wasps lay their eggs in the stems or branches of various plants. The larvae induce the surrounding plant cells to form a characteristic wart-like protuberance or gall.

Examine a gall and cut it open. What can you observe? What is the nature of the relationship between the plant and the wasp?

MOSQUITO AND MAMMAL

Examine a mosquito under low power, noting in particular the piercing and sucking mouthparts (*see* page 89). How would you describe the relationship between the mosquito and the mammal whose blood it sucks? How does this relationship differ from that between the mosquito and the malarial parasite?

NITROGEN-FIXING BACTERIA AND FLOWERING PLANT

Certain plants, particularly those belonging to the family Leguminosae (peas, beans, etc.) harbour nitrogen-fixing bacteria in their roots. The bacteria cause the cortical cells to proliferate forming a root nodule. Examine a transverse section of a root showing a root nodule and compare it with an uninfected root. Notice bacteria in the nodule cells. What do the bacteria and plant gain in this well-known mutualistic association? How does the presence of the bacteria affect the ecological distribution of the host plant?

HYDRA AND KERONA

Examine a specimen of *Hydra* under a binocular microscope. Often a small ciliate, *Kerona*, can be observed gliding over the surface of the hydra's body. Observe it in more detail under an ordinary microscope. What kind of relationship is this? What is the potential danger in *Kerona's* way of life, and how does this seem to be overcome?

FLEA AND DOG

The dog flea *Ctenocephalides canis* is adapted to live amongst the hairs close to the host's skin. If available, examine a live specimen in a closed tube. Examine a whole mount under the low power. In what respects is it adapted to its particular mode of life?

MYCORRHIZA

Many plants, particularly those that grow in nitrogen-deficient soil, show an association between their roots and a fungus. Such an association is termed a mycorrhiza. Examine a transverse section of the root of, e.g. pine, and notice the fungal network enveloping the root. Hyphal branches of the network penetrate between the cortical cells. Compare it with an uninfected root. Speculate on the nature of this relationship: what do the fungus and the host gain from it? How could you test your suggestions?

In the bird's-nest orchid (*Neottia nidus-avis*) the host is devoid of chlorophyll and the mycorrhizal fungus penetrates *into* the cortical cells. What are the benefits in this case?

HERMIT CRAB AND THE SEA ANEMONE

Observe a hermit crab in a whelk shell and notice the sea anemone *Calliactis parasitica* attached to the shell. What do you make of this association? Do you consider the sea anemone to be appropriately named?

HONEY BEE AND FLOWERING PLANT

Examine a worker bee (*Apis mellifera*) and a flower that is normally pollinated by it (*see* page 238). In what ways is the

Figure 33.4 The legs of the worker of the honey bee showing adaptations for gathering pollen.

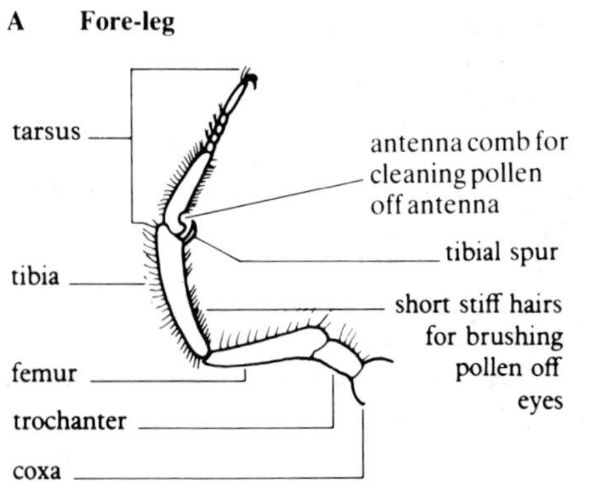

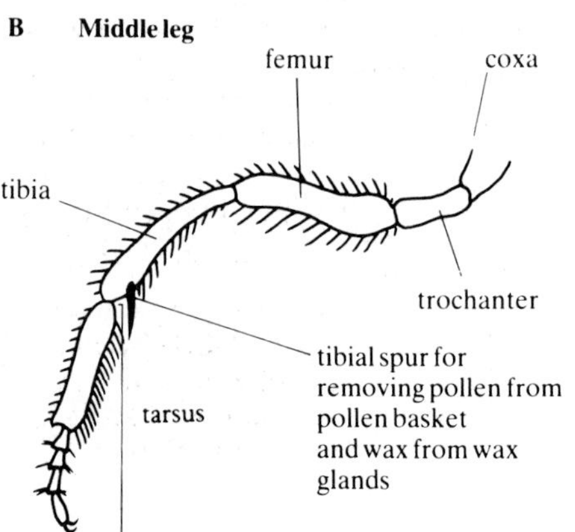

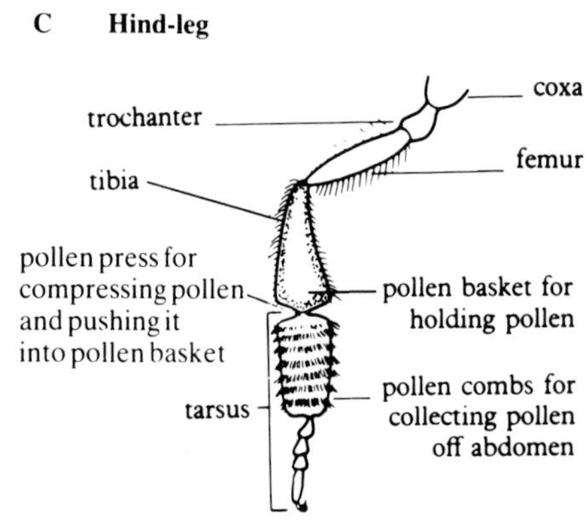

Requirements
Microscope
Binocular microscope
Hand lens
Slides and coverslips
Watchglass

Earthworm saline

Green hydra (*Chlorohydra viridissima*)
Live earthworm (or nephridium thereof)
Decaying earthworm
Aphids on green leaf
Blood smear with trophozoite stage of malarial parasite
Blood smear with trypanosomes
Plant galls
WM mosquito
Plant with root nodules
TS root with nodule
Hydra with *Kerona*
Live fleas in specimen tube
WM flea
TS root showing ectotrophic mycorrhiza
TS root without mycorrhiza
Live hermit crab with *Calliactis parasitica*
Honey bee (worker) entire
WM fore- and hind-limbs of honey bee
Bee-pollinated flower
Freshwater shrimp *Gammarus* with *Vorticella*
Lichen on bark
VS lichen (e.g. *Xanthoria*)

bee adapted for collecting pollen? Observe the three types of legs under the microscope and notice the pollen-collecting adaptations (Figure 33.4).

Does the flower show any special adaptations which facilitate its being pollinated by the bee?

How would you describe the association between the bee and the plant?

FRESHWATER SHRIMP AND VORTICELLA

Observe the head and/or anal regions of the shrimp *Gammarus* under low power and look for the stalked ciliate *Vorticella* attached to the surface of the shrimp's body. Is *Vorticella* found elsewhere? How would you classify this association?

LICHENS

Examine a sample of lichen attached to a piece of bark. Look at a vertical section of lichen (e.g. *Xanthoria*) under low and high powers. Notice the algal and fungal components of the organism. The algal cells are small and round and will be seen amongst the fungal hyphae towards the centre of the section. This represents the ultimate in mutualism. What does each gain? What effect has this association on the ecology of lichens?

How would you describe the relationship between the lichen and the tree on whose bark it grows?

For Consideration

(1) How clear-cut do you consider the distinction to be between the various associations considered in this investigation?

(2) In the course of your observations you have speculated on the nature of these associations. How would you test the validity of any hypotheses which you have formulated?

Questions and Problems

1 'Big fleas have little fleas
Upon their backs to bite 'em;
And little fleas have lesser fleas,
And so ad infinitum.'
Comment.

2 Define the term 'parasite'. Discuss the problem of deciding whether a given association is parasitic or not.

3 You have been commissioned to go to an African country to eradicate bilharzia. What will be the main thrust of your campaign, and why?

4 Give a general account of how parasites are adapted for a parasitic existence.

5 How do parasites and their hosts influence one another?

6 The following organisms, or organisms and tissues, may be found associated together:
(a) *Rhizobium leguminosarum* in the root of a leguminous plant.
(b) Active tubercle bacteria in alveolar tissues of the lung.
(c) *Zoochlorella* in the endoderm cells of *Chlorohydra*.
(d) Non-pathogenic species of bacteria in the rumen of a cow.
In each case describe the substance, or substances, which may pass from one organism to the other and comment on the possible significance of these exchanges.

(*AEB*)

7 Rats were infected experimentally with different numbers of the tapeworm, *Hymenolepis diminuta*. After 16 days, the mature worms were measured. The following data were obtained:

Number of worms per rat	**Mean mass per worm** (g)	**Mean number of eggs per gram of worm**
1	2.2	3.1×10^6
5	1.35	1.7×10^6
10	0.98	1.05×10^6
30	0.33	0.18×10^6

(a) Describe with comments the effects of crowding on the growth and reproduction of the worms, using graphs where appropriate.

(b) The gut of a human who is infected with the tapeworm *Taenia* never contains more than a single worm. Comment on this observation in the light of the data in the table above. *(OCJE modified)*

8 Show how a knowledge of the life cycle and physiology of a *named* parasite and its host can lead to the development of effective methods of controlling the parasite.

9 Suggest explanations for the following:

(a) Lichens can grow in places where few other organisms can survive.

(b) Certain termites can digest wood.

(c) Some species of flowering plant are devoid of all traces of chlorophyll and yet they survive.

(d) Many intercellular parasites flourish in the mammalian body and yet foreign tissue is rejected.

10 Compare the mode of life of a named endoparasite within its host with that of a mammalian foetus in the uterus. *(UL modified)*

11 Describe the methods by which parasites may be transmitted from one human being to another. How may such parasites be controlled? *(UL)*

12 Speculate on the possible evolutionary relationships between parasites, commensals and mutualists and between different kinds of parasites.

13 The polynoid worm *Arconoe* has two species **A** and **B**, each of which lives as a commensal on the surface of a particular species of echinoderm. **A** lives on the starfish *Evasterias troschelii*, whilst **B** lives on the holothurian (sea cucumber) *Stichopus californicus*. The two associations are highly specific, each species of worm living exclusively on its own particular host. If the worm is removed from its host it will climb back onto it.

(a) How would you confirm, beyond all reasonable doubt, that the association is commensalitic and not parasitic or mutualistic?

(b) Describe experiments which you would carry out to investigate the mechanism by which the worm associates with its own particular species of host.

34 Evolution in Evidence

Background Summary

1 Charles Darwin was the first person to put forward a theory of evolution based on firm scientific evidence.

2 Darwin's contribution was twofold: he put forward evidence supporting the idea of evolution and he formulated a plausible hypothesis explaining the mechanism of evolution.

3 Evolution reveals itself in the geographical distribution of animals and plants, comparative anatomy, taxonomy, embryology, cell biology, and palaeontology. Studies in all these fields furnish evidence for evolution.

4 Evidence for evolution is seen in **continental distribution**. For example, the distribution of mammals in the southern continents of the world, together with fossil evidence, suggests that their ancestors migrated there from the northern hemisphere, became isolated and then evolved independently.

5 Particularly cogent evidence for isolation followed by independent evolution is provided by the Australian fauna where the marsupials occupy the ecological niches filled elsewhere by eutherian mammals. This and certain other examples of distribution can be explained by **plate tectonic theory**.

6 Further evidence for isolation and independent evolution is provided by the distribution of organisms on **oceanic islands** such as the Galapagos archipelago. On the Galapagos islands, which were visited by Darwin during his voyage on the *Beagle*, the finches furnish particularly striking evidence for evolution.

7 The process of isolation followed by independent evolution depends on the establishment of natural barriers. These include mountain ranges, water, and various climatic factors.

8 From **comparative anatomy** the principle of **homology** emerges. This can be explained in terms of **divergent evolution** and **adaptive radiation** and provides evidence for evolution. A good example is the vertebrate pentadactyl limb.

9 In certain situations comparative anatomy can provide information which enables **evolutionary pathways** to be reconstructed. This is seen, for example, in the vertebrate heart and arterial arches. However, to gain an accurate picture of the evolutionary history of animals, the comparative anatomy of modern forms should be accompanied by a study of the fossils.

10 Groups with different evolutionary origins (phylogenetically unrelated groups) may appear to be similar as a result of **convergent evolution**. Superficially similar structures shared by such groups are called **analogous structures**, an example being the vertebrate and octopus eyes.

11 **Taxonomy**, the classification of organisms, is seen not so much as evidence for evolution as a consequence of it. The purpose of a natural classification is to reflect the degree of evolutionary affinity between different groups. A good example is seen in the classification of the chordates.

12 Sometimes the **embryology** of two seemingly unrelated groups reveals a phylogenetic connection which is not evident from studying the adult forms. Thus **comparative embryology** can provide important evidence for evolutionary affinities.

13 Cell biology also provides evidence for evolution. The basic similarity in the structure and functioning of cells, and the ubiquitous occurrence of many biochemical molecules, suggests a common ancestry for all animal and plant cells. Biochemical homology, established by techniques such as **serological tests**, protein sequence analysis and DNA hybridisation provides further evidence for evolutionary affinities between certain groups.

14 The most direct evidence for evolution derives from palaeontology, the study of fossils. Fossils take the form of petrified remains, moulds, impresssions and preservation in amber, asphalt, or ice.

15 Fossils can be dated by sedimentation data or, more accurately, by estimating the decline in radioactivity as, for example, in carbon dating.

16 From the fossil record evolutionary pathways can be reconstructed in detail as in the case of the evolution of horses, and the vertebrate ear ossicles.

Investigation 34.1
The vertebrate pentadactyl limb: an exercise in homology

Homologous structures may serve different functions but they are fundamentally similar to one another and are believed to share a common ancestry. An example of homology is provided by the pentadactyl limb of vertebrates. Animals possessing the pentadactyl limb include amphibians, reptiles, birds, and mammals.

The pentadactyl limb is so called because typically it terminates in the form of five digits. However, in the course of evolution it appears to have undergone considerable modification in different groups. These modifications have involved enlargement, fusion, degeneration or, in some cases, total loss of certain components.

Procedure

A generalised pentadactyl limb is shown in Figure 34.1. We shall examine the limbs of various tetrapods and observe the extent to which they conform to, or depart from, the idealised pattern shown in the diagram. In each case try to correlate the structure of the limb with the functions it performs.

RABBIT

1 Examine the fore- and hind-limb bones of a rabbit. Identify the component parts, regarding the carpus and tarsus as single units for the moment. To what extent does each limb depart from the ideal pentadactyl pattern? Why the differences?

2 Now examine the carpus and tarsus in detail. Are all nine component bones present? If not, what do you think has happened to them? Try to answer this for yourself *before* you look at Figure 34.2A. What functional explanation would you suggest for the modifications seen in the carpus and tarsus?

FROG

1 Examine the fore- and hind-limb bones of a frog. Again regarding the carpus and tarsus as single units, identify the component parts of each limb. To what extent do the fore- and hind-limbs depart from the ideal pentadactyl pattern, and how do they differ from each other? How would you explain the differences?

2 Now examine the carpus and tarsus in detail. In each case try to account for the nine component bones *before* looking at Figure 34.2B. How would you explain the structure of the carpus and tarsus in this animal?

BIRD

1 Examine the hind-limb of a bird, e.g. pigeon. This is more modified than either the rabbit or frog. Try to decide for yourself what has happened, and *then* look at Figure 34.2C. What are the functional reasons for the modifications in this case?

2 Now examine the fore-limb. This is even more modified. It is obvious that great reduction has taken place in the hand, but there is some controversy as to which particular components have been lost. Two different interpretations are given in Figure 34.2C. What do you think is the evidence for such views?

3 To explain the fore-limb skeleton in functional terms it is useful to examine an intact wing with the skin and feathers in position. Do this and try to interpret in functional terms the fore-limb's departure from the pentadactyl pattern.

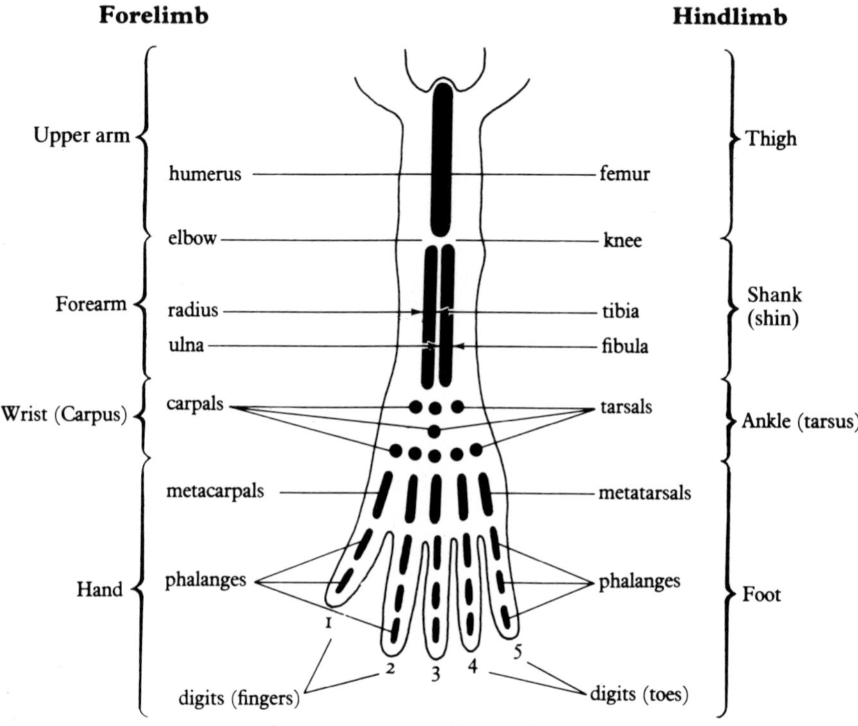

Figure 34.1 A generalized pentadactyl limb. This kind of limb is possessed by all terrestrial groups of vertebrates. The preaxial border (i.e. the edge of the limb which generally points towards the main axis of the body) is to the left, the postaxial border to the right. The fore- and hind-limbs both conform to the pattern illustrated: the nomenclature used for each is shown to the left and right of the diagram respectively. (*After* Grove and Newell, *Animal Biology*, University Tutorial Press).

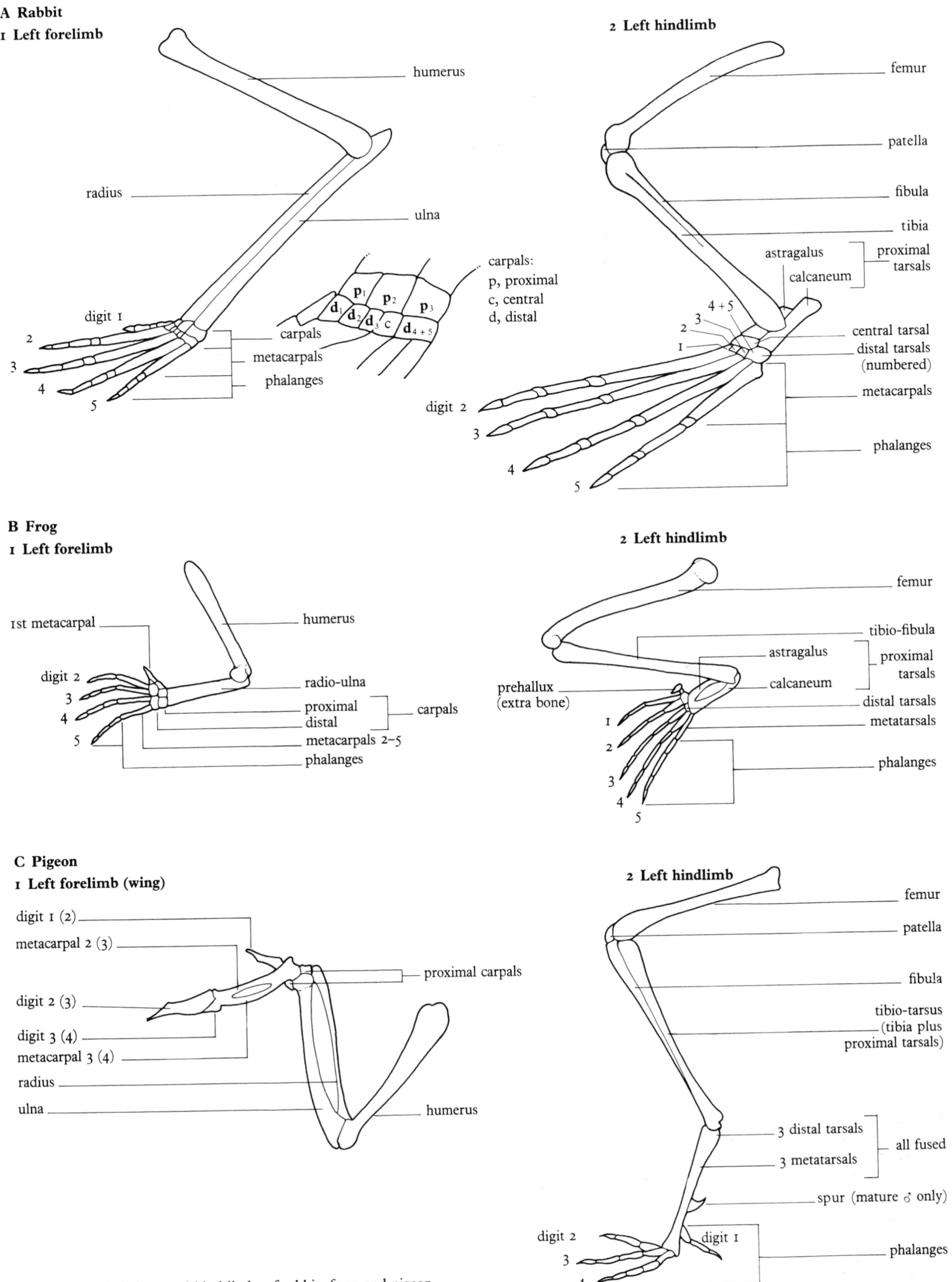

A Rabbit
1 Left forelimb
humerus
radius
ulna
carpals:
p, proximal
c, central
d, distal
p1
p2
p3
d1
d2
d3
c
d4+5
digit 1
2
3
4
5
carpals
metacarpals
phalanges
2 Left hindlimb
femur
patella
fibula
tibia
astragalus
calcaneum
proximal tarsals
4+5
3
2
1
central tarsal
distal tarsals (numbered)
metacarpals
phalanges
digit 2
3
4
5
B Frog
1 Left forelimb
1st metacarpal
humerus
digit 2
3
4
5
radio-ulna
proximal
distal
carpals
metacarpals 2–5
phalanges
2 Left hindlimb
femur
tibio-fibula
astragalus
calcaneum
proximal tarsals
prehallux (extra bone)
distal tarsals
metatarsals
phalanges
1
2
3
4
5
C Pigeon
1 Left forelimb (wing)
digit 1 (2)
metacarpal 2 (3)
proximal carpals
digit 2 (3)
digit 3 (4)
metacarpal 3 (4)
radius
ulna
humerus
2 Left hindlimb
femur
patella
fibula
tibio-tarsus (tibia plus proximal tarsals)
3 distal tarsals
3 metatarsals
all fused
spur (mature ♂ only)
digit 2
3
4
digit 1
phalanges

Figure 34.2 Left fore- and hind-limbs of rabbit, frog, and pigeon.

OTHER TETRAPODS

If available, examine the fore- and/or hind-limb bones of other tetrapods, or photographs of them, e.g. human, monkey, pig, horse, mole, bat, etc. In each case note the extent to which the limb skeleton departs from the pentadactyl pattern and interpret, in functional terms, the modifications you observe.

For Consideration

(1) Are you convinced that the pentadactyl limbs which you have examined share a common ancestry, or are you sceptical? What further information do you think you should have?

(2) If available, examine entire skeletons of rabbit, frog, and bird (*see* Investigation 21.3, page 204). What other structures besides the limbs appear to be homologous with each other? Compare such structures and try to explain the differences between them in functional terms.

(3) The bird's wing is covered with feathers. With what structures in other vertebrates might feathers be homologous? How might you test your suggestion? If time permits examine a feather under the microscope. What functions do feathers perform?

Requirements
Hand lens

Skeleton of fore- and hind-limb of rabbit
Skeleton of fore- and hind-limb of frog
Skeleton of fore- and hind-limb of bird (e.g. pigeon)
Intact wing of bird
Mounted skeletons of rabbit, frog, bird
Other limb skeletons as available

Investigation 34.2 Examination of the chordate characters

Evolutionary relationships can be seen in classifications. Provided it is based on homologous structures, a classification of animals and plants into groups reflects the evolutionary affinities between them.

A good example of this is provided by the chordates. The phylum Chordata includes all the vertebrates (fishes, amphibians, reptiles, birds, and mammals) together with several invertebrate groups (protochordates) which include *Amphioxus*, the lancelet. This wide range of animals is believed to be related phylogenetically on the grounds that they all share the six chordate characters. These are:

(1) A dorsally situated strengthening rod, the notochord, present as some stage during development.

(2) A hollow, tubular CNS on the dorsal side of the body immediately above the notochord.

(3) Pharyngeal clefts connecting the cavity of the pharynx with the exterior on either side of the body.

(4) A series of segmental muscle blocks (myotomes) on either side of the body.

(5) The anus, instead of being terminal, is situated some way in front of the posterior end of the body, thus leaving a post-anal tail which extends beyond the anus.

(6) Blood flows forwards in a ventral vessel and backwards in the dorsal vessel.

These features can be readily observed in, e.g. a fish, amphibian, and *Amphioxus*.

FISH

1 Examine the external features of, e.g. a dogfish or bony fish, and locate the cloaca (common vestibule receiving the anus, excretory, and genital openings) and post-anal tail. Function of the latter?

2 Strip off a piece of skin from the side of the body shortly behind the cloaca. Note the segmental muscle blocks (myotomes) separated by tough sheets of connective tissue (myocommata).

3 Examine a transverse section of a dogfish embryo through the pharyngeal region. How many chordate characters can you detect? Observe the notochord, dorsal nerve tube with small cavity, pharyngeal clefts lined by gills, dorsal and ventral aortae.

How would you describe the microscopic structure of the notochord? How does its structure relate to its function as a strong, but flexible, rod? What function is served by the pharyngeal clefts in the dogfish?

4 Examine a transverse section through the tail region of a dogfish embryo and compare with the previous section. How does this section compare with the previous one with respect to the chordate characters?

5 Examine a transverse hand section through the tail region of an adult dogfish. How does it differ from the embryo section? Explain the differences.

AMPHIBIAN

1 First compare the external features of a newt or salamander with a frog or toad. How many chordate characters can you observe in each case?

2 Examine a late tadpole of frog or toad (*see* page 260) and notice that it possesses certain observable chordate characters which are absent in the adult. What principle is illustrated by the differences?

3 Examine transverse sections of a tadpole through the head, pharyngeal, abdominal, and tail regions. Observe the occurrence (or otherwise) of the chordate characters in each section.

AMPHIOXUS

1 Examine a whole mount of *Amphioxus* noting the chordate characters, particularly the post-anal tail and the < shaped myotomes (Figure 34.3A).

2 Examine a transverse section of *Amphioxus* through the pharyngeal region. Most of the chordate characters will be clearly detectable. The pharyngeal clefts will appear as a series of perforations in the wall of the pharynx which is enclosed by a flap of the body wall called the **atrial fold** (Figure 34.3B).

How do you think the atrial fold is formed? The cavity created by it is called the atrium. Into this the pharyngeal clefts open. At the back of the pharyngeal region the atrium opens to the exterior by a pore, the atriopore.

Amphioxus is a filter feeder: water containing food particles in suspension is drawn by cilia into the pharynx and expelled through the pharyngeal clefts. As the water goes through the clefts food particles get caught up in mucus secreted by the endostyle organ and carried by cilia on the pharyngeal bars to the dorsal groove. Cilia lining the dorsal groove draw the mucus and food particles backwards to the intestine. Water leaves the atrial cavity via the atriopore.

Figure 34.3 Structure of *Amphioxus* as see under the microscope. The chordate characters are marked with an asterisk.

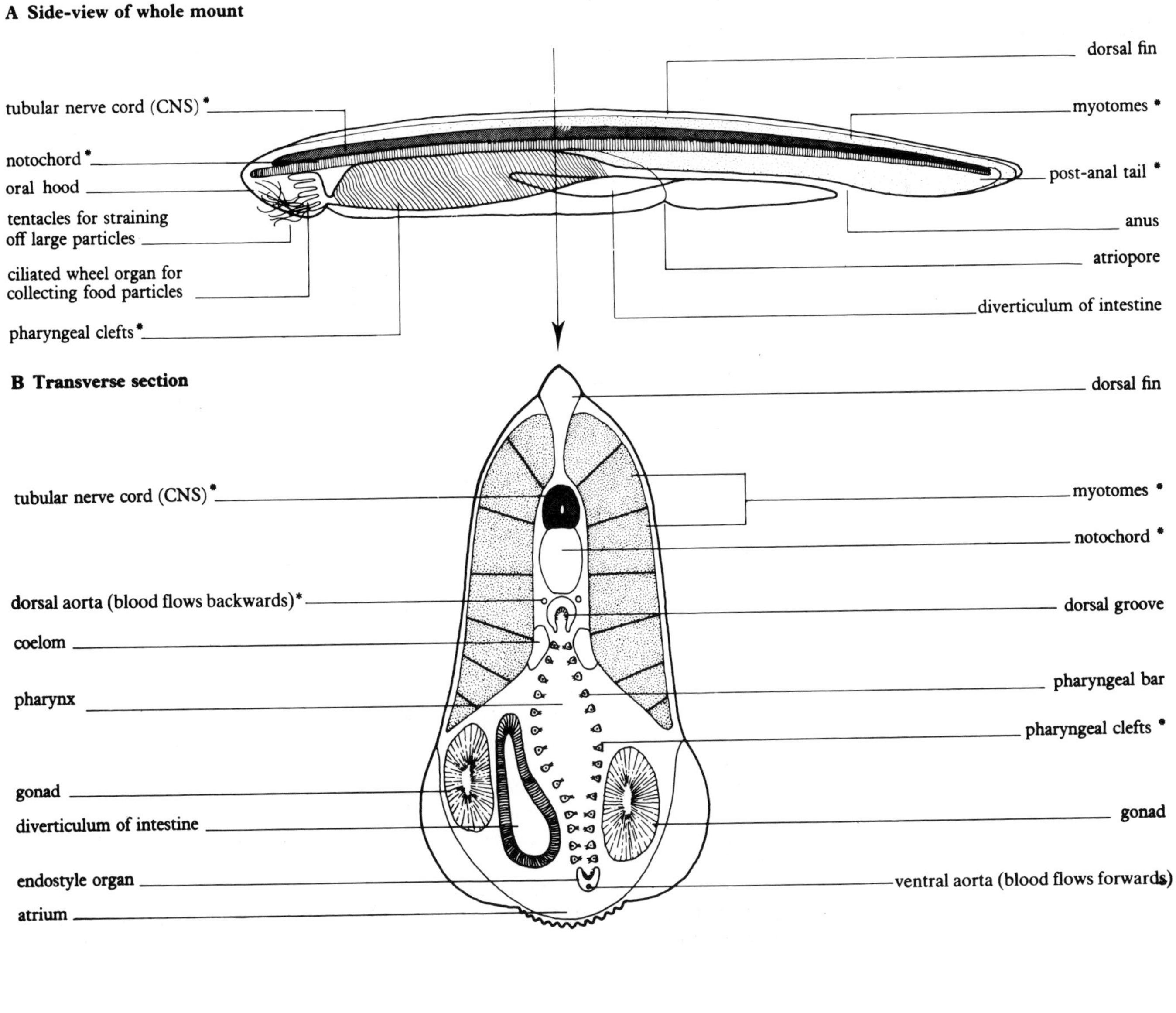

Requirements
Microscope
Scalpel and forceps

Dogfish or bony fish (entire)
Hand section of adult dogfish (tail)
Frog or toad
Salamander or newt
Tadpole internal gill stage
TS dogfish embryo (pharyngeal region)
TS dogfish embryo (tail region)
TS tadpole at various levels
WM *Amphioxus*
TS *Amphioxus* pharyngeal region

For Consideration

(1) From your observations of the chordate characters are you, personally, convinced that *Amphioxus* should be placed in the same phylum as the dogfish and frog?
(2) This phylum also includes *you*. What has happened to your chordate characters?
(3) What principle is illustrated by the fact that the pharyngeal clefts are used for respiratory gas exchange in fishes, but for filter-feeding in *Amphioxus*?
(4) *Balanoglossus* (the acorn worm) is a marine worm-like animal with a muscular proboscis which it uses for burrowing into sand and mud. It has pharyngeal clefts but the dorsal CNS is, for much of its length, and open groove rather than a closed tube; the anus is terminal; the body wall muscles appear to be unsegmented; the blood system is rudimentary, and the notochord is absent though a short structure with a similar microscopic appearance is present in the proboscis.

Do you think it is justified to include this animal in the chordates?
(5) What other information, besides that which you have obtained in this investigation, would you need to have in order to establish whether or not a given animal is a member of the chordates?

Questions and Problems

1 What kind of differences would you expect to find between the fauna and flora of an oceanic island and a comparably sized island on a continental shelf? Explain your answer. (*JMB*)

2 Dinosaurs belonging to the same genus have been found in North America, East Africa, South America and India. However, the *mammals* found in these areas belong to different genera. How would you explain these observations?

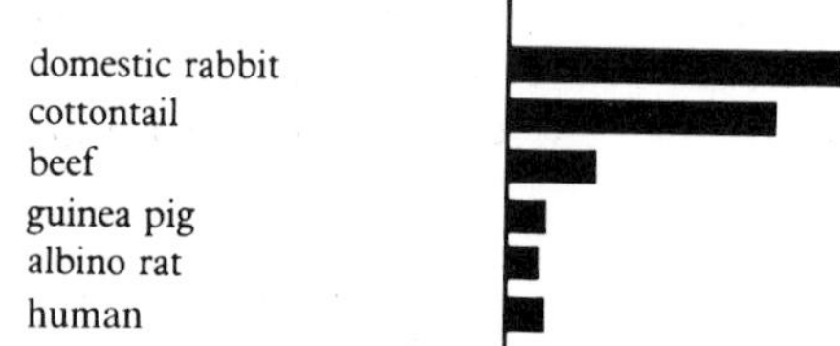

Figure 34.4 Results of serological tests on the domestic rabbit and other mammals. (*Based on* Moody, Cochran and Drugg).

3 In an attempt to investigate the evolutionary affinity betwen the domestic rabbit and various other mammals, Moody, Cochran, and Drugg carried out serological tests. Their results are summarised in Figure 34.4. The length of the bars represents the amount of precipitation in the tests.
(a) Describe the procedure by which you think these results were obtained.
(b) What do the results suggest to you?
(c) Consult a classification of mammals in a textbook of zoology. Do the results of the serological tests fit in with the classification?
(d) What further information might help to clarify the evolutionary relationships of these animals?

4 The haemoglobin molecule of mammals contains four polypeptide chains: two α and two β chains. Each α chain consists of 141 amino acids, and each β chain consists of 146 amino acids.

Analyses of the sequence of amino acids in the polypeptide chains of haemoglobin have revealed that gorilla haemoglobin differs from human haemoglobin with respect to two amino acids (one in the α chain and one in the β chain). However, horse haemoglobin differs from human haemoglobin with respect to 17 amino acids. Comment on these observations.

5 (a) What do you understand by the term 'adaptive radiation'? Illustrate your answer by reference to either the Australian fauna or to that of the Galapagos Islands.
(b) Construct a fully labelled diagram of the foot of the following hypothetical animals:
(i) a large swamp-dwelling reptile,
(ii) a tree-dwelling primate,
(iii) a large desert mammal,
(iv) an aquatic amphibian.

6 All vertebrates have genes which code for haemoglobin, fibrinopeptides and cytochrome **c**, but the genes and the amino acid sequences for which they code are not identical in different animals. Sequences of 13 bases from part of the messenger RNA coding for these proteins in sheep, horse, pig, cow and human are shown below. In these sequences the letters A = adenine, G = guanine, C = cytosine and U = uracil.

	Haemoglobin A	**Fibrinopeptide A**	**Cytochrome C**
Sheep	GAG GGG GGC AUU A	GCG UGG GGA ACC G	GCA GCU UAC ACG A
Horse	GAC GGG GGG AUU G	CAG AGA GGA ACA G	GCA GCU AAC ACC A
Pig	GGC GGG GCG AUU G	GGC AAA GGA ACG G	GCA GCU UAC ACG A
Cow	GGG GGG GGC AUU A	GCC CAG GGA CCC G	GCA GCU UAC ACG A
Human	CAC GGG GCG AUU A	GUG GGA GGA CCC G	AAU UCA UCU CUA C

(a) Work out the number of base differences between the RNA codes for each pair of organisms. There are ten comparisons to be made.

(b) Representing the five species by their initial letter (S, H, P, C and H), make a diagram in which the distances between the letters are proportional to the differences in the messenger RNA.

(c) Which two species seem most closely related (least different) according to this criterion?

(d) Which species seems most distinct from the others?

From the evidence of fossils and comparative anatomy of living species, the line which gave rise to humans (primates) probably diverged from that which gave rise to hoofed mammals as long as 250 million years ago. The ancestors of horses separated from those of pigs, sheep and cows approximately 55 million years ago. Since then, pigs have hardly changed in shape and size, but for at least 45 million years, they have been distinct from sheep and cows. Sheep and cows have recently undergone adaptive radiation; modern sheep and cows may have had a common ancestor within the last 6 million years.

(e) Compare your table of RNA base similarities with this evidence and discuss whether your data are compatible with these ideas.

(f) Do you regard this as evidence that evolution might have occurred? Explain your answer.

7 From fossils occurring in the Rocky Mountains, U.S.A., a biologist recorded the frequency of rodents and multituberculates. The animals belonging to these two groups are similar in size and have gnawing teeth, but rodents have only two front teeth whereas multituberculates have many.

The table below shows his data:

Millions of years ago	**Epoch**		**Rodents**		**Multi-tuberculates**	
			Genera	Species	Genera	Species
45		Late	13	31	0	0
50	Eocene	Middle	9	19	0	0
55		Early	4	12	3	5
60		Late	1	1	7	11
65	Palaeocene	Middle	0	0	6	17
70		Early	0	0	5	7

(a) Why were the Rocky Mountains a particularly favourable place for studying such fossils?

(b) How do you think the ages of the fossils were estimated?

(c) What conclusions would you draw from the data?

(d) Suggest explanations for the particular change in fauna which the data indicate may have occurred during the Palaeocene and Eocene epochs. (*SA*)

8 Discuss the usefulness (or otherwise) of the following features in assessing the evolutionary affinities of a plant:
(a) Its height.
(b) The absorption spectrum of its photosynthetic pigment.
(c) The number of petals in its corolla.
(d) The colour of its flowers.
(e) The degree of elaboration of its gametophyte generation.

9 The similarities between the fauna of different continents are cited as evidence for evolution, but so are the *differences* between them. How would you reconcile this apparent contradiction?

10 How would you convince a sceptic of the truth of the theory of evolution?

11 Make a list of the principal lines of evidence which support the theory of evolution. Which ones do you find the least convincing and the most convincing? Go on to discuss in detail *one* piece of evidence which you personally find most convincing.

12 'Evolutionary theory and religious belief are irreconcilable'. Discuss.

35 The Mechanism of Evolution

Background Summary

1 According to the Darwinian theory, evolution occurs by the **natural selection** of **chance variations**. In contrast, Lamarck's theory suggests that evolution occurs by the **transmission of acquired characters**.

2 Of the two theories Darwin's has stood the test of time. The Darwinian theory, updated by the findings of modern genetics, is referred to as **Neodarwinism**.

3 Darwin's theory depends on the existence of chance variation within species. Such variations may be **continuous** or **discontinuous**.

4 Continuous variation may be seen in **frequency distribution histograms** and generally approximates to a **normal (Gaussian) curve**.

5 Such variation may be attributed to reshuffling of genes resulting from the behaviour of chromosomes during meiosis, and new combinations established by fertilisation. Variation is accentuated by the fact that characteristics are often influenced by the cumulative effects of numerous genes (a **polygenic complex**) whose expression may be controlled by **modifier genes**. The effects of the latter may themselves be altered as a result of the behaviour of chromosomes during meiosis.

6 Discontinuous variation may arise through **mutations**. These may be caused by chromosomal abnormalities (**chromosome mutations**) or changes in the structure of the genes (**gene mutations**).

7 Mutation frequencies are comparatively low. However, the mutation rate can be increased by various **mutagenic agents**.

8 Mutations arise spontaneously and are relatively persistent. Usually they are harmful but sometimes they may confer beneficial characteristics on the individual.

9 Mutations are generally recessive at first, but they may become dominant in the course of time.

10 Types of chromosome mutation include **deletion, inversion, translocation, duplication,** and **addition**. The last may involve addition of one or more whole chromosomes as a result of **non-disjunction** during meiosis.

11 In extreme cases non-disjunction results in an organism containing one or more complete sets of extra chromosomes. This is known as **polyploidy**. In certain situations it is associated with beneficial characteristics, and may be an important mode of speciation in plants.

12 Beneficial characteristics may also result from **hybridisation** between closely related species or subspecies. The offspring may show varying degrees of **hybrid vigour**.

13 Gene mutations involve changes in the sequence of nucleotide bases in DNA. These may involve **substitution, insertion, deletion**, or **inversion** of one or more bases. Seemingly trivial changes may have far-reaching effects.

14 Mutations sometimes occur in an organism's non-reproductive cells. They are called **somatic mutations** and may result in **genetic mosaics**.

15 The conflict between organisms and their environment has been described as the **struggle for existence**. This results from **environmental resistance** as population numbers increase (*see* page 314).

16 Population growth is relevant to evolution because variation is greatest during periods of increase, and the mortality which results from over-population is differential (**differential mortality**). This is the basis of **natural selection**.

17 Natural selection is instrumental in holding species constant (**stabilising selection**), but, if the environment changes, it favours the emergence of new forms (**progressive** or **directional selection**).

18 Natural selection may be seen in action in various breeding organisms, e.g. the peppered moth, meadow brown butterfly, banded snail and toxin-tolerant grasses.

19 Some species possess two or more different types of individuals (**polymorphism**). Where the differences are genetic (**genetic polymorphism**), and the environment constant, the different morphs in a given population occur in more or less constant proportions, this constancy being maintained by selection.

20 The genetic constitution of a population is known as its **gene pool**. The Hardy–Weinberg principle states that the **gene frequencies** in a given gene pool are generally held constant. This **genetic equilibrium** is maintained by stabilising selection.

21 However, genetic equilibrium may be upset as a result of mutation, environmental change and selection, and the loss or gain of genes. Changes in genetic equilibrium are the basis of directional selection.

22 For new species to arise (**speciation**) some degree of **isolation** is necessary. Isolation need not necessarily be geographic, though this is often the first step in speciation. It may also be ecological, reproductive, or genetic, and these usually arise as a result of geographical separation.

23 Once two separated populations become reproductively or genetically isolated they may develop into new species. If subsequently they come to live in the same area again, they remain separate species.

24 Other types of selection may have been important in evolution. These include **sexual selection, kin selection** and (more controversially) **group selection**.

25 The principles of genetics and evolution are employed (sometimes unwittingly) by humans in **animal and plant breeding,** in which natural selection is replaced by **artificial selection**.

Investigation 35.1
Variation in a population of animals or plants

Requirements
Hand lens or binocular microscope if required
Squared paper

Variation provides the 'raw material' for natural selection. One way of investigating if evolution is taking place in a species is to study the occurrence of a variable feature in a population over a period of time, or in several different populations. Statistical techniques can then be used to determine whether or not there are significant differences between the populations.

Procedure

Studying the 'occurrence' of a particular feature means, in practice, determining the numbers of individuals within a given population showing the different variations of the feature. These numbers give us the frequencies. Plants lend themselves particularly well to this sort of investigation. Features suitable for analysis include: length of stem or flower stalk, length of petals, length of leaves, number of petals in a plant where this is variable (e.g. daisy), number of flowers per inflorescence, etc.

1 First select a feature which you would like to investigate in a particular population of plants. Specimens may be either measured in the field or collected and measured in the laboratory.

2 Score the frequencies on squared paper as shown in the hypothetical example in Figure 35.1. This gives you a frequency distribution histogram.

3 If you are investigating variations in a *number* (e.g. number of petals), then each number should be written along the horizontal axis of your frequency diagram. On the other hand, if you are investigating variations in, for example, a *length*, then it may be more appropriate to group the various lengths into classes (e.g. 10–15, 16–20, 21–25, etc.). The classes should be placed along the horizontal axis in your frequency diagram.

4 Obtain measurements from as large a sample of the population as possible. If time permits, do the same for a second population in a different locality.

Figure 35.1 An example of a frequency distribution histogram. Starting from the base, a cross is placed in the appropriate box each time a flower with a particular number of petals is encountered in the population. In this particular population seventy individuals were examined and recorded.

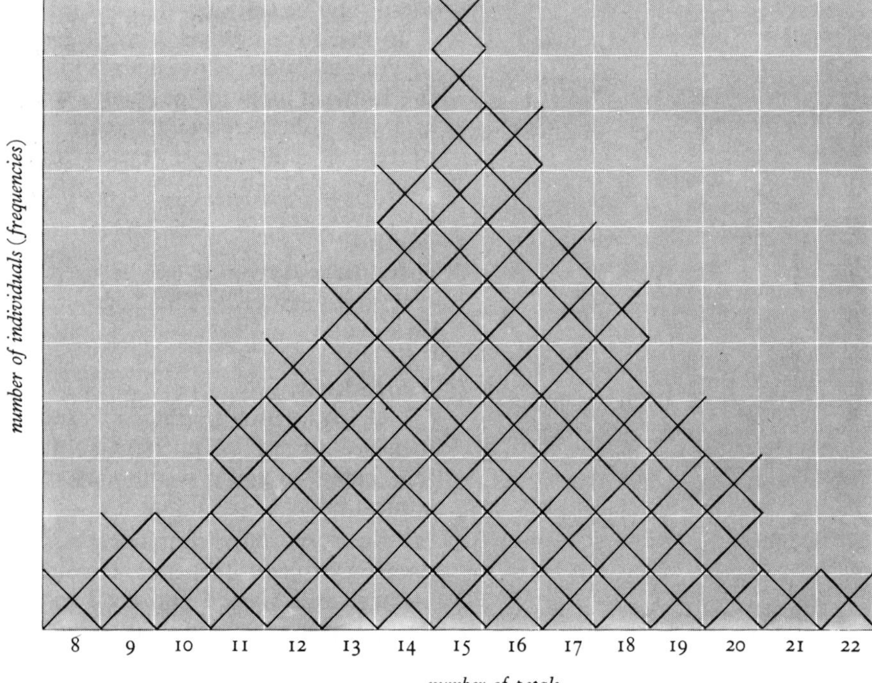

Analysis of Results

Refer to Appendix 6, page 393.

1 Construct a curve by joining the tops of the vertical bars in your frequency distribution histogram. Your curve should pass through the centre of the top of each bar.

2 Does the curve approximate to a curve of normal distribution? If not, suggest reasons for its failure to do so.

3 Calculate the arithmetic mean for your population. Is this the same as the mode in your histogram? If not, why not?

4 Now calculate the standard deviation. What percentage of the population departs from the mean by more than twice the standard deviation? What does this tell us about the population?

5 If you have obtained frequency data for two separate populations, calculate the standard error of the difference. Is the difference between the arithmetic means of the two populations less than, or greater than, twice the standard error? Conclusions?

For Consideration

(1) Suggest reasons why the 'class' represented by the mode in your histogram is the most common situation.
(2) If you were to continue with this investigation, what further observations and experiments would you carry out?
(3) Suppose a significant difference was found between the frequency data obtained in a given area in one year, and the frequency data obtained in the same area ten years later. How might this be explained?
(4) Suppose a significant difference was found between the frequency data obtained in two different areas. How might that be explained?

Investigation 35.2
Continuous and discontinuous variation in blackberry

The previous Investigation demonstrated the continuous variation which exists in a plant characteristic, such as length of petals or length of leaves. This variation has several causes. Firstly, different plants in a population may differ in genotype. Secondly, different plants may be growing in slightly different environments. Thirdly, different shoots on the same plant may receive different amounts of light, water, nutrients, or herbivore attack. To some extent, it is possible to distinguish between these different causes of variation in blackberry by a simple analysis of leaf shape.

Requirements
Gloves
Graph paper
Pencils
Polythene bags
Ruler with millimetre scale
Secateurs

Four different blackberry (bramble) plants

Procedure

1 Select four widely spaced plants of blackberry and identify them by the letters A–D. Ideally, the plants should not be growing in the same field under the same conditions, but should occupy a variety of habitats within 1 km of one another.

2 From each plant, select four stems distinguished by the numbers 1–4. From each stem, cut off four mature leaves at the base of the leaf stalk. Place each batch of four leaves into a separate labelled polythene bag.

3 In the laboratory, lay each leaf in turn on a flat bench. Measure the maximum length and the maximum width of the leaf blade (Figure 35.2) and record these measurements carefully. Return the leaves to their correct polythene bags.

4 When the measurements for all sixty-four leaves have been recorded, draw a scattergram of the results. On graph paper, draw a vertical axis representing the length of a leaf and a horizontal axis representing the width of a leaf.

5 Plot onto the scattergram sixty-four points, each representing one leaf, and identify the each leaf with the appropriate symbol (A, B, C or D) according to the plant which it comes from. Draw a circle around the sixteen points which represent each set of sixteen leaves from the same plant.

6 How much variation is there between the four different plants? If there are clear differences in leaf size or shape, a further comparison may also reveal consistent differences in other features such as leaf stalk length or spininess, and leaf colour or hairiness. Are these differences genetic or environmental?

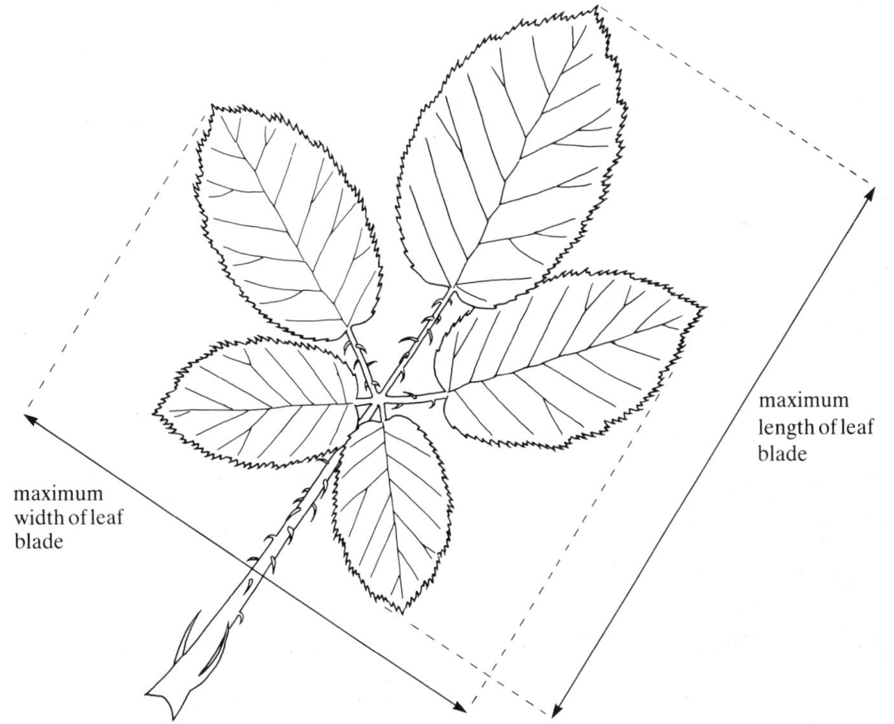

Figure 35.2 Leaf of bramble (*Rubus fruticosus*) with five leaflets, showing measurement of maximum length and maximum width of leaf blade.

For consideration

(1) Blackberries reproduce apomictically, which means that their seeds contain embryos produced by mitosis. Thus all the seeds produced by a blackberry plant should have the same genotype as each other, and their mother. Any mutation which has a major effect on the phenotype will create a new race. Do you think that these races ought to be called new species of blackberry?

(2) How much variation is there between different stems on the same plant, and between different leaves on the same stem? What might cause such variation?

(3) It has been suggested that somatic mutations, (i.e. mutations which occur during mitosis in the growth of a plant) might cause the genotypes of the different shoots on the same plant to differ. What advantages might this confer on the plant?

Investigation 35.3
Comparison of the growth of grasses in relation to nutrient stress

Individuals of some common grass species can be found growing in nutrient-stressed habitats. These habitats include roadside verges where the lead and salt concentration is high; spoil heaps resulting from mineral extraction or smelting, with high concentrations of lead, copper or zinc; and serpentine soils, high in nickel and chromium, low in calcium. It is possible that the individual grasses which grow on such soils have evolved tolerance to high levels of toxic ions. If so, their root growth should be faster than control roots grown in high concentrations of the same ions.

Procedure

You will compare the root growth of shoots (tillers) or seedlings of the *same species* of grass, one sample from the stressed habitat and the other from an unstressed habitat nearby.

EXPERIMENT WITH TILLERS

1 Label five volumetric flasks A to E. Into each flask pour calcium nitrate (v) solution up to the 995 cm^3 mark, leaving 5 cm^3 for the metal ion solutions.
2 Add metal ion solutions to the flasks as follows:
Flask A: 5 cm^3 of stock copper solution (giving a copper concentration of 2 mg dm^{-3})
Flask B: 5 cm^3 of stock zinc solution (giving a zinc concentration of 10 mg dm^{-3})
Flask C: 5 cm^3 of stock lead solution (giving a lead concentration of 12 mg dm^{-3})
Flask D: 5 cm^3 of stock nickel solution (giving a nickel concentration of 3 mg dm^{-3})
Flask E: no metal ion solution. This is your control.
3 Transfer each solution to a plastic container (e.g. sandwich box) labelled A, B, C, D or E.
4 Stretch a sheet of cling film over the top of the container.
5 Carefully detach from each plant a tiller bearing a basal node (Figure 35.3). Place each tiller through a hole in the cling film so that the base of the tiller is immersed in the solution. Each container should have five tillers of each variety. Record clearly on the side of each container the positions of the tillers of each variety.
6 Keep the apparatus in a well-lit warm spot for about two weeks. Aerate the solutions regularly with a pipette attached to a rubber tube leading from an aquarium pump. If no rooting has occurred within seven days, even in controls, it may be necessary to replace the nutrient solutions.
7 Measure in millimetres the length of the longest root attached to each tiller. Average the measurements for the five tillers of the same variety in the same metal ion solution.
8 Plot a bar chart of the average length of the longest roots against the metal ions.

EXPERIMENT WITH SEEDLINGS

1 Label ten 400 cm^3 plastic beakers A1, B1, C1, D1, E1, A2, B2, C2, D2, E2. Add to each 10 per cent Hoagland's nutrient solution without phosphate, and a raft of two layers of black alkathene beads.
2 To each of the beakers marked 1 add ten evenly spaced seeds of *Festuca rubra* var Dawson.
4 After 7-10 days, measure and record the lengths in mm of the longest root on each seedling. Then return the seedlings to their beakers.
5 After a further four days measure and record the longest root lengths again. Calculate the average increase in root length (in mm) in each beaker.
6 Make up metal ion solutions in volumetric flasks as in the tiller experiment but with Hoagland's solution (10 per cent) instead of calcium nitrate (v) solution.
7 Replace the original Hoagland's solutions in the plastic beakers with the metal ion solutions. Put copper in A1 and A2, zinc in B1 and B2, lead in C1 and C2, and nickel in D1 and D2.

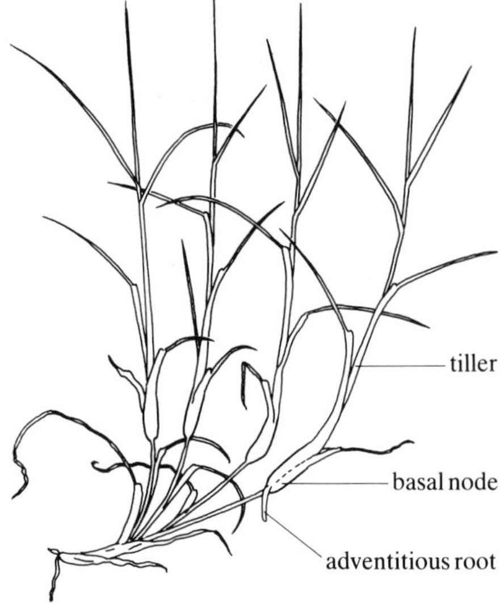

Figure 35.3 Vegetative part of a grass (*Festuca rubra*), showing it to consist of a series of shoots (tillers), each one with a node at the base. Each node is capable of producing adventitious roots.

Questions and Problems

13	19	20	19	18	19
21	17	16	14	16	17
15	15	12	19	15	13
11	16	14	16	18	16
16	15	17	15	19	16
15	13	15	16	15	16
14	15	15	14	12	13
19	19	20	18	19	18
19	18	18	14	19	14
14	20	15			

1 A sample of 57 rose hips was collected from several rose bushes growing in a hedgerow bordering a country lane. The length of each hip was measured. The results in millimetres are given in the margin.

(a) Rearrange the data to show the frequency of each length.

(b) Interpret these results in the form of a histogram.

(c) What general conclusions could be drawn from the histogram?

(d) Suggest *five* factors which could have produced the range of sizes evident in the data. Explain how each of these factors will have exerted its influence.

(e) Suggest *three* precautions which should be taken when assembling data for this type of investigation. (*AEB*)

2 (a) Figure 35.4A shows a set of human chromosomes in which a mutation has occurred.

(i) What is the nature of this mutation?

(ii) What appears to be the criterion by which the complete set of chromosomes has been arranged?

(iii) What is the sex of the person from whom this chromosome set has been taken? Give the reason for your answer.

(b) Figure 35.4B shows a cell at mitosis in which a mutation has occurred.

(i) Name the stage of mitosis shown in the photograph.

(ii) What is the evidence in the photograph that a mutation has occurred? (*AEB*)

A

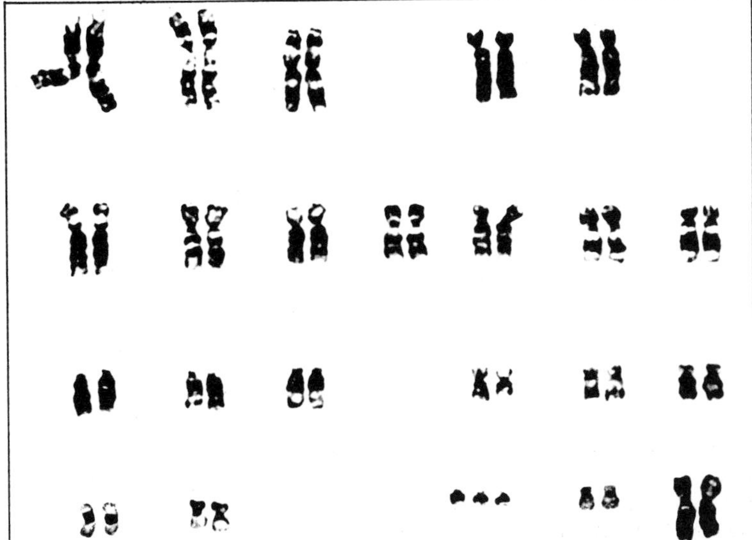

B

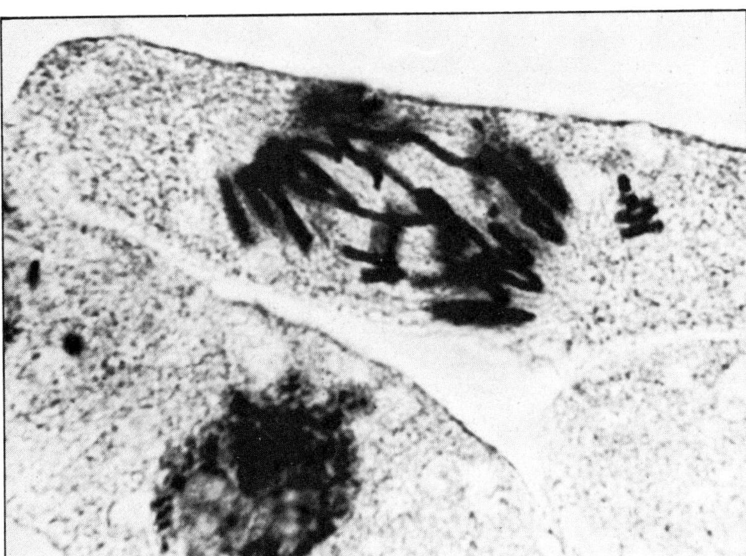

Figure 35.4 **A**, Set of human chromosomes in which a mutation has occurred. **B**, A cell at mitosis in which a mutation has occurred. (*Philip Harris Biological Ltd*)

3 In a certain plant, the flower petals are normally purple. Two recessive mutations have occurred in separate plants and have been found to be on different chromosomes. Mutation 1 (m_1) gives blue petals when homozygous (m_1m_1). Mutation 2 (m_2) gives red petals when homozygous (m_2m_2). Biochemists working on the synthesis of flower pigments in this species have already described the following pathway:

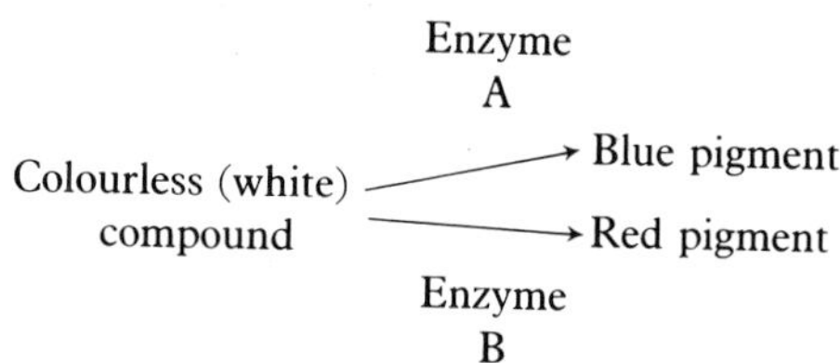

(a) Which homozygous mutant must be deficient in enzyme A activity?
(b) A plant has a genotype $M_1m_1M_2m_2$
  (i) What would its phenotype be?
  (ii) If the plant is self-pollinated, show, by means of a full genetic explanation, what colours of progeny are expected, and in what proportions?
(c) Why are these mutations recessive? *(CL)*

4 The sex chromosome constitution of human males is usually **XY**, but some individuals are abnormal in this respect. The data given below refer to three samples:
A Random samples of males.
B Mentally subnormal males confined to a state hospital under conditions of special security owing to persistent violent behaviour, and
C Males from the same hospital in a wing for patients suffering from various psychoses, some of whom were also mentally subnormal.

Sample	**Number in sample**	**Chromosome abnormality and incidence**			
		XYY	**XXY**	**XXYY**	**Others**
A	2000	1	0	0	0
B	197	7	1	1	3
C	314	9	2	1	4

Comment on these findings and discuss their significance. *(CCJE)*

5 The following are two examples of spelling errors, the first in a newspaper report of a speech delivered by the mayor of a certain industrial city (which will remain nameless), the second in a letter sent by a small boy at a boarding school to his parents:

IN CONSIDERING THE FUTURE OF THIS CITY, ONE MUST REGARD IT AS A HOLE

ON SUNDAY WE HAD ROAST BEEF FOR LUNCH AND THE HEADMASTER'S WIFE CALVED.

These errors can be taken as analogies to illustrate two types of gene mutation. Using hypothetical, or actual, examples, explain precisely the nature of each type of mutation. (Describe the chemical structure of genes in sufficient detail to make your answer clear.)

6 Cytochrome **c** is essential to most organisms since it takes part in aerobic respiration. In vertebrates it consists of a polypeptide chain of 104 amino acids which surrounds, and is attached to, a single haem group.

Cytochrome **c** is an ancient protein and its amino acid sequence has been established for at least forty different species, ranging from fungi to humans. The following data show the sequences of the first thirteen amino acids in the cytochrome c of selected vertebrates:

Human	gly-asp-val-glu-lys-gly-lys-lys-ile-phe-ile-met-lys
Tuna fish	gly-asp-val-ala-lys-gly-lys-lys-thr-phe-val-glu-lys
Rhesus monkey	gly-asp-val-glu-lys-gly-lys-lys-ile-phe-ile-met-lys
Chicken	gly-asp-ile-glu-lys-gly-lys-lys-ile-phe-val-glu-lys
Horse	gly-asp-val-glu-lys-gly-lys-lys-ile-phe-val-glu-lys

Each amino acid is coded for by three successive bases (= codon) in the segment of the DNA which codes for the cytochrome protein. The change from one amino acid to another in evolution could be due to changes in one, two, or all three bases in the relevant triplet.

TUT Phe	TCT Ser	TAT Tyr	TGT Cys
TTC Phe	TCC Ser	TAC Tyr	TGT Cys
TTA Leu	TCA Ser	TAA Stop	TGA Stop
TTG Leu	TCG Ser	TAG Stop	TGG Try
CTT Leu	CCT Pro	CAT His	CGT Arg
CTC Leu	CCC Pro	CAC His	CGC Arg
CTA Leu	CCA Pro	CAA Glu	CGA Arg
CTG Leu	CCG Pro	CAG Glu	CGG Arg
ATU Ile	ACT Thr	AAT Asn	AGT Ser
ATC Ile	ACC Thr	AAC Asn	AGC Ser
ATA Ile	ACA Thr	AAA Lys	AGA Arg
ATG Met	ACG Thr	AAG Lys	AGG Arg
GTT Val	GCT Ala	GAT Asp	GGT Gly
GTC Val	GCC Ala	GAC Asp	GGC Gly
GTA Val	GCA Ala	GAA Glu	GGA Gly
GTG Val	GCG Ala	GAG Glu	GGG Gly

Table 35.1 The genetic code for DNA.

(a) Use Table 35.1 to find the minimum mumber of mutations which would be required in each of the animals if their sequences were to be changed to that of the human.
(b) Discuss *in detail* the results which you obtain.
(c) Suggest the mechanisms by which the mutations could occur.
(d) Speculate on the reasons for the constancy of amino acids at some positions in the protein and their variability at others.

7 Tongue-rolling (the ability to roll the tongue longitudinally into a U-shape) is caused by a dominant allele. Tongue-rollers are either homozygous for this allele, or heterozygous. Non-rollers are homozygous recessive.

In a survey carried out in Baltimore it was found that out of 5000 people, 3200 could roll their tongues, where 1800 could not.

(a) What percentage of persons in the Baltimore sample are homozygous recessive for tongue-rolling?
(b) Calculate the frequency of the recessive allele in the population. In other words, what proportion of the alleles for the tongue-rolling trait in the population of Baltimore are recessive?
(c) Calculate the frequency of the dominant allele in the population.
(d) What percentage of persons in the Baltimore sample are homozygous dominant for tongue-rolling?
(e) What percentage of persons are heterozygous for tongue-rolling?
(f) What would you expect the answers to questions (a)–(e) to be in the next generation?
(g) What factor or factors might cause you to put forward a different answer to question (f)?
(h) What is the relevance of all this to the mechanism of evolution? (*BSCS modified*)

8 Phenylketonuria (PKU) is a disease which may result in deterioration of mental ability and ultimately death. It is determined by a single pair of autosomal alleles in which normal is dominant to PKU.

(a) If the incidence of PKU in the population was one in every 10 000 people, what proportion of people are carriers of the disease? (Assume that the population is in equilibrium with respect to these alleles.) Show details of your calculations.
(b) If the incidence of mutation to the recessive allele was 1 mutation per 10^4 cells, would this markedly affect the frequency of the PKU gene in the population over a period of time? Explain.

(*continued overleaf*)

(c) Would complete selection against homozygous PKU markedly affect the frequency of this gene in the population? Explain.
(d) It has been suggested that individuals exhibiting the PKU condition should not be permitted to reproduce. If all affected individuals in the population were sterilised, give three ways in which more affected individuals could appear in subsequent generations. *(SA)*

9 A farmer bought a herd of 600 sheep, taken from a freely breeding population, and later found that 150 of the animals had an economically undesirable feature, crinkly hair, caused by the recessive gene **cr**.
(a) What is the frequency of the undesirable gene in the herd?
(b) What proportion of the herd is likely to be heterozygous?
The owner then separates all those animals showing crinkly hair, and sends them for slaughter. He allows the remaining animals to breed freely.
(c) What proportion of the next generation of lambs would be expected to show crinkly hair? (From D. Harrison, *Problems in Genetics*, Addison-Wesley, 1970)

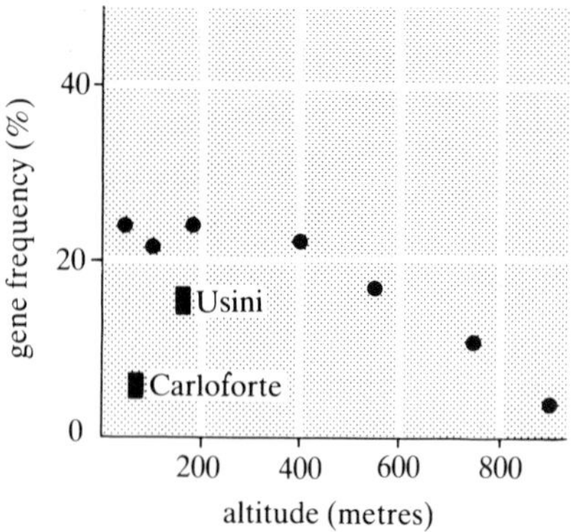

Figure 35.5 Diagram showing the frequency of the thalasaemia gene at different altitudes in Sardinia.

10 Thalassaemia is a disease similar to sickle-cell anaemia in which persons homozygous for a recessive allele show a severe, and often lethal, effect.

Figure 35.5 illustrates the correlation between altitude and the gene frequency for thalassaemia in a group of villages in Sardinia. Each dot shows the average gene frequency for thalassaemia in these villages at the altitudes indicated.

The gene frequencies for the towns of Carloforte (altitude 70 m) and Usini (altitude 180 m) are indicated in the same diagram by black rectangles. Usini is a small village in which the local dialect shows definite influences of the Catalon language (of Spanish origin). Carloforte was only founded in 1700 by fishermen from Genoa (also of Spanish origin).

In Sardinia malaria is endemic at low coastal altitudes.
(a) Why might the gene frequency of thalassaemia be so high in villages (other than Carloforte and Usini) below 800 m?
(b) Suggest explanations for the low gene frequency of thalassaemia in Carloforte and Usini. *(SA)*

11 In populations of white clover, allele **Ac** controls the production of a cyanide-forming substrate while allele **Li** controls the formation of an enzyme releasing the cyanide. The recessive alleles **ac** and **li** indicate that either substrate or enzyme is lacking.

Clover that contains both dominant alleles gives off cyanide when the leaves are crushed and may also evolve cyanide spontaneously at low temperatures.

Individuals which include **Ac** but not **Li** in their genotypes give off cyanide slowly when the leaves are crushed. Where **Ac** is not present in the genotype no cyanide can be evolved on crushing.
(a) From the above information suggest the likely genotypes of plants found (i) in a low-altitude field grazed by cattle, (ii) in a hedgerow verge seldom grazed and (iii) from the highest part of a mountain where the species can survive.
(b) Explain how natural selection would tend to retain a mixture of genotypes within the species as a whole. *(AEB)*

12 Pheasants were introduced on to two islands, one a hundred square miles in area and the other two square miles in area. Population counts gave the following results:

	Large Island		**Small Island**	
	Spring	Autumn	Spring	Autumn
1938	30	100	30	68
1939	81	426	59	299
1940	282	844	101	307
1941	705	1540	21	30
1942	1325	1898	18	24
1943	1129	1402	12	17
1944	1037	1463	6	7
1945	1089	1377	—	—

Comment on these figures. *(CCJE)*

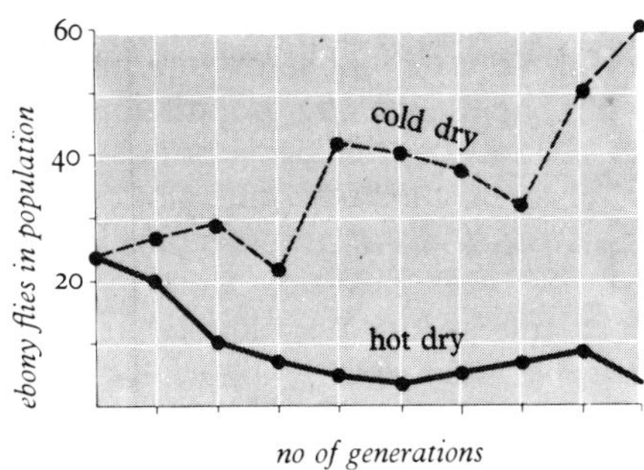

Figure 35.6 Graph showing the proportion of ebony flies in two populations of *Drosophila* kept under different temperature conditions.

13 Two populations of *Drosophila* initially containing an equal number of wild type and of individuals having the gene ebony (dark body colour) were kept in two boxes and under different conditions of temperature.

The graph shown in Figure 35.6 shows the changes with time of the relative proportions of ebony flies. Comment on these results. *(N.S.W. modified)*

14 Three populations of birds **A**, **B**, and **C**, live separately on three isolated oceanic islands. The birds all eat both insects and nectar, but have slightly different beaks and plumage as shown in Figure 35.7. The islands are swept throughout the year by strong prevailing winds from the north-west as shown in the figure.

Populations **A** and **B** can interbreed and produce fertile offspring. Population **B** can mate with population **C**, but the young are sterile. Matings do not occur at all, even under laboratory conditions, between populations **A** and **C**.

From your knowledge of the way evolution works, formulate an hypothesis to explain how successful breeding occurs between **A** and **B**, but not between **A** and **C**, or **B** and **C**. *(NSW)*

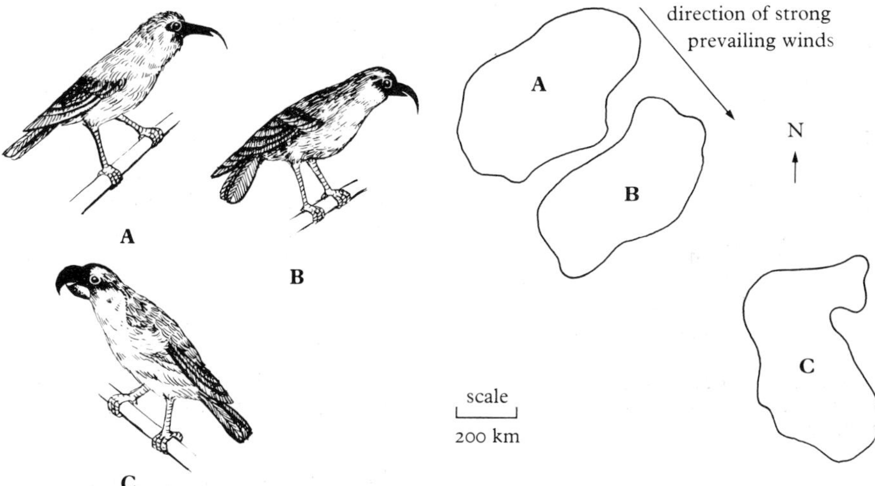

Figure 35.7 The birds **A**, **B**, and **C** which live on the three oceanic islands.

15 A species may be defined as a group of individuals, recognizably different from other species, which are able to breed amongst themselves, but not with individuals of another species. Sub-species are groups within a species, recognizably different from one another, but capable of interbreeding.

In Australia four species of the rosella parrot (*Platycercus*) are distributed as shown in Figure 35.8. The four species differ in the following respects:

P. icterotis: red head, yellow cheeks, underparts red.
P. eximus: red head, white and blue cheeks, red breast, bright-yellow belly.
P. adscitus: pale yellow head, white and blue cheeks, underparts pale blue.
P. venustus: black head, white and blue cheeks, pale yellow underparts.

Within each of the four species there is variation from one locality to another. In some cases the variations are sufficiently clear-cut for the variants to be regarded as sub-species.

Discuss how the situation described above may have arisen. What difficulties do you think are involved in trying to define the terms species and sub-species?

Figure 35.8 Distribution of the four species of rosella parrots in Australia.

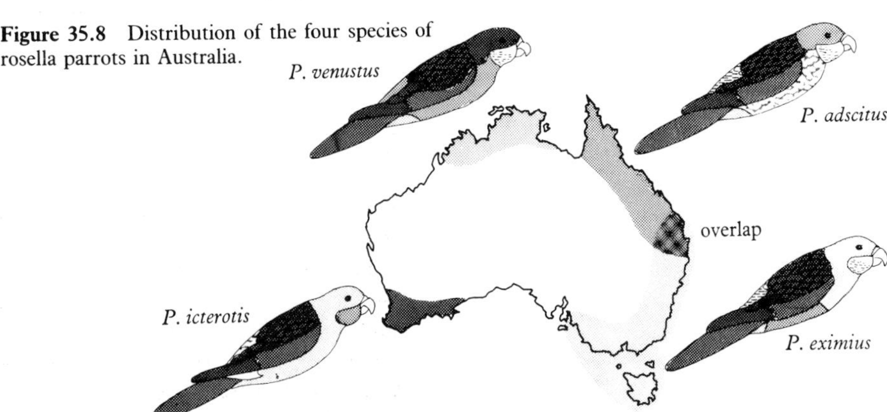

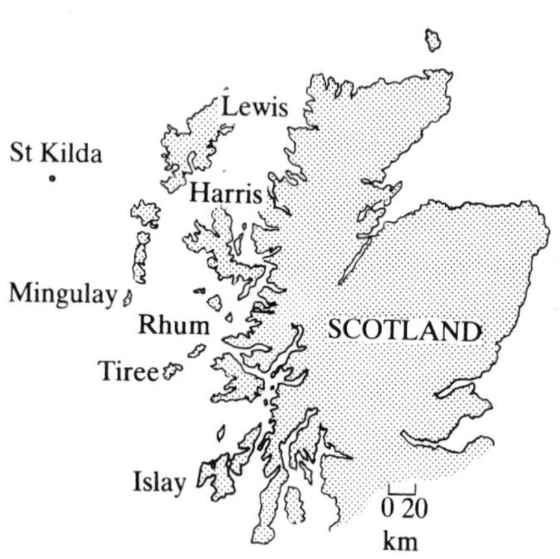

Figure 35.9 Islands off the west coast of Scotland.

16 The following data concern the distribution and characteristics of types of Fieldmice (*Apodemus*) on islands off the West Coast of Scotland (*after* Berry, 1969). The geographical positions of the islands is shown in Figure 35.9.

Name	**Location**	**Body length** (mm)	**Dorsal colour**
Apodemus hebridensis hebridensis	Lewis	96	Wood brown
Apodemus hebridensis nesticus	Mingulay	98	Pale brown
Apodemus hebridensis hamiltoni	Rhum	104	Pale brown
Apodemus hebridensis tirae	Tiree	102	Rufous
Apodemus hebridensis tural	Islay	94	Dark rufous
Apodemus hirtensis hirtensis	St Kilda	111	Pepper

(a) Using the data above as the basis for your answer, describe how the process of speciation is thought to occur.
(b) It is known that there are different degrees of interfertility between the races of fieldmice. What would you predict as the possible long term outcome of this varying degree of inter-fertility? *(O & C)*

17 The following table gives figures for breeding success in Arctic terns. Comment on the factors which seem to be important in controlling the production of young terns.

	Age of parents in years			
	3	4–5	6–8	*over* 8
1966–7				
No of pairs of birds	28	55	50	42
No. of eggs laid	41	86	93	65
% eggs hatched	31	38	48	53
% hatched eggs becoming fledglings	54	66	63	70
1968				
No. of pairs of birds	1	27	29	54
No. of eggs laid	1	36	45	80
% eggs hatched	0	41	31	27
% hatched eggs becoming fledglings	0	40	21	63

(OCJE)

18 In a woodland population of Great Tits the number of recaptures per brood after fledging has been used as a measure of survival rate among birds belonging to broods of different size.

Brood size	2	3	4	5	6	7	8
Recaptures per brood	0.20	0.51	0.60	0.75	0.82	0.87	0.83

Brood size	9	10	11	12	13	14
Recaptures per brood	0.86	0.91	0.83	0.98	0.80	0.72

The mean clutch size (number of eggs laid) is 8.6 and the mean brood size at fledging is 4.8 for all nests and 7.2 for unpredated nests. Comment on these figures. *(OCJE)*

Figure 35.10 Percentage of animals of different kinds surviving to a given age. The arrows indicate the time of first reproduction.

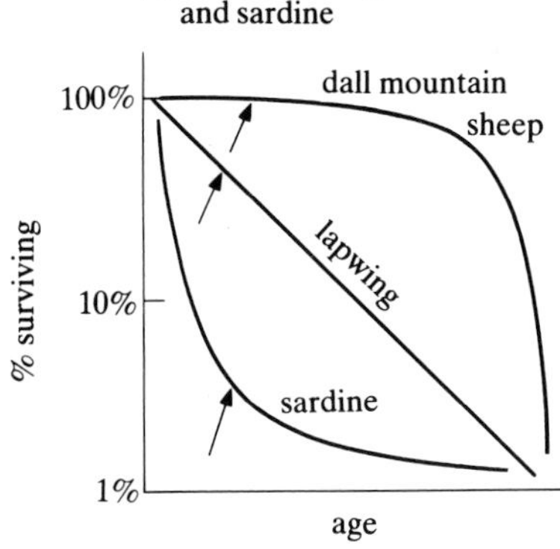

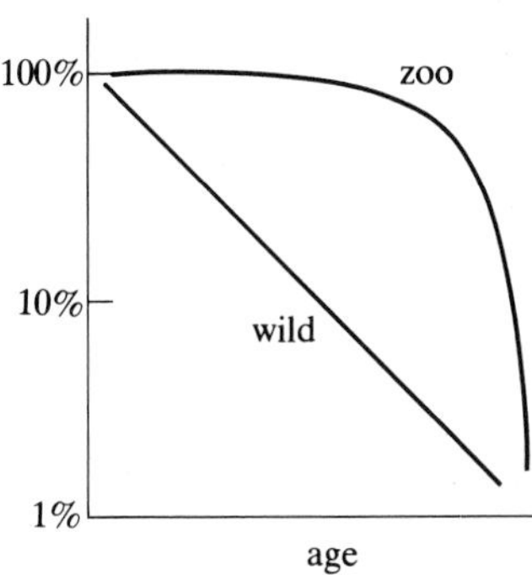

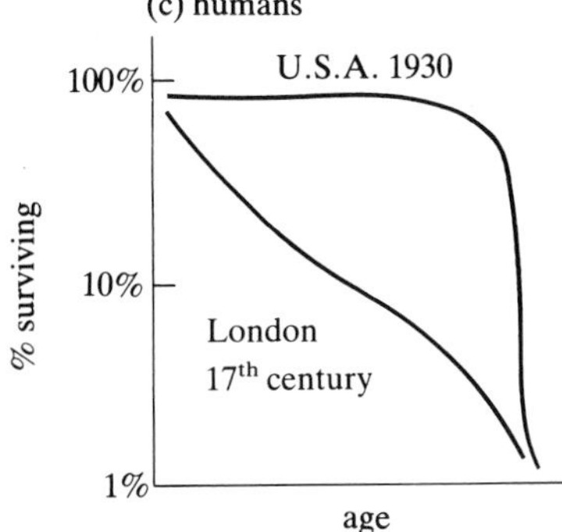

19 Figure 35.10 shows (a) the percentage of animals of different kinds surviving to a given age (the arrow indicates time of first reproduction); (b) shows the percentage of Night Herons surviving to a given age in the wild and in London Zoo; (c) shows the percentage of human beings surviving to a given age at two different periods of history. Comment on (b) and (c) in the light of the variation shown in (a). *(OCJE)*

20 Discuss the biological basis and implications of the newspaper report shown in Figure 35.11.

Weirdo, the rooster that kills cats

By IAN BALL in New York

A 17-YEAR-OLD Californian boy who has developed a flock of super-hens led by a 22lb rooster, named Weirdo, said yesterday he has been besieged with offers since stories about Weirdo gained international circulation.

Grant Sullens, of West Point, California, has received offers from governments, companies, chicken breeders and cockfight organisers.

He is hoping to increase his flock to more than 300 by the autumn so he can offer his breed of heavyweight hens to the world. By crossing and re-crossing the bigger members of various breeds he produced hens that grew rapidly, could survive the cold nights of the Sierra Mountains and "laid eggs like hell."

The only problem is that the super-roosters are unusually aggressive. Weirdo is so big and rough that he has killed two cats, crippled a dog and ripped through a wire fence to attack and kill one of his progeny, an 18lb rooster.

Flock of 40

Grant's superbreed now numbers 40—hens and roosters produced by Weirdo, many of them almost as big as he is. "I was lucky," he says. "Hybrids aren't supposed to be able to reproduce—but Weirdo could."

The youth's chicken breeding began seven years ago when his father won a lorry-load of chickens in a dice game at a bar he used to own.

Grant began selling eggs, and all was going well until the first snows of the winter began to fall on the Sierras. He lost more than 100 hens and roosters.

"Then somebody told me that Rhode Island Reds could stand plenty of cold," he recalled. "I threw some in and out I came with grey ones that laid eggs like hell."

Five thousands chickens later he had Weirdo. "I named him Weirdo because what else could you call something like that?"

Grant now has to decide who will look after his superchickens while he is away at university studying business administration.

Figure 35.11 The newspaper report referred to in Question 20. (Reproduced by kind permission of the *Daily Telegraph*, London).

21 (a) Explain the difference between inbreeding and outbreeding.

(b) Comment on the statement that 'inbreeding often results in lessened vigour, reduced size, and diminished fecundity and ultimately in inability of the stock to survive'. (Sinnott, Dunn, and Dobzhansky, 1952)

(c) Do laws prohibiting marriages between brothers and sisters make biological sense?

22 Write a letter to Charles Darwin bringing him up to date on the theory of evolution. *(OCJE)*

23 A deer with a neck
That was longer by half
Than the rest of the family
(Try not to laugh)
By stretching and stretching
Became a giraffe,
Which nobody can deny

Discuss.

36 Some Major Steps in Evolution

Background Summary

1 Pasteur, in his famous flask experiment, disproved, once and for all, the **theory of spontaneous generation**.

2 The **heterotroph theory** of the origin of life proposes that the first organisms to exist were heterotrophic. This is considered more likely than that the first organisms were autotrophs.

3 It is thought that the first step in the formation of living organisms was the synthesis of organic molecules from simple gases. This has been repeated in the laboratory under primitive earth conditions.

4 **Coacervates** give us a clue as to how the first organisms may have been formed.

5 Circumstantial evidence suggests that, at first, energy was obtained **anaerobically**. Present knowledge of cell structure and function provides a possible insight into how the first organisms may have fed and reproduced.

6 Further evidence suggests that in the course of time autotrophic nutrition developed, releasing oxygen into the atmosphere and paving the way to the development of **aerobic respiration**.

7 A transition from a prokaryotic to a eukaryotic cell structure may have occurred as a result of **endosymbiosis**.

8 The present day **flagellates**, a group of primitive protists, provide some evidence as to how the split into the animal and plant kingdoms may have occurred.

9 There are various theories as to how **multicellularity** may have arisen. In general multicellular organisms may have arisen by failure of cells to separate after cell division, or from a colonial or multinucleate intermediate.

10 It is possible that certain present-day animals may have evolved from sexually mature larvae of ancestral forms. The gaining of sexual maturity by a larva (**neoteny**) is known to occur in certain animals.

11 A major development in the evolution of both animals and plants has been the exploitation of dry land. For this to take place various anatomical and physiological changes were necessary.

12 Evolutionary trends in animals include the development of **triplobastic organisation**, **body cavities** (coelomic and/or haemocoelic) and **metameric segmentation**.

13 On grounds of comparative anatomy, embryology and biochemistry, the animal kingdom can be divided into the **annelid-mollusc-arthropod stock** and the **echinoderm-chordate stock**.

14 On the plant side, an early trend led to the separation of **reproductive** and **somatic cells**, and a later trend to the distinction between **sporophyte** and **gametophyte**. The great development of the sporophyte in flowering plants, with suppression of the gametophyte, is associated with adaptation to life on land.

15 In both animals and plants there have been trends towards larger size. This has sometimes been carried to excess as in the case of the dinosaurs the reason for whose demise is still hotly debated.

16 The evolution of the human species has been marked by the development of three salient features: an increased **mental ability**, manipulative **hands**, and **speech**. Humans have now entered upon a new phase of evolution, which may be called **psycho-social evolution**.

17 The evolutionary changes summarised above may have occurred gradually (**phyletic gradualism**) or in sudden jumps (**punctuated equilibrium**).

Investigation 36.1
The most primitive living organism?

One way of gaining an insight into what the earliest organisms may have been like is to look at the simplest organisms living to-day. These include the protists. Can you think of any others? In doing this one must bear in mind that, although it is tempting to regard these organisms as primitive, they are, themselves, the products of many millions of years of evolution and may be markedly different from their ancestors.

Procedure

Protists are a large group of microscopic organisms. Most biologists regard them as unicellular, i.e. single cells; however, some biologists prefer to think of them as acellular, i.e. organisms where the body is not subdivided into cells. The argument is academic.

1 Examine the following protists: *Paramecium* (*see* Investigation 3.3, page 27), *Euglena*, *Chlamydomonas*, *Vorticella* and *Amoeba* (*see* Investigation 3.4, *see* page 28). In what respects do they differ structurally? How does each one move and feed?

2 Which do you think is the most primitive of these five protists, and why?

3 If available, examine other protists from mixed cultures. Do any strike you as being more primitive than the five which you have examined in detail?

Requirements
Microscope
Slides and coverslips
Filter paper
Lens paper
Mounted needle

Vaseline
Noland's solution
Methyl green in ethanoic acid
Acetocarmine
Methyl cellulose
Stained yeast suspension (*see* page 18)
Silver nitrate solution (2 per cent aqueous)
Canada balsam

Euglena
Chlamydomonas
Vorticella
Amoeba
Paramecium

For Consideration

(1) What do you regard as the most important criteria to take into account in deciding which are the most primitive protists?
(2) From your knowledge of protists in general, do you think there are more primitive ones than those looked at here?
(3) Structurally more simple than the protists studied here are bacteria and viruses. Would you regard these latter as the most primitive living organisms?
(4) Critically evaluate the meaning of the word 'primitive'.

Investigation 36.2 Evolution of the multicellular state

The development of multicellularity was an important step in the evolution of both animals and plants. How did it arise? As in the previous investigation we may seek an answer to this question by looking at present-day forms. We can look, for example, at unicellular organisms to see if there is any tendency for them to become multinucleate or multicellular. Three common protists – *Microstomum*, *Opalina*, and *Pleurococcus* – show interesting tendencies which may shed light on this question. However, remember that when it comes to interpreting evolutionary history on the basis of modern forms, we can *never* say what actually happened; at best, we can only say what *may* have happened.

Procedure

1 Examine live specimens of the unicellular ciliate *Microstomum* under a microscope. How does it compare in size with other protists?

Irrigate the slide with methyl green in ethanoic acid. This stains the nucleus. How would you describe the shape of the nucleus? Suggest explanations for its shape.

2 Examine the unicellular flagellate *Opalina* under a microscope. This lives in the rectum of the frog and toad. It may be seen by removing the contents of the rectum of a fresh-killed host onto a slide in a drop of amphibian Ringer's solution. Irrigate with methyl green in ethanoic acid, or acetocarmine, to see the nuclei.

Examine a prepared slide of *Opalina*, noting the numerous nuclei.

What light does the nuclear condition shed on the question of multicellularity?

3 *Pleurococcus* is a simple green protist, found commonly on damp tree trunks, etc. Examine *Pleurococcus* under the microscope. Note that it occurs as a single cell, or as small groups of cells. What is the structural relationship between the cells where they occur in groups, i.e. are they stuck together or intimately united? What is the maximum number of cells in a group? Do the cells of a given group remain together permanently or do they tend to separate? How do you think the group condition arises?

4 Compare *Pleurococcus* with (a) the

Requirements
Microscope
Slides and coverslips

Methyl green in acetic acid
Acetocarmine
Amphibian Ringer's solution

Microstomum
Contents of rectum of frog or toad (for *Opalina*)
Pleurococcus
Chlorella
Spirogyra, *Chaetophora* and/or *Ulva*
Volvox and other colonial algae
Permanent slides of the above organisms

permanently unicellular organism *Chlorella*, (b) permanently multicellular algae such as *Spirogyra* (*see* Investigation 2.3, page 00), *Chaetophora*, and sea lettuce *Ulva*, and (c) colonial organisms such as *Volvox* and its less elaborate relatives *Gonium*, *Pandorina*, and *Eudorina*. The cells in these colonial forms are similar to *Chlamydomonas* (*see* Investigation 3.4, page 28).

Examine the above organisms alive under low and high powers.

For Consideration

(1) From your observations in this investigation summarise the possible ways the multicellular state may have arisen.
(2) Why is it unlikely that *Opalina*, itself, represents the ancestor of multicellular animals?
(3) There is a group of free-living flatworms called acoels whose cell membranes are incompletely formed. Find out as much as you can about acoels. Do you think they provide any clues as to how multicellular animals may have arisen?

Investigation 36.3
Dissection of the earthworm

Most of the features of a typical invertebrate can be seen by dissecting the earthworm. As a subject for dissection this animal has the added advantage of being soft-bodied and reasonably large. The organs are easily exposed with the minimum of cutting.

Procedure

1 Examine the external features of the earthworm, noting in particular those which show metameric segmentation, e.g. the constrictions (rings) between successive segments, and the chaetae (bristles). How many chaetae are there in each segment?

Note also the head, much reduced in keeping with the earthworm's burrowing habit, and the clitellum (saddle) which plays an important part in reproduction.

Be sure you can distinguish between the dorsal and ventral sides of the body: the dorsal side is darker and more rounded than the ventral side.

2 Pin the animal, ventral surface downwards, to the floor of a dissecting dish: put one pin through the body well posterior to the clitellum and one through the extreme anterior end.

3 Make an incision on the mid-dorsal side of the worm behind the clitellum. (Figure 36.1). With small scissors cut through the body wall along the mid-dorsal line to the extreme anterior end. Be careful not to dig down too deeply or you will damage underlying structures. If you pierce the wall of the intestine it will spoil your dissection.

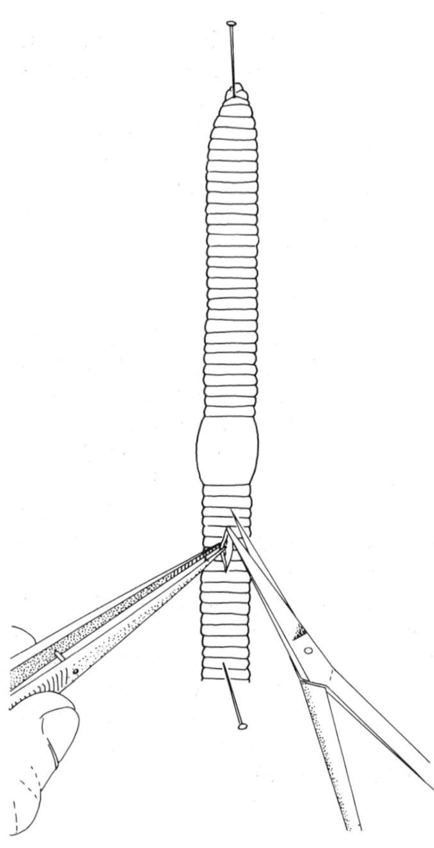

Figure 36.1 Dissection of the earthworm: making the first incision. (*After* H. G. Q. Rowett, *Dissection Guides, 5 Invertebrates*, John Murray 1953)

4 Cut through the septa between adjacent segments; deflect the body wall and pin it out on either side, starting at the anterior end and working backwards (Figure 36.2).

Cover your dissection with water: the organs will float up towards you and be easier to see.

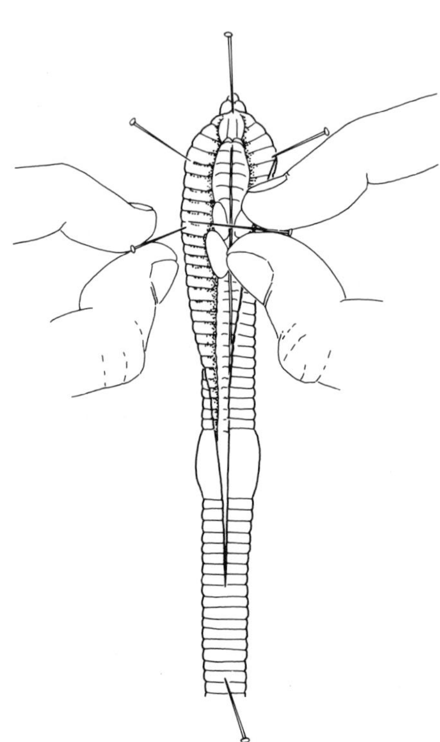

Figure 36.2 Dissection of the earthworm: pinning back the body wall. (*After* H. G. Q. Rowett, *Dissection Guides, 5 Invertebrates*, John Murray, 1953)

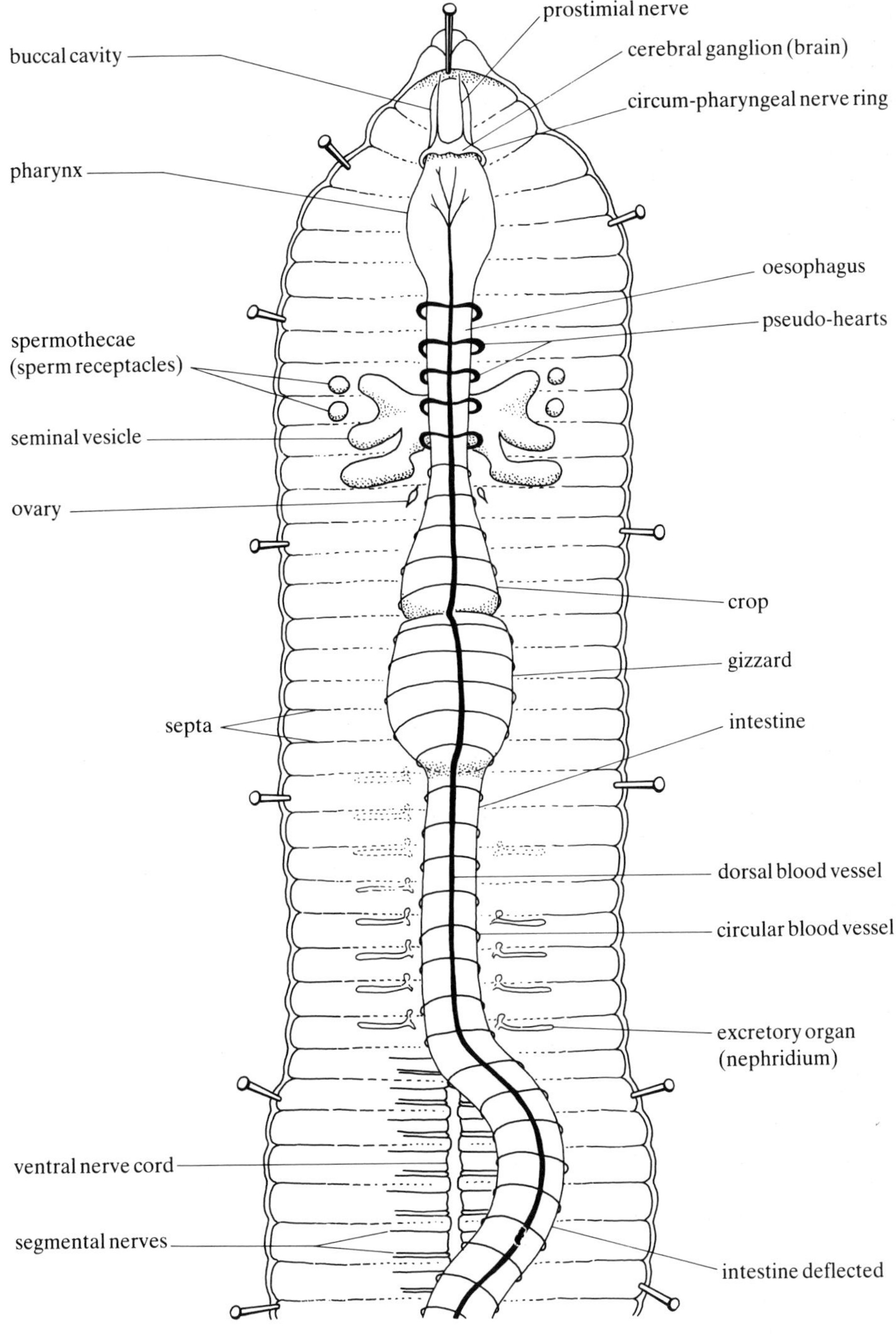

Figure 36.3 General dissection of the earthworm.

Requirements
Dissecting dish
Dissecting instruments
Binocular microscope or hand lens
Slide and coverslip

Freshly-killed earthworm

5 Identify the various structures shown in Figure 36.3. Notice the different regions of the gut, the dorsal blood vessel and pseudo-hearts, and the seminal vesicles and spermothecae.

Notice that the earthworm is as segmented internally as it is externally. Notice the septa between successive segments (corresponding to the external rings), and the excretory organs (nephridia), one pair in almost every segment.

6 Deflect the intestine to one side to reveal the ventral nerve cord beneath it. The nerve cord is swollen in each segment to form a segmental ganglion from which three pairs of segmental nerves pass outwards to the muscular body wall. The second and third segmental nerves are very close to one another. You will need a hand lens, or better still a binocular microscope, to see them clearly.

7 With a blunt seeker, push the pharynx to one side and locate the circum-pharyngeal nerve ring which runs from the cerebral ganglion to the first segmental ganglion (the sub-pharyngeal gangion) immediately beneath the pharynx. Note that the ventral nerve cord extends back from this ganglion.

8 Cut out a nephridium and mount it on a slide in a drop of water. Put on a coverslip and observe it under the microscope. The nephridium consists of a differentiated, twisted tube which runs from the body cavity to the exterior. You may see cilia beating in part of the tube.

For consideration

(1) The earthworm is described as metamerically segmented. What does this mean and to what extent is it shown by the earthworm's internal anatomy?
(2) The earthworm is also described as bilaterally symmetrical. What does this mean? Which structures in its body are bilaterally symmetrical and which structures, if any, are not?
(3) The earthworm's body cavity is called a coelom. What is a coelom and what are its functions in the earthworm?
(4) In what fundamental respects does the anatomy of the earthworm differ from that of a chordate such as *Amphioxus* (*see* page 343).

Investigation 36.4
Dissection of the cockroach

The cockroach demonstrates the main features not only of insects but also of the phylum to which it belongs, namely arthropods. It is slightly more difficult to dissect than the earthworm because, like all arthropods, it is covered by a hard cuticle.

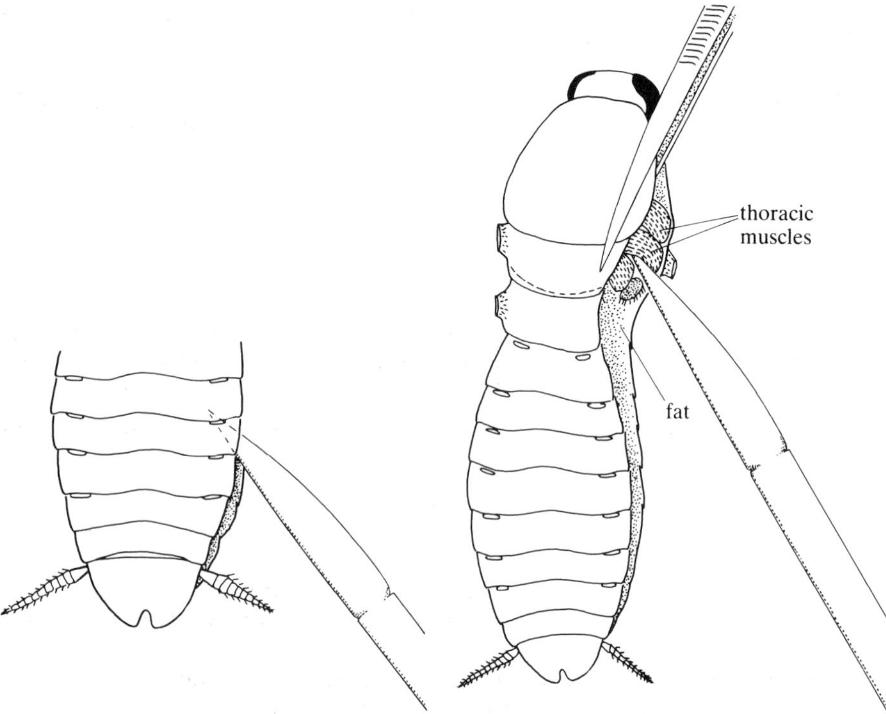

Figure 36.4 Dissection of the cockroach: separating the dorsal part of the cuticle from the lower part. (*After* H.G.Q. Rowett, *Dissection Guides, 5 Invertebrates*, John Murray, 1953.)

Figure 36.5 Dissection of the cockroach: cutting the flight muscles in the throax. (*After* H.G.Q. Rowett, *Dissection Guides, 5 Invertebrates*, John Murray, 1953.)

Procedure

1 You will be provided with a freshly-killed specimen. Examine the external features, noting in particular those features which are common to insects generally: head with compound eyes, antennae (feelers) and mouth parts; thorax with 3 pairs of legs and 2 pairs of wings; abdomen with anal cerci and external genitalia at the posterior end.

2 Remove the wings and with pins fix the cockroach, dorsal side uppermost, to the floor of a dissecting dish. Don't push the pins through the animal itself but angle them in such a way that they keep the body steady.

3 Starting at the posterior end of the abdomen, carefully cut through the membrane between the upper and lower parts of the cuticle (Figure 36.4) The upper (i.e. dorsal) part of the cuticle is called the tergum. Continue to cut forward as far as the anterior end of the thorax.

4 Cut through the dorso-ventral flight muscles in the thorax: they run from the tergum to the ventral part of the cuticle (Figure 36.5)

5 With a large scalpel blade deflect the whole of the tergum to one side. The heart, pericardium and alary muscles should come away with the tergum and be visible on its underside.

6 The abdomen contains a lot of fat. Carefully remove the fat so as to expose the gut and other organs in the body

Figure 36.6 (*below*) General dissection of the cockroach. (*After* H.G.Q. Rowett, *Dissection Guides, 5 Invertebrates*, John Murray, 1953.)

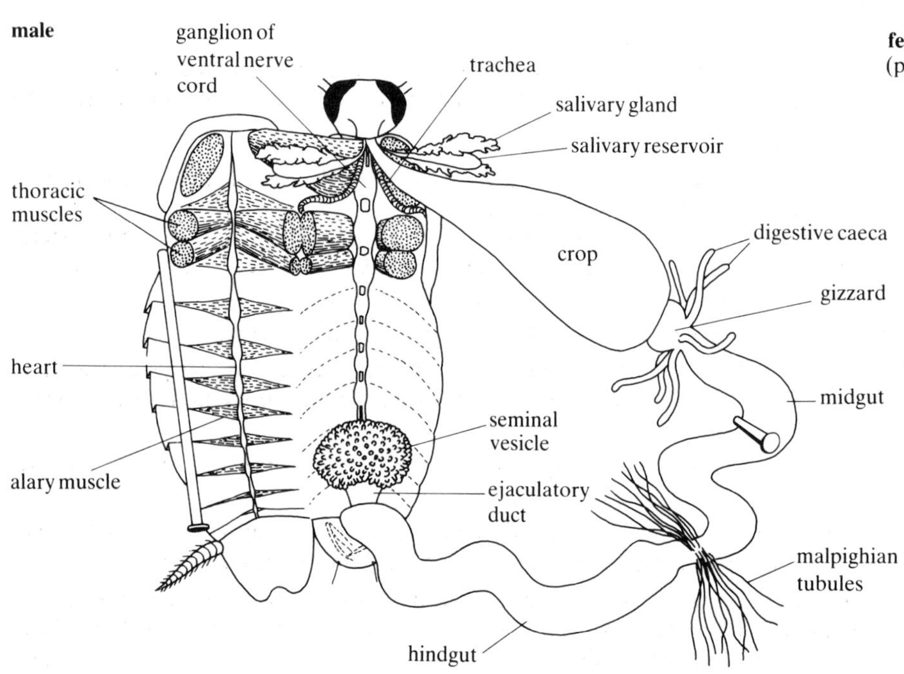

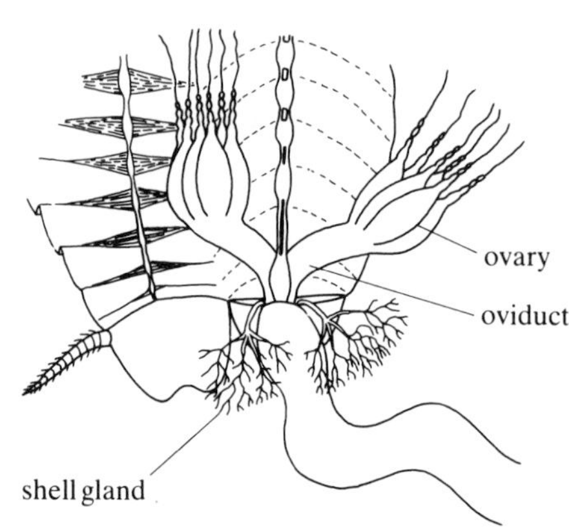

Figure 36.4 to 36.6 after H.G.Q. Rowett *Dissection Guides, 5 invertebrates*, John Murray 1953.

Requirements
Dissecting dish
Dissecting instruments
Pins
Binocular microscope or hand lens

Freshly-killed cockroach

cavity. Cover your dissection with water so that the organs float up towards you.

7 Unravel the gut and deflect it to one side so as to reveal the ventral nerve cord beneath.

8 Do such further dissection as is required to expose salivary glands at the anterior end and genital organs at the posterior end.

9 Your dissection should now look like Figure 36.6. Identify all the structures shown in the drawing.

For consideration

(1) Make a table comparing the main structural features of the cockroach with those of the earthworm. To what extent can the differences between them be related to their different ways of life?

(2) The cockroach's body cavity is a haemocoel. What is a haemocoel, how does it arise and what functions does it perform?

(3) In what respects is metameric segmentation shown *less* well by the cockroach than by the earthworm?

Questions and Problems

1 In 1953 Stanley Miller succeeded in synthesising certain biologically important compounds under primitive earth conditions. A certain newspaper headlined this achievement as '*Life created in a test tube*'. Write a letter putting the record straight.

2 Summarise the main steps in the heterotroph hypothesis for the origin of life, considering briefly the evidence for each of its propositions.

3 'Surely plants evolved before animals–they're so much simpler.' Discuss.

4 Giving due attention to caution, discuss the possible evolutionary significance of the following:
(a) The bodies of certain flatworms are incompletely cellularised.
(b) The larva of a certain amphibian becomes sexually mature and does not normally undergo metamorphosis into the adult.
(c) Flagellated collar cells are found in both the protists and the sponges.
(d) In flowering plants it is difficult to identify a gametophyte.

5 Why is it sometimes difficult to classify an organism as plant or animal? Use named examples to illustrate your answer wherever possible. *(O and C)*

6 Discuss the advantages to an animal of
(a) being triploblastic rather than diploblastic,
(b) having a coelomic body cavity,
(c) being metamerically segmented,
(d) possessing a thick cuticle.

7 Discuss the advantages to a plant of
a) having differentiated cells, b) undergoing sexual as well as asexual reproduction,
c) producing pollen rather than motile gametes, d) possessing a thick cuticle. *(CCJE)*

8 'The bigger the better.' Discuss.

9 Find out the name of one species of animal or plant which has become extinct during recorded history. What were, or might have been, the causes of its extinction?

Can you think of any animals or plants which might, by now, have become extinct but for the direct or indirect intervention of humans? Why do you think they were heading for extinction, and how have they been saved?

10 Speculate on the possible causes of the extinction of the dinosaurs.

11 Summarise the structural and physiological changes required for an aquatic animal to colonise dry land. What changes would be necessary for a plant to achieve the same thing? *(CCJE)*

12 What do we mean when we say that one group of organisms is more *primitive* than another? Illustrate your answer with examples.

13 By what criteria can the success of a group of animals or plants be assessed? What factors have contributed to the success of *either* insects, *or* mammals, *or* humans?

14 'Dinosaurs became extinct when their great size changed from being an advantage to a disadvantage. Man has reached a comparable point: he is too clever by half, and faces the prospect of extinction'. Discuss. *(CCJE)*

37 Classification and Diversity of Organisms

Background Summary

1 The number of species of living organisms which have been discovered runs into millions, so a system of classification is essential. The science and practice of classification is known as **taxonomy**.

2 Organisms as a whole are divided into **kingdoms**, which are further divided into **phyla, classes, orders, families, genera** and **species**. This system is called the **taxonomic hierarchy**.

3 As one progresses down the hierarchy, the range of organisms within each group decreases and the similarities between them increase.

4 A **species**, the smallest group in the taxonomic hierarchy, is a group of organisms which have numerous detailed features in common and which do not normally breed with other species. A species may be subdivided into **subspecies** or **varieties** which are capable of interbreeding.

5 An organism's scientific name is composed of the name of the genus followed by the name of the species, e.g. *Homo sapiens*, *Lumbricus terrestris*. This is called the **binomial system.** Scientific names are essential where precise identification is required, e.g. in medicine and agriculture.

6 For identifying organisms, **keys** are used. The most widely used are dichotomous keys in which organisms are split into successive pairs of approximately equal-sized groups on the basis of clearly discernible characteristics.

7 Characteristics used for identification include external features, cell structure and chemical constitution.

8 Three main types of taxonomy are practised: **orthodox taxonomy**, which aims to produce evolutionary (i.e. natural) classifications; **numerical taxonomy**, which aims to produce phenetic classifications; and **cladistics** which is based on a consideration of ancestry particularly the points at which different groups have diverged from each other.

9 The old system of splitting living organisms into two kingdoms (animal and plant) has been superseded by the **five kingdom system**. The five kingdom system splits living organisms into the Monera, Protist, Fungus, Plant and Animal kingdoms. Viruses are not included since they are generally considered to be non-living.

10 The **Monera kingdom** contains prokaryotic organisms, viz. Eubacteria (formerly Bacteria) and Cyanobacteria (formerly blue-green algae).

11 There is some difference of opinion as to which organisms should be included in the **Protist kingdom**. It invariably contains all unicellular eukaryotes, but in some classifications it also contains certain multicellular eukaryotes.

12 The **Fungus kingdom** contains an assemblage of eukaryotic saprotrophs and parasites, many of which are extremely important commercially.

13 The **Plant kingdom** contains multicellular eukaryotes which are usually sedentary and feed by photosynthesis, and the **Animal kingdom** contains multicellular eukaryotes which are usually motile and feed heterotrophically.

Investigation 37.1
Construction of an identification key

The diversity of organisms is prodigious and it is therefore necessary for each species to be named and formally described. Once this has been done, methods must be devised to identify unknown species. Identification keys are often used by biologists to determine the name of a species.

Principles involved

To illustrate how an identification key can be constructed, consider the following example. Nine students have the following features.

Alan – dark hair, blue eyes
Ann – auburn hair, brown eyes
David – dark hair, brown eyes
Elizabeth – auburn hair, blue eyes
Jane – fair hair, hazel eyes
John – fair hair, brown eyes
Pamela – auburn hair, green eyes
Philip – fair hair, blue eyes
Susan – fair hair, blue eyes

They are distinguished by sex, hair colour and eye colour. They can be classified into sub-groups as shown below, by splitting them into two groups at each stage.

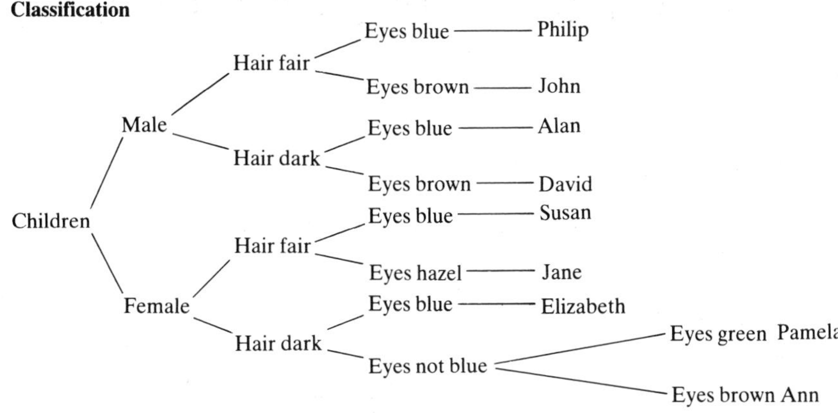

This diagram, known as a spider key, would enable a stranger to quickly determine the name of any student. However, in biology, the classification illustrated above is usually written down as a linear key. In this type of key there are two contrasting alternatives at each stage. Starting with the first pair of alternatives, you select one of the two statements as correct, and obey the instruction written down next to it (for example, go to 2). Then work your way down the page, choosing the appropriate statement in turn, until you reach the correct name for the individual you wish to identify.

Here is a linear key based on the classification of students above:

1.	Male	go to 2
	Female	go to 5
2.	Hair fair	go to 3
	Hair dark	go to 4
3.	Eyes blue	Philip
	Eyes brown	John
4.	Eyes blue	Alan
	Eyes brown	David
5.	Hair fair	go to 6
	Hair auburn	go to 7
6.	Eyes blue	Susan
	Eyes hazel	Jane
7.	Eyes blue	Elizabeth
	Eyes not blue	go to 8
8.	Eyes green	Pamela
	Eyes brown	Ann

Using the key above, determine the name of the brown-eyed boy with dark hair, and the blue-eyed girl with fair hair.

Exactly the same principles apply to the construction and use of keys for the identification of plants and animals. For instance, examine a flora, such as Clapham, Tutin and Warburg.

Construction of a key

1 With these principles in mind, write a dichotomous key to distinguish between eight different types of leaves which you have been given. Each leaf is identified by a letter. Using a *visible* characteristic, arrange the leaves in two groups of approximately the same size. Then, on the basis of a different character, divide each of these groups into two equal sub-groups, and so on. Express your classification as a spider key. Continue until each object is in a group of its own.

2 Now construct a linear key based on your classification. It must mention only characteristics which are easily observed. Use visible characters which you think are of biological importance. Try to avoid ambiguities. Instead of vague terms such as large and small, broad or narrow, use precise measurements such as length more than twice the breadth. Remember also that someone else may not judge hairiness or the various shades of green as you do.

3 Ask someone to check your key. Choose a specimen at random, cover its identifying letter, and see whether the specimen can be identified correctly, using only your key.

For consideration

(1) How much variation is there in the shapes and sizes of leaves on the *same* tree?

(2) To what extent can the following characteristics be modified by the environment (a) leaf area (b) the numbers of lobes or leaflets (c) leaf shininess (d) leaf hairiness (e) leaf shape?

(3) In view of your answer to (2), will your key distinguish between *any* two leaves taken from trees of different species? If not, modify your key to make it more generally useful.

Requirements
Eight leaves from different species – some simple, some compound – each labelled with a different letter.

Reference: A. R. Clapham, T. G. Tutin and E. F. Warburg, *Excursion Flora of the British Isles*, 3rd ed, CUP, 1981.

Investigation 37.2
Taxonomic hierarchy

Organisms are grouped together into sets, creating a hierarchy. Genera are grouped together into families, families into orders, orders into classes, classes into phyla (animals) or divisions (plants), and phyla or divisions into kingdoms.

It follows that, as one progresses *down* the hierarchy, the smaller the number of species belonging to each group and the more they have in common. Therefore a phylum may contain a large number of species, held together by certain fundamental features but at the same time displaying a wide range of variety. On the other hand, the different species in a genus may be so similar as to be indistinguishable except by an expert. In this exercise we shall look at the general truth of this statement.

Taxonomic categories	Taxa
Kingdom	Plantae
Phylum (division)	Tracheophyta
Class	Angiospermae
Order	Ranales
Family	Ranunculaceae
Genus	Ranunculus
Species	acris
Name	*Ranunculus acris* (common buttercup)

Table 37.1 How the common buttercup and its relatives fit into the classification of plants.

CLASSIFICATION OF A PLANT GROUP

Examine different species of a common plant growing in your part of the world. As an example, we can consider the genus *Ranunculus*, which includes the buttercup and its relatives. The way this group fits into the classification of plants is shown in Table 37.1.

1 Eleven species of *Ranunculus*, together with their common names, times of flowering, and habitats, are listed in Table 37.2. Examine specimens of some or all of these species, noting their similarities and differences. From your observations, what features cause them to be placed in the same genus? What are the differences which cause them to be placed in separate species?

2 *Ranunculus* belongs to the family Ranunculaceae. This family contains several other genera besides *Ranunculus*. These include:
Anemone, e.g. *A. nemorosa*: wood anemone
Caltha, e.g. *C. palustris*: marsh marigold*
Clematis e.g. *C. vitalba*: traveller's joy
Delphinium e.g. *D. ambiguum*: larkspur
Helleborus e.g. *H. foetidus*: stinking hellebore
Examine specimens of all or some of the above genera. What features do they have in common with *Ranunculus*, and how do they differ from it?

3 All these genera and species are placed in the same family because the structure of their flowers is so similar. What features of the flowers do they all have in common? Why are features of the flowers mainly used to distinguish

Table 37.2 Names, times of flowering, and habitats of eleven species of *Ranunculus*

Proper name	Common names	Time of flowering	Habitats
R. acris	Common buttercup Meadow buttercup	April-September	damp meadows and pastures
R. aquatalis	Water crowfoot	May-August	ponds, ditches, streams
R. arvensis	Corn buttercup Corn crowfoot	June-July	cornfields in chalky soil
R. auricomus	Goldilocks Wood crowfoot	April-June	woods
R. bulbosus	Bulbous buttercup	May-July	dry pastures, grassy slopes
R. flammula	Lesser spearwort	May-September	wet places
R. ficaria	Lesser celandine	March-May	woods, meadows, grassy bank, sides of streams
R. fluitans	Water crowfoot River crowfoot	June-August	fast-flowing streams and rivers
R. lingua	Great(er) spearwort	June-September	marshes, fens ditches
R. repens	Creeping buttercup	May-August	wet meadows, pastures and woods
R. sceleratus	Celery-leaved crowfoot	May-September	in and by slow streams, ditches and shallow ponds

**C. palustris* is also known as king-cup, golden cup, brave celandine, horse-blob, may-blob, mare-blobs, Mary-bud, soldier's button, and publicans and sinners. In parts of the U.S.A. it is called cowslip, a name which elsewhere is applied to *Primula veris*, a member of the primrose family (Primulaceae). This is a splendid example of how misleading the use of common names can be.

Taxonomic categories	Taxa
Kingdom	Animal
Phylum	Annelida
Class	Oligochaeta
Order	Terricolae
Family	Lumbricidae
Genus	Lumbricus
Species	terrestris
Name	*Lumbrious terrestris* (earthworm)

Table 37.3 How the earthworm and its relatives fit into the classification of animals.

Requirements
Ranunculus species (see Table 37.2)
Selection of species belonging to different genera of the Ranunculaceae
A few other angiosperms (*see* list in step 4)
Lumbricus species
Other oligochaetes
Representatives of other classes of annelids

References: A.R. Clapham, T.G. Tutin & E.F. Warburg *Excursion flora of the British Isles*, 3rd edn, CUP, 1981. W. Keble Martin, *The Concise British Flora in colour*, Ebury Press, 1975.

between orders, families and genera in flowering plants, instead of characteristics of the leaves and stems?

4 The Ranunculaceae is a family within the division Angiospermae. There are over two hundred families of angiosperms. These include the following:
Compositae, e.g. daisy, thistles, groundsel
Convolvulaceae, e.g. bindweed
Cruciferae, e.g. wallflower
Geraniaceae, e.g. geranium
Labiatae, e.g. dead nettle
Graminae, grasses
Leguminosae, e.g. pea, bean, clover, gorse, vetch
Primulaceae, e.g. primrose, cowslip
Rosaceae, e.g. strawberry, rose
Scrophulariaceae, e.g. speedwell, foxglove, snapdragon
Violaceae, e.g. violet, pansy.

Examine representatives from some or all the above families. In what respects do they differ from the Ranunculaceae and from each other? What features do they have in common which cause them to be placed in the same division of the plant kingdom, the Angiosperms?

CLASSIFICATION OF OTHER ORGANISMS

What you have done in this exercise is to look at a genus, then at the family to which that genus belongs, and finally at the phylum (division).

This can be done with any organism, though the procedure is easier for some organisms than for others. By way of contrast, try it with the earthworm (Table 37.3). In this case the genus is *Lumbricus*. First look at different species of *Lumbricus*; then look at other worms belonging to the same class (Oligochaeta). Then broaden your survey further to include the whole phylum (Annelida): this includes leeches, fanworms, ragworms and lugworms, as well as the earthworm and its relatives. What features do the various groups have in common? How do they differ?

For consideration

(1) Is it true of the phyla that you have examined in this practical that the similarities between organisms increase as you go down the taxonomic hierarchy?
(2) What explanation can you offer for the fact that some species are strikingly similar, others different?
(3) How would you explain the fact that in a natural classification, some organisms which appear to be similar are placed in different groups?
(4) Construct a dichotomous key which enables the different species of *Ranunculus* to be identified (see Investigation 37.1).
(5) What problems might arise if animals and plants were only called by their common names? Consult Table 37.2 and the footnote on page 368.

Investigation 37.3 Who's who in the five kingdoms

The five kingdoms are subdivided into phyla, which in turn are subdivided into smaller groups. The members of each phylum, though often displaying considerable diversity of form, are held together by certain features which they all possess.

The purpose of this investigation is to examine representatives of each major phylum. In doing this, you are urged to notice the variety within each phylum, but also the more obvious features uniting its various members.

Procedure

MONERA KINGDOM

Examine photomicrographs of the two phyla belonging to this kingdom: Eubacteria (formerly Bacteria) and Cyanobacteria (formerly Blue-green Algae). Why are they included together in the same kingdom? What distinguishes this kingdom from all the others?

PROTIST KINDGOM

Examine representatives of the following phyla under the microscope: Phytoflagellata (green flagellates, e.g. *Euglena*), Zooflagellata (non-green flagellates, e.g. trypanosomes), Sarcodina (*Amoeba*), Ciliophora (*Paramecium*), Sporozoa (malarial parasite). What are the main distinguishing features of this kingdom and the five phyla within it? Protists used to be included in the animal and plant kingdoms; why is it better for them to be put in a separate kingdom?

FUNGUS KINGDOM

Examine *Mucor* (pin mould) and *Agaricus* (mushroom) as two representative but contrasting fungi. What do they have in common? What other organisms belong to this kingdom, and what qualifies them for membership of it? Fungi used to be included in the plant kingdom; why is it better for them to be put in a separate kingdom?

PLANT KINGDOM

What are the distinguishing characteristics of the plant kingdom? Examine representatives of the following phyla (divisions): Chlorophyta (green algae, e.g. *Spirogyra*), Phaeophyta (brown algae, e.g. *Fucus* (sea weed)), Bryophyta (liverworts and mosses), Tracheophyta (ferns, conifers and flowering plants). From your own observations, try to determine the distinguishing features of each phylum.

ANIMAL KINGDOM

What are the distinguishing features of the animal kingdom? Examine representatives of the following phyla: Porifera (sponges), Coelenterata (Hydra, sea anemone, jellyfish), Platyhelminthes (planarian, tapeworm, fluke), Nematodes (roundworms, threadworms), Annelida (ragworm, fanworm, earthworm, leech), Mollusca (mussel, snail, octopus, squid), Arthropoda (crustacean, centipede and millipede, spider, insect), Echinodermata (starfish, sea urchin), Chordata (Amphioxus, sea squirt, fish, amphibian, reptile, bird, mammal). From your own observations, try to determine the distinguishing features of each division.

Requirements

Live and/or preserved organisms belonging to the kingdoms and phyla listed above.
Prepared slides where appropriate
Photomicrographs of Eubacteria and Cyanobacteria

For Consideration

(1) How would you explain the similarities that exist between the members of a phylum?
(2) How would you explain the fact that some phyla appear to have more in common than others?
(3) Have you encountered any cases where, in your opinion, two organisms that are in the same phylum ought to be in different phyla, or where two organisms that are in different phyla ought to be in the same phylum?

Questions and Problems

1 (a) Why do biologists classify organisms?
(b) Define and illustrate the terms phylum, class, genus and species with reference to any one plant or animal group with which you are familiar. *(O & C modified)*

2 What is meant by a natural classification? Give one example of a natural classification and explain the principles on which it is based.

3 Consider the following fruits: cherry, chestnut, coconut, grape, plum, tomato.
(a) Write down eight features each of which is possessed by some, but not all, of these fruits.
(b) Make a table summarising the presence or absence in the fruits of the features which you have listed.
(c) Make a further table which shows the *number* of features in your list which each pair of fruits, in every possible combination, have in common.
(d) On the basis of your table in (c), draw a branch-diagram (dendrogram) linking the fruits together at various levels of similarity.
(e) Do you think that your branch-diagram has any evolutionary significance? Explain your answer.

4 (a) What do you understand by a cladistic classification?
(b) Give two examples of cladistic classifications, one from the animal kingdom and one from the plant kingdom.
(c) Do you consider that such classifications are useful?

5 Given below is information from a biologist's notebook about twelve animals (**A**–**L**) in the phylum Mollusca, the group which includes snails, oysters, and octopuses:

A Has head; fleshy foot; one pair of tentacles; shell single and coiled; one pair of simple eyes; single gill on left side; lives between low-tide mark and 180 metres; active and carnivorous; separate sexes; internal fertilisation.

B Body compressed from side to side; shell in two halves, slightly coiled and held together by pair of adductor muscles; head rudimentary; no tentacles or eyes; one pair of sheet-like gills; common between high and low-tide marks in 'beds'; reduced foot secretes sticky threads for attachment to rocks; filter-feeder; separate sexes; external fertilisation.

C Shell single, internal and reduced; well developed head into which the foot is incorporated; mouth surrounded by ten tentacles with suckers; one pair of gills; large CNS; well developed eyes; marine; active swimmer; carnivorous; separate sexes; internal fertilisation.

D Mouth surrounded by eight prehensile tentacles; no shell; well developed head with eyes and large brain; foot incorporated into head; marine; active carnivore; separate sexes; internal fertilisation.

E Body flattened from side to side; rudimentary head with no tentacles or eyes; bivalve shell with one adductor muscle; left valve of shell larger than right and 'cemented' to rock; no foot; filter-feeder; separate sexes; some species hermaphroditic; external fertilisation; marine.

F Lives on land; herbivorous; head with two pairs of tentacles, the posterior pair bearing eyes; single coiled shell; no gills but has chamber which functions as lung; flat fleshy foot; hermaphrodite; internal fertilisation.

G Tubular shell open at both ends; no gills; head with numerous prehensile tentacles; no eyes; foot reduced and used for burrowing; found in sand and mud just below low-tide mark.

H Shell single, flattened and very slightly coiled and pierced by a row of holes; moderately well developed head with three pairs of tentacles, the posterior pair bearing eyes at their tips; large fleshy foot for attachment to rocks; numerous short tentacles (tactile) round edge of body; one pair of gills displaced to left by large shell muscle; occur from low-tide mark to depths of over 20 fathoms; feed on encrusting plant material; separate sexes; fertilisation external.

I Small head with no tentacles or eyes; numerous small gills on either side of body; large flat foot for attachment to rocks; shell consists of eight calcareous plates which, being separate, allow the animal to roll up like a woodlouse; lives under stones and rocks near low-tide mark; separate sexes; external fertilisation.

J Shell single, internal and reduced; head with two pairs of eyeless tentacles; pair of eyes just in front of posterior tentacles; hermaphroditic; internal fertilisation; single gill; elongated foot with flattened outgrowths used for swimming; marine.

K Much reduced foot; shell laterally compressed in two halves, one half flatter than the other; adductor muscle with striated fibres; no head but tentacles and simple eyes round edge of shell; can swim by repeatedly opening and closing the shell; filter-feeder; hermaphroditic; external fertilisation; one pair of gills.

L Occurs in fresh water; flattened body; shell in two halves; well developed muscular foot for burrowing; one sheet-like gill on either side of foot; much reduced head without tentacles or eyes; slow moving, filter-feeder; separate sexes; internal fertilisation.

(a) Make a classification of the animals, using whatever taxonomic procedure you feel is appropriate. Invent a name for each group, reflecting, if possible, the particular feature which distinguishes that group from others.

(b) Construct a key enabling each animal to be quickly identified by its code letter.

6 (a) By means of a table, place each of the following organisms into its correct kingdom, phylum and sub-group within the phylum. In each case state what you consider to be the most easily observed characteristic which shows what phylum and sub-group the organism belongs to:
Amoeba, Bee, Buttercup, Crab, Fanworm, Human, Millipede, Moss, Octopus, Pine.

(b) Which organism in the list is least like the other members of its phylum, and in what way(s) does it differ from them? How do you know that it belongs to this particular phylum?

(c) In the above list of organisms, common names are used. Does this matter?

7 There exists a rare animal called *Peripatus*. Its anatomical features include the following.
Head – 3 pairs of appendages with antennae,
Body – caterpillar-like,
Length – approximately 50 mm,
A thin chitinous cuticle covering the body, many pairs of non-jointed appendages ending in claws,
An open blood system,
A segmented nephridial excretory system,
Air tubes for gas exchange.
(a) This animal is difficult to classify. Why is this?
(b) What do these difficulties about its systematic position tell us about
(i) the nature of biological classification,
(ii) The process of evolution? *(O & C)*

8 'A practical system of classification is the first essential of all biological research'.
'It is useless and futile to try to classify animals and plants into groups and is of no more scientific value than classifying men according to their height or place of birth.'
Discuss these two views of biological classification. *(O & C modified)*

9 Nowadays it it generally agreed that living organisms should be split not into two kingdoms (animal and plant) but into five kingdoms.
(a) Give the names and diagnostic features of each of the five kingdoms.
(b) What are the merits of having five kingdoms rather than only two?
(c) What anomalies, if any, are there in the five kingdom system and how might they be solved?

Appendix 1 Additional Questions and Problems

1 The table below gives some figures for the metabolism of carbohydrates and lipids.

Energy source	Metabolic energy produced ($kJ\ g^{-1}$)	Metabolic water produced ($g\ g^{-1}$ food)	Oxygen consumed ($dm g^{-1}$ food)
Carbohydrate	17.2	0.56	0.83
Lipid	38.9	1.07	2.02

(a) From the above data give two reasons why animals store fat.
(b) Give two other reasons why animals might store fat.
(c) Why do lipids require more oxygen on a gram-for-gram basis for cellular oxidation than do carbohydrates?

The rugby-throated humming bird (*Archilochus colubris*) is one of the smallest of birds. It can hover, fly forwards and backwards, fly for 900 km non-stop and has a wing beat of 80-100 beats per second. The major levator muscle of its wings is peculiar in its cellular organisation in that it consists of only red myofibrils. It also has conspicuously large aggregations of mitochondria interspersed with lipid droplets between the myofibrils, a high concentration of myoglobin and an extensive blood supply.
(d) What is the significance of the large aggregations of mitochondria?
(e) What is the function of the myoglobin? *(CL)*

2 The following table gives the oxygen consumption of four selected animals.

Animal	Oxygen consumption ($mm^3\ kg^{-1}\ h^{-1}$)
Earthworm	60
Frog	150
Mouse, resting	2 500
Mouse, running	20 000
Butterfly, resting	600
Butterfly, in flight	100 000

Discuss the implications of these data with reference to gas exchange and transport systems, body temperature, and mode of life. *(O&C)*

3 (a) Distinguish between the terms 'action spectrum' and 'absorption spectrum'.
(b) In Figure A1.1 the three curves **A**, **B**, and **C** represent the action spectra for three different plant processes in which pigments are involved. Comment briefly on each curve, identifying the three processes (**A**, **B** and **C**) and naming the pigments involved.
(c) Discuss concisely the part played by the pigment(s) in any two of the processes outlined in (b) above. *(JMB-N)*

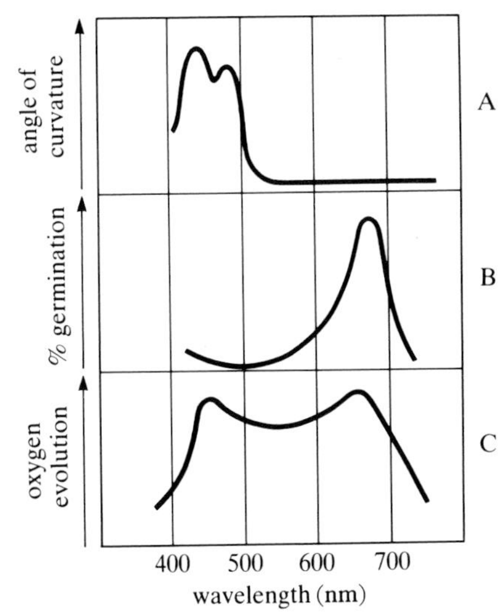

Figure A1.1 Action spectra for three different plant processes.

4 The cellular components of a cabbage leaf were separated into fractions in ice-cold isotonic buffer solution. The fraction containing chloroplasts was suspended in isotonic buffer solution containing dilute methylene blue, divided into four equal parts and treated as follows:

Part	Conditions	Colour of solution	
		After 5 mins	After 45 mins
1	Darkness at 5°C	blue-green	blue-green
2	Darkness at 25°C	blue-green	blue-green
3	Light at 5°C	blue-green	pale-green
4	Light at 25°C	pale-green	pale-green

(a) Outline a procedure for separating the chloroplasts from other cell organelles.
(b) State why it was necessary to suspend the cells in ice-cold buffer solution during the separation.

(c) Explain the purpose of adding methylene blue.
(d) Discuss the effects on the activity of the chloroplast suspension of
(i) temperature
(ii) light.
(e) Suggest **two** ways in which the design of the investigation could be improved. *(W)*

5 The mineral content of a water extract taken from the soil in a cultivated field was determined in April and September of the same year. The results are shown below.

Time	**Mineral content** (mmol dm^{-3})				
	NO_3^-	SO_4^{2-}	PO_4^{3-}	Ca^{2+}	Mg^{2+}
April	2.22	7.10	0.05	6.74	3.70
September	0.21	4.35	0.01	4.00	1.88

(a) Indicate **two** reasons for the decrease in the concentration of nitrates.
(b) It was found that the level of nitrate in April of the following year had increased to 2.72 mmol dm^{-3}.

Give **three** possible reasons to explain this increase.
(c) State the importance in plant metabolism of (i) calcium (ii) magnesium
(d) The concentration of phosphate in the soil appears to be low. In what ways could this affect plant growth?
(e) Some of the calcium **in the soil** was not readily available to plants. Explain—
(i) why this should be so;
(ii) how this calcium could subsequently be released and made available to plant roots. *(O & C)*

6 Figure A1.2 shows the growth and spread of the perennial plant *Ranunculus repens* (the creeping buttercup).
(a) Name the parts labelled **A** to **F**.
(b) The following results were obtained from a study of a population of this perennial plant in a given area over a period of two years.

At beginning of study	117 plants
New plants over 2 years	244 plants
Plants dead during 2 years	222 plants
Plants at end of study	139 plants
Original plants surviving to the end of the study	13 plants

(i) State **two** ways in which the number of plants could increase over the two year period.
(ii) Suggest **two** reasons for the high death rate.
(iii) Do these figures indicate that this population is stabilising? Give reasons for your answer.

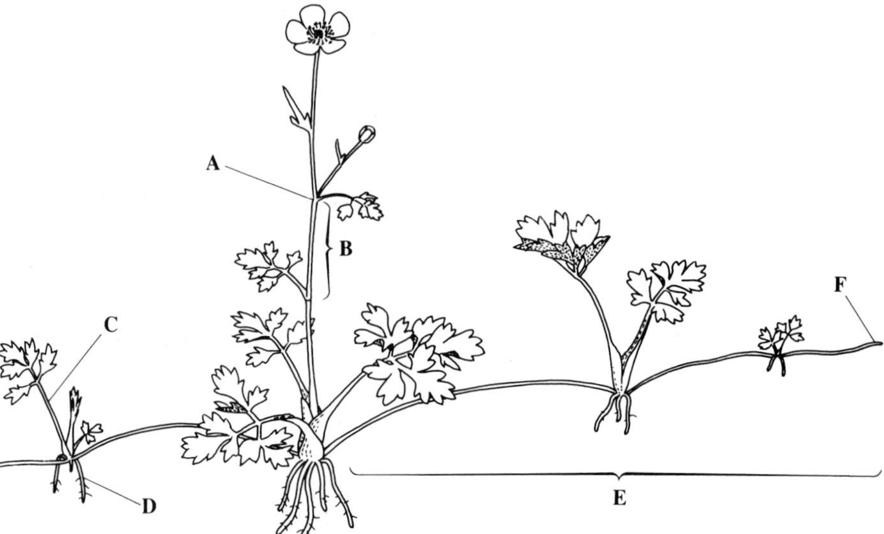

Figure A1.2 Diagram of *Ranunculus repens* (the creeping buttercup).

(c) Life span, ascertained in relation to density of plants, is shown in the table in the margin.

Plants per m^2	**Life span** (days)
50	105
100	90
150	82
200	72
250	60

Give reasons for this correlation.

(d) Outline an experiment you could carry out to test the validity of one of your comments in (c). *(O&C)*

7 Write short essays about *two* of the following statements:
(a) worker bees die after stinging an intruder;
(b) brightly coloured insects sometimes cluster together;
(c) some predators hunt in packs but most hunt alone;
(d) brain size is approximately correlated with body size;
(e) sessile organisms save energy;
(f) fungi are the only organisms which can completely break down lignin;
(g) there are hundreds of species of dandelion in Europe;
(h) conifers are well adapted to cold climates. *(OCJE)*

8 Why do organisms die? *(OCJE)*

9 What are the problems associated with increase in size in plants and animals? How have these problems been countered? *(OCJE)*

10 How has the use of radioactive isotopes contributed to biological knowledge? *(OCJE)*

11 Describe with full experimental details how you would investigate whether in human adults there is a relation between (a) cigarette smoking and heart rate and (b) cigarette smoking and tidal volume. Show how you would record your data and present your results. *(AEB)*

12 Outline the major discoveries which have led to the development of our concept of the gene. *(OCJE)*

13 Animal tissues are predominantly made of protein, whilst those of plants are mainly carbohydrate. Why is this so, and what problems arise because of this for herbivores? *(OCJE)*

14 (a) Describe briefly the principles of the following techniques: (i) electron microscopy; (ii) chromatography; (iii) X-ray diffraction.
(b) Describe, in detail, those features of a typical cell which have become better understood as a result of these techniques. *(CL)*

15 Give examples of processes in plants and animals that depend on diffusion of molecules. What type of mechanisms serve to transport substances when diffusion is not fast enough? *(OCJE)*

16 What are the functions of colour in plants and animals? *(OCJE)*

17 Why are the insects so outstandingly successful? *(CCJE)*

18 In what ways have animals and plants successfully co-operated in evolution and in what ways have they negatively responded to each other? *(CCJE)*

19 Explain why it is that (a) no animal is smaller than a shrew and (b) no flying bird is larger than a turkey. *(CCJE)*

20 Why do humans commonly cook their food? What happens to food when it is cooked? *(OCJE)*

Appendix 2 Advice to the Student

2.1 Keeping a Practical Notebook

It goes without saying that the student should keep a practical notebook as a personal record of his or her investigations and observations. For this purpose a hard-backed book with alternating plain and lined paper (A4 size) is recommended.

You will be constantly faced with the question of what to enter in your notebook. The following notes are intended as a guide.

Dissection

(1) Write a *brief* summary of your technique, stressing any special points of procedure which you discovered for yourself.
(2) Draw the relevant parts of the completed dissection and label the appropriate structures. (Advice on drawing is given below).
(3) Make sure your drawing has a heading, and indicate what view it represents, e.g. dorsal, ventral etc.

Microscopic work

(1) If you have made your own preparation (as opposed to using a prepared slide), give a brief account of your method.
(2) Draw the relevant parts of the object and label the appropriate structures.
(3) Be sure you state precisely what the object represents, e.g. whole mount, transverse section, etc.
(4) Give an indication of the scale.

Live specimens

Record your observations in the form of sketches and/or short notes, as appropriate. Get into the habit of recording your observations quickly and neatly, *while* you are observing the specimen. With experience you will learn to judge what is important and worth recording.

Experiments

Most students shudder at the thought of having to 'write up an experiment'. However, the labour is alleviated if you do as much of the writing-up as you can *during* the experiment. In biological experiments there are often odd moments when this can be done.

The format and presentation which you adopt in your notebook depends on the particular experiment. In general you should give an account of your **method**, a summary of your **results**, and a statement of your **conclusions**.

Note: The anatomical drawings in this manual are intended as a *guide* to help you identify structures which you yourself observe. You will gain very little by copying them direct into your notebook!

2.2 Drawing

Drawings are an aid to precise observations and for this reason they are an important part of laboratory work. The biologist is not expected to be an artist, but to become, in some degree, a draughtsman. Clear and accurate line drawings are preferable to rough sketches on the one hand, or to elaborately shaded pictures on the other.

First consider what you want to show. Then plan your drawing so the various parts are in proportion and fit on the page. Small marks indicating the length and breadth of the drawing are a great help in planning, and a faint outline can be rapidly drawn to show the relative positions of the parts. The final outline should be drawn with clean firm lines and details should be put in clearly with a sharp pencil. If important details are too small to be shown in proportion, they can be shown in an enlarged diagram at the side. Do not shade unless you are a competent artist, and only in special circumstances should it be necessary to use coloured crayons. It should be possible to make the drawing perfectly clear by the judicious use of thick and thin lines and careful cross-hatching. Get into the habit of making your drawings large and clear.

As important as the drawing is the **labelling**. This should be done neatly in pencil. Each label should be connected to the appropriate part of the drawing by a clear guideline or pointer. Do not label too close to the drawings, and never write on the drawing itself. Always make sure that each drawing is fully labelled before you leave it.

It is sometimes appropriate, particularly when drawing live specimens, to make short succinct notes close to the labels. Such **annotated drawings** are particularly valuable as they combine a record of structure with functional observations.

2.3 Dissection

The object of dissection is to reveal the anatomy, not to destroy it. In achieving this, there are certain rules which every biologist should observe:

(1) Instruments should be kept in good condition: always clean and grease them after use; cutting tools should always be sharp.

(2) Except in special circumstances, pin the animal to a board or to the bottom of a dissecting dish so that the body wall is stretched.

(3) Where appropriate dissect the animal under water; this supports its organs and facilitates the separation of its tissues.

(4) If you are not dissecting in water, keep your dissection moist at all times. If you wish to leave it for any length of time, cover it with a damp cloth.

(5) Consider before each cut what organ is being sought and where it is likely to be; never cut or remove anything without knowing what it is.

(6) In dissecting such structures as nerves and blood vessels, work along, not across, their course.

(7) When following a nerve or blood vessel cut upwards towards you, not downwards towards the object.

(8) Remove only those structures which, if left in position, would obscure the structures you want to expose.

(9) In the final stage of your dissection make sure all the structures that you wish to show are clearly displayed.

(10) In displaying your dissection make judicious use of pins to separate structures from each other.

2.4 Viewing Small Objects

Objects which are too small to be seen satisfactorily with the naked eye but too large for the ordinary microscope, may be observed with the aid of a hand lens or binocular stereo-microscope.

If you are using a hand lens, best results are obtained by having your eye as close to the lens as possible. Make sure the object is adequately illuminated against a contrasting background.

The binocular microscope operates on the same basis as a normal (monocular) microscope except that its magnification is less and, as it has two eye-pieces and two objectives, the image it gives is stereoscopic (three-dimensional). The distance between the two eye-pieces can be adjusted to suit the viewer.

Since it operates at comparatively low magnifications, the distance between the objectives and the specimen is sufficiently great for comparatively large objects to be placed under the binocular microscope. It is possible, for example, to place a dissection under the microscope, and indeed to carry out the dissection while looking through the microscope.

For gaining best results with a binocular microscope, it is important that the specimen should be correctly illuminated, preferably from a point-source of light, and that it is viewed against a contrasting background.

2.5 Measuring the Size of an Object under the Microscope

This can be done using an **eyepiece micrometer scale**. This is a glass scale mounted in the focal plane of the eyepiece so it can be seen in the field of view at the same time as an object is being examined under the microscope.

Obviously to be of any use the eyepiece micrometer scale needs to be calibrated. This can be done by placing a **stage micrometer** under the microscope. This is a glass slide on which is etched a series of vertical lines separated by distances of 1.0 mm, 0.1 mm and 0.01 mm. By superimposing the images of the eyepiece micrometer and stage micrometer scales, the former can be calibrated to the size of a given object viewed under the microscope can be accurately estimated.

When calibrating, adopt the following procedure. Put the stage micrometer on the stage of the microscope, and bring its lines into focus. Move the stage micrometer until one of its lines coincides exactly with one of the numbered lines on the eyepiece scale. Count the number of lines on the latter which fills the space between the line that you have selected on the stage micrometer and the next one.

If the distance between the two lines on the stage micrometer is 100 μm and it is found that x eyepiece divisions exactly fill this space, then the value of one eyepiece division is $\frac{100}{x}$.

It is now possible to purchase a 100 μm scale, printed in transparent film, that can be used as an eyepiece graticule and/or stage micrometer.

2.6 Preparing Material for Viewing under the Microscope

Temporary preparations

Observations on living material under the microscope are often very valuable. The material should be mounted in a drop of water, saline solution or glycerine on a slide and a coverslip applied. Anaesthetic fluids, fixatives, and stains may be introduced by a method called **irrigation**. A drop of the reagent is placed on the slide so that it just touches the edge of the coverslip. Fluid is then withdrawn from the opposite side of the coverslip by means of a piece of filter paper or blotting paper, and the reagent flows in to replace the fluid taken out. Care should be taken that there is always some fluid touching the coverslip to replace that removed. With delicate specimens be careful the organisms are not swept away by far too rapid a rush of fluid.

Permanent preparations

The making of permanent preparations is no substitute for examining living material. However, many structures are difficult to see in the living material. In such cases the processes of fixation, staining, and mounting can make the study of details much easier. The making of a permanent preparation involves the following processes:

Fixation. The purpose of this is to kill the living tissues with the minimum distortion, so as to permit subsequent staining and mounting of the preparations. Suitable fixatives include 70 per cent ethanol, aqueous methanol (formalin), and Bouin's fluid.

Staining. The purpose of this is to colour structures which would otherwise be difficult, if not impossible, to see under the microscope. Staining is normally carried out during the dehydration process at the appropriate ethanol concentration. This will vary with the stain used: aqueous stains should be used before dehydration; stains in 50 per cent ethanol after dehydration in 50 per cent ethanol, and so on.

Differentiation. The purpose of this is to sharpen the contrast between, e.g. nuclei and cytoplasm. It is advisable to examine the specimen under the microscope during the differentiation process.

Dehydration. The purpose of this is to remove all traces of water from the stained material. This is carried out by passing it through a series of ethanols of gradually increasing strength. The appropriate staining technique is interpolated into this series at the correct point.

Clearing. The purpose of this is to remove the ethanol and render the material transparent. Suitable clearing agents are xylene and clove oil; when completely cleared the material will sink to the bottom. If dehydration has not been complete a milky precipitate may be formed in the clearing agent, or the specimen may remain floating. In either case it must be returned to absolute ethanol until dehydration is complete. The specimen must not be placed in balsam until completely cleared.

Mounting. The purpose of this is to embed the material in a suitable medium for observation under the microscope. When the material is in the clearing agent a small drop containing it is placed on a slide, excess fluid is drained off with blotting paper, a drop of Canada balsam[1] is added and a coverslip applied. The slide should be left in a warm place: the balsam is dissolved in xylene and, as this solvent evaporates, sets hard so that the coverslip remains fixed.

The above procedures apply in general to the making of any permanent preparation. However, the details vary according to the material and the stain which is to be used.

The manipulations may be carried out either with the specimen on a slide (as in the case of smears or sections), or with the specimen in a watchglass (as in the case of complete organisms or pieces of tissue). In the former case the slide, with the specimen attached to it, is immersed for the appropriate time in a series of dipping jars. In the latter case the specimen is transferred from one reagent to another in a series of watchglasses.

When viewing the specimen under the microscope during the differentiation process, make sure the underside of the slide or watchglass is dry.

Several useful staining techniques are given below. For other techniques the reader should consult a handbook of microscopic technique.

Borax carmine

Specially suitable for whole mounts of animal material (i.e. solid pieces of tissue), this technique involves the use of a single stain.

Short method

(i) Transfer the specimen to 50 per cent ethanol, if not already in it.
(ii) Stain in **borax carmine** until the specimen is just thoroughly penetrated (about ten minutes).
(iii) Differentiate in acidified ethanol until the material is pale pink. While differentiating examine under the low power of the microscope. Nuclei should be pink against a light background. If understained return the specimen to borax carmine; if overstained leave in acidified ethanol.
(iv) Dehydrate in 90 per cent ethanol (ten minutes), and two successive lots of absolute ethanol (5–30 minutes each, depending on thickness of specimen).
(v) Clear in xylene.
(vi) Mount in e.g. Canada balsam, supporting the coverslip with strips of paper or celluloid if necessary. Leave on hotplate until balsam hardens.

Long method

Stain the specimen in borax carmine for up to 24 hours. Differentiate in acidified ethanol for between several days and six weeks. Examine the specimen under the microscope at intervals to determine the progress of differentiation. When the material is sufficiently differentiated, proceed as for the short method.

Borax carmine stains nuclei and cytoplasm pink, but since the acidified ethanol removes the stain more completely from the cytoplasm than from the nucleus, there will be a difference of colour.

Haematoxylin and eosin

This is a double staining technique in which the material is treated with two stains in succession. It is specially suitable for sections of animal material, and for smears.

(1) Bring the material to be stained into 50 per cent ethanol, if not already in it.
(2) Stain in **haematoxylin** until the specimen is dark blue (two to five minutes).

[1]Canada balsam, ready for use, is available in tubes from which it can be made to flow by gentle squeezing. Other mounting media, e.g. euparal, can be used instead of balsam. Smears and thin sections can be sprayed with tryolac spray which is, in effect, a liquid cover glass.

(3) Blue in tap water.

While blueing, examine under low power. Nuclei should be blue; cytoplasm light or colourless. If understained return the specimen to haematoxylin; if overstained differentiate in acidified ethanol.

(4) Dehydrate in 70 per cent, then 90 per cent ethanol (about three minutes each).
(5) Counterstain in **eosin** for two to five minutes.
(6) Replace in 90 per cent ethanol.

The specimen may be examined quickly under low power. Again make certain the underside of the slide is dry. If understained, return the specimen to eosin; if overstained leave it in the ethanol.

(7) Complete dehydration in absolute ethanol for about five minutes.
(8) Clear in xylene and mount in e.g. Canada balsam. Leave on hotplate until balsam hardens.

Safranin and light (or fast) green

This is a double staining technique which is suitable for botanical tissues, including sections. Fast green may be substituted for the light green: this has the advantage of fading less rapidly.

(1) Stain in **safranin** (ten minutes).
(2) Dehydrate in 50, 70, and 90 per cent ethanol, spending one minute in each.
(3) Complete dehydration in two successive lots of absolute ethanol (three to five minutes each).
(4) Counterstain in **light green** in clove oil (one minute).
(5) Clear and wash in clove oil (five minutes).

Examine under the microscope and if the material is understained with safranin, or overstained with light green, pass down through the ethanols and re-stain with safranin.

(6) Mount in e.g. Canada balsam and leave on hotplate.

Safranin and light green stain cytoplasm and cellulose green; lignified tissues and nuclei red; and chloroplasts pink.

Safranin and light green in cellosolve

It is possible to carry out the dehydration and double staining together in a single solution. This consists of **safranin and light green in cellosolve** and is available, made up ready for use, from certain suppliers.

(1) Stain and dehydrate in safranin and light green in cellosolve (five to ten minutes).
(2) Wash in cellosolve.

The cellosolve slowly removes the stain: watch under the microscope until the required intensity of staining is achieved.

(3) Transfer material into a mixture of equal volumes of cellosolve and xylene, then into pure xylene (two changes) for clearing.
(4) Mount in Canada balsam and leave on hotplate.

Appendix 3 Equipment and Apparatus

3.1 The compound microscope

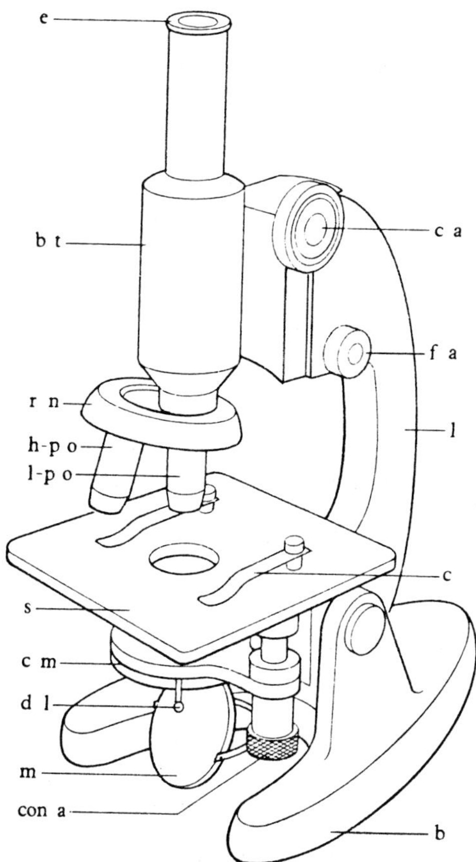

Figure A3.1 A typical compound microscope. e, eye piece; b t, body tube; r n, rotating nosepiece; h-p o, high power objective; l-p o, low power objective; s, stage; c m, condenser mount; d l, diaphragm lever; m, mirror; con a, condenser adjustment; b, base; c, clip; l, limb; f a, fine adjustment; c a, coarse adjustment.

Structures which are too small to be observed by other means are studied with the aid of the compound microscope. In this instrument light rays which have passed through the specimen are transmitted through two lens systems, the objective and eyepiece. A typical student microscope is illustrated in Figure A3.1.

The microscope is an expensive precision instrument and should be treated as such. When setting it up, adopt the following procedure:

Low power

Adjustment of lenses

(1) Place the microscope firmly on the table, not on books or papers. Set the microscope squarely opposite the source of illumination.

(2) The lenses must be quite clean. To test, hold them so that the light is reflected from their surfaces. Dirt or moisture should be removed by gentle wiping with a clean cloth or lens paper. Vigorous rubbing when grit is present scratches the lenses and makes them useless.

(3) Rack up the coarse adjustment until the objective lenses are about 20 mm above the stage. Turn the nosepiece so that the low-power objective is in use. Make certain that the objective has clicked exactly into line with the microscope tube.

(4) Note that the fine adjustment is a right-handed screw. Screwing in a clock-wise direction *lowers* the objective.

(5) Place the slide to be examined on the microscope stage.

(6) Looking at the microscope from the side, rack down the coarse adjustment till the low-power objective is about 5 mm above the slide. Then, looking through the microscope, rack up the coarse adjustment till the object is in focus. (When looking through the microscope NEVER rack downwards to focus an object unless you know *with certainty* that by focusing downwards a very small distance the image will come into view).

(7) Take great care to focus accurately in order to avoid eyestrain. Keep both eyes open. Get accustomed to using either eye.

Adjustment of illumination

(1) The whole field of the microscope should be evenly illuminated. The best source of illumination is natural daylight or a diffuse bulb. If a filament lamp is used, interpose a thin sheet of paper between the bulb and the microscope. A point source of illumination is suitable only for work with very high powers.

(2) Adjust the flat mirror until light from the source is thrown up the microscope.

(3) Focus the condenser. To do this, adjust it until an object placed just in front of the source of light, reflected by the mirror, is seen in focus at the same time as the object on the microscope slide.

Always use the condenser focused; *never* use the condenser with the concave mirror. The lenses of the condenser are adjusted to give optimum illumination only when focused with the *flat* mirror.

(4) If the condenser is not in use, illuminate with the aid of the concave mirror. This method of illumination is, for most purposes, inferior to that using the condenser.

(5) The purpose of the condenser is to increase the illumination and to bring rays of light from a wide angle to bear on the object. Have this in mind when you are adjusting it.

(6) Open or close the diaphragm to the required extent. The condenser should be used with the diaphragm as wide open as possible, without admitting too great an intensity of light. The *definition* of the image will then be at its best. If it is not possible to open the diaphragm widely without admitting too great a light intensity, place a sheet of paper between the microscope and the lamp.

N.B. A common cause of poor definition is that the object is over-illuminated. Best definition is often obtained by cutting down the light, not increasing it.

High power

Adjustment of lenses

(1) After the object is well defined under the low power, move the slide so that the part which is to be observed in greater detail is exactly in the centre of the field.
(2) Turn the nose-piece until the high-power objective clicks into place. The object should automatically come *approximately* into focus. If it does not do so, observe the microscope from the side, and rack the tube down until the lens is about one millimetre from the slide; then focus by racking *up*.

Adjustment of illumination

The diaphragm, etc., should be adjusted until the optimum intensity of illumination is obtained.

Magnification

(1) Do not use a higher power than is necessary. Far more can be made out with the low power in good illumination conditions, than under the high power with bad conditions. Also the larger the region of the object viewed in the field at the same time, the easier it is to interpret what is seen.
(2) Carry in your mind the degree of magnification. The following table shows the magnification given by typical lens combinations:

	Eyepieces		
	×6 (No.2)	×10 (No.4)	
Objective 16 mm (×10)	60	100	Magnification
Objective 4 mm (×40)	240	400	

(3) Always enter a *rough scale* with any drawings that you make, based on the degree of magnification and the apparent size of the object.

Oil immersion

If particularly high magnifications are required an oil-immersion objective lens may be used. This is a special optical system in which a fluid of the same refractive index as the lens itself, is placed between the objective lens and the specimen. The fluid permits a larger cone of rays to enter the objective from the object than is otherwise possible, and this increases the resolving power obtainable. The fluid used is generally cedar-wood oil. A drop of the oil is placed on the coverslip above the specimen and the objective is lowered until the lens comes into contact with the oil. The object is then viewed with appropriate illumination in the normal way.

Dark-ground illumination

For small transparent objects it is often best to view the specimen as a bright object against a dark background. This involves the use of dark-ground illumination. In this technique the direct light iluminating the object must not enter the objective: the only light rays entering the micrscope must be those which have been reflected or scattered by the object itself.

For low-power work this is achieved by interposing an opaque stop in the centre of the condenser. For high-power work a special dark-ground illuminator must be used.

Observations on living organisms under the microscope

Living organisms can be viewed under the microscope either on a slide or in a watchglass. The following points should be noted:
(1) Take care not to spill water on the stage of the microscope, and especially on the condenser.

(2) Take care not to wet the objective.
(3) When searching for organisms in a watchglass, place the latter on a slide. You can then move the slide easily on the stage and avoid the possibility of harming the condenser.
(4) *Never* tilt the microscope when there is living material on the stage.

Note: Rapidly moving organisms can be slowed down by mounting them in a viscous medium such as methyl cellulose, or in a very *small* drop of water which is allowed to evaporate. Alternatively they can be trapped in a meshwork of fibres made by pulling lens paper to pieces.

Cleaning the microscope

Like all scientific apparatus the microscope should be kept clean. Above all, it must be kept free from traces of water (particularly sea water), fixatives, stains and reagents which readily corrode the instrument. *See that the microscope is clean and dry and in good order when you put it away.*

Tracing faults

If good definition is not obtained:
(1) Is the slide clean?
(2) Is the objective centred?
(3) Are the lenses free from dirt and moisture?
(4) Is the condenser adjusted and focused?
(5) Is the diaphragm adjusted?
(6) Is the microscope squarely placed in front of a suitable source of illumination?
(7) Is the lens itself faulty? If so, report the fact.

3.2 The Phase-contrast Microscope

In normal microscopy structures in a specimen that would otherwise be transparent can be made visible by staining. However, these structures, by virtue of slight differences in density or refractive index, also produce invisible changes of phase in the light that passes through them. In phase-contrast microscopy these changes in phase are converted into corresponding changes of amplitude, resulting in a high-contrast image in which the distribution of light rays is related to the changes in phase. Provided there are variations in density or refractive index, any transparent object may be viewed this way. As fixation and staining are unnecessary, the technique can be used for examining living material that would otherwise be difficult or impossible to see.

Examining an object with phase-contrast involves placing a special annular disc beneath the condenser and using an objective fitted with a phase plate. Setting up the phase-contrast microscope can be a tricky business, particularly as the annuli and phase plates must be exactly aligned. However, several manufacturers are now producing student microscopes with built-in phase contrast equipment which is easy to handle and produces satisfactory results.

3.3 Centrifuge

A centrifuge is used to spin tubes which contain particles suspended in a liquid. In biology, tubes containing cell extracts are rotated around a vertical shaft, which is driven round and round by a motor. The particles in the tubes are subjected to a greatly increased gravitational force. They move away from the central shaft at a rate which depends on their density, and hence their size and molecular mass. They move through the liquid and are deposited at the base of the tube. The relatively clear liquid above the deposit is called the supernatant. The densest particles are deposited most rapidly. Repeated centrifugation of cell extracts, each time at a higher speed, is therefore widely used in cell biology to isolate particular organelles, e.g. chloroplasts, mitochondria, ribosomes or cell membranes.

The force tending to make a particle move in a centrifuge is proportional to $m\omega^2$, where m is the difference between the mass of the particle and the mass of an equal volume of liquid, and ω is the rate of spin in radians per second. Once the machine has been spinning at the same rate for a few seconds, all the particles will be moving towards the base of the tube, the heavy ones fast and the lighter ones more slowly. If the centrifuge is stopped after a minute of two only the massive particles will have been sedimented. If, however, the centrifuge ran for a few days, almost all the particles would have reached the plug of solid at the bottom. An increase in speed greatly increases the rate at which all the particles move away from the centre.

Precaution when using a centrifuge

It is most important that each centrifuge tube must be balanced against the tube opposite. Each pair should contain identical volumes of liquid. Their contents of cell walls and sand should be equalised before they are placed in the machine. Do not use tubes which are cracked; they are likely to break whilst being spun.

The centrifuge should never be operated with the cover open. This is not only to avoid injury to hands placed inside the machine. If a tube breaks when the lid is open, glass could be thrown a long way with considerable force.

If the machine vibrates excessively or makes a considerable amount of moise, stop it immediately. If a centrifuge tube breaks, remove all the fragments of glass and clean the centrifuge head thoroughly before you use the machine again.

3.4 The colorimeter

This instrument measures the density of the colour of a coloured solution. For example, it can be used to estimate the concentration of a compound solution, e.g. the intensity of the blue colour when iodine is added to starch, or the amount of haemoglobin in samples of blood.

A simple colorimeter is illustrated in Figure A3.2 When the coloured solution is placed in the instrument, light passes through the solution onto a photo-sensitive element. The amount of light passing through is registered on a meter scale. If the colour is dense, relatively little light passes through onto the photo sensitive element. On the other hand if the colour is weak, more light passes through. The readings on the meter scale vary accordingly.

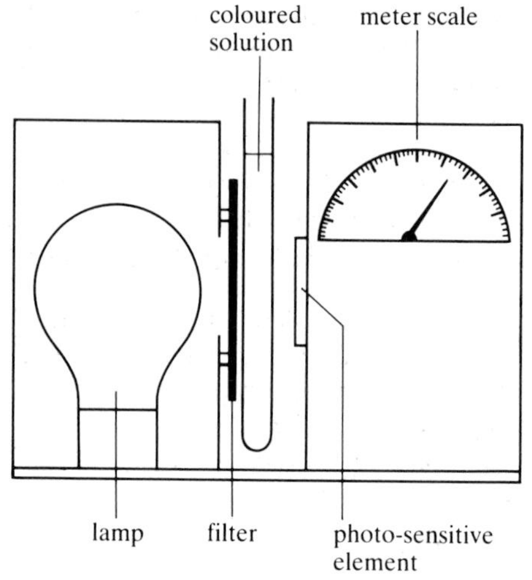

Figure A3.2 Diagram of a colorimeter. Using a microbalance to measure the mass of a leaf.

3.5 Kymograph

This apparatus usually consists of a vertical cylindrical drum, which can be made to rotate at a variety of speeds by either a clockwork or electric motor. It is used for recording movements, contraction of muscle, and so on. The speed can be adjusted according to requirements.

Movements can be recorded by a pen writing on white paper. Recording pens usually consists of a small well for holding the ink, with a narrow outlet to serve as the writing point. It is essential to use ink that does not clog: eosin is very satisfactory.

If kymograph recordings are to be of any value it is important to provide a **time scale.** With some kymographs the speeds at which the drum rotates are supplied, and a time scale can be worked out from this information. In cases where the speeds are not known, a time scale can be recorded on the revolving drum by means of a tuning fork vibrating at a known frequency (e.g. 100 s^{-1}): one of its arms is fitted with a point that will write on the revolving drum. Alternatively, and more expensively, an electrical time marker can be used: driven from the mains, the writing point of the marker will blip at a given frequency.

Now available on the market are chart recorders incorporating a kymograph, electronic stimulator, time marker, and various other accessories. The stimulators will give single pulses, or repetitive pulses ranging from 1 per ten seconds to 100 per second.

Separate stimulators are also available for use with kymographs.

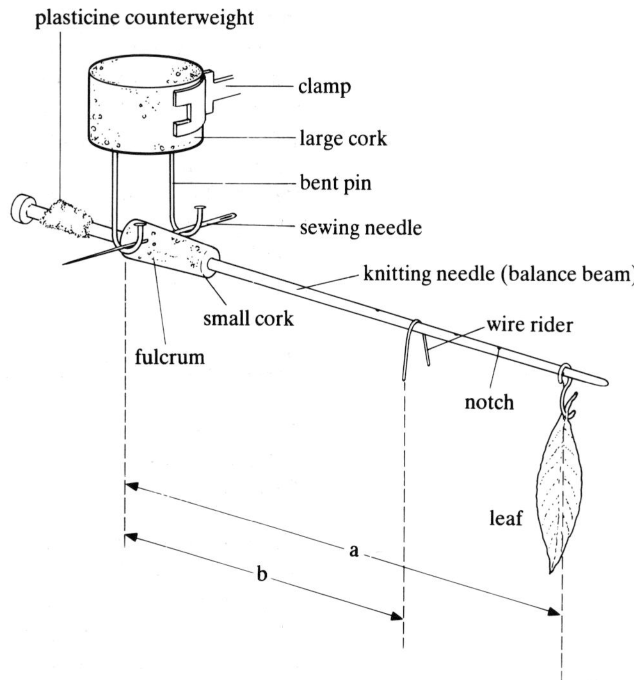

Figure A3.3 Using a microbalance to measure the mass of a leaf. (*Based on Revised Nuffield Biology, Practical Guide 3, Longmans*)

3.6 The microbalance

The microbalance is a simple but sensitive device which can be used to measure small changes in mass as may occur when, for example, water is lost from a transpiring leaf.

The balance beam consists of a knitting needle which moves on a wire fulcrum (Figure A3.3). A lump of plasticine is stuck onto the shorter end of the balance beam as a counterweight. At the longer end hangs a wire hook from which the object to be weighed is suspended. Behind the apparatus is clamped a piece of graph paper. On it is marked the position of the tip of the balance beam at the start of the experiment. The whole apparatus is set up away from air currents which can seriously upset the equilibrium of a sensitive microbalance.

Suppose you want to weigh a leaf. First suspend it from the hook and alter the amount of plasticine, and if necessary the position of the fulcrum, until the balance beam is more or less horizontal. Record its position by marking a line on the paper behind the tip. Then remove the leaf, making sure that the plasticine at the other end does not change in shape or position.

Place on the balance beam a wire rider, bent to fit into the notches in the beam. Slide it up and down the beam until the tip of the beam reaches the same horizontal position as before. Then measure the distances a and d from the fulcrum (Figure A3.1).

By moments, $ax = by$, where a = distance of the leaf from the fulcrum
b = distance of the rider from the fulcrum
x = mass of the leaf (as yet unknown)

Thus $x = \frac{by}{a}$ y = known mass of rider

The balance can be used in the following way to measure the rate of water loss of a transpiring leaf. Attach the leaf to the tip of the horizontal balance beam. Mark on the graph paper the position of the tip. Allow the leaf to lose water while still suspended from the balance. The tip of the balance beam will rise. After a known time, slide a rider up and down the notched beam until its tip returns to its previous position. Measure the distance (b) of the rider from the fulcrum at equilibrium. The mass of water lost = by/a as explained above.

Appendix 4 Ecological Techniques for Measuring the Environment

If you decide to measure some environmental variable in ecology, consider carefully how the data will be used. Will you be able to relate the environmental measurements to the distribution of the organisms concerned? Or will your data only be of interest to the Meteorological Office?

When you are planning your observations, arrange them if possible so that you can analyse them statistically (*see* Appendix 6, page 393). You may have to arrange your measurements at random in time or space. Several estimates of the same environmental variable may be needed to establish an average with a small standard error.

The most elegant way to collect the maximum quantity of environmental data in the shortest time with the minimum effort is to connect probes to a Vela or a microcomputer, which can be programmed to store the data as it is collected. Systems to collect micro-environmental data in this way can be bought from the usual biological supply houses.

4.1 Temperature

Many different types of thermometer are available. Glass thermometers are easily broken during carriage. Thermistors are more suitable for field use.

A thermistor is a small metal bead whose resistance changes with temperature. The thermistor is connected to a battery-operated meter which shows the temperature, on a dial or a digital scale.

Several thermistors can be connected in series to the same meter. By switching the meter from one thermistor to the next a large number of comparative readings can be taken in a short time.

4.2 Solar radiation, light intensity

Light intensity is measured most simply with a photographic light meter or a modern single lens reflex camera with through-the-lens metering.

To compare the light intensities at two or more places, you must be careful to arrange your samples in such a way as to provide a fair comparison. A cloudless day is ideal, and a uniformly cloudy day is acceptable. Do not make comparisons on a day of intermittent cloud.

Imagine that you wish to compare the light intensity at five sites in a wood. A suitable sampling technique would be to estimate the light intensity at each of the five sites in random order within a total time of five minutes. Half an hour later, repeat the measurements, in a differnt random order. Repeat at half-hour intervals and average the results. The significance of the difference between the light intensities at two different sites can be tested by a Mann-Whitney U-test or a t-test (*see* Appendix, page 398).

4.3 Wind Speed

Wind speed is most easily measured with a simple cup anemometer (Figure A4.1). Wind speed fluctuates considerably with time. When the wind speeds at two or more sites are to be compared, take one measurement at the same height at each place within as short a time as possible. Repeat this procedure at intervals.

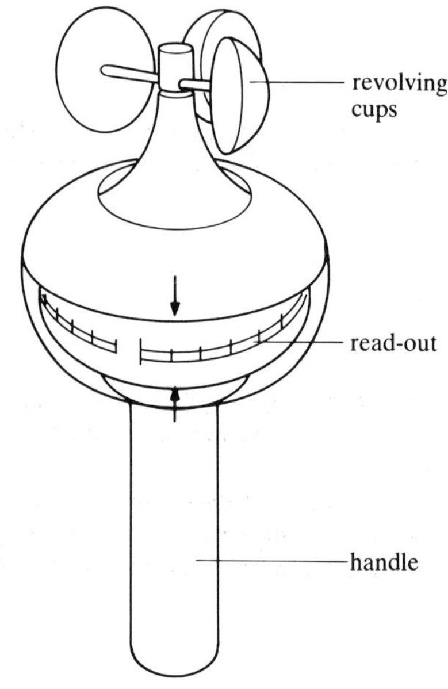

Figure A4.1 A cup anemometer which provides a direct read-out of wind speed. (*After* D. R. Slingsby and C. Cook, *Practical Ecological Techniques*, MacMillan, 1986)

4.4 Relative humidity

The classical method of measuring relative humidity with a wet and dry-bulb hygrometer is only suitable for crude ecological work and should be avoided if possible. Many smaller devices exist with a probe attached to a dial. Humistors are the best of all. These tiny devices work in a similar way to thermistors and the data are displayed on a battery-operated portable meter on a dial or in digital form.

If you wish to estimate the evaporative stress on an organism in a particular environment, it is often more valuable to measure evaporation directly.

4.5 Evaporation

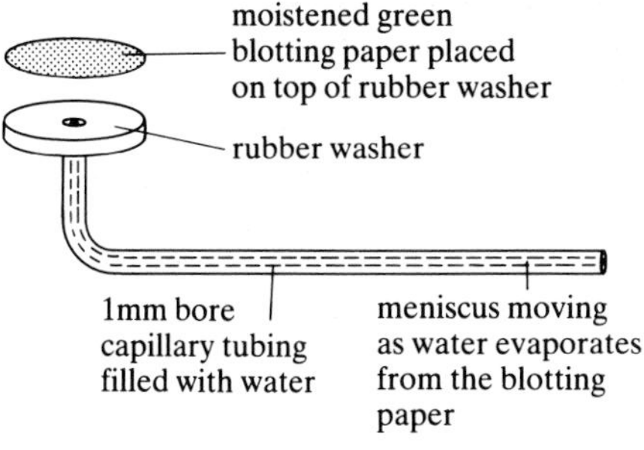

Figure A4.2 A simple evaporimeter for comparing the rate of evaporation in different environments. The rate at which the meniscus moves indicates the rate of evaporation.

Evaporation is easily measured with an evaporimeter (Figure A4.2). This device is an effective way to integrate the effects on evaporation of temperature, wind and relative humidity. Its use often makes unnecessary the collection of a mass of micro-environmental data.

The evaporimeter is a horizontal glass capillary tube bent upwards at one end. On this end is placed a rubber washer, flush with the cut surface of the tubing. The capillary tube is filled with water and a wet disc of green blotting paper is placed on top of the washer. The blotting paper connects to the water supply. As water vapour evaporates from the disc into the air, water is replaced from below. The rate at which the meniscus moves along the capillary tube measures the evaporating power of the environment.

4.6 Salinity

Chemical titration methods are messy and time-consuming. Use a conductivity meter. This measures the ability of a solution to conduct electricity. The more ions it contains, the better a solution conducts and the higher the conductivity in siemens (SI units for Ω^{-1}). This technique measures all ions, not just NaCl, but many different ions contribute to the low water potential of salt water.

To measure soil salinity, add to the wet or dry soil twice the mass of water and put the conductivity probe into the paste. Use the same dilution for all your samples and then you can validly compare readings. In analysing your results, you may be able to rank the sites in order of increasing salinity. Then you can use a non-parametric test (e.g. Kendall's coefficient of rank correlation) to work out whether a significant correlation exists between salinity and the numbers of a particular organism (*see* Appendix 6, page 395).

4.7 Oxygen concentration

The measurement of oxygen concentration in water is easy with an oxygen meter, which consists of a probe connected to a dial or a digial meter. Avoid time-consuming chemical methods. Borrow an oxygen meter instead.

4.8 Soil water content

Collect labelled samples from the field in closed containers (e.g. polythene bags). In the laboratory, transfer each sample carefully to a weighed beaker, crucible or specimen tube. Weigh again. Make sure that each sample is labelled.

Transfer the samples to an oven at 105 °C for 48 hours or until the mass of the containers becomes constant. Reweigh. Express the water content of the soil as a percentage of the original mass of the wet soil (more usual) or as a percentage of the mass of the dry soil.

4.9 Soil organic matter content

The simplest method is to heat very strongly a known mass of *dry* soil in a weighed metal crucible over a Bunsen burner. Turn the soil over from time to time with a spatula. After three or four hours the soil will have turned red and it can be reweighed. The loss of mass is loss of organic matter. Express it as a percentage of the original mass of the dry soil.

If a muffle furnace is available, set it at 800 °C for 4 hours. Bear in mind that high temperatures are unsuitable for chalk or limestone soils, since heat may decompose the calcium carbonate.

4.10 Soil nutrients

The levels of soil nitrogen, phosphorus, potassium and calcium are measured most easily for A-level work with a soil test kit, available from gardening shops. The kit also provides crude estimates of humus content and pH. A similar but more expensive kit is available from Griffins, the biological suppliers. Total soil nitrogen is very strongly correlated with soil organic matter content. The levels of ammonium, nitrite and nitrate in soils can be estimated with Merckoquant reagent sticks.

4.11 Soil pH

Stir up a moist soil sample with twice its own mass of distilled water, or a dry soil sample with 2.5 times its mass of distilled water. Allow the sample to settle for a few minutes, and then determine the pH with an electronic pH meter. Put the electrode carefully at the liquid-soil junction and wait for the reading to stabilise before you record it. Most pH meters adapted for soil use have a strengthened electrode.

If an electrical pH meter is not available, mix the soil sample with water as mentioned above, but test the liquid above the soil with Universal Indicator or pH paper, and read the pH off the colour chart.

Reference: W. H. Dowdeswell, *Ecology: Principles and Practice*. Heinemann, 1984.

Appendix 5 Projects

This Appendix is in two parts. The first part provides some advice about how to carry out a project. In the second part we list some suitable project topics and provide references to appropriate techniques.

5.1 Advice on Projects

The secret of a successful project is to select a topic which is interesting and yields interesting results. An infinite number of possible projects is possible. Most of them are not worth attempting. Be particularly wary of choosing a project which involves much identification or requires the collection of numerous environmental measurements. Descriptive projects can be valuable if carried out by an enthusiast, but remember that the best way to unravel cause and effect in biology is to perform experiments.

How to plan and execute your project

(a) Search for a topic which really interests you.

(b) Find a phenomenon, for example, daffodil flowers usually face away from nearby walls.

(c) Think about the phenomenon carefully and write down any explanations of it you can think of. At this stage discussion with friends, teachers or parents may provide ideas which had not previously occurred to you.

(d) Decide on a particular hypothesis to be tested. An hypothesis is a tentative explanation of the phenomenon, which can be tested by experiment or observation, for example, the flowerstalks of daffodils are positively phototropic.

(e) Decide what data you need, and how you should obtain it. Do not be too grandiose in your schemes. Beginners greatly overestimate what is possible in the time available. The analysis of the data and the production of the project report will take at least as long as the practical work.

(f) Consider now how you will present the data in your report. Will negative results be valuable? For example, if the flowerstalks of daffodils, in experiments, showed no tendency to grow towards light, could you still write up the project in an interesting manner?

(g) At this stage you should make a list of all the apparatus which you require and check that it is available.

(h) If possible, carry out a pilot experiment or make a trial set of observations. This will tell you if the snags in the experimental technique, suggest extra measurements which might have to be made, and enable you to predict how long the practical work will take. If your methods are unsuitable, a pilot study will expose the problems before you have invested too much time and energy in barking up the wrong tree.

Experimental design and sampling

Next you must consider how many experimental treatments to set up, or how many samples to collect. How should you arrange the collection of data in space and time? Where necessary you must include controls, replication (repeated attempts at the same experimental treatment), randomisation and analysis of results by statistical methods.

5.2 Suitable projects

Many of the investigations and questions in this manual, adapted as necessary, would make suitable projects.

In addition the following list of possible projects and references may be found helpful.

We would not claim that this list is exhaustive. Local conditions and the interests of teachers give the sorts of projects attempted by particular schools and colleges an idiosyncratic air. We list here topics which have yielded worthwhile projects for our students, and ideas culled from a variety of sources.

References

RNAB *Revised Nuffield A-level Biology* (1986); numbers refer to the seven practical guides (1-7) for the course.
K T. J. King, *Ecology* (Nelson, 1980)
F P. W. Freeland, *Problems in Practical Advanced Level Biology* (Hodder and Stoughton, 1985)
LT T. Lewis and L. R. Taylor, *Introduction to Experimental Ecology* (Academic Press, 1967)
GPA T. J. King, *Green Plants and Their Allies* (Nelson, 1983)
B A. P. Brookfield, *Animal Behaviour* (Nelson, 1980)
For advice on scientific method and techniques see:
G. H. Harper, *Tools and Techniques* (Nelson, 1984)

General

Pollen counts, made by exposing sticky slides to the atmosphere on several successive days, correlated with weather data and hay fever suffering.
Associative learning in animals (**RNAB**, 3).
Reproductive behaviour of sticklebacks or newts.
Colour change in chamaeleons in relation to their background.
Host-finding mechanisms in aphids.
Is the green hydra, *Chlorohydra viridissima*, completely dependent on its mutualistic association with Zoochlorella?
Analysis of territorial behaviour in birds, e.g. robin. (Ideal for keen bird-watchers.)
Reconstruction by serial sectioning of the pattern of vascular tissues in the transition from stem to root in a dicotyledonous plant.
Relationship between the internal structure and mechanical properties of stems and twigs.
Extra-sensory perception and psychokinesis in humans (**RNAB** 4). (Think carefully before you embark on a project in this field.)
Analysis of web-building by spiders as an example of innate behaviour.
Variation in willowherbs, *Epilobium* spp.
Variation in the size of pollen grains in different species of flowering plants.
The time and location of most active cell division in root tips.
Thin-layer chromatography of flower pigments in closely-related species (**F**).
In the snail *Cepaea nemoralis*, frequencies of different colour morphs and banding patterns in different habitats; effects of predation by thrushes (E. B. Ford, *Ecological Genetics* (Methuen, 4th edn. 1980).
Development of vascular system in broad bean plants of different ages (*see* Investigation 12.5, page 126; also **RNAB** 4).
Navigation of ants by pheromones (e.g. in trail-following) and polarised light.
The rate of fall of, and distance travelled by, winged seeds in relation to their structure.
Search for correlations on medical databases; for example, relationship of profession to age and cause of death.
Testing possible mutagens with respiration-deficient (RD) mutants of yeast (*Saccharomyces cerevisiae*) (P. W. Freeland, *Journal of Biological Education* No. 12, 1978; **GPA**).
Direction-finding in pond snails. (In general snails are good animals to work on: they are easy to keep, move slowly and don't answer back!)
Learning and colour/pattern recognition in relation to feeding behaviour of fishes.

Effect of light and/or temperature on the behaviour of fishes, amphibians or reptiles.

Stalking behaviour in cats. (In general many interesting projects can be carried out on pets, but be sure to adopt a rigorous scientific approach.)

Ecological

Energy budgets of stick insects of different ages (*see* Investigation 32.8, page 322; **RNAB**; R. J. Slatter *School Science Review*, November 1980).

Effect of trampling and burial on seed germination and establishment in *Plantago major* (Greater plantain).

Distribution patterns of nettles in relation to soil phosphate. (**RNAB**, 7).

Competition between different genotypes of *Drosophila* (**RNAB**, 7).

Growth curve in a population of unicellular alga assessed with a colorimeter or haemocytometer (**RNAB**, 7).

Soil pH and nutrient concentration around the bases of coniferous trees; effect on earthworm populations (**K**).

Biochemical oxygen demand (B.O.D.) and fauna in rivers at different distances from a pollution source (**K**).

Food web for a pond by examining gut contents and putting organisms together in pairs. (**RNAB**, 7).

Factors affecting the distribution patterns of different animal species, e.g. planarians, shrimps, barnacles, mussels.

Life tables for the holly leaf miner (*Phytomyza ilicis*) and its parasitic insects. (**RNAB**, 7; **LT**).

Comparison of diets of different species of snails and slugs by faecal analysis (**K**).

Testing for salt tolerance or lead tolerance in races of grasses collected from roadsides; comparison with normal races (**RNAB**, 7).

Pollination; flower constancy of pollinating insects; pollen identification from insects; flower preferences in relation to tongue length; role of flies in pollen-eating and pollination (**K; LT**).

Mosses and algae on north/south sides of walls or different levels up a salt marsh; distribution pattern in relation to desiccation tolerance (**K; GPA**).

Long term

Growth of duckweed (*Lemna* species) at different levels of added nitrate and/or phosphate to simulate eutrophication (*see* Investigation 32.9, page 324).

Growth of duckweed (*Lemna* species) at different levels of added detergent to simulate pollution.

Population dynamics of plants in permanent quadrats; death rates of seedlings and mature plants.

Increase in mass and length with time in an arthropod and non-arthropod.

How does the shell of a snail grow in size and shape as a snail becomes larger?

Birth and death rates of different leaves on the same plant or leaves on plants from contrasting habitats.

Mineral nutrient requirements of plants; water and sand cultures.

Tissue cultures of plants in sterile conditions on agar.

The effects of different water regimes on plant growth (**RNAB**, 7).

Inter-specific interaction between clover and grass; addition of fertiliser (**RNAB**, 7).

Life histories of insects isolated from galls.

Effect on bryophyte growth of varying nutrient concentrations in the substrate (**GPA**).

Effect of hair points on the water relations of mosses (**GPA**)

Pollination mechanism of Lords and Ladies, *Arum maculatum* (D. H. T. Jones, *Journal of Biological Education* 11, 253–260).

Physiological

Effects of various wavelengths of light, particularly red: far-red ratio, on seed germination, the tropic response, or phototaxis in Euglena (**RNAB**, 3; **B**).

Factors affecting aerial (adventitious) root growth in ivy.

Light compensation points of sun and shade plants.
Variations in salivary amylase activity with age, sex and diet (**F**).
Location of nitrate reductase and nitrite reductase enzymes in plants of different species (**F**).
Effect on various factors (physical and/or mental) on the pulse rate of the human.
Effects of inhibitors on active transport in *Elodea canadensis* (Canadian pondweed).
Influence of different wavelengths of light on the phototropic response of coleoptiles (**RNAB**, 4).

Applied

Effectiveness of antiseptics and/or disinfectants in destroying bacteria
Factors, internal and external, affecting the rate at which bread goes mouldy.
Effectiveness of biological washing powders in removing protein stains.
Damaging effects of fizzy drinks on human teeth.
Factors affecting the fermentation activity of yeast.
Different types of food-processing in relation to shelf-like. (Opportunities here for exploring the necessity and effectiveness of food additives.)
Analysis of cereal grain in relation to bread-making. (Recently a high-fibre white loaf has been developed. How?)
Tissue culture of fragments of crop plants as a means of propagating successful genotypes.
Construction of small-scale production unit for the synthesis of certain chemical products (biotechnology).
Effects of various treatments on the re-vegetation of trampled paths.

Important note

Project work must not be carried out in such a way as to cause any distress to an animal. The animal must not be wounded, poisoned, inflicted with a disease, or starved. For advice on what is ethically acceptable see *Recommended Practice for Schools Relating to the Use of Living Organisms and Material of Living Origin* (EUP, 1974) which is also quoted in *The Educational Use of Living Organisms* ed. Kelly and Wray (EUP, 1976).

There is now new legislation in this area, the Animals (Scientific Procedures) Act 1986, and many education authorities have introduced their own guidelines. For specific details of any licensing arrangements or other requirements refer to the Home Office and/or the local education authority. The Association for Science Education, the Institute of Biology and the Universities Federation for Animal Welfare have issued a joint statement entitled '*The Place of Animals in Education*' which can be found in *The Biologist*, (Volume 33, No. 5, November 1986. A reference list is included in this article.

Appendix 6 Statistical Tests

Several of the tests described here are not included in A-level syllabuses. Nevertheless, familiarity with these tests is valuable to A-level students in the analysis of data obtained in field courses, laboratory experiments or projects.

In experiments or projects the results are usually recorded as numbers. For example, suppose that plantains seemed more abundant in trampled area A than untrampled are a B. Random samples yielded the following numbers of plants per square metre: A 23, 28, 15, 31; B 35, 13, 7, 9. On average there were 22 plants per square metre in area A and 18 m^{-2} in area B. Is there a real difference between the densities of plantains in areas A and B? There is a danger that the experimenter might reach the wrong conclusions because feelings, expectations and hopes might influence his or her judgement.

Statisticians have developed 'significance tests' in order to answer objectively questions like this. Imagine that areas A and B really have the *same* density of plantains. This is called the **null hypothesis**. On the basis of a series of calculations on the data, one can assess the probability that average results of 22 and 18 plants per m^2 could have been obtained by chance, because of sampling error. After all, when you toss a coin ten times you may obtain by chance four heads and six tails, or three heads and seven tails. Such results occur 23% of the time in ten throws even with an unbiased coin.

In the case of the plantains the calculated probability level is 23%, or, as it is usually written, $P = 0.23$. In other words, if the null hypothesis was correct and the plantain density in the two areas was equal at 20 per m^2, there is a 23% probability that means of 18 and 22 plants per m^2 could have been obtained by chance. This probability value is above 5% ($P > 0.05$) and so, by convention, there is insufficient evidence that plantain density differs in the two areas.

If, however the probability value had turned out to be less than 5% ($P < 0.05$) the difference in plantain density in the two areas would have been 'statistically significant'. In that case the researcher might have continued the study by trying to find out how and why trampling favours plantains.

Various statistical tests have been designed, for use in different circumstances. You need not know the complex mathematical theory which underlies these significance tests. However, you need to know which test is appropriate for your data, how to do the calculations to obtain the probability value at the end, and how to interpret the resulting P value. Many modern hand-held calculators are or can be programmed to carry out these tests.

Use the key below to select the test you need. The main statistical tests which you are likely to need are summarised below the key. If none of them is appropriate to your particular data, or if the test you need is not included in this summary, then you should consult one of the references listed on page 409.

Key to tests

1 Data are counts of numbers of organisms in certain classes, or presence and absence . . . *go to* **2**

Data are measurements, continuously variable, or ranked . . . *go to* **5**

2 Observed data compared with expected proportions (e.g. genetic experiments) . . . *go to* **3**

Data in two or more discontinuous classes (e.g. presence and absence of one species, presence and absence of another); test for association between two classes required . . . *go to* **4**

3 No observed value below eleven . . . **Chi-squared test**

At least one observed value below eleven . . . **Chi-squared test with Yates' correction**

4 No observed value below five . . . **Chi-squared test on 2×2 contingency table**

At least one observed value below five . . . **Fisher's exact Chi-squared test**

5 Comparison of difference between means of two sets of measurements – *same* thing measured on both sets . . . *go to* **6**

Correlation between two sets of measurements on same organisms – *different* variables measured on each set . . . **Correlation coefficient** *or* **Kendall's coefficient**

6 Pairs of measurements *not* made on same individuals . . . **t-test** *or* **Mann-Whitney U-test**

Pairs of measurements made on the same individuals . . . **Paired comparison t-test** *or* **Wicoxon signed ranks test**

6.1 Chi-squared test

The chi-squared test enables us to assess the significance of differences between expected and observed results, and is particularly useful in the analysis of the results of genetic experiments. The null hypothesis to be tested is that there is *no* significant deviation between the expected and observed result.

The chi-squared value (χ^2) is a measure of the degree of deviation between an expected and observed result. The larger the deviation, the larger the χ^2 value. If the calculated χ^2 value exceeds that for P = 0.05, i.e. five per cent, (see the table on the next page), the observed results differ significantly from the expected. Don't be worried by the term 'degrees of freedom' – it is equivalent to the number of classes minus one.

$$\text{Chi-squared} = \text{the sum of } \frac{(\text{observed} - \text{expected})^2}{\text{expected}} \text{ for all classes of results}$$

Example involving two classes of results (one degree of freedom)

Suppose that in a genetic experiment where the expected ratio is 3.1, we obtain a total of 40 plants, 32 with red flowers, and 8 with white flowers.

	red	white
Expected numbers	30	10
Actual numbers	32	8

$$\chi^2 = \frac{(32 - 30)^2}{30} + \frac{(10 - 8)^2}{10}$$
$$= \frac{2}{15} + \frac{2}{5} = 0.53$$

A χ^2 value of 0.53 with one degree of freedom corresponds to a probability of between 0.30 and 0.50, i.e. between 30 and 50 per cent.

The difference between the observed and expected values is quite likely to be due to chance and so it is not significant. See Table A6.1.

Example involving three classes of results (two degrees of freedom)

Suppose that in a genetic experiment where the expected ratio is 1:2:1, we obtain a total of 80 plants, 22 with red flowers, 42 with pink and 16 with white (what circumstances might produce such results?)

	red	pink	white
Expected numbers	20	40	20
Actual numbers	22	42	16

$$\chi^2 = \frac{(22 - 20)^2}{20} + \frac{(42 - 40)^2}{40} + \frac{(20 - 16)^2}{20}$$
$$= \frac{1}{5} + \frac{1}{10} + \frac{4}{5} = 1.10$$

A χ^2 value of 1.10 with two degrees of freedom corresponds to a probability of between 0.50 and 0.70, i.e. between 50 and 70 per cent. The difference between the observed and expected values is again very likely to be due to chance and so it is not significant. It is regarded as not significant because the probability that the difference is due to chance exceeds 0.05 (five per cent).

The chi-squared test can also be applied to situations where there are four, five or more classes of results (i.e. three, four, or more degrees of freedom).

Table A6.1 Table of χ^2 values (based on Fisher)

Degrees of freedom	Number of classes	χ^2									
1	2	0.016	0.064	0.15	0.46	1.07	1.64	2.71	3.84	5.41	6.64
2	3	0.21	0.45	0.71	1.39	2.41	3.22	4.61	5.99	7.82	9.21
3	4	0.58	1.01	1.42	2.37	3.67	4.64	6.25	7.82	9.84	11.34
4	5	1.61	2.34	3.00	4.35	6.06	7.29	9.24	11.07	13.39	15.09
probability (P) that chance alone could produce the deviation		0.90 (90%)	0.80 (80%)	0.70 (70%)	0.50 (50%)	0.30 (30%)	0.20 (20%)	0.10 (10%)	0.05 (5%)	0.02 (2%)	0.01 (1%)

6.2 Correlation coefficients and Kendall's coefficient

Suppose two variables have been measured and we wish to know whether the two sets of measurements are related significantly. For example, is the number of growth rings in tree trunks proportional to their diameter? Are the numbers of the mayfly nymph *Ephemerella* in quadrats related to the proportion of sand in the substrate? Is the pollen count in Oxford air proportional to the pollen count in London air?

Calculations on such data yield a number between −1 and +1 called the correlation coefficient (symbol, r). If r = 0 the two sets of measurements are unrelated: a scatter diagram of one variable plotted against the other would show the points placed at random. If r = 1 one variable is directly proportional to the other and on a scatter diagram all the points lie on a straight line. If r = −1 the two sets of measurements are inversely related.

In practice r is generally an intermediate number and tables are consulted to assess its statistical significance. The null hypothesis is that the two variables are *un*related. If there is really no relationship between the two sets of figures (i.e. r = 0), what is the probability of obtaining the observed measurements by chance? If this probability is low (less than 5%) the variables are significantly associated.

Look up in a statistics textbook the method of calculating r and testing its significance. Programmes for microcomputers and hand-held calculators are readily available.

Another method is to use Kendall's τ. Tests such as this are based on ranking, are often more suitable for biological data than the older-established tests. They are simpler, quicker and easier to understand.

For example, the data below show gill mass and body mass in the crab *Pachygrapus crassipes*.

X Gill mass (mg)	159	179	100	45	384	230	100	320	80	220	210
Y Body mass (g)	14.4	15.2	11.3	2.5	22.7	14.9	1.4	15.8	4.2	15.4	9.5

Are gill mass and body mass related? The null hypothesis is that they are unrelated. How do we test the null hypothesis?

First, rearrange the pairs in numerical order of one of the variables, say X; and write the values for Y beneath, as shown in the table below.

X Gill mass (mg)	45	80	100	102	159	179	210	220	230	320	384
Y Body mass (g)	2.5	4.2	1.4	11.3	14.4	15.2	9.5	15.4	14.9	15.8	22.7
P	9	8	7	6	5	3	4	2	2	1	0
Q	1	1	0	1	1	2	0	1	0	0	0
P−Q	8	7	7	5	4	1	4	1	2	1	0

Now concentrate on the Y row, starting with the left-hand figure (2.5). Count the number of other figures in the Y row to the right which are larger than 2.5. Put this number in the P row, below the 2.5. Then, count the number of other figures in the Y row to the right of 2.5 which are smaller than 2.5 and put this number in the Q row beneath the figure 2.5. Repeat this in turn for each of the figures in the Y row as in the table shown above.

Calculate P−Q for each Y value and add all these P−Q values together. We shall call the total S. The sum S (in this case S=40), and the number of pairs of observations n, (in this case n=11), can then be substituted into the formula:

$$\tau = \frac{2S}{n(n-1)} = \frac{80}{11.10} = \frac{8}{11} = 0.73$$

Once τ has been calculated, the probability that the correlation is due to chance can be determined by looking up τ in statistical tables. The method used to assess the statistical significance of τ differs according to the number of pairs of observations (n).

When n is **10 or below** simply look up the value of S in the table below:

n	5	6	7	8	9	10	
S must exceed	10	12	14	17	20	22.5	to be significant at the 5% level

When n is **above 10** (as in the gill example) calculate the statistic τ as above, and then calculate the statistic t, as shown below for the gill data:

$$t = \frac{\tau}{2(2n + 5)/9n(n - 1)} = \frac{0.73}{(2 \times 27) \div (99 \times 10)} = \frac{0.73}{0.055}$$

$= 13.1$ standard deviation units from the mean

Look up this t value in tables of areas under the normal curve (*see* page 397). This provides the probability that a value of τ as large as 0.73 could have been obtained by chance from a set of data for which the correlation coefficient was actually zero.

In this case P = 0.0001 (0.01%). This is much less than 5% and so there is a significant correlation between gill mass and body mass in the crab.

6.3 Normal distribution, standard deviation and standard error

These are important statistics and are needed for the t-test (see later). Let us illustrate them with real data. Here are estimates for the density of wood for two different species, A and B:

Species	**Individual measurements**	**Sum**	**Mean** (average)
A	0.76, 0.74, 0.75, 0.72, 0.71.	3.68	0.736
B	0.68, 0.67, 0.72, 0.69, 0.66.	3.42	0.684

Standard deviation

The standard deviation is a measure of the extent to which the individual measurements vary around the mean. We can calculate the standard deviation (s) for the wood density of species A from the figures above by using the following formula:

$$Sx = \sqrt{\frac{\Sigma x^2 - \frac{(\Sigma x)^2}{n}}{n - 1}}$$

where Σ = sum of,
x refers to the individual values for the wood density of species A, and
n is the number of estimates of the wood density we have

Translated, the standard deviation (symbol s) of the wood density of species A =

$$\sqrt{\frac{(\text{sum of squared individual values of x}) - \frac{(\text{sum of x values})^2}{n}}{n - 1}}$$

$$= \sqrt{\frac{(0.76^2 + 0.74^2 + 0.75^2 + 0.72^2 + 0.71^2) - \frac{(3.68)^2}{5}}{4}}$$

$$= \sqrt{\frac{2.7102 - 2.7085}{4}} = 0.021$$

Similarly, the standard deviation of wood densities for species B is 0.023

Normal distribution

When measurements of a particular characteristic are made on a large number of individuals in a population, the numbers of individuals which exhibit a particular measurement often fall on a '**normal distribution curve**'. This is true, for example, of human intelligence. The curve is bell-shaped (Figure A6.1). Its position and width depend entirely on its mean and its standard deviation.

According to statistical theory, one standard deviation on either side of the mean encloses 68% of the area under the curve and two standard deviations enclose about 95% (Figure A6.1)

The two normal curves marked X and Y in Figure A6.2 are roughly the curves which we should expect if we had measured the densities of hundreds of samples of wood from species A and B.

Standard error

We used five estimates of wood density to estimate the mean density of the wood of species A (0.736). How reliable is this estimate of the mean? If we had measured the density of another five samples of species X, would their mean be 0.736 too? Probably not. Therefore we need an estimate of the degree of variation of our estimates of the mean.

According to theory, the estimates of the mean follow a normal distribution with standard deviation $\sqrt{s^2/n}$, where s is the standard deviation of the individual measurements, and n is the number of measurements from which the mean has been calculated. The wood samples of species A follow a normal distribution of wood density with a standard deviation of 0.021. The *mean* wood density, based on averages of five density measurements each time, follows a much narrower normal distribution curve with a standard deviation of $\sqrt{0.021^2/5} = 0.009$. This curve is also plotted on Figure A6.2.

The standard deviation of the mean is known as the **standard error** and must be clearly distinguished from the standard deviation of the individual measurements.

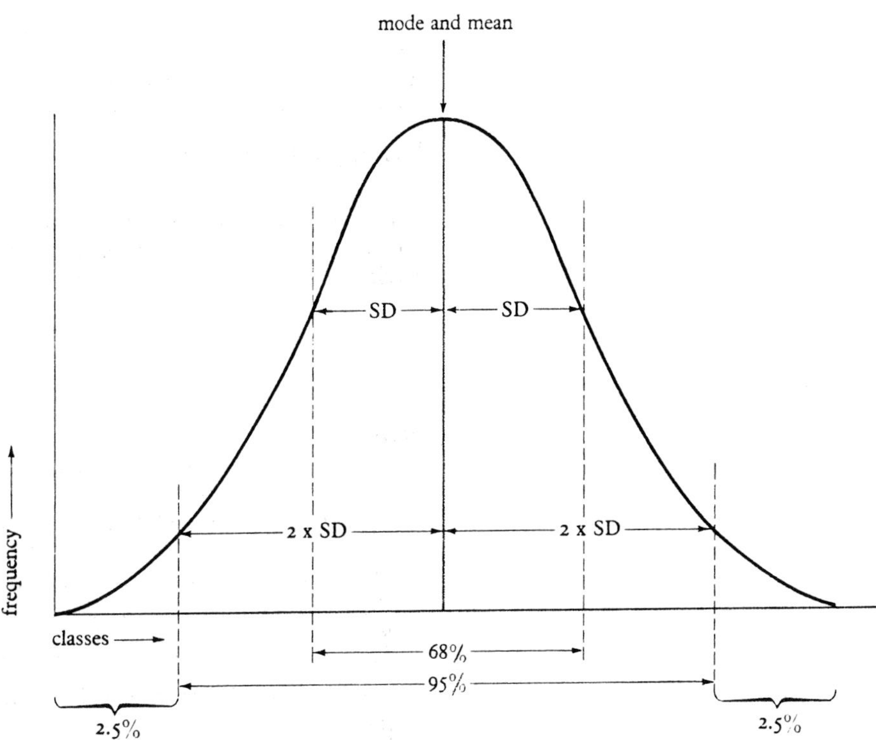

Figure A6.1 Diagram of normal distribution curve.

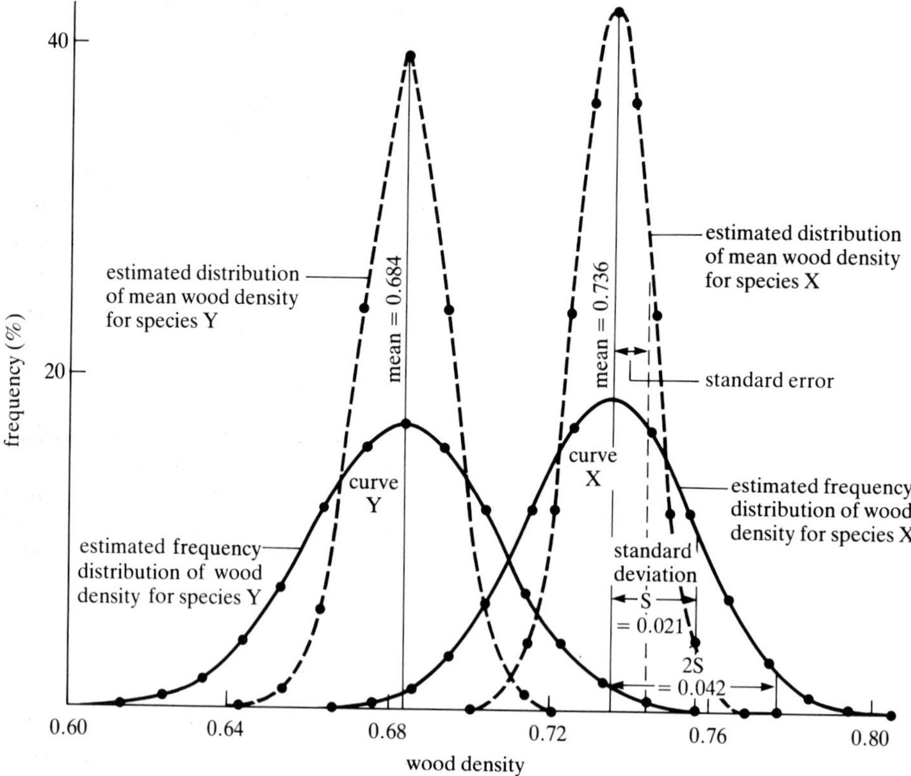

Figure A6.2 Normal distribution curves for the wood density data.

6.4 The t-test and the Mann-Whitney U-test

These significance tests are used when the same sorts of measurements have been made on two groups of organisms and we need to decide whether or not the means differ. For example, are the wood densities of species A and species B (see data above) significantly different? The null hypothesis is that they are *not* significantly different. The t-test is used when each of the two means to be compared is based on at least three individual measurements. When the number of measurements is seven or more the Mann-Whitney U-test can be used.

The t-test

Let's use the wood density figures to illustrate how to perform a t-test. First we must estimate the standard deviation of the whole population, i.e. all ten measurements of wood density from both species A (five measurements) and species B (five measurements).

To estimate the standard deviation of the population to which both means belong, you use the following formula:

$$s = \sqrt{\frac{\Sigma x^2 - \frac{(\Sigma x)^2}{n_x} + \Sigma y^2 - \frac{(\Sigma y)^2}{n_y}}{n_x + n_y - 2}}$$

As before, x refers to the individual values for the wood density of species A; y refers to the individual values for the wood density of species B; n_x is the number of measurements of x; n_y is the number of measurements of y.

For the X and Y wood density figures above:

$$s = \sqrt{\frac{2.7102 - \frac{(3.68)^2}{5} + 2.3414 - \frac{(3.42)^2}{5}}{8}} = 0.022$$

$$\text{Now } t = \frac{\text{mean of X} - \text{mean of Y}}{\text{standard error of mean}} = \frac{\text{mean of X} - \text{mean of Y}}{s\sqrt{\frac{1}{n_x} + \frac{1}{n_y}}} = \frac{0.736 - 0.684}{0.022\sqrt{\frac{1}{5} + \frac{1}{5}}}$$

$$t = \frac{0.052}{0.01379} = 3.77$$

Tables of t can be consulted to determine the exact level of significance for n_x+n_y-2 degrees of freedom. In this case, since t exceeds 2.3 (for 8 degrees of freedom) the means of X and Y are significantly different.

If there are **more than 32 individual values** calculate:

$$d = \frac{\text{mean x} - \text{mean y}}{\sqrt{\frac{s_x^2}{n_x} + \frac{s_y^2}{n_y}}}$$

The result is the number of standard errors apart of the two means. Consulting tables of the area under the normal curve, d needs to exceed 1.96 to be significant.

The standard deviations of the two means to be compared should be about equal. If the measurements are not normally distributed they can be made so by 'transforming' them before analysis to logarithms, arcsine, or square roots. It is easier to carry out a Mann-Whitney U-test.

Mann-Whitney U-test

The Mann-Whitney test is non-parametric i.e. it is based on ranking and can be used to compare two samples provided that there are at least seven individual measurements in each of the two groups being compared.

The data shows the percentage covers of the moss *Pleurozium schreberi* on ten anthills and ten random surrounding vegetation quadrats:

Ant-hills	10,	0,	19,	4,	0,	17,	7,	5,	2,	3
Surrounding vegetation	7,	8,	6,	7,	7,	57,	1,	7,	4,	20

Now write down for each figure its position in the rank order of the two samples together. If two or more numbers are the same, give each of them the same average rank for that number. There are twenty figures: 57 is the highest so it is ranked at position 20; 0 is the lowest so it is ranked at position 1.5 (average of 1 and 2). The full sequence should be as follows:

Ranks	Ant-hills	16,	1.5,	18,	6.5,	1.5,	17,	12,	8,	4,	5
	Surrounding vegetation	12,	15,	9,	12,	12,	20,	3,	12,	6.5,	19

The sum of the ant-hill ranks = R_1 = 89.5 and the sum of the surrounding vegetation ranks = R_2 = 120.5. Substitute in the following formulae:

$$U_1 = n_1 n_2 + 0.5n_2(n_2 + 1) - R_2 = 100 + 55 - 120.5 = 34.5$$
$$U_2 = n_1 n_2 + 0.5n_2(n_1 + 1) - R_1 = 100 + 55 - 89.5 = 65.5$$

Look up these values of U_1 and U_2 in tables. In fact when $n_1 = 10$ and $n_2 = 10$, either U_1 or U_2 would have to exceed 73 for the difference to be significant. Therefore in this case the difference between the percentage covers of the species on and off the ant-hills is not significant.

For a list of books on statistics, many of which contain statistical tables, *see* page 409.

Appendix 7 Advice for Technicians

A wide range of technical books, pamphlets and articles is now available to teachers and technicians on laboratory management and the technical requirements for A-level biology. The following two books are particularly recommended:
Peter Fry (editor), *Biological Science Laboratory Book: a Technical Guide* (Nuffield Advanced Science, 1971)
John Creedy, *A Laboratory Manual for Schools and Colleges* (Heinemann, 1977)

Other publications are listed on page 404.

The names and addresses of the principal biological suppliers in the United Kingdom are at the front of the book. It is essential to have copies of their current catalogues. They tell you what's available and serve as a useful source of information and ideas.
The following notes relate to specific requirements of this manual.

7.1 Sterilisation

It is necessary for instruments, culture media, and glassware to be sterilized for experiments involving micro-organisms, live embryos, tissue culture, etc.

Sterilisation is most efficiently and conveniently carried out in an **autoclave** or, failing that, a **pressure cooker**. For most purposes it is sufficient to sterilize at 6.7 kg (15 lbs) pressure for 20 minutes.

Instruments, pipettes, syringes, etc., should be wrapped in paper or metal foil before being autoclaved and left wrapped afterwards until required. Test tubes should be plugged with cotton wool beforehand and the caps of screw-topped bottles should be loose.

After unsealing, instruments can be quickly re-sterilised by heating in the flame of a bunsen burner or spirit lamp, or by dipping in 50–70 per cent ethanol.

Bench tops should be washed with an antiseptic, e.g. three per cent solution of lysol, before experiments are started.

For sterilisation of skin, swab the skin with cotton wool soaked in, e.g. 70 per cent ethanol. Alternatively use a pre-packaged medical swab obtainable from supplier.

7.2 Breeding *Xenopus laevis*

Use mature specimens, at least two years old. Keep them at room temperature in a tank with perforated cover. Feed them twice a week on mealworms, earthworms or liver and change the water whenever necessary.

Identification of sexes

Mature females are much larger than males and they have labia ('flaps') surrounding the cloaca.

Bringing the toads into season

Mature toads can be brought into season at any time of the year by injecting them with pregnyl (chorionic gonadotrophin) which is available from suppliers in ampoules of stated capacity.

The toads have to be treated with specific amounts of pregnyl. This should be injected with a hypodermic syringe into one of the dorsal lymph sacs. These are located in front of the row of 'stitch marks' in the lumbar region of the body. The toad should be held firmly

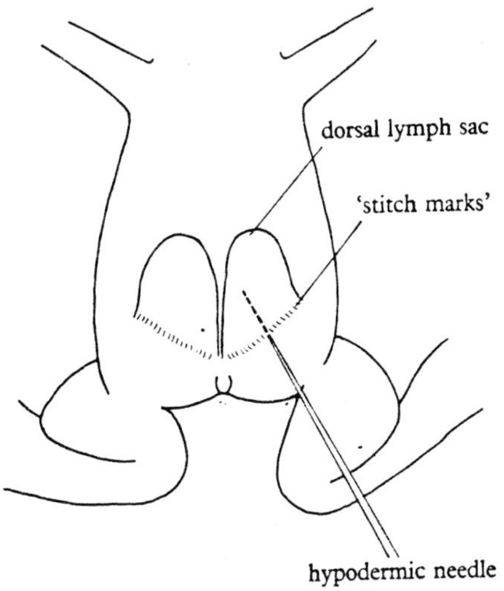

Figure A7.1 Injecting the African clawed toad *Xenopus laevis*.

and the needle inserted as shown in Figure A7.1. Keep the needle close to the skin so it does not penetrate the tissues beneath.

To allow for failure, inject at least three pairs of toads. Keep them in clean water in separate tanks at room temperature for 24 hours beforehand. For injection make up 500 international units (IU) of pregnyl in 1.0 cm^3 of distilled water or amphibian saline. Proceed as follows:

Primer injection

Two to four days before the eggs are required give the toads a primer injection of pregnyl: male–50 IU; female–100 to 500 IU.

Giving the female more than 100 IU may result in her spawning prematurely. Continue to keep the toads in separate tanks at room temperature.

Final injection

Twelve hours before the eggs are required give the toads a final injection of pregnyl: male–100; female–300 IU.

Put the male and female toad together in the same tank and, using a thermostatically controlled heater, maintain at a minimum of 22°C. The tank should measure at least 30 x 20 x 20 cm. Reluctant females can sometimes be encouraged to spawn by raising the temperature to (not more than) 28°C.

It may be found helpful to spread a sheet of muslin over the bottom of the tank and cover this with a single layer of smooth rounded stones. Eggs will fall between the stones where they will be protected, and can be lifted from the tank on the muslin sheet. Otherwise they must be lifted out individually with a wide pipette.

Keep the eggs in bowls at about 23°C.

Allow at least six weeks to elapse before injecting the same toads again. One or two preliminary injections two to three weeks before the eggs are needed may sometimes raise the chances of success.

Maintaining the tadpoles

The tadpoles should be kept in a tank at about 25°C. The water should be changed and the tank cleaned once a week. The tadpoles are herbivorous and can be fed on powdered nettle leaves (available from suppliers). Do not overfeed: the food should disappear within 24 hours.

At about the time of metamorphosis, when the tail begins to be resorbed, the tadpoles become carnivorous and should be fed on water fleas, small worms, etc., and, later, shredded heart tissue.

During metamorphosis it is advisable to oxygenate the tank and provide some means by which the young toads can climb out of the water.

7.3 Rearing Chick Embryos

Obtain newly laid fertile eggs from a supplier, not longer than ten days before they are required. To allow for infertility (which is generally around 15 per cent), more eggs should be obtained than are needed. Arrest development by keeping them in a refrigerator at 10–12°C.

If three-day embryos are required, move the eggs to an incubator 72 hours before the embryos are needed. If older embryos are needed, move the eggs to the incubator at the appropriate length of time beforehand.

The incubator should be maintained at a steady 38°C. It must have some means of ventilation and the atmosphere inside it should be kept moist by means of an open container of water.

The eggs should be placed sideways on a tray. They should be rotated laterally through 180° each day to prevent the embryo sticking to the shell. When the egg is turned the embryo and yolk sac will automatically roll round so the embryo lies towards the upper side of the egg.

7.4 Recipes for Biological Reagents

The reagents listed below are the more common ones that are constantly required for biological work. Details of other more specialized reagents are given at the ends of the particular laboratory investigations in which they feature.

Acetic orcein

Dissolve 3.3 g of orcein in 100 cm^3 of glacial ethanoic acid by gently boiling under reflux for about six hours. Filter. This gives a stock solution which can be stored.

When required for staining, dilute 10 cm^3 of stock solution with 12 cm^3 of distilled water. The diluted stain deteriorates quickly.

Ethanoic ethanol (acetic ethanol)

Three parts of ethanol to one part of glacial ethanoic acid.

Acetocarmine

To 45 cm^3 of glacial ethanoic acid add 1.0 g of carmine. Mix and add 55 cm^3 of distilled water. Boil. Cool and filter.

Benedict's reagent

Dissolve 173 g of hydrated sodium citrate and 100 g of hydrated sodium carbonate in approximately 800 cm^3 of warm distilled water. Filter and make the filtrate up to 850 cm^3. This is solution **A**.

Disssolve 17.3 g of hydrated copper sulphate in approximately 100 cm^3 of cold distilled water. This is solution **B**.

Add **B** to **A**, stirring as you do so. Make up to 1 dm^3 with distilled water.

Borax carmine

Dissolve 4 g of borax in distilled water. Add 3 g of carmine and boil for 30 minutes. Add 100 cm^3 of 70 per cent ethanol, allow to stand for two days, then filter.

Bouin's fluid

Mix 5 cm^3 of glacial acetic acid and 25 cm^3 of formalin (40 per cent methanol) with 75 cm^3 of a saturated aqueous solution of picric acid. The resulting solution will keep indefinitely.

Chloral hydrate solution

Dissolve 128 g of chloral hydrate in 80 cm^3 of distilled water.

Cobalt chloride paper

Dip a strip of filter paper, measuring approximately 2 x 5 cm, into a five percent solution of cobalt chloride. Dry and keep in a desiccator.

Cobalt thiocyanate paper

Drip a strip of filter paper, measuring approximately 2 x 5 cm, into a 25 per cent solution of cobalt thiocyanate. Dry and keep in dessicator.

Cotton blue in lactophenol

Dissolve 1 g of cotton blue in 100 cm^3 of lactophenol.

Eosin (alcoholic)

Dissolve 1 g of alcohol-soluble eosin in 100 cm^3 of 90 per cent ethanol.

Fabil

The following solutions are required:

Lactophenol: phenol (crystals), glycerol, lactic acid, and distilled water in equal parts by weight.

A Aniline blue: 0.5 per cent in lactophenol.

B Basic fuchsin: 0.5 per cent in lactophenol.

C Iodine, 3 g; potassium iodide, 6 g; lactophenol 1 dm^3.

To make up the stain mix the stock solutions in the proportions of **A**, 4: **B**, 1: **C**, 5. Allow to stand for 12 hours, then filter. The stain will keep indefinitely.

(Noel, A.R.A., *School Science Review*, Vol 47, No. 164, pp. 156–157).

Formalin

Commercial formalin contains approximately 40 per cent methanal (formaldehyde). For use as a fixative, add 90 cm^3 to 10 cm^3 of commercial formalin. The resulting 10 per cent formalin is suitable as a general fixative.

Glycerine

For mounting botanical sections use a concentration of five per cent. Prepare by making up 5 g of pure glycerine to 100 cm^3 with distilled water.

Haematoxylin (Ehrlich's)

Dissolve 2 g of haematoxylin in 100 cm^3 of absolute ethanol. This is solution **A**.

Add 3 g of aluminium potassium sulphate to 100 cm^3 of glycerol, 100 cm^3 of distilled water, and 10 cm^3 of glacial ethanoic acid. This is solution **B**.

Mix **A** and **B** and allow to ripen in an unstoppered bottle in bright daylight for two to three weeks.

Iodine

As a general stain for plant material, dissolve 1.0 g of iodine crystals and 2.0 g of potassium iodide in 300 cm^3 of distilled water.

Lactophenol

Dissolve 100 g of phenol in 100 cm^3 of distilled water without heating. Then add 100 cm^3 of lactic acid and 200 cm^3 of glycerine. Store in a brown glass bottle.

Light Green

Dissolve 1 g of light green in a mixture of 25 cm^3 of absolute ethanol and 75 cm^3 of clove oil. (Fast green which fades less rapidly, may be used as an alternative to light green).

Methylene blue

Mix 1 g of methylene blue, 0.6 g sodium chloride and 100 cm^3 distilled water.

Methyl green

Make up a 1 per cent solution of ethanoic acid in distilled water. To 100 cm^3 of this add 1 g of methyl green

Noland's solution

Dissolve 20 mg of gentian violet in a mixture of 80 cm^3 of phenol (saturated solution in distilled water), 20 cm^3 of formalin (40 per cent methanol) and 4 cm^3 of glycerol.

Phloroglucin (Benzene-1,2,3-triol)

Dissolve 2–5 g of phloroglucin in 100 cm^3 of 95 per cent ethanol. (The solution should be acidified with concentrated hydrochloric acid before use.)

Ringer's solution (frog)

To 1.0 dm^3 of distilled water add 6.5 g of sodium chloride, 0.3 g of calcium chloride, 0.2 g of sodium hydrogencarbonate and 0.2 g of potassium chloride. Dissolve.

Ringer's solution (earthworm)

Dilute frog Ringer's solution with distilled water (x6).

Safranin

Dissolve 1 g of safranin in 100 cm^3 of 50 per cent ethanol.

Schultz solution (chlor-zinc iodide)

Dissolve 110 g of zinc in 300 cm^3 of hydrochloric acid and evaporate to half the volume. In the course of the evaporation add a little more zinc to ensure complete neutralisation of the acid. Dissolve 10 g of potassium iodide in the least possible quantity of water and add 0.15 g of iodine crystals. Mix thoroughly and, if necessary, filter through glass wool. Keep in tightly stoppered bottle in the dark. (N.B. Dissolving zinc in hydrochloric acid results in the evolution of hydrogen. The evaporation should be carried out in an evaporating dish over a low flame.)

Appendix 8 Sources of Further Information

EXPERIMENTAL WORK: GENERAL

Biological Sciences Curriculum Study (BSCS) publications
Produced by the American Institute of Biological Sciences, the BSCS programme consists of three alternative texts and ancillary publications. The main texts are *Biological Science: an Inquiry into Life* (BSCS Yellow Version), *Biological Science: Molecules to Man* (BSCS Blue Version), and *High School Biology* (BSCS Green Version). Each is accompanied by appropriate laboratory blocks, teachers' guides, etc.

The BSCS programme provides a useful source of laboratory investigations for use in colleges and schools.

Nuffield Foundation Science Teaching Project: Revised Advanced Biology (Longman, 2nd edition 1985–6)
The new Nuffield A level publications include seven Practical Guides accompanied by a teachers' guide in two volumes.
Collectively they provide a magnificent source of material and ideas for those who like to try interesting new experiments.

G. D. Brown and J. Creedy, *Experimental Biology Manual* (Heinemann Educational Books, 1970)
This manual includes a wide range of experiments in microbiology, genetics, biochemistry, physiology, and behaviour. The instructions are clear and succinct.

P. Abramoff and R. G. Thompson, *An Experimental Approach to Biology* (Freeman, 1967)
Thirty-five laboratory exercises for first-year American college students. Some of the exercises, particularly those relating to cell biology, are useful.

G. Wald *et al*, *Twenty-six Afternoons of Biology* (Addison-Wesley, 2nd edition 1967)
This account of experiments featuring in the introductory biology course at Harvard University is full of useful ideas even though many of the experiments are demanding of apparatus.

P. W. Freeland, *Problems in Practical Advanced Level Biology* (Hodder and Stoughton, 1985)
A series of practical experiments with important theoretical implications. A separate edition contains specimen results.

EXPERIMENTAL WORK: GENETICS AND ANIMAL PHYSIOLOGY

J. J. Head and N. R. Dennis, *Genetics for O level* (Oliver and Boyd 1968)
Laboratory investigations, some too sophisticated for O level, run through this book (in green print). There are useful photomicrographs of mitotic and meiotic figures.

Gordon Haskell, *Practical Heredity with Drosophila* (Oliver and Boyd 1961)
In this useful little book the author explains how *Drosophila* should be handled and he suggests a series of suitable breeding experiments.

W. D. Zoethout, *Laboratory Experiments in Physiology* (U.S.A.: Mosby; U.K.: Henry Kimpton; 6th edition 1963)
Over 200 experiments in animal physiology (mainly mammalian), many of which are not unduly complicated.

R. B. Clark, *A Practical Course in Experimental Zoology* (Wiley, 1966)
Based on the author's own course, the experiments are designed for first-year university students in the U.K. Some of them can be adapted for more elementary use.

EXPERIMENTAL WORK: PLANTS AND MICRO-ORGANISMS

L. J. F. Brimble, *Intermediate Botany* (Macmillan, 1952)
This well-known text has suggestions for laboratory work at the end of each chapter, and a very useful classification of angiosperms at the end of the book.

W. O. James, *An Introduction to Plant Physiology* (Oxford University Press, 6th edition 1963)
In this classic textbook there is a section on laboratory work, consisting of a list of suggested experiments, at the end of each chapter.

W. M. M. Baron, *Organisation in Plants* (Arnold, 3rd edition, 1979)
There is an extensive series of experimental procedures in the appendix. In designing these the author spares us from unnecessary expense. Very useful.

Hans Meidner, S. Meidner and W. David, *Water and Plants* (Blackie, 1976)

J. Roberts and J. C. G. Whitehouse, *Practical Plant Physiology*, (Longman, 1976)
This describes several investigations suitable for class practicals or project work.

R. K. Pawsey, *Techniques with Bacteria* (Hutchinson Educational, 1974)
This book contains everything a teacher or technician needs to know about the culturing and handling of bacteria, and there are instructions for carrying out numerous experiments.

J. Williams and M. Shaw, *Micro-organisms* (Mills and Boon, 1976)
Less detailed than Pawsey but the practical exercises are particularly appropriate for schools.

EXPERIMENTAL WORK: ECOLOGY

D. P. Bennett and D. A. Humphries, *Introduction to Field Biology* (Arnold, 2nd edition 1974)
A general introduction to the practical aspects of ecology. Plenty of information on techniques and a useful section on statistical methods.

D. Slingsby and C. Cook, *Practical Ecology* (Macmillan, 1986)
A practical aid to carrying out practical field work. Full advice is given on the collection and analysis of data and writing up results.

T. Lewis and L. R. Taylor, *Introduction to Experimental Ecology* (Academic Press, 1967)
More advanced than the previous books but very useful to the teacher on both the practical and theoretical aspects of this subject. Full of ecological exercises and experimental data. There is a useful section on techniques, and keys to common land invertebrates.

W. H. Dowdeswell *Ecology: Principles and Practice* (Heinemann Educational, 1984)
Excellent summary of practical techniques in ecology, with descriptions of major habitat types and suggestions for projects. Highly recommended.

A. Darlington *The Ecology of Walls* (Heinemann Educational, 1981)
A fascinating summary which includes ideas for projects.

M. Collins *Urban Ecology* (Cambridge University Press, 1984)
A valuable resource book which contains many ideas for projects and class practicals in towns and cities.

S. D. Wratten and G. L. A. Fry *Field and Laboratory Exercises in Ecology* (Arnold, 1980)
Source of sophisticated ideas for quantitative practicals in the field and the laboratory.

S. A. Corbet and R. H. L. Disney (editors) *Naturalist's Handbooks* (Cambridge University Press, 1981–6)
These handbooks (on Grasshoppers, Insects and Thistles, Solitary Wasps, Insects on Nettles, Hover-flies, and Bumblebees) provide plenty of information and project ideas for A-level students.

DISSECTION

H. G. Q. Rowett, *Dissection Guides* (UK: John Murray, 1950–53; U.S.A.: Holt, Rinehart and Winston)
Clear line diagrams, accompanied by instructions, on dissection of the dogfish, frog, rat, and selected invertebrates; available separately or combined in a single volume.

J. T. Saunders and S. M. Manton, *Practical Vertebrate Morphology* (Oxford University Press, 4th edition 1969)
This advanced manual includes instructions on dissections of lamprey, skate, bony fish, salamander, lizard, grass snake, and pigeon.

W. S. Bullough, *Practical Invertebrate Anatomy* (Macmillan, 2nd edition 1958)
Contains instructions with diagrams on over 100 invertebrate species including microscopic ones. Instructions on dissection are given where appropriate.

ANIMAL HISTOLOGY AND EMBRYOLOGY

H. G. Q. Rowett, *Histology and Embryology* (John Murray, 3rd edition 1966)
Like her dissection guides, this book contains clear diagrams and a minimum of text. The book includes mammalian histology, the embryology of the frog and chick, and invertebrate histology.

W. H. Freeman and Brian Bracegirdle, *An Atlas of Histology* (Heinemann Educational Books, 2nd edition 1967)
A collection of photomicrographs, accompanied by labelled diagrams, of mammalian tissues and organs. Includes some useful notes and schematic diagrams. Eminently suitable for advanced classes in schools and first degree students.

W. H. Freeman and Brian Bracegirdle, *An Atlas of Embryology* (Heinemann Educational Books, 3rd edition, 1978)
Similar format to the previous book. Covers the development of *Amphioxus*, frog, and chick. Apart from some introductory notes on basic embryology, there is no text.

A. W. Ham, *Histology* (U.S.A.: Lippincott; U.K.: Pitman; 5th edition 1965)
Standard work of reference on mammalian histology in which microscopic structure is related to function. Full of useful information.

W. Bloom and D. W. Fawcett, *A Textbook of Histology* (Saunders, 8th edition 1962)
In this updated version of Maximow and Bloom's famous histology text, the fine structure of mammalian cells is integrated with traditional histology. Excellent for reference.

W. H. Freeman and Brian Bracegirdle, *An Atlas of Invertebrate Structure* (Heinemann Educational Books, 1971)
Here Freeman and Bracegirdles' expertise is brought to bear on the invertebrates. Very useful for interpreting difficult slides.

PLANT HISTOLOGY

A. C. Shaw, S. K. Lazell and G. N. Foster, *Photomicrographs of the Flowering Plant* (Longmans Green 1965)
Covering the stem, root, leaf, and flower, each photomicrograph is accompanied by a labelled line diagram. There is no text.

Brian Bracegirdle and Patricia H. Miles, *An Atlas of Plant Structure* (Heinemann, 2 volumes, 1971–1973)
A collection of photomicrographs, each accompanied by a labelled diagram, illustrating a wide range of plant structures from algae to angiosperms. Vol. 2 contains information on the gross anatomy of plants.

Mary-Anne Burns, *The Arlington Practical Botany, Book I Plant Anatomy* (Arlington Books, 1964)
A book of excellent drawings and notes in which emphasis is laid, not on topographical anatomy, but on the recognition of plant tissues.

C. J. Clegg and Gene Cox, *Anatomy and Activities of Plants*, (John Murray, 1981)
Photomicrographs and explanatory diagrams of flowering plants with an interesting text that includes some functional considerations.

ANIMAL AND PLANT TYPES

R. Freeman (Introducer), *Classifications of the Animal Kingdom, an Illustrated Guide* (English Universities Press, 1972)
A reasonably detailed and very well illustrated classification of animals. Its attractive layout makes it possible to see the wood for the trees.

M. A. Robinson and J. R. Williams, *Animal Types* (Hutchinson, 2 volumes, 1970–1971)
With modern biology courses paying so little attention to animal types, there is a need for a book which surveys the animal kingdom in a simple and attractive way. These two slim volumes fill the bill admirably.

W. M. Clarke and M. M. Richards, *The Locust as a Typical Insect* (John Murray, 1976)
If you keep locusts in the laboratory and use them for practical work, you will find this book indispensible. It covers the structure, life cycle, physiology and economic importance.

C. J. Clegg, *Lower Plants* (John Murray, 1984)
A thorough account of life cycles, well illustrated and containing much information on economic importance.

T. J. King, *Green Plants and their Allies* (Nelson, 1983)
A wide range of plant types are described, with illustrated life cycles and structure.

ANIMAL AND PLANT IDENTIFICATION

J. L. Cloudsley-Thompson and John Sankey, *Land Invertebrates* (Methuen, 1961)
An admirable little book, well illustrated with line diagrams and containing simple identification keys, eminently suitable for schools.

Helen Melanby, *Animal Life in Fresh Water* (Methuen, 6th edition 1963)
No keys, but very clear diagrams and excellent background information on the various animals surveyed.

John Barratt and C. M. Yonge, *Pocket Guide to the Sea Shore* (Collins, 1958)
A well illustrated survey of the organisms that live in rock pools, etc., on the sea shore.

W. Keble Martin, *The Concise Flora in Colour* (Ebury Press and Michael Joseph, 2nd edition 1965)
This best-selling survey of the families of flowering plants is beautifully illustrated with the author's own paintings.

A. Leadley-Brown, *Ecology of Soil Organisms* (Heinemann, 1978) and *Freshwater Ecology* (Heinemann, 1986)
Two useful books, covering a wide range of organisms.

M. Chinery, *A Field Guide to the Insects of Britain and Northern Europe* (Collins, 2nd edition 1976)
A comprehensive guide.

Aidgap Keys/Field Studies Council. These are available for many groups of British animals and plants, for example Water plants, Brown seaweeds, Diatoms, flies, crabs and slugs. Available from The Richmond Publishing Company, Orchard Road, Richmond, Surrey TW9 4PD

Also useful for identification purposes are the *The Observer's Books* (Warne), *Wayside and Woodland Series* (Warne), and Collin's Pocket Guide Series.

USE OF THE MICROSCOPE

C. A. Hall and E. F. Linssen, *How to use the Microscope* (A. & C. Black, 6th edition 1968)
Sun-titled *A Guide for the Novice*, this is a practical introduction to microscopy with no physical background. There is a useful section on the use of the hand lens and simple (single lens) microscope.

L. C. Martin and B. K. Johnson, *Practical Microscopy* (Blackie, 3rd edition 1958)
Concise account with explanation of the physics of different types of microscope, including the phase contrast, polarizing, and electron microscopes.

J. D. Cassartelli, *Microscopy for Students* (McGraw-Hill, 1969)
A very practical book by an experienced microscopist who, as technical representative of a well-known manufacturer, is familiar with the kinds of questions asked by biologists at all levels. Includes sections on the phase contrast and stereomicroscopes.

HISTOLOGICAL METHODS

R. R. Fowell, *Biology Staining Schedules for First Year Students* (H. K. Lewis, 1964)
A concise summary of various zoological and botanical staining procedures. Very useful.

Biological Stains and Staining Methods (British Drug Houses Ltd.)
Short booklet (50 pages) full of information on stains and histological procedures, including methods suitable for bacteria.

C. F. A. Pantin, *Notes on Microscopical Technique for Zoologists* (Cambridge University Press, 1946)
For anyone who wishes to prepare wax sections, this little book is indispensable. In addition to staining techniques, there are clear instructions on narcotization, fixation, dehydration, impregnation, and embedding.

Ann Preece, *A Manual for Histologic Technicians* (U.S.A. Little, Brown & Co.; U.K. Churchill-Livingstone, 3rd edition 1972)
Emphasising the mastering of histological skills, this book is particularly aimed at the technical student. A range of staining procedures are summarised in an extensive appendix.

Edward Gurr, *A Practical Manual for Medical and Biological Staining Techniques* (Leonard Hill, 2nd edition 1956)
This book has become a classic since it was first published in 1952. An excellent source of information on all manner of staining techniques.

J. B. Gatenby and H. W. Beams, *The Microtomist's Vade-Mecum* (Churchill, 11th edition 1950)
A mine of information on zoological and botanical staining procedures, covering just about all aspects of the subject. Recommends the best methods to adopt for specific tissues.

GENERAL LABORATORY TECHNIQUES

Peter Fry (Editor), *Biological Science—Laboratory Book: a Technical Guide* (Penguin, 1971)
One of the Nuffield Advanced Science publications. It contains instructions for teachers and technicians on culture methods, chemical recipes, and apparatus.

John Creedy, *A Laboratory Manual* (Heinemann Educational, 1977)
A mine of information on the management of the school laboratory and the preparation of material for practical work.

James J. Needham *et. al*, *Culture Methods for Invertebrate Animals* (Dover Publications, 1937)
Compiled by the American Association for the Advancement of Science, this is an old book, but it contains a wealth of information on the rearing and maintenance of a wide range of invertebrates.

P. Hunter-Jones, *Rearing and Breeding Locusts in the Laboratory* (Anti-Locust Research Centre, 1966)
For anyone who wishes to keep locusts in the laboratory this booklet (only 12 pages) is indispensable.

The UFAW Handbook on the Care and Management of Laboratory Animals (Livingstone, 1967)
One thousand pages on every conceivable aspect of keeping and handling animals in the laboratory. Edited by the staff of the Universities Federation for Animal Welfare. Useful to have around!

G. H. Harper, *Tools and Techniques* (Nelson, 1984)
This is not a technician's handbook but an introduction to the principles underlying biological methods. Ideal for people who wish to understand, as well as know how to use, biological apparatus.

Association for Science Education, *Safeguards in the School Science Laboratory* (John Murray, 8th edition 1981)
It is essential to have this book readily at hand and to take note of its recommendations. It is available from the Association for Science Education.

P. J. Kelly and J. Wray (editors), *The Educational Use of Living Organisms* (English Universities Press, 1976)
This book deals with the humane usage of living organisms in schools and contains a summary of the current legal requirements.

JOURNALS AND PERIODICALS

The School Sciences Review (published by the Association for Science Educations) and *The Journal of Biological Education* (published by the Institute of Biology) contain much useful information on experimental work suitable for advanced work in schools and equivalent levels.

Some of the teaching notes from back numbers of *The School Science Review* have been brought together in book form. Published by John Murray, several titles are already available and others are scheduled for the future.

Also recommended is the *Investigation in Biology Series* (Heinemann Educational Books). These moderately priced books contain much helpful information on laboratory work.

QUESTIONS AND PROBLEMS

Joseph J. Schwab (Supervisor), *BSCS Biology Teachers' Handbook* (Wiley, 1963)
This book contains 44 *Invitations to Enquiry*, involving the formulation of hypotheses and interpretation of data in a wide range of investigations.

Garrett Hardin, *Biology: Its Principles and Implications* (Freeman, 2nd edition 1966)
Some of the questions and problems at the ends of the chapters are stimulating and thought-provoking.

S. W. Hurry and D. G. Mackean, *Enquiries in Biology* (John Murray, 1968)
Seven investigations involving interpretation of experimental evidence and data. The investigations include muscle action, breathing, photosynthesis, and moulting in insects. There is a teachers' guide.

J. M. Eggleston, *Problems in Quantitative Biology* (English Universities Press, 1968)
If you like grappling with quantitative data and numerical problems, you will enjoy this book. The problems cover a wide range of topics, including physiology and genetics.

Students are also advised to examine past examination questions. Past papers are generally obtainable from the offices of the various examining boards or from certain booksellers.

Margaret K. Sands, *Problems in Plant Physiology*, (1971), *Problems in Animal Physiology* (John Murray, 1975) and *Problems in Ecology* (Mills and Boon, 1976)
These three books contain a wide range of problems.

These three books contain a wide range of problems involving interpretation and analysis of data. In each case there is a teachers' edition with answers.

Revised Nuffield Advanced Biology, *Study Guides I and II* (Longman, 1985-6)
The Study Items, most of them involving interpretation of data, are particularly useful. The accompanying narrative places the Study Items in context.

P. W. Freeland, *Problems in Theoretical Advanced Level Biology* (Hodder and Stoughton, 1985)
A collection of questions of the kind one finds in current A-level examination papers, with answers at the back.

QUANTITATIVE METHODS

F. Clegg, *Simple Statistics* (Cambridge Educational, 1982)
An entertaining introduction to statistics written in a simple style—ideal for those who dread statistics!

O. N. Bishop, *Statistics for Biology* (Longman, Microcomputer edition 1983)
A well-known book now updated to cover microcomputers.

R. C. Campbell (1974) *Statistics for Biologists*. 2nd edition. (Cambridge University Press)
Clear explanations of non-parametric methods.

D. C. Carter et al. *Mathematics in Biology*. (Nelson, 1981)
A general introduction to the use of mathematical techniques in biology with many practical examples.

R. E. Parker *Introductory Statistics for Biology*. *Studies in Biology 43*, (Arnold, 1973)
Advanced but concise. Each chapter is followed by a series of problems.

R. R. Sokal and F. J. Rohlf *Biometry*. *Statistical Tables* (Freeman, 1981)
All the tables you need (and lots that you don't) for statistical analysis.

SOFTWARE MANUFACTURERS

Longman Micro-Software, 62 Hallfield Road, Layerthorpe, York Y03 7XQ
Cambridge Micro Software, C.U.P, The Edinburgh Building, Shaftesbury Road, Cambridge CB2 2RU
IRL Bioscience Software, IRL Press, Southfield Road, Eynsham, Oxford 0X8 1JJ.
Nelson Computing, Thomas Nelson & Sons Ltd., Nelson House, Mayfield Road, Walton-on-Thames, Surrey KT12 5PL.
Chelsea Science Simulations, c/o Edward Arnold, Woodlands Park, Avenue, Woodlands Park, Maidenhead, Berkshire SL6 3LX/41, Bedford Square, London WC1 3DQ
Longman Micro Software Unit, Longman House, Burnt Mill, Harlow, Essex CM20 2JE.
B.B.C School Software, B.B.C Publications (Schools), P.O. Box 234, London SE1 3TH.
Philip Harris Biological Ltd., Oldmixon, Weston-Super-Mare, Avon BS24 9BJ.
Science Education Software, Unit 4, Marian Mawr Industrial Estate, Dolgellan, Gwynedd LL 40
AVP Computing, Hocker Hill House, Chepstow, Gwent NP6 5ER

Index